James Bond After Fleming

The Continuation Novels

by

Mark Edlitz

Cover design by Sean Longmore. Illustrations by Pat Carbajal.

This book is not authorized or endorsed by Ian Fleming Publications, Eon Productions, or any copyright holder. This work is not intended to be a replacement or stand-in for any of the continuation Bonds. I implore you to put this book down and head to your neighborhood bookstore or library if, at any point, you feel the urge to read a Bond novel.

This book is dedicated to Suzie, the Wise
Ben, the Adventurous
and Doug, the Fierce

TABLE OF CONTENTS

FOREWORD

Bond Beyond Fleming
by John Peel

You people don't know how lucky you are.

I remember my first James Bond book. I was about 12 years old, and visiting one of my grandfathers. He had his own "to read" pile in a cupboard (a bit like mine, only mine is about 100 times larger...), and he'd give it away when he finished a book. (My other grandfather had his own stash, but it was comic books, and that's a whole other story.) Since I happened to be around, Granddad gave me his latest discard. He wasn't exactly into wondering whether books were age-appropriate; he just knew I loved to read, so he handed over *From Russia with Love*. (It was the Pan paperback edition, with lots of lovely photos from the film on the cover.) I didn't have a clue what it was, but once I finished it, I knew I wanted more. Luckily, there was a terrific second-hand bookshop near where I lived, and they had several other James Bond books in the window—at least, they did until I bought them.

I devoured them (except *The Spy Who Loved Me*, which seemed rather silly to me), and then moved on to *Thrilling Cities* and *The Diamond Smugglers*. And that was it.

I then discovered that Ian Fleming was dead, and there would be no more James Bond books.

Ever.

At the time, there were other book series I was into, and it was hard enough to have to wait six months—or even a year!—for the next one. But... *forever*?

It was a huge disappointment for me. Of course, I could (and did) re-read the existing books again and again, but it wasn't the same as stumbling across one I had never seen before, snatching it up feverishly and sitting quietly away from everyone simply living the story.

And then came the strange, wonderful news: there was, after all, going to be more James Bond. A new book had been written: *Colonel Sun,* by Robert Markham. Actually, everybody knew that "Robert Markham" was Kingsley Amis, so I've never understood that decision. An extract was printed in a national newspaper to whet everyone's appetites, and we were promised that this was just the first of a series.

Bond was back! I was still too young to be able to afford a hardcover book, so I signed up for it at my local library. I had to wait several long, impatient weeks because plenty of other people were clearly as addicted as I was. And then I got to read *the new* James Bond.

And it was kind of a letdown, really. I wasn't the only person to think that, clearly, because the promised sequels never did show up, and I went back to re-reading Fleming. (I do now own a hardcover copy of *Colonel Sun*. I've never opened it. I don't want to relive that particular disappointment.)

And then…

Well, if you're reading this book, then you know what "and then…" means. Several dozen *new* James Bonds over the years! And thankfully, many of them are not disappointing at all. Even better news—there are new Bond books turning up on a fairly regular basis. Teenaged me would have loved it. Aged me does love it.

Like I said, you people don't know how lucky you are!

You don't have that terrible wait.

"The future of James Bond is going to require far more thought than I have so far devoted to him."
IAN FLEMING[1]

PREFACE

I'll begin with a confession. Before writing this book, I had not read every single James Bond continuation novel. I am somewhat embarrassed to admit that there were gaps in my Bond continuation knowledge, as I am not a casual Bond fan. I've carefully followed the movie series since the 1970s and I've written two other books about James Bond—*The Many Lives of James Bond* and *The Lost Adventures of James Bond*. Granted, those works largely focused on the movies, as well as the comics, video games, and radio dramas rather than continuation stories. I offer my shameful secret to, hopefully, put you at ease. If you haven't read every Bond sequel book yet, don't worry, we'll go on this journey through every Bond continuation novel together.

Ian Fleming's James Bond.
Illustration by Pat Carbajal

"The name joined all the others in the cemetery, carved in stone."
ANTHONY HOROWITZ, *With a Mind to Kill*[2]

INTRODUCTION

Ian Fleming wrote twelve original Bond novels and two collections of short stories. Despite the cultural importance of Fleming's 14 books, they represent just a fraction of the Bond novels. Since Fleming's death, his estate has authorized the publication of 27 Bond novels, 1 biography, 1 novella, 9 books about the teenaged Bond, 3 novels about M's secretary Miss Moneypenny, 1 concerning Bond's nephew, a planned trilogy about the next generation of agents in the Double O division, and 8 short stories (5 about the adult Bond, 1 about the teen Bond, and 2 about Moneypenny). These post-Fleming works are referred to as continuation novels.

Bond continuation and spin-off authors include Sir Kingsley Amis, John Pearson, Christopher Wood, John Gardner, Raymond Benson, Sir Sebastian Faulks, Sir William Boyd, Jeffery Deaver, Arthur Calder-Marshall, Charlie Higson, Steve Cole, Samantha Weinberg, Anthony Horowitz, and Kim Sherwood. There are more than 50 Bond continuation works, and this volume will explore them all.

I write about the books chronologically and group them into different eras by author. For instance, Benson's era spans from 1997–2002 and Anthony Horowitz's is from 2015–2022. I do not separate the different works into different groups or rankings. To wit, I don't devote one section of the book to continuation novels, another to spin-off works, and yet another to novelizations. Separating the books into categories could inadvertently signal to the reader that one category of work is somehow more important than another. To do so, would inadvertently bestow a lower status, for instance, to the *Young Bond* or *Moneypenny Diaries*. I believe those spin-off series are just as worthy of consideration as the continuation novels that feature stories about the adult 007. Of course, we all have our favorite Bond books. Nevertheless, no work is inherently more worthy than another.

There are some inherent challenges with defining eras. Bond film actor eras are generally discrete. For instance, Timothy Dalton's era is from 1987–1989 (*The Living Daylights* to *Licence to Kill*), Pierce Brosnan's runs from 1995–2002 (*GoldenEye* to *Die Another Day*), and Daniel Craig's spans 2006–2021 (*Casino Royale* to *No Time to Die*). Unlike the movies, the eras of continuation authors can overlap. For instance, Higson's first Young Bond book *SilverFin,* and Samantha Weinberg's first Miss Moneypenny book *Guardian Angel* were both published in 2005. The final books in their respective series were published in 2008. I keep each section of their work more or less self-contained to avoid ping-ponging back and forth between writers. I believe this method will make it easier for you, the reader, to track the progression of an author's run. There are exceptions. In 2023, Higson wrote *On His Majesty's Secret Service*, a novella about the adult Bond which is not part of his Young Bond series. I place Higson's novella after Sherwood's 2022 *Double Or Nothing*.

My objective is to look at each author's approach to interpreting the Bond character, place the novel in the Bond literary canon, scrutinize each author's stated ambitions, and interpret how they achieved them. For instance, one of Gardner's stated goals was to update Bond's tradecraft from Fleming's 1950s/1960s to the then-current 1980s/1990s. Higson's stated aim was to chart the changes in Bond's attitudes as he progressed from adolescence into young adulthood. Each author's works are considered on their own merits and ambitions.

Each novel or short story has a dedicated chapter that includes a summary, observations, and commentary on what each author was trying to achieve with each book and a breakdown of how each author has handled Bond's character and history. These sections feature information about Bond's History, Personal Life, Inner Life, Tastes, Work Methods, and Continuity Nods, which examine how Bond writers allude to events from Fleming's novels or other facets of the Bond world.

The chapters also include subcategories such as Meaning of Title, Chronology, Bastard Meter, and Eggs. Those labels are largely self-explanatory, with the possible exception of the last two, which are meant to be whimsical. "The Bastard Meter" is intended to show how frequently Bond is described as a bastard across most eras. For instance, sometimes he is a plain old bastard and other times he is a "selfish" or an "elusive" one. Eggs cite the occasions when Bond orders his favorite breakfast. What can I say? The spy likes his eggs.

The dates provided correspond to the UK release of the books; frequently the novels are published in the US at roughly the same time. There are, however, several noteworthy cases in which the US release comes later than the UK release. For example, *Double Or Nothing* debuted in the US in April 2023 after being launched in the UK in September 2022. A few of the books—like the last two Moneypenny Diaries by Weinberg and *Danger Society: The Young Bond Dossier*, which includes Higson's short story "A Hard Man to Kill"—have not yet been published in print editions in the United States. All of Weinberg's novels and Higson's short story are available as e-books.

This book follows the essential scholarship of Raymond Benson's *The James Bond Bedside Companion* (1984) and Andrew

Lane and Paul Simpson's *The Bond Files* (2002). Their works are indispensable. *The Bond Files* provided a roadmap on how to approach analyzing the complete series. I have sought to build on Benson, Lane, and Simpson's books and to write about every Bond continuation novel and spin-off ever written from 1965–2023, a 58 year period.

My book is comprised of two parts. Part One is a potted history of the Bond continuation novels. Part Two is a survey of each continuation and spin-off novel. I've included summaries and observations about each work. If you are already familiar with the source material, feel free to skip those recaps.

In the novels that followed Fleming's own, Bond has been stripped naked and dunked into cold Artic water, attacked by a tarantula bat while showering, served a sandwich filled with spiders, married a woman under gunpoint, saved Miss Moneypenny from kidnappers, rode a battlecruiser with Margaret Thatcher and George H.W. Bush, and investigated the mystery of who killed his son. Bond has battled nefarious organizations named The Union, The Scales of Justice, the Brotherhood of Anarchy and Secret Terror, and Children of the Last Days. He's squared off against villains like Zoltan the Magyar, Maximilian Hepworth Blade, serial killer David Dragonpol, Æthelstan of Wessex, and confronted henchmen named Tree-Trunk, Mimic, and Caber. He's charmed Cindy Chalmer, Easy St. John, twin sisters Heidi and Hedy Taunt, Roan Power, Felicity Willing, and Jeopardy Lane. The spy has gone undercover as a mercenary, computer expert, journalist, and, unexpectedly, as a pornographic video salesman. This book charts his ongoing adventures.

I hope you enjoy this volume and that it inspires you to read (or re-read) the wealth of Bond literature out there.

What is a Continuation Novel?

Given that this book explores the James Bond continuation novels, it would probably be wise for me to define a few basic terms, even though some might seem self-evident. A continuation novel is a new work in an existing series that is written by someone other than the creator, often after the original author's death. In other words, it continues the adventures of an author's character. For instance, Arthur Conan Doyle created Sherlock Holmes; a Sherlock Holmes novel not written by Doyle is a continuation novel.

A spin-off novel is a book that features a supporting character from the main character's series. Carrying on with the Holmes example, a book about Detective Inspector Lestrade, the Scotland Yard detective, is a spin-off.

A novelization is a book based on a film or television series, as opposed to a previously published book which was later adapted into. In the former, the film came first; in the latter, the book came first. To wit, author Alan Arnold novelized Chris Columbus' screenplay of *Young Sherlock Holmes*.

The same holds true of the Bond series. Anthony Horowitz's *With a Mind to Kill*, which is set shortly after Fleming's last Bond novel, is a continuation novel. Samantha Weinberg's *Moneypenny Diaries: Guardian Angel*, a book about M's secretary, is a spinoff. Christopher Wood's *James Bond and Moonraker*, an adaptation of the Eon film *Moonraker* is a novelization. So far, so good.

PART ONE: THE HISTORY OF BOND CONTINUATION NOVELS

"When Bond Stops"

When exploring the James Bond continuation novels, two licenses must be considered. The first is, of course, Bond's license to kill. This license has captured audiences' imagination since Ian Fleming's first novel, *Casino Royale* in 1953. Since then, Fleming's Bond books have sold more than a hundred million copies.

The other is the copyright license. It may not be nearly as exciting or glamorous as Bond's, yet it's the reason that Bond's adventures can continue in movies and books. Here is a brief, but vital, overview of the Bond copyright.

When Ian Fleming created Bond in early 1952, he became the copyright holder for all rights to the character.[3] That same year, he acquired Glidrose Productions for tax purposes and assigned the rights to the character he would later use in his debut novel, *Casino Royale* (1953). Glidrose, a shuttered theatrical production company, derived its name from its founders, John Gliddon and Norman Rose.[4] This strategy allowed him to ease his tax burden; otherwise, he would owe an astronomical 91% of his earnings to the government.[5]

Fleming sold the right to turn his books into movies to different parties. Harry Saltzman picked up the film and television rights to the bulk of Fleming's books in 1961. Saltzman partnered with Albert R. Broccoli and formed the holding company Danjaq that licenses Eon Productions, the film company, to make the Bond movies. Eon produced their first Bond film, *Dr. No,* in 1962. Since then, Eon Productions has continued to produce Bond movies with various actors, from Sean Connery to Daniel Craig, playing the secret agent.

There were two Bond movie outliers—*Casino Royale* and *Thunderball*. In 1954, Gregory Ratoff, an actor and producer, bought the rights to *Casino Royale*. When Ratoff died, producer Charles K. Feldman acquired the rights and made the 1967 spoof *Casino Royale* with David Niven and Woody Allen. In 1999, the *Casino Royale* film rights were acquired by Eon.[6] Kevin McClory, who, along with Fleming and Jack Whittingham cooked up the plot to *Thunderball*, originally held the rights to Bond's water-bound adventure. McClory partnered with Broccoli and Saltzman to co-produce the 1965 film adaptation of *Thunderball*, but he retained the film rights to the story. After McClory died in 2006, his estate sold his rights to Eon in 2013. Now, Eon controls the rights to the Bond films and television series but shares them with various studio partners.

The book rights to the character are similarly complicated but equally important. In 1964, Fleming sold a 51 percent interest in Glidrose to a London-based sugar company called Booker McConnell (and its president, Sir Jock Campbell, a friend and golfing companion), for £100,000.[7] That would be more than £2 million in today's money.

The deal was unprecedented for the time. It was nearly unheard of for a living author to sell the underlying copyright to their work to a third party. The *New York Times* cheekily suggested that Fleming was selling *himself*. In an article titled "Author Sells Himself," the *New York Times* estimated that the deal "works out at around $173 an ounce" for Fleming's flesh.[8]

After the lighthearted opening salvo, the *Times* clarified that the sale was for Fleming's literary rights only, film and television rights were excluded, and Fleming would retain creative control of his work. As Ian's wife Ann explained, [Fleming sold] all the book royalties forever and ever, keeping 49 percent of the shares—a minority share, so that the estate gets a tax dividend whenever they choose to declare it, which isn't a fortune, really. Taxation being what it is."[9]

The paper's joke about Fleming selling himself suggests how unprecedented this agreement was. The *Times* concluded the article with the assessment, "As far as is known, he is the first author to be 'taken over' as an investment by an industrial group."[10] According to Fleming, the overall purpose of the deal was to "have some capital *when Bond stops*"[11] [emphasis mine].

Despite Fleming's pessimistic prediction, Bond didn't stop. The resilient agent not only persisted but interest in his adventures only increased. In 1997, the Ian Fleming Estate purchased back the rights from Glidrose and since then they have gained total control of the literary copyright. Over the years, Glidrose has gone by different names, including Glidrose Productions, Glidrose Publications, Ian Fleming (Glidrose) Publications, and finally Ian Fleming Publications.

Throughout the decades, various figures have overseen Fleming's literary interests. In addition to Fleming himself, Michael Howard and Wren Howard, the heads of Jonathan Cape and the original publishers of the Bond novels, oversaw the character. Ann Fleming, Peter Fleming, and Peter Janson-Smith (Ian's wife, brother, and literary agent, respectively), were all board members at Glidrose. Eventually, Peter Fleming became the company's chairman. Following Peter Fleming, Janson-Smith became the company's chairman and Nichol Fleming, Ian's nephew, served as the Head of Estate, until his death in 1995.[12] Ian Fleming publications noted, "As Chairman, [Janson-Smith] oversaw and developed the early post-Fleming continuation novels...He nurtured the subsequent books by John

Gardner and by Bond expert Raymond Benson, while never losing sight of the original Fleming books...He protected the Fleming rights with fierce loyalty."[13]

After he retired, Janson-Smith was succeeded by Fleming's nieces, Lucy Fleming and Kate Grimond (neé Fleming), who led the Estate. After Kate Fleming stepped down, Ian's nephew Fergus Fleming took over as chair. Corinne Turner joined Ian Fleming Productions in 1988; she serves as the managing director and runs the operation for the Fleming Estate. In 2021, Simon Ward joined IFP as its publishing director.

Ian Fleming Publications has multiple goals in publishing the continuation novels. The new works protect the copyright, generate income, and ensure the longevity and popularity of Bond, as envisioned by Ian Fleming. The decision to publish the first Bond continuation book was not necessarily an obvious one, nor was it universally agreed upon by the Fleming family.

Modern audiences are intimately familiar with multiple artists reinterpreting other people's characters. For instance, George Lucas no longer controls the intellectual property of *Star Wars*. Instead, Disney does. In 2012, Lucas sold the rights to his space series to Disney for a deal valued at more than $4 billion. Since then, Disney has produced multiple feature films, television series, comics, and cartoons without involving Lucas. When Fleming died in 1964, that kind of transaction was decidedly less common.

Ian's wife, Ann Fleming, was not a Bond fan. In fact, long before his death, Ann encouraged Fleming to stop writing his spy novels. When Fleming died, his widow had strong reservations about publishing continuation novels. Ann wanted to protect Fleming's legacy, and she worried that other writers would change the nature of her late husband's creation. She wrote to Lord Jock Campbell, the chairman of Booker who had a controlling interest in Bond, to express her displeasure with the enterprise. "Though I do not admire Bond, he was Ian's creation and should not be commercialized to this extent."[14]

There is also some reason to believe that Ann Fleming thought that continuation Bonds would dilute her existing rights. A January 11, 1965 letter from Ronald Aiken, the lawyer for a prospective continuation novelist reads, "I think the question that is worrying Mrs. Fleming's Lawyers is that further stories about 'James Bond' not written by the late Ian Fleming may in some way derogate from the rights in the originals novels and character."[15] Aiken added that neither he nor Ann agreed with this legal argument, but this letter sheds additional light on her concerns.

Regardless, Ann continued to resist giving her consent to sequel works. In a 1966 interview, she further explained her reasoning, acknowledging that she felt "rather emotional about it" but more than that she felt like a continuation Bond "couldn't come off."[16] She reinforced her stances by indicating that her late husband seemed to agree with her. Ann cited a letter that was written by the widow of Fu Manchu novelist Sax Rohmer, asking if Ian Fleming would consider writing a new novel about the criminal mastermind. Ann reported that Ian "did not think this could ever be done."[17] However, after Fleming's death, other writers began using Bond's name without authorization. One such rogue work was *007—With Love from Hell*, a novel by a Japanese writer who had previously been hired to translate Fleming's novels from English to Japanese.[18] Similarly, a Bulgarian writer named Andrei Gulyashki shopped his own Bond adventure in England, Bond's home turf.[19] Gulyashki, author of a series of books about Avakoum Zahov, a spy/super detective in the vein of Sherlock Holmes, wanted to pit Zahov against James Bond in a new book, and sought Glidrose's permission to do so. On February 4, 1966, *Time* magazine reported that Gulyashki, whom they described as "Communism's answer to Ian Fleming," intended to call his opus *Avvakum Zahov Meets James Bond*.[20] Glidrose demurred and didn't grant Gulyashki permission. In turn, Gulyashki barely disguised the identity of Bond and, in 1966, published *Avakoum Zahov versus 07*. The Fleming estate had to confront the issue of these pirate Bond works.

Fleming's nephew, James Fleming, concluded that the experience with the ersatz Bond "rattled the Fleming estate, which was beginning to make big money from the films and books. To keep their hands on the golden goose," they would need to protect their copyright.[21] Duff Hart-Davis, the author of *Peter Fleming*, a biography of Ian's brother, similarly concluded, "The only effective way of suppressing these plagiarists, the Glidrose board decided, would be to produce a 'continuation Bond' book of their own, and so to saturate the market with a form of an authorized sequel.[22]

Peter Fleming, like Ann, was initially against the notion of continuation novels, but eventually relented. Hart-Davis published a portion of a 1966 letter in which Peter laid out the case for the continuation novels, "The Bulgarian [writer who is attempting to shop his Bond manuscript] against whom Glidrose are taking all possible preventive measures, is not himself an important phenomenon. What is important is the alacrity with which publishers have jumped at the chance of cashing in on piracy...This brings out the importance of Glidrose either publishing, or at least having up its sleeve, a Continuation Bond, the existence of which would deter a respectable publisher going forward with a competing work.[23] Ann relented, albeit reluctantly, writing Lord Campbell on April 13, 1967, "Since Peter Fleming agrees to the counterfeit Bond, I am prepared to accept his judgment. Though my distaste for the project is in no way altered."[24]

Glidrose's first effort was not a proper Bond continuation novel but a spin-off about 007's nephew James Bond, Jr. The result was the 1967 adolescent-adventure book *The Adventures of James Bond Junior 003½*. The book's cover suggests that R. D. Mascott is the author. However, the front material allows that "R. D. Mascott is the pseudonym of a well-known British author." Mascott's true identity was a mystery for decades but was eventually revealed to be English novelist Arthur Calder-Marshall. 007 doesn't appear in the book, and *The Adventures of James Bond Junior* is not considered to be the first continuation novel. That honor goes to Kingsley Amis.

Glidrose approached Amis, who demonstrated an understanding of Bond in his books *The James Bond Dossier*, an enthusiastic appraisal of Fleming's writing and Bond, and his tongue-in-cheek manual *The Book of Bond or, Every Man His Own 007*, both published in 1965. Amis, as a self-described "Fleming addict," indicated that Fleming himself approved of the *Dossier*.[25] Amis even got a chance to meet his literary hero, recalling, "I let him see the typescripts of *The James Bond Dossier* before I sent it to the publisher for his comments. [Fleming] kindly took me out to lunch—it was nice, quite expensive."[26] Amis met Fleming on at least one other occasion, this time over dinner at Fleming's house with Ann in attendance. Of the July 1964 meal, Ann recalled, "I suspected he wrote of Ian to further his own sales, but it seemed a genuine admiration, he thinks Ian should write a straight novel."[27]

After Fleming's death from a heart attack in 1964, Glidrose prepared to posthumously publish *The Man with the Golden Gun.* However, Fleming died before he could revise the manuscript. So Glidrose consulted Amis for his input. Among other suggestions, Amis recommended changing the dynamic of the villain's relationship with Bond and having Francisco Scaramanga sexually attracted to the agent. Glidrose didn't implement the story ideas but it's telling that Glidrose thought Amis understood Bond enough to ask him to help edit Fleming's final novel.

In 1967, Glidrose needed to select an author to write the first Bond continuation novel. Given Amis's relationship with Glidrose and his passion for the subject matter, it was only natural that they turned to Amis. From Amis's perspective, writing a Bond novel wasn't something that he previously contemplated. Amis said, "I had never even thought of writing a James Bond story myself, but right out of the blue came this invitation from Glidrose. The idea appealed to me and after some meetings, I decided to go ahead."[28] Young Bond novelist Charlie Higson argued, "With his in-depth knowledge of the material, Kingsley was the perfect choice to carry on the Bond legacy."[29]

Some people in Amis' inner circle were surprised that Amis accepted the writing assignment. Along with his two essay-style books, his continuation novel would mark his third Bond-associated book. Amis's son, Martin Amis, observed, "I'm really astonished that the bug hit him so hard. I mean, he was 43 or 44. That's the time when a novelist is at the height of his energy and to have this three-book divagation from what you would normally be working on. I was just struck again and again by how kind of boyish it all was."[30]

Glidrose's original plan was to have Amis, and all subsequent authors use a shared pseudonym. Amis elaborated on the rationale of using a nom de plume to the 007 fan magazine *Bondage*, "It was considered possible that other writers might like to have a crack at it. And so it would be there for all other writers doing sequels in a few years—it would be less confusing if they all had the same pseudonym. No attempt to persuade the public that it was the same man, but it would be more convenient to market the books and so on."[31] The name "George Glidrose," named after the company, was offered. Alliterations aside, George Glidrose didn't have the requisite punch and the pen name was rejected. Ultimately, the estate settled on the name Robert Markham.

Simultaneously, it seems that Geoffrey Jenkins, a South African journalist and novelist, was pressing Glidrose for permission to write his own Bond novel. Jenkins was a colleague of Fleming and had pitched 007's creator an idea for a Bond book. According to Jenkins, Fleming told Jenkins to write the book and, later, when Jenkins shared the outline with Fleming, Jenkins declared that Fleming "was most enthusiastic about it."[32] Jenkins maintained that because he had Fleming's blessing, he had the authority to write a continuation novel.

Whatever Fleming might have felt about the Bond novel is the subject of conjecture. However, Glidrose was very much against the idea. Peter Fleming's biographer, Duff Hart-Davis, contended that Glidrose was essentially forced to allow Jenkins to write his novel. If they didn't, he would write it without their consent. In a letter to Glidrose, Jenkins warned, "Unless therefore, formal consent is forthcoming in the very near future, I shall write the novel whether or not is it granted.[33] Likely considering that they would have more control over the book if they entered into a contract with Jenkins, Glidrose permitted Jenkins to write a Bond continuation novel. However, when Jenkins' book, now called *Per Fine Ounce*, was submitted to Glidrose, the estate was not at all enthusiastic about the book and they exercised their contractual right not to publish it.

If Ann Fleming had gotten her way, Amis's manuscript, *Colonel Sun,* would also have been rejected. She felt that Amis didn't capture the spirit of Fleming's writing. Glidrose decided to publish the manuscript anyway and *Colonel Sun*, the first Bond continuation novel, was launched on March 28, 1968. That same year, Glidrose Productions changed its name to Glidrose Publications.

Ann was clearly not pleased with the decision. To voice her displeasure, she wrote an unfavorable review of the book for the *Sunday Telegraph*. However, fearing libel, the paper decided not to print it.

An excerpt of *Colonel Sun* was published in the April 1968 edition of *True*, which advertised itself as "The Men's Magazine." The cover boasted, "James Bond in a New Novel with New Girls and a New Villain," alongside the offer that readers could "Win a Sporty Car!" The intro to the excerpt declared, "Since the death of James Bond's creator, Ian Fleming, 007 fans the world over have waited for the return of their hero. Now, reincarnated by a distinguished British novelist, James Bond lives again."

Despite *Colonel Sun*'s success, Glidrose elected not to immediately publish another Bond continuation as they had originally planned. In fact, the next Bond novel that was published was not an original Bond novel. Instead, it was a pseudo-biography of the agent called *James Bond: The Authorized Biography of 007*, written by John Pearson, Fleming's official biographer, and published in 1973.

The next two Bond literary works were novelizations of Bond movies. Glidrose didn't instigate the idea or even select the author, Eon did.[34] The Bond movie producers selected Christopher Wood to novelize his own screenplays of 1977's *The Spy Who Loved Me* and 1979's *Moonraker*. Wood's novelizations were titled *James Bond, The Spy Who Loved Me,* and *James Bond and Moonraker*, respectively to distinguish them from Fleming's originals.

It wasn't until about 13 years had passed that an original Bond novel would be published. In 1980, a year before Ann Fleming's death, Glidrose decided the time was right to publish a traditional sequel Bond novel, not just one based on an Eon film. First, they needed to decide who would take the mantle. According to Janson-Smith, Glidrose didn't want to approach another literary darling like Amis.[35] Such an author would be less likely to write a series of books and presumably, they would be harder to manage.

Glidrose approached John Gardner, a respected British spy novelist and a former Royal Martine, to take up the mantle. Gardner was hired to write not one but three consecutive Bond novels. It was something of a risky venture for both parties. Gardner recalled, "I was conscious by that time that everyone was taking a gamble. When I met Glidrose, I was even more conscious just how much a gamble the idea was...When they drew up the contracts it was for three novels, but because it was such a risky venture there were let outs all the way down the line, which meant that they had to pay me even if I didn't write the books, or if at any time they didn't like what I had written and I was not prepared to change it, then the books would not necessarily [be] published."[36]

Happily, Glidrose accepted Gardner's manuscript and *Licence Renewed* was published in 1981. *Licence Renewed* was followed by *For Special Services, Icebreaker*, and *Role of Honour*, all *New York Times* best sellers. Neither Glidrose nor Gardner expected their relationship to be so fruitful. Each time, Gardner was contracted to write a new cycle of three books. As Gardner explained, "The three book contract became six, then six became nine, and nine became twelve."[37] In total, Gardner wrote 14 original Bond novels and 2 novelizations before he stepped down in 1996, after the publication of his last original Bond novel *COLD*.

After Gardner's last Bond novel, Glidrose selected Raymond Benson, the first American, to write a Bond novel. Like Amis, Benson was a Bond fan and Fleming devotee. Benson wrote a highly praised critical survey and appreciation of Fleming's novels called *The James Bond Bedside Companion*. The 1984 book also included a look at Fleming's life and an overview of the Eon films. However, Benson had never written a novel before. The Texan had, however, written plays and Bond text-based video games. To make sure Glidrose agreed with his approach Benson first obtained approval of his outline and continued submitting chapters as his novel progressed.

Benson didn't continue Gardner's approach to the character. Instead, Benson brought back Bond's various vices (drinking, cigarettes, multiple sexual partners) and put Fleming's Bond into situations that resembled Eon's movies. Benson's approach was dictated, in part, by Glidrose. The author said that he was "told that I should do my best to blend elements of the literary Bond with elements of the more widely known cinematic Bond."[38]

Benson's approach was successful and from 1997 to 2002, Benson wrote six original Bond novels, three Bond novelizations, and three short stories that appeared in *TV Guide* and *Playboy.* In addition to his original Bond novels, Benson has contributed immeasurably to Bond scholarship and he has interviewed key figures including continuation authors Kingsley Amis and John Gardner, as well as

Glidrose chairman Peter Janson-Smith. It was during Benson's era (in 1999), that Glidrose changed its name to Ian Fleming Publications.

After Benson's tenure ended, there was a six-year pause on Bond continuation novels. During this period, Ian Fleming Publications concentrated on spin-off works. Their first effort was a five-book series by Charlie Higson that looked at Bond's teenage years. Higson's fast-paced books ran from 2005 to 2008 and concentrated on Bond's time at Eton College, a boarding school in Windsor, England.

During that same period, Samantha Weinberg authored a spin-off series called *The Moneypenny Diaries* which included three novels and two short stories about M's secretary, Miss Moneypenny. Not only did Weinberg give Moneypenny a first name—Jane—but she also provided Her Majesty's secret servant with a rich inner life. Weinberg successfully blended the incidents in Fleming's novels with real historical events.

A new era of Bond continuation novels—with a different strategy—was about to begin. Ian Fleming Publications would no longer select a single author to write a series of adult Bond books as they had done with Gardner and Benson. Instead, they would engage a series of authors to write one Bond book apiece. This new approach would ensure that each new book would be heralded as an event.

This new series of books would ignore the movie Bond focusing instead on Fleming's version of the character. Not coincidentally, this new tactic coincided with Ian Fleming's centenary. Ian Fleming Publications made the somewhat unlikely choice of engaging Sebastian Faulks to write the first book in this new cycle.

Faulks was known in literary circles for writing the French Resistance novel *Charlotte Gray* (1999) and, his 600-plus page book about the early stages of psychiatry in the late nineteenth and early twentieth centuries, *Human Traces* (2005). He would later write his self-described "modern-Dickensian novel" *A Week in December* (2009). It was Faulks' unlikely background that appealed to Ian Fleming Publications. As Lucy Fleming explained, "We didn't want a thriller writer. We wanted someone who would read Ian's books and see how he did it. [Faulks] has thought himself into Ian's mind."[39]

Sebastian Faulks kicked off the modern era of Bond novels with *Devil May Care* (2008), a best-seller that was set in the mid-1960s. As part of the conceit of the book, Faulks would "write in the style of Ian Fleming." After reading all of Fleming's books chronologically, Faulks made two important decisions about the plot and setting. He recalled, "The way I attacked it was trying to think of something the villain could do that wasn't gold, wasn't diamonds, wasn't bird droppings—which is what Dr. No is incredibly into. And I thought, well, what about drugs? Because I'd already decided it was going to be a period piece. And I figured the last novel was set in 1965, and Bond was in a very bad way and needed time to get back on full form, so it had to be 1967."[40] So Bond must stop the villainous Dr. Julius Gorner from fortifying his drug empire before he can weaponize it to destroy the fabric of the United Kingdom.

Devil May Care was a huge success for Ian Fleming Publications. *The Guardian* declared "James Bond Smashes Sales Figures," and reported that *Devil May Care* sold over 44,000 copies in four days, and that the special edition that cost £750 sold out all 300 copies in just two hours.[41] Some reports suggested that ultimately Faulks' novel sold nearly 300,000 copies.[42]

Faulks made it clear that he wouldn't be writing a follow-up. Faulks emphatically stated, "One tribute, one centenary, one book."[43] So the question remained, if Faulks wasn't going to write another Bond, what would Ian Fleming Publications do? When asked by *The Sunday Times* about future novels, Faulks suggested that a variety of other novelists could each write a one-off adventure.[44] For a time, that did seem like the path that the Fleming Estate was following.

Faulks was followed by American author Jeffery Deaver's *Carte Blanche* (2011). In it, Bond is stuck in the center of the action as two Sudanese warlords fight for control of the land and an unseen villain uses food insecurity to try to gain ultimate power. Deaver, the second American to write a Bond novel, didn't set his story in the 60s as Faulks did; instead, he set his story in the 21st century. Deaver told me, "I wanted the book to be contemporary, modern-day, I wanted younger readers, to the extent that there are still younger readers, to experience a Bond story the way I had experienced a Bond story." Unlike Amis, Gardner, Benson, and Faulks' novels, Deaver's *Carte Blanche* is not tied to Ian Fleming's continuity. Instead, Deaver rebooted the entire series and wrote what could serve as a brand-new literary continuity.

In 2012, William Boyd was selected to write the next one-off Bond adventure. Boyd returned Bond to Fleming's timeline and set his novel, *Solo* (2013) in 1969. In *Solo*, Bond is celebrating his 45th birthday when he's assigned to go to West Africa to put an end to a civil war. Boyd revealed to me, "I had this ambition to create a portrait of James Bond drawn exclusively by Fleming. The novel is told entirely from Bond's point of view." *The Guardian* and *The New York Times* suggested that Boyd's writing was as good or better than Fleming's.

In 2014, six years after Higson's last Young Bond novel, Steve Cole continued the series with four books that covered Bond's first term at Fettes College in Scotland and his gradual pull into a career in intelligence work.

Ian Fleming Publications then selected Anthony Horowitz to write the next adult Bond novel. Horowitz's *Trigger Mortis* (2015) is set shortly after Fleming's *Goldfinger,* which was widely embraced by critics and Bond fans. As such, he was invited back for another Bond novel *Forever and a Day* (2018), a prequel to Fleming's first Bond novel. The final book in Horowitz's trilogy was *With a Mind to Kill* (2022), a sequel to Fleming's last book. Horowitz's trilogy depicts Bond at three critical stages of his career—a novice spy, an accomplished agent at the height of his powers, and a burnt-out man longing to get out of the nasty spy game.

In 2022, Ian Fleming Publications launched another spin-off series. Kim Sherwood's *Double Or Nothing* (2022) explored three other agents in the Double O division. Bond is largely absent from the narrative; he's missing in action. Still, his presence is felt throughout the book. Because Bond wasn't going to be the focus of *Double Or Nothing*, Sherwood needed to determine who would be. To find her answer, Sherwood researched the modern intelligence community. "This was kind of developed as an idea within intelligence agencies, particularly post-911 when intelligence agencies realized just how monocultural they were, and how diversity could be a strategic asset. So that was really interesting, and that made me think 'Well, it's kind of an invitation to widen out this world and create a more inclusive and modern and realistic and representational MI6. So I thought, 'Well, if I have this more diverse, inclusive, MI6, I can create heroes from all sorts of different backgrounds, and hopefully invite more readers to see themselves as the hero of the story. So we can have a female 00, we can have a black gay 00, we can have a Muslim 00—people bringing in their different perspectives as an asset to the team."[45]

In October 2022, Ian Fleming Publications announced that they would take over publishing responsibilities for Fleming's original Bond novels, effective Spring 2023. In March 2023, the Fleming Estate approached Young Bond author, Charlie Higson to write a story that would coincide with King Charles III's coronation. Higson told me, "[Ian Fleming Publications] said that we should probably want to avoid anything about a villain trying to stop the coronation. I thought, surely that's got to be the plot. Someone is going to try to stop the coronation or assassinate him before he's crowned." The result is the novella *On His Majesty's Secret Service*, which Higson wrote in about a month.

Ian Fleming Publications' newsletter, which is signed by Moneypenny, granted there were some publication bumps along the way. Moneypenny acknowledged, "Agent Higson's book had to overcome various hurdles to be released—not least, logistical issues regarding getting stock out of warehouses and into shops during a bank holiday and coronation." Proceeds for the book went to the National Literary Trust, a UK-based charity promoting literacy. Quite unexpectedly the book became a hit, making the *Sunday Times* best seller list. A short four weeks after its launch, Higson's *On His Majesty's Secret Service* entered its second printing.

In addition to the continuation novels, the Estate has authorized the publication of non-fiction works related to Bond's world. Although those projects fall outside the remits of this volume, they include Henry Chancellor's *James Bond: The Man and His World, the Official Companion to Ian Fleming's Creation* (2005), and two books by Fergus Fleming—*The Man with the Golden Typewriter: Ian Fleming's James Bond Letters* (2015) and *Shaken: Drinking with James Bond and Ian Fleming, the Official Cocktail Book* (2019).

Ian Fleming Publications' partnership with Eon Productions resulted in the creation of Chris Moore's Dutch novelizations of *Octopussy* (1983) and *A View to a Kill* (1985), four Find Your Fate game-novels, loosely based on the Roger Moore film *A View to a Kill*, and six *James Bond Jr.* novels, adapted from the animated series by John Peel and published in 1992.[46]

Their work with Dynamite Entertainment has resulted in numerous original Bond comics, as well as adaptations of Fleming's novels. In addition, they have also sanctioned the production of a series of radio plays with Toby Stephens as 007.

On August 12, 2023, the 59th anniversary of Fleming's passing, Ian Fleming Publications announced that they would start republishing the Bond continuation books under their imprint. Amis' *Colonel Sun*, Pearson's *James Bond: The Authorised Biography*, and Benson's *Zero Minus Ten* were the first three selections.

The significance of the Fleming Estate and Ian Fleming Publications taking control over the Bond books is an important moment in the history of the character. It represents the family retaining ownership and control of Fleming's significant cultural creations, which he shortsightedly sold ownership of in 1964, roughly 59 years earlier.

As long as Bond remains a vital cultural figure, Ian Fleming Publications will likely continue to publish Bond continuation novels and spin-off works that endeavor to stay true to Fleming's protean creation.

PART TWO: THE CONTINUATION WORKS

THE BIRTH OF THE CONTINUATION SERIES

"Continue, my dear friend.
It is interesting for me to see this new Bond."
IAN FLEMING, *Casino Royale*

KINGSLEY AMIS' TENURE—PART ONE
1965

Kingsley Amis wrote *The James Bond Dossier* (1965), a literary review of Fleming's Bond novels, *The Book of Bond or, Every Man His Own 007* (1965), a wry guide for would-be Double O agents, and the continuation novel, *Colonel Sun* (1968).

THE BOOK OF BOND OR EVERY MAN HIS OWN 007 (1965)

Author: Kingsley Amis

Pseudonym: Lt.-Col. William "Bill" Tanner.

In Brief: A tongue-in-cheek manual on how to live the James Bond lifestyle.

Meaning of Title: The title references the books of the Bible, such as the Book of Job.

Chronology: Set after the events of *The Man with the Golden Gun*.

Operation: Not applicable.

Bastard Meter: Not applicable.

Eggs: Eggs Benedict and *Eggs en Cocotte*, aka baked eggs.

Insight into Bond: "There are three main types of men in the 00 Section: double-firsts, gay-soldiers of fortune, and men who count life lost for $1,000 a year."

Summary: Bond's colleague Bill Tanner offers prospective Double O agents insight into how to live like 007.

Commentary: *The Book of Bond or Every Man His Own 007* is not a continuation novel. Instead, it's a spin-off book proffering a tongue-in-cheek manual for prospective field agents. Written from the perspective of Lt.-Col. William "Bill" Tanner, M's chief of staff and Bond's closest friend in the service, it extends the continuity of Fleming's novels and suggests that all of Bond's adventures really took place. Granted, *The Book of Bond* is not generally considered part of the Bond canon. After all, it is a reference guide to Fleming's novels and a sardonic form of literary criticism. Still, because Tanner, the author of record, treats Bond as a real person, *The Book of Bond* can be read as an "in-universe" work.

The Book of Bond was published in the United Kingdom in hardcover by Jonathan Cape and in the United States by The Viking Press in 1965. A Pan edition followed in 1966. It was a means for Jonathan Cape to publish high-quality Bond-related material without selecting a Bond continuation author to write a new installment. It also gave the publisher a way to spotlight Fleming's own novels, which are listed at both the beginning and end of the book. To further bolster the claim that the Book of Bond was a legitimate sequel work, Cape and Pan engaged Fleming's paperback-cover-creator, Raymond Hawkey, to lend his talents to the cover design.

The slim paperback, at only 111 pages, covers various categories, including chapters on Bond's drink, food, smoking, looks, exercise habits, clothing, accessories, car, places that he has visited, gambling habits, as well as his views on M and women. For instance, in the drink section, Tanner recommends that would-be Bonds drink no more than half a bottle of hard alcohol. He estimates, "This is adequately devil-may-care without being too sodden."[47] On food, Tanner suggests, "Your position here is being a gourmet while pretending not to be" and, concerning vehicles, he suggests that "talk lovingly and nostalgically about your first car."[48] On smoking, Bond "never got on with people who didn't smoke or who frowned on it."[49]

Witticisms aside, the book is a heavily annotated guide to Bond's character as described by Fleming. Each category cites references from each of Fleming's novels and refers the reader to the appropriate chapters in each. It's as if Amis stripped out all the plot from Fleming's works and just extracted Bond's tastes, peccadilloes, vices, and personal interests. Young Bond author Charlie Higson observed, "Explaining how why and what to wear, eat drink and gamble, Kingsley's books about Bond are not only a humorous homage to Britain's most enduring fictional spy but also a testament to Amis' unlikely obsession with Fleming and his glamorous imaginary world."[50]

It seems *The Book of Bond* was an offshoot of Amis's research on *The James Bond Dossier,* his 1965 appraisal of Fleming's novels. In *The Life of Kingsley Amis*, biographer Zachary Leader reported on Amis' research methodology for the *Dossier*. Leader wrote, "On the dust jacket of each novel he carefully anatomized its contents, in notes such as 'B[ond] smiles 13 times by p.165' or 'description of nasties 107-8."[51] I have a hunch that Amis took the research he conducted for the *James Bond Dossier* and repurposed it for *The Book of Bond.*

Amis didn't originally intend to write a book-length examination of the Bond novels; instead, he planned to write an appraisal of spy novels in general. In 1963, he told publisher Curtis Brown that he wanted to start with a "major article" on Bond. So, he took his Bond novels with him on vacation, read through them, and took copious notes. The proposed article proved to be too expensive and, arguably, too important for a single article. So Amis bypassed his agent and usual publisher and took the book directly to Jonathan Cape, home of Fleming's work.

Amis finished the manuscript for the *Bond Dossier* in May 1964, and began working on his Bond follow-up, *The Book of Bond,* shortly after that.[52] The majority of *The Book of Bond* was written during Fleming's lifetime. After Fleming's death, publisher Cape postponed its publication until after *The Man with the Golden Gun* (released posthumously) so that Amis could incorporate elements from Fleming's final novel. Amis and Fleming's books were published in quick succession—*Man with the Golden Gun* on April 1, 1965, and *Bond Dossier* two months later on June 1st. *The Book of Bond* came out that fall.[53]

The hardcover edition of *The Book of Bond* includes a reversible dust jacket. The front side comprises the expected information about the title and the author. On the back side, a joke title reads *The Bible to be Read as Literature.* This alternative cover also falsely claimed the book was edited by Terence Cumberland Oates, and promised an introduction by Clarence Bunion. The alternative title alluded to a scene in *Goldfinger*, in which Bond retrieved a book from his suitcase called *The Bible Designed to be Read as Literature*, in which his Walther PPK was hidden.

Amis might have unknowingly predicted a new era in publishing Bond novels. *The Book of Bond* ends with Tanner encouraging Double O agents to join forces and work together. He argued that when multiple agents join forces, "a new era in 007 research and activities will be inaugurated."[54] Tanner (or Amis) was correct in suggesting that "a new era" was forthcoming. The new era would not take the form of additional guidebooks. Instead, continuation works would take hold.

Along with the *Bond Dossier, The Book of Bond* set the stage for Amis to write the first post-Fleming Bond book. It also proved that Amis was a Bond and Fleming expert, and established a working relationship between Amis and Fleming's publisher.

Continuity Nod: All of Fleming's novels are referenced throughout the book.

Bond's History: Little is revealed, save for a lunch that Bond shared with Tanner in Piccadilly Circus at a restaurant named Scott's. Both Bond and Tanner ate crab and had black velvet cake for dessert.

Bond's Personal Life: Bond is a good golfer, but his swing is rather flat.

Bond's Inner Life: "What really appeals to [Bond's aesthetic sense], such as it is, is modern luxury trains, antique trains, ocean liners, ocean-going yachts, casinos, cards, birds, and fish. And girls, of course."

Bond's Tastes: Bill Tanner suggests that Bond sticks to hard liquor, and avoids soft drinks; he is a gourmand but pretends not to be. Bond avoids friendships with non-smokers, gaudy clothes, and eating with women at his home.

Bond's Work Life: According to Tanner, each week sixty would-be spies submit applications to the British Secret Service; most of those applications are for the Double O Section. However, the Secret Intelligence Service (SIS) does not recruit through this method. So one of Tanner's jobs is to write rejection letters to these would-be agents. Bond keeps a cyanide pill hidden in the handle of his razor. 007 knows five different ways to kill a man with a single blow.

Assorted Observations:

- Tanner references seven-time Bond movie actor Sean Connery.
- Amis employed an alias for two of his Bond books: *Colonel Sun* and *The Book of Bond or, Every Man His Own 007*. In the United Kingdom, his name only appears in *The James Bond Dossier*. The US edition gives Amis' name on the cover.

ARTHUR CALDER-MARSHALL'S TENURE 1967

Arthur Calder-Marhsall wrote the Bond spin-off children's book *The Adventures of James Bond Junior 003½.*

THE ADVENTURES OF JAMES BOND JUNIOR 003½ (1967)

Author: Arthur Calder-Marshall

Pseudonym: R. D. Mascott

In Brief: 007's nephew, James Bond Junior, suspects his new neighbor of stealing gold bullion and concealing it on his property.

Alternate Title: *003½: The Adventures of James Bond Junior*

Meaning of Title: Refers to the nickname of 007's nephew, who possesses some of the same admirable qualities as his uncle.

Chronology: Set during the 1960s.

Operation: Barker

Bastard Meter: James Bond's bastard level is not addressed.

Eggs: Two fried eggs.

Insight into Bond: "He was alone. He would always be alone." Written about James Bond Junior, but it also applies to 007.

Summary: James Bond Junior is the son of Flight Captain David Bond and Mrs. Bond. The Bonds live in England, on the border of Kent and Sussex. David and Mrs. Bond need to immediately leave town so that they can look after Mrs. Bond's sister who lives in Africa. Although his parents prefer James to accompany them, they reluctantly agree to let him stay home, under the care of their housekeeper, Mrs. Raggles.

Mrs. Frame owned Hazeley Hall, a private estate close to David and Mrs. Bond's home, until her recent death. Mrs. Frame used to tease James about being the nephew of James Bond 007, the famous spy. Similarly, local children and their parents know of 007's exploits and they have given James Junior the nickname of 003½.

James has never met 007, but his uncle sent him a sheath knife as a gift.

Hazeley Hall had recently been put up for auction. The Bonds attempted to purchase the land, but they were outbid by a private speculator named Mr. Merck. While his parents are away, James wants to explore the property and hunt for its treasures.

As soon as his parents leave town, James rushes to Hazeley Hall and discovers that the property is now protected by barbed wire and guard dogs. Unable to gain entry, James then decides to visit his friend Squirrel Joram. To save time, he cuts through the land owned by Sir Cuthbert Conningtower, a local resident. Along the way, he spots a young Irish girl crying over the body of her dead dog. The Irish girl picks up the carcass of the dead animal and runs away.

Bond continues his trek and spots some men on the land and he then calls after them and announces that he wants to meet Mr. Merck, but the men ignore him. The Irish girl comes out of the house. Bond tries to get her attention, but an adult woman grabs the girl and brings her back inside.

James returns home and tells Mrs. Raggles that Merck changed the public path into a private one. Mrs. Raggles is unconcerned. James goes into his father's study and retrieves the auction catalog for Merck's newly acquired estate, and discovers that Merck was legally within his right to make the path private. James wonders if Merck purchased the property with the express purpose of sealing off the land to the public.

James convinces the local mailman, Nobby Scales, to let him accompany Nobby to Hazeley when he drops off their mail. When Nobby delivers the mail to Hazeley, he's warned never to return. As Nobby gets back into his truck, a guard dog rushes him. While trying to flee, Nobby accidentally runs over the dog with his truck. Nobby begs James not to tell anyone what happened. Nobby explains that if anyone found out that he brought James with him on his mail rounds, he would be fired. James agrees not to tell a soul.

Sometime later, James goes into town and spots the Irish girl at a store. Offering her candy, James learns that the girl's name is Sheelagh Smith. Sheelagh explains that she loves drawing, but she cannot afford drawing materials. James explains that Mrs. Frame, the previous owner of the estate, let him keep art supplies at Hazeley Hall. If James can get back in, he could recover the materials and then give them to Sheelagh.

James meets up with his friends Squirrel Joram, Bobbie Maws, and Bill Asher, who collectively call themselves the Pride of Lions.". With Mrs. Frames' permission, the Pride used to play on her property.

However, now that Merck has bought it, they are unable to continue their games. The boys decide to irritate Merck by taunting his dogs and making them bark all night. They call their scheme Barker's Operation.

That night, James and his friends go to the farmhouse and try to create a nuisance, but only find one dog and it refuses to bark. James speculates that the other dog has been moved to protect another nefarious operation. On their way to Hazeley Hall, the boys spot a car being driven by Sir Cuthbert. James notices that the blonde woman in the passenger seat is not Cuthbert's wife, Lady Conningtower. James wonders what Cuthbert is doing with this mysterious woman.

James, Bobbie, and Bill make it to Hazeley Hall and see a series of camouflaged trucks entering the property. James notices that even though it's dark, the trucks do not have their lights on. James believes something is amiss.

James returns home to tell Mrs. Raggles what he discovered. Much to his chagrin, Mrs. Raggles does not believe that there is any wrongdoing. Raggles warns James, "I'm not going to have any of that 007 nonsense in this house." Ignoring Mrs. Raggles' admonishment, James decides to call Sir Cuthbert and enlist his help. When Lady Conningtower answers, James innocently informs her that he saw Sir Cuthbert driving his car earlier that night. Lady Conningtower is surprised by the information. So, when she asks James if her husband was alone, James does not mention the blonde woman in the car. Lady Conningtower takes the message, assuring James that she will have her husband call back the next day.

The following morning, James meets up with Sheelagh so that he can give her his art supplies. At the farm, James notices a lapse in the security at Hazeley; the space between the two areas is not fenced in. Sheelagh appears and introduces James to her new dog who she calls Satan.

James and Sheelagh break into the garden and cottage and locate the art supplies. He wraps them up to give them to Sheelagh. James asks Sheelagh to draw what she sees on the property. Unbeknownst to Sheelagh, James plans to use her drawings of Hazeley as a de facto map of the property, which he can use to sneak inside.

The next day, James reads a newspaper article detailing a robbery worth two million pounds of gold. The robbery took place about 40 miles away from Hazeley Hall. James tells Mrs. Raggles about the trucks he saw last night and theorizes that they might have been carrying the stolen loot. Mrs. Raggles tells Bond that unless he has evidence, no one will believe him.

In town, James encounters Sir Cuthbert who offers to give him a ride back up the hill in his Jaguar. While driving, Cuthbert explains to James that he wasn't driving last night so there is no way that James could have seen him. James doesn't argue with this obvious lie. James tells Cuthbert about the gold and the trucks, but Cuthbert doesn't buy young Bond's theory. Instead, Cuthbert tells James to ask 007 for help. James leaves the conversation feeling dejected.

James goes for a hike near Hazeley Hall. Along the way, he sees Merck in the passenger seat of a truck, heading to the ammunition dump. Soon after, James spots Sheelagh with her dog. Sheelagh confides in James and explains that her mom is missing and her dad ran off. Now, she lives at the farm with Auntie Mo, who is the girlfriend of Merck's driver Donal. Sheelagh's job is to tend to the guard dogs.

At the farmhouse, Sheelagh kisses James and shows him her drawings, including an illustration of Merck's girlfriend. James buys the drawing from her for a guinea.

That night, James tells Mrs. Raggles about his mounting concerns. Raggles suggests that James should wait until his parents return home so that he can enlist their help. Not wanting to wait any longer, James grabs his camera and decides to get proof that Merck stole the gold. James sneaks out of his house to investigate.

James heads to the ammunition dump and sees the guard dogs. The dogs' presence at the dump suggests that Merck is hiding something there, possibly gold bullion. James tries to sneak in and take photos, but the dogs are alerted to his presence. Merck arrives, produces a gun, and fires blindly into the bushes. James gets away and discovers that Donal and his men are searching for another gang who have come to steal the gold bullion. James escapes by swimming through a lake and channels, eventually taking refuge behind a waterfall. Once Bond passes through the water, the guard dogs will not be able to catch his scent. The water-soaked Bond stays in his hiding spot all night and catches a terrible cold.

James returns home and finds that Mrs. Raggles is up, waiting for him. James doesn't care if he's in trouble as in his mind, he's proven that Merck is hiding something in the ammunition dump. Mrs. Raggles listens to James's story, puts him to bed, and then calls Sir Cuthbert to tell him what she's learned about Merck.

When James wakes up the next day, Mrs. Raggles is listening to a radio report indicating that the criminals were apprehended, and the gold was recovered. The report praises Sir Cuthbert for cracking the case.

A doctor arrives, examines James, and concludes he has pneumonia and a torn ligament in his ankle. The doctor teases James that he will have to do something pretty impressive in his life if he wants to compete with the likes of 007.

A few days later, James is visited by Sir Cuthbert. Cuthbert claims that he was investigating the case based on the recommendation of Audrey Wedderburn (the blonde woman who is revealed to be his mistress). James is suspicious and believes that Cuthbert is unfairly claiming credit for the case.

Later, James recovers and visits Sheelagh, who says that she's leaving the area and is going back to stay with her mom. It turns out that her mother was in prison for shoplifting and has now been released. Due to the publicity of the gold bullion case, Sheelagh and her mom were able to reunite.

The Bonds return home. The criminals who stole the gold are prosecuted to the fullest extent of the law and the property on which Hazeley Hall sits is broken up into smaller lots and sold off at auction. This time, the Bond family can afford some of the land. So they buy the plot containing the stables, the garden, and the cottage. James decides that he will use the cottage as his secret lair from which he can solve future cases.

Commentary: Surprisingly, the first post-Fleming Bond novel was not about 007; instead, it was about his young nephew. In 1967, Jonathan Cape published *The Adventures of James Bond Junior 003½,* which was retitled *003½: The Adventures of James Bond Junior* for the American edition. *The Adventures of James Bond Junior* is an adventure book that is squarely aimed at young readers; the inner flap indicates that it's "a story for boys and girls aged 8-14." The spin-off book is not unlike the Hardy Boys mysteries book series in which the teenage brothers get embroiled in adult-sized mysteries.[55]

The book is filled with sympathetic observations about being a child in a world controlled by adults. For instance, "The advantage of being young may be that you find out things which no grownup could get to know. The disadvantage is that no grownup is prepared to believe you." Despite its strengths, *The Adventures of James Bond Junior* is still not widely read, even among Bond aficionados.

According to the cover of the book, the author is R.D. Mascott. However, Mascott is a pseudonym. *James Bond Junior*'s true author has been a long-standing question in the Bond community. *007 Forever*, a now-defunct fan site, described it "as a frustrating and perplexing question. For a Bond fan, it was an intriguingly elusive mystery, like asking, 'Who killed JFK?'"[56] Similarly, Jake Rossen observes in his article "No One Knows Who Wrote This James Bond Novel," "For Bond fans, what started as a passing bit of trivia grew into a literary forensics cold case."[57] The cold case dates back to the 1960s.

A publisher does not traditionally advertise the fact that a pseudonym has been used. Glidrose let the cat out of the bag in the "About the Author" section of the book. In it, they reveal that "R.D. Mascot is a pseudonym of a well-known British writer."

Over the years, many well-known authors became suspects. Kingsley Amis and Roald Dahl, the beloved author of *Charlie and the Chocolate Factory* and the screenwriter of *You Only Live Twice,* were both thought to have written *The Adventures of James Bond Junior.*

The list of subjects has shrunk over time, and it has been a long-held suspicion that Arthur Calder-Marshall, a critic, biographer, essayist, and novelist authored the book, but that's never been confirmed. However, while writing my book *The Lost Adventures of James Bond*, I was able to verify, via his family members, that the book's true author is Calder-Marshall. Both Anna Calder-Marshall, his actress daughter, and Tom Burke, his grandson and an actor, confirmed that Calder-Marshall wrote *The Adventures of James Bond Junior.*

It is worth noting that *The Adventures of James Bond Junior* is more nuanced and adult-themed than a typical adventure book. For instance, James Bond Junior discovers that Sir Cuthbert Conningtower, an esteemed member of the community, is having an extramarital affair. Additionally, despite his efforts in recovering the gold and bringing the villains to justice, young Bond walks away with only a limited victory. In the end, the adults do not give young James the credit he deserves for solving the case. Instead, the philandering Sir Cuthbert takes the glory.

Even though James Bond Junior is not recognized for his bravery or his help in bringing the criminals to justice, Mascott gives the boy high praise: "The way this schoolboy had bucked everyone in this blind drive to find what was hidden in [the estate] was as good as anything that precious 007 had done."[58]

The Adventures of James Bond Junior set the stage for other spin-off adventures set in Bond's world. In 1991, Eon produced *James Bond Jr.*, the animated TV series about 007's nephew, which was also adapted into a series of books and comics. Similarly, the Young Bond novels, written by Charlie Higson and then Steve Cole, are a series of nine books published over a twelve-year span that explores 007's exploits as a teen. The first Young Bond novel, *SilverFin* (2005), was later adapted into a graphic novel by Higson. The comic book company Dynamite Entertainment published *James Bond Origin* (2018–2019), a twelve-issue series about seventeen-year-old Bond's adventures in World War II. The series spanned Bond's time as a student at Fettes College to his service as a Lieutenant in the Special Branch of the Royal Navy. The series concluded long before Bond rose up the ranks to Commander, let alone becoming a Double O agent.

Continuity Nod: The stolen gold bullion that consumes James Bond Junior's thoughts could be a reference to Auric Goldfinger's interest in gold.

Bond's Family History: *The Adventures of James Bond Junior* takes liberties with 007's ancestry. In the novel *On Her Majesty Secret Service*, Bond tells a genealogist that he has no relatives or children."[59] Fleming seems to confirm Bond's account in *You Only Live Twice*. In the obituary for the presumed-dead agent, M writes that Bond has "no relative living."[60] Whereas 007 is an only child in Fleming's work, Mascott extends the spy's family tree. 007 has a brother named Captain David Bond who is a commercial pilot; a sister-in-law who is only referred to as Mrs. Bond (no first name is given), a co-sister-in-law named Penny, and a nephew who shares the same name.

James Junior laments that he never met his uncle and that his parents never see him either; it appears that 007 "was always on some mission or other."[61] The fact that James Junior never sees his uncle might have been included to explain why 007's brother and his family are never mentioned in Fleming's work. However, it does make Bond seem like a poor uncle.

The Apple Doesn't Fall Far From the Bond Family Tree: James Junior shares some qualities with his famous uncle. Like 007, James Junior is resourceful, compelled to uncover secrets, and trusts his instincts. Sir Cuthbert, who attempts to undermine and thwart James Junior, grudgingly acknowledges that the boy shares "something of your uncle's flair." Mrs. Raggles, his housekeeper, lovingly suggests that he is a "proper little devil," a description that might also apply to 007.

James Junior and 007 have several traits in common. For instance, James Junior trains in judo and carries a sheath knife, a gift from his uncle. Like 007, James Junior has two keen interests, women and playing the detective. Both seem to prefer the latter. Both understand how difficult it is to balance relationships and the responsibility they feel to complete their assignment. Calder-Marshall explains, James Junior "felt torn. He would have liked to play with Sheelagh. He liked [her] almost as much as to play the detective. But to do both was hard." 007 and his nephew are more interested in their mission than they are in ladies. James chooses to solve the mystery rather than prioritize his blossoming relationship with Sheelagh. Moreover, James Junior manipulates her to accomplish his mission. Calder-Marshall explains, "He realized that he had an opportunity to use Sheelagh to spy on her own people." It's a grown-up but calculated decision. While James Junior contends that he's "only a schoolboy," he has the makings of a spy.

Bond's Work Methods: Apparently, Bond does not keep his career as a spy very secret. Throughout the book, different characters tease young James about his famous uncle. Even the housemaster at his school in North Yorkshire, England inquiries about the association. "'Tell me, what's it like, James, being overshadowed by 007?'"[62] Bond is famous in the book, even though the identity of a secret agent shouldn't be known by school kids.

It's worth noting that the 1991 animated series *James Bond Jr.* employed a similar conceit in that the identities of 007 and his nephew James Bond Junior were known to the villains and Junior's classmates. Because the target audience of *The Adventures of James Bond Junior* and *James Bond Jr.* were adolescents, it's sometimes best to take these matters at face value. Nevertheless, there are other instances in the franchise when 007 steps into the public spotlight. Among them, in Fleming's novel, *You Only Live Twice*, the presumed-dead agent's obituary appears in the newspaper, and we learn that Bond briefly appeared on television newscasts in both John Gardner's novel *Icebreaker* (1983) and Raymond Benson's short story "Live at Five" (1999).[63]

Bedtime for Bond: The complete accounting of the origins of the 003½ moniker is still unknown. However, there is some evidence to suggest that it was initially an advertising initiative. It appears that before the release of *The Adventures of James Bond Junior 003½,* at least one 003½ product was available for purchase. During the height of Bondmania, manufacturers slapped "James Bond" or "007" on an overwhelming number of products and called it a day. Some products like Corgi's Aston Martin DB5 or Multiple Toymakers' attaché case were natural extensions of the brand. However, just as many peculiar retail tie-ins went on sale in the early to mid-1960s. In his book *Ian Fleming: The Complete Man*, Nicholas Shakespeare reported that the makers of the Bond films approved the sale of 007-branded cosmetics, hair dye, lingerie, and kid's pajamas with the number 003½ emblazoned on them. In the instance of the pajamas, it could be that a creative marketing executive thought of the 003½ label as a way to justify the Bond connection and advertise their product to children. Thus 003½ was born. Once 003½ was established in the marketplace, it was only natural that a book would follow.

James Bond Junior Spin-Off Series: It's possible that the Bond movie producers were considering adapting the book *The Adventures of James Bond Junior* into a live-action production. On Sunday, July 10, 1966, *The New York Times* reported that Eon was turning the book into a television series or a film. According to the article "Pint-Sized Bonded Stuff on Tap," the project was conceived as "a comedy-adventure about a 10-year-old boy—003½—who is not crazy about girls but is just as clever as Bond." *The New York Times* also reported that Eon was meeting with writers to discuss the adaptation. The July 22, 1967, edition of *The Book Seller* similarly reported that Saltzman "plans to make a series of television feature films based on the book."[64] *The Book Seller* article offers no added information so it's possible that they were simply restating the *New York Times* piece.

Setting aside that the story appears in the *New York Times*, there are reasons to take the account with a grain of salt. For starters, why would the sole source of information for the article go unnamed? It is possible that the project was real and that someone from Eon was not authorized to talk about the adaptation but did so for their own reasons. Alternatively, these kinds of generic stories are sometimes planted by someone hoping to jump-start a project with a little positive press buzz. If that were the case, then the story could have been planted by someone with a personal stake in the adaptation. Of course, it is possible that Eon had hoped to adapt the book, but nothing came of the project, as is often the case.

Irrespective of the veracity of the articles, it's interesting to note that the spin-off book about Bond's nephew was being discussed as a possible series or film. Had it come to pass, then I imagine that *The Adventures of James Bond Junior* would occupy a greater space in Bond lore than it does now.

KINGSLEY AMIS' TENURE—PART TWO
1968

COLONEL SUN (1968)

Author: Kingsley Amis

Pseudonym: Robert Markham

In Brief: Bond must rescue M who has been kidnapped by the sadistic Colonel Sun Liang-tan of the People's Liberation Army.

Meaning of Title: Refers to Bond's titular adversary.

Chronology: Set after *The Man with the Golden Gun.*

Operation: Not applicable.

Bastard Meter: Not applicable.

Eggs: Not ordered by Bond.

Insight Into Bond: "He knew instantly that he had not gone soft, that at need he was the same efficient fighting machine as ever.

Summary: James Bond is playing golf with his friend and colleague Bill Tanner. Bond and Tanner are unaware that they are being surveilled by a man wearing sunglasses. After the match, Bond goes to M's house and discovers intruders who hold Bond at gunpoint and show him his unconscious drugged boss. The intruders inject Bond with a hypodermic needle. Bond overpowers them, and escapes from the house, but passes out before he can seek help.

When Bond comes to, he learns that M has been kidnapped. The only clue to the identity of the kidnappers is a piece of paper found in the wallet of one of M's abductors. The paper contains the names and numbers of what appear to be women, "Christiana," "Vasso," "Antigone," and "Paris." The Secret Service correctly concludes that the names are clues to the kidnappers' destination and since they are all Greek, M has been taken to Greece. However, given the ease with which they decoded the paper, they also deduce it has been left intentionally to lure Bond to the villains. Still, Bond has no choice but to follow the clues.

M awakens in Greece and meets his captor Colonel Sun Liang-tan, head of China's People's Liberation Army.

Bond heads to Greece but with no additional clues, he has to wait for the enemy to find him. Sitting at a bar, Bond spots a Turkish man strong-arming a Greek woman. Knowing that it might be a trap, Bond nonetheless steps in and scares the Turkish man away. Bond invites the woman for a drink. She accepts and introduces herself as Ariadne Alexandrou. The drinks turn to dinner and then to an impromptu tour of Greece, including the Acropolis. Suddenly two men approach. Ariadne warns Bond that the men are enemies and Bond overcomes them.

After the fight, Ariadne tells Bond that she was assigned to bring Bond to two other men. However, when the two men approached, and they failed to provide the correct recognition signal, she knew that they were adversaries who wanted to abduct Bond. Ariadne tells Bond that she wants to introduce Bond to someone. Bond acquiesces.

Ariadne, a Greek communist, takes Bond to meet a Russian named Gordienko and his associates Tzimas and Markos. Gordienko tells Bond that they are planning to detain Bond for a few days and then let him go. Gordienko is under orders to protect Bond, not harm him. Gordienko explains that they are on the same side, and he suggests that they team up to defeat whoever it was that tried to kidnap him. Gordienko also reveals that he is planning an unspecific "event" that is to take place within three days. As the conversation continues, they hear a noise. Tzimas investigates the disturbance, but he is killed in the process. Markos is also slain as Bond, Ariadne, and Gordienko manage to escape.

The next day, Bond and Ariadne agree to join forces. Bond wants to visit the bookshop that a former Double O agent named Stuart Thomas used to run. However, when Bond arrives at the bookstore, he discovers that it has been burnt down. Later, Bond asks Ariadne about the "event" that Gordienko mentioned. While she won't reveal the exact nature of it, she does tell Bond that it will take place on Vrakonisi Island, about 120 miles away. They try to enlist the aid of Niko Litsas, a sailor who served under Ariadne's father in the fight against communism, to take them to the island. They tell him that their mission is to aid Greece, Russia, and Britain. At first, Litsas refuses to help them, as he believes Bond might be a communist. When Litsas learns that Von Richter, a Nazi, has also been inquiring about transportation to the island, Litsas agrees to help Bond and Ariadne. Bond, Ariadne, and Litsas board his ship, the *Altair*.

On the *Altair*, Ariadne reveals that a secret international conference is going to take place in Vrakonisi. Delegates from Russia, Greece, and other countries will be in attendance. The Chinese government wants to disrupt the conference, kill the delegates, and frame the British for the massacre by dumping Bond and M's dead bodies on the island. Once Bond and M's corpses are discovered, it will seem like the English are responsible for the attack, diminishing English prestige. Simultaneously, Russia will be blamed for failing to protect their conference. As a result, the region will become unstable, and China will have an opportunity to step in and take control. Tensions will rise, and the stage will be set for a third world war.

Arriving at the island, Bond, Ariadne, and Litsas go into town and learn that Von Richter is there and that he has a cottage on the east end of the island. Bond wonders, if the conference will take place on the west end of the island, then what is the connection to this cottage on the opposite end?

Bond keeps watch and eventually spots Von Richter transporting men and a small trench mortar. Bond doesn't comprehend how the small weapon could possibly topple the venue where the conference is being held. He follows Von Richter to a meeting with Colonel Sun.

A Russian security agent discovers Bond. Niko kills the agent and Bond escapes. To avoid being caught, Bond, Niko, and Adrianne switch from the *Altair* to a smaller vessel, the *Cynthia*. They enlist a local fisherman, Ionides, to pilot the *Altair* in one direction while the *Cynthia* goes in the opposite direction. The Russians capture the *Altair* because they think Bond is hiding there. Under threat of death, Ionides tells the Russians how to find the *Cynthia*. Soon thereafter, the Russians track down Bond's boat. Unable to fight back, Bond swims to shore. Once on dry land, Bond is captured.

Bond is brought to Colonel Sun and is reunited with M. Sun tells Bond that he's going to torture the agent for the sheer pleasure of it. Sun also tells Bond he will use Von Richter's weapon to assassinate the delegates, so it will be associated with British warfare. Bond deduces that Sun will be using the trench mortar to kill everyone at the conference.

Colonel Sun begins the torture by stabbing a metal skewer into Bond's ear and sticks another skewer up his nostril. Colonel Sun directs Luisa Tartini, an Italian woman whom Sun has abused, to sexually humiliate Bond. Instead, she unfastens Bond's restraints and slips him a knife. Seizing on the opportunity, Bond takes Luisa's knife and stabs Sun in the back.

Bond leaves the cellar, locates M, and the two escape the compound. Then, Bond finds Von Richter, who has started firing the trench mortar at the delegates. Bond tries to attack Von Richter, but 007 trips and is momentarily vulnerable. Niko arrives, shoots Von Richter, and saves 007.

Bond returns to Sun's headquarters and discovers that Colonel Sun is still alive. Bond tracks him down. Sun threatens to blow up both himself and Bond by detonating a mortar. Before Sun can do so, Bond fatally stabs his adversary. Sun's plan has failed, and the delegates are safe.

For his bravery, Bond is offered the Order of the Red Banner, a Soviet military decoration. As a Double O agent, Bond cannot accept. Before he goes back to London, Bond and Ariadne agree to enjoy each other's company.

Commentary: As discussed earlier, before Fleming's death in August 1964, Kingsley Amis had been working with Glidrose and Cape on two Bond-related books—*The James Bond Dossier* and *The Book of Bond or Every Man His Own 007. The James Bond Dossier* was an astute appraisal of Fleming's Bond novels. His second volume, *The Book of Bond*, was a tongue-in-cheek guide to living the Bond lifestyle. In both works, Amis displayed his unbridled enthusiasm and affinity for Fleming's work.

Prior to *The James Bond Dossier*, Amis had been working for publisher Victor Gollancz Ltd. However, he opted to use Fleming's publisher Jonathan Cape for this Bond-related work. In a letter to Gollancz on May 1, 1964, Amis explained his reasoning, "I don't think that this is all your sort of book in several ways. I'm pretty sure in my own mind that you have very little time for Fleming and the Fleming cult; at the very least, your heart wouldn't be in it...The hearts of Jonathan Cape would be very much in this venture, and, as you well know, they have an immense Fleming distribution machine already functioning."[65] In the same letter, Amis assured Gollancz that working with Cape would be a strictly one-off venture. However, that's not the way things panned out; *The James Bond Dossier* led to *The Book of Bond*, which led to *Colonel Sun.*

Given his working relationship with Cape on Bond-related books, Amis was the natural successor to Fleming. Amis' biographer Zachary Leader reported that Tom Mashler, publisher and managing director of Cape, originally suggested that Amis write the first Bond adult sequel.[66] Although the publisher had previously invited Amis to edit a science-fiction anthology[67] that didn't come to pass, and Mashler seemed eager to persuade Amis to work with Cape. Perhaps, Mashler reasoned, that once Cape established a productive relationship with Amis, the author might be tempted to collaborate with them again. And that's exactly what happened. After *Colonel Sun*, Amis worked with Cape on several non-Bond books, including *I Want it Now* (1968), *The Green Man* (1969), *Girl 20* (1971), *Ending Up* (1974), and *Jake's Thing* (1978).

Colonel Sun has two undeniable highlights. The first high point is the daring kidnapping of M. Not only does it start off the novel with an exciting sequence, but it also signals a change in the nature of the novels. In *Colonel Sun*, M's function in the story significantly increased. M is no longer simply outlining Bond's adversary and giving orders. Now, M is the object of Bond's mission.

In some ways, Amis was following Fleming's instinct. In Fleming's previous book, *The Man with the Golden Gun*, a brainwashed Bond tries to kill M, and in *Moonraker*, Bond goes to M's private club to help him out on a personal matter. So the increased importance of M in *Colonel Sun* was a natural progression. It also raises the stakes. Not only does Bond need to save the Chief of the Secret Intelligence Service, but M is Bond's father figure and this is an opportunity to make amends for past transgressions.

Incorporating M into the story to that extent was a fresh idea when *Colonel Sun* was published in 1968. Since then, Eon's movies have taken a page from Amis' book. Starting with the Pierce Brosnan era and moving through Daniel Craig's tenure, the Eon films have followed Amis' lead and made M a greater focus. Brosnan's third outing, *The World Is Not Enough*, also features the kidnapping of Judi Dench's M.

The other standout sequence in *Colonel Sun* is an extended sadistic torture scene. After shackling Bond to a chair in a small cellar in Greece, Colonel Sun thrusts metal skewers into Bond's head via his ear and nose. The agonizing scene leaves Bond spent, exhausted, scared, and near death—at one point, he vomits. It's arguably the most visceral torture scene since *Casino Royale* when Bond was beaten in the groin with a carpet-beater. The memorable sequence, in which Colonel Sun asks a woman to sexually assault a helpless Bond, comprises a full chapter of the book and is appropriately titled "The Theory and Practice of Torture." One aspect that makes the scene so memorable is that Colonel Sun is not attempting to extract any information from Bond. Instead, Sun is torturing 007 for the sheer pleasure of it.

Colonel Sun Goes to the Movies: The terrifying torture scene from the book was adapted for the big screen in *Spectre*. A few passages of dialogue from Amis' book were included in the movie. Viewers with keen eyes may have noted that the acknowledgments section of the credits include a thank you to the Estate of Kingsley Amis. To date, *Colonel Sun* is the only continuation novel to have been openly adapted—even in this limited way—to an Eon production.

Continuity Nod: Bond is still recovering from the wounds he incurred from Scaramanga's derringer in the previous book *The Man with the Golden Gun*. Bond is still driving the Bentley and there is a fleeting reference to the events of *You Only Live Twice* and his trip to the USSR, which occurred between Fleming's eleventh and twelfth novels.

Bond's History: As a kid, Bond enjoyed John Buchan's book *The Thirty-Nine Steps* and was fascinated by the character who could "hood his eyes like a hawk." Bond identifies more with his Scottish side than his English one. Since the events of *Man with the Golden Gun*, Bond has been on two minor missions—one in New York and the other in Hong Kong.

Bond's Personal Life: Bond frequently plays golf at Sunningdale New Course and has a group of three friends who he regularly sees. A love-struck Bond asks Ariadne Alexandrou to come back to London with him. She declines.

Bond's Inner Life: When *Colonel Sun* begins, Bond's mental health is causing him the most concern. 007 wonders if he's going soft. His work life isn't as challenging as it used to be; his missions aren't as challenging. Bond is also suffering from nightmares. In one, a formless creature chases him, and trees explode in puffs of fire. The agent fears that he might not have the edge he needs. Over the course of the novel, Bond is put to the test and emerges rejuvenated.

Bond's Work Methods: When Bond is being tortured, he tries to control the situation using two methods, one practical and the other mental. Bond uses breathing techniques to control the pain. He also tries to create a mental wall between him and the pain.

Book Cover: The original *Colonel Sun* book cover is a striking illustration. It features a naked female figure, but her head is replaced by an oversized ear and nose; a giant floating blood-shot eye floats above her in the background; a volcano spews smoke and morphs into a dragon, and a gun melts. The cover is one of the most arresting images among all the continuation novels. Yet, I suspect that, at the time, potential readers were confused by Tom Adams' surrealistic cover design, which was a severe departure from Richard Chopping's realistic covers of Fleming's books.

Spelled in symbols—Bond is back

THE REINCARNATION of James Bond, blunt instrument of the British Secret Service, is complete.

As long promised, the late Ian Fleming's dauntless, dissolute hero returns to the bookstands this Spring in a new adventure, Colonel Sun.

The literary kiss of life was applied by novelist Kingsley Amis. And this (below) is the book jacket designed to propel the new-image Bond into the best-seller lists. The jacket was painted by Tom Adams and is surrealistic by intent. Publishers Jonathan Cape wanted a new-look facade for the Amis Bond.

To elucidate: The setting is a volcanic Greek island, the broken columns aloft Bond's rather fluid Walther PPK lending the Grecian touch. Smoke from the volcano reveals Colonel Sun as a Chinese villain and the sex-and-sadism background so necessary to true Bondage is clearly symbolised. No new Bond for old, however.

"Amis has captured all the old Fleming flavour," say Cape.

Except that Amis does not appear on the jacket as Amis. He lurks under the pseudonym Robert Markham. He wants to keep his Bond books distinct from his Amis writings.

Adams, incidentally, says his cover design is a pastiche of Magritte and Dali.

Cape have been approached several times with offers to buy the original.

Tom Adams' *Colonel Sun* book cover art is highlighted in an article that includes a sneak peek at the "new-look façade for the Amis Bond. Adams was inspired by the work of Salvador Dali and René Magritte. Courtesy of Robin Harbour

Adams' effort might have been designed as a deliberate parting from previous covers. It could have been a way to signal to readers this was a modern Bond novel of the late 1960s having shed the old-fashioned trappings of the early 1950s, when *Casino Royale* was first published. However, despite the undeniable artistry of Adams' work, the cover does not, on its face, suggest the world of the literary Bond. Nor does the cover link Amis's novel to Fleming's. If the publisher aimed to suggest that *Colonel Sun* was a direct continuation of

Fleming's novels, then a Dali-esque cover might not have been the most consumer-friendly choice.

Granted, it's an arresting image and one that might not be out of place in an opening credit sequence of an Eon Bond movie. Adams also created the covers of dozens of Agatha Christie novels so selecting him as the cover artist made sense. Ironically, while Adams' cover is not in the style of Fleming's previous books, he was initially hired in 1961 by Cape to produce a cover for John Fowles's *The Collector* in the style of Chopping, Fleming's go-to hardback cover designer.[68]

Assorted Observations:

- The Daily Express published a faithful adaptation of *Colonel Sun* as part of its ongoing James Bond comic strip series. This is the only continuation novel to have been adapted into comic strips. The story was leisurely told over 219 strips from December 1, 1969 to August 28, 1970.[69]
- The front of the *Colonel Sun* cover design was repurposed in 1970 by Ballantine Books for *Timepivot* by Brian Ball. However, they used Tom Adams' art without notifying or paying him. Being gracious, Adams said that he tried to take their actions as a form of praise for his work.[70] Bond expert Brad Frank noted that the back of the art was used on another Ballantine sci-fi book, *To Open The Sky* by Robert Silverberg.
- The book reads like a love letter to Greece and Amis's research and trip to Greece undoubtedly had a significant effect on the writer. Much of the book is made up of observations and facts about Greek culture, food, attractions, and its people, all in the Fleming-vein.
- Stuart Thomas, a Welshman and a retired Double O agent, used to carry the 005 designation. He has since run a bookshop in Greece. However, that was his last cover, as Thomas dies in *Colonel Sun*.

POST AMIS YEARS

After the release of *Colonel Sun*, Glidrose did not immediately put their plan into place to publish another continuation Bond under the Robert Markham pseudonym or, for that matter, under any other name. There were several factors against Glidrose immediately commissioning another Bond continuation novel. The reviews of *Colonel Sun* were mixed; sales were robust but apparently not at blockbuster levels; and, from the start, Ann Fleming was vehemently against a single Bond continuation, let alone a series.[71] Given the struggle to bring *Colonel Sun* to fruition, it seems likely that Glidrose needed more time before embarking on the next Bond novel, with or without Amis. After all, *Colonel Sun* had succeeded in one of Glidrose's primary goals; its publication helped protect the Bond copyright and it established that Glidrose was the only entity that could instigate and authorize the publication of a new Bond literary work.

GEOFFREY JENKINS' TENURE (circa 1968)

PER FINE OUNCE

Unpublished

Author: Geoffrey Jenkins

In Brief: While the Double O Section is on the verge of being disbanded, Bond travels to South Africa on a mission that involves gold.

Meaning of Title: Refers to an ounce of pure gold.

Chronology: Presumably set after *The Man with the Golden Gun.*

Background: Kingsley Amis was not the only Bond author Glidrose had engaged to write a Bond continuation novel; there was another. In 1966, Glidrose hired Geoffrey Jenkins to write a Bond novel. Jenkins was a suitable choice. He was a writer for the *Sunday Times* and a Fleming associate. However, after Jenkins turned in his manuscript, Glidrose was said to be sufficiently dissatisfied with it, that they canceled plans for its publication. The reason for the refusal to publish the manuscript appears to be that Glidrose simply didn't like it. According to Fleming's agent and one-time Glidrose Chairman, Peter Janson-Smith, "I thought it was extraordinarily badly written."[72]

However, it's seemingly unlikely that the general public will be able to read the manuscript and decide for themselves. The full manuscript has seemingly been lost to time. However, 18 pages are known to exist. In 2010, MI6-HQ, the authoritative James Bond fan website, published two pages of original extracts—pages 86 and 87. From those two pages, we know that there was a briefing scene between Bond, M, and a new character named Sir Benjamin, a financier of some sort.

From those pages, we can also surmise that a recovered "gas cylinder," planted by a Soviet agent, was meant to be discovered (possibly by Bond) and its true purpose was to destabilize the British pound. Bond is making a case that an incident involving a "bullion broker" is connected to "gold flights." The gold flights start in Angola and go to London, where the South African government will supply a fighter escort for part of the trip, and the British and American governments will seemingly provide coverage for the rest of the trip. Bond sums up the entire affair as "finger-on-the-tit stuff." Bond worries that if the gold flights are disrupted and a plane is lost, then the UK pound and American dollar would be devalued. M, who is clearly frustrated with 007, rejects Bond's theory that the discovered gas containers and the gold flight are related.

The Bond of the movies has a fraught relationship with his superior. However, the Bond of the novels is largely respectful to the man and his office. So it's notable that, in *Per Fine Ounce*, Bond and his superior would clash so openly:

> Bond stood up, looking down from across the desk into the old sailor's face. "I'm sorry, sir."
>
> M put down his pipe. "Sorry about what, 007?" The voice was ominous.
>
> "In just over two months this department won't exist," he said...."You recalled me because the Treasury wanted help. Fair enough. But do you think you'll get anything more than an appreciative minute for today's discovery? Do you really think they'll reprieve your department because of a couple of piddling things like soda-water syphon cylinders?"

And that's where the published two-page extract ends. However, novelist and Bond expert Jeremy Duns contacted Jenkins' estate and was given access to additional pages. In his essay "Gold Dust," Duns revealed the rest of the scene. They begin with M's mounting exacerbation with Bond. "I am ordering you, 007." Bond heard the sharp intake of breath from Sir Benjamin behind him. "'And I', said Bond, 'am for once refusing that order..."[73] It's a shocking exchange for the literary Bond. The argument heightens and Bond tells Sir Benjamin that he is going to follow up on his instinct, "To the point of resigning." The extract ends with Bond flying to South Africa. "James Bond, for the first time, was going on a mission without the blessing of M."[74]

Beyond the villain's plot, these two jam-packed pages offer other insights. In his meeting with M, Bond also refers to the fact that the Double O Section will be phased out in two months. On the second page, there is a reference to the fact that Bond has been "recalled." It's hard to say for certain, but the line suggests that Bond was inactive or wasn't being used in the traditional capacity. One small character detail is revealed. On the second page, after Bond makes an impertinent remark, Jenkins writes that Bond "regretted the pain he saw in the face [of one] whom he admired above anyone he knew." From the extract, the reader is meant to understand that the outcome of Bond's mission will impact not only England but America as well.

The two pages are marked up, as if someone were making notes or corrections.

Those two pages, of course, do not answer every question about the novel. For instance, some Bond scholars indicated that the book was about diamond smuggling, a topic Fleming wrote about in his non-fiction book *The Diamond Smugglers* (1957). Others suggested that it was about gold. The term "fine ounce" is a reference to the purity of gold.

Decades later, the Jenkins estate commissioned South African writer Peter Vollmer to expand on Jenkins' concept and write a new story unconnected to James Bond and published it in 2014 under the name *Per Fine Ounce*. In the foreword to Vollmer's *Per Fine Ounce*, the publisher stated that Fleming and Jenkins spoke about setting a Bond novel in South Africa against the backdrop of diamond smuggling. So it's possible that the story was intended to touch upon both gold (a topic that Fleming covered in *Goldfinger*) and diamonds (see Fleming's *Diamonds Are Forever*). The two pages that originally appeared on MI6 were reprinted in the introduction to Vollmer's *Per Fine Ounce*.

Vollmer's novel concerns the hijacking of gold bullion and missing nuclear weapons. The character of Bond has been removed and replaced with Commander Geoffrey Peace, who like 007, is an MI6 agent. Peace appears in other Jenkins's books. However, Vollmer's *Per Fine Ounce* is not intended to serve as a substitute for Jenkins' unpublished work. In an interview with the Bond fan website *Artistic Licence Renewed*, Vollmer clarified, "They sent me a synopsis of the novel Per *Fine Ounce* that Jenkins had written. I wrote back telling my agent that I couldn't write a novel similar in content to Jenkins due to copyright issues but submitted my own synopsis for another book, which had no similarity with Jenkins' *Per Fine Ounce*, in the hope of writing another South African spy thriller altogether, i.e. my version of *Per Fine Ounce*, but without reference to Bond or any 007 Bond characters."[75]

Throughout this book, I cite the publication date of each continuation novel. Obviously, that's not possible for an unpublished work like *Per Fine Ounce*. Yet, it is helpful to place *Per Fine Ounce* somewhere in the Bond continuation novel history. The seeds for the story might have started in 1961 when Jenkins lunched with Fleming. By 1965, Jenkins had written an outline for the story. He had expected Ann Fleming to give her approval by February 24th; however, much to his mounting frustration, he did not receive it then.[76] In May 1966, Jenkins received word that he could go forward with his story[77]. By June 1966, he was already writing it,[78] and in August 1966, he received a contract to write it.[79] So, it's possible that a draft of the manuscript existed as early as the fall of 1966. Duns believes that Jenkins submitted the manuscript in early 1967. Irrespective of when Jenkins submitted *Per Fine Ounce* to Glidrose, it wouldn't have been a finished work. Jenkins would still have had to entertain notes from both Glidrose, Cape, and the American publisher.

Even if Glidrose were inclined to publish *Per Fine Ounce*, I believe that it would have been released after *Colonel Sun*; after all, Amis had gained notoriety for his non-Bond work. If my theory is correct and Amis's book was a blockbuster success and Glidrose wanted to quickly put out another Bond novel on the heels of *Colonel Sun*, then at the earliest, *Per Fine Ounce* would have been published in the fall of 1968 or more likely, 1969. The 1969 date would have continued the traditional pattern of one Bond book a year pattern that Fleming established. Conversely, if *Colonel Sun* had been a runaway success and Amis wanted to write a second Bond book, then publishing a book by an alternate Bond author (i.e. Jenkins) in between Amis's first and second work might have been confusing to the public.

MI6-HQ reported that, under the terms of the deal, Jenkins would receive £5,000 when he signed the contract and another £5,000 when he completed it. He would also be entitled to one-half of Glidrose's 2.5% shares for any film or television adaptation, the result of which was expected to be over £100,000. Jenkins would not get any share of merchandising.[80]

Getting a hold of the manuscript would be a dream for any Bond fan. However, at the moment, there is no indication that the work still exists. Per Duns, the contract required Jenkins to supply Glidrose with four copies of the manuscript.[81] If Jenkins followed the letter of the contract, then at least four copies of the manuscript would have been produced. Glidrose's Janson-Smith believes that the manuscript was returned to Jenkins to avoid any charges of plagiarism later on. Unfortunately, the Jenkins estate cannot locate a copy of it. As such, it appears that one of the first James Bond continuation novels has been lost to time.

NOT YOUR TRADITIONAL BONDS

"In his particular line of business, peace had reigned
for nearly a year. And peace was killing him."
IAN FLEMING, *From Russia with Love*

JOHN PEARSON'S TENURE
1973

John Pearson, the author of The Life of Ian Fleming, wrote the book, *James Bond: The Authorized Biography of 007* (1973).

JAMES BOND: THE AUTHORIZED BIOGRAPHY OF 007 (1973)

Author: John Pearson

In Brief: James Bond tells a biographer his life story.

Alternate Title: *James Bond: The Authorised Biography*

Meaning of Title: Signals that the novel takes the form of a biography.

Chronology: Contemporary with events taking place in multiple periods. Set roughly 11 years after the events of *You Only Live Twice* (Bond's son is 10 years old in the book, plus Suki's 9-month pregnancy). Bond is 52 years old and the major events throughout Bond's life are recounted.

Operation: Octopussy.

Bastard Meter: Gone, as in the "bastard is gone." Honeychile Rider refers to Bond as a bastard of the male chauvinist variety.

Eggs: Boiled, scrambled, and Benedict.

Insight into Bond: "He had the look of someone who had suffered and who was wary of the pain's return."

Summary: John Pearson, author of *The Life of Ian Fleming*, is on a plane to the Bahamas to interview James Bond, a real-life spy and the subject of Fleming's novels. During the flight, Pearson reviews the events that brought him to this unusual assignment. After writing Fleming's biography, he received a letter from a woman in Vienna named Maria Künzler, who was romantically involved with Fleming. Astonishingly, Künzler claimed that she also knew James Bond.

Intrigued that Bond was a real figure, Pearson sets out to find out more. Pearson manages to track down a few old Etonians who knew Bond. Then, he receives a letter indicating that Künzler has died, and she has instructed her estate to send Pearson a photograph of a young Bond.

After the photo arrives, Pearson receives a call from Mr. Hopkins, who works with the Ministry of Defense. Pearson and Hopkins meet in person and Hopkins tells Pearson to stop looking into 007's past. Later, Hopkins' colleague, a man named Urquhart, also instructs Pearson to stop his investigation.

Urquhart contacts Pearson again but this time he has a proposal. Urquhart suggests that Pearson write Bond's memoirs. According to Urquhart, other journalists have also discovered that Bond is a real person. So to control the story, SIS will allow Pearson to write Bond's biography. Pearson accepts the invitation and agrees to fly to the Bahamas to meet Bond where he is recovering from a bout of acute hepatitis and mental and physical exhaustion. For Bond, participating in the project gives him a chance to show that he's ready to return to duty.

In a series of interviews, Bond tells Pearson about his life. Bond says that he was born in November 1920 in Wattenscheid, Germany. 007's father Andrew Bond is an engineer who worked for an electrical engineering company called Metropolitan-Vickers. Andrew and his wife Monique had two sons, Henry and James both of whom attended Kings College School.

Bond discovers that his mother, Monique, is being unfaithful to his father. She starts acting paranoid and believes that the Russians are watching her. Monique has a mental breakdown and Andrew sends her to a sanitorium. When she returns home, Andrew decides to take her on a vacation to Switzerland; his goal is to rekindle their love for each other. During the trip, Bond and his brother, Henry, stay with their grandfather. While away, Bond's parents die in a climbing accident. Aunt Charmian breaks the news to Bond and Henry. She agrees to look after the children in her home in Pett Bottom, Kent.

Under Charmian's care, Henry and James enroll at Eton, where Henry succeeds but Bond struggles to fit in and bristles against the classism. Bond has a love affair with the seventeen-year-old half-French sister of a school chum. Henry reports their love affair and Bond is kicked out of school and enrolls at Fettes College in Edinburgh, Scotland.

007 in his fifties looks back in
James Bond: The Authorised Biography.
Illustration by Pat Carbajal

Bond goes to Paris where he visits a brothel and loses his virginity, his wallet, and passport. Bond reports the thief-prostitute to Madame Marthe de Brandt who returns the stolen goods. Bond and Marthe have an affair. Next, Bond meets a man named Maddox, a military attaché at the British Embassy. Maddox tells Bond that Marthe is using her position in the brothel to steal the military secrets of her clients and sell them to the intelligence community in Berlin. Maddox tells Bond that Marthe must be killed. Even though Bond loves Marthe, he agrees to eliminate her. Afterward, Maddox tells Bond that Marthe was innocent. Maddox informs a guilt-ridden Bond that he can make amends for his wrong deeds by serving his country and working for him.

Bond's first mission is to beat a skilled Romanian card player who is breaking the bank at a casino in Monte Carlo. Professional cardsharp Steffi Esposito teaches Bond the basics of card trickery. Together they figure out that the Romanian is wearing a pair of glasses with special lenses that reveal the number and suit of the cards. Bond beats the Romanian at his own game, gaining a reputation for himself in the process.

Maddox sends Bond to Berlin for another assignment that results in Bond's first kill. Bond goes to a hotel and pretends to be having an affair with a beautiful blonde woman. Their true purpose is to secretly trade documents. Bond and the woman participate in the ruse several times. One night, Bond enters the room only to find an assassin. For the first time in his life, Bond kills a man in self-defense.

Later, Bond travels to Moscow to meet a scientist named Fedyeov. Bond tells the scientist that he can defect to England. The man, who knows he's being watched, refuses the offer. Shortly after the meeting, the scientist is murdered. Bond, who drew unwanted attention to the scientist, feels indirectly responsible for his death.

The story shifts back to the present day. Bond introduces Pearson to Honeychile Rider, who has been married twice and is going by the name Mrs. Schultz. As they continue the interview, Bond recalls his time as a lieutenant in the Royal Navy, where he served in Naval Intelligence under Ian Fleming. For his part, Fleming is working as a personal assistant to the Director of Naval Intelligence, Admiral Godfrey.

Fleming gives Bond an assignment—eliminate a Japanese cipher named Shingushi in New York. Using a long-range rifle, Bond kills the cipher. After the war, Bond is a bit aimless, finding comfort in the arms of various women.

Bond returns to Pett Bottom to spend time with his Aunt Charmian. In 1946, Sir Miles Messervy invites Bond to join his department on a probationary period. M sends Bond to Washington, DC on attachment to the O.S.S. In DC, a congressman's wife fancies Bond. Even though her affection is not returned, the scandal causes Bond and his department embarrassment. As a result, Bond is kicked out of the service.

Maddox recruits a jobless and rudderless Bond to work for him and the British Secret Service in France. Bond spends four years based in Paris but goes on a series of short-term assignments in Africa, Morocco, Guinea, the Niger River, and Senegal.

In Paris, Bond falls in love with Maddox's wife, Regine. Regine is quite fond of Bond, but she doesn't reciprocate his feelings. Maddox sends Bond on a mission to Oran, Algeria where a man named Descaux gets the jump on Bond and beats him mercilessly. Descaux tells Bond the thrashing is a warning to stay away from Maddox's wife. Bond meets up with Ian Fleming who tells Bond that he should return to London.

In London, Fleming meets with M and tells him that Bond would make an effective agent. M takes Fleming's advice and invites Bond to rejoin the service and become a member of his Double O unit. Bond accepts. To become field-ready, Bond undergoes three months of training. Bond buys a flat in Chelsea and, following Charmian's advice, hires May as his housekeeper.

Bond's missions as a Double O agent take him to Jamaica where he confronts the cult of Kull, and to Greece where he uses mines to takedown a gunrunner ship. He is asked to help facilitate the defection of a KGB agent. However, he is not only a KGB agent; he's a member of SMERSH, who has been sent to kill Bond. Between missions, Bond also goes on the assignments depicted by Fleming in *Casino Royale* and *Live and Let Die*. On yet another assignment, Bond kills SMERSH member Colonel General Grubozaboyschikov.

As the mission and body count rise, so does SMERSH's obsession with the death of 007. SMERSH attempts to assassinate Bond in London. Bond gets away but a woman Bond was dating is badly wounded. Fearing that Bond has become a high-value target, M suspends him. Bond returns to his flat where May tells Bond that he missed a call from Fleming.

Fleming, a trusted advisor to M, has come up with a plan to reinstate Bond. Fleming will write a series of novels about Bond. The resulting popularity of Fleming's thrillers would convince the enemy that Bond is a fictional character and not an agent of Her Majesty's Secret Service. The outrageous plan is put into place and Fleming writes a fictionalized version of Bond's adventures. Sometimes the stories are accurate reflections of what really happened and sometimes Fleming takes liberties with the facts. The ruse works and SMERSH is thrown off guard. As a result, Bond is reinstated.

In the present day, Bond tells Pearson that he was initially wary of Fleming's plan to turn his life into pulp stories. Eventually, Bond seems to come around and recognize their value. In fact, it was Bond who told Fleming to name the villain in *Moonraker* after his childhood dog, Drax. Bond reveals that Fleming completely fabricated the plot for *Moonraker,* unlike with the other novels. Then, Bond lives out the adventures of *From Russia with Love* and *Dr. No*.

M gives Bond another assignment—tracking down 009 who was last seen in Hungary but has now gone missing. Previously, 009 was in possession of a top-secret list of names of members of the resistance group. Bond needs to find 009—or more critically, the list. Bond travels to Hungry and finds that 009 has been killed, his throat slashed. Bond also meets a woman named Nashda who has memorized the contents of 009's list. Bond successfully escorts Nashda to London so that she can share her secrets.

A series of missions follow; Bond battles Goldfinger, then Blofeld (*Thunderball*), and meets Vivienne Michel (*The Spy Who*

Loved Me). M's friends confide to Bond that they believe M, who is receiving calls from an unidentified person, is being blackmailed. Bond and Tanner trace the calls to a flat in Kensington that belongs to Del Lungot, an Italian photographer. Bond recovers the blackmail photographs. Later, Bond learns that the photos were taken during M's brief interest in naturism (non-sexual public nudity) and that his boss was not engaged in any impropriety.

Bond lives through the adventures depicted in *You Only Live Twice* and *The Man with the Golden Gun*. Bond reveals that he has a 10-year-old son named James. By now, Fleming's book *Dr. No* has been adapted into a major motion picture starring Sean Connery.

In the present day, Bond and Pearson near the end of their interviews. Pearson has enough material to write 007's biography. Bond and Honeychile make plans to marry. Before their event, Bond receives word that his old enemy, Irma Blunt, is still alive and is plotting a fiendish plan to unleash hundreds of infected rats in major cities. Bond leaves Honeychile at the altar to track down Blunt.

Background: *James Bond: The Authorized Biography of 007* is not a typical Bond continuation novel, nor is it, as the title suggests, strictly a biography. Instead, it's a novel in which John Pearson is both the author and a character. The fictional Pearson is a witness to Bond's life and coaxes the reluctant agent to candidly recount his personal and professional history. Curiously, the idea of *The Authorized Biography of 007* didn't come from Ian Fleming Publications, nor from Pearson or Cape, the traditional publishers of Bond novels. Instead, the prospect of a Bond biography came from a competing publisher, Sidgwick & Jackson.

Exactly who at Sidgwick & Jackson cooked up the idea is not known. Pearson has given two slightly different accounts. In a 2006 interview with Hank Reineke for *007 Magazine*, Pearson recalled, "I had done *The Life of Ian Fleming* a few years earlier which was a big success—it sold a lot. I had a very good publisher called William Armstrong [who worked at Sidgwick & Jackson]. He was sort of a publishing industry 'genius' at that time. He suddenly came up with this great idea. He rang me out of the blue and said, 'I've got a great idea for a book for you.' I'd never been published by these people before. They were called Sidgwick & Jackson, a rather small publishing house that was famous for publishing Rupert Brooke [an English poet] and nothing much else. Armstrong was trying to build 'the list' up, I think, and suggested the idea for *The Life of James Bond.* I said, 'You must be joking!'"[82] In a later interview, Pearson ascribed the idea to Frank Pakenham, the head of the independent publisher Sidgwick &

Jackson.[83] Of course, it's possible, if not likely, that both Pakenham and Armstrong discussed the matter before approaching Pearson.

Even with Sidgwick & Jackson's enthusiasm for the project, Pearson could not immediately begin writing his book. There was a hitch; Sidgwick & Jackson did not own the rights to the Bond character. As such, Sidgwick & Jackson sought and was granted permission from Glidrose to write the book. As to be expected, Sidgwick & Jackson had to pay Glidrose a licensing fee, which Pearson characterized as modest.[84]

In the interview with *007 Magazine*, Pearson described the context in which *The Authorized Biography* was written. The author explains that faux biographies were popular at the time. Philip José Farmer wrote two such tomes about a pair of pulp heroes: 1972's *Tarzan Alive: A Definitive Biography of Lord Greystoke* and 1973's *Doc Savage: His Apocalyptic Life*. Similarly,1974's *The Seven-Per-Cent Solution: Being a Reprint from the Reminiscences of John H. Watson, M.D. The Seven-Per-Cent Solution* is purportedly "written" by Holmes's trusted colleague, but it was authored by Nicholas Meyer. Meyer would later become a successful writer-director of Star Trek movies and would also, for a brief stint, join the writers' room of Eon's *Tomorrow Never Dies* for a brainstorming session. Like *The Seven-Per-Cent Solution, The Authorized Biography of 007,* fills in gaps between the novels and short stories.

Originally, Pearson envisioned a different form than *The Authorized Biography* eventually took. Pearson wanted to write a typical biography that would tell the full story of Bond's life, including his death. The chairman of Ian Fleming Publications, Peter Janson-Smith, didn't like that approach. Janson-Smith told Raymond Benson, "Originally Pearson's idea was that Bond was dead and so this was a complete biography, a clear indication that he wanted to write a book as if this was it and that was the end of Bond. I put my foot down and said, 'No, you've got to have Bond in retirement being interviewed or reminiscing to a friend."[85] Pearson agreed to the new approach and Janson-Smith permitted him to write the book.

Commentary: Once it was determined that Pearson was going to write a biography of Bond, he needed to answer two related questions. One, if Bond were real, how did Ian Fleming come to pen his adventures? Two, why would SIS encourage Bond to tell his version of events to his biographer?

In both instances, Pearson turned to Fleming for the answers. A throwaway line in *You Only Live Twice* links Bond, the character, to Fleming, the author. In the novel, Bond is presumed dead, and M writes an obituary for the agent. In the obituary, M details Bond's parents, his early days, and his work as an agent. Fleming curiously added that Bond became "something of a public figure with the inevitable result that a series of popular books came to be written around him by a personal friend and former colleague of James Bond." Here, Fleming is stating Bond was a real figure and the subject of his novels and film series.

The line was, of course, a throw-away joke. The winking line also became the basis for Pearson's Bond biography. Fleming provided Pearson cover by suggesting that the Bond of the novels wasn't just a character in the novels; he was also a real figure who went on actual missions for SIS. The line also establishes that Bond and Fleming were friends.

Even if Bond and Fleming knew each other, that doesn't answer the question as to how the author came to write about Bond's secret missions. Nor does it address why SIS would allow Bond to recount his missions to a journalist. The answers to both questions were once again provided by Fleming. In the obituary, M wrote "If the quality of those books or their degree of veracity, had been any higher, the author would certainly have been prosecuted under the Official Secrets Acts." Here it's important to remember that Fleming, in real life, was constantly mocking his talents as a writer. So it's a fair assumption that the obituary was referring to Fleming. Therefore, Pearson reasoned, Fleming could be a character in Bond's biography. Pearson, who had written a biography of Fleming and knew him, was in a unique position to create a sympathetic, accurate, and playful sketch of Fleming.

Hidden with that same line was a third clue that would inform Pearson's approach. In the obit, M challenged the accuracy of Fleming's books. This line about the "veracity" of the novels gave Pearson permission to expand the events in the novels and sometimes challenge and contradict them. Now, Pearson had the cover to stick to the novels or veer from them as he saw fit.

The above unique stew helped create a Bond continuation novel that was like no other. It wasn't a straightforward adventure. Instead, the book offered a meta-commentary on Bond and Fleming. It's a unique mix that is specific to Pearson's knowledge and personal interests. It's not an approach that any other Bond writer would (or should) take. Accepting the premise—that Bond has been asked to share all the secrets of his trade—does require a little suspension of disbelief. If the reader is willing to go along with it, then there is a great deal of fun to be had. Glidrose head, Janson-Smith, was pleased with the final result. Janson-Smith said, "It has been a very underrated book. I think it's very good.[86]

Between Novels: Pearson filled in the gaps about what happened to Bond between adventures. For instance, Pearson described the dissolution of his relationship with Tiffany Case, following his time when he squared off against the Star Spangled Mob. Bond and Tiffany moved in together. Bond thought that their relationship could progress toward marriage. However, boredom crept into their relationship. That wrinkle could be expected. Perhaps less expected was Pearson's contention that Case and May, Bond's housekeeper, didn't get along. Case and May's relationship becomes so fractured that Tanner cautions Bond that he must choose between them. May stays; Tiffany goes. It's Tiffany who, ultimately, makes the final decision. On a trip to the embassy with Bond, Tiffany meets a man named Nick who eventually asks Tiffany to marry him. Tiffany agrees and Bond is left alone.

Pearson also details what happened following *From Russia with Love*, when Rosa Klebb kicks him with a poison-tipped shoe-knife. Fleming's novel ends with Bond seeming to lose consciousness, his future uncertain. After Klebb was taken into custody, she swallowed a cyanide pill so she wouldn't be of any value to SIS, her sworn enemy. In *The Authorized Biography of 007*, Pearson counters that Bond never passed out and that his friend René Mathis arrived quickly and administered aid until help came. Fleming alluded to the story in *Dr. No* but Pearson brings it to life.

Fleming and Bond: As noted, Ian Fleming is a central figure in *The Authorized Biography of 007* and a key figure in Bond's life. Fleming's name appears nearly 300 times in the novel. By contrast, Miss Moneypenny's name is evoked in only 14 instances. Pearson posits that Fleming and Bond knew each other. They became friends and their lives intersected. Around the age of ten, Bond caught a glimpse of Fleming, when the writer was working for Reuters and was covering a trial that Andrew Bond was part of. It is the sight of the dashing Fleming who spurs Bond to consider becoming a journalist. It was Fleming who effectively scouted Bond and suggested to M that James would be an effective secret agent. When Bond is disgraced and kicked out of the service, it's Fleming who tells M that he should give Bond a second chance. Out of deference to Fleming, M agrees. Most significantly, "Bond believes [Fleming] all but saved his life" by publishing novels that confused the opposition.

Pearson delineates the differences between Fleming and Bond. Fleming was a "dreamer," whereas Bond is a "man of action." Fleming is "witty, sociable" and Bond is solitary and blunt.

Fleming cultivated an air of laziness but was, according to Pearson, a diligent writer. The book is about cover stories. And Fleming's cover is that he didn't take his writing seriously.

According to Pearson, Bond is toying with writing a book on self-defense. After hearing the idea, Fleming encouraged the agent to author the book and Fleming even proposed a title—*Stay Alive!*

Bond's Got a Bone to Pick with Fleming: During the conversations between Pearson (the literary figure) and Bond, 007 expresses his frustration with the way that he's depicted in Fleming's novels. Bond was so upset with how he's portrayed in *Casino Royale* that he declined to read *Live and Let Die*, Fleming's follow-up. Bond believes that Fleming more or less got the facts right about his missions, but took liberties with some of the other details in Bond's personal life. For instance, Fleming wrote that Bond got kicked out of Eton because of an incident with the maid. In *The Authorized Biography of 007*, Pearson allows Bond to correct the record. He was in love with a young woman who was not a maid, but the half-sister of one of Bond's friends. Fleming wrote that Bond smoked seventy cigarettes a day. Bond disputes the number and said that he smoked considerably less.

Bond's History: Bond spotted his mother Monique having an affair with another man. Eventually, Bond's father, Andrew, discovers the relationship and emotionally pulls away from her. Monique's betrayal and Andrew's reaction to it were too much for the impressionable son. As Pearson explains, James "could not forgive her for rejecting him. In years to come a lot of women were to pay the price for this rejection."

Continuity Nod: The entire book weaves in stories and incidents from each of Fleming's novels.

Bond's Early Life: In his early days, Bond and his family moved around a lot. Bond grew up in Germany, Egypt, France, and Russia, and had a French au pair. He grew up in a reasonably affluent home and there were plenty of servants around. At first, Bond wanted to follow in his father's footsteps and become an engineer. Of course, that didn't come to pass. While living with his aunt, he once spent an entire afternoon patiently waiting for a rat to emerge from a barn so that he could shoot it with his air rifle.

Bond's Family Tree: Bond's parents met each other through mountain climbing. Andrew spotted Monique while she was climbing a mountain, and Andrew was taken with her. Bond's mom and dad had a more complicated relationship than Fleming's books suggest. Pearson writes about their fraught dynamic and her bouts of depression which put a strain on them. A depressed Monique went to the mountains to kill herself. Andrew chased after her, but he wasn't able to save her. Instead, they both fell to their death. Bond doesn't know if Monique's death was a suicide or an accident that occurred while Andrew was trying to rescue her.

In the *Authorized Biography of 007*, we learn that 007 has an older brother, Henry Bond. They are opposites. Henry is studious, Bond is apathetic. They have a contentious relationship, even by the standards of normal sibling rivalry. It is Henry who reported Bond's inappropriate relationship with the maid and who is responsible for Bond's expulsion from Eton. Other family members include Archie Bond, Bond's grandfather on Andrew's side, Uncle Gregor, and his Great-Uncle Ian who includes Bond in his will. Bond uses those funds to buy his apartment, his flat on King's Road. His mother's family includes Bond's cousin, Victor Delacroix, who lives in Italy.

Bond has a ten-year-old son named James, who is a spitting image of his father. When Bond found out that he had a son, he returned to Tokyo and offered to marry Kissy Suzuki but she declined his offer. Bond is proud of his son, but Pearson suggests that Bond only sees him occasionally. Still, James Jr. has met Bond's mother's side of the family. Bond plans to enroll his son at Eton in two years.

Bond's Inner Life: At the start of the novel, Bond is not in fighting form. Instead, he's facing a crisis of confidence; he's spent both emotionally and physically. The process of talking to "Pearson" gives Bond a new lease on life and a renewed vitality.

Bond doesn't consider himself an Englishman; he thinks of himself as a Scotsman. When Bond dies, he wants his ashes to be scattered in Scotland.

Bond is a combination of his parent's defining traits. Bond picked up his father's need for order and his mother's passion and romance. Bond resents all father figures. Bond rarely worries. For him, worry is money paid in advance for a bill that never comes due.

Bond's Personal Life: Pearson provides details that Fleming would avoid—including Bond's birthday (November 11, 1920) and his address (30 Wellington Square). When Pearson interviews Bond for the book, the agent is said to be 52 years old.

Bond has retained a few mementos of his dead parents. In addition to keeping a photograph of his mother (and Marthe de Brandt) on his dressing table, he has also held on to two of his father's "silver-backed brushes."

Pearson gives May a last name—McGrath—and establishes that May comes into Bond's employ at the suggestion of Aunt Charmian. Bond didn't just spend time with Aunt Charmian when he was in his teens. Even as an adult, he would often return and visit her.

Bond's Romantic Life: Tracy wasn't the first woman Bond had made plans to marry. In the spring of 1941, Bond was engaged to a woman named Muriel, the sister of an officer that Bond knew. The twenty-two-year-old was quite taken with Bond. They reserved a room at the Dorchester and Bond was uncharacteristically nervous about spending the night with her. As a way to ease his nerves, Bond went to the bar for a drink. At the bar, Bond runs into Ian Fleming. Fleming tells Bond that it's time to return to work for M. At first, Bond is reluctant to go back but Fleming persists. Bond relents and agrees to return. Because he's going back into action, Bond tells Muriel that they should hold off on their marriage. Muriel acquiesced.

From Pearson's book, we learn how Bond became a skilled lover (due to his relationship with Marthe de Brandt), and card player (under the tutelage of a card sharp named Steffi Esposito). Bond's first murder took place at the Hotel Adlon in Berlin. Bond was on his way to meet a contact (and make love to her) when he's surprised by an assassin (dressed as his contact) who has been employed to kill Bond. Bond is forced to kill the man in self-defense.

Bond's Tastes: Bond thinks that his housekeeper May makes a delicious breakfast. However, May is lacking in preparing a suitable lunch or dinner. So Bond tries to have a large breakfast so that he can avoid her other inferior meals. Bond enjoys a swim in the morning. He used to read Eric Ambler mysteries for pleasure. Pearson's choice of reading material is consistent with Fleming's. In *From Russia with Love*, while on a plane 007 is reading Ambler's *The Mask of Dimitrios.*

Bond's Work Methods: M helped form the Double O Division and when he invited Bond to join it, the division was in its infancy, only three months old. At first, Bond is reluctant to join the Double O Division. Bond's impression of the division is that they are a kind of "murder squad." It's only after learning the broader nature of the division, that Bond agrees to serve. Bond needs to believe in the cause; he's not simply an assassin for hire. After he joins, he goes through a wide-ranging three-month training program that includes finding out how much physical pain he can endure. Double O agents are entitled to four months of vacation time, although Bond rarely uses it. After Bond completes his assignment at Royale-les-Eaux (*Casino Royale*), a grateful M grants the spy an additional three weeks' leave.

1951 was a bad year for the Double O Division. In that single year 003, 008, and 0011 were all killed in action. Pearson establishes that Bond was not the first person to be given the 007 designation. Originally the code belonged to an agent who was killed in the line of duty. The number remained unused until M assigned it to Bond.

Bond is wary of being inside submarines, which he likens to steel coffins. In cases where he is simply a button man, he prefers not to know too much about his target. Keeping himself in the dark ensures that he doesn't humanize his mark. Bond's vices are ignored by the service because he gets results. Pearson argues "In [Bond's] business, failure was the only sin against the Holy Ghost."

The Origin of Bond's Scar: Fleming's Bond has a three-inch scar on his face. Though Fleming frequently referred to the scar he never explained how Bond received it. Pearson does. While driving Marthe's car, Bond sends the car, with him and Marthe in it, into the river. She dies; he suffers a gash on his face. Thus, a scar is born.

Final Line: The concluding sentence of Pearson's novel is "The bastard is gone." It's spoken by Honeychile, and it refers to the moment when Bond skips out on his pre-wedding celebration and sets out to go after Irma Bunt. The line echoes "The bitch is dead," the final sentence of *Casino Royale.*

Assorted Observations:

- A villain explains that there will be "No deals, Mr. Bond." That same phrase would become the title of John Gardner's sixth Bond novel, *No Deals, Mr. Bond.*
- A passage in the book anticipates a scene in the Bond film *Never Say Never Again*. In both *The Authorized Biography* and the Connery film, Bond's life is saved when he chooses to spend an intimate moment with a woman in *her* hotel room; thus avoiding his own hotel room bed, which has a bomb planted under it.

CHRISTOPHER WOOD'S TENURE (1977–1979)

Christopher Wood, a novelist and screenwriter, wrote the James Bond novelizations *James Bond, The Spy Who Loved Me* (1977) and *James Bond and Moonraker* (1979).

JAMES BOND, THE SPY WHO LOVED ME (1977)

Author: Christopher Wood

In Brief: Bond teams with Soviet agent Anya Amasova to retrieve two stolen nuclear submarines.

Meaning of Title: James Bond is a spy, and a woman believes that he loves her.

Chronology: Contemporary. After *The Man with the Golden Gun*.

Operation: Armageddon

Bastard Meter: Unaddressed.

Eggs: Scrambled and fried.

Insight Into Bond: "We are spies. It is a dirty business. We try to believe that the end justify the means but we are never sure."

Summary: At a beachside hotel, Anya Amasova pines for her lover Sergei Borzov, who is sunning himself on a nearby beach. Borzov returns to the room and reminds Anya that he is being called away for work. Borzov answers the phone and informs Anya that she must return to Moscow immediately.

In a cabin in the mountains in Chamonix, France, James Bond spends time with Martine Blanchaud, a woman he met while gambling. Bond looks out the window and notices tracks in the snow. Realizing Martine has set him up Bond flees the cabin and skis away as SMERSH agents descend on him. The enemy agents, who include Anya's lover, try to eliminate 007, but Bond kills them.

Anya Amasova is called into SMERSH's headquarters in Moscow. Colonel-General Nikitin, the head of SMERSH notifies her that Sergei has been killed in action while attempting to assassinate a

British agent. After breaking the news to Anya, Nikitin gives Anya a new assignment.

In Regent's Park, M informs Bond that the HMS Ranger, a nuclear-powered ballistic missile submarine, has disappeared. M believes that a traitor to the crown tracked the sub and sold its coordinates to the enemy. M also explains that someone in Cairo is prepared to sell the blueprints of a sophisticated tracking system to the UK. M instructs Bond to go to Cairo and get the blueprints. As a first step, Bond should contact a man named Aziz Fekkesh.

Bond pays a visit to Fekkesh's home in Cairo and meets his lover Felicca. Bond quizzes her about Fekkesh's whereabouts. A gunman shoots Felicca. Bond chases after the gunman and kills him. Bond returns and discovers that Felicca is still alive but in critical condition. Before she expires, Felicca tells Bond that Fekkesh can be found at the pyramids.

Bond goes to the pyramids where he spots Fekkesh, as well as Anya and two Russian men. Bond also sees a giant man with stainless-steel teeth (Jaws) bite into Fekkesh's neck killing him. Bond searches Fekkesh's body for the blueprints, but doesn't locate them. Bond examines the dead man's appointment book and discovers that Fekkesh is scheduled to meet with a man named Max Kalba the following Thursday. While searching Fekkesh for further clues, Bond is knocked unconscious.

When Bond wakes up, he discovers that he's tied up to a chair and is being held by the Russians. His captors ask Bond about the location of the blueprints. When Bond says that he doesn't know where they are, the Russians torture him by sending an electric current to his genitals. Anya enters the room and tells them to stop the torture, as that method will likely kill Bond. Instead, she recommends that her men drug the agent. The guards untie Bond, who seizes the moment, overpowers them, and escapes.

Later, Bond goes to the Mujaba Club to locate Max Kalba, the man with whom Fekkesh had an appointment. At the club, Bond meets Anya. Then, Bond locates Kalba and expresses his interest in buying the blueprints for the tracking system. Anya appears and says that she too is interested in acquiring them. Kalba produces a metal canister containing the blueprints, but he is called away before he can sell them. Jaws kills Kalba. Bond leaves Anya and discovers Kalba's dead body. Jaws tries to escape but before he can get away, Bond and Anya stow away in his vehicle. Jaws drives to a desolate ancient city. Once there, Bond and Anya leave the vehicle, battle Jaws, recover the microfilm containing the blueprints, and escape.

Bond meets up with M in Egypt where Bond sees M's Russian opposite and Anya. Bond and Anya are told to work together to retrieve the missing British and Soviet submarines, the *HMS Ranger,* and the *Potemkin*. They examine the microfilm that the agents recovered and see the symbol of the Stromberg Shipping Line, which is owned by Sigmund Stromberg.

Posing as Mr. and Mrs. Robert Sterling, a marine biologist and his wife, Bond and Anya go to the shipping line to investigate Stromberg. Stromberg lectures Bond about the importance of the oceans and reveals his plans for a vast submersible structure that can sustain life indefinitely. After the meeting concludes, Stromberg orders Jaws to eliminate Bond. While driving away from the meeting, Bond is attacked by Stromberg's men. Bond evades them driving his Lotus into the water. Then, Bond activates the car's underwater mode, and the high-tech vehicle transforms into a submarine. As Bond pilots the car deeper underwater, he discovers a massive structure similar to the model in Stromberg's office.

Back at the hotel, Anya receives a message from her superiors indicating that Bond killed her lover Sergei. Bond and Anya board a submarine named the *Wayne* and meet Commander Carter of the US Navy. On the *Wayne*, Anya reveals that she knows that Bond killed Sergei and, when the mission is over, she will eliminate Bond.

The Navy submarine sails into Stromberg's waters and discovers a giant supertanker called *The Lepadus*. Stromberg's men attack the *Wayne* and Commander Carter is forced to surrender. Bond, Anya, and the crew of the *Wayne* board *The Lepadus*

Once onboard *The Lepadus*, Bond and Anya are discovered and brought to Stromberg. Stromberg reveals his master plan; he intends to use the US submarine to attack the Russians. Simultaneously, he will use a Russian submarine to shoot the Americans. Each country will blame the other and World War III will start. Stromberg's ultimate goal is to destroy the world and start a new order beneath the sea. Stromberg invites Anya to join him in this new world order. Anya refuses but Stromberg takes her with him regardless. Stromberg's guards take Bond away.

Bond escapes and frees Commander Carter and his men. A battle rages between the Marines and Stromberg's forces. Bond makes it to Stromberg's control room and Bond instructs a naval officer to change the trajectory of the submarines' missiles. Instead of firing at the US and Russia, the submarines will destroy each other. Bond sets out to rescue Anya, who is still in Stromberg's clutches in his underwater stronghold named the *Atlantis*.

Bond boards the *Atlantis* but the now-free Commander Carter is under orders to fire on it. Carter's missiles begin to destroy the *Atlantis*; a portion of the structure falls on Stromberg, killing him. While the *Atlantis* sinks, Bond faces off with Jaws, gets the better of him, and then saves Anya. Bond and Anya escape.

Shortly after that, Bond convalesces in his home. Anya visits Bond. They spend a romantic night together.

Background: Ian Fleming's novel *The Spy Who Loved Me* and the Eon film of the same have virtually nothing in common. The novel is told from the point of view of Vivienne Michel, a Canadian woman who is terrorized by two small-time gangsters in a motel in upstate New York. The Roger Moore film, co-written by Christopher Wood and Richard Maibaum, is about an extraordinarily wealthy industrial magnate named Karl Stromberg who wants to destroy the world.

The differences between Fleming's novel and the movie can't be chalked up to the usual changes that take place in the filmmaking process. When Eon bought the rights to Fleming's works, he stipulated that they couldn't adapt the poorly received *The Spy Who Loved Me*. Later, Fleming's Estate permitted Eon to use the title in an entirely new plot. This discrepancy between Fleming's novel and the movie went further to novelizing the film, as the story did not previously exist in book form. Given that the story had never been published in a book before, the difference between Fleming's book and the film provides further justification for novelizing the film.

Because novelizations were popular with readers at the time, Eon needed a book that more accurately reflected the events in the 1977 film. So they turned to Wood to novelize his own script. In the novelization, Wood expanded and revised his story, clarified plot points, and deepened his characters. The novelization was published under the title *James Bond, The Spy Who Loved Me* to try and differentiate it from the original Fleming novel *The Spy Who Loved Me.* A photograph of Roger Moore and the advertising copy, "The Book of the Film!" drove the point home.

Commentary: *James Bond, The Spy Who Loved Me* brings the movie Bond closer to the literary one. A standout sequence of the novelization is a torture scene that does not appear in the film. In the scene, Bond is captured by the Russians, who mistakenly believe that Bond has the blueprints for a coveted tracking system. To induce him to give them the blueprints, the Russians pull Bond's pants down and wire his manhood to a heavy-duty battery. Between questions, the men turn on the battery, which sends an electric current to Bond's loins. The pain, needless to say, is excruciating. Given the relatively graphic nature of the torture, it couldn't appear in a Bond film. The torture scene also recalls a similar moment in the novel *Casino Royale*, in which Le Chiffre assails Bond's groin with a carpet beater. According to Bond scholars David Lowbridge-Ellis and Thomas Mason, the idea for the scene originated with Richard Maibaum's original treatment, and it survived at least two of Wood's drafts before it was cut. However, Wood was clearly taken by the idea and he incorporated it into his novelization.[87]

There are other notable changes from the film to the novelization. In the novelization, Anya's superiors tell her that Bond killed her lover. In the film, she figures it out on her own, which is a stronger character choice. Jaws' fate is more ambiguous in the novelization. In the film, Jaws is shown to definitively survive the shark attack. In the novelization, Wood does not reveal what happened to Jaws. A reader could reasonably infer that the shark got the better of the assassin. As an aside, Wood's writing is occasionally enigmatic; he requires that readers pay attention to follow the action. To wit, Wood doesn't even identify the predator by name. Instead, he refers to it as a "relentless triangle." It's up to discerning readers to determine that the "triangle" is a shark.

In both the movie and the novelization, Bond skis off a mountain and then deploys his parachute with the Union Jack emblem. However, the way the event is handled in each medium is different. In the movie, it's a big, heroic moment with soaring music. In the novelization, the outrageous stunt is downplayed. In the book, the jump is witnessed from the point of view of an old man in the nearby town. The old man says, "Ils sont fous, les anglaise" which roughly translates to, "They are crazy, the English." In this instance, Wood's goal is to tone down the deliciously over-the-top film moment and translate it into something closer to a Fleming book. Granted, Fleming probably wouldn't have written the stunt in the first place, but Wood is attempting to filter the movie Bond through its creator's lens.

There are other differences between the film and novelization. In the film, Stromberg's first name is Karl, the supertanker is called *The Liparus*, and Anya is a KGB operative. In the novelization, Stromberg's Christian name is Sigmund, the tanker is *The Lepadus*, and Anya is an operative of SMERSH, the arm of the KGB that kills Western spies. The film's General Gogol, head of the KGB, has been replaced by General Nikitin, the head of SMERSH who also appears in the novel *From Russia with Love.*[88]

Additionally, the film kicks off with an action beat; an attack on a British ballistic-missile submarine, followed by the news that a Soviet nuclear submarine has also disappeared. The novelization picks up more quietly; with Anya lying in bed while her lover suns himself on the beach outside. The central emotional relationship in the film is Anya's love-hate relationship with Bond. In the novel, Wood gets inside Anya's mind and helps chart her feelings for him, as well as her eventual decision not to eliminate the man she has sworn to kill.

We should refrain from attributing every deviation from the film exclusively to Wood. Some of these elements might have come from uncredited writers or other filmmakers who worked on the movie. Nonetheless, even if he didn't cook up the ideas, it doesn't diminish Wood's achievement. The pleasure of Wood's novelization is not necessarily the story itself but the way that he tells it.

Continuity Nod: When Anya uses a needle hidden in her ring to incapacitate Bond, his thoughts immediately return to SMERSH agent Rosa Klebb who hid a poisoned knife in her shoe.

Bond's History: When he was a child, Bond used to have a Scottish nanny. When the nanny wanted to shoo someone away, she would announce it is "bye-byes time."

Bond's Personal Life: May, Bond's Scottish housekeeper does not appear in *The Spy Who Love Me* nor in any of the Eon productions. However, she does briefly appear in the final chapter of *James Bond, the Spy Who Loved Me*.

Bond's Inner Life: Bond plays cards because the tension of the game paradoxically relaxes him. Bond prefers a hard-won victory to one that comes with little effort. For Bond, the start of an assignment is similar to the start of a love affair.

Bond's Tastes: As with Fleming's Bond, Wood's Bond relishes his breakfast.

Bond's Work Methods: Bond's training dictates that while being tortured, it's helpful to distract yourself by concentrating on an object in the room. Bond implements this technique by focusing his attention on a model in a pin-up calendar. Even though the method isn't entirely effective, it does mitigate the pain and helps him survive the ordeal. Bond is indifferent to killing. He considers it a part of his job and he eliminates people without passion. As such, he essentially bares no ill will for those who try to kill him. In Bond's point of view, it's simply their job. Expressing his philosophy about work, Bond reasons, "We are spies. It's a dirty business. We try to believe that the ends justify the means, but we are never sure. We kill, and we hope that others will live."[89]

Notable Character: Jaws is given the name Zbigniew Krycsiwiki and a backstory. In it, Jaws was born in Poland to a father who was a strongman in a circus and a mother who was a warden in a woman's prison. In 1972, Krycsiwiki's jaw was broken by the police with clubs during a bread riot. Left for dead, Krycsiwiki stowed away on a vessel owned by Stromberg. After he was discovered, Stromberg became fascinated with Krycsiwiki's oversized body and arranged to have a doctor restore his jaw and teeth with steel components. However, during the operation, Krycsiwiki's vocal cords were damaged and Krycsiwiki was rendered mute.

Human Shield: Roger Moore's James Bond is a hero. So, it is particularly shocking when the movie Bond uses a woman to shield himself from gunfire, as he seems to do in *The Spy Who Loved Me.* In the movie, Bond searches for a black market trader named Fekkesh at his home. Instead, Bond meets Fekkesh's secretary Felicca. Employing his standard protocol, Bond charms Felicca to learn her employer's whereabouts. As they talk, Felicca realizes that Stromberg's henchman, Sandor, has a gun trained on her. Felicca cries out, "No," begging for her life and simultaneously warning Bond of the threat. Sandor fires and a shot rings out. Based on the film's blocking, it appears that Bond moves Felicca between him and the gunman. As a result, Felicca is fatally wounded, and Bond is unharmed. Surprisingly, Bond seems to use Felicca as a human shield.

Bond's film history seems to report that Bond is not above putting a woman in harm's way to save himself. Sean Connery's Bond uses a woman to block an attacker in *Goldfinger*'s pre-title sequence. In the film *Thunderball*, Connery's Bond performs a similar act when he uses Fiona Volpe to block a bullet intended for him. However, in both instances, the women were villains, not innocents caught up with the wrong man, as is the case with Felicca. Given Bond's cinematic history, some Bond fans believe that the scene in *The Spy Who Loved Me* is just another example of Bond doing what he needed to do to survive. At least, that's the theory.

To shed light on the filmmaker's intentions, I turned to the screenplay. The stage direction in the script reads: "The gun is fired. BOND, holding FELICCA, flings her and himself on to the floor beside the divan. He turns her over. She is dead—a red stain spreading across the back of her dress."[90] Clearly, in the script, Bond tried to save Felicca but failed. So what accounts for the common belief that Bond used Felicca as a human shield?

There are a few possibilities. One, the filmmakers departed from the script and wanted viewers to think that Bond sacrificed Felicca to save himself. It's possible that they thought Bond's action, albeit decidedly unchivalrous, would show that 007 is one tough bastard. Similarly, in the next scene, Bond throws the killer off the roof after extracting critical intel from him. At this moment, 007 is hardly behaving as a gentleman spy. Yet, Bond killing an unarmed man who is no longer a threat would become a defining moment in Moore's era. Moore would get praise for a similar moment in *For Your Eyes Only*.

However, I don't personally believe that the filmmakers intended it to seem as if Bond played a hand in Felicca's death. If Bond knowingly killed two unarmed people in two back-to-back scenes, it would hardly seem heroic. Instead, I think that the filmmakers tried to simplify the scene by eliminating the stage direction where Bond jumps behind a divan. It's possible that the divan on set was not a suitable prop that would have allowed 007 the proper cover. Or the filmmakers were falling behind that day and wanted to cut down on a few moments, and the divan beat was the first to go. Case closed. Well, not quite.

Wood's novelization provides another possibility. In Wood's book, Bond is not there to charm the information out of Felicca. Instead, he's there to intimidate her. In a very un-Roger Moore-like threat, the novelization Bond says, "'I didn't come here to make love to you.' ... He yanked her roughly to her feet and shook her until her dress dropped off her shoulders. 'Don't think I wouldn't hurt you.'" In the next moment, Bond sees the glint of the gun, hears the sound of the shot, and finds the woman in his arms. For a moment, even Bond is confused by what happened. Wood clarifies, "Bond threw himself sideways, still using the girl as an unintended shield."[91] Here, Wood is splitting the difference. Bond is not deliberately killing Felicca to save himself. Instead, he is the unintended beneficiary of her death. Not only does the novelization add critical information regarding the question of the "human shield" debate, but it also provides Wood with a second draft of his work.

Assorted Observations:

- Wood eliminates the character of Naomi (Caroline Munro), Stromberg's pilot. Instead, Jaws pilots the helicopter.
- Woods also doesn't refer to Anya Amasova as Triple X.
- SMERSH employs about 60,000 people.

JAMES BOND AND MOONRAKER (1979)

Author: Christopher Wood

In Brief: Bond is sent to investigate the hijacking of Hugo Drax's space shuttle, the *Moonraker.*

Meaning of Title: Refers to the hero's name and the object of his mission.

Chronology: Contemporary. Set after the events of the novelization *James Bond, The Spy Who Loved Me.*

Operation: Not applicable.

Bastard Meter: Unaddressed.

Eggs: Sunny-side-up, but not served to Bond.

Insight Into Bond: Smoking was also, for Bond, part of the ritual of flying, and he enjoyed his rituals.

Summary: A 747 airplane, transporting the *Moonraker* space shuttle, is highjacked. Early signs suggest that the Russians are the responsible party, but M is not convinced. So he instructs Bond to find out if there is more to the story than meets the eye. Bond starts his inquiry by visiting the manufacturer of the shuttle, Hugo Drax.

At the Drax Corporation, Bond meets Drax's pilot Trudi Parker and then Drax himself. After pleasantries, Drax tells Bond to tour the plant with Dr. Holly Goodhead. As part of the tour, Bond enters a centrifuge unit, a device that simulates the experience of breaking the earth's gravitation field. The centrifuge unit, which is rigged to kill Bond, spins out of control. Bond uses a wrist dart gun (previously provided by Q) to disable the contraption.

That night, Bond visits Drax's pilot, Trudi. Trudi tells Bond that Drax has been working on a top-secret project in his laboratories but recently the project has been relocated. After sleeping with Trudi, Bond infiltrates Drax's study and breaks into his safe. There, Bond finds secret plans that include a blueprint for a globe, a small cylindrical object, and a glass vial. Bond takes photos of the evidence. Bond leaves Drax's study but is spotted by Drax's enforcer, Chang.

The blueprints from Drax's safe display the name Venini Glass. So Bond goes to Venice to investigate the company. At Venini Glass,

Bond finds cylinders identical to the cylindrical object that he removed from Drax's safe. Later, Bond spots Holly who says that she is in Venice for a scientific conference. Holly reveals that Trudi has been killed.

Bond returns to Venini Glass and discovers vials similar to the ones that he spotted in the safe. Bond removes a vial, but, in his haste, he doesn't return it to its original position. When the scientists return, they knock over the precariously placed vial, causing it to break and release a deadly toxin. The nearby scientists inhale the toxin and die. Then, Drax's henchman Chang confronts Bond; Bond and Chang fight, and Bond kills his opponent. Later, Bond and Holly meet up. Holly reveals that she is working with the CIA. They agree to work together to uncover Drax's plan.

Bond accompanies M and Frederick Gray, the Minister of Defense to Drax's lab. They discover that the lab has been transformed into a private chamber. Knowing Bond was coming, Drax got rid of any damning evidence. After the meeting with Drax, Bond gives M the vial that he previously removed from the lab and tells him to have it tested.

Drax hires Jaws to replace Chang. Then, Jaws attacks Bond and Holly on a cable car. They manage to get away from Jaws, but they are captured by other enemy operatives posing as emergency medics. Bond escapes but Holly remains in their clutches.

Q analyzes Drax's vial, and discovers that it contains a nerve gas that will kill humans but is harmless to wildlife. Q explains that the formula for the gas is made from a rare orchid that can only be found in Axhazoco, in the Amazon jungle. Bond is sent to Axhazoco to investigate.

Bond travels upriver and locates Drax's hidden city, which is staffed by exceptionally attractive men and women. Bond is captured and brought to Drax and Holly, who is Drax's prisoner. Drax explains that he is going to unleash the vial which will cause sterility and eventually kill off most of the human race. Then, Drax will inhabit space with a group of perfect physical specimens, a new master race.

Drax attempts to kill Bond and Holly by placing them beneath the *Moonraker* space shuttle, one of six preparing for lift-off. Bond and Holly escape and board the *Moonraker*. The *Moonraker* launches and takes them to a giant space station. The space station is using a blocking device so that it cannot be detected.

Once onboard, Bond and Holly explore the space station and turn off its cloaking device. They are captured and Drax launches the capsule containing the virus to Earth. With the cloaking device off, the space station is visible again. Acting on a tip from General Gogol of the Soviet Union, the United States send in the space marines. A battle takes place between Drax's army and the Marines. During this time, Jaws realizes that Drax is going to wipe out the human race and he changes allegiances. Bond triggers his wrist-dart gun and shoots Drax and then ejects him into space.

Bond and Holly board Drax's space shuttle, which is equipped with a laser gun. They fly to the three spheres of nerve gas that have already been released and shoot them down before they reach Earth. To celebrate saving the planet, Bond and Holly make love in outer space.

Commentary: As Christopher Wood had previously done with *The Spy Who Loved Me*, the writer novelized his screenplay for *Moonraker*, Roger Moore's outer-space-themed adventure. As was the case with *The Spy Who Loved Me*, *Moonraker* has little in common with Fleming's novel of the same name. Hugo Drax, the antagonist of the *Moonraker* movie, is one of the many general parallels between the book and movie. However, taken as a whole, they ought to be regarded as distinct works.

Wood's assignment was to ignore Fleming and write a faithful adaptation of the Eon movie. From that modest metric alone, Wood succeeds. The author also manages to add some fun touches and expand on some story elements that were not present in the feature film.

In the film, Bond locates Drax's jungle fortress relatively quickly. In the novelization, it takes Bond over four days to find Drax's hidden stronghold. During that time, Bond is lost in the jungle. His resources are dwindling, along with his chances of survival. By chronicling Bond's four-day ordeal, Wood ratchets up the tension and increases Bond's jeopardy. The new sequence is a welcome addition to the story.

Wood's novelization restages Jaws' assault on Manuela, Bond's Station VH contact in Rio. In the movie, Jaws assaults Manuela during Carnival. Bond leaps at the steel-tooth killer to save Manuela just as the behemoth is about to kill her. Then, partygoers drag Jaws away. Jaws appears to voluntarily give in and merge in with the crowd. In the novelization, when Bond launches himself at Jaws, the agent's steel-capped heels hit Jaw's teeth, creating a spark. Then, the partygoers put up a wall between Bond and the murderer. Jaws is prevented from attacking Manuela; he doesn't just voluntarily halt his assault. Here, Wood is trying to frame Jaws as an unstoppable killing machine. He doesn't choose to soften the character.

As the scene continues, Bond cradles Manuela in his arms and puts her in a taxi driven by a man in a skeleton suit. Bond suggests that the driver give up cigarettes as, "They're bad for your health." Bond's closing quip about not smoking recalls other Moore-era Bond witticisms. I was curious if this quip was in Wood's original draft, filmed, and then discarded. However, the line doesn't appear in the revised screenplays dated May 19, 1978, or in an earlier but undated draft. Its absence from both scripts makes me think that Wood wrote the line expressly for his novelization.

Wood also departs from the film's climactic ending, which features a massive space battle between Drax's army and the United States Marines. In the movie, the battle is the central focus but, in the novelization, Wood gives Bond a new objective. Bond must destroy a laser gun turret poised to mow down the marine's shuttle. To successfully embolize the weapon, Bond must don a space suit and travel outside of the space station. Bond's spacewalk tops the already outlandish events in the Eon film. Unlike his *Spy Who Loved Me* novelization, where Wood makes the proceedings more realistic, in *James Bond and Moonraker,* Wood leans into the absurdity of 007 in space.

Wood not only gives, but he also taketh away. Wood eliminates Jaws' love interest Dolly from the novelization. In the movie, Jaws' new-found love for Dolly causes the assassin to switch sides and help Bond. Some fans find their relationship charming, but others think that the love-struck Jaws lost his menace. Judging from Dolly's elimination from the novelization, I suspect that Wood falls into the latter camp.

The erasure of Dolly also alters Jaws' reasoning for changing sides. In the film, Jaws helps Bond as a means to save Dolly who wore glasses and, therefore, would not be accepted into Drax's new world order. Yet, in the novelization, because there is no Dolly, Jaws switches sides out of an act of self-preservation, not love. This modification robs Jaws of a nice character arc.

In the film, the attack on Drax's pilot by his vicious Dobermanns takes place (more or less) on-screen. In the novelization, the mauling sequence is not depicted. Instead, the reader learns about it when Bond does, after the fact. Then, Wood uses that moment to add a shade of Bond's character that is largely absent from 007's onscreen adventures—remorse. Bond feels responsible for Trudi's death. He knows that Drax had her killed because she was helping Bond. With few exceptions, the movie Bond is, on the surface, indifferent to death. Bond knows that it's a part of his job and that sometimes his associates pay with their lives for the greater good. In *James Bond and Moonraker*, 007 is grief-stricken by Trudi's demise. Wood takes the reader inside Bond's thoughts: "Bond felt like throwing up. Just a few days before he had been making love to the girl. Now she was dead."

Wood uses the novelization to provide a little information about Bond's boss. In the Eon films, M's full name is not revealed. In *James Bond and Moonraker*, M is identified as Admiral Sir Miles Messervy, K.C.M.G. The name is consistent with the one Fleming provided in his novel *The Man with the Golden Gun*. When entering a room that might contain a highly toxic virus, M is forced to don a gas mask. The act of putting on the protective gear reminds M that he had to wear a similar mask during his service in World War II.

Despite the strengths of Wood's *Moonraker* novelization, one gets the sense that he was slightly less invested in it than when he was writing *James Bond, The Spy Who Loved Me*. Wood's first effort retells the Eon movie version through a Fleming-esque lens. However, *James Bond and Moonraker* is closer to a traditional novelization. Or as Bondologist Calvin Dyson puts it, the novelization "felt like Christopher Wood was writing the Bond book that was in him" but *James Bond and Moonraker* lacked that special something "extra to make it work as a novel in its own right."[92] That's not to say that the novelization is without reward. It's simply that Wood delivered a more traditional novelization the second time around.

Continuity Nod: Bond suggests that he deserves a respite after battling Stromberg (*James Bond, the Spy Who Loved Me*).

Bond's Personal Life: Wood includes excerpts of Bond's medical examination. The report suggests that Bond smokes about 60 cigarettes a day and drinks daily. As a result, his "liver is becoming palpable." The doctor's report suggests that Bond is smoking and drinking less than he used to. However, Bond might argue with the veracity of that report.

Bond's Inner Life: Wood's apparent goal in *James Bond and Moonraker* is to strip Bond of his cinematic-super-hero status and humanize him a bit. To that end, Wood repeatedly refers to Bond's mental state; he reveals that 007 often experiences fear. For instance, "Bond was tortured by the fear that he... was ploughing into some limitless wilderness," "Bond suddenly felt frightened," "Feeling no other sensation beyond numbing fear," and "Fear ran through him like a fast-moving current." At one point, Bond's fear is so overwhelming that it becomes "physically painful." Moore's 007 is decidedly less afraid. In the same scene, Bond calls on God to intervene and end the torture. It's something akin to prayer.

Bond's Tastes: Bond enjoys rituals. For him, smoking on an airplane is one of the enjoyable parts of flying.

Bond's Work Methods: Before the novelization began, Bond received training on how to free-fall without a parachute. Bond's one-day training comes in handy when Bond is thrown from a plane and needs to remove a parachute from the co-pilot, who seems to want to keep it.

Assorted Observation

- In the movie, Drax's pilot is a French woman named Corinne Dufour, played by Corinne Cléry. In the novelization, she is an American called Trudi Parker. Cléry was cast because *Moonraker* was made as part of a British-French co-production. As such, a certain number of characters needed to be played by French performers.[93] I've reviewed an undated script from Wood's in which the pilot is called Trudi Parker. Because his novelization wasn't bound by the same restrictions as the production, Wood restored his original idea for the character.

THE REBIRTH OF THE SERIES

"Bond remembered the dictum of the pros:
"It's never too early to start winning."
IAN FLEMING, *Goldfinger*

JOHN GARDNER'S TENURE
1981–1996

John Gardner wrote 16 Bond books—14 original Bond novels and 2 film novelizations. His impressive output of Bond books surpasses the output of Fleming, Bond's creator. Gardner's record is also unlikely to be surpassed. His work includes *Licence Renewed* (1981); *For Special Services* (1982); *Icebreaker* (1983); *Role of Honour* (1984); *Nobody Lives For Ever* (1986), *No Deals, Mr. Bond* (1987), *Scorpius* (1988); *Licence to Kill* (1989 novelization); *Win, Lose or Die* (1989); *Brokenclaw* (1990); *The Man from Barbarossa* (1991); *Death Is Forever* (1992); *Never Send Flowers* (1993); *SeaFire* (1994); *GoldenEye* (1995); and *COLD* (the 1996 novel was also released as *Cold Fall*).

In his sixteen-year tenure, Gardner turned out a new book almost every year. The one exception was in 1985 when Gardner took a year off after his fourth novel *Role of Honour*. However, Gardner made up for it in 1989 when readers were treated to two Bond books—an original tale (*Win, Lose or Die*) and a novelization (*Licence to Kill*).

Gardner revealed to *The New York Times* how he got the gig, recalling, 'Apparently Glidrose had a list of six candidates, and I was at the top. I supplied them with four possible narrative outlines, they picked one of them and asked me to do certain things. What they wanted was for me to think in terms of Bond having been on ice for a while, but being quite up to date about what's been going on in the world during the past two decades."[94] Still, Gardner knew that he might not be universally embraced for his approach. He told *People Magazine,* "[Bond is] a household name. Fans know how he cuts his fingernails, so the writer is a target for nitpickers. Mr. Fleming is a very difficult act to follow."[95] Gardner was correct on that score, but over the years he has amassed a dedicated and loyal following.

LICENCE RENEWED (1981)

Author: John Gardner

In Brief: James Bond is sent to investigate a physicist who is determined to set off six nuclear reactors if his ransom demands are not met.

Meaning of Title: The Double O branch has been disbanded but M unofficially renews Bond's license to kill. The title also alludes to the fact that the era of Bond continuation novels has begun again.

Chronology: Contemporary. Set after Fleming's novels, in the then-present 1980s.

Operation: Meltdown

Bastard Meter: Not mentioned concerning Bond.

Eggs: One boiled egg.

Insight into Bond: "You're a man of vigour who lives for danger."

Summary: James Bond intends to share a romantic evening with a married woman at his new cottage outside of London. Bond has been called back to work, though. M informs Bond that the Double O branch is being shuttered. However, M insists that Bond will covertly continue on as a Double O agent. M briefs Bond on Franco Quesocriado, a terrorist who is on the loose and is somehow connected to Dr. Anton Murik, a renowned nuclear physicist. M tasks Bond with finding out what Franco and Murik are up to. To prepare for the assignment, Bond looks into Murik's life and learns that the scientist has invented a new kind of power reactor that is supposedly safe. However, the scientific community thinks Murik's reactor is suspect. M informs Bond that he can meet Murik at the horse races on Gold Cup day.

Bond goes to the Gold Cup and locates Murik who is there with bodyguard Caber, his girlfriend Mary-Jane Mashkin, his ward and fashion model Lavender Peacock. Bond notices that Lavender is wearing a pearl necklace. As a way of ingratiating himself with Murik, Bond steals the pearls, pretends to "find" them, and then returns them to Lavender. To show his gratitude, Murik invites Bond to his home, Murik Castle where he will be holding the Highland Games, a series of games and festivities. Bond tells Murik that he's a mercenary who is looking for work. Murik indicates that he might have a job for Bond.

Bond goes to Murik's Castle in Murcaldy, Scotland and plants a listening device in the castle. Then he has dinner with Murik, Lavender, and Mary-Jane. After the meal, Bond returns to his room and uses the bug to eavesdrop on a conversation Murik is having with Franco Quesocriado. During the call, Murik lays out his plans for Operation Meltdown, which concerns the hostile takeover of nuclear reactor sites in England, France, Germany, and the United States. Murik also explains that he wants a woman killed but does not reveal her name. Then, Bond is visited by Mary-Jane. She makes a pass at Bond, which he declines. Later, Lavender goes to Bond's room. She tells Bond that she's suspicious of Franco, who frequently meets with Murik.

Bond armed with a FN Browning 1903 9mm in *Licence Renewed.* Illustration by Pat Carbajal

The next day, at the Highland Games, Murik arranges for Bond to wrestle Caber. Caber is the stronger man but, with the aid of a knock-out gas from Q'ute (a member of Q Branch), Bond wins the match. Murik is impressed. Later, Murik gives Bond a tour of his castle, which includes a room filled with old weapons. Murik explains that he is going to demonstrate to the world the dangers of nuclear energy by taking over six nuclear control rooms. If the world powers do not meet his demands, he will cause a nuclear meltdown. Murik plans to use the ransom money to construct his own safe nuclear reactor. Franco laments that he is supposed to split the money with Franco. If Franco is out of the way, then Murik will get the entire sum. Murik hires Bond to eliminate Franco.

Later, Bond feels that he has enough information to share with M and tries to escape in his Saab. However, Murik's men catch Bond. Murik brings Bond to his dungeon, where he injects Bond with a drug, tortures him with high-frequency white noise, and interrogates him.

The next day, Murik flies Bond to Rivesaltes, France. Bond escapes from Murik's men and tries to inform M of Murik's plan. However, before he can brief M, one of Murik's goons attacks Bond. Although Bond gets the upper hand and dispatches the enforcer, he realizes that it's up to him to stop Murik from killing a woman, whose identity is still not unknown.

Bond rushes to the Palais des Rois de Majorque, where Lavender is walking the runway in a fashion show. Once there, Bond sees that Franco is getting ready to shoot someone. Bond rushes Franco, but the terrorist gets a shot off. The stray bullet kills Mary-Jane. In turn, Bond kills Franco. Then, Caber captures Bond.

Bond is brought to the airport where he and Murik board a plane that will function as the control center for Operation Meltdown. Bond learns that Lavender and not Mary-Jane was Franco's intended target. Murik explains that he plans to kill Lavender because she is the true heir to his title, finances, and estate.

Murik sets his main plan in motion. His six teams take control of the six nuclear control rooms around the world. Disguising his identity, Murik announces to the world that if he isn't paid $50 billion in 24 hours, he will cause a nuclear incident. Bond knocks out Murik, calls off the strike, and then fights Caber. Bond throws Caber off the plane and returns to find that Murik is missing.

Sometime later, Bond meets with M who informs Bond that authorities have captured the six teams who took control of the nuclear power plants. However, there is still no sign of Murik. Bond has a hunch that Murik will return to his castle. M authorizes Bond and Tanner to go to the castle.

Bond and Tanner go to the castle and discover Murik has returned and is in possession of the documents that prove Lavender is entitled to Murik's estate, title, and their family funds. Murik tries to kill

Bond but, using Murik's ancient weapons, Bond kills him and retrieves the documents.

Weeks later, Bond meets up again with Lavender who has now reclaimed her family's estate and title. Bond and Lavender make plans to see each other again.

Commentary: In 1981, John Gardner revealed to *The New York Times* he had been Glidrose's top choice to write the first traditional Bond novel since 1968's *Colonel Sun*. It's no mystery why he was on the list. Gardner wrote a series of Boysie Oakes spy novels and a pair of novels about Sherlock Holmes' adversary Professor Moriarty. The Moriarty books demonstrated that Gardner could write stories that were based on another author's character. The popularity of the Oakes series proved that Gardner could craft a compelling spy yarn. It should be noted that the eight Boysie Oakes books were not straightforward spy yarns. Oakes is an inverted-Bond character, an operative who is a coward and abhors violence.

Like Fleming, Gardner had a military background. Before becoming a writer, Gardner was a member of the Royal Marines in World War II. Gardner's military service no doubt also suggested that he could credibly write about the clandestine world of the secret service.

Before setting out to write his novel, Gardner needed to decide what period Bond should exist in—should his novel be set in the mid-to-late 1960s, and follow the events of *The Man with the Golden Gun,* or should it be set in the then-present, the 1980s? After all, *Colonel Sun* was set in Fleming's period (and the then-present day). Both Gardner and Glidrose felt that the present-day setting would be more accessible to readers.

Neither Gardner nor Glidrose wanted to change the essential nature of Bond's character, they wanted him to stay consistent with Fleming's writing. Gardner explained that they wanted to preserve Bond's personality while bringing the world around him up to date to reflect contemporary mores and geopolitical issues.'[96] Once the broad details were agreed upon, Gardner needed to craft a story that would meet the Fleming Estate's approval. Gardner recalled, "I supplied them with four possible narrative outlines, they picked one of them."[97]

By changing the setting from the mid-1960s to the early-1980s, Gardner needed to account for Bond's activities since *Golden Gun*. In some ways, he also needed to explain why there were no new Bond stories since Fleming. If Bond had gone through an important mission or faced off with a spectacular villain, then that story would need to have been written and published. Gardner efficiently addressed both issues by indicating that Bond had been relatively inactive in the intervening years, having only gone out on a handful of missions. Otherwise, he had largely been performing clerical and other duties that had kept him out of the field.

Gardner also needed to establish Bond's character, or at least, Gardner's version of Bond. Gardner's Bond is largely consistent with Fleming's Bond. Gardner's Bond plays golf, socializes with Bill Tanner, is particular about his meals and what he wears, and carries on romantic relations with married women.

Yet, Gardner's Bond has not been frozen in time. Instead, Gardner's Bond has made some modest changes. For instance, Bond has traded in his Walther PPK for a 9mm Browning, prefers his Saab 900 Turbo to his Bentley, and, while retaining his flat off King's Road in Chelsea, has also acquired a new place, a small cottage south of London. At the cottage, Bond drinks champagne and carries on his affairs. While he is still very much a bachelor, the cottage's proximity to one of his lovers was instrumental in his acquiring the property. For the Bond of the 80s and 90s, that's a true demonstration of love and commitment.

Gardner contended that these changes were essential. Gardner wrote, "Believe me when I say that unless I was going to slavishly reproduce Fleming's Bond I was always going to get knocked simply because I wasn't Fleming. Many people did not take the point that all fictional characters have to grow and strengthen. To allow Bond to have remained static in a changing world as some seem to desire—would, I still believe, have been death."[98]

The spy game had changed since Fleming wrote about it in the Sixties. Gardner's goal was to update the technology and Bond's working methods so that they would be consistent with modern practices. Gardner also created a new colleague for Bond, a member of the Q Branch named Ann Reilly (aka Q'ute). Reilly and Bond develop a flirtatious relationship. Happily, M, Miss Moneypenny, the Armorer, and Tanner all still work for SIS whose cover business is still called Transworld Consortium.

When *Licence Renewed* begins, M informs Bond that the Double O division has been mothballed. Going forward, Bond will be a part of a new secret division, named the Special Section, which reports only to him. As he has before, M will give Bond assignments and Bond will carry them out. In other words, while everything has changed, nothing has changed, really. Bond will continue to keep the world safe from maniacs who want to control it.

Continuity Nod: Gardner makes several allusions to Fleming's work. Gardner references the cigarette case that blocked a bullet in *From Russia with Love*, and the scar on his hand that he earned in *Casino Royale.* There is also a blink-and-you'll-miss-it allusion to Bond's special relationship with Felix Leiter.

Bond's History: As a schoolboy, Bond listened to the popular music of the time. Bond describes his Scottish father as a "true Highlander." Gardner's Bond has a father named Archie who achieved the rank of Colonel. Of course, in Fleming's novels, Bond's father's name is Andrew and not Archie. I suspect that the differences in names were just a slip and it was not a deliberate attempt to change the established facts.

Bond's Personal Life: Fleming's Bond is a heavy drinker and smoker. Gardner's Bond has cut back considerably on both vices. Bond's favorite sport is golf. Gardner describes Bond as a "staunch monarchist." Even though sticking to a routine is dangerous for a secret agent, Bond is a creature of habit in his personal life. Bond performs daily exercises that challenge his body and his mind, including a Japanese discipline called Kata.

Bond's Inner Life: Bond is getting restless. He's considering retiring and "going private." It's not just that Bond welcomes danger (although he does), it's just that work provides Bond with a sense of "real purpose." As established by Fleming, Gardner's Bond does not like killing. However, he considers it a part of his job and once he does take someone's life, he does not think about it afterward.

Bond's Work Methods: As noted, Gardner was a member of the Royal Marines commandos, and had first-hand knowledge of military operations. As such, he wanted to make Bond operate in a manner befitting a trained operative. For instance, Gardner describes Bond's methods for sweeping his room for electronic devices. Elsewhere, Bond reminds himself not to get too close to a man with a gun and that it's better to keep at least one leg-length away from an adversary. Bond even has a counter-intuitive method for fleeing danger—walk, don't run. This way it looks like he is one of the crowd.

The movie Bond just seems to have infinite knowledge of all arcane matters. Like Fleming, Gardner takes a different approach. Before heading out on a mission, Bond spends a considerable amount of time learning new skills or brushing up on a new subject. For instance, as part of an upcoming operation, Bond will need to clandestinely steal a necklace from a woman while she's wearing it. So, before going into the field, Bond studies the art of pickpocketing. Unlike the movie Bond, Bond doesn't already possess the required specialized skills; he needs to learn them.

Bond's flat in Chelsea and his new cottage south of London both contain two sets of phones—a white phone for personal use and a red one for special communications to his office. Bond goes to the shooting range weekly and takes courses on combat skills every month.

It's Not Cute: Gardner provided the assistant quartermaster Ann Reilly with the nickname of Q'ute—obviously a play on Q, Bond's armorer from the movies. However, the name was a late addition to the writing process. In the first draft of the *Licence Renewed* manuscript, the armorer was a woman named Q. However, because Q is the name of Eon's character and not Fleming's, who is called Major Boothroyd, Ian Fleming Publications needed Eon's permission to use any character named Q. According to Gardner, Eon declined the request. Because the manuscript was nearly complete, Gardner thought that the easiest thing to do would be to change the character's name from Q to Q'ute.[99] For his part, Gardner says that he wasn't "trying to be clever" and he calls the pun "unfortunate."[100]

Gardner's impulse to make Q a woman anticipates Eon's decision to cast Judi Dench as M in *GoldenEye*. For some, the cutesy name Q'ute diminishes Reilly's character. The character Q'ute appeared in the *Daily Express* comic strip *The Paradise Plot* (1981), which was written by Jim Lawrence and illustrated by John McLusky.[101]

Assorted Observations:

- Gardner's working title for *Licence Renewed* was named after the villain's codename—*Warlock.*[102]
- Bond is not superstitious but is mindful of the meaning of potential omens.
- When the pilot instructs passengers to fasten their seatbelts, 007 quotes Bette Davis in *All About Eve,* joking that it's going to be a bumpy ride.
- Bond does not need an alarm clock. Instead, he can wake himself up at the appointed hour.
- *Licence Renewed* sat on the *New York Times* bestseller list for three months. It was also Gardner's best-selling Bond book.[103]

FOR SPECIAL SERVICES (1982)

Author: John Gardner

In Brief: Bond must discover if Markus Bismaquer, a wealthy ice cream manufacturer, is connected to the newly reconstituted SPECTRE, which is being led by Blofeld. Bond is aided on this mission by Felix Leiter's daughter, Cedar Leiter.

Meaning of Title: The President of the United States sends Bond the gift of a .38 revolver with the barrel of the gun inscribed *For Special Services*. According to Gardner, Ian Fleming himself was given a similar gift from William Donovan, the head of America's Office of Strategic Services (OSS), the precursor to the CIA.[104]

Chronology: Contemporary. Set after *Licence Renewed.*

Operation: Heavenly Wolf and HOUND.

Bastard Meter: None, as applied to Bond.

Eggs: Sunny side up.

Insight into Bond: "His smile was touched with sadness."

Summary: While providing security on a commercial airline flight, Bond thwarts a terrorist attack. Before dying, one of the terrorists reveals that he is a member of SPECTRE, the evil organization which SIS thought had ceased operations. In Louisiana, Blofeld, the leader of SPECTRE, discusses his plans for a secret operation dubbed HOUND.

Back in London, Bond is carrying on an inter-office romance with Anne Reilly, a member of Q Branch. Then, Bond meets with M who introduces him to Cedar Leiter, Felix's daughter. Cedar is a CIA operative who will join 007 on his next mission. M briefs Bond on Markus Bismaquer, a wealthy businessman with a legitimate ice cream operation, who aspires to overthrow the United States government. M also reveals that SIS has come into possession of a letter signed by Blofeld. They wonder how Blofeld can be the head of SPECTRE when Bond apparently killed him in Japan (*You Only Live Twice*). M tasks the agents with finding out if Bismaquer is in league with SPECTRE.

Bond and Cedar travel to New York where Bond poses as an art dealer selling a rare set of William Hogarth prints. At the hotel, Bismaquer's men, including Mike Mazzard, force themselves into Bond's room.

To throw SPECTRE off their scent, Bond and Cedar first drive to Washington, DC. In DC, Bond and Cedar are nearly killed when they board a sabotaged elevator. However, the duo escape.

Using the number that Mazzard provided, Bond calls Bismaquer at his home in Amarillo, Texas and arranges to show him the Hogarth prints. Bond and Cedar travel to Bismaquer's compound. The compound is heavily fortified and protected by armed guards. It's so large that a monorail is used to reach it. At Bismaquer's ranch, Bond and his host discuss the prints. Then, Bond meets Bismaquer's wife, Nena. Nena and Bond form a connection. Nena takes Bond around the property and shows him a secret entrance that allows passage to a large conference center. Nena also tells Bond that she knows his prints are forgeries. Later, Bismaquer makes Bond a bet. If Bond can win a car race, then he will give him $2 million but if he loses, then Bond must give Bismaquer the prints at no charge. Bond accepts the wager.

Elsewhere, SPECTRE advances its plans regarding the Space Wolves, the laser-firing satellites that can destroy other satellites.

Armed with his Heckler and Koch VP 70
For Special Services
Illustration by Pat Carbajal

That night, Bond sneaks out of the ranch and surveys the compound. Bond discovers a working ice cream plant and observes two of Bismaquer's workers eating ice cream laced with mind-controlling hypnotic drugs. Under the drug's influence, the workers are highly susceptible to following any command that Bismaquer issues.

The next day, Bond enters a car race against Bismaquer's partner, Walter Luxor. During the race, Luxor tries to kill Bond by throwing an incendiary device at him but Bond evades the threat and wins the race. After the race, Bismaquer explains that he is hosting a large conference on his property the next day so Bond will have to leave the estate. Bond returns to his cabin to find it teaming with lethal harvester ants. He burns down the cabin to destroy the ants.

Later that night, Bond meets Nena who tells them that a large amount of the ice cream will be shipped out that night to an undisclosed location. Bond wonders if the ice cream is laced with the drug that makes people highly susceptible to commands. Bond suspects that Bismaquer is the new Blofeld. Bond and Nena make love. Still later, Bond sneaks into the conference center, finds a hiding place, and waits for the conference to begin.

The next day, members of SPECTRE assemble. Bismaquer announces to the crowd that Blofeld is in their midst. Bismaquer talks about a high-tech space laser called the Particle Beam Weapon and a satellite system that can defeat other satellites called the Space Wolves. Whoever controls the Particle Beam Weapon and the Space Wolves would control space and could threaten any country in the world. SPECTRE plans to break into NORAD headquarters and steal the computer tapes, and microfilm that will enable them to control the satellite system. Bismaquer explains that his company will supply NORAD with his drug-laced ice cream. Once the NORAD personnel eat the ice cream, they will do Bismaquer's bidding.

Bond tries to escape the compound and relay Bismaquer's plan to his superiors. He is captured before he can get away. Bond is brought to Bismaquer and forced to take the mind-controlling drug. Under the drug's influence, Bond thinks he is a four-star general named General James A. Banker. The real Banker has clearance to enter NORAD headquarters.

Bond/Banker and Mike Mazzard go to NORAD headquarters. Claiming that they are there for an inspection, they are granted entry. At NORAD, Bond/Banker learns how to control the Space Wolves satellites. It turns out that Bismaquer has developed feelings for Bond and had previously supplied him with the antidote. So the agent is no longer under the influence of the drug. Bond warns the American soldiers that the NORAD base is under attack. With Bond's help, the Americans thwart SPECTRE's attack.

Bond returns to Nena who tells him that Cedar Leiter has been taken to SPECTRE's headquarters in Louisiana. Nena and Bond fly to

Louisiana to save Cedar. In SPECTRE's headquarters, Bond sees Nena killing Bismaquer. Nena confesses to Bond that she is actually Blofeld's daughter and that she's the new head of SPECTRE. Nena attempts to shoot Bond but before she does, giant pythons grab hold of her. Felix Leiter arrives and shoots Nena in the head.

Bond and Cedar go to New Orleans and plan to go on vacation together. Felix gives his blessing for a relationship and the President of the United States sends his thanks to Bond.

Commentary: Blofeld is dead. Long live Blofeld. With apologies to Messieurs Goldfinger, Scaramanga, and Largo, Bond's most memorable adversary is SPECTRE leader Ernst Stavro Blofeld. Not only is Blofeld a worthy opponent with a brilliant criminal mind but Bond also has a vendetta against him. He's responsible for Bond's wife's death. So when Bond goes up against Blofeld, it is personal.

When John Gardner was creating an adversary for Bond to face, he could not pit 007 against Blofeld. Fleming had killed off his rival in *You Only Live Twice*. Still, Gardner wanted to make Blofeld the central villain of *For Special Services*. So Gardner needed to answer the question, how could he bring back Blofeld without violating Fleming's continuity? That question is the central mystery of the book. Gardner waits for the second to last chapter of the book to provide an answer. It turns out that "Blofeld" is not Ernst Stavro Blofeld, but his daughter, Nena. And it is Nena who is out for revenge. As the new head of SPECTRE, Nena has concocted a plan to destroy 007, the man who killed her father.

Before Gardner reveals Nena's identity, he offers up other suspects. Potential culprits include Nena's husband Markus Bismaquer, who Bond has been sent to investigate, and Walter Luxor, Bismaquer's partner whose skin is so translucent that it looks like he has a skull for a face. Gardner uses the villain's last name almost as a title when Bismaquer and Luxor are thought to be the new Blofeld. As if, whoever becomes head of SPECTRE is called "Blofeld," as a tribute to the villainous mastermind and as a way to confuse the opposition.

Gardner's trick of having Nena Blofeld as "Blofeld" is a technique that works in a book. In a movie, filmmakers would have to go to greater lengths to prevent the audience from figuring out the mystery, keeping the character in the shadows for most of the story and using a voice control box to disguise their voice. In a novel, Gardner can use gender-neutral pronouns to keep the reader guessing.

The battle between Bond and Nena Blofeld is short-lived. As soon as Gardner reveals her identity, he immediately kills her off.

Surprisingly, it is not Bond who does the honors. Instead, Nena's pet python puts the squeeze on her and Felix Leiter shoots her in the head. There is nothing wrong with killing off Bond's central adversary at the end of a novel. In fact, Fleming frequently did the same. However, in this instance, Gardner might have been better served by letting Nena escape and allowing Bond to confront her in a later novel.

For many fans, it is a thrill to see Blofeld's return. Blofeld is to Bond what Moriarty is to Holmes. Before writing *For Special Services*, Gardner had already authored two Moriarty books, *The Return of Moriarty* (1974) and *The Revenge of Moriarty* (1975). I imagine that Gardner was eager to try his hand at his version of another iconic baddie. Gardner makes Nena the first central female that Bond has gone up against. In the past, women have been secondary villains but never the brains behind the operation. Nena Blofeld is not the only second generation of Bond characters. Gardner also introduces readers to Cedar Leiter, the daughter of his old friend Felix. Cedar, like Felix, is a CIA operative.

Gardner reveals the return of SPECTRE. In the opening scene, Bond thwarts a terrorist attack on a plane and kills an enemy with a knife. Before dying, the critically wounded terrorist repeats a word that sounds like "Inspector." As the man repeats himself, "inspector" becomes "In...spector" or "spector" or "SPECTRE."

Gardner also crafted a few set pieces for 007, including an escape from a falling elevator, a car race, and a ride on the villain's private monorail system. These action beats bring to mind Bond's cinematic escapades.

Continuity Nod: Gardner references Lavender Peacock (*Licence Renewed*) and several of Fleming's former heroines, including Tracy di Vicenzo, Vesper Lynd, Kissy Suzuki, Honey Rider, Tiffany Case, Domino Solitaire, Pussy Galore, and Gala Brand. Gardner reveals that Brand is now married. She even exchanges Christmas cards with Bond. Past Bond villains such as Blofeld and Mr. Big are also name-checked. Bond recalls how Leiter was maimed by a shark (*Live and Let Die*).

Bond's History: Bond's nanny used to tell Bond that "promises are like pie crust—made to be broken."

Bond's Inner Life: Bond is not overly emotional. However, he is not without feelings. He feels a tinge of regret after killing an enemy agent that he only meant to injure, and he feels a pang of jealousy for the villain's wife to whom he is attracted.

Bond drives his Saab, his Silver Beast.
Illustration by Pat Carbajal

Bond's Personal Life: Bond smokes low-tar cigarettes that have been made especially for him. Bond loves New York, preferring it to London. His beloved Saab is nicknamed the Silver Beast. Bond's best friend describes him as a "swashbuckling Lothario." The memory of his late wife still haunts him, but sex provides him a measure of comfort.

Bond's Tastes: The chicken pot pie that Bond consumes is the best he has ever eaten and the martini that a SPECTRE agent offers 007 is among the best he's ever tasted. Even so, Bond generally prefers the martinis that he prepares himself to those that others make for him. Bond loathes greetings in which he has to kiss someone on the cheek. The human contact that Bond gets when he makes love to a woman leaves him "refreshed and cleansed."

Bond's Work Methods: To keep his shooting skills sharp, Bond routinely practices his fast-draw dueling methods at Q Branch firing sessions. When recreating a disguise, Bond believes that modest changes are more effective than trying to remake an entire face or body. Changing one's walk is also a helpful method. Bond's instructors taught him that if he crimped the fuse of a detonator with his teeth, he would eventually lose them. Bond ignores this advice and uses his teeth anyway. In the end, Bond's pearly whites are no worse for wear.

Assorted Observations:

- Bond's primary weapon is a Heckler & Koch, but he also carries a backup Smith & Wesson.
- Bismaquer, the villain, is bisexual.
- Cedar Leiter is referenced in the anthology comic book *Reflections of Death* (2020). In it, Bond calls Felix Leiter, who refers to Cedar as his oldest daughter.

ICEBREAKER (1983)

Author: John Gardner

In Brief: Bond teams up with agents from the CIA, KGB, and Mossad to stop the rise of a neo-Nazi group who are conducting assassinations and dispensing armaments from their hidden base on the Russia-Finland border.

Meaning of Title: Icebreaker is the name of a joint operation between Britain, America, the Soviet Union, and Israel.

Chronology: Contemporary. Set after the events of *For Special Services*.

Operation: Icebreaker.

Bastard Meter: Straight-forward "bastard."

Eggs: Scrambled.

Insight into Bond: "There was no time for a death duel. Even 007 knew when the odds were stacked against him."

Summary: The National Socialist Action Army (NSAA) conducts a series of assassinations against members of the communist party from various countries, including Britain and America.

In Helsinki, Bond pays a visit to his longtime friend and lover Paula Vacker. At Paula's apartment, Bond is attacked by Finnish assassins. After neutralizing the attackers, Bond asks Paula how the assassins knew how to find him. Paula says that the only person who knew Bond was coming is her friend Anni Tudeer.

Back in London, Bond and M discuss the attack. M also orders Bond to join Operation Icebreaker, a joint mission with the CIA (United States), Mossad (Israel), and KGB (Soviet Union) in Finland, near the Finland-Russian border. The goal of Icebreaker is to stop the NSAA, which is founded on Nazi beliefs, from assassinating communists and distributing weapons. The head of the NSAA is a Finnish Nazi officer named Aarne Tudeer who has changed his name to Count Konrad von Glöda. Bond is told to go to a hotel in Madeira, Portugal and meet other members of his team. Then, he will travel to the Arctic Circle where the operation will take place.

Bond goes to Portugal where he meets CIA agent Brad Tirpitz, KGB operative Nicolai "Koyla" Mosolov, and Mossad operator Rivke Ingber. Bond learns that the NSAA has an ordinance depot called Blue Hare where they distribute the weapons and a base of operations called the Ice Palace. Their mission is to go to the base, gain intelligence on NSAA's activities, and put an end to them.

Before Bond leaves for the mission, he visits Paula's flat. He discovers that her home has been ransacked and that she's not there. Searching the apartment, Bond finds two medals awarded to a Nazi officer named Aarne Tudeer, a relative of Anni Tudeer, Paula's friend. Bond pockets the medals.

Back at the hotel, Bond receives an envelope from M which contains a photo of Anni Tudeer. He also learns that Anni is a Mossad agent who goes by the name of Rivke Ingber. Bond meets up with Rivke and confronts her. Rivke confesses that her real name is Anni Tudeer and that she is the daughter of Aarne Tudeer, the Nazi. Rivke tells Bond that while she knows Paula Vacker, the two have not spoken to each other in years. If what Rivke is saying is true, then another operative is at large posing as Anni.

Bond packing heat in *Icebreaker.*
Illustration by Pat Carbajal

Bond and CIA agent Brad Tirpitz meet. Tirpitz tells Bond that he has reason to believe that the KGB agent intends to kill both of them. Bond and Tirpitz make a pact to stick together. Later, in the hotel, Bond sees Count Konrad von Glöda (aka Aarne Tudeer) and his wife, the Countess. Bond receives a call from Paula Vacker warning him that Rivke is marked for death. Elsewhere, Rivke runs over a landmine while skiing down a mountain. Bond and Tirpitz rush to save Rivke and arrange for her to get emergency medical care at a local hospital.

Bond calls the hospital but Rivke isn't there. It turns out that the ambulance drivers were actually disguised enemy agents who kidnapped her. Tirpitz tells Bond that he's worried that KGB agent Kolya is behind her abduction. Tirpitz tells Bond not to trust Kolya.

Bond, Tirpitz, and Kolya travel by snowmobile to NSAA's ordnance depot called Blue Hare. Along the way, Tirpitz's snowmobile blows up, apparently killing him. However, the explosion was just Tirpitz's ploy to trick Kolya who seemingly had plans to kill both Bond and Tirpitz.

Bond and Kolya reach Blue Hare. Once they arrive, Bond is captured by Paula Vacker. Bond learns that CIA agent Tirpitz is also working for NSAA. Count von Glöda tortures Bond to learn the whereabouts of one of the NSAA soldiers who has been previously captured by the British. Eventually, Bond passes out.

Bond wakes up to discover that he's being held in a room with Rivke. Count von Glöda arrives and thanks Bond for cracking during the torture and providing him with the information he needed. When Count von Glöda leaves, Bond tells Rivke that he's not sure what he said while being tortured. However, he hopes that he didn't reveal the fact that Count von Glöda's soldier is being held in SIS's headquarters. Suddenly, Paula enters the room, shoots out the lights in the room, and then kills Rivke. Paula explains that Rivke is a double agent working for Count von Glöda. Paula says that the lights were bugged, and Bond has just revealed the soldier's location to Count von Glöda. Paula also reveals that she's a member of the Finnish Intelligence and Security Agency.

Paula sneaks Bond out of the compound. Meanwhile, a Soviet-led airstrike on Blue Hare and the enemy's base of operations destroys the facilities and apparently kills Count von Glöda in the process.

Bond and Paula celebrate the success of their mission by getting a hotel room together. They are interrupted by KGB agent Mosolov, who reveals that he is working with Count von Glöda. Bond kills Mosolov and then goes after the count who is trying to flee the country. Bond and Count von Glöda draw guns and shoot each other. Bond kills the count but takes two bullets in his chest.

Later, M visits Bond in the hospital. Bond learns that CIA agent Brad Tirpitz wasn't a double agent working for Count von Glöda. Instead, Tirpitz was a triple agent working with SIS who had been assigned to infiltrate the count's organization. M also confirms that Mossad agent Rivke Ingber was in league with Count von Glöda and that KGB agent Kolya Mosolov had been selling arms to the count. Bond asks his nurse out on a date. After she accepts, Paula enters and says that she'll be the one to take Bond out. Pleased by the attention, Bond goes to sleep.

Commentary: You cannot write a Bond book without a little torture. It is not that the writing process is torturous, although it undoubtedly has its challenges. It's just continuation authors often have to invent a unique way for the villain to inflict pain on 007. Fleming's Le Chiffre used a carpet beater on Bond and Amis' Colonel Sun inserted a metal spike into the spy's ear canal. If Gardner wanted to compete with these two seminal scenes, then he'd have his work cut out for him.

For my money, Gardner invents a memorable way to torment Bond. Largely set in snowbound and cold Finland, Gardner's Bond must face the elements, Jack London style, in this Artic assignment. Despite wearing proper winter clothes, the freezing temperatures are nearly unbearable. So when Count Konrad von Glöda captures Bond and strips him naked, the reader knows that 007 is in grave danger. Even before the torture begins, Bond feels the bitter blast of the cold. That is only the beginning of the spy's ordeal. The enemy carves a hole in the ice and dunks the naked agent into the freezing water. Then, they raise him up, let him freeze, and then dunk him back into the water. Count von Glöda treats 007 as if he were a human tea bag.

Gardner illustrates the psychological effects of the punishment on Bond's psyche. In the scene, the enemy is trying to get Bond to reveal information to them about the whereabouts of one of their operatives. As the torture progresses, Bond becomes less and less in control of his critical thinking. Eventually, he's unsure of what he's revealed to the enemy and what he has kept secret.

As a way of withstanding the torture, Bond tries to concentrate on a location that is both warm and that will give him a measure of serenity. Bond chooses the countryside and a series of images rush through his head—a summer day, a bumble bee, the sound of farm machinery, hay, and so on. In another telling moment, Bond sings, "Sumer is icumen in, Sing, cuckoo..." The exact origins of the song are unknown, but it appears to be a British folk song called "Sumer is icumen in" also known as the "Cuckoo Song." The 13th Century tune roughly translates to "Summer has come in." The inclusion of the song is an interesting glimpse into Bond's psyche and tastes. The refrain is presumably something he learned as a child and it provides him with a quantum of solace.

Bond withstanding torture in *Icebreaker.*
Illustration by Pat Carbajal

The intense torture scene provides insight into Bond's character that might not have been as effectively revealed in other circumstances. If Bond revealed the same details while on a date, it wouldn't have had the same impact. This way, the images float through Bond's head in an almost lyrical way. It's more effective to have Bond cling to these memories as a way to stave off the torture.

Icebreaker contains Gardner's most labyrinthine plot yet. The story is filled with not only double-crosses but triple-crosses as well. To make it easier for the reader to follow the plot, Gardner limits the number of key characters—three agents from various intelligence organizations, a villain, and his daughter. More characters than that would no doubt make the story hard to track. In subsequent novels, Gardner would make his plots even more complex.

Continuity Nod: Bond recalls being questioned by Austrian police officers after Tracy's murder. Gardner makes passing references to SPECTRE and CIA agent Brad Tirpitz sends Bond best wishes from Felix and Cedar Leiter (*For Special Services*). Bond compares Count von Glöda to other ruthless adversaries such as Drax, Goldfinger, and Blofeld, as well as his daughter Nena (*For Special Services*). In this instance, Gardner can bolster his own creation's evil standing by comparing them to Fleming's all-star lineup of baddies. KGB operative Nicolai Mosolov works for the intelligence organization formerly called SMERSH.

Bond's History: Drinking beef tea as an adult reminds Bond of his parents who gave him the drink during his frequent bouts of flu which either kept him at home or in the school nurse's office.

Bond's Inner Life: When M instructs Bond to work with a team of agents, Bond bristles. As Gardner correctly points out "Bond was not a team man."

Bond's Personal Life: Bond has an interest in sailing, jazz, and Eric Ambler's books. He has been having an intermittent relationship with a woman in Helsinki named Paula Vacker. Despite their repeated time together, Bond has failed to discover that Vacker is also a spy.

Bond is aware that May, his housekeeper, does an excellent job of caring for him. When he needs it most, May will send an exhausted Bond to his room and provide him with a light supper to eat in bed. When someone moves fast, she often says that they move "like greased lightning."

Bond's Tastes: Bond enjoys a soup that contains reindeer sausages and when Bond wants to give himself a treat, he will book the honeymoon suite at the Inter-Continental.

Bond's Work Methods: From time to time, Bond trains with the Royal Marines' Special Boat Squadron so the agent can stay up to date on their tactics and weaponry. Some of the exercises require him to "live off the belt," a term which means that 007 can use only the tool that can be stored in his equipment belt to survive.

Bond was taught that he should never use a knife to defend himself. Instead, the knife is only an offensive weapon. As a way to escape from captivity, Bond briefly considers dressing in a female nurse's uniform and posing as her. However, he dismissed the idea because it was not practical.

Because an agent will sometimes need to sleep at inopportune moments, Bond has developed the skill to take a catnap virtually on command. Bond also uses pneumonic devices to remember scores of phone numbers and he can fire a gun with either hand.

Bond has developed methods to endure freezing temperatures. For instance, Bond is "constantly flexing his finger" so that it does not go numb. This way, Bond is always battle-ready.

Assorted Observations:

- After the villain tortures 007, he thoughtfully tells Bond that he hopes that the experience has not rendered him impotent.
- During the war in the Falkland Islands, an unidentifiable Bond briefly appears on television.

ROLE OF HONOUR (1984)

Author: John Gardner

In Brief: Bond pretends to resign from SIS so that he can work for the enemy, a SPECTRE agent who is using computer games technology to execute criminal and terrorist enterprises.

Meaning of Title: Bond's cover is that he is a disgraced Secret Service agent whose honor has been called into question.

Chronology: Contemporary. After the events of *Icebreaker*.

Operation: Down Escalator.

Bastard Meter: Unmeasured.

Eggs: Poorly prepared, nearly inedible.

Insight into Bond: "He was trained as a loner, one who acted without others, one who relied on himself."

Summary: With computer-like precision, a group of thieves pull off a series of audacious robberies, including the Kruxator art collection that is valued at a billion dollars.

In London, Bond receives an inheritance from his late Uncle Bruce that is worth a quarter of a million pounds. M calls Bond into his office and tells him that he's aware of Bond's windfall and that SIS has concocted a scheme to use Bond's newly founded wealth for their own purposes. SIS will suppress the real origin of Bond's money and leak that Bond embezzled the funds from the service. Bond will pretend to resign in disgrace. When the enemy learns that Bond is a free agent, they will attempt to hire him for their nefarious purposes.

M reveals that their true target is the presumed dead, Dr. Jay Autem Holy. M explains that Dr. Holy faked his death and has recently resurfaced under the name Jason St. John-Finnes, a computer game expert who is living in England. The resurfaced Holy is using sophisticated computer simulations to plan criminal and terrorist enterprises. As a first step, Bond is tasked with going to Monte Carlo, Monaco so that he can learn computer programming from Persephone "Percy" Proud, a CIA agent and the ex-wife of Dr. Holy. Once Bond knows coding, the spy can work for Holy.

At a hotel in Monte Carlo, Bond meets Percy who reveals that she only married Dr. Holy as part of her assignment with the CIA. At the time, Holy had been working for the Pentagon and a plane carrying him and a general named Joseph Zwingli went down, presumably killing both of them. During the month-long training session, Bond and Percy become intimate. One night, they spot General Joe Zwingli, who is also thought to be dead. Zwingli is holding court with Tamil Rahani, an American-Lebanese chairman of Rahani Electronics.

Bond meets and befriends Lady Freddie Fortune, a friend of St. John-Finnes (aka Dr. Holy). Bond tells Lady Fortune that he's looking for work in a computer-related field. Lady Fortune suggests that Bond approach St. John-Finnes at a dinner party that he and his wife, Dazzle, are having.

At the dinner party, Bond meets with St. John-Finnes (aka Holy) who has read about Bond's departure from the Secret Service. Holy indicates that he might have a job for Bond. Holy also tells Bond about his sophisticated computer war simulation programs that can be used to train soldiers for battle. Bond also meets computer programmers Cindy Chalmer and Peter Amadeus.

When Bond returns to his hotel, he finds Cindy Chalmer, who reveals that she's a CIA agent who is working with Percy Proud. Cindy gives Bond hard disks containing two simulations that she swiped from Holy. Bond learns that the disks contain a training program for the Kruxator Collection art theft. Cindy tells Bond that Holy is working on a secret program called The Balloon Game.

While driving the next day, Bond realizes that he's being followed. Bond attempts to lose the tail but he's captured, drugged, and brought to Erewhon, a training camp for terrorists. Bond meets Tamil Rahani, the electronics mogul working with Holy. Rahani hires Bond and reveals that his organization plans to orchestrate and execute criminal and terrorist operations for a price. Rahani has an assignment for Bond in London, but first Bond must participate in his war games. Bond accepts but discovers that he's been given blank ammunition, whereas his opponents have live rounds. Bond kills the men and earns a place working for Rahani.

Holy informs Bond about a secret radio frequency called EPOC (Emergency Presidential Orders Communications). EPOC is a system that allows the President of the United States to receive and give military instructions, including nuclear strike instructions, to the army. For the program to work, the order has to come from an area where US satellites know the President to be. The Russians utilize a similar system. Bond's first assignment is to go to London and get the EPOC frequency number and give it to Holy. Holy reveals that he's working for SPECTRE.

Cindy Chalmer meets up with Bond and gives him a computer disk that contains a program called the Balloon Game. The next day, Bond meets with Holy who tells Bond that he knows Cindy stole the Balloon Game program. However, the disk that she took was a decoy. Bond denies knowing anything about the disk. Holy puts Bond to the test by playing against him in a computer-generated recreation of the American Revolution. Bond wins.

Bond travels to London so that he can meet M and obtain the EPOC frequency numbers. M informs Bond about the theft of the Goodyear airship called the *Europa*. M suspects that Holy will use the *Europa* to get close to the American President's location in Geneva, where he is attending a summit. Once there, Holly will send a signal for Ploughshare, a code that will cause the two nations to deactivate their nuclear weapons. If the Ploughshare signal is sent, then America and Russia will be defenseless against hostile nations with nuclear firepower. This initiative is called Operation Down Escalator.

Bond returns to the enemy and gives them the EPOC codes. Bond and Holy travel to the city of Lausanne and board the *Europa*, which Bond will be co-piloting. During the flight, the command to disarm the nuclear codes is sent to the United States. Rahani tells Holy that the plan is only to use the code on the Americans and not the Soviets. Holy, who feels duped, goes after Rahani, who in turn, kills Holy. One of Rahani's men kills General Zwingli. Rahani, the new head of SPECTRE, escapes by parachuting away.

Bond and Percy celebrate the successful completion of their mission by going to Greece together. In Greece, SPECTRE agents try but fail to kill Bond and Percy who subsequently abruptly end their vacation. They know that they can't enjoy their time together when Rahani, the new head of SPECTRE, is still at large.

Commentary: Speed counts. One of the many elements an author can use to create a captivating novel is manipulating the duration of an event. To wit, a fistfight can be dispensed with in a single sentence—"Bond punched out Goldfinger." Or their physical contest can be described in detail for several pages. "Bond's clenched fist found no perch on Goldfinger's chin. The gold-loving villain ducked and avoided 007's haymaker. He countered with his own strike." And so on.

Authors, arguably, have more flexibility about the length of an event than filmmakers. For instance, when the movie Bond checks his room for surveillance bugs, the process takes about 20–30 seconds. Any more than that bores viewers. However, when Gardner's Bond sweeps his room for devices, Gardner describes the activity in detail. He takes the reader through each step. However, that's not the end of it. Later, Bond has to leave his room again and when he returns, Bond sweeps his room a *second time* for bugs. A second sweep is not something a general movie audience would tolerate. Instead, they'd want the filmmakers to move on to the next scene. To be clear, in this case, Gardner dispenses with the second sweep in a sentence. This way, he doesn't bog down the action and it's logical that a second sweep is required. It's telling that Gardner seems to take great pleasure in bringing up this unexpected fact. In each instance, Gardner reveals aspects of Bond's tradecraft and methodology.

In *Role of Honour*, Gardner finds a new way to send Bond on a mission. Typically, M briefs Bond on his assignment, and then Bond assumes a cover identity to carry it out. In *Licence Renewed,* Bond plays the part of a mercenary who is looking for work. In *For Special Services*, Bond posed as an art expert in possession of rare prints that the villain sought. In *Role of Honour*, the mission's success rests on the villain knowing Bond's identity. This way, SPECTRE agents will actively recruit him. Four novels into Gardner's run, it's an effective way for him to mix up the formula.

There are some downsides to the operation. Bond's "resignation" makes the newspapers and Bond is outed as a spy. What might be an ingenious plan for this mission, might have far-reaching consequences. Secret intelligence agencies should generally refrain from making public the identity of their operatives. Granted, Bond's outing is not front-page news, and his photo is not published. Moreover, most enemy countries and evil organizations seem to have a file on Bond anyway. If that's the case, then M hasn't published anything that isn't already known. In *You Only Live Twice*, M published a fake obituary as a way to fool the world into thinking that Bond is already dead. As such, Bond is already something of a public figure who lost a measure of anonymity long ago.

Continuity Nod: Cindy Chalmer, who is working with the CIA, asks Bond if he remembers Fort Knox (*Goldfinger*). Bond is still haunted by memories of his dead wife Tracy and thinks about Ernst Stavro Blofeld and his daughter Nena (*For Special Services*).

Bond's History: As a child, Bond's school rooms tended to be dusty and he learned about the American Revolution. When he was sixteen years old, Bond went to Lake Geneva and had a brief relationship with a local waitress, and spent a week in Montreux with friends.

Bond's Inner Life: When Bond is happy, he sings. In one instance, he croons "Rolling Home," a sea shanty about a sailor who is happy on payday. The snippet of the song that Gardner writes about is the part where the protagonist has two pence in his pocket that he can spend or lend, as he goes rolling home. Gardner doesn't quote the entire song. The other verses apply to Bond. In the shanty, the sailor is happy because "No cares have I to grieve me" and "No pretty little girls to deceive me." In other words, the sailor is happy because he has no family and no relationships to lay claims on him. It's a fitting song for Bond, even if the agent doth protest too much.

So perhaps it shouldn't be a complete surprise that Bond experiences a touch of sadness while singing the song. In the final lyric of the song, the sailor gleefully sings that he has "No pence to send home to my wife-poor wife." However, Bond is not able to sing this final line. It reminds him of his deceased wife, Tracy, who he still mourns. Her memory doesn't simply provide sadness, the thought of her still haunts him.

Bond is not the super confident agent of Eon's movies. After spending a month learning computer code with Percy, he feels "uncharacteristically inadequate" while saying goodbye to her.

Bond needs a jolt of adrenaline to keep him engaged with life. 007 "long[s] for some kind of action—a craving that he slaked with too many late nights, the excitement of the gaming tables, and a lukewarm affair with a girl he had known for years—a small romance that gutted out like a candle after a few months." The only thing that will supercharge Bond's life is a mission. However, Bond's passion for work isn't limited to thrill-seeking. For Bond, being a Double O is a calling.

Bond's Personal Life: Bond comes into a generous inheritance from his Uncle Bruce, his father's younger brother. Bruce is a new name on the family tree. In *The Adventures of James Bond Junior*, Arthur Calder-Marshall established that Bond's brother was named David, and in *The Authorized Biography of 007*, Pearson provides the name Henry as Bond's brother. Bruce, David, and Henry are said to be from Bond's father's side.

There are a few possibilities for the multiple names of Bond's uncles. One, Bond's father had several brothers. Two, some of these uncles are not strictly relatives. Instead, they are just good family friends who have earned the title. Although, that doesn't seem to be the case. Three, Gardner made a mistake, and no one caught the error. Four, Gardner didn't read *The Adventures of James Bond Junior* and/or *The Authorized Biography of 007* and, even if he did, Gardner wasn't beholden to them. *The Adventures of James Bond Junior* and *The Authorized Biography of 007* are considered spin-off works and not continuation novels. As such, they haven't necessarily earned the status of canon.

There are good reasons to limit the number of Bond's family members. A key component of Bond's character is that he is a loner and an orphan. If Bond had a vast family, he would have a large support network. An adult Bond mustn't have surviving family members. If he maintained a close relationship with Uncle Bruce, it would lessen Bond's pain and sense of isolation.

Putting aside the circumstances surrounding the sudden appearance of a new family member, it's also worth briefly looking at what Bond's uncle's existence can tell us about the spy. Gardner clarifies that Bond has never seen Uncle Bruce. So Gardner's Bond willfully remains alone and cut off from any surviving family. If Bond did crave family, he could have sought out Uncle Bruce and forged a relationship with Bruce when he was still alive. Instead, Bond separates himself.

In *Role of Honour*, Uncle Bruce is a device to provide Bond with a significant amount of new-found wealth. In the novel, SIS uses the influx of cash as a pretext for their operation in which they pretend to discredit and dishonor 007. Gardner could have provided Bond with other ways to have gotten the money. Bond could have won it at the gambling tables, or an enemy agent carrying a suitcase full of money. Instead, Gardner chose to connect the money to a family member, and in doing so, Gardner created a small character moment that further revealed a little more information about Bond's ancestry.

Bond's Tastes: Bond uses his inheritance to buy a new Bentley Mulsanne Turbo. In future books, Bond would often continue to drive a Saab. However, putting Bond behind the wheel of a Bentley harkens back to the 4 ½-liter Bentley that he drives in Fleming's novels.

Bond's Work Methods: In Gardner's previous book, *Icebreaker*, Bond made a near-fatal mistake failing to sweep a room for listening devices. As a result, he inadvertently reveals secret information to the opposition. Fortunately, in *Role of Honour*, Bond has learned from his mistakes. This time, he double-checks for bugs before speaking to an ally.

A secret agent doesn't get time off. So even when Bond is not on assignment and he's puttering about in London, he must always remind himself to behave as though he were in the field.

Bond's ASP 9mm in *Role of Honour.*
Illustration by Pat Carbajal

It takes Bond a full month of training to learn computer code before he starts his mission.

Before they are placed in the field, agents meet with psychiatrists who identify and eliminate mannerisms, such as head tilts or adding flourishes to letters or underlying names while signing off on notes.

Gardner also provides a little insight into SPECTRE's operational methods. For instance, when SPECTRE agents tail Bond, they work in groups of five. The operatives can be adult men or women, or even a child or student. Those five operatives change daily, and they never use a tail car more than once.

Assorted Observations:

- At the start of the novel, Bond is under disciplinary action. However, the reasons for this action are not disclosed.
- Bond enjoys driving through France.
- For Bond, winning any game is a matter of honor.

NOBODY LIVES FOR EVER (1986)

Author: John Gardner

In Brief: When SPECTRE puts out a contract on 007's life, Bond must evade numerous assassination attempts by the world's best hitmen. Bond must also rescue Miss Moneypenny and his housekeeper, May, from kidnappers.

Alternate Title: *Nobody Lives Forever*

Meaning of Title: Eventually, everyone dies, including the villain who is suffering from a terminal illness that will kill him in about four months.

Chronology: Contemporary. Set in 1985, after the events of *Role of Honour.*

Operation: Not applicable.

Bastard Meter: Standard bastard.

Eggs: Scrambled and served with a bottle of Taittinger champagne at Bond's request as a "last meal."

Insight into Bond: "You strike me as a fast cars, horses, and women kind of fellow."

Summary: While on vacation, Bond witnesses three suspicious events—the death of two passengers on a ferry, an explosion on the highway, and a robbery of a woman. Bond saves the woman who introduces herself as Principessa Sukie Tempesta. Meanwhile, Bond's beloved housekeeper May has been suffering from bronchitis and is under Doctor Kirchtum's care at the Klinik Mozart in Salzburg, Austria. Bond places a call to the clinic, and discovers that Miss Moneypenny is visiting May.

Bond goes to his hotel in Switzerland and encounters Sukie Tempesta. Over dinner, Sukie tells Bond that her car broke down and that she's heading for Rome. Bond is also traveling to Rome, and offers her a ride. Later, on a phone call, Bill Tanner warns Bond that he's in danger and that when he arrives in Rome, he should meet with Steve Quinn, the local contact.

In Rome, Quinn tells Bond that SPECTRE has put out a contract on the agent's life. The contract states that whoever kills 007 within the next three months will get 10 million Swiss francs. The contest called the Head Hunt, was ordered by SPECTRE's head Tamil Rahani who only has a few months to live and wants to see Bond dead before he shuffles off this mortal coil. Enemy operatives who have picked up the contract include SPECTRE and SMERSH agents.

Bond calls Doctor Kirchtum, the director of the health clinic, who tells Bond that May and Moneypenny have been kidnapped. Bond tells Sukie Tempesta that he needs to go to Austria. Sukie tells Bond that she has made arrangements to meet up with her friend Nannette "Nannie" Norrich. Reluctantly, Bond agrees to take Nannie with them.

After picking Nannie up, Bond realizes that they're being followed by a silver Renault. When the Renault attacks Bond's car, Nannie pulls out a concealed gun and shoots the gas tank, causing the vehicle to explode. Nannie reveals that she is a member of NUB, the Norrich Universal Bodyguards agency.

Bond's trip with Sukie and Nannie continues but they are stopped and questioned by Inspector Heinrich Osten. Osten brings Bond to an old apartment building and locks him inside a room. Using the tools in his belt, Bond escapes and discovers that Osten has been murdered. Acting on a tip from the Austrian Foreign Ministry and Security Department, Kommissar Becker arrives at the apartment. Becker tells Bond that he's the target of a headhunt and that Moneypenny and May will only be returned safely if Bond surrenders himself. Becker also reveals that SPECTRE agents transported May and Moneypenny out of the country. Bond receives a call from Dr. Kirchtum who, repeating orders from SPECTRE, instructs Bond to go to the hotel Goldener Hirsch in Vienna and await further instructions.

Bond travels with Sukie and Nannie to Vienna. At the hotel, Bond takes a shower and is attacked by a hybrid vampire bat. Bond grabs his baton and bludgeons the bat to death. Bond receives another phone call from Kirchtum, who tells Bond to go to the George Cinq Hotel in Paris.

On the way to Paris, Bond travels to the Mozart clinic and overhears Steve Quinn, who is working for SMERSH, plotting with Kirchtum against Bond. Bond gets the drop on Quinn. Bluffing, Bond tells Quinn that if he doesn't cooperate then the SIS will kill his wife. Bond instructs Quinn to signal to SPECTRE that their scheme is going according to plan. Bond learns that the winner of Operation Head Hunt is supposed to decapitate Bond's head and take it to Key West, Florida.

Bond pretends to go to Paris, where Quinn's confederates are waiting for him. Instead, he goes to Florida. There, Bond is intercepted by Quinn and Kirchtum who force the agent to board a ship. It turns out that Bond thought that he had successfully coerced Quinn into working for him. Instead, Quinn turned the tables on Bond.

Sukie and Nannie arrive, kill Quinn and Kirchtum, and rescue Bond. Bond learns that SPECTRE's operations are being conducted on Shark Island. When Bond and Nannie arrive on Shark Island, they locate Tamil Rahani, the new SPECTRE leader. Before Bond can attack Rahani, Nannie stops him. Nannie reveals that she's part of Head Hunt. Her assignment was to keep Bond alive until he could be brought to Rahani. Nannie explains that they will use a guillotine to cut off Bond's head.

Rahani needs medical care before Bond's headectomy can take place, Rahani's doctor orders the nurse to administer him an injection that, as a side effect, will knock him out for an hour. While Rahani sleeps, Bond is taken to a detention cell to wait. Bond sneaks out of his cell, enters Rahani's room, and plants explosives under Rahani's hospital bed. Then, Bond returns to his cell.

Later, Bond is brought to the operating room, where his head will be chopped off. When Rahani's bed is raised to watch the procedure, it triggers the explosive device and kills Rahani. Then, Bond kills Nannie by chopping off her arms with the guillotine. Bond escapes with Moneypenny and May. SPECRE's headquarters goes up in flames, apparently putting an end to their operations. Later, Moneypenny and May recuperate, and Bond goes on a romantic vacation with Sukie.

Commentary: *Nobody Lives For Ever* represented a change in the publication schedule for Gardner's Bond books. Gardner's first four Bond books were published yearly, from 1981-1984. One book a year is a tremendous pace for any writer to sustain. For years, Fleming had a similarly relentless output. Starting in 1953, Fleming's first seven novels came out yearly. It wasn't until 1960 that Fleming took a break from the Bond novels and instead published *For Your Eyes Only*, a collection of five short stories. Those short stories weren't entirely original. Four of them were ideas for a television series that never came to fruition and the fifth entry was a piece that he kept in his proverbial drawer but was never published. Repurposing old ideas is one sign that Fleming was feeling the strain of the grueling writing schedule.

Given the demands of writing a new Bond novel a year, it's understandable that Gardner would request a modest break so that he could recharge his creative batteries. There are other benefits to taking a brief pause in the yearly output. A once-a-year release makes each Bond book less of an event and could hurt potential sales. Still, it's not like Gardner took the year off completely; 1985 marked the publication of his 500-page novel *The Secret Generations* the first book in his trilogy about the creation of the Secret Service.

The extra time seems to have paid off. Gardner came up with a strong premise for *Nobody Lives For Ever*—SPECTRE has ordered a hit on 007 and a group of international assassins are gunning for him. SMERSH (now called Department Eight) is among those who are trying to give Bond an early retirement. Fleming aficionados will recall that SMERSH were the baddies in *Casino* Royale, *Live and Let Die, From Russia with Love,* and *Goldfinger* and SPECTRE was up to no good in *Thunderball*, *On Her Majesty's Secret Service*, and *You Only Live Twice*. In his novels, Fleming usually kept SPECTRE and SMERSH's operations discrete. In Gardner's *Nobody Lives For Ever* the two competing enemy organizations found a way to work for the same goal—Bond's demise.

After four previous Bond novels, Gardner continued to refine his approach to the series. Following Gardner's second novel, *For Special Services*, some fans complained that he prematurely killed off Nena Blofeld, an interesting new character, and the daughter of Ernst Stavro Blofeld. It might have been wiser to have Nena survive the novel and return in a future work. Gardner seems to have taken that criticism to heart. *Nobody Lives For Ever* marks the return of Tamil Rahani, the SPECTRE head and villain of Gardner's previous Bond. Rahani thinks that landing hard on his spine after jumping out of the airship with a parachute in the previous novel, *Role of Honour*, is what caused his cancer. Rahani, therefore, holds Bond responsible for his terminal illness. This history explain's Rahani's motivation for Bond's head.

Bringing back Rahani is a good instinct. By reusing Rahani, an established character, Gardner doesn't have to start from scratch. The reader is already familiar with him and is rooting for his demise. Yet, it doesn't mean that Rahani will stick around indefinitely. By the story's end, Bond blows the villain to smithereens. After terrorizing Bond for two novels, Rahani's death is even more emotionally satisfying.

Usually, Bond is given an assignment to complete on behalf of Her Majesty's Secret Service. In *Nobody Lives For Ever*, Gardner switches up the formula. In his fifth Bond novel, the mission becomes personal when SPECTRE operatives kidnap May, his beloved housekeeper, and Moneypenny, M's secretary.

Before the abduction occurs, Gardner establishes how important May is to Bond. May has been suffering from severe bronchitis attacks. So Bond pays for her treatment at a pricey medical facility in Salzburg, Austria. While she's away, a doting Bond regularly calls the clinic and checks in on her. At first, May's health condition doesn't seem germane to the story. Gardner slowly reveals his endgame. During one call, May is not available to talk to Bond. Later, Bond tries again and she's still not available. Bond doesn't begin to suspect something is wrong until after a couple of calls go unanswered. When Gardner finally reveals that May has been abducted, her disappearance has an impact on the reader. However, to make matters worse, Moneypenny is also missing. Now, Bond's personal mission is to ensure the safe delivery of both May and Moneypenny.

One must consider Gardner's decision to have both May and Moneypenny snatched. Certainly, May's abduction would have been enough. The addition of Moneypenny isn't really necessary. In the previous four books, Gardner spent time establishing Bond's relationship with May. Conversely, Gardner's Moneypenny appears fleetingly. I suspect that the inclusion of Moneypenny was a concession to readers who are more familiar with Lois Maxwell's winning performance in the movies than Gardner's novels. One could argue that kidnapping both women doubled the stakes. From a story perspective, the number of hostages is immaterial. In a different kind of novel, Bond would have to make a difficult choice to save just one of them. Instead, he saves both of them in rapid succession.

Nobody Lives For Ever is a fun read, but the story has a plot hole that is a little hard to overlook. There are several instances where Bond is cornered and is about to be killed but then he is miraculously saved by an unknown third party. Bond's savior isn't a colleague. Instead, the guardian angel is a SPECTRE agent who is tasked with preventing another outfit from killing Bond. As a result, the SPECTRE agent is always saving Bond's life, meaning Bond is never really in grave danger or at least the danger is muted. Gardner tries to make that plot contrivance work. So not only is SPECTRE trying to kill Bond off, but they are simultaneously trying to save money by not paying the bounty on Bond's head. In theory, it's a nice double-cross. As an organizational policy, it's penny-wise and pound-foolish. After all, Bond has been a thorn in their side for long enough. Paying the full freight would be in SPECTRE's best interest in the long run.

Continuity Nod: Colonel Tamil Rahani, head of SPECTRE returns. Rahani's illness was caused by the injuries he sustained while escaping from Bond's clutches in *Role of Honour*. Bond's ex-father-in-law Marc-Ange Draco (*On Her Majesty's Secret Service)* is dead before the novel begins. Gardner doesn't elaborate on the circumstances of Draco's death but readers can infer that he didn't die of natural causes. It is later revealed that the reports of his death were not true. In Raymond Benson's *Never Dream of Dying,* readers learn that Draco is still alive.

Bond's History: As a "young man" (possibly in his twenties), Bond visited Lake Maggiore and Locarno, Switzerland, and spent a memorable night with an Italian countess. By the book's end, Bond will have shared the bed with Sukie Tempesta, yet another Italian aristocrat.

Bond's Inner Life: Gardner describes Bond as "a man of habit, Bond did not normally like change." Regardless, Bond allows himself a few minor changes, such as updating his soap, shampoos, and his cologne.

Bond's Personal Life: As noted, Bond has taken an active role in restoring the health of May, who has suffered through a couple of bronchitis attacks. In some ways, the passages that show Bond's care for his housekeeper are some of the most personal and intimate sections of any post-Fleming Bond book. Many of the novels, reveal Bond's character by showing the romantic love that he feels for the women in his life. In *Nobody Lives For Ever*, Bond reveals something that is best categorized as a kind of familiar love. May has become a quasi-mother figure to Bond. Apparently, the feelings are mutual. After he saves May, his beloved housekeeper, indicates that she is eager to get back to her kitchen and looking after Bond.

Bond doesn't listen to much Mozart, has read Hemingway's *To Have and Have Not*, and he's not a religious man. Trying everything he can to save May and Moneypenny's lives, Bond acknowledges that he could use "all the help the angels could provide." Uncharacteristically, the agent tries to pray for their safe return.

Bond's Work Methods: Gardner tells us that Bond "had never believed in coincidences." Being wary of coincidences is a sensible rule for secret agents to follow. Bond employs an aggressive technique to prevent an enemy vehicle from fleeing. In the movies, police shoot at the tires. Bond, though, was taught to shoot the gas tank. According to this reasoning, a car with flat tires may still be able to escape, but a car that has caught fire is less likely to do so.

Bond knows that in a firefight, to reduce the size of the enemy's target, it's best to stand sideways. He believes that when interrogating a man in the field, it's best to keep the conversations brief. The longer you talk the more likely it is that your enemy will find a way to escape or attack.

Despite his considerable skill in the field, Bond might need a refresher course in frisking a potential threat. Because Bond is such a "gentleman," he neglects to properly pat down Nannie Norrich, the bodyguard looking after Sukie's safety, who kept a gun strapped to her inner thigh. Had Nannie been an immediate threat, she could have used the gun to kill Bond. Still, Bond's kindness to women has its limits. To get the traitorous agent Steve Quinn to talk, Bond arranges to have Steve's wife held against her will. Bond threatens that if Quinn doesn't talk, he will have his wife killed. Quinn doesn't realize that Bond is bluffing; but given the circumstances, he will stop at nothing to save Moneypenny and May and complete his mission.

In the movies, Bond kills his enemies and leaves it to someone else to clean up his mess. In Gardner's books, sometimes the agent needs to clean up his own mess. For instance, when Bond kills a vampire bat in his hotel bathroom, Bond uses rubber gloves and antiseptic to rid the place of any signs of struggle and bat guts.

Assorted Observations:

- In *Nobody Lives For Ever*, Bond appears on television, via a file photo, indicating that the agent has been killed in a car crash. In *Role of Honour*, Bond appeared in the papers and is spoken about in the House of Commons. Sometimes, the life of a secret agent isn't so secret.
- Bond takes two Benzedrine tablets along with his coffee to help him stay up and alert. Bond famously used Benzedrine in Fleming's novels too.
- Gardner's fifth Bond novel was originally published under the title *Nobody Lives For Ever* in the United Kingdom and as *Nobody Lives Forever* in the United States. Recent editions have opted for the American title.

NO DEALS, MR. BOND (1987)

Author: John Gardner

In Brief: After two assets are brutally murdered, Bond must protect the remaining members of Operation Cream Cake, a former initiative in which five German civilians attracted enemy operatives, learned their secrets, and gave them to the British.

Meaning of Title: Bond will not be able to talk or negotiate his way out of the villain's clutches.

Chronology: Contemporary. Set after the events of *Nobody Lives For Ever*.

Operation: Cream Cake and Seahawk.

Bastard Meter: Bastards aplenty, but not about Bond.

Eggs: None served.

Insight into Bond: "With luck and his expertise combined, he had a chance—though a slim chance—of winning."

Summary: As part of Operation Seahawk, Bond travels by submarine to the East German coast to secretly retrieve two young German women. Bond is successful but one of his compatriots dies in the process. Five years later, Bond lunches with M at Blades. M tells Bond that the two women he rescued were part of a failed operation called Cream Cake, consisting of two other women and one man. The five assets, known as "Emilies," worked for the West German government. The British Government used the Emilies as "honey pots" to seduce and extract intel from high-value officials, including Colonel Maxim Smolin, a member of the East German intelligence service. Following Bond's mission, SIS provided the Emilies with secret identities and new lives. A short time ago, two of the Emilies were brutally murdered and their tongues were cut off by the KGB. The three surviving Emiles are in danger. They include Ebbie Heritage, who is living in Dublin, Heather Dare, who owns a beauty salon in England, and Jungle Baisley, whose whereabouts are unknown. M tasks Bond with locating the remaining Emilies and keeping them alive.

Bond goes to the Mayfair Hotel to find Heather Dare and explains that he is there to save her. Heather tells Bond that Ebbie's lover was a man named Colonel Maxim Smolin. To keep Heather safe, Bond instructs her to travel with him to Ireland where they can retrieve Ebbie. Before they can leave, they are attacked by Mischa, an enforcer of General Konstantin Chernov, the Chief Investigating officer from the KGB agency Department Eight (formerly SMERSH). Bond and Heather get away.

Bond and Heather go to Ireland and meet up with Norman Murray, a local police Inspector who is Bond's old contact and gambling companion. Later, Bond and Heather spot Colonel Smolin, one of the Emilies' targets. Bond and Heather attempt to flee Dublin but they are stopped by Colonel Smolin and his men.

Smolin takes Bond and Ebbie to a Victorian neo-Gothic castle where they meet one of Smolin's formidable housekeepers, Ingrid, who is also a KGB agent. Later, Smolin brings Bond to a room to be interrogated and tortured. Once alone, Smolin reveals that he defected to England five years ago. Bond doesn't believe the claim but Smolin explains that his defection was known only by a few, including M and that if he were lying Bond would have already been killed. Now, Smolin needs to help Bond before his deception is discovered. Smolin then warns Bond about General Chernov.

Ingrid bursts into the room and says that she's been listening to the entire conversation. Ingrid commands her three German Shepherds to attack Smolin and Bond. Bond manages to overcome the dogs, but he's wounded in the process and passes out.

When Bond awakens, he discovers that he and Smolin are being held captive. Bond uses the equipment in his belt to break out of the room. As General Chernov arrives by helicopter, Bond, Smolin, Heather, and Ebbie escape. Because Chernov is looking for four people, the group breaks up into two; Bond and Ebbie go to one hotel, and Smolin and Heather go to another.

Later, Bond calls Smolin and Heather's hotel and learns that they checked out early. Bond checks the listening devices that he previously-planted at Smolin's castle and discovers that General Chernov is making plans to go to Hong Kong where Jungle Baisley and Captain Susanne Dietrich (another target) are heading. In Hong Kong, Baisley and Dietrich are expected to go to Cheung Chau Island, the location of a GRU house. [GRU is the Soviet's foreign military intelligence agency].

Bond and Ebbie are captured by General Chernov's men and are told that they will be brought to Three Sisters Castle in Dublin, a location controlled by the KGB and GRU. But before they can arrive, Inspector Norman Murray saves Bond and Ebbie. Then, Bond takes Ebbie with him to a safe house in Paris where he meets with Anne Reilly of Q Branch. Reilly gives Bond equipment for his mission.

Anne Reilly from Q Branch.
Illustration by Pat Carbajal

Bond and Ebbie travel to Hong Kong to track down Jungle Baisley. In Hong Kong, Bond meets up with Big Thumb Chang, an old contact, who provides Bond with a gun. Later, Bond meets Agent Swift, who has instructions from M. Swift says that there was a double agent in Operation Cream Cake. Bond is ordered to find out the traitor's identity and eliminate them.

Bond and Ebbie make their way to Cheung Chau Island. Once on the island, Bond plants the equipment that Anne Reilly gave him in Paris. Bond and Ebbie are captured by General Chernov's men, and brought to his house. Ebbie is taken to a cell with Heather Dare, Maxim Smolin, Jungle Baisley, and Captain Dietrich.

Chernov forces Bond to participate in a test of his skills. Armed only with a gun with four bullets, Bond has to evade and kill four well-armed operatives who have six hours to kill him. When the contest begins, Bond quickly retrieves the tools and weapons that he previously planted on the grounds and them to kill the four enemies.

Bond makes his way back to Chernov's house and encounters Heather Dare who reveals herself to be the double agent. Before Heather can kill Bond, he takes her gun and uses it on her. Bond's old friend Norman Murray is also exposed as a double agent. Bond kills Murray, captures Chernov, and then passes out. Having completed the mission, Bond wakes up in a hospital room.

Commentary: In *No Deals, Mr. Bond*, Gardner continues to alter the nature of Bond's missions. Usually, Bond's assignments are officially sanctioned efforts. As such, Bond is afforded all the support in the field that SIS can muster. But in *No Deals, Mr. Bond*, Gardner puts Bond on an unofficial mission forcing the SIS to take a hands-off approach. He is unable to turn to the SIS for support. Instead, Bond must rely on his cunning or personal connections that are not as trustworthy or reliable as those of the services. With the aid of some sketchy characters, such as Big Thumb Chang, who provides 007 with firearms, Bond successfully achieves this task.

Gardner also creates a twist on "The Most Dangerous Game," Richard Connell's 1924 short story, about a big-game hunter who hunts and kills humans on his remote island. In the thrilling climax of *No Deals, Mr. Bond*, General Konstantin Chernov tasks four men who are sentenced to death, known as Robinsons, with killing Bond. If the Robinsons kill Bond, they are pardoned. Three of the Robinsons are equipped with guns and one of them is given a dagger. Bond is only given a Luger Parabellum and four rounds of ammunition. Because four rounds equal just one shot for each Robinson, Bond must make each shot count. One Robinson opts to also go after Bond with a morning star, a medieval weapon with a spiked ball mounted on a shaft. The passages where Bond thwarts and kills the Robinsons are fast-paced and exciting.

Gardner's books demand that readers pay close attention. Gardner will explain a pertinent fact about an operation, but he won't necessarily repeat it. He expects the reader to retain the information. Gardner also requires the reader to keep track of a character's multiple aliases and codenames. For example, Colonel Smolin's codename is Basilisk and General Chernov also goes by Blackfriar. In *No Deals, Mr. Bond,* five Germans have defected to the East and are now living under assumed names. So each character has their original name and their new name. Franz Belzinger now goes by Jungle Baisley and his nickname is Ward. Bond's contact's name is Norman Murray but 007 refers to him as Big Mick. And Irma Wagen and Emilie

Nikolas have changed their names to Heather Dare and Ebbie Heritage. Sometimes, their cover names have cover names. To wit, Emile Nikolas has a cover name of Ebbie Heritage and Ebbie has a series of rotating cover names, including Elizabeth Larke and Elizabeth Sparrow. Even the two murder victims in the inciting incident of the story go by multiple names. Franziska Trauben, whose cover name is Bridget Hammond, is occasionally called Franzi and, Eleonore Zuckerman, aka Millicent Zampek, sometimes goes by Elli. So, to follow the story, the reader must retain multiple names for a single character.

Even Bond goes by additional names or aliases—at least five in total. Of course, there's 007. But in *No Deals, Mr. Bond*, the agent has an operational name of Seahawk, the codename of Predator, he books tickets on an airline as Boldman, and his old gambling buddy calls him Jacko.

Continuity Nod: When Bond goes to Blades to meet M, the agent sees a porter, whose father worked at the club when Bond played cards against Hugo Drax (*Moonraker*).

Bond's History: Bond's childhood nanny used to say, "First come, first served."

Bond's Inner Life: Bond experiences a rare moment of bliss in which he is "at peace with the world," taking in the springtime air, hearing May's humming, and finishing his breakfast.

Bond's Personal Life: While Bond is not normally thought of as a movie buff, he has seen Fritz Lang's *Metropolis* and Bond's specific-mission cryptonym, The Seahawk, is likely derived from the 1940 Errol Flynn movie *The Sea Hawk.* The agent also knows a few bawdy drinking songs including "The Jolly Tinker," about a group of wanderers who earn their keep by fixing pots, pans, and utensils, and "The Old Monk of Great Renown," about a randy castrated monk who is sowing his wild oats. In a moment of cheekiness, Bond offers to recite the lyrics to M. As to be expected, M doesn't take Bond up on his impertinent offer.

Bond's Work Methods: To avoid being followed, Bond will avoid driving straight forward for longer than half a minute, a variation on a pilot's admonition to never fly straight for more than 30 seconds. When coming up with an alias, he finds it best not to use common names like Smith, Jones, Green, or Brown. Those names will generally attract more attention than a slightly more inventive alternative. Bond is not a master of accents, but he can convincingly get by with an Irish lilt. When walking with a person he's not quite sure he can trust yet, Bond will walk two paces behind them, and slightly to the left. The spacing is close enough so that Bond can keep an eye on them, but far enough so that they can't effectively attack him. When being interrogated, Bond not only tries to make his mind blank, but he also tries to fill it with useless information. The idea is that if he's actively thinking about unimportant facts, then the critical information will be harder for the enemy to retrieve, as it will be deeper in his subconscious mind.

Bond was taught to choke an enemy with one hand, not two. 007 has also been trained in how to defeat an animal attack—punch them in the groin.

Bond keeps a safe house in Paris, which has a desk drawer with a false bottom that contains about a thousand francs, and he has arranged a standing cover story with Tom and Maria Hazlett, his alibi couple. In the event he's caught, Bond can provide the enemy with a fake cover story and Tom and Maria know to corroborate it.

Assorted Observations:

- For reasons that I haven't been able to discern, Bond is "deeply suspicious of rugs."
- Gardner makes a passing reference to Bond continuation author Kingsley Amis.
- The working title of the book was *Tomorrow Always Comes.*[105]

SCORPIUS (1988)

Author: John Gardner

In Brief: Bond is dispatched to look into the murder of a well-connected woman who had recently joined the Meek Ones, a deadly religious cult that is run by the world's most dangerous armaments trader, Vladimir Scorpius.

Meaning of Title: Refers to the villain's last name.

Chronology: Contemporary. Set after the events of *No Deals, Mr. Bond.*

Operation: Last Enemy.

Bastard Meter: None.

Eggs: Boiled for three and a third minutes by May.

Insight into Bond: "Someone once called you a blunt instrument. I find you are more than a bludgeon."

Summary: In London, Emma Dupré runs from an unseen threat, falls into the River Thames, and drowns.

In Hereford, England, Bond has recently finished training exercises with the Special Air Service. Sergeant "Pearly" Pearlman is engaged by Bond to drive him back to London. Along the way, assassins attempt to kill Bond, but Pearlman helps Bond escape danger.

In London, Bond meets with M and Chief Superintendent Bailey. M explains that the body of Emma Dupré, a friend of the daughter of one of SIS's auditors, was dragged from the Thames. Bond has been brought in because his phone number was discovered on Emma's body. Emma was mixed up with a cult named the Society of Meek Ones, led by Father Valentine who is believed to be an arms dealer named Vladimir Scorpius.

M tells Bond that Trilby Shrivenham, the daughter of an SIS auditor, is also connected to the Meek Ones. Trilby was addicted to heroin and Father Valentine helped her get clean. Trilby's grateful father gave Father Valentine advice on how to set up a credit card company, which he later named Avante Carte. Emma was carrying her

Avante Carte card when she was killed. M instructs Bond and Bailey to go meet with Trilby and ask her about Emma and The Meek Ones.

Bond and Bailey meet Trilby at her home and discover that she's still under the influence of The Meek Ones. As if being possessed, Trilby chants, "The meek shall inherit the earth" and "The blood of the fathers will fall upon the sons." Bond consults with M, who arranges for Trilby to be placed under the care of neurologist Sir James Molony (in *The Man with the Golden Gun*).

After reading a file on Scorpius, Bond concludes that the arms dealer underwent considerable plastic surgery to hide his true identity and has reemerged as Father Valentine. Only their shared wristwatch and virtually matching earlobes serve as physical indicators that Scorpius and Valentine are the same person.

Bond investigates Avante Carte, Father Valentine's company. They are creating high-tech credit cards encoded with electronic chips. However, the chips are flawed; they can be unscrambled and used to illicitly move funds and destabilize banks. At Avante Carte's office, Bond meets receptionist Harriett Horner. Bond attempts to apply for a card but Harriett tells Bond that the cards are not available to the public; they are by invitation only. When three men attack Bond, Harriett helps Bond and defeats the attackers. Harriet explains that she isn't a receptionist; instead, she's an undercover agent of the United States Internal Revenue Service.

Bond drops Harriett off at a safe house and returns to the clinic to visit Trilby. A seemingly possessed Trilby again chants "The meek shall inherit the earth." Bond receives word that Harriett's safe house has been attacked. Bond rushes to the safe house and discovers that Harriett is unharmed and that one of the attackers, Ahmed el Kadar, has been captured.

Bill Tanner informs 007 that M blames him for unwittingly leading the attackers to the safe house. Ahmed el Kadar is questioned by Bond, who discovers that The Meek Ones have orchestrated yet another attack. Just then, Bond receives word that a suicide bomber has killed former Prime Minister Lord Samuel Mills.

M and Bond meet with London based CIA liaison David Wolkovsky. Wolkovsky claims he knows nothing about Harriett's IRS operation into Scorpius on British soil. After the meeting, M wonders if Wolkovsky might be secretly working for Scorpius. M asks Pearlman, the SAS agent who drove Bond to London, to stay and help out with the investigation.

Bond and Harriett investigate the Meek Ones' operation in Pangbourne, England and they learn that a mole tipped off The Meek Ones about Bond's movements. Bond meets with el Kadar, the man who shot up the safe house. With the help of truth serum, el Kadar confirms that Father Valentine is actually Scorpius. Bond learns that for a price, The Meek Ones will perform any terrorist attack, even if it means taking their own lives in the process.

Bond hides Trilby at M's safe house. Ann Reilly explains how smart chips in credit cards can be used to bankrupt an enemy or make an ally wealthy beyond compare.

SAS Sergeant Pearlman takes Bond hostage. Pearlman explains that his daughter Ruth is being exploited by The Meek Ones. Scorpius is using Ruth to blackmail Pearlman into betraying Bond and the SIS. But instead of helping Scorpius, Pearlman enlists Bond's help to save Ruth and bring down Scorpius. Pearlman reveals that Scorpius is hiding out on Hilton Head Island off the coast of South Carolina. Bond agrees to help the distraught father. As part of the plan, Bond will pretend to be Pearlman's prisoner and Pearlman will take Bond to Scorpius.

Bond and Pearlman arrive in America and meet David Wolkovsky, the CIA agent, who Bond now believes was the mole inside SIS. Bond is taken to Hilton Head, where he meets Scorpius and is shown a prayer hall where The Meek Ones perform their ceremonies. Pearlman reunites with his daughter. Scorpius insists that Bond marry Harriett Horner. To bide for time, Bond agrees to the shotgun wedding.

Bond has dinner with Scorpius and his now-wife Trilby. Over dinner, Scorpius reveals his intention to use The Meek Ones to kill all of Britain's leaders.

Later that night, Bond and Harriett are forced to marry. Later, the newlyweds try to break out of their room, but they are trapped in a chamber. Bond and Harriett escape the chamber of scorpions, traverse a swamp filled with moccasin snakes, and make it to the sea, where they are rescued by CIA agent David Wolkovsky. Shortly after, Harriett dies from the snake bites that she sustained while escaping.

Bond forces Scorpius to follow the same dangerous path that killed Harriett. En route, Scorpius is bitten by the lethal snakes. Even though Scorpius is dead, his plan to use The Meek Ones to kill political figures is still in motion. Bond realizes that the British Prime Minister is meeting the American President at the White House.

Bond goes to the White House and discovers that Ruth Pearlman and Chief Superintendent Bailey are trying to kill the President and the Prime Minister. Bond thwarts the plot and kills the potential assassins. With the mission over, M grants Bond a leave of absence. Reluctantly Bond agrees, but he's eager to return to duty.

Commentary: *Scorpius* is John Gardner unleashed. Gardner's first six novels were somewhat in keeping with Fleming's efforts. His previous works were an attempt to follow Fleming's template while modernizing Bond's tradecraft and technology. In those books, Bond fought SPECTRE and SMERSH and squared off against Blofeld, all Fleming's creations. But in his seventh work, Gardner subverts what readers could expect out of a Bond novel, or more specifically, out of a Gardner Bond novel.

In *Scorpius*, Gardner alters the type of mission that Bond is given. Instead of going up against a government agency, like SMERSH, Bond has to look into a well-connected woman who was murdered. She's been caught up with a religious cult called The Meek Ones. The Meek Ones follow the most extreme views of the major religions of the world, including the Christian Bible, the Jewish Torah, and the Muslim Koran. Bond needs to look into the sect, which is controlled by Father Valentine, a charismatic and dangerous leader. Valentine is not just the leader of the cult; he has a dual life. He's also known as Vladimir Scorpius, the world's leading arms dealer. I suspect that making Scorpius an international arms dealer was Gardner's way of raising the stakes and providing a reason for Bond's involvement in the case.

Religion wasn't absent from Fleming's books. Voodoo played a part in *Live and Let Die*, but there's something about a group of religious extremists that feels like it's out of Bond's normal beat. The cult seems to be a topic that Fleming would have avoided. But it's something that clearly fascinated Gardner. Gardner's cult followers are so devoted to Valentine that they will do anything he commands them to, even if it means dying to obey his commands. So, Valentine sells their services as a kind of "rent a terrorist" business.

And then there's the demonic possession. Gardner also references a scene out of the supernatural horror film *The Exorcist.* In it, Bond is intending to interrogate a potential witness. But instead, he discovers that she's been possessed, or something close to it. When she tries to talk, another voice emanates from within her.

But that's not necessarily the most curious part of the book. In *Scorpius*, the villain Scorpius forces Bond to marry Harriett Horner, an IRS agent working on the case for the Americans. The shotgun ceremony is a way for the villain to exercise his power over 007. But, by Gardner's design, there's something farcical about the ceremony. A forced wedding might be included in a comic book or an episode of the 1960s *Batman* TV series, but not in a Fleming Bond book. But that's precisely Gardner's point; he's not going to continue to try to follow in Fleming's footsteps. Instead, he needs to chart his own path.

Something peculiar happens to Bond during the ceremony. He hallucinates and sees a vision of his slain wife, Tracy, on the altar with him. But Bond hasn't been drugged and he's not being hypnotized. Instead, Bond has, in some ways, summoned her from his subconscious. He's never gotten over her loss. So, he imagines that she's there with him and they are about to be married all over again.

Gardner sets the climax of the book in The White House. Bond needs to stop Scorpius' extremists from killing the President of the United States and the British Prime Minister, who are appearing at a joint event at the People's House. Bond is given clearance by the Secret Service, to carry a gun, guard the President, and identify the threat. The plot to kill the President and Prime Minister could be the focal point of a book, but instead, Gardner uses it as a kind of afterthought. He shoehorns this plot twist into the final chapter. But for Gardner, it's the cherry on his sundae which is already filled with cult leaders, demonic possessions, and a forced marriage.

Gardner also includes a cruel twist of fate for Bond. At great cost, Bond and Harriett escape Scorpius' lair. They eventually make it to the rescue team, but Harriett dies in the process. The head of the team tells Bond that the SIS knew about 007's location and that they were conducting a rescue effort. In other words, had Bond remained in his prison and not tried to escape, then Harriett would still be alive. In a sense, it is Bond who killed Harriett.

Feeling culpable for Harriett's death causes Bond to snap and behave mercilessly towards Scorpius. Instead of directly killing Scorpius Bond shoots him in the hand, and then the foot. Then, he forces Scorpius to follow the same path through the marsh that killed Harriett. The implication is that even though Bond's wedding to Harriett was a farce, the ordeal was too much in some ways for the emotionally wounded agent.

Continuity Nod: Bond was previously a patient of neurologist Sir James Molony, who Bond visits at times of great stress. Bond visited Molony in *The Man with the Golden Gun,* after the agent was programmed to kill M. Molony also appears in Fleming's *Dr. No*, *On Her Majesty's Secret Service,* and *You Only Live Twice,* when he counsels M on how to handle a grief-stricken Bond. As Andy Lane and Paul Simpson point out in *The Bond Files,* Molony is being used more like a psychiatrist here and less as a neurologist, his chosen specialty.

Bond's Personal Life: When Bond needs a tailor in Hong Kong, he prefers to go to Bel Homme. He's back to driving his beloved Bentley.

The Saab 900 does appear in the book, but it's the bad guys who are behind its wheel.

May is very intuitive to Bond's moods and knows when to keep her distance from a grumpy 007. Bond does not enjoy the company of women who cry.

Bond has read Eric Ambler's spy thriller *Doctor Frigo* and Peter Wright's *Spycatcher: The Candid Autobiography of a Senior Intelligence Officer* (1987), a memoir of his work at MI5 but he prefers Ambler's non-fiction work. Gardner has his hero making a few movie-Bond style puns. After his car is attacked on the highway, Bond jokes that traffic was murder.

Bond's Inner Life: Bond is a bit on edge and short-tempered, barking at one colleague, "Don't be stupid."

Bond's Work Methods: As referenced in other Gardner books, Bond must participate in regular training exercises. In *Scorpius*, Bond is taking part in an extended survival and endurance exercise. The nature and the objects of the training exercises change daily, sometimes he needs to complete a course within a certain time frame, and other times he's trying to evade someone.

Bond can get a direct line to M by using a private code, allowing him to sidestep Moneypenny on occasion. If the spy needs to get rid of a dead body, he only needs to place a call to the Disposal Unit and the cleanup crew will clean up Bond's handiwork. Bond rents a security box in banks all over the world (Paris, Rome, Vienna, Madrid, Berlin, Copenhagen, and of course London) to hold documents that provide him with different aliases or "lives."

Gardner also provides a little more insight into SIS operations. SIS is going through an audit, the result of which will impact the Double O Division for years to come. The process, mired by politics and favoritism, is stressful for M and underlines the agency's reliance on funding to do their work. SIS has several safe houses in England, including one in Kilburn that is deliberately designed to look like it's dilapidated. SIS also maintains a facility called Scatter that M uses for private meetings. Of minor note, Moneypenny usually leaves the office around 6 p.m. However, in other Gardner novels, she will stay much later when necessary.

Gardner also provides insight into a technique that Bond uses to avoid thinking about all the men he killed. It's not simply that Bond compartmentalizes that aspect of the job; instead, he chooses to misplace it in a way. He removes it from his memory in a way that he describes as having it “missing from your mind.” Otherwise, holding on to it too tight will get him killed.

Assorted Observations:

- Playing off documents that are normally classified as for his *eyes* only, M hears information that is for his *ears* only.
- Gardner references Fleming again when the villain says, “Someone once called you a blunt instrument.”
- In *On Her Majesty’s Secret Service*, Blofeld underwent surgery to disguise himself. That operation included changing his earlobes. Scorpius also undergoes a similar surgery but keeps his earlobes unaltered. It’s a decision that leads to Scorpius’ cover being blown.
- A murdered woman is found to be carrying a credit card named Carte Blanche, which is coincidentally the title of Jeffery Deaver’s Bond novel.
  Bond’s favorite actor is Sean Connery and he’s watched Connery’s film *The Untouchables* multiple times.

A Note about the publication order of *Licence to Kill* and *Win, Lose or Die*:

Both *Win, Lose or Die* and the *Licence to Kill* novelization were published in 1989. *Win, Lose or Die* is customarily listed first in multiple bibliographies and in official websites from the license holders, as well as in *James Bond: The John Gardner Years*, the 2013 collection of Gardner's novels. That doesn't seem to be correct, though. William Kanas, a Bond expert, alerted me to this issue and Bond scholars Jon Gilbert, John Cox, and Brian McKaig have convinced me that he is right. Let me highlight some of the evidence that they have shared with me.

Gilbert's esteemed (and heavy) *Ian Fleming and James Bond: Manuscripts in The Schøyen Collection* reports that the British trade edition of *Licence to Kill* was published in April 1989; the Signed Limited edition came out in May 1989. Trade publications *Kirkus* and *Publisher's Weekly* list the publication date of *Win, Lose or Die* as July 24, 1989 and July 1989, respectively.

McKaig sent me a series of photos that back up the claim that the novelization hit bookstores first. The inside cover of the Charter US edition of *Licence to Kill* lists its publication date as June 1989. The back of the novelization includes an advertisement that *Win, Lose or Die* is "Coming Soon" suggesting the original novel had not yet been released. (Kanas also sent me this advertisement and my copy includes the same.)

John Cox showed me a clipping from the UK paper, *Wales*, with a May 28, 1989 review of *Licence to Kill* and a May 24, 1989 review of *Licence to Kill* from the *Cincinnati Post* indicating that Win, Lose or Die would be released in July[106]

The US Berkley edition of *Win, Lose or Die*, places the book in July 1989. The August 1989 edition of *Private Eye* magazine reviewed *Win Lose or Die*, released the previous month.

Before the book went to press, Penguin Random House confirmed their imprint Charter Books published *Licence to Kill* on June 1, 1989, and Win, Lose or Die on July 24, 1989, in the US.

In short, I now believe that *Licence to Kill* initially came out in limited editions in April and May 1989; it was widely released in June 1989; and *Win, Lose or Die* followed in July. In light of the aforementioned, I am placing *Licence to Kill* before *Win, Lose or Die*.

LICENCE TO KILL (1989)

Author: John Gardner

In Brief: Bond goes rogue to get vengeance on the drug lord who mutilated his friend, Felix Leiter.

Alternate Title: License to Kill (with an "s").

Meaning of Title: Refers to Bond's authority to kill, at his own discretion, in the line of duty.

Chronology: Contemporary. Set sometime after *Live and Let Die* and possibly after *Scorpius.* However, Gardner doesn't consider *Licence to Kill* to be part of his Bond canon. In the introduction to the novelization, Gardner writes that "it has absolutely nothing to do with my series of James Bond books."[107]

Operation: Not applicable.

Bastard Meter: Bond is referred to as a bastard by various people, including a CIA agent, a Hong Kong Narcotics officer, and the main villain.

Eggs: None.

Insight into Bond: "In spite of the fear that engulfed him, Bond began to laugh."

Summary: In the Florida Keys, James Bond, Felix Leiter, and Sharky are on their way to Felix's wedding when they learn that drug kingpin, Franz Sanchez, is entering the country. Felix has been gunning for Sanchez so the group changes course to pursue him. After successfully apprehending Sanchez, Felix marries Della Churchill.

At the wedding, Bond meets DEA agents Hawkins and Ed Killifer, and a mysterious woman named Pam. As a token of their esteem, Felix and Della give Bond an inscribed lighter. Elsewhere, the DEA transport Sanchez to jail in an armored van. When the van reaches a bridge, it crashes through the guard rails and plunges into the water below. In a daring underwater escape, Sanchez's men free him.

At the airport, Bond learns that Sanchez is on the loose. Bond quickly returns to Leiter's home and finds that Della has been killed and that Leiter has been mauled by a shark. Sharky arrives and Bond asks him where someone would keep a shark. Sharky brings Bond to the Ocean Exotica Warehouse where Bond, posing as a marine biologist, meets Milton Krest. Bond spots a discarded white rose that Leiter wore on his tuxedo. Leiter's rose is proof that he was taken to and maimed at the warehouse.

Later that night, Bond returns to the warehouse. Killifer, the local agent, gets the drop on Bond and confesses that he was given $2 million to help Sanchez escape. Killifer plans to kill Bond by dropping him through a trapdoor and feeding him to a shark. When Sharky arrives and distracts Killifer, Bond kicks Killifer through the trap door, where the corrupt DEA agent is eaten by a shark.

The next day, two MI6 agents locate Bond and take him to M at Ernest Hemingway's house. M instructs Bond to cease his vendetta and return to the Service. When Bond refuses, M revokes Bond's license within the service. Bond flees before the MI6 agents can take him into custody.

Bond spies on Milton Krest, the man he met at the warehouse. Krest is on board his boat, the *Wavekrest*. Searching for Sanchez, Bond boards the boat and meets Sanchez's abused lover, Lupe Lamora. Bond learns the Krest's men are transporting hundreds of thousands of dollars of drug money. Bond kills Krest's men and confiscates the drug money.

Bond sneaks into Leiter's home and retrieves a floppy disk that Leiter had hidden behind a photo of Della. When Bond inserts the disk into Leiter's computer, he learns that Leiter has an upcoming meeting with "P. Bouvier" at the Barrelhead Saloon. Bond goes to the bar and discovers that P. Bouvier is actually Pam, the woman he met at Leiter's wedding. One of Sanchez's men, Dario, spots Bond and Pam. After getting into a fight with Sanchez's men, Bond and Pam flee aboard a nearby boat. Bond hires Pam, an army pilot, to fly him to Isthmus City, where Sanchez keeps his base of operations.

Back in London, Moneypenny tells M that she's worried for Bond's safety. M instructs Moneypenny to get Q Branch on the phone.

Bond spies on Sanchez and spots William Truman-Lodge, Sanchez's financial expert and Heller, an ex-Green Beret captain, who is the head of Sanchez's security. Pam tells Bond that Sanchez keeps his money at Banco de Isthmus. Bond uses the money he confiscated from Krest's operation to open an account in the bank.

Bond goes to the casino and sees that Sanchez is hosting a big event. Among Sanchez's guests are Kwang and Miss Loti, from Hong Kong. Bond meets Sanchez and tells the drug lord that he's looking for work. Sanchez assures Bond that he'll consider his request. Bond returns to his hotel and discovers that Q is waiting for him. Q supplies Bond with the equipment that he'll need on the trip, including a sniper rifle and explosives.

That night, Sanchez hosts an event for the world's most successful drug lords where Sanchez offers to sell franchise rights to drug territories around the world. Kwang, apparently another drug lord, requests to see Sanchez's operation. Later, Bond prepares to shoot Sanchez with a sniper rifle but Kwang and Loti stop him. They explain that they are undercover narcotics agents from Hong Kong who have infiltrated Sanchez's drug empire. Suddenly, Sanchez's men storm the place, kill Kwang, and Loti and knock Bond unconscious.

After awakening in Sanchez's residence, Bond meets with him and tries to make the drug lord suspicious of his own men. Bluffing, Bond tells Sanchez that Kwang and Loti were recruited to assassinate him by one of his closest confidantes. Sanchez boasts that his men are loyal, but he still wants to pay a visit to Milton Krest, one of his key drug smugglers. Bond and Sanchez confront Krest, who swears his loyalty to Sanchez. Sanchez kills Krest, who he believes is lying.

Sanchez takes Bond and the drug lords to the Olimpatec Meditation Center. The Center is a front for Professor Joe, a televangelist, who is using his television show to send coded messages to drug lords around the world. The Center is also where the drugs are manufactured. During a tour of the facilities, Bond learns that Sanchez has developed a method to transport cocaine by hiding it in oil. Gas tankers, like the six scheduled to leave the Meditation Center that day, will transport the oil.

Bond starts a fire in an effort to destroy the Center and interfere with operations. Dario tries to stop Bond but Bond kills Sanchez's enforcer by dropping him into a grinder. The six gas tankers carrying drugs leave the facility and Sanchez escapes in a car. Pam pilots Bond to the tankers. Bond jumps from the plane onto a tanker, commandeers the tanker, and uses it to destroy four of the five other tankers. Bond leaps from his tanker to Sanchez's, dumping its gasoline to stop its progress.

Sanchez tries to kill Bond with a machete; the two fight and it appears that Sanchez is going to kill Bond. Before striking the killing blow, Sanchez asks Bond to explain to him why he destroyed his drug empire. Bond reveals that he did it to exact revenge on Sanchez for ordering Felix Leiter to be mauled. Then, Bond produces the lighter that Leiter gave him and sets Sanchez ablaze.

Later, Bond speaks with Leiter who is on the way to recovery. Bond reassures his friend that the suffering he is experiencing will pass in time. Leiter lets his friend know that M will allow Bond to return to the service. Then, Bond meets up with Pam and they enjoy a celebratory kiss.

Commentary: Gardner's *Licence to Kill* is a faithful adaptation of Timothy Dalton's second and final Bond film. Gardner sets the story within Ian Fleming's continuity. Therefore, the events of the novelization take place after *Live and Let Die.* In Fleming's second book, Felix Leiter is fed to the sharks, survives, and is given a prosthetic leg and arm. However, the filmmakers didn't include that scene in their 1973 movie adaptation. Instead, the gruesome incident was adapted in 1989's *Licence to Kill.* So Gardner faced a choice in addressing the mauling in his novelization. He could either ignore the fact that Leiter was injured in Fleming's novels, or he could elect to have Leiter go through the same terrible experience twice. Cheekily, Gardner chose the latter option. He explained, "I felt that we should keep it for real [and remain faithful to Fleming]. They didn't in the movie. I thought, what the hell. Let's keep it correct."[108]

Shark attacks aside, Gardner is not strictly faithful to Fleming's continuity. Bond first encountered Milton Krest in the short story "The Hildebrand Rarity." Yet in the *Licence to Kill* novelization, Bond meets Krest for the first time. While there are differences between the Krest of the short story and the novelization, there are enough similarities to conclude they are essentially the same character. As Bondologist Calvin Dyson noted it seems arbitrary that Gardner followed the Leiter continuity but ignored Bond's previous meeting with Krest.[109]

Still, Gardner might have had a good reason for this discrepancy. Gardner might have thought that even casual Bond fans would remember Leiter's run-in with the shark in *Live and Let Die*. Felix's injuries are referenced in the rest of his appearances in the novels but they might not have read the Fleming short story "The Hildebrand Rarity." In fairness to Gardner, the 1960 short story is less well known than Fleming's widely read second novel. Also, Gardner would have to have gone through more gymnastics to explain away the second encounter with Krest and that would have felt like déjà vu, all over again. Or Gardner could have changed Krest's name and made him an entirely different character. However, that would mean straying from the film to such an extent that it would likely take Gardner outside of the mandates of his novelization. I suspect that because Gardner needed to adhere to the plot of the film, he decided to have a little fun at Leiter's expense; continuity be damned.

Licence to Kill is the first film and novel about Bond going rogue. In both, Bond countermands orders, leaves the service, and avenges his friend's slaughter. Although Bond has used less-than-orthodox tactics in the past to complete his objective, this is the first time that he has set his own mission. The film sympathizes with Bond and frames his righteous anger and resignation as heroic. However, Gardner's book highlights the negative impact of Bond's decisions. For instance, Bond inadvertently and fatally compromises a secret Hong Kong police mission to break up Sanchez's drug empire. Gardner's book makes it clear that if it wasn't for Bond, the Hong Kong police would have stopped Sanchez on their own. The film touches on this point but not to the same extent as Gardner's work. Bond's goal to stop Sanchez would have been more effective if Bond stayed home in London and let the Hong Kong police bring Sanchez to justice. In the end, Gardner's Bond realizes his error and accepts that M was right to revoke his license to be in the service.

In the film, Felix Leiter's new bride Della kisses Bond on the mouth. The smooch could be read as a friendly gesture between two friends, or it could mean that Della was making a pass at Bond. The film is unclear about the meaning of the kiss and how well Della and Bond knew each other before the wedding festivities. Gardner provides insight into that moment. In the novelization, Della is definitively coming on to Bond and Bond rebukes her advances. Gardner establishes that Bond and Della are old friends. Gardner also implies that they were intimate years before.

Gardner reframes the scene in the movie in which Bond speaks to an ebullient Leiter who seems to have quickly moved on from his bride's brutal murder. In Gardner's adaptation, Bond comforts his old pal who is still grieving, "The pain goes with time, Felix…I've been there, old buddy. Never leaves you, but it does get easier." Gardner's Leiter takes a moment to compose himself before responding.

Gardner fleshes out a scene in which Bond says goodbye to Lupe Lamora. After Lupe asks him to stay with her in Isthmus City, Bond dismissively rejects her offer. In the movie, Lupe comes across as naïve for thinking that a relationship with Bond is possible. In the novel, Gardner makes it clear that Lupe thinks Bond can keep her safe; after all, she just ended an abusive relationship. Gardner's Bond is less dismissive of Lupe; instead, he lets her down easy when he confesses, "Nobody's ever really safe with me." His response is a sober admission.

The tie-in includes a scene that was cut from the movie. In it, Bond searches through a briefcase that Q Branch gave him for his Istanbul trip. He finds a gun concealed in the case's fake bottom. Disappointed because he initially believes it to be a Walther PPK, 007 is relieved when he sees that it is instead a P38K, a more effective weapon. The PPK is typically connected with the movie Bond, but

Gardner had a valid reason for the weapon upgrade. When a Royal Bodyguard attempted to use a PPK to defend Princess Anne and her husband from being kidnapped, the firearm jammed. Later, it was removed from service. Gardner concluded that Bond ought not to use one either.[110]

Trying to make the super heroic movie Bond into a plausible literary one requires some finesse. Gardner tries to make the action a little more realistic than the movies, such as an audacious stunt in which an oil tanker goes on its side wheels to avoid being hit by a missile. Gardner explains that Bond "swore that he actually heard the [missile] pass underneath the cab and the tanker, but in his heart, he knew this might be an exaggeration." In other words, Gardner presents the events as the film did but he implies that the film did not accurately depict the events as they happened to the literary Bond. Or elsewhere, when Bond uses a helicopter's winch to hoist a plane in mid-air, Bond laughs at the situation. Bond thinks that he must look like "some movie stuntman doing a particularly daring act for the cameras." It's a meta-moment where Gardner reminds the viewer that they are reading a novelization of a movie.

The novelization isn't completely faithful to the movie. In the movie, M seems to completely abandon his rogue agent. However, in the novel, M acknowledges that Bond needs help and he provides Bond with a measure of support by alerting an operative in Isthmus to keep an eye out for Bond. M states that he "alerted our man in Isthmus" in the film, but it has a more ominous tone there. Gardner's characterization of M's orders is a nice departure from the film and suggests that M, at least, has some understanding and appreciation for Bond's need to bring Sanchez to justice. Plus, I suspect bringing down Sanchez's empire is in Britain's best interests as well.

Personal Life: The night before Leiter's wedding, Bond throws a debauched bachelor party for his old friend. All these years later, Bond is still stinging from Tracy's death. But now, Bond has found a way to cope with it. He finds that the "pain goes with time" and the loss "never leaves you, but it does get easier."

Continuity Nod: Bond's travel documents display the name James Boldman, the same cover identity that he uses in *Nobody Lives For Ever; No Deals, Mr. Bond; Scorpius; The Man from Barbarossa; Death Is Forever*; and *COLD*. Gardner also explains how Leiter came to lose his leg (*Live and Let Die*). The author might have been referencing *On Her Majesty's Secret Service* when he notes that Bond did *not* have all the time in the world to select a woman to hit on at Felix's wedding.

Bond's History: As noted, Bond is an old friend of Della Churchill, the woman who Felix Leiter marries. Bond knew Della before Felix met her.

Bond's Inner Life: Bond does not believe in omens.

Bond's Personal Life: Bond has dramatically cut down on his intake of both liquor and cigarettes. These days, while Bond enjoys the occasional martini, he prefers a good wine. He has cut his cigarette smoking habit down to five a day. Gardner's Bond loves jazz music and is a member of a private club in London, which is not Blades.

Bond's Work Methods: Bond keeps his business cards, with different cover identities on him, in a silver card case. Bond employs a tradecraft technique known as "round-the-houses" or "dry cleaning" to make sure that he's not being followed.

Assorted Observations:

- Bond is friends with David Wolkovsky, a Key West resident who performs restoration work on buildings. In *Scorpius*, Gardner used the same name for a CIA operative. Based on my reading of the text, they are two separate characters who share the same name.

WIN, LOSE OR DIE (1989)

Author: John Gardner

In Brief: Bond must defend a Royal Navy aircraft carrier holding a conference of international leaders from an attack by the terrorist group BAST.

Meaning of Title: At least three meanings. First, WIN and LOSE are the names of two operations. Second, while Bond may ultimately succeed, others don't lose, they die. Third, a terrorist who thought his side would win, instead lost and died.

Chronology: Contemporary. Set after the events of *Scorpius*, in the late 1980s.

Operation: WIN, LOSE, Landsea, and Sleeping Beauty.

Bastard Meter: Not determined.

Eggs: Sunnyside up. Elsewhere, Bond prepares himself a four-egg omelet.

Insight into Bond: "We're TS Eliot's 'Hollow Men,' we are also rust-stained dinosaurs. Our day has come and gone."

Summary: A terrorist group called BAST (Brotherhood of Anarchy and Secret Terror) attacks a Japanese oil tanker near the Gulf of Oman. BAST is successful in this operation which they have dubbed WIN, but they sustain heavy casualties.

At SIS, M notifies Bond about Landsea '89, a joint training mission between the British Royal Navy and the United States Navy; it will take place on the air carrier *HMS Invincible*. The exercise might be disrupted by BAST, who have recently performed terror attacks all over the world. The four leaders of BAST are Bassam "The Viper" Baradj (the prime leader), Ali Al "The Snake" Adwan, Abou "The Man" Hamarik, and Saphiis "The Cat" Boudai. M believes that the attack on the Japanese tanker is a rehearsal for an assault on the *Invisible.* Bond will go undercover and make sure that BAST doesn't disrupt the exercise. To facilitate the mission, M relieves Commander Bond of his duties in the Foreign Office and promotes him to the rank of Captain RN (Royal Navy).

For over eight months, Captain Bond trains on jets along with other Royal Navy personnel, including Felipe Pantano. During one of Bond's practice flights, someone fires a live missile at him. When Bond reports the incident, his claims are met with disbelief. Felipe Pantano and his aircraft vanish on the next practice flight.

Bond meets Clover Pennington, a member of the Women's Royal Naval Service, aka Wrens. Clover and Bond go out to dinner together. Elsewhere, Petty Officer Engineer Blackstone befriends two men named Harry and Bill at a local bar. Blackstone tries to impress his new friends by telling them about the Royal Navy's secret naval turbine engines.

When Bond meets with M and Bill Tanner, they tell him that BAST has sent an operative to kill him. To ensure his safety, M instructs Bond to go on holiday. Bond reluctantly agrees to go to Ischia, an island in Italy.

In Italy, Bond goes to his villa and meets Beatrice Maria da Ricci, who is in charge of maintaining the property. Later that night, Bond wakes up to investigate a noise. He sees Beatrice carrying a gun and assumes that she's the threat. Beatrice tells Bond that there is an intruder on the grounds. Bond looks into it but only hears the sound of a car fleeing the scene. When Bond returns, Beatrice reveals that she's an intelligence officer who has been assigned to protect him.

Back in Plymouth, Harry and Bill coerce Petty Officer Blackstone into sharing more classified information. Later, they go to a brothel where Blackstone's intimate acts are recorded.

Back in Italy, Bond and Beatrice grow close. Bond visits a local jeweler to buy Beatrice a gift. They spend Christmas together and their relationship deepens. But their romance is short-lived. A car bomb goes off apparently killing Beatrice. M arranges for Bond to be brought back to safety.

Bond returns to the *Invincible*. On board the ship are representatives of the Soviet Union and the US Secret Services, Nikola "Nikki" Ratinokov and Edgar Morgan, respectively. Nikki and Morgan are there to ensure that the upcoming meeting between the Prime Minister of the United Kingdom, the President of the United States, and the head of the Soviet Union goes smoothly.

Bond is informed that Morgan, one of the Americans, was murdered, and his body was discovered by one of the Wrens, Sarah Deeley. Bond examines the dead body and sees that Morgan's throat was cut. Bond interrogates members of the crew and tries to determine who killed Morgan. He discovers that Deeley's name does not appear in the Wren files and, therefore, she must be an imposter.

Bond arrests Deeley for the murder of the American. Deeley tries to stab Bond with a knife, but a young marine overpowers her.

Bond is told that naval intelligence officer, Dan Woodward, has been dispatched to replace the dead Secret Service agent. Woodward is abducted by BAST while traveling to the ship, and BAST strategist Abou Hamarik adopts his identity and boards the ship.

The dignitaries for the Steward's Meeting board the *Invincible*; they include President George H.W. Bush, Prime Minister Margaret Thatcher, and Chairman Mikhail Gorbachev. The three world leaders discuss the reduction of nuclear weapons. Meanwhile, Petty Officer Blackstone sabotages the ship's turbine engines. Elsewhere, Nikki Ratinokov tells Bond that she thinks Woodward is an imposter. To confirm Nikki's story, Bond asks headquarters to send him a photo of the real Woodward. Later that night, Bond and Nikki make love.

The next day, Bond reviews a photo of the real Woodward and sets off to arrest the imposter, Abou Hamarik. Hamarik resists and kills Nikki, but he is overpowered by a Secret Service agent. A Petty Officer tries to sink the *Invincible* by causing an explosion. The ship's personnel contain. Bond briefs the heads of state on the attack and suggests that they seek safety at a naval base in Rota, Spain. The leaders agree to go to Spain but insist on continuing with their talks.

The *Invincible* arrives at Spain. When Bond exits the ship, he is shocked to see the presumed-dead Beatrice Maria da Ricci. Beatrice tells Bond that her death was a ruse to confuse BAST. Bond receives word that Prime Minister Thatcher and President Bush and Chairman Gorbachev have been kidnapped and are being held for a ransom of $600 billion.

Clover Pennington arrives and reveals herself to be "The Cat," one of the four heads of BAST. Clover explains that all meals and drinks on the ship were drugged. When the crew members passed out, BAST kidnapped the world leaders. This operation was called Sleeping Beauty.

Bond is taken to a cell, but he breaks free by strangling one of the Wrens. Felipe Pantano, the missing pilot and secret member of BAST, commences an aerial attack on the *Invincible*. To escape, Bond steals a jet and shoots down the enemy fighters. Bond's aircraft suffers damage, so he uses an ejector seat to escape. A helicopter takes Bond to safety.

Bond receives a message from BAST leader, Bassam Baradj, that if the $600 billion ransom is not paid by 6 a.m., world leaders will be killed. Operatives determine that the message was sent from Gibraltar.

Bond flying a Sea Harrier
in *Win, Lose or Die.*
Illustration by Pat Carbajal

Bond boards the *Invincible*, and overpowers Clover who takes him to the world leaders, all of whom are safe. Bond and Beatrice go to Gibraltar to track down Baradj. They discovered that Baradj is hiding in what appears to be a small town but is actually a military training facility. Just as Baradj has the upper hand and is getting ready to kill Bond, Beatrice kills the BAST leader.

Bond and Beatrice take a trip to Spain. He believes Beatrice has the potential to be his true love. He is painfully aware that his previous partners perished too soon.

Commentary: Before John Gardner started his career as a writer of thrillers, he served with Britain's Fleet Air Arm, one of the branches of the Royal Navy, and Royal Marines, the United Kingdom's naval commando force. They don't just operate on the sea; both the Fleet Air Arm and Royal Marines have pilots who take to the air to defend their vessels and attack the enemy. Gardner was also a member of the Royal Marines 42 Commando. Given his military background, one gets the sense that Gardner was chomping at the bit to write *Win, Lose or Die*, which takes place on a British aircraft carrier and ends with Bond piloting an aircraft and participating in a dogfight with an enemy plane. In many ways *Win, Lose or Die* continues to be an extension of

Gardner's passions and interests. It's replete with information about spy craft and the latest technology.

Gardner is aware that he's writing for an audience who might not be familiar with the Royal Navy's operations. So, Gardner must lay a lot of groundwork for the book to make sense to the layman. He has to explain the inner workings of the Navy, what an aircraft carrier is, how it works, and how it can be defeated. Gardner also outlines Bond's training regimen as the spy refreshes his knowledge of jet piloting.

Gardner isn't satisfied exclusively with writing a military thriller. Gardner mixes things up and jumps genres by inserting a quasi-locked room mystery into the book. In a locked room mystery, a crime is committed in a room and the murderer can't get in or out of the crime scene undetected. That's not quite what happens in *Win, Lose or Die* because the murder takes place on an aircraft carrier in the North Sea, but the entire vessel serves as a quasi-locked room. Following in Miss Marple and Hercule Poirot's footsteps, Bond plays the part of a detective. Bond interrogates the suspects, and questions their whereabouts, opportunity, identity, and motives. Bond doesn't feel up to the task and he acknowledges that he's "not Sherlock Holmes." Nevertheless, he solves the crime and apprehends the perpetrator.

In Gardner's previous book, *Scorpius*, the life of the unnamed President of the United States is saved. At the time, Ronald Regan was the President, but Gardner didn't refer to him by his name. This time, Gardner is more explicit. When Gardner wrote *Win, Lose or Die*, President George H.W. Bush, Prime Minister Margaret Thatcher, and Chairman Mikhail Gorbachev were in power. Because the summit involves leaders from the United States, the United Kingdom, and the Soviet Union, Gardner not only references the leaders but he also has them appear in the book as characters. Moreover, Gardner concocts a scenario where Bond personally meets each world figure. For some readers, this touch adds a touch of authenticity, but others are challenged to suspend their disbelief.

Gardner also experiments with the organizational structure of the evil organization. Typically, there is one leader. In *Win, Lose or Die*, there are four—Bassam Baradj (the prime leader), Abou Hamarik, Ali Al Adwan, and Saphiis Boudai. Their respective codenames are The Man, The Viper, The Snake, and The Cat. Changing the hierarchy from one evil leader to four is another way in which Gardner continues to experiment with the formula.

Continuity Nod: In *Colonel Sun,* a member of M's household staff is named Chief Petty Officer Hammond. In *Win, Lose or Die*, Gardner states that Hammond has since retired.[111] As Hammond and his wife were murdered in *Colonel Sun*, this could be classed as a mistake by Gardner or, perhaps, a different continuity. When M suggests that an operation can take place during Christmas, Bond notes that he doesn't have any real family and then recalls the time that he spent with Tracy at Christmas (*On Her Majesty's Secret Service*).

Bond's History: Keeping with the Christmas theme, the adult Bond does not take pleasure in the holiday. However, that might be because his favorite Christmas memory came from when he was a child before his parents died. He had measles and chicken pox, so they purchased him an air pistol while he was recovering. Bond describes those moments as his "final taste of love." Gardner references Bond's pre-Double O days when he served in the conflict in the Falkland Islands. Bond's primary mission was to arrive before the violence erupted and to help train civilians.

Bond's Inner Life: Bond is still reeling from witnessing the violent death of his new love, Beatrice Maria da Ricci—a car bomb apparently blew her to pieces. It turned out to be a ruse but Bond was convinced he had witnessed her demise. In the last chapter, Bond is traumatized by the incident. He replays her death in his head and can't escape "the agony of knowing that he lost her." He is unable to escape the visions of his murdered allies, such as Edgar Morgan, whose throat is nearly severed. Hearing specific words and seeing objects connected to his mission trigger Bond, who is somewhat reluctantly seeing a therapist. For instance, the word "cat" conjures up his BAST foe, while the site of an automobile conjures up Beatrice being ripped to shreds. He tries to downplay the personal toll on him by saying it's only a "touch of horrors" to use the term offered by his "shrink." However, Bond is clearly shaken, even though Beatrice is back in his life. This is arguably the most vulnerable Gardner's Bond has ever been.

Bond relishes the "privileges of rank" and he seems to get pleasure out of issuing orders to those below him. When someone of a lower rank tries to leave the room without Bond's permission, 007 snaps, "Sit down! I haven't said you can leave." Granted, in the military everyone operates under a set of rules and a chain of command. In this case, Bond is deliberately trying to demonstrate his authority to someone with whom he has an adversarial relationship. But still, Bond comes across as terse. Gardner acknowledges that Bond is sometimes too class-conscious. Few things give Bond greater pleasure than being at sea.

Bond is not overly superstitious but he's mindful of signs. For instance, he sees what appears to be a reflection of a spear in the water and he wonders if it's an omen about his assignment.

Bond starts to fall in love with Beatrice and wonders if their relationship will lead to marriage. As a sign of his growing esteem, he buys her diamond-encrusted jewelry with a gold clasp. Bond hasn't made a similar purchase for a woman in quite a long time. But Beatrice "had started to command his heart" and Bond is open to allowing the relationship to blossom. At the end of the book, Beatrice tells Bond that she loves him, and he responds in kind. Despite their blossoming romance, Beatrice does not appear in Gardner's follow-up, *Brokenclaw*. However, she does return in Gardner's last Bond novel, *COLD*.

Bond's Personal Life: Bond is a creature of routine and he's trained himself to be a light sleeper, especially in the field. Bond doesn't often cook for himself; he greatly prefers that food be prepared and served to him. But in a pinch, Bond makes himself a four-egg omelet and a tomato salad for an early dinner.

Bond's Work Methods: At the start of *Win, Lose or Die*, Bond's job responsibilities are largely administrative. Bond resents that he is still an active member of the Royal Navy, and that he has been sidelined from taking part in any mission. He'd much rather formally return to the Foreign Affairs office, where he can conduct assignments as a Double O agent. Bond knows at least 403 ways of killing someone and at least 21 ways of faking his own death.

Assorted Observations:

- The climax of 1989's *Win, Lose or Die* takes place in Gibraltar, the site of 1987's *The Living Daylights'* pre-title sequence.
- Bond's not always the dapper spy. As a part of a disguise, Bond dons a fishing hat.
- Gardner includes two footnotes in the book. One describes Bond's involvement in the Falklands War and the other clarifies the use of naval slang.

BROKENCLAW (1990)

Author: John Gardner

In Brief: Bond is sent to investigate a possible connection between Brokenclaw Lee, a charismatic mob boss who supplies information to Chinese Intelligence, and the disappearance of naval experts working on a submarine detection system. Along the way, Bond discovers that Brokenclaw is working on a scheme to destabilize the American dollar by manipulating the stock market.

Meaning of Title: Refers to the name of the villain.

Chronology: Contemporary. Set a year after the events of *Win, Lose or Die*.

Operation: Curve and Jericho.

Bastard Meter: Unregistered.

Eggs: Eggs served with bacon, not to Bond's satisfaction. Elsewhere, Bond orders eggs Benedict.

Insight into Bond: "Sometimes I think the Grim Reaper sits on your shoulder, 007. One day he'll catch up with you."

Summary: In Victoria, British Columbia, two men try to abduct Commander Robert Allardyce. Allardyce is killed while trying to escape. Elsewhere in Victoria, Bond has finished playing golf, when he spots a team of security guards. Reading the security team's lips, Bond discovers that they are working for Lee Fu-Chu, who is also known as Brokenclaw Lee. He also learns that a member of their detail recently killed someone. Intrigued, Bond follows Brokenclaw to a museum. There, Brokenclaw, who has Native American and Chinese heritage, donates an ancient totem.

Bond returns to London and tells M that he's eager to start a new mission. M believes that Bond needs more rest since the last assignment, and he recommends that 007 visit California.

Bond travels to San Francisco. Once there, Bond realizes that a man is following him. In Chinatown, four thugs with bats appear and kill the man. Back at his hotel, Bond is visited by FBI agents Wood and Nolan, who want to talk to Bond about the murder of a fellow agent.

Bond goes to their office and learns that the dead man was an FBI agent who was assigned to protect Bond.

Bond is taken to meet M at the Naval Station Treasure Island in San Francisco Bay. M informs Bond that the FBI blames 007 for the death of their agent. M introduces Bond to his new partner, Commander Ed Rushia, a US Naval Intelligence officer. Bond and Rushia's mission involves two new submarine systems; one that detects submarines and another that counters the first one. These two systems are known as LORDS and LORDS DAY. M explains that a group of naval experts who have built the technology, including Commander Allardyce, have gone missing. Bond and Rushia will find the missing naval experts and investigate Brokenclaw whose sobriquet comes from the fact that his thumb is on the wrong side of his hand. They will be aided by Lieutenant Commander Wanda Man Song Hing of the US Navy and Naval Intelligence Officer, Sue Chi-Ho, aka Chi-Chi.

Over dinner, Wanda tells Bond that her father, Tony Man Song Hing, owed Brokenclaw $1 million. So, as a perverse form of payment, her father "gave" Wanda to Brokenclaw. Wanda agreed to the proposition as a way to infiltrate Brokenclaw's organization and report on his activities to the navy. Wanda reveals that Lee is in possession of naval secrets, which he intends to give to the Chinese intelligence agency for whom he is working. Wanda explains the procedure for transferring the documents: two couriers, Peter Argentbright and Jenny Mo, will fly to the United States, stay with the courier's contact, Myra, at her apartment in New York City, and then take possession of the documents. To get the naval secrets, Bond and Chi-Chi decide to intercept the couriers and take their place.

Bond and Chi-Chi undergo minor surgery to make them look more like couriers. Then, Bond and Chi-Chi travel to New York City and go to Myra's apartment. Their cover is quickly blown because Myra knows what the real Jenny Mo looks like. Chi-Chi grabs Myra by force and Bond interrogates her. Myra tells Bond that the Chinese government has forced her to work on their behalf. Myra also reveals that her parents saved the life of Hung Chow H'ang, who later became the head of Chinese Intelligence.

Bond and Chi-Chi go to JFK Airport and meet Brokenclaw's enforcer, Bone Bender Ding. Bone Bender takes Bond and Chi-Chi to a private jet that will take them to his boss. SIS attempts to track the plane.

Bond and Chi-Chi are brought to Brokenclaw's estate, hidden somewhere in California. Brokenclaw tells Bond that there is a location in Washington State's Chelan Mountains where indigenous people have lived. Brokenclaw visits there to commune with his ancestors. Still posing as a courier, Bond explains to Brokenclaw that he will need to turn the documents into microdots. Then, Bond will go to a bank and arrange payment for them. Brokenclaw accepts this proposal and informs Bond that Chinese Intelligence Officer, Hung Chow H'ang, will be arriving the next night. Bond and Chi-Chi will need to pull off their plan before Hung Chow H'ang arrives or their cover will be blown.

Later, Brokenclaw brings Wanda's father, Tony, to the house and tells him that he knows his daughter is spying on him. As punishment, Tony is fed to a pack of wolves.

Bond discovers that Brokenclaw is not only interested in submarine detection technology, but he is also going forward with Operation Jericho, a plan to sabotage the New York Stock Exchange. Brokenclaw will collapse the value of the dollar and destabilize the world markets. Bond also learns that the missing naval experts are being held in Brokenclaw's home. Commander Rushia, Bond's ally, figures out where 007 is being held.

The next day, Bone Bender takes Bond to the bank to arrange payment to Brokenclaw. However, unbeknownst to Brokenclaw, the bank is a CIA front. The FBI men deliberately break Bond's cover because they continue to hold Bond responsible for their colleague's death. Bond contacts M who tells Bond that the SIS and the Navy have called for an airstrike on Brokenclaw's base. Bond tells M that he's returning to Brokenclaw's home so that he can save Chi-Chi and the other naval experts.

When Bond arrives, Brokenclaw informs him that while Chi-Chi was being tortured, she revealed that Bond is a spy. As punishment, Brokenclaw ties Bond to a post, strips him naked, and attempts to feed him to the wolves. However, the wolves ignore Bond. It turns out that Commander Rushia had secretly drugged the animals to make them docile.

The Navy and SIS arrive in time to save Bond and free the hostages. Then, Bond and Chi-Chi become intimate. Later, Bond goes out on an errand. But when he returns, he finds that Chi-Chi has been kidnapped. Bond discovers an FBI pin on the floor and realizes that agents Nolan and Wood participated in Chi-Chi's abduction.

Bond suspects that Brokenclaw is hiding out in the Chelan Mountains in Washington State, in an area where Brokenclaw visits to spend time to reconnect with his culture. Bond travels to the mountains and tracks down the villain. Brokenclaw challenges Bond to participate in a painful ritual ceremony that involves nailing pegs into Bond's body. If Bond wins the contest, then he and Chi-Chi can go free. The two warriors compete in the ritual that ends with them shooting arrows at each other. Brokenclaw's arrow narrowly misses his target but Bond's arrow pierces Brokenclaw's throat, killing him. Bond is taken to the hospital for treatment. Chi-Chi is happy to help him recover.

Commentary: It must be said, John Gardner has a wicked sense of humor. In a direct conflict of wills, Bond typically prevails because he is physically stronger, mentally smarter, or more determined than his opponent. However, in *Brokenclaw*, Bond prevails because he is weaker than the other guy.

At the end of *Brokenclaw*, Bond competes with Brokenclaw in an exhausting race. At the end of the competition, Bond and Brokenclaw square off and fire arrows at each other. Brokenclaw shoots his arrow first, with deadly precision. However, at just the last moment, a tired Bond's legs give way, he hunches over, and the arrow sails over his head. Had Bond not been so exhausted, he would have remained erect, and the arrow would have gone through his skull. Making Bond win because he's the physically weaker of the two is Gardner in his purest and cheekiest form.

After a mission, Bond is usually worse for wear. Being shot, stabbed, strangled, and battered is not unusual for the spy. Typically, his healing takes place between books. But Gardner takes a different approach in *Brokenclaw*. After Bond survives his torture ceremony, Bond is sent to the hospital. There, over a period of a month and a half, the agent goes through five painful operations. At first, Bond is unable to walk. But eventually, he gains the power to use his legs. Gardner further explains that Bond will need a full year of physiotherapy before his body heals. Some might argue that seeing the toll it takes on Bond, as it would any person, would ruin the illusion of the books and make him less of a fantasy figure. Arguably, that's Gardner's intention in using the last few pages of the book to describe Bond's recovery. It's a way of grounding the fantasy.

Continuity Nod: Bond refers to the health farm that M sent him to, as depicted in *Thunderball*. Gardner also references the events of *Win, Lose or Die* where Bond's rank is raised to that of a Captain.

Bond's History: Bond tells Chi-Chi that he lost his virginity at 14. In his short story "From a View to a Kill (1960)," Fleming previously established that the momentous event took place at 16, so either Gardner overlooked that bit of information or Bond is strategically lying. When Bond was a student, his school would serve fish on

Fridays, usually cod. The cod was cooked so badly that he swore to himself that he would only eat the best meals when he grew up.

Bond's Personal Life: Bond's housekeeper May describes Bond as a bit of a busybody who is forever putting his nose into other people's business. She warns him that "curiosity killed the cat." Bond lives by the advice that someone gave him about how to get over a heartbreak. He accepts that there is "nothing you could do about it, except put your hands in your pockets and walk away." There's a fatalism in that sentiment which is consistent with Gardner's depiction of Bond.

Bond shares how he handles breakups and getting dumped by a woman who has fallen out of love with him. A wise man told him to "put your hands in your pockets and walk away" rather than wallow in the muck of his emotions.

Bond has tablets that will put him to sleep in two minutes. He appears to be carrying them for personal purposes. I can't be positive, though, because he does share them with a nervous person who is in his protection.

Bond's Inner Life: At the start of *Brokenclaw*, Bond mostly performs administrative work. And it is slowly driving him mad. Bond threatens M that if he doesn't put him back on active duty posthaste, then he's going to resign and go private. If Bond is serious about being a hired gun, then Gardner's Bond isn't a spy solely as a means to serve his country. Instead, he does it because he loves danger. Other passages support this theory. Elsewhere, Bond acknowledges to himself that he has the "mind of an adventurer." Bond also worries that he has lost his adventurous spirit but once he's exposed to danger, he seems to believe that he rediscovered it. That adventurous spirit is "more precious to him than life itself."

Bond claims that he is not overly superstitious except he does have an aversion to quoting Shakespeare's *Macbeth* and hearing the saying, "Eat, drink, and be merry for tomorrow we shall all die." Still, Bond might be disassembling, as he showed superstitious tendencies in Gardner's previous original novel, *Win, Lose or Die*.

Bond's Tastes: In atypical fashion for Gardner's Bond, the agent eschews coffee and, instead, orders tea. Still, the agent has never opted for High Tea. He does, however, like a good crumpet. He enjoys wearing moccasins that he orders from Lily Shoes, a store in Hong Kong. Bond is starting to enjoy the taste of American wine. Bond has memorized passages of *Alice's Adventures in Wonderland* and he also references quotes from the Bible that he finds meaningful. He appears to occasionally play Trivial Pursuit, a board game meant to test one's trivial knowledge and is adept at the tile-based game Mahjong.

Bond's Work Methods: Because of the time he spent with Ebbie Heritage in *No Deals, Mr. Bond*, Bond can lip-read. In *Brokenclaw*, he puts those tools to work when he reads the lips of a security team who are up to no good. Had Bond not met Ebbie and learned a new skill, then the villain might have gotten away with his scheme. For me, that's an excellent use of continuity. Instead of simply referencing a past event, our hero retains and utilizes the new set of skills.

Bond is suspicious of M. He doesn't believe that M sent him on vacation to recuperate. Instead, Bond thinks he's there as a prelude to an assignment. Later, Gardner notes that when Bond is in the thick of the mission, he doesn't trust anyone, not even M. These are fleeting moments. But it's a notable aspect of their relationship.

Bond watches a man get beaten to death by four men with bats. Later, he learns that the man was an FBI agent. Still, Bond doesn't show remorse. Instead, he insists that an important rule is "self-preservation." It's a decidedly unheroic, but realistic, viewpoint. In Bond's defense, he didn't know that the man was an FBI agent; instead, Bond had good reason to believe that the man was a threat.

Bond will fall asleep across the doorway while holding a gun to prevent someone from secretly sneaking into his hotel room or private residence. Bond's instructor taught him that, above all, he is an English gentleman. Not only should he live like one, but he needs to die like one too. He shouldn't beg for his life or reveal classified information, even under the most grueling torture.

Assorted Commentary:

- Gardner makes more pop culture references than he has done in the past. Bond watches Johnny Carson on *The Tonight Show*, and, at some point, has watched *Star Wars*, *Dirty Harry*, and Woody Allen movies.

THE MAN FROM BARBAROSSA (1991)

Author: John Gardner

In Brief: James Bond and Mossad agent, Pete Natkowitz, are sent to infiltrate the Scales of Justice terrorist group which are putting a war criminal on trial as a smokescreen for their true plans to destabilize the Soviet Union and install their own leader as president.

Meaning of Title: The code name for Adolf Hitler's invasion of the Soviet Union was Operation Barbarossa. The titular "man" was a key figure in that operation.

Chronology: Contemporary. Primarily set after the events in *Brokenclaw.* September 28, 1941 marks the prelude with the bulk of the story happening decades later between December 26, 1990, and mid-January 1991.

Operation: Barbarossa and Fallen Timbers.

Bastard Meter: Not gauged.

Eggs: Boiled for three and one-third minutes.

Insight into Bond: "Bond thought he sounded a shade smug and almost instantly regretted it."

Summary: In the 1941 prelude, over thirty-three thousand Jews are massacred in Babi Yar, Kyiv. Nazi commander Paul Blobel, along with his deputy Josif Vorontsov, lead the massacre. Years later, Blobel is charged with war crimes but Voronstov escapes. In 1990, a man named Joel Penderek is kidnapped by a terrorist organization called the Scales of Justice in Hawthorne, New Jersey. The Scales of Justice announce that Penderek is actually the Nazi Voronstov and demand that the Soviet Union put Voronstov on trial for his war crimes.

In London, M tells Bond that the KGB has requested assistance from Britain and Israel to look into the disappearance of Penderek. Bond will represent British interests and Pete Natkowitz will serve as Israel's agent. Later, M, Bond, and Bill Tanner compare a photo of the Nazi Voronstov to private citizen Penderek and wonder if the Scales of Justice kidnapped the wrong man. According to Israeli intelligence, the real Voronstov has been living in Florida under the name Markus Liebermann. More recently, Voronstov/Lieberman has also been kidnapped. General Yevgeny Yuskovich, a Red Army general with close ties to the KGB, is a relative of the Nazi Voronstov. Additionally, SIS intelligence indicates that two French secret service agents—Henri Rampart and Stephanie Adoré—have arrived in London.

Bond pays a visit to Stephanie Adoré to find out what she's doing in England. Adoré reveals that she was sent by the French Intelligence Agency to test the British Intelligence. When Bond leaves Adoré's apartment, French operative Henri Rampart tries to run Bond over with his car.

The Scales of Justice issue a statement indicating that if Voronstov is not put on trial within a few days, a high-ranking member of the Soviet Union will be executed.

Bond and Natkowitz travel to Moscow and meet Boris Stepakov, a KGB agent. Bond, Natkowitz, and Stepakov travel to a dacha, a small Russian cottage. Later, Stephanie Adoré and Henri Rampart arrive at the dacha and tell Bond that the French government has kidnapped the real Voronstov (the man from Florida) and is keeping him safe. The French and English are both united in their goal to bring the Scales of Justice down. Professor Vladimir Lyko, a KGB informant, who also works for the Scales of Justice, explains that the Scales of Justice are now going to conduct a televised Nuremberg-esque trial of Voronstov as a means to embarrass the Soviet Union for their past and current treatment of Jews.

Bond, Natkowitz, and KGB agent Nina Bibikova are brought to a suburb in Moscow, drugged by the Scales of Justice, and transported to a "hotel" in the Arctic Circle named Hôtel de la Justice. Bond and Natkowitz pose as crew members who are there to help televise the trial.

The military tribunal of Penderek begins. During the trial, the Scales of Justice agents and professional actors pose as Holocaust survivors and recount the real horrors of the Holocaust. The Commander-in-Chief of the Red Army, General Yevgeny Yuskovich, serves as the judge. Joel Penderek from New Jersey goes along with the ruse and pretends to be Voronstov. At first, Bond cannot figure out why Penderek is pretending to be a war criminal. Bond eventually learns that Penderek and Yuskovich are working together and the trial is really a tool to help overthrow the current President and install Yuskovich.

The trial continues and Soviet forces attack the hotel. A dead body thought to be Bond's is found during the raid. M is informed of Bond's apparent death and a funeral is held for the fallen agent.

Yuskovich escapes, boards a minesweeper, and keeps Natkowitz, Adoré, Rampart, and Stepakov as prisoners. The vessel contains a Scamp, a Russian mobile launching system, and a Scapegoat, compatible nuclear missiles, which Yuskovich intends to supply to Iraq. Yuskovich plans to frame the English and French Governments by making it appear that they are selling weapons to Iraq, America's enemy. In response, Iraq will fire nuclear missiles at Washington, DC.

Bond reappears in the submarine; he had fooled the enemy into thinking he was killed by dressing a dead operative in his own clothes and decimating the man's face so that he couldn't be identified. Bond disguised himself and posed as the enemy agent. Now, Bond rescues his comrades, Natkowitz, Adoré, Rampart, and Stepakov, who have been held prisoner. The Russian Navy kill Yuskovich and the threat against Washington is averted.

Bond returns to London. M informs 007 that he has been awarded the Order of Lenin.

Commentary: *The Man from Barbarossa* could be said to begin the third era of Bond novels. In the first era, an evil organization or madman plans is working against British interests, and Bond must put an end to it. *Licence Renewed* and *For Special Services* fall into this category. In the second era, Gardner used the general formula but spoofed the spy series in some way. For instance, in *Scorpius*, Bond witnesses a possible satanic possession and, later, the villain forces Bond to marry another agent. For his tenth original Bond novel, Gardner tries something completely different. It is his most personal effort and, according to the author, it's his favorite.

In *The Man from Barbarossa*, Bond is sent to infiltrate the terrorist group the Scales of Justice, who are televising a mock war crimes tribunal with actors playing Holocaust victims recounting real atrocities. Bond's role in the proceedings is to serve as a TV cameraman. As such, Bond is merely a witness to the proceedings. For substantial portions of the book, Bond isn't shaping events or driving the plot. Instead, other characters take over and become the focus and impact of the narrative. Gardner deliberately sidelines the spy. Bond is not the one man—one Spartan—of the past books where a single figure can change history.

Gardner is not the first author to experiment with the template of a Bond novel. Fleming also mixed up the Bond formula in his fifth novel, *From Russia with Love*. Bond does not appear for the first third of the book. In his place, Fleming provides readers with an inside look at SMERSH. In *The Spy Who Loved Me*, 007 does not arrive until about two-thirds of the way into the book. Moreover, the book is not told in the third person, as was typical for Fleming's novels. Instead,

Fleming wrote the novel in the first person from the viewpoint of a young Canadian woman named Vivienne Michel, who recounts her life story.

Ostensibly, the Scales of Justice are the villains of *The Man from Barbarossa,* and they bear a surface similarity to SPECTRE in that both organizations rely on terror and extortion. Here, the Scales of Justice threaten to kill an innocent every day until their demands are met. So, they're no angels. However, they are not the true enemy of the book; instead, the Nazis are the ultimate evil. From 1941 to 1945, the Nazis killed six million Jews and untold homosexuals, Polish, Afro-Europeans, and people with disabilities in violent and horrific ways.

In *The Man from Barbarossa*, Gardner details some of those methods and attempts to shine a light on the Nazis' brutality and their systematic attempts to eliminate world Jewry. These real-world events are shocking and deeply upsetting. Therefore, because the book uses genocide as its backdrop, it is a radical departure from Gardner's previous escapist efforts.

Whether a Bond novel, which is typically a source of entertainment, is the proper medium to describe the horrors of the Holocaust may depend on the reader's preferences. Nevertheless, the subject that Gardner raises is unquestionably worthy of consideration and attention.

Bond's History: A previous mission took Bond to Switzerland, where Bond and Nigsy Meadows, an MI6 agent, worked together to bring down a Soviet agent who was laundering money that would support UK-based Soviet networks. Years ago, Bond killed a man in Los Angeles by running him off the road. The man was stalking a woman and was going to embarrass Bond's intelligence community. So Bond was ordered to get rid of him. The entire operation was performed without the knowledge or permission of the US government.

Bond's Inner Life: Bond is understandably "deeply depressed" by the nature of the mission and listening to the catalog of atrocities committed by the Nazis. Bond and Nina Bibikova become so close during the mission, that the agent begins to think of Nina as his wife.

Bond's Personal Life: Bond no longer has a flirtatious relationship with Miss Moneypenny. Instead, she's more like a sister to him. Bond still has a working command of Russian.

Bond's Tastes: Bond has an appreciation of high-level stage magic, and he believes that spies, like magicians, both share the need to perfect sleight of hand. [Gardner was a stage magician during World War II and, after the war, he briefly served as a magician with the American Red Cross. He was also a member of the Magic Circle, a magician's society.]

As a boy, Bond read *The Prisoner of Zenda* and adventure books by Dornford Yates. Bond read *The Wind in the Willows*, likely as a child, and Fyodor Dostoyevsky's *Crime and Punishment.* Bond quotes Tolstoy to himself and finds personal meaning in the author's quote "What a strange illusion it is to suppose that beauty is goodness." Except for Homer, Bond doesn't like poetry. He knows the American blues song "Blues in the Night."

Surprisingly, Bond has a favorite denim jacket, replete with leather patches. Bond might tolerate the unexpected fashion choice because the patches conceal his survival equipment.

Bond's Work Methods: Rather than reading briefing files on computers, Bond prefers studying hard copies. For him, the "old ways" are the best. Bond is well-known to most intelligence agencies the world over. During the mission, Bond heeds M's advice to "never discount the impossible." When possible, SIS instructs Bond to neutralize enemy agents rather than kill them, lest they be replaced by an even worse threat. The devil you know.

Assorted Observations:

- Pop culture references in the book include Barry Manilow's "Could It Be Magic?"
- M doesn't always let others do the dirty work. Instead, the head of SIS rolls up his sleeves, gets his hands dirty, and personally conducts an interrogation.
- This might be the only Gardner Bond book where the storyline heavily relies on historical context. The book is set in the time leading up to Desert Storm, the 42-day US military operation that freed Kuwait from Iraqi domination. Given that, the section discussing Iraq is particularly relevant at the time. The book was released in the United States in May 1991, following the end of Desert Storm in February 1991.
- Bond is awarded the Order of Lenin for his work on the mission. He asks M to hold on to the medal for him.
- From time to time, Bond is asked to lecture new MI6 agents. He describes his job as "nine-tenths boredom followed by one-tenth sheer terror."

DEATH IS FOREVER (1992)

Author: John Gardner

In Brief: Bond teams up with CIA agent, Easy St. John, to find out who is killing off a shuttered spy network. Along the way, Bond discovers a scheme to kill twelve world leaders as they ride a train through the Channel Tunnel, the rail between England and France, and install a Stalinist regime in their place.

Meaning of Title: A reference to a passage in *Diamonds Are Forever*, where Fleming writes, "Nothing is forever. Only death is permanent. Nothing is forever except what you did to me."

Chronology: Contemporary. Set after *The Man from Barbarossa*. In the fall of 1992.

Operation: Not Applicable.

Bastard Meter: Standard bastard.

Eggs: Served as an omelet. Also, a sandwich stuffed with venomous spider eggs is served to Bond in an effort to murder him.

Insight into Bond: [Upon the start of a new mission.] "He already felt that strange mixture of excitement and fear fluttering in his belly."

Summary: Ford Puxley, a spy by the code name of Vanya, is run over by a car and killed in Frankfurt. In Berlin, Elizabeth Cearns, a CIA agent whose cryptonym is Eagle, is shot with a cyanide pistol.

In London, M meets with Bond and Elizabeth "Easy" St. John, an untested CIA agent who has been assigned to work with Bond on a new mission. M explains that Vanya and Eagle were killed using antiquated KGB methods. M reveals that the two of them were part of Cabal, a network of spies that was created during the Cold War. Cabal had many enemies, including Markus Wolf, the head of East Germany's foreign intelligence service, and his chief deputy Wolfgang Weisen. After Cabal disbanded, its agents dispersed throughout Europe. The surviving ten members include Praxi Simeon, aka Sulfur, Heini "Harry" Spraker, aka Tester, and Oscar Vomberg, aka Mab. However, Sulfur and Mab might be collaborating with the enemy. Bond and St. John will assume the identities of Vanya and Eagle to learn more about Cabal.

Bond and Easy travel to Berlin and go to the Bristol Hotel Kempinski, a pre-arranged meeting point between Eagle and Praxi Simeon, a surviving agent. Later, Bond enters Easy's hotel room to discover that she is being held at gunpoint by Mab. Mab tells Bond and Easy that he knows that they are not Vanya and Eagle. Bond overpowers Mab, who reveals that Praxi Simeon issued the command "Nacht und Nebel," aka "Night and Fog," a pre-arranged code that caused Cabal agents to disband and flee. Mab tells Bond that he will return to the hotel with Harry Spraker, a spy with the codename Tester.

Bond meets with Tester in the hotel lounge. Tester informs Bond that Mab was thrown under a train and killed. After Mab's death, the only three surviving members of Cabal are Tester, Karl Kuckuck (aka Ariel), and Praxi.

Bond, Easy, and Tester, travel to Paris by train to meet Praxi. On the train, they spot Klaus Korngold, an agent of Stasi, the former German intelligence agency. Tester knocks him out. Bond is confronted by two other enemy agents, Felix Utterman and Hexie Weiss, who have captured Harry Spraker and drugged Easy. Bond kills the enemy agents and frees his allies.

When the train arrives in France, Bond instructs Easy to meet him at the Sofitel Hotel near Orly Airport. Bond spots Spraker being followed by a man who he dubs The Jockey. Bond watches as The Jockey greets Spraker as if they were old friends.

Bond is contacted by someone claiming to be Praxi Simeon, the missing Cabal agent. Bond uses an identifier code to prove that she's Praxi. Praxi gives Bond twenty-four hours to leave Paris.

When Bond attempts to contact Spraker at his hotel, he is informed that Spraker has been killed. Bond provides the SIS with Praxi's number and uses it to determine her home address.

Bond goes to Praxi's home. Praxi introduces Bond to a man she claims is Harry Spraker. Praxi plays a recorded message in which the surviving Cabal agent, Ariel, instructs her to meet her in the French village of Montmartre at a restaurant.

Praxi, Tester, Easy, and Bond head to Easy's safehouse in Paris. Late that night, Ariel arrives. Ariel explains that Wolfgang Weisen is a zealot who idolizes Joseph Stalin, the former head of the Soviet Union. Because Cabal opposed Stalin's ideology, Weisen wanted to eliminate them. Weisen sent his operative Axel Ritter to pose as Harry Spraker. Praxi produces Eagle's diary, which confirms that Eagle was having an affair with Cabal member August Wimper.

Bond, Easy, Praxi, and Spraker decide to go to Weisen's home in Venice on separate planes. When Bond boards his plane, he finds that he's seated next to Alex Ritter, the man who has been posing as Harry Spraker. Once they land, Bond goes into the restroom. When Ritter follows him in, Bond knocks him out.

Bond arrives in Venice and meets August Wimper, who was Eagle's lover before she was killed. Wimper says that Eagle's diary is a fake because she destroyed it as a security measure. Wimper produces a letter from M, indicating that Wimper is who he claims to be and should be trusted.

Bond takes a boat to the Hotel Cipriani in Venice. At the hotel, Bond receives a note indicating that Easy was taken hostage. Later, Bond learns that Wimper has also abducted Harry and Praxi. Bond has dinner with Wimper who says that Weisen is staying at his private palazzo nearby.

Bond and Wimper infiltrate Weisen's palazzo and find Easy, Praxi, and Harry. Weisen and his men stop Bond from escaping. Bond is confronted by Weisen who admits to killing the members of Cabal to bring the Communist Party back into power. Weisen alludes to a plan that he is enacting the next day that will take place in Calais, France.

Bond, Easy, Praxi, and Harry are taken to a cell. Using the belt that Q Branch has supplied, Bond and company break out. During their escape, Bond and Easy profess their love to one another. Weisen's men are alerted to the breakout. Easy is shot and killed.

Bond and Praxi head to Calais in the hopes of uncovering more of Weisen's plan. Bond sees a television report indicating that twelve European world leaders, including the British Prime Minister, will head from France to England via the Eurotunnel. Weisen highjacks the train. Bond orders French authorities to cut the electricity to the tunnel, thereby stopping the train's progress. Bond catches up with Weisen and signals to the authorities to turn on the electricity. When Weisen touches the rail, he is fatally electrocuted.

Bond and Praxi attend Easy's funeral in America. Then, they return home to spend time together. In Bond's flat, he is attacked by Monika Haardt, Weisen's lover who is seeking revenge. Bond kills Haardt in a knife fight but he is severely wounded. Bond is taken to the hospital, where he recovers.

Commentary: James Bond has seen enough death. Fleming established that Bond accepts that killing is a part of his duty and he does it without passion. Still, 007 has blood on his hands; he has shot, stabbed, and strangled scores of adversaries. In *Death Is Forever,* he is starting to feel the weight of those lives lost. As Gardner puts it, Bond is "still not completely used to it." In fact, he has come to think that killing people, while necessary, is immoral. So Bond has developed strategies intended to buttress himself from the burden of guilt. For instance, while in the act of killing someone, Bond will only focus on his technique. That could mean concentrating on his breathing, stance, or when firing a gun, bullet grouping. Bond is able to distract himself from the murder by focusing on the practical steps in front of him.

There is a limit to the effectiveness of this strategy. All this murder sickens him. It makes his stomach turn. When he shoots one agent, Bond notes that "most of his face had ceased to exist." When Bond recalls killing a SMERSH agent who might have been a mother, the "vivid mental picture brought bile into his mouth." After watching an enemy agent die, Bond observes, "You can go from life to death in the twinkling of an eye." So wanting to avoid another death, the spy shows a moment of mercy. Against another agent's wishes, Bond opts not to kill an adversary; instead, he coldcocks his opponent and leaves him on the floor. However, this decision could put Bond at greater risk. Even though his adversary is temporarily neutralized, he might return and cause further bloodshed.

Despite his desire to avoid unnecessary carnage, Bond faces circumstances where he cannot show mercy. At the end of the book, Bond needs to stop Stalin-acolyte Wolfgang Weisen from accomplishing his plan to kill world leaders on board a train. When Weisen and his four men get off the train and touch the third rail, Bond has the electricity restored violently executing Weisen and his toughs. For four lurid paragraphs, Gardner describes in detail the gory impact that electricity has on human flesh. After witnessing their death and smelling "burned and charred" flesh, Bond "retched and vomited." At that moment, their death was too much for Bond to stomach. It's a moment that humanizes the spy.

There are instances where Bond considers his own mortality. In the last few pages of the book, 007 gets into a harrowing knife fight with the villain's lover Monika Haardt. During the battle, Bond is aware that he is up against a more skilled opponent and that she will likely kill him. Haardt is faster, better trained, and she's out for revenge. During the fight, she knocks Bond into a wall, breaking his nose. Realizing that he met his match, Bond accepts that he will be killed in the line of duty. Gardner reveals, "Somehow he knew this was the end." Of course, Bond does not die. With more than a little luck, he defeats Haardt. Even though he has survived, there is still a cost to pay. The weight of his job has caught up with him. He can only find rest in his sleep, "where there was no death and no violent ends."

Bond's misgivings about his job are not the focus of *Death is For Ever*. Gardner's Bond is not experiencing a mid-life crisis or a crisis of faith. Gardner sparingly weaves these small moments of introspection throughout the book. A line here and a few sentences there. One gets the sense that by the time his next adventure rolls around, he will have compartmentalized those feelings once again.

Continuity Nod: When Praxi worries that she is marked for death, Bond comforts her by explaining that they have, "All the time in the world" (*On His Majesty's Secret Service*). But Bond regrets the turn of the phrase as it reminds him of the pain that he felt after Tracy's death. Gardner also refers to Bond's other mission involving a spy ring, which could be an allusion to Gardner's *No Deals, Mr. Bond*.

Bond's History: A light switch in Bond's childhood home was brass. So when Bond sees a similar switch in the enemy's house, it brings back an array of childhood memories. Riding on a train also reminds Bond of his childhood. However, Gardner does not describe what those recollections are. Bond is reminded of a naval song called "We're Off to Samoa, By Way of Samoa."

Bond has traveled to Venice many times in the past. When 007 is in Venice, he likes to admire the Grand Canal. Bond has also conducted several meetings in the Tuileries Gardens in Paris; those meetings involved an asset in the Russian Embassy and another meeting where he had to evade SMERSH. In France, he's also eliminated two SMERSH agents at the Louvre.

Bond's Personal Life: Bond still does his daily exercise routine which consists of physical and mental exercises. Before making love, Bond acknowledges that he always practices safe sex. Bond loves Paris and he is as familiar with the city as he is with London.

Even Bond's personal life requires him to apply his knowledge of spy craft. As such, the spy will never go directly to his own house. Instead, he will park his car 10 minutes away and walk home, ensuring that he is not being followed.

Thanks to a thrilling knife fight, Gardner provides us with a peek into Bond's home décor as Bond and his adversary try to stab each other with pointy objects while navigating his furniture. The battle provides a little ad-hoc tour of Bond's living room which is filled with books (including some rare first editions, purchased as investments). The room also has a fireplace, an Empire desk, a restored leather settee, various antique pieces, and a forged J.M. Turner painting.

Bond's Inner Life: Despite his globetrotting, Bond is still somewhat of a nervous traveler; the flight attendant's safety demonstration makes him a little uneasy. Bond briefly wonders if his suspicion of others, which has risen to a level of paranoia, has bled into his personal life. Still, he knows that the cost of turning "blameless men and women into assassins" is part of the "invisible card index a spy carries for life."

Bond's Tastes: Bond prefers taking the train to travel by airplane; he would rather see the countryside than sit "cooped up in a metal shell, thirty-five thousand feet above the earth." Bond knows the lyrics to the 1925 blues song "Coffin Blues," which he thinks about after making love to Easy. "Coffin Blues" is a plaintiff, mournful song about a person standing over a lover's coffin, trying to ease their broken heart. It's an upsetting idea to contemplate after performing a loving act.

Bond's Work Methods: In addition to always carrying his gun, four additional clips, and a commando dagger, Bond travels with three passports and associated identities. Bond has stayed at the safe house in Switzerland many times.

For Bond, fatigue does not dull his senses; it sharpens them. Bond and M have worked out a code that allows M to alert someone if a new contact is to be trusted. If M trusts the contact, the code word is "Byline" but if he does not then the code word is "Crossroad."

Bond can learn many telephone numbers with the aid of a color-coding system that he employs. Even though he did not learn it in a class or with an instructor, Bond has come to learn that overtipping can be a useful tool in the field; a greased palm works wonders.

Bond considers himself a decent but not necessarily highly skilled climber. When possible, Bond avoids gun fights in confined spaces, like homes or buildings; he greatly prefers to have them outside. He learned the art of knife fighting from a Spaniard.

Assorted Observations:

- During their adventure, Bond falls in love with Easy.
- Discussing thriller writing, Easy references a passage that says that a character has the "rugged good looks of Sean Connery."
- Bond notes, "Someone once said I looked like Hoagy Carmichael with a cruel mouth." That someone is, of course, Fleming who made the comparison in several of his novels.
- Bond is awarded medals from the French and English governments and the Queen wants to make Bond a knight, but he must refuse the honor.
- Bond survives an unusual attack; he's served a sandwich that is filled with poisonous spider eggs.

NEVER SEND FLOWERS (1993)

Author: John Gardner

In Brief: Bond is dispatched to look into a string of brutal killings that appear to be related to a well-known actor. The serial killer must be stopped before he can target the Royal family at Euro Disney.

Meaning of Title: As a calling card, the killer leaves a single luminous white rose, with red tips on each petal.

Chronology: Contemporary. Set in 1993, after the events of *Death Is Forever*.

Operation: Not applicable.

Bastard Meter: None.

Eggs: Bond cooks himself eggs; but Gardner doesn't indicate how they are prepared.

Insight into Bond: "People don't often actually give me presents."

Summary: Five prominent figures are murdered—General Claudio Carrousso in Italy, Archie Shaw, a politician in London, Pavel Gruskochev, a writer in Paris, Mark Fish, a CIA agent in Washington, DC and Laura March, an anti-terrorist agent in Switzerland. Each murder scene has a single, red-tipped white rose left as the assassin's calling card.

In London, M instructs James Bond to go to investigate Laura March's murder in Switzerland. Bond travels to Switzerland, and meets Swiss intelligence agent Fredericka "Flicka" von Grüsse. Bond and Flicka travel to Interlaken to visit the hotel where March was staying when she was murdered. They meet the hotel's manager Marietta Bruch. According to Marietta, Laura made yearly trips to the hotel with her brother David March. Yet, something doesn't sit right with Bond; David March was a serial killer who passed away from a brain tumor years ago. The agents wonder, if David March is dead, then who was Laura meeting?

The hotel manager takes Bond and Flicka to Laura's room where they find a letter to her dead brother David. Bond faxes Laura's letter to London to have it authenticated and locks the original in the safe in his room. That night, while Bond and Flicka are making love, a maid comes into the hotel room and interrupts them. The maid apologizes and leaves. The next day, Bond attempts to retrieve Laura's letter from the safe, but it's vanished. At first, Bond accuses Flicka, a rival agent, of stealing it but then he realizes that the maid is actually the thief. Bond informs SIS about Laura's missing letter.

Bond and Flicka travel to Grindelwald, Switzerland to meet Bodo Lempke, the police detective who is investigating Laura's death. Bond, Flicka, and Bodo travel to the mountain where Laura was killed. On the mountain, they find a CO2 cartridge, which suggests that the killer used a gas-operated rifle to shoot Laura. Bodo reveals that Laura's killer had one appearance going up the mountain (tall and with a beard) and another going down (short and clean-shaven). Bodo says that Laura's killer checked into the hotel under the name of David Docking. Bond and Flicka return to the hotel and find Bill Tanner waiting for them. Tanner explains that M is furious that Bond lost Laura's letter. As a result of Bond's carelessness, M recalls Bond.

Back in London, M tells 007 that he is being suspended for two reasons; Bond lost the letter and the hotel guests complained that Bond and Flicka were too loud when they made love. As a result, Bond has embarrassed the service. Bond denies the charges and says that he's being set up by the hotel manager. M puts Bond on leave but, with a wink, suggests that the agent check his office safe before leaving. In the safe, Bond discovers a file concerning information about assassinations that took place in Italy, Paris, Washington DC, and London. Bond interprets the file as a cue from M to keep working on the case.

Bond returns home and discovers an unsigned letter mixed in with his mail. The note instructs Bond to visit Brown's Hotel if he wants to learn more about Laura March.

At the hotel, Bond meets MI5 operative, Carmel Chantry, who worked with Laura March. Carmel tells Bond that March was dating a well-known actor named David Dragonpol. Carmel also explains that anti-terrorist agent, Gerald Grant, failed to properly vet March and uncover that her brother was a serial killer. Carmel posits that Grant used the hotel manager to discredit Bond and get him taken off the case.

Later, Flicka phones Bond and tells him to turn on the television. On the news, he sees that Carmel Chantry has been killed at her hotel. More alarming, the composite picture of the killer looks remarkably like Bond.

Flicka tells Bond that David Dragonpol is planning to open an interactive theater museum at his castle on the Rhine River in Germany. When Bond calls the hotel, they confirm that Carmel

Chantry checked out. Bond reads the newspaper and realizes that the dead woman is not Carmel but someone who looks like her. When Bond and Flicka visit the West End Central Police Station, Detective Chief Superintended George Daily reveals that the slain woman was not Carmel.

The next day, Bond and Flicka attend Laura March's funeral. At the funeral, the agents find a single, red-tipped white rose, the killer's calling card. The rose definitively links March's murder to the four other assassinations. Flicka reveals that David Dragonpol's sister Maeve Horton grows similar white roses in her garden. Bond calls Dragonpol and arranges to meet him at his castle.

Bond and Flicka go to the castle and meet Dragonpol, who greets them disguised as Richard III, using a wig and putty for a fake nose, demonstrating the actor's ability to assume any identity. Dragonpol's sister Maeve Horton is also present. Dragonpol announces that he intends to build a Disney-inspired museum. Bond refers to a moment in a performance the actor gave in the play, *The Merchant of Venice*. Dragonpol claims that he remembers the moment. However, Dragonpol doesn't realize that Bond made the story up to test the actor. Dragonpol failed, suggesting that he is hiding something.

Dragonpol gives Bond and Flicka a tour of the grounds, including Maeve's garden, which features red-tipped white roses, the same kind discovered at the five assassinations. Dragonpol tells Bond to stay away from the great tower, as it is not safe.

Bond asks Dragonpol about Laura March. Dragonpol claims that he ended their relationship after learning that Laura's brother was a serial killer. Dragonpol also talks about his recent travel movements, which included trips to Italy, Paris, Washington DC, London, and Switzerland, the same locations where the murders took place. However, Dragonpol can prove that he arrived in the cities a day after the murders.

Bond and Flicka determine that because there is sufficient evidence to connect Dragonpol to the murders, they can leave the castle. They are stopped by Dragonpol's butler, Lester. Flicka knocks Lester out.

Bond and Flicka make their way through the house and enter Dragonpol's Disney-inspired Museum of Theatre, a living museum and testament to theater throughout the centuries. They sneak into the tower and discover a map containing potential targets in Milan, Athens, and Paris, as well as the initials PD, H, and W.

Bond and Flicka leave the castle and then take a flight to Milan, a possible target. Once they arrive at the hotel, Bond has a surprise visit from Bill Tanner. Tanner tells him that Dragonpol sometimes travels under the name David March, Laura's brother.

Bond and Flicka meet up with M and Gianne-Franco Orsini, M's opposite in Italy. M informs Flicka that she's been let go by her service because of the complaints about her at the hotel. M offers her a job with SIS.

Bond and Flicka return to the hotel and find Laura's colleague Carmel Chantry in their room. Carmel says that she can lead the agents to Dragonpol and that it was Laura March and not Dragonpol who ended the relationship. Laura broke up with him because he was going through a nervous breakdown. In turn, Dragonpol killed Laura.

Carmel calls Bond and Flicka and tells them to meet her on the roof of the Duomo di Milano, a cathedral in Milan. Bond and Flicka go to the cathedral and see that Carmel has been captured by Dragonpol. A shot rings out and Dragonpol is killed by his twin brother Daniel.

Bond meets with Daniel Dragonpol who explains that David Dragonpol went completely insane and became a serial killer. David intended to kill again, and his targets were Princess Diana, and her sons Prince Harry and Prince William.

M tells Bond that the case is closed, and Bond can take a brief respite. Bond is troubled by the fact that when the police searched David Dragonpol's home they didn't find the killer's rose calling card.

Bond and Flicka decide to vacation in Athens. Upon arrival at their hotel, they receive a call from the SIS indicating that Daniel Dragonpol is missing. Bond and Flicka attempt to get their car, but it car explodes. A red-tipped rose is left nearby.

Bond and Flicka return to Milan. Bond realizes that David is alive and is impersonating his brother, Daniel. Because David is on the loose, it means that the royals are in danger. M informs Bond that Princess Diana is taking her sons to Euro Disney in France. Now, Bond must find Dragonpol and keep the royal family safe.

Bond goes to Euro Disney and catches up with Dragonpol, who is wearing an explosive vest. The two men fight and Bond knocks Dragonpol into the water. Bond shoots a barrel of explosives that Dragonpol had smuggled into the park and this sets Dragonpol ablaze, killing him.

Back in London, Bond meets up with Flicka who tells Bond that Dragonpol's sister, Maeve Horton, is now in custody after having tried to kill Princess Diana. Bond and Flicka go to M's office where M announces that Bond and Flicka will be working together on future missions. M notices the chemistry between Bond and Flicka and he wonders if they will ever marry. Bond jokes that if he and Flicka were to tie the knot, he would ask M not to send flowers.

Commentary: *Never Send Flowers* is one of Bond's most unusual missions; it begins with an Uzi-wielding nun and concludes with the agent going mano-a-mano with a serial killer in Euro Disney. Of course, Bond's cinematic adventures have taken him to interesting locales, including a hollowed-out volcano (*You Only Live Twice),* Fort Knox (*Goldfinger*), an underwater lair (*The Spy Who Loved Me*), the cliffs of Gibraltar (*The Living Daylights*), the Scottish highlands (*Skyfall*), and even to outer space (*Moonraker*), but Euro Disney might well be the most unlikely setting for a Bond plot to date.

In *Never Send Flowers*, John Gardner continues to experiment with the form of a Bond novel. Gardner removes Bond from the spy genre and inserts him into a mystery and serial killer yarn. In it, Bond is on the hunt for a serial killer, who takes out prominent figures, such as a famous general, a noted politician, and a writer. At first blush, Bond versus a serial killer seems like an unlikely combination. However, *Silence of the Lambs* came out the year before Gardner wrote *Never Send Flowers,* as noted by John Gardner expert Brian McKaig. So serial killers were à la mode.

Gardner offers a double dose of serial killers—David Dragonpol and David March. Dragonpol is an actor and a master of disguise; he is the true villain of the story. Offered as a red herring, March is the sibling of Laura March, Dragonpol's murder victim. March is a violent offender who keeps his victim's heads as souvenirs. Gardner doesn't hold back when describing March's handiwork. "The head had literally been hacked off;" another victim's "head had been severed—possibly with an axe and a saw;" and "the heads were in large jars…floating in formaldehyde turned pink from the blood which had flowed from the terrible ragged necks." There's even the suggestion of an inappropriate relationship between Laura and her sibling who she describes as "my brother, my lover." All of this gets to Bond who gets so scared that the "short hairs rise on the back of his neck."

Gardner's villains may have been influenced by Thomas Harris' serial murderer Hannibal Lecter, but Gardner's hero is definitely modeled after Arthur Conan Doyle's renowned detective. Bond's partner Flicka refers to him as "Sherlock" and, elsewhere Bond unconvincingly protests, "I'm not playing Sherlock Holmes." However, Bond is playing detective—interviewing suspects, figuring out clues, and trying to understand the lead suspect's personal psychology. At one point, Bond deduces "My guess is that the mother had a dominating personality."

There are a few passages that might be satirizing Bond's reputation for being a lothario. Bond is brought into M's office where his bosses accuse him of making too much noise while making love with Flicka in a hotel room. According to M, six guests complained about the volume of Bond's lovemaking. M accuses Bond of "rutting like animals," making "noise of the brute beasts of the field," and having "some kind of orgy going on in [his] suite." The noise was so loud that the incident was reported to the police. Bond is so incensed at the allegation that he tells M that he will go on leave until the service clears his name. I suspect that Garnder was trying to bring a little levity to an otherwise horrifying genre story.

In many novels, Bond falls in love. However, those romances don't usually progress beyond the final page. In *Never Send Flowers*, Bond thinks that their relationship might evolve into something more long lasting. To demonstrate his feelings, Bond buys Flicka a diamond ring. Flicka immediately wants him to put the ring on her left hand, signaling a plan for marriage. Surprisingly, Bond does want to marry Flicka, but he wants to wait until the mission is over before making that commitment. After all, he knows, "Women with whom I get deeply involved have a tendency to meet what bad novelists call an untimely end." Even M recognizes the spark between Bond and Flicka. M queries, "James do I sense the possibility of wedding bells...?" Bond is uncertain, but he allows that it's a possibility. Ultimately, their relationship does survive the mission and it will continue to develop in Gardner's next book, *SeaFire*.

Disney World: The climax of *Never Send Flowers* takes place at Euro Disney where Dragonpol sets his sights on Princess Diana and her two young children, Prince Harry and Prince Edward. Bond goes to Euro Disney to search the park for potential threats. In doing so, Bond takes in the attractions and the rides in the park. And, to my surprise, he loves it.

Bond's History: According to M, Bond consistently and frustratingly forms romantic relationships with the female foreign intelligence agents with whom he's paired. Gardner indicates that Bond has gotten to know many actors throughout his life. Gardner doesn't indicate if these encounters are work-related. As a child, Bond played a game of tag at school called "He" and "Chain He," which was just like tag but more violent.

Continuity Nod: Bond's remark, "There was a time when my briefcase was a lethal weapon" is a reference to *From Russia with Love.* M tells Flicka that she should visit Shrublands, a health clinic that Bond was ordered to go to in *Thunderball.* Bond recalls, "I went there once and it almost killed me." While looking at Flicka, Bond's thoughts turn to Tracy: "For a second, he saw the face of someone else, long lost, instead of Flicka, then it was gone."

Bond's Inner Life: Given that his parents died in a mountain climbing accident, Bond has a healthy fear of mountains. Bond recites a line from a poem by Thomas Gray's "Elegy Written in a Country Churchyard" that resonates with him, "And leave the world to darkness and to me." It's an interesting and character-revealing line.

Bond's Personal Life: Sadly, Bond admits that "people don't often actually give me presents." So he's touched when Flicka buys him a pair of cufflinks. When it comes to women, Bond seems to prefer those who demand "nothing of him and give only affection" in return. Through the course of the book, Bond falls deeper in love with Flicka. It's not only her great beauty that appeals to him, but also her ability to handle herself when things get rough. Flicka knocks out an enemy with such force that she seems to have killed him. Bond is genuinely impressed. Soon thereafter, Flicka handles herself in another scrape, and Bond swoons, "You always as vicious as this, Flick?"

Gardner gives a little more information about May, Bond's housekeeper who is away visiting her nephew and his wife in Scotland. Gardner describes her as "old-fashioned" and someone who despises plastic utensils and Bond puts his trash in an "old and heavy Victorian all-metal rubbish bin." When May is away, he cooks curry for himself.

Bond's Tastes: Bond doesn't consider himself much of a theater fan, but he knows the chorus to Aristophanes' *The Frogs,* and he's impressed by David Dragonpol, the actor-cum-killer, and has seen him perform on stage. Bond also quotes Shakespeare's *Henry V*, "Oh, for a muse of fire."

Bond sings, briefly. The agent croons two lines from the musical *Kiss Me Kate* that reference a mountain in Switzerland, the location of a victim's murder spot. He also provides insight into Cole Porter's takedown of musical comedies. Bond seems to know his poetry. He recalls a poem from the 17th Century called "Upon Julia's Clothes" by Robert Herrick. The poem includes the line "how sweetly flows, the liquefaction of her clothes."

Bond's Work Methods: Bond has a sixth sense, an "antennae" that alerts him when he's being followed or watched. Bond generally likes to operate solo but when he does need a partner, he looks for someone “decisive, tough, and uncompromising.” One of Bond’s former instructors gave him advice on how to choose a place to live. “You either live out in the open, with a lot of flat ground between you and the rest of the world, or you choose a street with only one entrance or exit.” Bond’s flat in King’s Road is on a cul-de-sac, in deference to the advice. His apartment is still equipped with a red phone, a secure line that he uses for work.

Assorted Observations:

- Bond quips “The things I do for England,” a line that he also says in the film *You Only Live Twice*.
- Disney plays a key role in *Never Send Flowers*, but Gardner also references the Magic Kingdom in *For Special Services, Nobody Lives For Ever,* and *Scorpius.*

SEAFIRE (1994)

Author: John Gardner

In Brief: James Bond and Fredericka von Grüsse look into Sir Maximilian Tarn, a philanthropist and industrialist who wants to revive the Nazi party.

Meaning of Title: The villain's plan, known as SeaFire, is to torpedo a tanker carrying oil and gasoline.

Chronology: Contemporary. Set in the spring of 1994, after the events of *Never Send Flowers*.

Operation: SeaFire

Bastard Meter: A bastard, who broke his opponent's jaw.

Eggs: Served with ham.

Insight into Bond: "He was a man of action, happy only when he was out there in the midst of danger, almost like a person with a death wish."

Summary: On a cruise ship in the Virgin Islands, James Bond is on vacation with Fredericka "Flicka" von Grüsse, his partner and fellow agent. Their time together is interrupted when terrorists attempt to take over the ship. Bond and Flicka kill the terrorists. Soon, a torpedo fires on the ship, interrupting their journey once more. The cruise ship, which is owned by businessman and philanthropist Sir Maximilian "Maxwell" Tarn, is damaged but Bond and Flicka survive.

Bond and Flicka return to London. The Double O Division has been reorganized and renamed Two Zeros. M is no longer in charge. Instead, Two Zeros is overseen by a management group called MicroGlobe One, aka The Committee.

Bond and Flicka attend a briefing of The Committee to discuss the owner of the cruise ship, Sir Maxwell Tarn. Tarn is not only a businessman and philanthropist, but he is also an arms dealer who has been using his legitimate companies to launder money. The Committee is concerned that Tarn purchased a Victor II Class Russian submarine for use in his operations. The Committee instructs Bond to contact Tarn and tell him that he has information that will benefit him.

That weekend, Bond and Flicka, who are now living together, travel to Cambridge and check into the hotel where Tarn is staying. Bond meets Tarn and his wife, Trish Nuzzi. Bond attempts to use a cover name, but Tarn knows 007's real identity. Bluffing, Bond claims that he quit the service. When Bond has a moment alone with Tarn's wife, she warns the agent not to trust her husband.

Bond returns to the hotel and discovers that Flicka is being held by Tarn's security guards, Mr. Cuthbert, and Mr. Archibald. Cuthbert and Archibald draw their guns and demand that Bond and Flicka accompany them.

Bond and Flicka are taken to a Victorian home by Tarn's thugs and handcuffed to a radiator inside. Cuthbert and Archibald are joined by a woman named Beth. The trio leave the property. Bond breaks free of the radiator, looks out the window, and sees Max Tarn. Then, Tarn and company leave. Bond finds the nearest phone and calls Bill Tanner. Tanner tells Bond that Tarn and his wife, Trish, were killed in a car accident.

The next day, the newspapers report on Tarn and Trish's death. Bond believes that Tarn faked his own death, killed his employees, and planted their bodies in his car, hoping to fool the police. Soon after, M learns from an informant named Peter Dolmech that Tarn might be in hiding in his villa in Seville, Spain.

Bond and Flicka travel to Seville to meet M's contact Peter Dolmech. When Bond and Flicka get to the meeting place, they see Dolmech there with a satchel in tow. Bond spots two men riding a Harley motorcycle. The passenger shoots and kills Dolmech and takes the informant's satchel. Riding his motorcycle, Bond chases after the two hitmen. Bond kills the hitmen and retrieves the satchel.

Bond and Flicka spend the next week trying to locate Tarn, who is still in hiding. Bond receives word that M is ailing. When Bond visits his boss, M gives him a note that was in Peter Dolmech's bag. The letter indicates that Trish Nuzzi is heading to Jerusalem, Israel, and will be staying at the King David Hotel. M tells Bond to go to Israel, find Trish, and contact Mossad agent, Steve Natkowitz.

Bond and Flicka travel to Israel and meet Natkowitz. Then, they meet Mr. Archibald and Mr. Cuthbert, Lady Tarn's bodyguards, who are revealed to be women named Anna and Cathy. They also meet Lady Tarn who has been recently beaten by her husband's enforcer Conrad "Connie" Spicer. Lady Tarn tells Bond that her husband is anti-Semitic, and aspires to become the new Adolf Hitler. Because Lady Tarn is a quarter Jewish, Tarn despises her. Additionally, Lady Tarn states that Tarn employs an assassin by the name of Beth and has bases of operations in Seville, Spain, and San Juan, Puerto Rico. Tarn uses the San Juan operation to hide illicit cargo. Lady Tarn thinks Tarn might be in his family home in Wasserburg, Germany.

That night, Bond gets a call from Israeli agent Steve Natkowitz who tells Bond that Lady Tarn has left Israel and is now on her way to Paris. Bond and Flicka return to London. Bond receives a call from Cathy, Lady Tarn's bodyguard, who claims to be in Paris. Using an advanced caller ID unit, Bond determines that Cathy is calling from London, not Paris.

The next day, The Committee tells Bond that Tarn is now in London in a place called Hall's Manor. Also with him are Connie Spicer and the assassin, Beth. Bond tells The Committee that he wants to go to Hall's Manor and find Tarn. The Committee reluctantly agrees and Bond and Flicka travel to Hall's Manor and surreptitiously enter the residence. There, they find Lady Tarn hanging from a rope.

Later, Bond and Flicka spend time together and grow closer. Bond asks Flicka for her hand in marriage. She accepts his proposal.

The Committee gives Bond permission to travel to Germany to track down Tarn and investigate his claim on his former estate Tarnenwerder. Bond travels to Germany and meets Tarn's lawyer Fritz Saal. Saal explains that his brother Helmut Saal, another lawyer, oversees Tarn's account. Saal worries about the rise of Nazi ideals and reveals that Tarn is holding an event at Tarnenwerder that night.

That night, Bond goes to Tarnenwerder and sees Tarn hosting an event where three hundred men, women, and children are in attendance. Tarn gives a speech where he praises Hitler and announces his intention to follow in the Nazis' path.

Later that night, Bond sneaks back to Tarn's lawyer's office, where he checks their files for information about their client. 007 discovers an application for Tarn to become a German citizen. Bond learns that there is a traitor in The Committee, when he plays a voicemail left on the lawyer's answering machine, tipping off the lawyer about Bond's movements. Bond takes the tape with him. On his way out of the office, a woman attacks Bond who ably defends himself.

As Bond drives away, three cars chase him. Unable to fully shake them, Bond jumps out of his car, which sails off the cliff. The enemy assumes that Bond has been killed.

Bond returns to London and calls for a meeting with The Committee. Bond plays the answering machine message that reveals that The Committee's head is a traitor and has been supplying Tarn with intelligence from the start. The Committee's head is taken to an interrogation room, where he quickly confesses to the crimes and the Prime Minister appoints Lord Harvey to be the new head of

MicroGlobe One. Bond asks The Committee to go to Puerto Rico, where Tarn has a warehouse filled with illegal arms. Bond offers to go off the books to investigate Tarn.

Bond pays a visit to the ailing M. M tells Bond that he is considering stepping down shortly and he asks Bond to consider taking over his position. Bond does not accept the offer, but he says he will consider it.

The next day, Bond and Flicka travel to Puerto Rico. There, they meet up with Felix Leiter, who is working with the Americans to stop Tarn. Later, Felix makes friends with three of Tarn's employees, Rex Rexinus, a marine biologist, Dr. Vesta Motely, another biologist, and Professor Afton Fritz, a biochemist. The trio invites Felix and company to their laboratory which is located on a ship named *Mare Nostrum*.

The next day, Bond, Flicka, and Felix head to the *Mare Nostrum*, where the scientists work on an experimental foam that is designed to clean up oil spills. However, the foam does not work yet. The scientist tells Bond that San Juan has large caves, which can hide boats. Bond wonders if Tarn's newly acquired submarine is hidden in one of those caves.

Later, Bond, Flicka, and Felix head to Tarn's villa and locate the submarine in a nearby cave. Bond, Flicka, and Felix return to the *Mare Mostrum* and talk to the scientists. Bond hears Tarn coming so he hides. Tarn arrives with Lady Tarn's bodyguards, Cathy and Anna, and another enforcer, Connie Spicer. Tarn announces that he is arranging for a public demonstration of the automatic anti-oil pollution system (AAOPS), the experimental foam. As part of the demonstration, Tarn is going to use his submarine to attack an oil company's supertanker. Because the AAOPS does not work yet, the scientists worry that Tarn will pollute the Caribbean Ocean. Tarn will watch the attack from El Morro, an old fortress.

Bond tells Flicka that he's going to go to Tarn's submarine to prevent it from attacking the supertanker. Flicka goes back to her hotel, where she sees Maurice Goodwin, Tarn's fixer, and Tarn's assassin, Beth. Beth knocks Flicka out and takes her to Tarn's residence.

Bond locates the submarine, infiltrates it, and then plants explosives inside. Before Bond can leave the submarine, Tarn's men arrive. Unable to escape, Bond hides in a cramped hatch. Then, the submarine sets sail. When Tarn's enforcer Rollen discovers Bond's hiding spot, Bond kills the man.

The sub arrives near its destination. However, before it can attack the oil supertanker, Bond's explosives set off, forcing the submarine to surface. Bond kills Connie Spicer, escapes the submarine, and makes his way to dry land.

On the shore, Bond is discovered by Captain Jim Dodd, a member of the Britian's Special Air Service. Bond and Dodd make their way to El Morro, the local fortress where Tarn intended to watch his plan unfold. Bond and Dodd launch an assault; Bond shoots Tarn with a flare, causing a chemical explosion and burning the would-be Nazi.

Bond and Dodd head to Tarn's villa to search for Flicka. At the villa, Bond battles and defeats Beth. Then, Bond finds Flicka who is alive but badly wounded. A distraught Bond professes his love for Flicka. Bond tells the injured Flicka that she will be okay. However, her fate is uncertain.

Commentary: For Bond, it is a time of change. His personal and professional lives are in flux. Job wise, Bond's department is going through a huge transformation. Normally, Fleming's Bond would report directly to M, the chief of the Secret Intelligence Service. During those meetings, M would brief Bond, and Bond would mostly (but not entirely) carry out his orders as he saw fit. Gardner's Bond did the same, but he was more subject to M's authority and other political or governmental pressures. Bond nevertheless operated as a mostly independent operator. With *SeaFire*, everything is altered.

In *SeaFire*, 007's division has been restructured. M is not the head anymore. Instead, Bond answers to a group of security and intelligence chiefs, including the Chief of Intelligence, the Chief of the Security Service, the Minister of Related Home and Foreign Affairs, and even a police commissioner. Therefore, whenever Bond devises a strategy to eliminate the enemy—in this instance, millionaire businessman and philanthropist Max Tarn—the spy must make his case to the Watch Committee. Not surprisingly, the Committee does not usually agree with Bond's methods, conclusions, or attitudes. Whereas Bond and M were largely on the same page about the mission objectives and how to achieve them, the Committee does not hold Bond in high regard.

Even M can do little to protect his favorite agent. Not only is he ailing but there has been a shift in the political system. Although M is a member of the Committee, he has been sidelined. M is no longer the sole authority; instead, he is but one of many voices.

Because of his deteriorating condition, M is working from his home where a nurse tends to his needs. From time to time, Bond visits M's residence to offer and receive strategic counsel and company. It's during these visits that Bond witnesses the start of his old chief's demise. Without being maudlin, Gardner implies that M's life is coming to an end. As such, M begins to plan for the future, and he wants to name his successor. The chief asks Bond to take over when he retires. Bond does not accept M's offer, but he does agree to give it thoughtful consideration. Bond already oversees the current group of agents so taking a more formal role would be a natural progression. However, the job would take him out of the field and Bond is not sure if he has the temperament or desire to accept the offer. It should be mentioned that, despite the text, Gardner had no intention of killing M. Gardner explicitly declared in a 1994 letter to Bond scholar Bill Kanas that M would survive.

There are other changes to Bond's department. There is not a single character reference to Bond as 007. The department is now called Two Zeroes. Thus OO agents become 00. The changes go beyond cosmetics rendering. It seems that the agents have been stripped of their license to kill and they no longer have the authority to take a life in the line of duty.

Bond is also going through changes in his personal life. Gardner's earlier novel *Never Send Flowers* introduced agent Fredericka "Flicka" von Grüsse, an agent, and their relationship is heating up. In *SeaFire*, Bond and Flicka are living together and are falling in love. Bond tells his old friend, Felix, "It's the real thing this time." It's so substantial that the relationship is heading towards marriage, a topic that was broached in *Never Send Flowers*.

Gardner suggests that Bond's feelings for Flicka run deeper than those he had for Tracy di Vincenzo, his slain bride. Gardner writes "His feelings for Flicka seemed to him to be an entirely novel experience. She was also responsible for a deeper commitment from him—a mature understanding of what a man and woman could share: something that had little to do with sex, and much more concerned with their entire lives. Two people blending together as one."

Bond refers to Flicka as the woman of his dreams. One of the reasons that their relationship works, according to Bond, is because she is a fellow agent who understands the demands of 007's profession. As a result, Bond does not feel any pressure to return home for dinner if he's been called away for a mission.

Their relationship is not built to last. By the book's end, Flicka is severely injured. When Bond finds her, her face is shattered and while Bond comforts her, it's not clear if Flicka will pull through. Bond promises to love for "tomorrow and for all time," but their future is uncertain. One of the SAS officers notes that they thought they saw him crying. Despite seeing it with his own eyes, the officer dismisses the idea because Bond is not that kind of man. However, Bond was likely shedding a tear, and the ending evokes the last passages of *On Her Majesty's Secret Service* when Bond cradles and weeps over Tracy's dead body.

For Bond purists, the idea that Flicka is more important to Bond than Tracy are fighting words. For many Bond fans, Bond's feelings for Tracy, or Vesper for that matter, can never be matched, let alone surpassed. However, Gardner's inclusion of that belief is Gardner's way of trying to prevent Bond's internal life from being frozen in amber. It's Gardner's way of showing Bond's emotional progress. Gardner's instinct, although not necessarily one that is embraced by Bond fans, is the natural evolution of an author who has written more original Bond novels than Fleming, his creator.

Bond's History: Bond makes a reference to his grandmother who he describes as "sainted." She also used to say that something was "quicker than hell would scorch a feather." Bond indicates that he came from a middle-class family and that any wealth that he has acquired is a result of dragging himself "up by my bootstraps." Bond has been to Jerusalem multiple times; it's a city that he loves.

Continuity Nod: Bond's past lovers return to his memory, almost like ghosts that "float in and out of Bond's mind." Gardner concludes that Tracy is the only person that Bond truly ever loved. Still, other specters include Vesper Lynd, Honeychile Rider, Domino Vitali, and Kissy Suzuki. None of the love interests from Gardner's tenure are mentioned in this thought.

Gardner references *Live and Let Die* and how Felix Leiter came to lose his leg and arm. Gardner cheekily refers to the event that maimed Leiter as an "argument with a shark." Bond asks his old friend about his daughter, Cedar, with whom Bond worked in *For Special Services*. There appears also to be a reference to Bond's ride on a submarine in *No Deals, Mr. Bond*.

Bond's Personal Life: Bond and Flicka spend several nights a week watching a classic movie. They often play a game where they test each other's knowledge of film trivia. When going to bed, Bond does not fret over the day's concerns; he can fall asleep quickly. When they sleep together, they sometimes spoon. Gardner does not specify if Bond is the big spoon or the little spoon.

Bond's Inner Life: Bond suggests that he had a level of personal comfort while fighting in the Cold War. However, when that suddenly ended, it was Bond who was sent out into the cold. Bond gets an inordinate thrill by driving a motorcycle. He climbs the walls when he is not working in the field. A "man of action, he's only happy out there in the midst of danger, almost like a person with a death wish."

Bond's Tastes: Bond's interest in jazz is mentioned, as is Bond's general lack of interest in movies and theater. He knows a rhyming poem about fleas called "Siphonaptera" by Augustus De Morgan and another called "The Scribe" by Walter de la Mare, about resilience and the triumph of the spirit. The latter includes the stanza "My worn reeds broken. The dark tarn dry." Bond enjoys visiting Cambridge more than he likes Oxford, in part, because of Cambridge's architecture.

Bond's Work Methods: Bond's new position in the restructured service requires him to take a pay cut. He's now only earning one-third of what he used to make. Bond keeps a sign on his desk saying: Beware, the End is Nigh. It's his way of reminding himself that he's disposable and about to be put out to pasture. Bond fantasizes about retirement, but he also claims that he's never quit in the middle of a mission. Bond is given a new personal secretary named Chastity Vain.

Even though Bond and Flicka make an excellent team sometimes Bond insists on going it alone. For 007, sometimes "one against many works better than two." Bond's sixth sense to tell if he's being followed is referenced again and his knack for requesting the right equipment from Q Branch is akin to a "second sight." Bond has learned techniques to use his car as a weapon. Bond is so fluent in German that he can pass as a native speaker.

Assorted Observations:

- In *The Man from Barbarossa*, Bond works with Mossad agent Pete Natkowitz. In *SeaFire*, Bond works with Steve (and not Pete) Natkowitz. When introducing Steve, Gardner describes Steve as a "familiar figure." It is possible, that Gardner misremembered the Israeli agent's first name when writing the character in *SeaFire*. Alternatively, Bond could know two different Mossad operatives whose last name is Natkowitz.
- The banter between Mr. Cuthbert and Mr. Archibald is similar to that of Mr. Wint and Mr. Kidd, the gay assassins in the movie *Diamonds Are Forever.*
- Actor Christopher Cazenove narrated the *SeaFire* audiobook. Cazenove also played Bond in a 1973 documentary called *Omnibus: The British Hero* in which two scenes from Fleming's novels were reenacted. He would also narrate Gardner's last Bond book, *COLD*.

GOLDENEYE (1995)

Author: John Gardner

In Brief: When the GoldenEye weapons system is stolen, Bond is sent to recover it before it is used to topple England's financial institutions and communication systems. Along the way, Bond discovers that his old friend and ally, Alec Trevelyan, is now his enemy.

Meaning of Title: GoldenEye is the name of a space-based electromagnetic secret weapons system developed by the Soviet Union.

Chronology: Contemporary. The opening operation is set in 1986 and the rest of the novelization is set in the then-present 1995.

Operation: Cowslip.

Bastard Meter: None for Bond.

Eggs: Boiled. Served with whole wheat bread and marmalade.

Insight into Bond: "What had he become, he asked himself. Was he just a killing machine? Did his superiors let him get away with all kinds of excesses both on and off missions because they understood the kind of strain his work produced?"

Summary: In 1986, James Bond, 007, and Alex Trevelyan, 006, are sent to destroy an underground factory capable of producing a deadly biological virus. In the process, Colonel Ourumov apparently kills Trevelyan, but Bond succeeds in destroying the factory.

In 1995, Bond goes to a casino in the south of France and meets Xenia Onatopp, formerly of the Soviet Union, who is in the company of US Navy Rear Admiral Charles Farrel. Following a hunch, Bond observes Onatopp as she meets Admiral Farrel on a Janus Corporation-leased yacht. On the yacht, Onatopp kills Farrel by crushing him to death with her legs. Bond secretly boards the yacht and discovers Farrel's dead body. Then, Bond witnesses a demonstration of a Tigre helicopter that employs cutting-edge stealth technology. Onatopp and Colonel Ourumov steal the helicopter from a French warship.

In London, Bond speaks to the new M, a woman Bond does not hold in high regard. Bond is informed by M that the Tigre helicopter was discovered in northern Russia, close to the Severnaya Station, a former site for the Soviet Union's weaponry command and control, replete with weapons of mass destruction. M explains that the station is still operational.

Thirty minutes earlier, piloting the stolen Tigre helicopter, Onatopp and Ourumov land at Severnaya Station. There, Onatopp and Ourumov use the GoldenEye control disk to perform a test with the GoldenEye weapon, a system that can send electromagnetic pulses to virtually any location on the planet. Also at the station are computer programmers Natalya Simonova, who operates the satellite, and Boris Grishenko, who can hack into virtually any computer. On Ourumov's orders Onatopp guns down everyone in the control room and then uses the weapons system to target the base. Ourumov takes the GoldenEye disk and leaves the station before it is destroyed. Most of the workers are killed but Natalya and Boris get out in time.

Back in the present, the English and American satellites experience a service disruption. M informs Bond that MI6's surveillance has detected that the Tigre helicopter fled and an unidentified woman escaped before the site was destroyed. Because Onatopp killed Admiral Farrel in a yacht leased to the Janus Crime Syndicate, M authorizes Bond to travel to their base in St. Petersburg. She orders Bond to locate the GoldenEye and find out who stole it.

Natayla locates a computer and sends Boris a message; they agree to meet at a church. Later, when she arrives, Xenia Onatopp drugs her.

Bond flies to St. Petersburg where he meets CIA agent Jack Wade. Wade tells Bond that a Janus operative lives on an armored train and that Janus' main competition is Valentin Zukovsky. Bond decides to meet Zukovsky and asks for his help in taking on Janus.

Back at his hotel, Bond goes swimming. Onatopp appears, seduces Bond, and during sex, attempts to crush him with her legs. Bond gets the better of her and learns that Janus will be at Statue Park. At the Park, Bond discovers that his old friend Alec Trevelyan is alive and working with the Janus Crime Syndicate. Trevelyan's men shoot Bond with a stun gun. Bond wakes up inside the stolen Tigre helicopter with Natalya. They discover that two missiles are heading their way. Bond triggers the eject button and they get out before the missiles make impact. Trevelyan's men seize Bond and Natalya and take them to an interrogation cell.

In the cell, Bond meets the Minister of Defense, Viktor Mishkin. Ourumov enters, takes Bond's pistol, and kills Mishkin, setting Bond up to be blamed for Mishkin's murder. Ourumov abducts Natalya and flees in a car. Bond escapes, steals a tank, and chases after them.

Ourumov and Natalya join Trevelyan and Onatopp in the armored train and try to escape. Bond uses his tank to obstruct their exit, causing the tank and the train to collide. Entering the train, Bond shoots Ourumov in the head and saves Natayla, but Onatopp and Trevelyan get away. Bond and Natalya are trapped in the train, which Trevelyan is going to blow up. Natalya uses the train's computer to learn that Boris is hiding in Cuba and then they get free of the train with the GoldenEye disk. Bond and Natalya meet up with Wade who gives them tickets and fake passports to get to Cuba.

Once in Cuba, Bond and Natalya try to find Trevelyan's base of operations by surveilling the area in a plane but they are forced to land when their plane is hit by rockets. Suddenly, Onatopp rappels down from a helicopter and tries to crush Bond with her legs. When he's unable to break free, Bond fires a gun at the helicopter, which ascends with Onatopp still attached to it. Onatopp dies when the helicopter inadvertently crashes her into tree branches.

Bond and Natalya infiltrate Trevelyan's base and make plans to target the antenna and transmitter which will send instructions to the satellites. Trevelyan orders Boris to use the GoldenEye system to transfer large sums of money from the Bank of England to his. Trevelyan's guards capture Bond but Natayla finds her way to the mainframe computer room, which cools the vast network of computers. Once inside, she hacks into the system.

Bond is brought to Trevelyan who reveals that he's going to use the GoldenEye system to decimate all of England's electronic data, including tax, criminal, and land records. The guards capture Natalya and take her to the control room. Boris inadvertently triggers Bond's pen which is equipped with an explosive device. When the pen goes off, Bond and Natalya escape.

Bond heads to the transmitter to destroy it. Meanwhile, Boris begins to regain control of the system. Trevelyan catches up to Bond and the two men fight. Bond knocks Trevelyan from a great height onto the satellite dish and uses explosive devices to destroy the transmitter. In the control room, the liquid coolants overheat, explode, and kill Boris.

Mission accomplished and out of danger, Bond and Natalya share an intimate moment, as Jack Wade and the US Marines belatedly arrive for backup support.

Commentary: *GoldenEye* is John Gardner's second novelization, and his second to last Bond novel. Although Eon's *GoldenEye* was Pierce Brosnan's first Bond film, Gardner did not establish Brosnan as the new 007 in his book. Instead, Gardner placed *his* Bond into the movie's plot and tried to remain faithful to his characterization of the agent. For instance, Gardner's Bond isn't as cavalier as Brosnan's; he has a much harder edge. Gardner's Bond has "never forgotten that a license to kill is also a certificate to die." Unlike Brosnan's Bond, Gardner's Bond has flecks of gray in his hair. He also feels somewhat emasculated when taking orders from M. When she directs him to take a seat by pointing, Bond thinks, "Sit. Good dog."

Gardner preserves elements of his own continuity. For instance, the Bond of *GoldenEye* thinks about his lover, Flicka von Grüsse, who was gravely injured at the end of Gardner's previous novel, *SeaFire*. In *GoldenEye,* Gardner reveals her fate—Flicka is still alive, but she may never regain her ability to walk. It should be noted that *GoldenEye* doesn't entirely line up with Gardner's continuity. For instance, Bond holds the rank of a Commander in the novelization, but he is a Captain in Gardner's original works. Similarly, in the novelization M is a woman but in Gardner's books that precede and follow it, M is a man.

Gardner's *GoldenEye* is a largely faithful adaptation of Eon's seventeenth Bond movie. As with many novelizations, Gardner fills in the blanks between scenes, fills in plot holes, and elaborates on character motivations and relationships. For instance, in the movie, when Bond and Natalya escape from the train they need to get from St. Petersburg to the Caribbean. The film uses a dissolve to signal their move from one location to the next. In the novelization, Gardner can take the reader through each step. In Gardner's version, after Bond and Nataly escape the train, they walk a few miles, meet a singing beggar (to whom Bond gives some money), take refuge in a restaurant, make contact with CIA agent Jack Wade who outlines their extraction plan, don a disguise (Natalya dressed as a school girl, wearing white knee socks), fly to Puerto Rico, meet with another CIA agent, and so on.

In the movie, Brosnan's Bond swims in the hotel's pool. No reason is given for Bond's dip. In the novelization, Gardner provides a motive for this swim; Bond is actually tricking his enemies into believing that he's defenseless. Gardner also makes sure to flesh out Natalya and strengthen her character. For instance, Bond teaches her the art of bluffing an adversary. Gardner allows her to put Bond's teaching into practice.

The Bond novels are for adults. As such, Gardner makes the sex scenes more graphic than they are in the PG-13 film. When Bond and Natalya make love, Gardner writes, "She felt his hands slide under her buttocks, pressing, stroking and kneading them as he bent his mouth to kiss first one breast and then the other. Her hands guided him down and he slid into her, thick and long so that she lifted her buttocks in his hands and let out a sharp breath of pleasure." Bond and Xenia Onatopp have sex in the novelization, whereas in the film, they just grapple.

The film *GoldenEye* established that Onatopp gets a sexual thrill when killing men. Her method is to asphyxiate them with her thighs. Gardner's book makes Onatopp's arousal even more explicit. Gardner details that "at the moment of his asphyxiation, Xenia Onatopp cried out in her own final and conclusive orgasm." She is so turned on by the prospect of death that even after she kills Admiral Farrel, she continues to have intercourse with his dead body. After the admiral's death, Onatopp is "still rubbing herself against his corpse." It's a wonder that Gardner was able to insert a little necrophilia in this merchandising effort.

In keeping with the dynamic of the Eon films, Bond and M do not get along. As with the film, M views 007 as a misogynistic dinosaur and a relic of the Cold War. In turn, Bond believes that she is a numbers cruncher. Still, through their interactions, the new M earns Bond's grudging respect.

Absent from the novelization is a revealing snippet of dialogue in the beach scene in which Bond talks unemotionally about his decision to kill his old friend 006. Natalya, says, "How can you be so cold?" James Bond replies, "It's what keeps me alive." Natalya counters, "No. It's what keeps you alone." When I interviewed screenwriter Bruce Feirstein for my book *The Many Lives of James Bond*, he indicated that the exchange was a late addition to the script. So it's possible that Gardner was given an early draft of the script on which to base his novelization and did not have an opportunity to include it.

Moviegoers receive their first excellent sight of Brosnan as Bond when 007 surprises an enemy spy in the bathroom. The introduction is a bit of a send-up and a way to provide a good-natured poke at the gentleman spy. Gardner eliminates the light-hearted moment from his novelization.

In the film, Bond's bungee jump off the dam is a thing of beauty. It's graceful and balletic. In the novel, the maneuver causes Bond to feel a sense of vertigo, this intense sensation is an unwelcome first for 007. Gardner also emphasizes Bond's uncertainty in performing the daring feat, as well as the strain on Bond's body.

Bond's Personal Life: Bond swims to stay fit and to relieve himself from the tensions of the day. 007 and 006 used to date the same women.

Bond's Tastes: Bond doesn't like ice in his bourbon; he claims it ruins the drinks. Obviously, the spy feels differently about the use of ice in other libations.

Bond's Work: Every five years, Double O agents have to go through a rigorous evaluation, which includes proving driving and boating competency. During an operation, Bond can go to sleep at will and can even sleep while standing. Bond does not like to wear disguises. More than any physical discomfort he might feel while wearing a disguise, Bond detests acting.

Bond's History: Bond recalls a previous mission to St. Petersburg, Russia during the Cold War. Even though he was considered the enemy, he admired the city's beauty and architecture.

Credit Where Credit is Due: The movie *GoldenEye* was written by Jeffery Caine and Bruce Feirstein, with a story by Michael France. Oddly, Feirstein's contribution to the film is not noted on the novelization's title page. Instead, the text indicates that only France and Caine wrote the script. This error suggests that the novelization was completed and sent to the printer before the film's writing credits were finalized.

Assorted Observations:

- Bond's mission at the start of the novel is called Operation Cowslip.
- After the outgoing M retired, Moneypenny reluctantly agreed to stay on and help the incoming M with the transition to her office.
- Samantha Bond, who played Miss Moneypenny during the Brosnan era, narrates the audiobook.

COLD (1996)

Author: John Gardner

In Brief: Bond must ascertain how a terrorist attack on an airline relates to COLD, a new criminal organization that seeks to violently eradicate all organized crime in the United States in order to impose its Puritanical beliefs and, ultimately, topple the government.

Alternate Title: *Cold Fall*

Meaning of Title: COLD is an acronym for the criminal organization Children of the Last Days.

Chronology: Contemporary. Set in the Spring of 1990 after the events in *Brokenclaw*, and in 1994, picking up immediately after the events in *SeaFire.*

Operation: Blizzard.

Bastard Meter: "That bastard Bond."

Eggs: Served as an omelet, and elsewhere as well as a farm-fresh egg.

Insight into Bond: "Death, fire, shooting, and all those other charming pieces of gratuitous violence seem to follow you around like an untrained Rottweiler."

Summary: In 1990, a flight from England to Washington, DC is blown up. In London, M informs Bond that his former lover, Principessa Sukie Tempesta, is believed to have been traveling on the plane; she is presumed dead. The downed airplane is owned by British millionaire, Harley Bradbury. M directs Bond to travel to Washington, DC, where investigators are examining the plane's wreckage.

In Washington, Bond meets Sukie, who, it turns out, is alive. She was not on the plane. Sukie tells Bond that she received his note requesting her to come to DC. Bond tells her that he never sent the note.

Bond and Sukie sleep together. Sukie tells Bond that she is widowed but that her stepsons Luigi and Angelo know Harley Bradbury, the owner of the downed aircraft. Sukie invites Bond to spend time with her family in Rome.

At the plane's inspection site, Bond meets Bradbury and Special Agent Eddie Rhabb and learns that the explosive material was manufactured in the United States. So far, no terrorist organization has claimed responsibility for the bombing.

Bond receives a voicemail message from Sukie beseeching him to remember the acronym COLD. However, she is cut off before she can complete the call. When Bond tries to contact Sukie, he learns that she was killed in a car explosion.

Bond meets with FBI agent Eddie Rhabb who explains that Sukie was unaware that the family that she married into is part of an Italian crime family. Bond and Rhabb travel to Quantico, Virginia, home of the Marine Corps Base. Bond meets FBI agent Toni Nicoletti, who had been working undercover in the Tempesta crime family and later became Luigi Tempesta's mistress. Toni also explains that Luigi recently discovered that his wife, Giulliana, had been having an affair with Harley Bradbury. They speculate that the Tempesta family could have destroyed Bradbury's airplane for revenge. Rhabb tells Bond about Children of the Last Days (COLD), a right-wing organization intent on wiping out organized crime. Rhabb has evidence that the Tempestas are working with COLD.

Bond flies to Italy and goes to the Tempesta Villa, where he meets Luigi Tempesta, his brother Angelo, and their wives Giulliana and Maria. The family tells Bond that their deceased stepmother, Sukie, used to speak fondly of Bond, who they know is a spy. The Tempesta family suspects that Sukie was killed by General Brutus Clay, a retired general who controls a militia. General Clay wanted to marry Sukie, but she continually rebuffed his advances. The Tempestas tell Bond that he can find General Clay in the mountains of Idaho. FBI agent Toni Nicoletti warns Bond that the Tempesta family might be trying to eliminate Bond by sending him after Clay.

That night, Giulliana Tempesta tries to seduce Bond, who rebuffs her advances. Her husband Luigi bursts through the door carrying a gun. Toni saves Bond by shooting Luigi with a tranquilizer. Bond and Toni flee the villa.

Bond and Toni go to a local safe house, where they meet FBI agent Rhabb, and M. M informs Bond that his new mission is to determine if General Brutus Clay is working with COLD. That night, Toni and Bond make love.

The next morning, agent Rhabb informs Bond that M has been kidnapped. Later, Rhabb explains that M's abduction might have been a way to lure Bond to the United States.

Bond flies to Idaho and phones General Clay to request that their meeting take place later at a graveyard. Then Bond meets an agent named Felicia Heard Shifflet and the duo travel to the graveyard. Clay arrives with a squadron of choppers. Clay reveals that he is working with COLD and that the Tempesta crime family wants to kill Bond. Clay also reveals that they have kidnapped M and placed him on one of the choppers. Bond and Felicia steal the chopper that M is in and take flight. Clay's men take to the air and an air battle ensues. Bond brings down Clay's chopper, but his aircraft is destroyed in the process and Bond crashes into the water. Bond passes out as he's being rescued and he is brought to a hospital.

Bond in an aerial assault in *COLD.*
Illustration by Pat Carbajal

When Bond wakes up, he learns that M is safe, and Felicia has died. Agent Rhabb informs Bond that although they have not located Clay's body, he is most likely dead. Bond and M fly to Washington, DC together.

The next year, Harley Bradbury's company files for bankruptcy, and two years later, in 1992, the bombers who planted the explosives on the plane are apprehended. In 1993, Bond partners with Fredericka "Flicka" von Grüsse but during their mission, Flicka is severely injured (*SeaFire*).

In 1994, Bond visits M at his home named Quarterdeck. Bond then pays Flicka a visit at the clinic where she is in a coma and may never wake up. Later, Bond receives a package from Italy, which contains a cassette tape. On the tape is a recording from Beatrice Maria da Ricci, an agent he worked with on a previous mission (*Win, Lose or Die*). Beatrice tells Bond to go to Geneva so that she can talk to him about COLD.

Bond looks in on M who reveals that he is being forced out and that a new M will replace him. M tells Bond that COLD plans to impose its Puritanical values on the world by eliminating all illegal activities.

Bond returns to his flat in Chelsea when he receives a call from Flicka's doctor. The doctor says that Flicka briefly regained consciousness, made an oblique reference to Bond, and then relapsed into her coma. The doctor asks Bond to come to Geneva to see Flicka. After the phone call, the doctor calls someone and informs them that Bond took the bait.

Bond flies to Geneva and meets up with Beatrice da Ricci at her hotel; Special Agents Farmer and Allen are also there. Bond suspects that agents Farmer and Allen are crooked. With the help of the FBI, Bond has Farmer and Allen arrested. Agent Rhabb informs Bond that Farmer and Allen were working for the Tempesta crime family. Beatrice says that she is now working undercover, posing as a member of the Tempesta family's household staff. She tells Bond that the leaders of COLD will soon be holding a secret briefing at the Tempesta's villa.

Bond and Beatrice go out to dinner and then make love. Later that night, agent Rhabb informs Bond that Flicka succumbed to her injuries and has died.

Bond, Beatrice, and Rhabb plan the raid on the villa. Eddie has proof that Sukie is still alive. However, Eddie fears that she is working with COLD.

Bond, Beatrice, and Rhabb fly to Italy so that they can begin their raid on the Tempesta's villa. Bond parachutes in, breaches the house, and locates Sukie. Sukie admits that she was the one who detonated the bomb on the plane, killing a passenger who was blackmailing COLD. Sukie explains that COLD plans to forcefully eradicate all criminal activity in the United States. Sukie reveals that General Brutus Clay survived the helicopter battle and that she intends to marry him. Sukie's sons-in-law Luigi and Angelo appear. Sukie tells Luigi and Angelo that she wants Bond to give her away at the upcoming wedding ceremony. Then, Bond is thrown into a locked room with Beatrice, who has also been captured.

Bond is forced to give Sukie away during her marriage to General Clay. A security guard named Roberto keeps an eye on Bond. Bond knocks Roberto out but spares his life. When the reception ends, a secret meeting of COLD begins. General Clay announces that Operation Blizzard will commence in New York on Christmas Day. As part of the plan, COLD will kill law enforcement agencies and military personnel and explode a bomb in Times Square, New York. Then they will attack Washington, DC, and assume control of the White House and the Capitol. General Clay anticipates that COLD's actions will eventually lead to a second Civil War.

As the COLD meeting ends, a group of elite officers infiltrate Tempesta's villa. Bond and his security guard Roberto discover that General Clay killed Sukie. Clay explains that Sukie killed her previous husband and he feared that she might harm him too. Clay tries to escape but Bond and Beatrice catch up to the general and neutralize him.

Bond and Beatrice return to England. Bond is informed that M has retired and that the new M is a woman. Bond and Beatrice go to Bond's flat. Bond plays a voice message from the former M, in which he suggests that he was forced out of the job. Looking out his window, Bond sees two service members approaching. Bond knows that he is being called to meet the new M. Bond places Flicka's ashes in his bedroom and tells Beatrice that he would like to continue their relationship. Bond tells himself that this moment does not represent the end of anything; instead, it is the beginning of a new chapter in his life.

Commentary: John Gardner says, "Goodbye, Mr. Bond" with *COLD*, his sixteenth and final Bond novel. In *COLD*, Gardner concludes his sixteen-year epic run of Bond adventures, usually publishing a new original story or novelization at a rate of one a year. In wrapping up his last novel, Gardner clears the deck for the next continuation author. Most notably, in *COLD*, Gardner kills off Fredericka "Flicka" von Grüsse, Bond's love interest from the past two original Bond novels, *Never Send Flowers* and *SeaFire*. In *Never Send Flowers*, Bond met Flicka and was besotted by her. In *SeaFire*, their relationship deepened, and the duo made marriage plans. Then the villain, neo-Nazi Maximilian Tarn's henchwoman Beth, severely beat and tortured her. In the final passages of *SeaFire*, Flicka's odds of survival are unknown. The book ends with a cliffhanger—will Flicka live?

COLD does not immediately answer that vital question. Instead, the first half of the novel is set in 1990, a few years before the previous book, *SeaFire*. As such, Flicka's fate will remain a mystery until *COLD* skips ahead to 1994, 137 pages later. By then, the question about Flicka's health is no longer pressing. Eventually, Gardner reveals the truth about Flicka. Gardner explains that after her encounter with Tarn, Bond brought Flicka to an SIS-run facility where she was operated on by doctors. She survived her injuries but slipped into a comma. Still later, Bond learns that Flicka has succumbed to her injuries. By this time, Bond has already prepared himself for her death. He might mourn her, but Bond is not overcome with grief. Neither Bond nor the reader is asked to shed a tear for her passing.

Without any context, Flicka's death and Bond's reaction to it might strike readers as if something is amiss. Not only did Gardner spend two books building up Bond and Flicka's relationship, but their upcoming union was also a culmination of all of Gardner's previous novels. So the handling might come across as perfunctory. However, Gardner knew that *COLD* would be his last Bond novel. The next Bond writer could not have his Bond caring for an injured Flicka. Nor could he have Flicka make a miraculous recovery and marry Bond as they had planned.

I initially suspected that had Gardner written a seventeenth Bond the plot of *COLD* might have unfolded differently. Bond might have wedded Flicka, and the reader might have seen Bond navigate married life as a spy. In *COLD*, Gardner suggests that before meeting Beatrice Bond was faithful to Flicka. It seems that Gardner's Bond does not consider marriage to be like a room with an unchanging view that would always pall, as Fleming described it. Gardner had other plans. In his 1994 letter to Bond fan Bill Kanas, the author revealed that he was not going to marry off the agent. Instead, 007 would remain a bachelor.

Had Gardner continued, we might have seen the agent navigate the perils and bureaucracy of MicroGlobe One and the changing nature of the Secret Service. If Gardner continued with his series, Bond could have continued as the head of his division. Not only supervising and overseeing the training of new agents but also serving beside them. He might have even accepted M's offer to take over for him.

The next Bond author, Raymond Benson, needed to start his run with a clear deck. Starting from scratch makes sense as both a creative and business decision. It would be somewhat unfair to expect Benson to pick up the story threads of the previous author. Moreover, because Benson's novel would be the first in a new series, it would likely interest new Bond readers who were either unfamiliar with Gardner's work or who did not read Gardner's entire run.

Not only did he write more Bond novels than Fleming, but he also wrote more original stories than Benson, Faulks, Boyd, Deaver, and Horowitz combined. Gardner's work might be somewhat controversial among Fleming purists, but the totality of his work deserves examination and consideration. Gardner might not have written the novels the way Fleming set out to, but they reflect his tastes and passions. To paraphrase Frank Sinatra, Gardner did it his way.

Continuity Nod: In Gardner's Bond novel, Bond brings back love interests from previous adventures, including Fleming's Jill Masterson (*Goldfinger*), Kissy Suzuki, and Tracy Bond. Gardner also includes his own creations, such as Sukie Tempesta (*Nobody Lives For Ever*), Beatrice Maria da Ricci (*Win, Lose or Die*), and Fredricka von Grüsse (*Never Send Flowers* and *SeaFire*). Beatrice informs Bond "I want to win. I don't want to lose or die," which is a reference to the book in which they were introduced. Gardner alludes to the time that Bond's housekeeper, May, was kidnapped (*Nobody Lives For Ever*).

Bond's History: Early in his career, assassinations were a significant part of Bond's assignments. The agent has made many night jumps. Bond once strangled a man to death on a beach in Italy as part of his mission. When in Venice, Bond used to like visiting a store that made handmade paper.

Bond's Inner Life: When Bond thinks he might be suffering from hypothermia and drowning, he considers the possibility that he is dying. As he loses consciousness, Bond wonders if the angels are pulling him across the river Styx.

Bond's Personal Life: In a gesture of intimacy, Bond holds hands with Toni Nicoletti, an agent he only recently met, on the flight from the United States to Rome. Bond is a strong swimmer and has not had a cigarette in years. Bond wakes up every day at 7:30 AM and then exercises, which includes twenty push-ups and leg lifts.

Shortly after Flicka's severe injury, Bond starts to emotionally separate himself from her. Bond thinks that Flicka would rather die than be unable to walk for the rest of her life. Once Bond comes to this conclusion, he begins to *hope* that she will die. Like Bond, Flicka's work is what brought purpose to her life. Without it, life is hollow. Bond also knows that he cannot be her caretaker, despite his love for her. That's not to say that Bond is indifferent to Flicka's situation. Before her death, Bond would visit her at the hospital on a daily basis.

Instead of attending Flicka's funeral when she eventually passes away, he keeps working on his current mission. He acknowledges that his decision "sounds cold and ruthless" but he believes he must stop Tarn from conducting his fiendish plans. After defeating Tarn, Bond keeps Flicka's ashes in his apartment for a brief period before scattering them in the Jungfrau mountains in Switzerland, a location where the two once made passionate love.

Bond believes that he has only truly loved four women; Tracy and Flicka are named but the other two are not specified. One is presumably Vesper Lynd. However, I'm not certain that Gardner counts her. In his sixteen book run, I only found three instances where he refers to Vesper by name. Gardner could be referring to Easy St. John to whom Bond professed his love in *Death Is Forever.*[112] I believe the fourth woman is possibly his current flame, Beatrice Maria da Ricci. Later in *COLD*, Bond believes that Beatrice, "could easily have been the love of his life." Still, Bond acknowledges to Beatrice that they both know that their relationship will not last. (And it does not. She goes unmentioned in the next continuation novel.)

Bond's Tastes: Gardner notes that Bond is "fastidious" about how he dresses. M thinks that Bond is rather "fussy" when it comes to his food preferences. Bond quotes from Peter Pan when while listening to driving directions, he asks, "Straight on till morning?" Bond is familiar with Elton John and his song "Tiny Dancer." He listens to music on his Walkman. Bond also recites the opening lines of a "vulgar limerick" that begins with the line (not quoted) "There once was a barmaid named Gail."

Even though Bond craves a vodka martini, he decides that ordering one would be out of place in the dive bar where he's meeting his contact. Instead, he orders a Red Dog beer, which was just introduced to the market in 1994, the year that the book is set and two years before *COLD*'s publication.

Bond's Work Methods: M strongly detests when his agents use coarse language. As such, M rebukes Bond when the agent describes jet-skiing as "bloody bumpy." Bond jokingly describes his job as that of a mail carrier with a license to kill, "Nor rain of bullets, nor sleet of nerve gas, nor hail of fire, nor death of night, shall halt the males from SIS, I must get through." Years ago, Bond took a water-survival course. When Bond failed at a task, the instructor shouted, "This is not a bloody water carnival, Bond. Do it properly, man!"

Assorted Observations:

- *COLD* was released as *Cold Fall* in the United States and was split up into two parts—"Cold Front 1990" and "Cold Conspiracy 1994."
- M's last command in the Royal Navy was on the HMS *Repulse*. The bell from the battlecruiser hangs outside M's residence.
- Bond notes that the TV service in his hotel is provided by a cable company by the dubious name of Spectravision. Undoubtedly, Gardner is pointing out that the word SPECTRE seems to be contained within.
- Fleming's former agent and Chairman of Glidrose was Peter Janson-Smith. The name of a former member of the Security Service's Watchers Division is Peter Janson, whose cover name is Smith. As *COLD* was Gardner's final Bond novel, he included Jason-Smith's name as a tribute.

RAYMOND BENSON'S TENURE
1997–2002

When John Gardner completed his impressive run of original Bond stories, it was time for Glidrose to select a new author. They faced a similar difficulty in finding a new continuation author when Fleming passed away. In that case, they enlisted Kingsley Amis, a noted author and Bond fan who wrote an admired critical study of Fleming's work. This time, they turned to Raymond Benson, a respected Bond expert.

Benson was not yet a noted author, but he did write the seminal *The James Bond Bedside Companion* (1984 and subsequently updated in 1988), a comprehensive examination of the novels and the films, as well as featuring an overview of Fleming's life. By the time Glidrose hired him, Benson had also written the role-playing game *You Only Live Twice II—Back of Beyond* (1986) and two text-based computer games: *A View to a Kill* (1985) and *Goldfinger* (1986).

He then parlayed his appreciation of Fleming's prose and vast knowledge of 007 into success as a six-time Bond novelist: *Zero Minus Ten* (1997), *The Facts of Death*, (1998), *High Time to Kill* (1999), *DoubleShot* (2000), *Never Dream of Dying* (2001), and *The Man with the Red Tattoo* (2002).

Benson novelized the screenplays for *Tomorrow Never Dies* (1997), *The World Is Not Enough* (1999), and *Die Another Day* (2002) and published a trio of Bond short stories: "Blast from the Past" (1997), "Midsummer Night's Doom" (1999), a tongue-in-cheek piece for *Playboy*, where Bond encounters Hugh Hefner at one of the magazine founder's hedonistic parties, and "Live at Five" (1999) for *TV Guide*. He also wrote the unpublished Bond short story "The Heart of Erzulie" (2001).

"BLAST FROM THE PAST" (1997)

Author: Raymond Benson

In Brief: Bond investigates the death of his only child, James Suzuki, who was killed by his old foe, Irma Bunt.

Meaning of Title: Key figures from Bond's past resurface.

Chronology: Contemporary. Set at least twenty years after the events of *You Only Live Twice*.

Operation: Not applicable.

Bastard Meter: None.

Eggs: Scrambled, and served at the hospital. As such, they are "intolerable."

Insight into Bond: "Bond was aware he needed to grieve, and that it would happen sooner rather than later. He wouldn't allow himself to dwell upon it too long, lest he start to blame himself. Save it all for another day, he ordered himself. For now, relish the victory."

Summary: In London, James Bond is naked in bed with Kate, a close friend of his housekeeper May. The next morning, Bond receives a letter from his son, James Suzuki, who is living in New York and needs help. Bond flies to the United States to aid his son.

Bond goes to James Jr.'s apartment building and notices a homeless woman outside. He enters the apartment and discovers his son's dead body.

Soon after, British Secret Service agent Cheryl Haven questions Bond about his son's death. At the apartment, Bond discovers an envelope addressed to him that contains a key to a bank's safety deposit box, perhaps a clue to the identity of the murderer. Bond and Haven decide to go to the bank and search the contents of the deposit box.

Entering the bank, Bond spots the same homeless woman who was outside his son's building. The bank manager gives Bond and Haven access to the safe deposit room. When a bank employee opens the lock box, a bomb is triggered. Bond and Haven run outside to safety as the smoke fills the room.

Outside the bank, Bond spots the homeless woman entering a car. Bond steals a taxi and chases after her. After a high-speed car chase through the streets of New York, Bond follows the woman to a warehouse. He sneaks into the warehouse, while Haven gets help.

Once inside, Bond is knocked out. When he comes to, he sees Irma Bunt, an old enemy (*On His Majesty's Secret Service*), and her two hoods. Bunt reveals that she survived Bond's attack on Blofeld's castle (*You Only Live Twice*) and that she killed Bond's son as a means of getting revenge for the death of her lover, Blofeld. Before Bunt can kill Bond, Haven arrives, shoots one of her goons, and apprehends the other. Bond chases after Bunt, who shoots 007 in the leg. Bond returns fire and kills Bunt.

Bond is taken to a hospital and undergoes surgery. Haven visits the hospital and makes love to the recovering agent.

Background: Benson authored the short story "Blast from the Past" for the January 1997 issue of *Playboy* as a way of commemorating the start of his tenure of Bond novels.

Commentary: James Bond's son was doomed from the start. There was no chance that James Suzuki, son of 007 and Kissy Suzuki, would live to see another day. James Jr. was fated to death as soon as Raymond Benson decided he wanted to include him in the short story "Blast from the Past." According to Benson, Ian Fleming Publications did not (and still does not) own the rights to the character; Eon did (and does).

In an extensive interview with *007 Magazine*, Gardner explained why he couldn't include Bond's son in a novel, "I'm not allowed to do it! Glidrose has sold it to Broccoli! When Glidrose signed the contract for *James Bond Jr.* there was a clause in the contract that included the rights to 'any offspring of James Bond.' I can use any of the characters I want, but I cannot use [his child].[113]

Regardless, Benson wanted to include Bond's son in his short story. So he came up with an ingenious solution. If James Suzuki was not a living breathing character and was instead a corpse, Benson could incorporate Bond's offspring into the story. And that's what he did.

In "Blast from the Past," when 007 receives an urgent message from James Jr., the agent rushes to New York to provide help. However, when Bond arrives at his son's apartment, he finds that James Jr. has been murdered. It turns out that the letter from James Jr., was actually a lure, a means of bringing Bond to New York, so that Irma Bunt could kill him.

Let us go back to the birth of Bond's son, both literally and figuratively. At the end of 1964's *You Only Live Twice*, Fleming revealed that Kissy was pregnant, but that Bond was unaware that he was an expectant father. What ultimately happened to 007's son was a delightful topic of discussion for Bond fans. They wondered if Kissy ever gave birth to a child and if Bond ever learned about the existence of his progeny. Thirty-three years after Fleming's book, Benson addressed the issue.

According to Benson, Kissy gave birth to a boy and named him James after her father. At some point, Kissy tracked down Bond and told him about his son. Bond stayed in touch with her and financially supported the child. The short narrative starts with Kissy already deceased. Bond and James Jr. see each other from time to time but they are hardly close. James Jr. only has one photo with him of his father. Bond's son is a banker and lives on the Upper East Side of New York on 75th Street and First Avenue. James Jr. uses his mother's last name, not Bond's. James Jr., like his dad, is a charmer. Because James Jr. is half-Japanese, he experiences his share of racism, including from the super of the building in which he lives.

Of course, Benson was not the first author to address the fate of Bond's son; John Pearson also offered his version of events in *James Bond: The Authorized Biography of 007*. It was Pearson who provided the name of 007's progeny. John Gardner also wanted to try his hand at fleshing out Bond's relationship with his son, but given the rights issue, Gardner was told he could not address it in his work.

"Blast from the Past" is an exciting short story and contains a strong enough idea that it could have been the basis for an entire novel or novella. The fate of James Jr. merits its own volume. However, it speaks of Benson's talent that the reader is left wanting more.

Continuity Nod: The short story functions as a sequel to *On Her Majesty's Secret Service* and *You Only Live Twice.* As such, there are references to key events from both books throughout. Operation Thunderball is briefly mentioned.

Bond's Inner Life: Bond realizes that the thing that has kept him alive all these years is not his body or a weapon, it's his mind. Killing Bunt and avenging the death of Tracy and James Jr.'s death provides Bond with a measure of closure.

Bond's Personal Life: Bond maintains his morning ritual of push-ups, leg lifts, and cold showers. When he is in between assignments, Bond plays golf and cards, reads for pleasure, and romances women.

Bond's Tastes: Bond's sitting room is filled with books, and he works at his Empire desk. He has a subscription to *The Times.* However, the décor in his house is decidedly outdated.

Bond's Work Methods: Bond continues to use his Walther PPK even though it is no longer standard issue for agents. Bond practices driving with his right hand and shooting with his left. As a matter of protocol, relatives of SIS agents who are based in foreign countries are assigned a case agent. Family members are instructed to contact their case agent monthly.

Differences in Versions: When "Blast from the Past" was originally published in *Playboy* in 1997, it was abridged due to space issues. The story was later published in its entirety in the 2008 anthology, *The Union Trilogy*, which collects three of Benson's novels. Benson playfully refers to this unabridged edition as the "director's cut." As such, there are differences in the texts. The *Playboy* version starts with Bond receiving the letter that sends him on his mission. The director's cut opens slightly more leisurely with Bond in the arms of a woman and provides a glimpse into the spy's morning routine.

In both versions, Bond does not seem to have a strong relationship with his son. However, the nature of that dynamic changes depending on which version you read. In the director's cut, Benson established that Bond's son "rarely" speaks to his father. You might get the impression from reading the director's cut that Bond and his son are somewhat estranged from one another and that the younger Bond does not wish to maintain a relationship with his father. Benson also explains that part of the reason Bond does not stay connected with his son is that it dredges up painful memories of Tracy's death. These key details were omitted by *Playboy*'s editor.

I do not want to suggest that Bond is completely absent from his son's life or that James Jr. is suffering. Bond knows his son's home and work numbers by heart, indicating that they are not completely out of touch. In the director's cut, it is clear that Kissy met a man and remarried; therefore, James Jr. did have a father figure in his life, even if it was not his birth father.

There are other notable differences between the two versions. In the director's cut, Benson notes a resemblance between Bond's murdered wife, Tracy, and the special investigator, Cheryl Haven, with whom Bond teams up. No such comparison is made in the *Playboy* edition. The running theme of "Blast from the Past" is that Bond is haunted by the ghosts of the past and is looking for closure. His time with Haven helps provide that resolution. The *Playboy* edition of the short story is a fun, fast-paced short story but the director's cut, which preserves original Benson's vision, is a richer experience.

Assorted Observations:

- Because "Blast from the Past" appeared in *Playboy*, the short story contains some risqué elements. For instance, while shaving Bond with a poisonous blade, Bunt masturbates; for her, the torture has an erotic quality.
- Irma Bunt reveals that she and Blofeld did not mean to shoot Bond's wife Tracy; the bullets were intended exclusively for 007.
- Bond's facial scar is now only barely visible.

ZERO MINUS TEN (1997)

Author: Raymond Benson

In Brief: Bond is sent to Hong Kong on the eve of its transfer from the UK to China to investigate if a shipping firm called EurAsia Enterprises is linked to a string of terrorist incidents.

Meaning of Title: Bond has ten days to complete his mission before China takes back control of Hong Kong from the British.

Chronology: Contemporary. Following the events of John Gardner's last Bond novel.

Operation: Not applicable.

Bastard Meter: "Coldhearted" and "Bloody."

Eggs: Scrambled but not ordered by Bond.

Insight into Bond: "Living so close to death was what invigorated him and gave him the edge that had managed to keep him alive for so many years."

Summary: James Bond is attacked by two apparent assassins at his home in Jamaica. He gets the better of the duo, who are revealed to be SIS agents taking part in a training exercise. Bond is called back to England to deal with an emergency.

Three days earlier, in England, members of a Chinese Triad unload crates from a cargo vessel that was shipped from Hong Kong. The local police discover that the crates are filled with heroin. A gunfight breaks out, and the police kill the Triad members.

The next day in Hong Kong, shipping magnate and CEO of EurAsia Enterprises, Guy Thackery, is attending an event at a floating restaurant named the *Emerald Palace*. Thackery announces the retirement of John Desmond, the company's lawyer. Three albino brothers rig the boat with explosives. When Thackery leaves the party to go to his office, the vessel blows up. The next day, a nuclear bomb goes off in Western Australia.

Bond and M discuss the events over the last three days, as well as the fact that in ten days, on July 1, 1997, Hong Kong will no longer be under British control; it will revert to China. M informs Bond a lawyer who worked for Thackery named Gregory Donaldson and two

Chinese officials have been murdered. Their deaths might be linked to Thackery's company EurAsia Enterprises, a legitimate shipping business that operates out of Hong Kong. M tells Bond that the cargo vessel containing the heroin is owned by EurAsia and that the Chinese men who were unloading the crates were part of a Triad named San Yee On. Bond suspects that the bombing in Australia is related to the bombings in Hong Kong and England but M isn't convinced. M tells Bond to go to Hong Kong to investigate the connection between EurAsia and the Triads. Before he leaves for Hong Kong, Bond visits the Quartermaster who supplies Bond with a shoe that contains a variety of hidden gadgets.

Bond travels to Hong Kong and meets T.Y. Woo, 007's local contact. Woo tells Bond that the leader of the Triad group Dragon Head is a businessman named Li Xu Nan. Woo tells Bond that Guy Thackeray plays mahjong, a title-based game, at Lisboa Hotel and Casino.

Bond goes to the casino and plays mahjong with Thackery. At first, Thackery is winning but Bond suspects that his opponent is cheating. Bond and Woo work out an elaborate system of sending signals, which allows Bond to beat Thackery. Bond, who is assuming the identity of a journalist reporting Hong Kong's transfer to China, is invited by Thackery to attend tomorrow's press conference. Bond accepts the invitation. Thackery excuses himself to go to the washroom. When he's gone, three Chinese men attack Bond and Woo. Bond defeats the men but when he searches for Thackery in the bathroom, he discovers that Thackery has escaped via a hidden trap door.

The next day, Bond tells Woo that he wants to meet Li Xu Nan, the head of the Triad Dragon. Woo informs Bond that he might be able to find Li Xu Nan at a nightclub called The Zipper. At the Zipper, Bond meets a dancer named Sunni Pei. Sunni and Bond quickly form a bond. 007 tells her that he wants to meet Li. Sunni says that Li poses as a legitimate businessman, and he would never admit to being a member of the Triad. Sunni identifies Li who is sitting with his three albino bodyguards to Bond. Bond asks Sunni to arrange an audience with Li.

Posing as a journalist, Bond asks Li for an interview. Li tells Bond that he does not have any information about the Triads or about the various attacks. On his way out of the club, Sunni slips Bond a piece of paper that indicates that because she helped Bond, she's in danger.

Bond agrees to hide Sunni at her mother's place. When they get there, they discover that Sunni's mother is dead. At the apartment,

Bond battles a series of Chinese thugs. Bond is victorious but they wound him with a cleaver. Sunni reveals that she is what's known as a Blue Lantern, someone who has been accepted into the Triad but who hasn't gone through the initiation process yet. Bond takes Sunni to the local safe house where they meet T.Y. Wong and his son, Chen Chen.

The next day, Bond attends Guy Thackeray's press conference where Thackeray announces that he is leaving the company and selling 59% of the shares of his company to China. Following the announcement, Thackeray attempts to drive away in his car but a bomb goes off, apparently killing him.

Bond chases after the bomber but the assassin kills himself by jumping off the building. Bond returns to the safe house but discovers that it's been destroyed. Bond calls Bill Tanner at SIS. Tanner tells Bond to look into the connection between EurAsia and the Triads.

Searching for clues, Bond investigates EurAsia's warehouse where he discovers a small boat called a sampan. After sneaking into the office, Bond finds a bag full of heroin and finds a folder marked Australia, which includes details about a gold mine. Spotting Li Xu Nan and the Triad Bond concludes that Li is using the warehouse as part of his smuggling operation. Bond also surmises that Guy Thackeray learned about the illegal activities and was killed before he could report it.

Bond follows Li to a condemned building where a Triad initiation ceremony is taking place. Bond is captured and brought to Li Xu Nan. Li tells Bond that a Chinese general named Wong killed Thackeray. Li also explains that his great-grandfather had a secret agreement with Thackeray's great-grandfather. As part of the contract, Li's grandfather would eventually take control of EurAsia. That agreement was memorialized in writing, but it is now in General Wong's possession in China. By suppressing the document, Wong is set to control EurAsia, a multi-billion dollar company. Li makes a deal with Bond—recover the contract that shows that Li has a stake in the company, and he will cancel the death warrant on Sunni.

Bond flies to China where he poses as James Pickard, an attorney representing EurAsia and who needs to verify the authenticity of the contract. Bond meets General Wong and inspects the document. During the meeting, two guards bring in T.Y. Woo, Bond's partner. When Wong asks Bond if he knows Woo, Bond disavows his ally. Wong accuses Bond of being a spy.

Wong tortures Bond by beating his naked body with a cane. When Wong leaves, Bond removes a knife that was hidden in his shoe and uses it to kill the guards and escape. Bond discovers that Wong had Woo killed. Bond finds General Wong, kills him, and retrieves the coveted contract.

Bond returns to Hong Kong and surrenders the contract to Li who tells Bond that he is going to end his heroin operation and run EurAsia as a legitimate company. From Li's office, Bond calls M and updates her on the mission. 007 reports that Thackeray, the Triads, and General Wong are all working together. Then, Bond retrieves a map of EurAsia's goldmine in Australia and decides to investigate the mine personally.

As the clock ticks closer to the Chinese takeover of Hong Kong, Bond flies to Australia with Sunni. En route to the mine, a bomb explodes in Honk Kong's Victoria Harbor, a response to General Wong's murder.

Bond enters the EurAsia operation and discovers the sampan boat he had previously seen in Hong Kong. Bond and Sunni enter EurAsia's mine and discover reactors that can be used to help produce material for atomic bombs. Guy Thackeray, who was thought dead, arrives. Thackeray explains that he faked his own death and planned to live secretly in Australia on the money he earned from divesting his stakes in EurAsia. Because he is no longer able to run his beloved company, he is going to get revenge on both Britain and China by exploding a bomb in Hong Kong. Britain and China will blame each other and a conflict with ensue.

Thackeray tells one of his albino enforcers, Mr. Chang, to take Bond on his plane to a remote area of Australia. Once there, Chang will kill Bond and hide his body. Bond kills Chang and takes control of the plane but crash lands in a remote area of Australia. Bond survives but he has less than 24 hours to get to Hong Kong and locate the bomb before it goes off.

Bond flies to Hong Kong and meets with Li, who believes that a bomb might be planted in the harbor. Bond realizes that the device is probably on the sampan boat that he found in EurAsia's warehouses. Bond searches for it while a group of Triads battle with Thackeray's men. Thackeray shoots Li Xu Nan, killing him. Bond catches up to Thackeray. The two men battle and Bond eventually kills his adversary by drowning him. At the last minute, Bond locates and disarms the bomb.

Later, Bond talks to M who agrees to help Sunni escape Hong Kong and relocate to a safer place. Soon after, China peacefully takes control of Hong Kong.

Commentary: Raymond Benson's first Bond novel *Zero Minus Ten* is written with confidence and an appreciation for Ian Fleming's work.

Yet, *Zero Minus Ten* doesn't require the reader to have much existing knowledge of Fleming's books. Instead, it's easy to imagine that the intended audience is a Bond fan more familiar with the Eon movies. In fact, Benson has said that his and Glidrose's conceit is that he would take Fleming's Bond and insert him into the plot of an Eon film. It's a tightrope act that Benson expertly walks and it's a path that previous and future continuation authors wouldn't have to navigate.

In structuring his novel as an Eon movie, Benson provides plenty of action. There is even a quasi-pre-title sequence where Bond faces off with two apparent assassins (Michael and Stephanie Lane) who are revealed to be Single O agents that are taking part in a training mission. After Bond gets the better of both agents and the exercise is over, Bond is called away for duty. Before he leaves, Stephanie joins Bond in the shower. "Naked, she pushed back the shower curtain, and got in with him." One can almost imagine the scene fading to black and the opening credits rolling on an Eon film.

Many of the Bond films end with Bond and a group of soldiers raiding the villain's stronghold. That scenario played out in various Bond films such as *You Only Live Twice*, *On Her Majesty's Secret Service*, *The Spy Who Loved Me*, and *Moonraker*. Similarly, *Zero Minus Ten* concludes with Bond and his temporary allies, the triads, storming the villain's vessel, the *Taitai*. In keeping with the Eon films in which Judi Dench played M, Benson's M is a woman with short grey hair. Before briefing Bond on his latest gadgets, Major Boothroyd, the armorer instructs Bond, "Now pay attention, 007." It's the same phrase that Q uses in the Eon movies.

While aspects of *Zero Minus Ten* are in keeping with the Eon films, Benson's novels also owe a lot to Fleming's novels. Benson describes an extended Mahjong game between Bond and Guy Thackeray, which recalls the card games in *Casino Royale* and *Moonraker* and the golf match in *Goldfinger*.

Fleming seemed to delight in finding new ways to torment Bond. The passages in *Casino Royale* where Bond is stripped naked and tortured are perhaps the most remembered examples. Benson writes a similar scene in which a naked Bond is told to bend over and grab his ankles before being thrashed with a cane. It's an effective and frightening passage.

When writing his Bond novels, Fleming would draw on his background as a journalist and he would teach his readers about other cultures and customs. Similarly, Benson displays his knowledge of Hong Kong, China, triads, and even the Australian tradition of walkabouts. *Zero Minus Ten* is an assiduously researched effort.

Benson's Bond, like Fleming's, is not superhuman. As such, there are numerous times throughout the book when Bond must take a moment to catch his breath or even apply ointments to his wounds. The movie Bond would never stop moving for that kind of self-care. Yet, Benson's Bond needs all the help he can get.

Benson keeps *Zero Minus Ten* in continuity with both Fleming and Gardner. Benson references the carpet beater torture in *Casino Royale*, Oddjob in *Goldfinger*, and past loves Vesper Lynd and Tracy di Vicenzo. He also refers to the ASP pistol that Gardner's Bond used, as well as Gardner's heroines Fredericka von Grüsse (*Never Send Flowers*), Harriett Horner (*Scorpius*), and Easy St. John (*Death if Forever*).

Benson's use of continuity is to acknowledge the previous books but not to be limited by them either. So Benson's Bond no longer uses Gardner's ASP pistol. Instead, he's packing a Walther PPK, as Fleming's Bond does. Benson makes Bond a Commander again after Gardner promoted 007 to the rank of Captain.

Benson contends that his writings belong in a different continuity than Gardner's so the allusions to Gardner's works are intended to be playful nods. Nonetheless, readers can reasonably infer that Benson's Bond experienced Gardner's adventures.

In *Zero Minus Ten*, Benson establishes that Bond is a senior agent, and that time has marched on. As such, Bond's previous secretaries Loelia Ponsonby and Mary Goodnight have retired and have been replaced by Helena Marksbury, who hails from Wales.

Benson's depiction of the personal cost of Bond's decisions is what makes *Zero Minus Ten* so intriguing. In one scene, the terrorist Bond is chasing shoots a guard and takes a woman hostage. Bond realizes his pursuit precipitated the guard's death and jeopardized the woman. Later, posing as a lawyer, Bond meets Colonel Wong, a Chinese extremist. During their meeting, one of Wong's thugs brings Bond's Hong Kong contact, T. Y. Woo, into the room. Bond, attempting to preserve his own cover, denies knowing Woo. He knew that his disavowal of Woo could potentially get Woo killed. So he blames himself. Of course, Bond is not responsible for the death of the security guard or Woo. If the assassin wasn't stopped, he would have killed many more people and if Bond blew his cover, then both he and Woo would have been murdered. Despite these mitigating factors, Bond bears the full weight of their deaths.

Continuity Nod: After kicking an agent in the groin during a training exercise, Bond quips about the time he was assaulted with a carpet beater (*Casino Royale*). When Bond is being caned, he thinks back to the same event. There are additional references to Bond's past secretaries Loelia Ponsonby and Mary Goodnight and his trip to New York with Felix Leiter (*Live and Let Die*). When Bond visits the Wanchai District, he's near the Bottoms Up club, the topless bar he went to in the movie *The Man with the Golden Gun.* Benson playfully notes that Bottoms Up has been in existence since the 1970s, which is when the Roger Moore film was made. When Bond's ally Sunni Pei mentions that she went to Las Vegas in her youth, Bond notes that he's been there before (*Diamonds Are Forever*).

Bond's History: Bond has been to Hong Kong before and seems to have preferred casinos and restaurants.

Bond's Inner Life: Death is such a part of his profession that the agent has found a way to cope. "James Bond had lost many friends during his career with the Secret Service. He had learned long ago how to deal with it and turn the pain into an asset that contributed to his self-made shell—the hardened, tough armour that protected him from the inevitably maddening, and conceivably fatal, aspects of consciousness called human emotions." In short, Bond has learned to bury his emotions. It's how he dealt with Leiter's maiming in *Live and Let Die,* Darko Kerim's death in *From Russia with Love*, and Quarrel's death in *Dr. No.* It may make him seem callous but Bond's "self-made shell" not only dulls his emotions, but it also makes him a better agent.

Bond's Personal Life: Bond's office is sparsely decorated. However, a watercolor of the clubhouse at the Royale St. George Golf Course hangs on the wall and a picture of him and Felix Leiter, which was taken at a New York City bar, sits on his desk. Bond plays golf and tennis with Bill Tanner. Even though Sir Miles Messervy recently retired from the service, Bond and his former boss have formed a personal friendship. Bond frequently visits Messervy at his home near Windsor Great Park. Despite their close relationship, Bond has to fight the urge to address the former-M as "sir."

Bond still lives in Chelsea, off King's Road and he has a second home in Jamaica which is called Shamelady. Benson implies that Shamelady is actually GoldenEye, Fleming's house in Jamaica where he wrote his novels. Bond is not a nervous flyer, and he can easily fall asleep when traveling on a plane. Bond considers himself chivalrous, isn't religious, is fairly conversant in Cantonese, and knows a smattering of Mandarin.

Bond's Work Methods: Bond knows many forms of combat but when in the thick of it, he relies on a single fighting discipline and sticks with it. Bond believes that a good way to learn about a potential adversary is to compete against them in a game.

Bond took a desert survival training course. As a way to withstand torture, Bond tries to focus his attention on something external, like a stain on a bedsheet in the room where he's being hit. When that fails, he fantasizes about places he likes, like his new house in Jamaica and his flat in Chelsea. When an opponent is beating the stuffing out of him, Bond finds a way to persevere by willing "himself to turn the pain into energy."

Assorted Observation:

- The Cantonese phrase for 007 is "Ling Ling Chat."

TOMORROW NEVER DIES (1997)

Author: Raymond Benson

In Brief: James Bond and Chinese Agent Wai Lin team together to take down a media mogul who is attempting to incite war between the United Kingdom and China.

Meaning of Title: *Tomorrow* is the name of the media baron's newspaper:

Chronology: Contemporary. After the events of Gardner's *GoldenEye* novelization.

Operation: Not applicable.

Bastard Meter: A bastard who steals a MiG-29 airplane.

Eggs: A brown egg.

Insight into Bond: "He thought that he had experienced what others called love maybe three or four times in his life. The rest of the time it was purely lust, and in a few extreme cases, perhaps intense infatuation."

Summary: On the border of Afghanistan and Pakistan, cyberterrorist Henry Gupta attends an arms bizarre. Gupta is there to purchase a secret device that is encased in a red box. British Admiral Roebuck and Bill Tanner are monitoring the arms bazaar alongside the newly appointed M. Roebuck hurriedly orders an airstrike, but British monitoring spots a nuclear missile on a MiG-29 aircraft. James Bond sneaks into the bazaar and steals the aircraft carrying the nuclear weapon, ensuring that the device does not go off. Gupta acquires the red box and flees the area. As Bond flies away, a British cruise missile destroys the bazaar.

Elsewhere, Elliot Carver's Carver Media Group Network, the second-largest news company in the world, records and reports the news via satellites. Carver's newspaper is called *Tomorrow.*

In the South China Sea, the HMS *Devonshire*, the British Royal Navy ship, receives word that they are violating international law by entering Chinese waters. Checking their instruments, the British Navy confirms that they are not operating in Chinese territories. Believing that the British are spying on them, the Chinese instruct their pilots to fire upon the *Devonshire*. Simultaneously, a German named Stamper orders a guided submersible drill, a Sea-Vac, to attack the *Devonshire*. Then, Stamper sends a group of divers to steal cruise missiles from the downed ship while he records the action from a control room.

In Hamburg Germany, Carver stands in the Carver Media Group Network control room. Also there is Henry Gupta, the cyberterrorist from the arms bazaar. Via satellite, Stamper shows Carver footage of seven cruise missiles they salvaged from the Devonshire.

Two days earlier, Colonel Wai Lin, a spy and a member of the People's External Security Force, attends a briefing near Beijing, China. General Koh informs Lin of Russian low-frequency radar technology, which might make Chinese military vehicles as covert as those of the United States and Russia. Koh explains that General Chang has stolen the radar technology and hidden it in tea crates. Lin is instructed to find the shipment.

Back to the present day. Wai Lin infiltrates the Xiang Warehouse and searches the records for information on the whereabouts of the tea crates. She discovers that Mr. Deng, the warehouse manager, has the info she seeks.

Later, Lin poses as a prostitute in the nightclub district. Mr. Deng spots and propositions her. When Wai Lin and Deng go to his apartment, she sees a photograph of Deng and General Chang, who sent her on the mission. Lin realizes that she has been set up. Deng tries to shoot Lin, but she overpowers him. Lin searches the apartment and learns that the missing tea crates were sent to the Carver Media Group Network in Hamburg, Germany.

In England, Bond drives his Aston Martin to Oxford. He goes there to meet Professor Inga Bergstrom, who is teaching him Danish. Inga and Bond's relationship is not strictly professional. Moneypenny calls Bond and tells him to return to duty.

When Bond arrives at the Ministry of Defense, Admiral Roebuck and M debate the dangers of sending the British Fleet to China. M contends that the Chinese government is being set up. However, the Atomic Clock Signal Encoding System (ACSES), a tool used to guarantee the accuracy of the data transported to and from satellites, indicates there was no malfeasance.

Elliot Carver's *Tomorrow* newspaper reports that the British sailors on the *Devonshire* were shot dead by the Chinese government. In reality, Carver knows that his men performed the execution.

M, Bond, and Tanner head back to London. On the way, M reminds Bond that Henry Gupta obtained a device that works with satellite technology and because Carver's news network owns satellites, there might be a connection. M orders Bond to fly to Hamburg and investigate Carver, who is now married to Bond's former lover, Paris Carver.

Once in Hamburg, Bond goes to a car rental place where he meets with Q, who is posing as a car rental employee. Q provides Bond with a BMW, which has been outfitted with special gadgets and can be operated remotely.

Bond goes to the Carver Media Group Network building and attends a party. There, Bond meets Wai Lin, posing as an employee of the Bank of Hong Kong. Bond also claims he is a banker, but Wai Lin knows he is lying. Bond and Lin meet Elliot Carver and Paris. Paris spots Bond and slaps him, explaining that she used to date him. Bond tries to get under Carver's skin by making veiled accusations about satellites and the recent incidents at sea.

At his newsroom, Carvers announces the opening of his new broadcasting facility with regional centers around the world, including Saigon. Nearby, Bond tells Paris that he suspects that Carter engages in illegal activity. As they speak, a guard tells Bond that he has a phone call. The guard takes Bond to a room where three other guards are waiting for him. One beats Bond with a Billy Club, but Bond turns the tables and gets the better of them. As he escapes Bond runs into Wai Lin. They both acknowledge that they are not bankers. Bond uses a lit cigar to set off the building's fire alarms, allowing them to escape in the commotion.

Carver confronts Paris and voices his suspicions about Bond. Paris covers for Bond. When Carver becomes physically abusive, Paris decides to leave him.

Wai Lin gives Bond the slip and uses the computer to try to find out more about him, but she comes up short.

Bond returns to his room at the Kempinski Hotel Atlantic. Later that night, Paris comes to his room to tell him that she left Carver. They briefly talk about old times and kiss.

At Carver's building, Carver learns that Bond is a spy and that Paris has left him. Carver calls for "The Doctor."

Back at the hotel, Paris and Bond lie naked together. Paris recalls meeting Bond seven years ago in Paris. At the time, she was a professional model and he claimed he was a banker. Although she was deeply in love with him, he left without any explanation. Paris tells him how he can enter the Carver Media Group Newark building undetected.

Bond goes to the Carver building and sneaks in. Bond locates Henry Gupta's private office. Inside, he finds the hidden wall safe and breaks into it using Q's gadget. Bond discovers the red box that Gupta purchased from the underground market inside the safe; inside the box is the ACSES device.

Bond leaves Gupta's office and spots Wai Lin as she inadvertently sets off the security alarm. Meanwhile, Paris is still in Bond's hotel room. Carver and Stamper force their way inside. Carver accuses Paris of being disloyal to him.

Back at the Carver building, Bond and Wai Lin are being shot at by Carver's men. Bond uses stacks of newspapers to topple the guards. Wai Lin escapes.

Bond returns to his hotel room and finds Paris' dead body. Distracted, an assassin named Dr. Kaufman trains his pistol on Bond. A television reporter announces that Paris Carver has been found dead in a hotel room, along with the body of an unidentified man. Dr. Kaufman explains that he needs the red box from Bond's car before he can kill the spy. Kaufman explains that Carver's men have inadvertently triggered Bond's car alarm. Bond says that he can turn off the alarm with his phone. Kaufman grabs Bond's phone, activates it, and receives an unexpected electrical shock. Bond grabs Kaufman's gun and shoots him with it.

Bond enters the parking garage and sees that Carver's men are still trying to break into his car so that they can retrieve the red box. Using the remote control device, the car comes to Bond, who jumps into it and drives away. Carver's men chase after him but Bond tricks the chasing cars into driving off the building.

Carver takes his corporate jet from Germany to Saigon. Bond arrives at the US Air Force base in Japan and meets his CIA contact Jack Wade and Dr. Greenwalt, a scientist who developed the ACSES device. When he tests the device Greenwalt concludes that someone tampered with it. The tests suggest that the *Devonshire* was deliberately tricked into entering Chinese waters.

Wade arranges for Bond to conduct a High Altitude Low Opening jump from a plane into the waters of the South China Sea, near Vietnam. After Bond lands in the water, he investigates the wreckage of the *Devonshire*. Bond confirms that the Devonshire was in Chinese territory but it did not fire on the Chinese Navy. He also finds evidence of a missile attack, which suggests that the *Devonshire* was destroyed by an underwater vessel. While continuing to investigate the wreckage, Bond sees another diver, who turns out to be Wai Lin. The wrecked ship starts to shift and sink further into the ocean. Bond and Lin manage to escape before the ship becomes their watery tomb. Bond and Lin make their way to the surface and are rescued by a Vietnamese fisherman. Stamper appears, kills the fisherman, and captures Bond and Wai Lin.

Meanwhile, the British Fleet sends six ships to the South China Sea. The Chinese fleet reacts by mobilizing their fleet placing the two countries on the brink of war.

Stamper brings Bond and Lin to Carver's headquarters in Saigon, where they spot General Chang. The spies are brought to Carver's office. Bond tells Carver that he and Wai Lin have revealed Carver's plans to their superiors. Carver tells Stamper to stab himself in the leg. Stamper does so, but he is unfazed; his pain and pleasure sensors are reversed. Carver confesses that he is starting a war between the British and the Chinese to increase viewership to his news network. Bond baits Carver, calling him names and attacking his reputation and status. When Carver lunges at 007, Bond and Lin jump out the window, holding onto a giant banner as it lowers them safely to the ground.

Bond and Wai Lin steal a BMW motorcycle and are chased by one of Carver's helicopters. Eventually, the helicopter seems to pin them down. Bond and Wai Lin launch their motorcycle directly into the copter, bringing it down.

Now safe, Lin handcuffs Bond to a pipe and tells him that she is going to handle Carver on her own. Bond quickly frees himself and decides to track her down. Together they can stop Carver. Bond realizes that he is developing feelings for Lin.

Soon after, Wai Lin goes to a bicycle shop, but she is spotted by one of Stamper's men. The man attempts to call in Lin's location to his superior, but Bond stops him before he can pass on the information. Bond goes into the shop and sees Lin knocking out three of Carver's toughs. One of the assailants trains his gun on Lin and is about to shoot her when Bond intervenes. Bond kills the man and saves Lin.

Bond and Lin agree to team up. They trade intelligence that they have gathered and conclude that the British *Devonshire* and the Chinese fighter planes were destroyed by Carver's stealth boat. Lin flips a switch, and the rack of bicycles moves away, revealing a sophisticated computer and hidden munition depot. Lin checks the news stories for unusual activity and learns that there were three unexplained deaths in Ha Long Bay in North Vietnam. The agents file a joint report and send it to their superiors.

Carver, Henry Gupta, and Stamper board the *Sea Dolphin II*, Carver's stealth boat. When Bond and Wai Lin reach Ha Long Bay, a local fisherman points to an island and says that all the locals avoid it. Lin pays the fisherman $5 thousand to take them to the island. Bond and Lin make love on the boat.

The next day, Bond and Lin board a raft and make their way to land. They locate and board Carver's ship. Bond and Lin separate and place mines in strategic places throughout the vessel. A security camera spots Wai Lin. Carver instructs Stamper to find Lin and kill Bond. Stamper captures Lin and brings her to Carver. Meanwhile, Bond begins his assault on Carver's men. As the agent makes his way through the ship, he also rigs homemade explosive devices.

Tensions between the British and Chinese fleets rise as the combat aboard the ship rages. Carter believes that their conflict will make for excellent television. Bond locates Carver, who reveals that he has captured Wai Lin. Bond shoots one of his homemade bombs, causing it to explode. Carver and his men run for cover. The blast gives Wai Lin a chance to try to escape but Stamper grabs her. The explosions wreak havoc with Carver's stealth technology revealing their position to the British and Chinese. Now, the Chinese government understands that the British did not intentionally invade their waters and they call their fleet back.

The British fleet turns its attention to Carver's ship and plans to attack it. Meanwhile, Bond and Stamper fight but Stamper is too powerful for Bond. Elsewhere, Wai Lin takes out more of Carver's men, including Gupta. Carver orders his men to launch a missile at the British fleet. However, Stamper is positioned exactly in the trajectory of the missile. So when the missile launches, it blows Stamper up. Simultaneously, the Chinese government arrests General Chang. On his ship, Carver observes a news report announcing that he has been reported missing and has been charged with fraud. The Sea-Vac drill crashes into the newsroom and kills Carver.

Bond and Wai Lin flee the sinking ship and take refuge on separate inflatable rafts. The Royal Navy searches for Bond but the spy remains hidden. He would prefer to stay the night with Lin than be rescued. Bond climbs into Lin's raft and they embrace.

Commentary: 1997 marked the publication of two Bond works by Raymond Benson, the original novel *Zero Minus Ten* and *Tomorrow Never Dies*, the novelization of Pierce Brosnan's second Bond film. Happily, Benson does not slavishly follow the plot of the movie; instead, he provides an alternate version of the story. His most significant narrative change is to increase the presence of Wai Lin, the Chinese agent who is very much Bond's equal.

Benson modifies the structure of the story. Lin appears for the first time 30 minutes into the film, and the audience meets her when Bond does. In the novelization, she is introduced after the inciting incident, the destruction of the *Devonshire* and the theft of its warheads. Usually, in the Bond movies, following the world-shattering event, M meets with 007, briefs him on the incident, and then sends him off on his assignment. By giving Wai Lin that post-incident moment, Benson defies the reader's expectations and uses that moment to introduce Wai Lin.

The author provides Wai Lin with a backstory, describes her various skills, the languages she knows, and establishes that she was at the top of her stealth training course. She finds greater enjoyment in her work than anything in her personal life, a quality she shares with Bond. Benson has Wai Lin's superior provide her with information about a separate incident, involving stolen Russian low-frequency radar technology, and instructs her to find it. Benson's choices have the overall effect of strengthening Wai Lin's character and demonstrating that she is at least as capable as Bond.

Benson's novelization also provides additional insight into Bond's relationship with Paris Carver. Benson explains that the two met when she was a fashion model in Paris. At the time Bond was dating another woman, but he was taken with Paris and their relationship lasted a couple of months. The breakdown of the relationship was due to two factors—one emotional and one practical. The first is Bond's aversion to closeness and the second is that Paris was a security risk. As a model, she was always getting her photo taken. One night at a fashion show, Bond was standing too close to her, and his photo was also captured. Obviously, secret agents must remain out of the public eye, so he left her. Bond will repeat this pattern of falling in love with security risks in Benson's fifth original Bond novel *Never Dream of Dying*, with Tylyn Mignonne, a model turned actress.

Even though readers learn more about Paris, Wai Lin is given the greatest prominence. The development of Wai Lin's narrative has one unforeseen effect. Bond's relationship with Paris does not appear to be a key relationship in his life. Instead, it comes across as more of a fling, at least from Bond's point of view. Even though Paris thought that she might marry Bond, there is little to indicate that he felt the same way. It is Lin, though, who comes to mind when Bond thinks of major women in his life and long-term partnerships.

Still, Benson is not suggesting that Wai Lin and Bond's romance will develop into anything serious. Instead, Benson sets up Lin and Bond as equals who share similar views on their profession and sexual dalliances. Neither operative wants a committed relationship. Stil, neither is above enjoying the other's company and gratifying their carnal desires. Moreover, Bond and Lin are an effective team. They can sense each other's movements and have a near-telepathic relationship when things go sideways. For instance, in one scene Bond and Lin are captured by Carver's men. For a moment, they consider fighting back. With a subtle eye gesture, they decide to delay their escape and instead learn more about Carver's plan. Benson explains that "somehow they were able to read each other's thoughts." Elsewhere, Benson writes that Lin had "read [Bond's] thoughts."

Benson also aims to add a little realism to the outsized fantasy of the Bond movies. To wit, there is a sequence in both the movie and novelization where Bond and Lin are nearly trapped in a sunken vessel. In the movie, Bond uses his oxygen tanks to quickly ascend. Benson's Bond goes to the surface of the water in stages, to avoid the bends. One stage takes nearly 30 minutes. Elsewhere in the book, Bond is forced to wear the clothes of a local fisherman. Benson notes that the man's shoes are a little too small for Bond's feat. It is a throwaway moment, but it does create a little verisimilitude to the proceedings.

Benson also gives Elliot Carver a medical condition, TMJ (temporomandibular joint), and a backstory. According to Benson, Carver's mother died during his birth and his father Lord Roverman, a married newspaper tycoon, did not want to raise him. So Carter was raised by Chinese foster parents who took him in. When Carver grew up, he found his father and blackmailed him. Lord Roverman, tried to pay him off with a thousand pounds, but Carver refused. Later, Carver met a slow-witted German boy named Stamper and his handler Mr. Schnitzler. The trio discovered that Lord Roverman was unfaithful to his wife. So they paid his mistress £6 hundred to film her making love with Roverman. Carver extorts Roverman into giving him the paper business upon his death. As a means to expedite Roverman's death, they framed him for murdering his mistress. Rather than risk a public scandal, Roverman killed himself and Carter came into his inheritance.

Benson provides readers with a potted history of Fleming's Bond. Bond's education at Fettes, the incident with a maid, and his service in the Royal Navy are all referenced. In this way, Benson is aligning the Bond of his novelization with Fleming's work.

Continuity Nod: Benson states that Bond has been in love three or four times. However, he does not specify with whom. Presumably, Vesper and Tracy are two of the women. Benson also references Bond's friend Felix Leiter who doesn't appear in the narrative. Staying consistent with Fleming, Benson's Leiter has left the CIA, now lives in Texas, and works as a freelancer.

Bond's History: Bond did not get good grades in school; he was restless and too easily bored. When Bond was seventeen years old, he would hunt for octopus and crabs in the Caribbean with his friend Ramsey. Benson alludes to Bond's brief tenure at Eton and the events that led to him being kicked out of the school, as well as the death of Bond's parents. Before he was a member of the Secret Service, Bond visited Hamburg with a group of Royal Navy sailors; their trip included a visit to the red light district.

Bond's Inner Life: Benson describes Bond as a "restless soul." Bond is aware that his attitudes towards women are out of date and are a touch chauvinistic. Yet, he does not consider himself a misogynist. Bond believes that if he has a fault with women, it's that he puts them on a pedestal and tries to satisfy them excessively.

Bond's Personal Life: When writing about Bond's personal life, Benson keeps to the facts as established by Fleming. However, he does not mind putting his own spin on the movie Bond's history. For instance, in *You Only Live Twice*, Sean Connery's Bond tells Moneypenny, "You forget, I took a first in Oriental Languages at Cambridge." In his novelization, Benson playfully suggests that Bond was telling a little fib to Moneypenny. It was Bond's way of flirting with Moneypenny and trying to make himself seem more accomplished and also to reconcile the fact that Bond cannot decipher the Chinese keyboard later in the story.

Bond's Tastes: Irrespective of the number of times that Bond scuba dives, he is always in awe of sea life, plants, and animals.

Bond's Work Methods: Bond has been trained to drink plenty of water before a HALO jump. He learned stealth techniques while training in Canada, and he only teases Q because he is exceedingly fond of his colleague.

In order to better prepare him for his assignments, Bond routinely takes training courses. He took a course on how to fly the Soviet's twin-engine fighter Mikoyan MiG-29. Bond also attended a stealth training camp in Canada and does sit-ups to stay in shape.

Assorted Observations:

- Benson gives Paris Carter a maiden name, McKenna. She did not have one in the film.
- According to Bill Tanner, he would resign if James Bond were to die in the line of duty.

THE FACTS OF DEATH (1998)

Author: Raymond Benson

In Brief: After M's boyfriend is slain, Bond investigates a string of terrorist attacks using a deadly toxin that is linked to the Decada, a group founded on mathematical concepts.

Meaning of Title: The facts of death are that once you're gone, there's no correcting mistakes or redeeming yourself.

Chronology: Contemporary. Set after the events of *Zero Minus Ten.*

Operation: Not applicable.

Bastard Meter: Standard bastard.

Eggs: Scrambled.

Insight into Bond: "The threat of death hanging over you is what really makes you tick. Without it, you're unhappy."

Summary: Prologue. In Los Angeles, Carl Williams unexpectedly dies following a blood transfusion. Carl's wife, his caregiver, and others with whom he had contact also pass away. In Tokyo, Hiroshi Nagaza receives leukemia treatment, which calls for a blood injection. Nagaza boards a train after the treatment and he, along with everyone else on the train, dies.

In the Republic of Cyprus, James Bond investigates an incident in which 12 soldiers were killed by a biological weapon. Painted on the wall next to their dead bodies is the number "3." A small statuette of the Greek god of the sea, Poseidon, is discovered nearby. The soldiers' deaths are connected to two other recent incidents—the death of SIS agent Christopher Witten and the deaths of a squadron of men. Numbers "1" and "2" were found near their bodies, as well as a small statue of the Greek god Hera near the second victim. Bond speculates that the statuettes left near the second and third victims were intended to link the deaths to ancient Greece.

Bond meets Niki Markos, a member of the Greek National Intelligence Service who has been sent to investigate the three terrorist attacks, which are tied together by the use of chemical and biological agents.

During a shower, Bond is nearly sprayed with a deadly chemical agent, but he jumps out before it causes him any harm. Then, he spots an enemy agent fleeing the area and chases after him. When the enemy agent jumps into a helicopter, Bond holds onto the bottom of it as it flies away. The enemy shoots at 007, who is forced to let go of the helicopter and dive into the sea below. Piloting another helicopter, Niki rescues Bond. Later that night, Niki and Bond make love.

Back in London, former M, Sir Miles Messervy, invites Bond to a party at his house that night. Later, Bond goes to his office and learns that a different chemical agent was used in each of the three attacks. The perpetrator is now being referred to as the "Number Killer" because they leave numbers by the scene of their crimes. Later, Bond meets with the new M who tells him that the chemical agents were smuggled in frozen sperm vials.

That night, Bond goes to Miles Messervy's house and speaks to Sir Miles, the new M, Barbara Mawdsley, and meets M's boyfriend, British diplomat Alfred Hutchinson. Bond, M, and Hutchinson agree to meet the next day, because Hutchinson has critical information about the Number Killer case. Later that night, Bond receives word that M's partner, Ambassador Hutchinson, was killed by a chemical agent.

Bond goes to M's residence, consoles his boss, and inspects Hutchinson's body. In Hutchinson's overcoat, investigators uncover a small statuette of Ares, the Greek God of war and the number "4." Hutchinson is the Number Killer's fourth victim, and the two objects are his calling card. M instructs Bond to investigate the Number Killer's first two sets of victims in Greece and Cyprus.

On the Greek Island of Chios, the Decada, an evil organization whose methods and philosophies are based on mathematical principles, is meeting. The Decada's leader, the Monad, reports that they successfully killed their fourth target (Hutchinson) but that he was not carrying the critical information that they were seeking. The Monad explains the importance of a Tetractys, a triangle shape consisting of ten points—each point stands for a terrorist attack. The Monad announces that they have conducted the first stage of four attacks. The next phase will be three attacks, then two, then one, a total of ten. Then, they will repeat the process and conduct more strikes in the same pattern.

Back in London, M tells Bond that they have not been able to find Alfred Hutchinson's son, Charles Hutchinson, who lives in Texas. Bond flies to Texas to find him. The girlfriend and coworker of Felix Leiter, Manuela Montemayor, picks up Bond at the airport and takes him to Leiter's home.

At Leiter's, Bond reunited with his old friend and learns that Charles Hutchinson works as a representative fertility clinic named ReproCare. The sperm bank is owned by BioLinks Limited and has ties to a group of militants who call themselves the Suppliers. Leiter tells Bond that he can meet Ashley Anderson, the physician in charge of ReproCare at a local restaurant.

At the restaurant, Bond observes a meeting between Dr. Ashley Anderson and a minor criminal named Jack Herman. Bond meets Dr. Anderson who tells the agent that Charles Hutchinson is one of their couriers and if Bond goes to the clinic, she can supply Bond Hutchinson's location. Bond visits Hutchinson's office and sees that it has been ransacked. He hides when Dr. Anderson and Jack Herman enter the office. Bond overhears them saying that the files did not have the files. Herman leaves the office and goes to the parking lot. Bond slips into the back of Herman's truck. Then, Herman drives to Hutchinson's mansion which looks like a Greek temple.

At the mansion, Bond sees Charles Hutchinson, Jack Herman, and a bodybuilder from Greece (later identified as Vassilis). They search Alfred Hutchinson's computer for information, but they do not find it. When Bond is spotted, he escapes on a motorcycle. Herman chases after Bond in his truck. Bond jumps from his motorcycle to the truck, points his gun at Herman, and demands that he stop the vehicle. Ignoring Bond, Herman speeds up and tries to kill both of them. Bond jumps off the truck before it goes sailing off the cliff.

The next day, Bond goes to the fertility clinic to meet Dr. Ashley Anderson. The receptionist tells Bond that Dr. Anderson is running late. When the receptionist is not looking, Bond sneaks into the clinics and overhears Dr. Anderson talking about a trip someone is making to the United Kingdom. Anderson tells the caller not to open the vials he will be carrying.

Bond meets with Dr. Anderson who tells the agent that Charles Hutchinson is in Italy. Bond knows that Charles Hutchinson is still in Texas and, therefore, Anderson is hiding something. Later, Bond sneaks back into the clinic and finds a folder on a computer marked "Shipping" and finds an address in Bastrop, Texas. Dr. Anderson appears and aims her Colt .38 at Bond. She tells him that the clinic is using its sperm vials to transport deadly chemical and biological agents. She claims that Charles Hutchinson traveled the globe for the militant group, the Suppliers, transporting these chemical weapons. Anderson threatens to blow up the clinic with Bond in it. Bond disarms her and escapes before the building blows up and kills Anderson.

Bond provides the FBI with the address of the Suppliers, which he gleaned from the clinic's computer while he was snooping around.

The FBI raids the Suppliers' Texas-based property and finds a barn full of biological and chemical weapons.

The Decada and the Number Killer enact the next phase of their plan—three more attacks in Cyprus. Each attack is accompanied by the appearance of small statuettes and the numbers 5, 6, and 7, each representing the number of the attack. The Monad reports that the sixth attack was not entirely successful, as their plan to poison the citizens of Cyprus through their food was uncovered. The Monad accuses Charles Hutchinson of being a traitor and alerting the police to their plans. Charles confesses that he betrayed the Decada because they killed his father, Alfred. The Monad reveals that Alfred's death was necessary since he was ready to inform the authorities of Decada's secret plans.

Leiter tells Bond that the house which looks like a Greek Temple is owned by Konstantine Romanos, a respected mathematician and a tycoon. Romanos is related to a bodybuilder named Vassilis. Romanos was a teacher at the University of Texas during the time that Alfred Hutchinson was a guest professor there. M tells Bond to go to Athens, find Charles Hutchinson, and investigate Romanos.

Bond meets Hutchinson's lawyer, Manville Duncan, who tells Bond that his client is up to no good. Duncan also explains that since Hutchinson's death, he has assumed his client's diplomatic responsibilities.

Bond goes to Athens where he meets up with Niki Mirakos, the Greek Agent. They agree that the goal of the Number Killer is to inflame relations between Turkey and Greece over Cyprus. Niki explains that Konstantine Romanos is the owner of a pharmaceutical company called BioLinks Limited, which is based in Athens. Romanos is also a member of the Pythagorean Society, an organization that follows the teachings of the Greek philosopher Pythagoras.

Bond and Niki go to the location where SIS agent Christopher Whitten was found. There, they discover the body of Charles Hutchinson. Bond and Niki visit the Pythagorean Society, where they learn that the followers believe that the universe can be explained by studying numbers. At the society, Bond spots a photo of Konstantine Romanos and Alfred Hutchinson.

Bond and Niki have dinner. After dinner and on the drive home, enemy agents try to kill Bond and Niki. Bond defeats them. Later, Bond and Niki make love.

Bond calls Sir Miles Messervy who reveals that Alfred Hutchinson's father, Richard, is said to have absconded with Nazi gold. Bond and Niki visit Melina Papas, the president of BioLinks but

Papas does not reveal anything to them. After Bond and Niki leave, Papas makes plans to leave town. Meanwhile, the Decada continue to implement their plan; the death toll rises, as people in London, New York, Los Angeles, and Japan die from a mysterious disease.

Bond goes to the casino where he plays baccarat against BioLink's head Konstantine Romanos. Bond wins and talks to Romanos who strikes Bond as unhinged. Then, Bond meets Hera Volopoulos, a Greek woman who is secretly a member of the Decada. Bond goes with Hera back to her place. After they make love, Hera poisons Bond's food. Bond passes out and wakes up in the trunk of his car where he is being brought to the ruins of Mycenae, Greece. Bond tries to escape but Vassilis Romanos, the strong man stops him. The two fight and eventually Bond kills Vassilis. Bond finds Vassilis' notebook which reveals that the next event will take place at the village of Monemvasia at eleven a.m.

Hera confronts Bond and confesses that she's the Number Killer. At the point of a gun, Hera takes Bond to Romanos' yacht, the *Persephone*. On the yacht, Romanos reveals that he's Monad, the head of the Decada. Romanos said that his ultimate plan is to get revenge on Turkey for their political actions towards Cyprus. In turn, Turkey will act against Greece and war will break out. Romanos claims that he and Hutchinson used Hutchinson's Nazi Gold for their personal ambitions. However, Hutchinson reconsidered, and he was going to expose the Decada's secrets, so Hera killed him.

Bond escapes from the boat, calls the local authorities, and warns them of Decada's plan to use members of the Greek military to attack Turkey or Cyprus with a virus. Then, Bond calls M and tells her that Ambassador Hutchinson might have been a member of the Decada.

M calls Bond and remembers that when Hutchinson was dying, he kept asking for M's "hand." She now realizes that he was actually asking for her handbag, which held an envelope instructing her to go to a bank's safety deposit box. The box holds intel about the Decada, as well as details about an upcoming meeting with the President of Turkey. Bond figures out that Hutchinson was murdered so that Duncan, who would provisionally become the ambassador, could meet the Turkish President and eliminate him.

The next day, Duncan and Hera meet and fortify plans to kill the President of Turkey with the deadly virus. Hera tells Duncan that after the assassination she will become the head of the Decada. Duncan draws his gun, but Bond is faster, and he shoots and kills Duncan. Niki arrives and prevents Hera from killing the president, but Hera gets away.

Bond tracks the Decada to an ancient temple. At the temple, Bond finds Hera, Romanos, and BioLinks president Melina Papas. Bond learns that they are going to detonate a warhead over Istanbul. The explosion will end the fragile peace and instigate conflicts all over Europe, Asia, and the Middle East. Bond learns that Ambassador Hutchinson was not a member of the Decada. Hera shoots Romanos and says that she is going to be the new leader. The Decada have created a deadly virus that they have sent to medical clinics throughout the world. Once the virus has spread and reached critical impact, the Decada will ransom off the cure for it.

The Decada place Bond in a trap. The only way out is for him to solve a complicated mathematical puzzle. Hera leaves with a suitcase containing the virus. Bond solves the math problem, diffuses the bomb, and escapes with his life.

Hera leaves in a helicopter and Bond follows suit in a Blackhawk. Bond uses a Stinger launcher to bring down Hera's helicopter. After he successfully grounds the helicopter, Bond recovers the suitcase filled with the virus. The Centers for Disease Control can use the virus to find a cure. Bond provides M with closure by telling her that Hutchinson was not a member of the Decada.

Commentary: *The Facts of Death* represents Raymond Benson's first effort to create an evil organization in the vein of SPECTRE. Benson's sinister cabal is called The Decada, a cult based around mathematics. The Decada's key symbol is that of a triangle. The number 10 serves as the focal point for their terrorist strikes, which are carried out in groups of five, four, three, two, and finally one. The Decada's tenets are inextricably linked to Greece, the birthplace of the Greek philosopher and mathematician Pythagoras. Therefore, it's reasonable to assume that Benson would have created a different crime syndicate if he had not set the book in Greece. Instead, he would have invented a different sinister outfit.

The Decada have such faith in their love of mathematics that they allow Bond to defuse a bomb by cracking a mathematical riddle. The correct answer to their equation will dictate which of the three wires of the bomb Bond can cut. Little does the Decada know, but 007 has a head for figures. Bond solves the equation and saves the day. Having the hero figure out which wire to cut is an old trope. Benson reverses the reader's expectations. In the end, Bond learns that he should not cut any of the wires. The bomb will only switch off if 007 takes no action.

Benson's Bond continues to be a mixture of Fleming's and Eon's. Benson's Bond has the same internal feelings and demeanor as Fleming's original, but he also possesses the movie Bond's cavalier attitude towards women. Benson's Bond is a ladies' man with a "girl in every port" and who women instantly find irresistible. For instance, when Hera Volopoulos draws a gun on Bond, he uses his charm to disarm her, and they kiss shortly after. The action is also in keeping with Eon's movies. In one scene, Bond clings to the bottom of a villain's helicopter as his adversary tries to flee. Similarly, 007 hangs outside a helicopter in a couple of Bond movies including the already-made *For Your Eyes Only* (1981) and the not-yet-conceived *Spectre* (2015).

The observation that Benson's novels have a movie-like quality might seem like a criticism to some Fleming purists. Still, it was a tactic that 007's creator himself employed. When describing *Moonraker*, Fleming stated, "I originally thought of this novel as a film."[114]

As an Ian Fleming aficionado, Benson incorporates Fleming's characters into his writings. He doesn't discard them. For instance, in *The Facts of Death*, the current head of SIS is Barbara Mawdsley. Just because Sir Miles Messervy is no longer the head of the SIS, it doesn't mean that he disappeared from existence. Benson keeps Messervy as a presence in Bond's life. The duo continue to stay in contact although there is a suggestion that Bond is seeing his old boss with less frequency than in the previous novel. In *Zero Minus Ten*, Bond visited M "often" but in *Facts of Death* his visits occur "sometimes." However, the frequency of the visits might have been affected by Bond's work schedule and not because their relationship cooled down. In one scene, Bond attends a party at Sir Miles' house. At the party, Benson creates a scenario that was not possible in the Eon films—there's a brief exchange between the old M and the new one. At this moment, it's as if Bernard Lee shared screen time with Judi Dench.

Benson is a proud Texan. So it is only fitting that he sets part of the *Facts of Death* in his beloved state. In those scenes, Bond is a fish out of water—drinking frozen margaritas, doing shots of Tequila, and eating Tex-Mex food. I wouldn't be shocked if some readers were taken aback by the idea of Bond consuming a frosty beverage. However, when Fleming's Bond traveled to foreign countries, he would routinely eat the local cuisine.

The Facts of Death is a Fleming-esque title. Fleming's titles, such as *Live and Let Die* and *You Only Live Twice*, used common phrases and twisted them. Similarly, the expression "the facts of life" is altered so that it becomes "the facts of death." Originally, Benson wanted to call his second novel *The World Is Not Enough*, after Bond's family crest. However, Glidrose rejected the title. Yet, Benson was able to use it as the title for the closing chapter. Of course, in 1999,

The World Is Not Enough would become the name of Pierce Brosnan's third Bond movie.

Continuity Nod: When Bond goes to Greece, he recalls his earlier visit where he battled Colonel Sun (*Colonel Sun*). Bond's contact is the son of Darko Kerim, Stefan Tempo; he remembers his conflict with Red Grant on the Orient Express (both *From Russia with Love*). M recounts the time when Bond played cards against Drax (*Moonraker*). There is a reference to Bond's trip to Texas in which he investigated Ernst Stavro Blofeld's daughter, Nena Bismaquer (John Gardner's *For Special Services*).

Bond's History: Bond's worst subject in school was math.

Bond's Inner Life: Bond has encountered death so many times, that he treats it as if it were an old friend; life without the possibility of death, for Bond is boring. Bond is aware that he suffers from melancholy; he no longer tries to fight the feelings; instead, he accepts and welcomes them.

Bond's Personal Life: Bond has a housekeeper in Jamaica named Ramsey. As in Fleming's novels, May is his housekeeper in England. His Chelsea flat is furnished with an ornate desk and white and gold wallpaper, which belonged to the previous owners. Bond moved in but did not change his surroundings. Bond has two phones in his house. A white one for his personal life and a red one for work emergencies. Bond knows some Greek, enough to read but not enough to speak it.

Bond's Tastes: Bond rarely goes to the movies; so he's missed such popular films as *Reservoir Dogs*, *Natural Born Killers*, and *Basic Instinct*.

Bond's Work Methods: Bond teaches a class at the service called "How to Turn Everyday Items into Deadly Weapons." He puts his skills to the test by throwing a key card at an opponent. The title of Bond's class might be a reference to Ricky Jay's book *Cards as Weapons*. In addition to playing the henchman Gupta in *Tomorrow Never Dies*, Ricky Jay was a noted magician who was able to throw an ordinary playing card into a watermelon.

MIDSUMMER NIGHT'S DOOM (1999)

Author: Raymond Benson

In Brief: James Bond attends a party in the Playboy mansion in order to recover stolen secrets that are being sold to the Russian Mafia.

Meaning of Title: A reference to the name of the party that Bond attends at the Playboy mansion, as well as the William Shakespeare play *A Midsummer Night's Dream.*

Chronology: Contemporary. Set in 1999.

Operation: Not applicable.

Bastard Meter: None for Bond.

Eggs: None.

Insight into Bond: "He normally disliked disco dancing. He preferred the more traditional ballroom and big band swing."

Summary: In London, Bond meets with Barbara Mawdsley, M, who informs the agent that there is a leak in the Ministry of Defense. Government secrets have been stolen by a defense ministry staffer and given to her rock star husband Martin Tuttle. The staffer has recently confessed that Tuttle will be selling documents to the Russian Mafia at a party at the Playboy Mansion in Los Angeles. M instructs Bond to retrieve the documents and apprehend Tuttle's contact.

Miss Moneypenny informs Bond that attendees of Playboy's annual soiree, Midsummer Night's Dream, must wear pajamas or lingerie.

Bond flies to Los Angeles, and goes to the Playboy mansion where he meets the magazine's founder, Hugh Hefner. In the mansion's library, Hefner tells Bond that he doesn't know the identity of Tuttle's contact and gives Bond a pen with a transmitter hidden inside.

Posing as a Playboy attorney, Bond attends the party where he meets playmate Victoria Zdrok, who is wearing a pearl necklace, and her boyfriend Russian movie producer Anton Redenius. Victoria invites Bond to dance. Bond inspects her pearl necklace while dancing after Victoria reveals that Anton wants her to wear the necklace in a movie that will film in Russia.

Bond and another playmate, Lisa Dergan, meet Martin Tuttle, the rockstar who Bond has been sent to investigate. Bond gives Tuttle the pen with the transmitter inside when Lisa requests his autograph.

Still holding the trick pen, Tuttle moves to another area of the party. Bond eavesdrops on Tuttle who is having a conversation with Redenius, the Russian filmmaker. Tuttle demands payment for the secrets that he previously delivered. Instead of paying Tuttle, Redenius's henchman Estragon strangles Tuttle with a garrote. Overhearing the struggle, Bond races to save Tuttle but Estragon attacks him. The two wind up fighting in the pool where Bond drowns the henchman.

When Playboy security shows up, Bond orders them to detain Redenius for being a spy. Redenius demands proof. Bond destroys Victoria's pearl necklace to reveal a tiny microfilm cartridge that was concealed inside. Because the pearls weren't as smooth as real pearls should be, Bond recognized they were phony. Security arrests Redenius and Bond takes possession of the microfilm.

After a brief conversation between Bond and Heffner, a Playboy Bunny leads Bond to the grotto where they can share a more private moment.

Commentary: The premise of "Midsummer Night's Doom"—Bond meeting Hugh Heffner—is intentionally a parody; it's written in the tradition of 1962's *Alligator* by Christopher Cerf and Michael K. Frith and 1963's *Bond Strikes Camp* by Cyril Connelly. Benson refers to it as an apocryphal story not meant to be considered part of the canon. Instead, it's written as a bit of a lark.

The short story was published in 1999 as a way to commemorate *Playboy* magazine's 45th anniversary issue. Bond and Playboy go back quite a bit. *Playboy* has a history of publishing Fleming's own short stories, such as "The Hildebrand Rarity," "Octopussy," and "The Property of a Lady" and the novels such as *You Only Live Twice* and *The Man with the Golden Gun* were serialized in the publication.

Playboy has published interviews with Fleming and actors who have played Bond, including Sean Connery, Pierce Brosnan, and Daniel Craig. Bond actresses such as Tanya Roberts, Barbara Carrera, Kim Basinger, and Maryam d'Abo have appeared in pictorials, often timed to the release of the latest Bond movie. In *On Her Majesty's Secret Service,* while Bond is pulling off a heist and trying to break into a safe, he settles down to read a copy of *Playboy*, the men's magazine. Benson's own *Zero Minus Ten*, *The Facts of Death*, and *DoubleShot* were previewed in the magazine.

Continuity Nod: When Moneypenny informs Bond that he needs to wear pajamas to the party at the Playboy mansion, the agent responds, "You must be joking." Bond responds in the same way when Q tells him that his Aston Martin has an ejector seat in *Goldfinger*.

Bond's History: Bond enjoys fishing with friends in Jamaica. He previously met Hugh Hefner a long time ago in Jamaica.

Bond's Tastes: When Hugh Hefner says that "gadgets and girls" are his two biggest interests in life, Bond says that he can relate to that worldview. Bond had a subscription to *Playboy* magazine, but he let it lapse. The agent doesn't enjoy rock music or disco dancing, but when called upon, 007 can bust some moves on the dance floor. He prefers ballroom and big-band swing dancing. While in Los Angeles, he drives a Jaguar XK8 Coupe. I believe that the Jaguar is a rental and not the same vehicle he uses in Benson's *The Facts of Death.* Bond relishes wearing a nice pair of pajamas.

Bond's Work Methods: Apparently, Q Branch didn't properly equip Bond on this mission. So Hugh Hefner supplies the necessary gadgets for Bond to complete his assignment. Bond is one of just three Double O agents to have received a first in the SIS's underwater combat course. He can hold his breath for "an extraordinary amount of time."

Assorted Observations:

- Bond encounters several celebrities in the story, including singer Mel Tormé, actors Tony Curtis and Robert Culp, *M*A*S*H* writer Larry Gelbart, and athlete Jim Brown.
- Doug Redenius, the movie mogul, was named after the co-founder of The Ian Fleming Foundation. His fellow co-founders Dr. Michael L. VanBlaricum and John Cork are referenced in *Zero Minus Ten* and *DoubleShot*, respectively.
- The short story's final line, "Then he brought his mouth ruthlessly down on hers" paraphrases the last sentence in *Goldfinger*, "His mouth came ruthlessly down on hers."

HIGH TIME TO KILL (1999)

Author: Raymond Benson

In Brief: James Bond must scale the third-highest peak in the world to find a downed aircraft that contains a formula that allows planes to travel at Mach 7 speeds.

Meaning of Title: The title alludes to the fact that much of the action occurs at a high altitude on Mount Kangchenjunga.

Chronology: Contemporary. Set about two months after *The Facts of Death.*

Operation: Not applicable.

Bastard Meter: Selfish bastard.

Eggs: Served scrambled and not cooked properly, and elsewhere Bond fantasizes about eating May's correctly prepared scrambled eggs.

Insight into Bond: "He had let his loins do his thinking for him once again."

Summary: James Bond and his secretary Helena Marksbury are on holiday in the Bahamas. Bond and Helena attend a dinner party at the home of the former Governor of the Bahamas where Bond learns that the Governor is being blackmailed by a mysterious organization called The Union. The Union has warned the Governor that they will expose his involvement in an unlawful real estate transaction if he does not pay them. Bond agrees to help the Governor get out of this mess. Shortly after their conversation, The Union slits the Governor's throat.

Back in London, Bond plays golf with Bill Tanner at the Stoke Poges Golf Club. At Stoke Poges, Bond meets Dr. Steven Harding, who works at the Defense Evaluation and Research Agency, as well as Royal Air Force Commander Roland Marquis, Bond's rival from Eton. Bond and Tanner agree to play golf against Marquis and Dr. Harding. Bond and Tanner lose the competition.

Harding goes to work at the defense and research agency and speaks to his boss, Dr. Thomas Wood. At their laboratory, they are testing Skin 17, a formula that allows planes to travel at speeds of Mach 7. After the successful test, the formula is placed on a microdot, a way to reduce a text to such a small size that it is nearly undetectable. RAF officer Roland Marquis arrives and shoots Dr. Wood. Marquis and Harding take possession of the microdot, which contains the secret formula, and burn down the lab.

At SIS HQ, Bond advises Helena Marksbury that they should call it quits on their romance now that their vacation is over, and they are back at work.

In Brussels, Harding meets with a surgeon named Dr. Lindenbeek who outlines a surgery in which the microdot could be attached to a pacemaker and inserted into a person's body. Lindenbeek illustrates the operation by drawing it on a sheet of paper. Later, Lindenbeek conducts the surgery on Lee Ming.

Bond and Roland Marquis attend a briefing about the Skin 17 formula, which is worth billions. In order to find Dr. Harding and locate the formula, Bond is dispatched to Brussels, and M dispatches 007 there to locate Harding and retrieve the formula.

Once in Brussels, Bond meets his local contact, Gina Hollander. Bond goes to Harding's hotel room and discovers a drawing of a man's body with a small rectangle drawn on his left breast. As Bond is snooping, Harding enters the room, accompanied by two men, Basil and Lee Ming, the surgeon. Bond and Basil fight but Harding escapes with Lee Ming.

The next day, When Bond first meets Dr. Lindenbeek, he questions him about the drawing. Lindenbeek tells Bond that the Union forced him to insert the microdot into Lee Ming's body.

Elsewhere, Lee Ming has left Brussels and is traveling to Tibet. From there, he can escape to China. Three Nepalese nationals kidnap Lee and take him to an airport, where they board and hijack a small plane. The plane encounters a terrible storm, and crash-lands into the world's third tallest mountain, Kangchenjunga.

M informs Bond that he will join a team that is assigned to climb the mountain and retrieve the microdot.

Elsewhere, The Union is headed by a man known as Le Gérant. Le Gérant informs his group that Lee, who has the microdot, has been kidnapped, by an unknown enemy.

Le Gérant claims that Harding was complicit in Lee's disappearance. Despite Harding's denial, Le Gérant has him assassinated. Le Gérant adds that he has made arrangements for the microdot to be retrieved. In order to get it, The Union will have to work fast; the British, Chinese, and Russian mafia are all sending teams to recover the microdot.

Bond travels to Kathmandu, Nepal where he meets Zakir Bedi, a local operative. Later, a sniper tries to kill Bond but shoots Bedi instead. Bond chases after the sniper, who falls from the roof and breaks his neck while trying to escape. Bond is certain that a SIS leak is the only way the enemy could have learned of his whereabouts.

Bond meets with the climbing team, which includes Otto Schrenk, a last-minute addition. Another member of the team is Dr. Hope Kendall, who will look after any injuries the climbers sustain and Sergeant Chandra Bahadur Gurung, from Nepal. Roland Marquis, Bond's school rival, will serve as the team leader. Bond worries that there is a traitor in their large climbing group.

Bond and the team climb Kangchenjunga over the next few weeks. They face dangerous elements and climbing sicknesses as they slowly ascend. Sergeant Chandra realizes that the Chinese team is gaining on them. Bond and Chandra sabotage the Chinese supplies so that they cannot continue with their climb. Shortly after that, Bond and Chandra are shot at by an unseen sniper.

Bond's group continues their ascent up the mountain. Later, Schrenk's tent catches fire. Schrenk says that the destruction of the tent was related to a fire that he started to boil water. His ice-climbing crampons come loose from his boots as Bond continues his journey, nearly killing him. When he reaches safety, Bond speculates that Schrenk intentionally set fire to his camp so that he could cause a distraction and sabotage Bond's climbing gear.

The climb continues but Dr. Kendall gets sick, so she is forced to return to a lower height on the mountain. Bond checks in with his colleague Bill Tanner. Tanner tells Bond that 007's secretary Helena Marksbury has gone missing and she is likely the leak. Tanner reveals that there is a traitor in his climbing group but that their identity is unknown.

Bond's team finally reaches the plane. Bond finds Lee's frozen body, cuts it open, and retrieves the microdot.

Schrenk knocks Bond unconscious but, before he can eliminate 007, Roland shoots Schrenk. Roland escapes with the microdot and Chandra chases after him. Bond passes out and wakes up to find Dr. Kendal trying to revive him. She tells Bond that nearly everyone in their climbing party has been killed.

Roland sells the microdot to the Russians for a total of $4 billion. After the sale, Chandra confronts Marquis, but Marquis turns the tables and kills Chandra by causing him to fall off the mountain.

Bond and Hope Kendal track Roland to the top of the mountain. Bond gets the drop on Roland, who is delusional from mountain sickness. Bond retrieves the microdot and leaves Roland to die.

Bond and Hope work their way down the mountain. Bond is stopped by Paul Baak, one of the members of their climbing party.

Baak, who is a Union operative, tries to take possession of the microdot but Bond and Hope overcome Baak and then knock him off the mountain.

Days later, Bond is back in London meeting with M who informs Bond that he is up for a commendation. Bond thanks her but declines. M admonishes Bond for his improper relationship with Helena Marksbury, which resulted in her being compromised.

Later still, Bond is at home when Marksbury calls. Marksbury tells Bond that she is in a hotel in Brighton and that Union members are watching her. Bond races to the hotel to protect her but he is too late, Marksbury's throat has been slit. Bond acknowledges a hard truth; while he is sorry that Marksbury has been killed, he is already largely indifferent to her death.

Commentary: Mountain climbing is an integral part of James Bond's origin story. Bond became an orphan when his parents were killed in a climbing accident. So it is only fitting that Benson's third original Bond novel, *High Time to Kill*, would be centered around climbing. Bond's mission is to retrieve military secrets which are in a plane that has crashed towards the top of a mountain. A substantial portion of the book consists of the expedition and the preparation for it. The dangerous ascent provides a surprising variety of threats—not only from the elements and the innate peril of mountain climbing but also from enemy operatives, some of whom are embedded in Bond's team.

As anyone who has read Jon Krakauer's book *Into Thin Air: A Personal Account of the Mt. Everest Disaster* can tell you, mountain climbing is a dangerous business. Coincidentally, Benson and Krakauer's books were both published in the same year. Krakauer's book was released in October 1999, while Benson's was released a bit earlier, in May. Benson takes great care in describing the hazards of mountain climbing and the variety of threats that Bond faces. They include altitude sickness, frostbite, snow blindness, high-altitude cerebral edema, and high-altitude pulmonary edema. If Bond's body does not betray him, then the mountain can get him through extreme cold, avalanches, and snowstorms. There is also the physically grueling act of climbing, which itself has inherent risks.

Benson ratchets up the threats by including not one but two traitors within Bond's climbing group. Moreover, 007 is not the only interested party who is trying to get the formula. The Russian mafia, the Chinese, and the Belgians have also sent climbing teams to get to the plane first. So, it is also a race.

Still, writing about mountain climbing is not without its pitfalls. Many adventure stories work best when the hero is facing a ticking clock. For instance, in *Zero Minus Ten*, Bond only has 10 days to meet his objective. Similarly, the events in *Moonraker* take place over just 5 days. However, mountain climbing is a slow endeavor. The human body needs to acclimate to rising altitudes. As such, Bond's effort to climb the mountain takes him weeks. Still, Benson keeps the action fast-paced, even if the climbing itself sometimes needs to be deliberately controlled.

As engaging as *High Time to Kill* is there is arguably one missed opportunity. As noted, Bond's parents died in a mountain climbing accident. Despite referencing that tragedy in his previous novels, Bond does not mention it in this mountain-climbing-themed book, where it is most relevant. Bond would undoubtedly think about his parents in this scenario. Perhaps, he would wonder if history would repeat itself and he would suffer the same fate as them.

In Fleming's books, Bond faces off with the terrorist organization SPECTRE. In *The Facts of Death*, Benson created the Decada, an evil cabal, based on mathematical principles. Now, in *High Time to Kill*, Benson offers The Union, another crime syndicate. Whereas SPECTRE is often involved in ambitious world-ending schemes, The Union has less ambitious goals, they are often a mercenary outfit who can be hired for a fee. Benson likens SPECTRE to a "corporation," but The Union is more of a "guerrilla" outfit. The Union are known to slash the throats of their enemies from ear to ear. They cut so deeply that their victims' heads are nearly cut off.

In the Eon films, members of SPECTRE wear specifically designed rings that have an Octopus on them. The rings are a way to clandestinely signal to other operatives that they belong to the same organization. Yet, as cool as the rings are, they stand out too much. After all, once SIS is aware of the rings, they can also immediately recognize a SPECTRE agent. In *High Time To Kill,* Benson puts his own spin on the secret signal—each Union agent must have a tattoo burned on the back of their retina.

Benson also finds interesting and unexpected use of SIS's supporting players. In Benson's first novel *Zero Minus Ten*, the author introduced Helena Marksbury as Bond's new secretary and she reappeared in *The Facts of Death*. When *High Time to Kill* begins, Marksbury and Bond are carrying on a secret inter-office romance. Bond even takes Marksbury with him on a vacation to the Bahamas. When they return to the office, Bond thinks it's best if they discontinue their romance. The entanglement causes hurt feelings, awkward moments, and talk of Marksbury transferring out of her assignment. It's the kind of break-up conversation that usually happens between novels, off-screen as it were. Benson does not intend to use

Marksbury simply as another woman that Bond loves and leaves. Instead, she is integrated into the overall narrative.

Throughout *High Time to Kill*, the enemy is one step ahead of Bond and they know his whereabouts and his plans. This causes SIS to suspect that there is a traitor in the ranks. In a twist, that turncoat is revealed to be Marksbury, who is being blackmailed into helping the enemy. In the last chapter Marksbury, who has gone missing, calls Bond for help. He rushes to her hotel room, but arrives too late. She has been killed, her throat slashed. Bond is often riddled with guilt about how the women in his life often face tragic endings. However, the deaths of those women, are not usually Bond's fault. Instead, they meet their grim endings because the world of espionage is a dangerous business. In this instance, Bond is partially to blame. Marksbury would not have been a target for the enemy if he had not broken protocol and had an affair with his assistant.

Continuity Nod: Bond recalls battling Blofeld Francisco Scaramanga. He reminisces about Mary Goodnight, his previous secretary, with whom he had an affair. Goodnight appears in Fleming's last three novels, *On Her Majesty's Secret Service*, *You Only Live Twice,* and *The Man with the Golden Gun*. Benson also reintroduces the former Governor of the Bahamas who appeared in Fleming's short story "Quantum of Solace."

Bond's History: The villain of the story is Roland Marquis, an old-school rival. Not only did Roland beat Bond in a wrestling match (although he had to cheat to win) but Roland also stole Bond's girlfriend from him.

Bond's Personal Life: Bond wonders if his "hardened heart" is the thing that prevents him from developing a relationship with women. Even Bond knows that he is not very good at maintaining contact with women after the mission is over. Bond informs Dr. Hope Kendall that he probably will not keep in touch with her rather than making promises he will not keep. Regardless, he wants to try. There is little chance of a long-distance romance, though. When Hope leaves Bond at the airport, she does not look back to get one last look at him. Instead, she just keeps walking, face forward. It's a sign that Hope is also not emotionally committed to maintaining the relationship. Like *Moonraker*'s Gala Brand, Hope doesn't see Bond as a long-term romantic partner.

Bond reacts negatively to praise, which he finds disturbing. As a form of respect, Bond makes sure that he always follows the local customs.

Bond used to have an affair with a married French film star; their relationship ended when she left for East Asia to shoot a movie.

Bond's Inner Life: Benson's Bond, like Fleming's, suffers from melancholy, which Bond considers to be a "bittersweet companion." His personal demons, in his opinion, are the only thing that can provide him with comfort. Bond admits that he is leading a "wretched solitary" life by the book's conclusion, and expresses little hope.

Bond's Tastes: Bond loathes drinking tea, driving in convertible cars, and he rarely goes to the movies. He enjoys reading, though, and has been poring over books by John le Carré and a former FBI agent about criminal profiling.

Bond's Working Methods: M secretly considers Bond to be her best agent, although she would never tell him that. Bond routinely works with an instructor to ensure that his shooting is still top-notch. His instructor will never admit it, but Bond is the best shot in SIS. An Instructor in *Moonraker* made a similar observation. Bond rejects another trainer's advice to never think that you are better than your opponent. For Bond, his belief in himself that he will remain victorious provides the psychological edge that he always needs.

Assorted Commentary:

- Retirement has been good for Sir Miles Messervy. Though his medical status might have contributed to his leaving the Secret Intelligence Service, Messervy's health has improved considerably.
- Bond's teenage sweetheart is named Felicity Mountjoy.
- A doctor gives Bond a prostate exam.
- Bond has sexual intercourse on the side of a mountain, 7900 meters above sea level.
- Benson uses the name George Almond for an amateur artist in the book. In real life, Almond provided illustrations for several Bond-related works, including for the Bond fan magazines, *Bondage* and *007*.
- *High Time to Kill* is the first book in Benson's Union Trilogy, a series of books that is connected by its central adversary—The Union.
- The working title of *High Time to Kill* was *A Better Way to Die.*[115]

"LIVE AT FIVE" (1999)

Author: Raymond Benson

In Brief: Bond helps an Olympic skater from the U.S.S.R. defect on live television.

Meaning of Title: The action is captured by a local news crew, and is aired live at five.

Chronology: Contemporary. Flashback is set before Raymond Benson's novels, during the Cold War.

Operation: Not applicable.

Bastard Meter: None.

Eggs: None.

Insight into Bond: "Bond was never one to wallow in nostalgia."

Summary: Bond is on his way to a date with a beautiful woman at the bar in the Ritz Hotel in London. He recalls a past mission.

Flashback to Chicago, years ago. Bond watches a Russian Olympic skater Natalia Lustokov practice. Natalia wants to defect from the U.S.S.R., but she is being watched by her coach and two bodyguards. Max, an FBI agent, and Janet Davies, a local reporter covering the event, are also present.

Bond puts on his ice skates and joins Natalia on the ice. The bodyguards spot Bond, get on the ice, and try to put the agent out of commission. Bond fights back and incapacitates the men. Natalia's coach grabs his gun and shoots at Bond. The shot misses Bond, but the gunfire causes panic. In the chaos, Natalia vanishes.

Two hours later, Bond joins the FBI agent and Natalia at a safe house, from which she will defect. They watch a news segment depicting Bond's brawl on the ice.

Back to the present day, Bond arrives at the Ritz hotel and takes a seat at the bar next to reporter Janet Davies.

Commentary: Wherever James Bond goes, chaos follows. In his wake, Bond leaves dead bodies, wrecked cars, sunken boats, and derailed trains. In his defense, the destruction of property is a fair price to pay if it means that lives are saved. Benson's short story "Live at

Five" proposes that the mayhem is not always a byproduct of the mission; it can be essential to its success.

In "Live at Five," Bond must aid in the defection of Olympic ice skater Natalia Lustokov. The plan is that Lustokov will try to get away during skating practice. But she is watched like a hawk by her coach and two bodyguards. So James creates a bit of a ruckus. First, skating with her and nailing a series of tricky maneuvers. However, Natalia's bodyguards do not want anyone near the prized skater, so they jump on the ice and try to grab Bond. Bond is having none of that. So he knocks the guards into each other, causing them to all fall. Bond dispatches the coach when he enters the rink and chases after Bond. While the bodyguards, the coach, and even Benson's readers are focused on Bond, Lustokov slips away.

Benson's ploy is an effective one. Benson effectively uses the action on ice as a magician might use a flash of fire, as a means to misdirect the viewer from Bond's ultimate goal, to aid in the defection of the Olympic star. While all the other characters' attention is on Bond, they lose track of where Lustokov is on the rink. It's during this time that Lustokov sneaks away and is picked up by the American authorities who whisk her to safety.

Bond vs the bumbling guards is the kind of action sequence that would not be out of place in a Roger Moore Bond movie. The set piece—Bond on ice taking on a series of goons—recalls a similar scene in *For Your Eyes Only.* Unlike the Bond movies, there are no jokes or one-liners in the short story. In fact, Benson does not give Bond any dialogue. Instead, the agent is silent throughout.

At least, Bond does not speak in the version of the story that was published in *TV Guide* in 1999. For space reasons, the magazine cut the framing device in which Bond is on his way to a date with Janet Davies, the news reporter who covered the event. In the unedited text, later collected in the anthology book *Choice of Weapons*, Bond does have one line of dialogue—"Is this seat taken?" It's a question he poses to Davies.

There is another significant difference between the two texts. In the version that appears in *TV Guide*, Davies was simply reporting on the Olympic skater. In the complete version, it is implied that she was an accomplice in the defection.

Bond's Personal Life: Bond is an expert skier, but he considers himself to be merely an adequate skater. Still, he can keep up with the Olympic skater and together they perfectly perform a few tricky moves, including a jump named the salchow. He can also fight while ice skating.

Bond's Work Methods: Bond gets a measure of joy and personal satisfaction for completing the mission.

Assorted Observations:

- The FBI agent who helps Bond is named after Benson's son Max.
- The local reporter, Janet Davies, was named after the Chicago-based broadcaster Janet Davies.

THE WORLD IS NOT ENOUGH (1999)

Author: Raymond Benson

In Brief: Bond is sent to protect M's family friend, Elektra King, from a madman who once kidnapped her.

Meaning of Title: Bond's family motto.

Chronology: Contemporary. After the events of the *Tomorrow Never Dies* novelization.

Operation: Not applicable.

Bastard Meter: Bastard Bond, as thought by the villain Renard.

Eggs: Bond does not order any.

Insight into Bond: "You're nothing but a dim-witted bouncer at a fancy English club run by your betters. Too busy chasing the member's daughters."

Summary: Bond is sent to recover Sir Robert King's money in Bilbao, Spain. Bond has been asked to procure the funds, as a personal favor to M who is friends with King and his daughter Elektra. Bond meets with the banker, Lachaise, who is going to facilitate the transaction. Lachaise's associate Giulietta da Vinci gives Bond a case full of King's cash. Bond demands that Lachaise give him the name of the man who killed 0012. Before he can provide it, Lachaise is killed by Giulietta who escapes. Lachaise's men nearly kill Bond, but an unknown sniper shoots them, saving Bond.

At MI6, Bond meets with M and Sir Robert King, who is wearing a lapel pin. King inspects the recovered money, touching it. After King leaves Bond fixes M a drink and notices a strange chemical reaction occurring in the ice that King just handled. Bond realizes that the money in the briefcase must have been coated with a chemical that could cause a deadly explosion. Bond chases after King but it's too late. A bomb goes off at MI6 headquarters, causing the wall of the building to collapse. Bond spots Giulietta, the woman from Spain. Bond boards Q's boat and pursues her down the River Thames. Giuletta climbs into a hot air balloon and tries to get away but Bond closes in. Rather than be captured, Giuletta kills herself, injuring Bond's shoulder in the process.

M calls a meeting where she demands that her top agents look into King's murder. Bond's arm injury prevents him from being on active duty. Bond seduces his doctor who gives him the all-clear to return to work. When Bond meets with Q, the Quartermaster gives the agent the equipment he needs for the mission and introduces Bond to his colleague, "R." Q leaves through a trap door in a literal cloud of smoke, after offering parting advice.

Bond looks into Elektra King's kidnapping and discovers that the ransom figure that King paid for Elektra's return was the same amount that Bond recovered in Spain.

M tells Bond that Elektra's kidnapper is an anarchist named Victor "Renard" Zokas. Previously, 009 shot Renard in the head. Renard survived but the bullet remains. Nowadays, the bullet is killing the terrorist, but it is also making him stronger and immune to pain. M instructs Bond to protect Elektra.

Bond flies to the Caucasus and meets Elektra King, who is now the head of her father's oil company. Elektra's company is building an 800-mile pipeline that bypasses Iran, Iraq, and Syria. Bond joins Elektra on a site visit where there is a dispute with the villagers about the location of the pipe. The villagers claim that the pipe is being built on their sacred land. Elektra agrees to reroute the pipe, a move that will cost millions of dollars. But Elektra insists that rerouting the pipe is the right thing to do.

Elektra and Bond go skiing together but an assassination attempt on Elektra interrupts their enjoyment. Bond protects Elektra and kills the would-be assassins who are operating Parahawks, Russian military snow vehicles. When Bond examines the assailants' equipment, he discovers an engraving of the Russian Atomic Energy Department and concludes that Renard is responsible for the assault.

Bond and Elektra go to Baku, Azerbaijan where King Industries is conducting business. They visit the Casino L'Or Noir where they meet Valentin Zukovsky, the proprietor. Zukovsky is an ex-KGB agent who has helped Bond before. Bond asks Zukovsky how Renard got a hold of the Parahawks that the assassins piloted when they attempted to kill Elektra. Instead of answering, Zukovsky points out that Elektra is having a grand time while gambling.

Bond checks on Elektra, who is placing large bets without any fear of the consequences. She explains, "There's no point in living unless I can feel alive." Elektra makes a wild bet and loses $1 million.

Elektra's security expert Sasha Davidov meets with Renard and Dr. Mikhail Arkov, of the Russian Atomic Energy Department. In a show of force, Renard injures Davidov's hand. When Arkov expresses some concern about the mission, Renard kills him. Handing over Arkov's ID, Renard tells Davidov to fill in for the now-dead Arkov.

Back at the hotel, Bond sees that Davidov's hand has been damaged. Bond follows Davidov and finds Arkov's body in the back of his car. Then, Bond follows Davidov to a small airfield where he finds a military transport plane. Bond kills Davidov, takes Arkov's ID, and boards the plane, which flies to Kazakhstan. At his destination, Bond sees a Land Rover with the Atomic Energy Department logo on it. It's the same logo that the men who tried to kill Elektra had on them.

Posing as Dr. Arkov, Bond meets Christmas Jones, a nuclear physicist. Jones does not trust Bond, but she tells him to meet his colleagues at the bottom of the mine shaft. There, Bond catches Renard planting a bomb. When Bond threatens Renard, the villain replies, "There is no point in living if you can't feel alive." It is the same phrase that Elektra used. Colonel Akakievich arrives on the scene with two soldiers who capture Bond. Renard squeezes Bond in the shoulder, the exact spot where he was injured. Before Renard can kill Bond and Jones, they escape. Renard takes the tracking card out of the bomb so that neither he nor the bomb can be found.

Back at MI6, Robinson informs M that Colonel Akakievich is most likely to blame for stealing the bomb and that the Russian Atomic Agency has reported that Dr. Arkov has vanished. Elektra calls M and pleads with her to come to Baku.

When M arrives, Bond meets with her and voices his growing suspicions of Elektra. Bond notes that both Elektra and Renard used the same phrase, suggesting that they are in league with each other. Bond suspects that Elektra told Renard about his shoulder injury. He argues Elektra is suffering from a case of Stockholm Syndrome. M disagrees with Bond. M receives word that Renard has a transporter plane and a nuclear bomb. Bond believes that Renard is going to put the bomb in the pipeline. Bond and Jones rush to diffuse it.

Bond and Jones enter the pipeline and find the bomb. Bond suspects that the bomb does not have nuclear power. So he instructs Jones to let the device detonate so that Renard will believe Bond perished in the explosion.

Elektra accuses M of telling her father not to pay the kidnappers. Elektra accuses M of being more concerned with catching her kidnappers at the expense of her safety. Elektra confesses that she helped arrange her father's death.

Bond contacts MI6 and learns that M and Elektra are missing. Elektra takes M to the Maiden's Tower, a structure just off the coast of Istanbul where she reunites with Renard.

Bond and Jones meet up with Valentin Zukovsky. Bond asks Zukovsky about his dealings with Elektra. Zukovsky admits that the million dollars that Elektra lost at the tables were payments for military equipment that his nephew is delivering to her in Istanbul.

Renard takes control of a Russian nuclear submarine that was delivered to him by Zukovsky's nephew, Captain Nikolai. Renard takes control of the submarine and kills Zukovsky's nephew. While in jail, M uses a location card, which was taken from one of the bombs, to signal her location to MI6.

One of Zukovsky's men changes allegiances, captures Bond, and brings him to Elektra. Elektra tortures Bond, who is fastened to a wooden chair. Before Elektra can kill Bond, Zukovsky arrives to save Bond and avenge his nephew's death. Elektra shoots Zukovsky, who dies after freeing Bond. Bond kills Elektra and chases after Renard.

Bond boards the submarine and finds Jones. Together, they locate Renard who is planning to blow up the submarine with a nuclear bomb. Bond kills Renard by causing a plutonium rod to impale the villain's heart. Bond seals off the bomb so that there will be no radiation leakage. Bond and Jones escape in a nearby boat as the submarine explodes and descends to the sea floor.

Later, M returns to London; she is ready for duty. Bond and Christmas enjoy the fireworks over Istanbul.

Commentary: Benson's novelization *The World Is Not Enough* faithfully adapts the story by Neil Purvis and Robert Wade and the screenplay by Purvis, Wade, and *GoldenEye* writer Bruce Feirstein. As Benson did with the *Tomorrow Never Dies* novelization, he fleshes out the characters' backstory and their relationships with one another. For instance, in the Eon film, audiences learn that Victor "Renard" Zokas kidnapped Elektra King. Elektra exhibited symptoms of Stockholm syndrome during the period and appeared to develop feelings for Renard. Benson takes the reader inside that dynamic and also elaborates on how Renard came to kidnap her. In Benson's novelization, he explains that Renard became obsessed with Elektra. Benson also expands on Elektra's relationship with her father. Benson describes how Elektra felt abandoned by her father and M's decision not to pay the kidnapper's ransom (pocket change to her family) and instead used her as bait to capture the criminals.

In the novelization, Benson also fleshed out Elektra's relationship with M. After Elektra's mother died of cancer, M became a surrogate mother to Elektra.

The novelization provides additional weight to Elektra's death and Benson gives her a touching final moment. After Bond shoots her, a fatally wounded Elektra sings a lullaby. It's a tender and deserved moment. Elektra is the story's villain, but she also suffered at the hands of her kidnapper. Her death is not a triumphant victory for Bond. Instead, it's a sad ending to a once-promising life.

Benson also helps chart the progress of Bond's personal and professional relationship with the "new" M. Bond's relationship with M in the first sixteen Eon films was essentially static. In the Brosnan era, their relationship has an arc. In *GoldenEye*, Bond and M are largely antagonistic towards each other. By the end of that film and throughout *Tomorrow Never Dies*, they have both warmed to each other. In *The World Is Not Enough*, they have mutual respect and fondness for each other. In the novelization, Benson reveals that Bond hopes that M reciprocates his feelings.

Benson heightens the stakes in Bond's pre-title mission to recover a briefcase full of cash. In it, Bond questions a banker about the death of an unspecific MI6 agent. In the book, Benson reveals that the fallen agent was actually 0012. Without that crucial detail, the assignment seems better suited to an "errand boy" (the chapter's title) rather than a Double O agent.

There are a few snippets of dialogue that made it to the novelization that were cut from the film. Bond's "things we do for England" joke about making love to his doctor so that he could be cleared for active duty and M's remark that "the world is not populated by madmen who can hollow out volcanoes, fill them with big breasted women, and threaten the world with nuclear annihilation" were omitted from the final cut.[116] The "things we do for England" is a joke that appeared in the film *Thunderball*. In it, Bond had to make love to an enemy agent, so the line made sense. However, it does not quite work when it is about a woman that Bond has been intimate with in the past. The "hollow out volcanoes" line was written by Bruce Feirstein, and because he referenced it in an interview I conducted, I believe it is one of his favorites.[117]

Bond's Inner Life: In both Eon's film and Benson's novelization, Elektra asks Bond about what he does to survive. In both mediums, Bond replies that he takes pleasure in great beauty. In the film, audiences accept the answer. In the novelization, Benson clarifies that Bond's response is only a bluff and a way to deflect from his true feelings.

Personal Life: Bond has suffered many losses. As a result, he has "given up" on love. To move beyond grief, he has learned to always look towards the future, never the past. This sentiment echoes his thought process in *From Russia with Love,* "Never job backwards." In the films, it sometimes seems that Bond just magically speaks a little of nearly every foreign language. Moviegoers are left to wonder how Bond became such a cunning linguist. Benson explains how. Bond studies languages of his own accord.

Bond's Tastes: Bond appreciates and respects Eastern philosophy. Bond drives an Aston Martin and a BMW and not Fleming's Bentley. This is in keeping with the film's continuity.

Bond's Work Methods: The death of a Double O agent always sends ripples throughout the entire organization. Benson likens it to a death in the family. When M is kidnapped, Bill Tanner becomes the acting head of the agency. To enter MI6 headquarters, Bond must always pass through a careful security screening. In addition to his Walther PPK Bond carries a throwing knife, which he keeps concealed and strapped on his back.

Assorted Observations:

- Screenwriter Bruce Feirstein's credit was mistakenly left off of the *GoldenEye* novelization.
- In the novelization, Benson implies that Zukovsky might have survived his wounds. In the film, he perishes.
- Not all additions to the story were Benson's inventions. Some of the scenes and lines and dialogue were in the script that he was novelizing. Some of those scenes were shot and deleted from the final cut.[118]
- The villain Victor Zokas has multiple nicknames. He is alternatively known as Renard, the anarchist (as his goal is chaos), and the fox, as he is as stealthy as one.
- 0012 had only been an agent for a short while before he was killed in Omsk, Russia. Bond and 0012 were only casually acquainted. 009 is on a mission in East Asia.

DOUBLESHOT (2000)

Author: Raymond Benson

In Brief: James Bond must stop a lookalike enemy agent from conducting a plot to assassinate the prime ministers of Britain and Spain at a peace summit. If Bond fails, a former bullfighter who is now a mafia boss will be elected governor of Gibraltar, and Bond will be held accountable for the murders.

Meaning of Title: Bond's doppelganger or "double" is committing a series of crimes and terrorist acts in London and Tangiers. The title also alludes to two female CIA agents who are identical twins.

Chronology: Contemporary. Set two months after the events of *High Time to Kill*.

Operation: Not applicable.

Bastard Meter: An elusive bastard.

Eggs: Disappointingly prepared.

Insight into Bond: "James Bond exercised his license to kill and pulled the trigger. He felt no remorse, but it didn't give him any satisfaction either. He felt absolutely nothing."

Summary: [The book begins *en media res*, in the middle of things.] James Bond is apparently under the mind control of Nadir Yassassin, a member of the for-hire terrorist group The Union. Yassassin has ordered Bond to infiltrate a meeting between Britain and Spain's Prime Minister. The Union plans to kill the Prime Ministers, pin the blame on Bond, and install Domingo Espada, a former bullfighter with political ambitions, as the new Governor of Gibraltar. Bond appears ready to carry out The Union's sinister plot.

Two weeks earlier. In Northern Africa, The Union holds a meeting of their terrorist group. Among those in attendance are its leader, Le Gérant, and his lieutenants, Julius Wilcox, Jimmy Powers, and Yassassin. Le Gérant explains that Espada wants to hire The Union in his bid to rise to power. Espada's ally Margareta Piel, aka Praying Mantis, will aid their plan. Le Gérant intends to hire mercenary Peredur Glyn to eliminate 007.

In England, Bond is suffering from headaches and blackouts that stem from injuries that he recently sustained in the Himalayas (*High Time to Kill*). At dinner in a Chinese restaurant, Bond finds a disconcerting message in his fortune cookie—Meeting Your Double Means Certain Death. After dinner, Bond sees a vision of his dead wife, Tracy. Soon thereafter, Bond sees a man on the street who looks like him. Later, Bond blacks out and wakes up at home.

Bond goes to his office and investigates the death of Helena Marksbury, his assistant who was murdered by The Union (*High Time to Kill*). He calls Felix Leiter, and asks him to look into the whereabouts of three Union operatives, Samuel Anderson, James Powers, and Julius Wilcox. Bond receives a package that contains a pornographic magazine that was mailed to him from a local adult bookshop in Soho.

007 goes to New Scotland Yard to visit Detective Inspector Howard, who is tasked with investigating Helena's death. Detective Howards tells Bond that they do not have any leads in the case but mentions that the owner of Helena's building is a man named Michael Clayton who, with his partner Walter van Breeschooten, owns several bookshops in Soho.

In Spain, Domingo Espada and Margareta Piel meet with Union operative Yassasin. Yassasin tells Espada that The Union will help Espada kill the British and Spanish Prime Ministers. After the meeting, Espada, a former bullfighter, kills a disloyal employee by having a bull gouge him.

Bond goes to the pornography shop in Soho and learns the location of van Breeschooten's office address. Bond visits van Breeschooten's office and discovers that he has plans to fly from London to Morocco that night. Then, Bond overhears van Breeschooten talking to his associate, Michael Clayton, about Le Gérant's plans to move The Union headquarters out of Casablanca.

Following another panic attack, Bond returns to his office. There, he hears a message from Felix Leiter informing him that Union lieutenant Samuel Anderson is dead, but his associates James Powers and Julius Wilcox are alive and operating out of North Africa.

Bond reports what he knows to Detective Howard of Scotland Yard and M. M tells Bond that he lacks the objectivity to work on the case and advises Bond to take some time off and go to Jamaica. Bond uses his SIS computer to find out that Clayton and van Breeschooten have booked a flight to Casablanca and have a stopover in Tangier, Morocco. Ignoring M's orders, Bond books a flight to Tangier that is scheduled to depart the next day.

Later that night, Bond tries to contact Dr. Kimberly Feare, who is treating him for the blackouts and anxiety attacks, but she is unavailable. So, 007 tracks Feare down at a restaurant and then follows her home. After explaining his symptoms to the doctor, Feare invites Bond up to her apartment so that she can examine him.

After the examination, Feare tells Bond that the medication he has been taking is not reducing the size of the lesion on his brain that he sustained in the Himalayas. Feare instructs Bond to double his dosage. As their attraction grows, Bond and Feare succumb to their impulses.

Bond wakes up the next day in Feare's apartment and discovers that her throat has been slashed with a kitchen knife. Realizing that he is being framed for murder, Bond panics and leaves her flat. Then, he takes the plane to Tangier.

At a Union meeting, Le Gérant announces that Bond is heading to Tangier, just as he planned. Le Gérant also says that when Union agents van Breeschooten and Clayton arrive they will go to their terrorist training camp in the mountains.

When Bond reaches Tangier, he visits an old friend, Latif Reggab, at his home. Bond asks Reggab if he knows Le Gérant's true identity. Reggab suspects that the Union head could be a Corsican named Olivier Cesari. Reggab shows 007 surveillance photos of Clayton and van Breeschooten at the terrorist training camp.

Back in London, Tanner informs M that Dr. Feare is dead, and Bond is missing. They decide that 001 will provide protection during the upcoming meeting between the British and Spanish Prime Ministers regarding the sovereignty of Gibraltar.

In the Spanish village of Ronda, Margareta Piel enters the hotel room of Robert Rojo, a man who absconded with one of Espada's sex slaves. Piel makes love to Rojo and then kills him. That night, Bond and Reggab visit the Union's terrorist training camp. At the camp, Bond recognizes a man from the adult bookshop in Soho. Bond confronts Clayton and demands the address of the Union headquarters. After Clayton divulges the information, Bond kills the Union agent who Bond blames for his secretary's death.

The next day, Bond reads a newspaper report concerning a terrorist attack on a ferry that resulted in the death of several British tourists; the killer looks suspiciously like Bond. The police try to apprehend Bond but he escapes. In London, M watches footage of the attack and notes the striking resemblance to 007.

Bond takes a train to Casablanca. On the train, he meets an American named Heidi Taunt. They strike up a conversation and agree to meet for dinner that night. Later, Bond tries to talk to Heidi, but she ignores him. Still later, Bond sees Heidi on the train but this time she is glad to see him. A little bit later, he bumps into Heidi again and this time she is cold to him. Bond does not know what to make out of her erratic behavior. That night, Bond shows up to dinner and sees Heidi waiting with her identical twin sister, Hedy. Bond realizes that he has been mistaking the two throughout the day.

The next day, Bond finds and kills Walter van Breeschooten, the Union lieutenant who played a part in Helena's death. Checking van Breeschooten's pockets Bond discovers two tickets to a bullfight in Malaga, Spain. He also finds a map of Spain with an X over a town close to Marbella. As Bond plans his next move, the nearby Union's headquarters is blown to smithereens. The police spot Bond. With Hedy's help, he gets away.

Hedy takes 007 to Heidi at the CIA's Casablanca headquarters. Heidi identifies her and Hedy as CIA agents who are working on a shared cover of "Hillary Taunt." Heidi further explains that she and her sister were sent to find Bond and take him back to London. Bond tells them that Domingo Espada is somehow involved in the murder of Dr. Feare and the shooting of British tourists. He shows them the map, which they say identifies Espada's home. They agree to work together to stop the Union. Bond checks in with M and informs her that Michael Clayton, a recruiter for Union operatives, has a cousin in London. Bond and the Taunt twins agree to go to Spain via the CIA's boat.

In London, Detective Inspector Howard tells Bill Tanner that they have forensic evidence proving that Bond killed Dr. Feare. Tanner tells M that Bond is acting as Domingo Espada's bodyguard. Believing that Bond has turned, M gives Tanner the authority to have 001 kill Bond.

In Spain, Bond and the Taunt Twins meet Javier Rojo, a bullfighter and brother of Robert Rojo who Espada had killed. Bond tells Javier that Espada is part of a plan that is somehow linked to the Union and the Gibraltar summit. Union member Jimmy Powers secretly follows Bond.

In his speech, Domingo Espada discusses the Gibraltar conference that will take place the next day. Espada also asks for volunteers to join his security force. Then Javier Rojo enters the ring, and the bullfight starts. Javier is distracted by one of his banderilleros wearing a red outfit and is impaled by the bull as a result. The banderillero looks like a dead ringer for Bond. Margareta knocks Bond out and takes him to Espada's estate.

Jimmy Powers enters the King's Chapel in Gibraltar and hides a cache of weapons inside. Later, Margareta Piel shows Bond a closed-circuit television that displays a private dinner that Espada is hosting. During the dinner, Espada explains that the assassin who will kill the two Prime Ministers looks exactly like Bond.

Bond learns that the medication that he has been taking has been tampered with. Instead of relieving him of pain from the head trauma, the medication is causing him to experience panic attacks and blackouts. Bond also learns that The Union performed plastic surgery on a mercenary named Peredur Glyn so that he would resemble Bond. It was Glyn who carried out the series of terrorist while posing as Bond in order to frame him.

Bond is taken to a bullring, where he is forced to fight a bull. Bond acquits himself well but then Peredur Glyn jumps into the ring. Bond and Glyn fight each other until Bond passes out, apparently killed.

Margareta meets a man whom she believes to be Glyn. Glyn explains that he needs to meet up with Hillary Taunt. Two hours later, Glyn calls Margareta and explains that there has been an emergency. When Margareta arrives, Glyn is covered in blood. He shows her the dead body of Hillary Taunt, who he says he accidentally killed. Later, Margaret and Glyn meet up and make love.

The next day, Estrada, Margareta, and the rest of the Union operatives prepare for the attack on the Gibraltar summit. As part of the plan, Glyn will kill the two Prime Ministers and then Margareta will murder Glyn. When the conference begins, Margareta realizes that the man she thought to be Glyn is actually Bond. Regardless, Margareta insists that Bond carry out the assassination. The British Prime Minister enters the room, along with 001. Just then, Heidi Taunt enters and shouts for everyone to get down. As gunfire breaks out, 001 saves the British Prime Minister. Simultaneously, Bond, Heidi and Hedy Taunt take out the rest, including Espapda, Margareta, and Powers. Yassassin is taken into SIS custody and interrogated.

Later, Bond explains to M that he posed as Glyn and faked Hillary Taunt's death. Sir James Moloney, a neurologist who works with the SIS, explains how the Union exploited Bond's physical and emotional weaknesses through the medication that he was taking. Bond undergoes surgery which resolves his mental health issues. Heidi and Hedy Taunt meet up with Bond and the three of them get frisky.

Commentary:

Even though Alfred Hitchcock never directed a Bond movie, his impact on the series is clear. The airplane attack in From Russia with Love could almost be lifted from Hitchcock's North by Northwest, in which Cary Grant is similarly threatened. Raymond Benson effectively applies Hitchcock-like motifs to Bond's adventures in his novel *DoubleShot*.

Hitchcock's theory of suspense is something that the Bond filmmakers have closely followed. According to Hitchcock, if a bomb goes off without the audience first knowing about it, then the audience is surprised. In this instance, the audience experiences a fleeting sense of excitement. However, if the audience is aware of the bomb before it explodes, the tension increases as they anticipate the detonation. Hitchcock favored suspense over surprise because suspense keeps the audience emotionally invested for a longer time. Many Bond movies have their own version of a ticking bomb. *Goldfinger*, *Octopussy,* and *GoldenEye* are among the Bond films that have an actual ticking clock.

Despite having an impact on the movies, Hitchcock has minimal influence over the continuation novels. Raymond Benson's *DoubleShot* is a notable exception. Benson's book draws from Hitchcock's "Wrong Man" plot device in which an innocent person is wrongly accused of murder. The innocent party spends the rest of the movie on the run from the authorities, while they track the real killer, and prove their innocence. Hitchcock films that include that plot device include *The 39 Steps, Strangers on a Train*, the aforementioned *North by Northwest*, and the appropriately titled *The Wrong Man.* In *DoubleShot*, Bond wakes up next to the dead body of a woman. Bond panics and flees the scene. For the rest of the book, Bond is on the run, trying to clear his name while the police, CIA, and SIS question his innocence. Things get so dire for Bond that M authorizes 001 to eliminate him.

Hitchcock's films also explore the notion of doubles. Doubles can be lookalikes (*The Wrong Man*), have split personalities (*Psycho*, *Shadow of a Doubt*), or pose as someone else (*Vertigo*). In *DoubleShot*, Benson incorporates some of these tropes. At first, Bond thinks he sees his own double on the street. As the plot unfolds, the agent realizes that he is not seeing things. Bond eventually learns that The Union enlisted an enemy agent to undergo plastic surgery so that they could look like Bond's doppelganger. At one point, Bond poses as his own double and attempts to infiltrate the enemy.

In the end, Benson makes Bond his own worst enemy. Bond and his double face off in a fight to the death. It is Bond vs "Bond," where Bond eventually comes out on top. Bond's allies are also doubles. Heidi and Hedy Taunts are twin sisters and CIA agents who operate under the shared identity of "Hillary Taunt." They alternate playing Hillary and can confuse the enemy by switching parts.

The archetypal Hitchcock hero is a flawed character who is often consumed by their own guilt. Notable examples are *Vertigo*'s James Stewart and *Spellbound*'s Gregory Peck. In *DoubleShot*, Bond feels responsible for the death of Helena Marksbury, his personal secretary. Hitchcock's heroes sometimes also suffer from a psychological condition; *Marnie*'s Tippi Hedren is a kleptomaniac; Stewart's character suffers from a fear of heights, and Peck's has a phobia of parallel lines. Similarly, Bond suffers from intense anxiety. Although, in 007's case, Bond's paranoia is brought upon by drugs that he has unwittingly taken.

DoubleShot serves as a sort of preface to Benson's post-Bond works. After Bond, Benson mostly shied away from the spy genre though he didn't entirely give it up (see *Splinter Cell* and "Ghosts"). Rather, Benson's non-Bond novels frequently center on mystery (*The Mad, Mad Murders of Marigold Way*), suspense (*The Secrets on Chicory Lane*), crime (*Blues in the Dark*), and even the paranormal (*Destiny: A Ghost Noir*). Putting aside Benson's oeuvre, Bond fans can look at it as a Bond and Hitchcock as a fun hybrid.

Continuity Nod: Bond thinks he sees his deceased wife, Tracy, but her presence is really the consequence of a reaction from taking tainted medicine. Bond's mental state following the death of his wife and his subsequent trip to Japan to seek revenge on Blofeld are mentioned. Bond's housekeeper May is name-checked but she does not turn up. Felix Leiter briefly appears and provides Bond with intelligence about the opposition. Not only are the events of Benson's previous novel *High Time to Kill* referenced, but the Union's failure in the Himalayas regarding their Skin 17 project, is the catalyst for their actions in *DoubleSh*ot. Margareta Piel, a Union operative, describes Bond's mouth as "somewhat cruel," which is also how Fleming described it.

Bond's History: Bond has been to Tangiers on multiple occasions.

Bond's Personal Life: Bond enjoys swimming in a private cove at his house in Jamaica, where a local named Ramsey works as a housekeeper and cook. Since the death of Helena Marksbury in the last novel, Bond has refrained from sex. He does not watch television as he thinks doing so is a form of torture.

Bond's Inner Life: Bond feels like he is "drowning" in depression. He is also suffering from anxiety, which is causing him to drink more. The strain on Bond causes the agent to wonder if it is time to retire, "Had his career finally come to an end?... Was it time to give it up? Had he begun to pay the price for living on the edge for so long?" He even wonders if he's lost his mind and is going insane. He is also experiencing hallucinations, delusions, and paranoia.

Bond's Tastes: Bond is a regular at a Chinese restaurant in London and he likes his food to be prepared particularly spicy, something that this restaurant has not been able to reliably achieve. Bond (like Fleming) does not like tea but, as a sign of respect to his host who is serving it, Bond feigns appreciation for the beverage. Bond is usually in the driver's seat, so when he's in the back seat of the car, he feels a special pleasure in not being in charge for once.

Bond's Work Methods: Bond notes that the SIS accountant has a stressful job. Bond accepts his role as a "blunt instrument of death" and when he kills a man he has learned to "shut himself off from every possible emotion" so that he can perform his duties "coldly and objectively." Bond's photographic memory and his ability to quietly move (run, jump, etc.) quickly are great assets to his work as a spy. 007 and 001 know each other.

Assorted Observations:

- Benson uses the name John Cork as an alias. Cork is a notable Bond scholar who has written several Bond books and has produced numerous extras for Bond DVDs.
- Further indication of Benson's appreciation for Hitchcock is demonstrated by the title of his 2017 short story "The MacGuffin," a reference to the item that the characters in the story are after.

NEVER DREAM OF DYING (2001)

Author: Raymond Benson

In Brief: James Bond must stop Union head Le Gérant from exploding a bomb at the Cannes Film Festival. 007 also reunites with his former father-in-law, Marc-Ange Draco, who is secretly seeking revenge.

Meaning of Title: A reference to the proverb that if you dream of dying, you just might die in real life.

Chronology: Contemporary. Set after the events of *DoubleShot.*

Operation: Not applicable.

Bastard Meter: Standard level bastard.

Eggs: Scrambled.

Insight into Bond: "His steely reserve was a façade that he had perfected with years of experience. The reality was that he was only human and was susceptible to pain, fear, and anxiety like anyone else. What made him different was how he acted under the pressure."

Summary: James Bond is with his old ally René Mathis and the French national police force at a movie studio in Nice. Mathis and Bond are there to observe the police's raid on the terrorist group The Union, whose leader is known by the alias Le Gérant. The police believe that Union member Julius Wilcox is moving arms out of the studio. Suddenly, a bomb goes off; the entire operation is merely a ruse to lure the French police into a trap. A gunfight ensues. To prevent The Union members from getting away, Bond shoots at a barrel of gasoline, which causes a tremendous explosion. Union members are killed but so are several civilians. As a result of the fiasco, Bond is recalled to London, and Mathis is suspended.

Four months later, René Mathis is at a casino in Monaco; he's trying to learn Le Gérant's true identity by following up on a lead on his own initiative. Mathis observes a blind man named Pierre Rodiac who he suspects might be the Union leader. Mathis also thinks that the new owner of Bisset Film Studios, Léon Essinger, is in league with The Union. The Union is believed to have acquired a new explosive material, CL-20, developed by the US Air Force and stolen from the

French government. Rodiac is traveling on a yacht registered to Emile Cirendini, a member of the Corsican mafia.

Union lieutenant Julius Wilcox meets with Léon Essinger. The Union has helped Essinger in the past, now it's time for Essinger to return the favor.

In London, Bond meets his new assistant, Nigel Smith. Then, M tells 007 that his new assignment will involve Goro Yoshida, a Japanese billionaire with terrorist ties. However, Bond requests to stay on the hunt for The Union. M reluctantly agrees and gives the agent two weeks to find out information on Le Gérant.

Union strategist Nadir Yassasin is being held in prison. The prison's eye doctor spots an unusual lesion on Yassasin's retina. Soon thereafter, Union operative Staff Officer Evans slits Yassasin's throat. An examination reveals that Evans has the same tattoo on his retina. Bond interrogates Evans, who reveals that Union members are required to get the same tattoo as a secret identifying mark. The procedure is carried out in Paris by an ophthalmologist.

Near Japan, in the Kuril Islands, Corsican mafia member Emile Cirendini meets with Japanese billionaire Goro Yoshida. Yoshida agrees to send The Union a considerable sum of money.

Mathis goes to Corsica, France to investigate Le Gérant and Emile Cirendini. There, Mathis discovers a cave that Cirendini uses as a covert entrance to the shipping center for his company Corse Shipping. Mathis goes to Corse Shipping and finds a crate belonging to the US Air Force, from whom the CL-20 was recently stolen.

M tells Bond to go to Paris to investigate a patient of the ophthalmologist who has a Union tattoo on their retina. Q gives Bond a camera that can be used to detect the tattoo.

In France, Bond meets Bertrand Collette, the new head of station. Collette reveals that the Union's ophthalmologist is Doctor Didier Avalon. Bond goes to the doctor's office and the doctor reveals that he performed the surgery on studio head Léon Essinger.

In Corsica, Mathis searches for Pierre Rodiac, the suspected head of The Union. A restaurant owner tells Mathis to meet Annette Culioli, a *mazzeri*, a person who has a special ability to predict a person's death. The *mazzeri* tells Mathis that she does know Rodiac but he appears in her dreams as a wolf and he resides on an island in southern Corsica. The next morning, the British Embassy in Tokyo is blown up on Goro Yoshida's orders.

Léon Essinger holds a press conference with his wife Tylyn Mignonne, an actress turned model. When Bond breaks into Essinger's office, he locates a file containing a movie's budget and learns that Essinger's company is using Corse Shipping to import soft drink canisters from Corsica. He also finds a torn-up photo of Tylyn in the trash.

Bond looks over the production budget for Essinger's film and discovers that special effects coordinator Rick Fripp is being paid $5 million—more than the stars of the film earn. Collette tells 007 that Tylyn, a wealthy former model, is holding a fashion show the next day for her clothing line at the Louvre.

Mathis follows Annette Culioli's cryptic clues to the location of Le Gérant's house where he is discovered, captured, and brought to Pierre Rodiac, who is revealed to be Le Gérant. After forcing Mathias to send Bond a letter, Le Gérant tortures the French agent.

Posing as a journalist from a British pop culture magazine, Bond attends Tylyn's fashion show. After the show, Bond meets Tylyn and takes her to a nearby café, where they get to know each other better. Tylyn invites Bond to visit her at her studio in Mougins, France. Bond notices that a security guard from the party has been following them.

A day later, the suspicious security guard confronts Bond and demands that he come with him. Bond refuses and tries to get away in his Aston Martin but he is followed by three vans and is not able to escape. Suddenly, Marc-Ange Draco, Tracy's father and Bond's ex-father-in-law, intervenes and saves Bond. Draco, who is part of the Corsican mafia, tells Bond that he remarried and had a daughter but both his wife and daughter were killed. Draco tells Bond that he knows Le Gérant's true identity. He also explains that Le Gérant gambles in Monte Carlo every Thursday, where he uses the alias, Pierre Rodiac. Draco reveals that The Union is now in league with Goro Yoshida, the Japanese businessman turned terrorist that M wanted Bond to investigate.

Bond goes to Tylyn's studio where they go horseback riding and spend time getting to know one another. Bond uses Q's gadget camera to confirm that Tylyn does not have a tattoo on her retina and, therefore, is not a member of The Union. Bond and Tylyn make love. Later, Tylyn invites Bond to visit her on the set of her movie in Corsica.

Bond travels to Monte Carlo so that he can spy on Le Gérant. Bond decides to make contact with Le Gérant by challenging him to a game of *chemin de fer*. After the game, Bond runs into Tylyn, who invites him to join her on a chartered cruise that Léon Essinger arranged. Bond notices that Essinger, who is carrying a case full of money, is meeting with Julius Wilcox, a Union lieutenant.

Bond travels to Nice, France and meets Bertrand Collette who provides Bond with a sport boat, the *Ariel,* from Q Branch. Then, Bond boards the yacht that Essinger and Tylin will be using. In Chicago, Goro Yoshida's followers cause another explosion.

Back in France, Bond watches Tylin and Essinger while they work on the film. Later, Bond decides to check the equipment of the special effects man, Fripp and discovers that it has been shipped by Corse Shipping. Bond opens one of the crates and discovers the stolen CL-20 explosives. Fripp catches Bond, so 007 knocks him unconscious, scans his eyes, and learns that he is a member of the Union. Later, Bond runs into Union member Julius Wilcox, who in turn, tells Le Gérant that Bond is a British agent. Le Gérant instructs Essinger to kill Bond.

The next day during filming, Essinger's goons try to assassinate Bond. Bond tries to get away in one of the boats that the film's crew was using but the boat is blown to smithereens. The Union mistakenly thinks that 007 has been killed.

Bond contacts Nigel Smith who has received the letter from Mathis. Smith reads the letter, which indicates that Le Gérant and Mathis are in Calvi, France. In order to investigate the Corse Shipping complex, Bond and Collette board a sailboat. Bond pilots the *Ariel* to a cave which serves as a secret entrance to Corse Shipping complex. Bond breaches the complex and discovers pressurized soft drink canisters, film cans, and a detonator. When Bond returns to Collette, he discovers that the Frenchman's boat has been destroyed and Collette is injured. Bond takes Collette to a nearby hospital.

Bond goes to his hotel and finds his former father-in-law Marc-Ange Draco waiting. Draco tells Bond that Léon Essinger is a member of The Union. Draco provides Bond with the address of the *mazzeri* with whom Rénee Mathis met. Elsewhere, Tylyn tells her husband Léon that she wants a divorce. Léon agrees to the divorce on the condition that Tylyn attends the premiere of their film in Cannes. Prince Edward and Princess Caroline will also be in attendance.

Bond meets with the *mazzeri* who tells the agent where to find Le Gérant. Searching for the still-missing Mathis, Bond goes to Le Gérant's residence. He sneaks inside the house but is captured and thrown into a cell with Mathis, who has been blinded by The Union. Bond and Mathis discuss the case and determine that Essinger is using the movie production to smuggle the explosive materials.

Bond is brought to Le Gérant who unwittingly reveals the Cannes Film Festival will be the target of the Union's next bombing. Le Gérant explains that Goro Yoshida is funding the operation. Le Gérant tortures Bond by burning his eyes with a laser.

Back in the cell, Bond catches a rat and fashions a weapon out of his bones. When a guard enters, Bond uses his makeshift weapon to kill the guard. Mathis is too weak to flee, so he beseeches Bond to leave without him. Bond agrees but promises to return and save him. Bond manages to get hold of a beverage supply truck and speeds out of the estate.

Holding up to laser eye torture
in *Never Dream of Dying.*
Illustration by Pat Carbajal

Bond goes to the Cannes Film Festival to thwart Le Gérant's plans to blow up the festival. When he arrives, the gala event is about to begin. Princess Caroline and Prince Edward are in attendance. Bond searches for an explosive device, possibly hidden in one of the soft drink canisters that Essinger's company is importing. Bond is unable to locate the explosive.

Bond finds Fripp and demands that the special effects coordinator reveal the location of the explosives. Before Fripp can talk, Essinger shoots at Bond and Fripp flees. Bond hands Essinger over to the local authorities and then catches up with Fripp. After a battle, Bond kills Fripp. Meanwhile, Essinger kills his guard and escapes in a van with Julius Wilcox. Bond catches up with the van and demands that Essinger call his Union contact and instruct him not to activate the bomb. Essinger complies and takes out his phone to make the call. Bond realizes that Essinger intends to use his cell phone to remotely set off the device. Under the threat of a gun, Essinger relinquishes his phone to Bond and confesses that the bomb is hidden in a film can in the projection booth. Bond alerts the French police, who locate and deactivate the device.

Bond and the French police raid Le Gérant's house and save Mathis. During the raid, Bond locates Mathis and frees him. Then,

Bond tracks down Le Gérant but before Bond can kill him, Marc-Ange Draco intercedes. Draco confesses that he and Le Gérant are half-brothers through marriage. Draco reveals that his wife and child were killed in the explosion that Bond caused at the movie studio in Nice (at the beginning of the novel). Since then, Draco has sought revenge. Bond uses the light in Boothroyd's camera to temporarily distract Draco and then Bond shoots his former father-in-law, killing him in self-defense.

Commentary: *Never Dream of Dying* is Benson's third and final novel in his Union trilogy. In his two previous novels, *High Time to Kill* and *DoubleShot*, Bond had been searching for the identity of Le Gérant, the leader of the Union. In *Never Dream of Dying*, Bond finally discovers that Le Gérant is a blind man whose real name is name Pierre Rodiac. He also learns that Le Gérant is the half-brother of Marc Ange-Draco, Bond's former father-in-law.

Benson's three novels form a compelling arc that brings to mind Goldfinger's adage that "Once is happenstance. Twice is coincidence. Three times is enemy action." In each book of Benson's trilogy, Le Gérant's prominence comes to the fore. Le Gérant's Union was a shadow organization in *High Time to Kill*. Once Bond thwarted their plans, in *DoubleShot*, the Union's primary goal was to eliminate Bond. And Bond's efforts to stop their plans and figure out their identity become the central focus of *Never Dream of Dying*.

Draco is not the devil-may-care man that Bond fans recognize from Gabriele Ferzetti's winning performance in the movie *On Her Majesty's Secret Service*.[119] Instead, Draco is the tough-minded head of a crime syndicate. Since the death of his daughter, Tracy, he has gone through challenging times. Draco's wife and daughter have been murdered. Draco blames Bond for his role in their deaths and plots to kill his former son-in-law.

Draco holds Bond responsible for these tragedies and his reasons for revenge are understandable. Even though Draco wants to kill 007, Bond still cannot quite bring himself to terminate his former father-in-law. It is only when Draco shoots at Bond that the agent's instincts kick in and Bond returns fire. For Bond, the decision to pull the trigger is not a conscious one; it is a reflective action.

Never Dream of Dying is told from multiple perspectives. As with most Bond novels, the action cuts between Bond investigating the villains and the bad guys devising and executing their schemes. However, Benson also gives René Mathis nearly as much to do as Bond. Mathis, who appeared in *Casino Royale, From Russia with Love* and *Thunderball*, is a fan favorite character. As is the case with Draco, his star has fallen. After a botched raid, Mathis has been sidelined in his French intelligence division. Given the importance of the case, Mathis decides to suss out Le Gérant's identity on his own accord. Mathis tracks the Union head to his home. Mathis pays dearly; he is caught, tortured, and blinded. When Bond is later captured and thrown into a cell with Mathis, the weakened Mathis tells Bond to escape on his own. It seems that Mathis has given up. In the end, Mathis finds his fire again. When the chips are down and Bond is about to be overcome by the enemy, the unsighted-Mathis shoots and kills the Union operative, saving Bond.

Benson introduces elements of spiritualism and psychic phenomena into the book. He explains that a type of psychic called *mazzeris* can see someone's death in their dreams. In *Never Dream of Dying*, a *mazzeri* named Annette Culioli is able to locate Le Gérant through her dreams where he takes the form of a wolf. The *mazzeri* is not the only character with visions. Le Gérant, who is described as a blind prophet, has dreams as well. Through his visions, Le Gérant learns that Bond, who has taken the form of a stag, has escaped from the dungeon that he had been placed in. Later, Bond has a similar dream in which, as a stag, he is chased by Le Gérant, a wolf. *Never Dream of Dying* is not the only book where Bond enters the world of spiritualism. In *Live and Let Die*, Solitaire is a gifted fortune-teller.

Bond falls in love with Tylyn Mignonne, a fashion model turned actress. He believes that she is one of the most beautiful women that he's ever seen. Throughout most of their relationship, Bond is posing as a journalist from a pop-culture magazine called *Pop World*. He lets down his guard enough to tell Tylyn about his deceased wife and to form a deep connection. Benson writes, "This was one of those uncommon occurrences when he had to admit that he was falling in love." By the book's end, Bond tells Tylyn that he loves her, and he seems to mean it. Bond is not responding to Tylyn's declaration; he says it first. Later, he tells her, "I fell in love with you for a number of reasons." Ultimately, Bond is not ready to give up his life of danger for her and she's not prepared to continue on a relationship that started with lies. Benson presents the relationship as a significant one.

Continuity Nod: Important characters from Fleming's books, René Mathis and Marc-Ange Draco, play major roles in *Never Dream of Dying*. Benson references the fact that Mathis saved Bond's life in *From Russia with Love*. He also alludes to Bond's trip to Japan in *You Only Live Twice* and Blofeld is name-checked. The loss of Bond's virginity is established by Fleming, expanded on by Pearson, and reinforced by Benson. He also briefly alludes to his Bond books *High*

Time to Kill and *DoubleShot* when M makes mention of the "business in the Himalayas" and "the affair in Gibraltar."

Never Dream of Dying also evokes the film franchise. In addition to the movie-worthy action set pieces, the book features an Aston Martin and a female M, who like Q implores, "Would you pay attention, Double O Seven." Riffing on a line from *Thunderball*, Bond quips, "Someone probably lost a dog." After sustaining an injury, Bond's ally vents, "The things I do for England," which is a line from the movie *You Only Live Twice*.

Bond's Personal Life: Bond offers that he has rarely been dumped by a woman; it is usually he who prematurely ends relationships.

Bond's Inner Life: Despite all his years on duty, Bond still gets nervous on missions. However, he does not mind those feelings of anxiety. They help keep him focused on the task at hand. Bond avoids contacting Draco after Tracy was killed because doing so would have brought up difficult memories that James was not ready to face.

Bond's Tastes: Bond has seen Alfred Hitchcock's horror classic *Psycho.*

Bond's Work Methods: Much to Bond's dismay, he is assigned a male personal assistant, Nigel Smith. Prior to that, the only other time he had a male assistant was when he was in the Navy. It took Bond six months to recover from the injuries he sustained in *DoubleShot.* Since then, 007 has taken a stealth course so that he can run, jump, walk, swim, hit, and even murder a man silently.

Assorted Observations:

- An assassin from the Bronx is named Schenkman. Richard Schenkman, a filmmaker, was the publisher of the 007 fan magazine *Bondage*. Benson names an ophthalmologist Dr. David Worrall after the co-writer of *The Essential Bond: The Authorized Guide to 007.*
- In one of the more memorable moments of the book, Bond kills a rat with his mouth. Then, he uses the rat's skeleton to fashion a weapon out of its bones. Bond stabs the weapon into the guard's chin, killing him.
- One of the actresses who attends the Cannes Film Festival is Carole Bouquet. In *For Your Eyes Only*, Bouquet played Bond woman Melina Havelock.

Tylyn was named after Playboy Playmate Tylyn John.

THE HEART OF ERZULIE (2001)

Unpublished in its original form.

Author: Raymond Benson

In Brief: In Haiti, Bond's search for his missing housekeeper puts him on the trail of a serial killer on the loose.

Meaning of Title: A reference to the Haitian love goddess Erzulie.

Chronology: Contemporary. Presumably, set after *Never Dream of Dying.*

Operation: Not applicable.

Bastard Meter: None.

Eggs: Sunny side-up eggs.

Insight into Bond: "Most of the time he preferred to live like a hermit at his secluded home."

Note: The original protagonist in Raymond Benson's 2001 short story "The Heart of Erzulie" was James Bond. Bond was replaced with CIA operative Brock Fuller in Benson's 2015 rewrite. More on that later. For now, I ask that wherever you see Brock's name stated in the forthcoming synopsis, please replace it with Bond's.

Summary: Brock Fuller is fishing in the waters of Haiti. When he returns home, he discovers that his dependable housekeeper, Stephane Moon, is not there. In the morning newspaper, Brock reads two disturbing news items about a spate of missing persons and a serial killer on the loose in Haiti.

Stephane's sister Cherry Moon arrives and asks Brock for his help in locating her missing brother. Cherry explains that Stephane owes money to a local racketeer named Emo Tuff. Fearing for his life, Stephane might have sought sanctuary with Jeremiah Priest, a local who makes his living performing voodoo rituals for the tourists at the Temple of Erzulie.

Brock and Cherry go to The Temple of Erzulie. At the temple, they meet Stephane's friend, Judas, a performer in Priest's show ritual. Brock and Cherry are invited by Judas to the evening performance.

Before the performance, Brock and Cherry have dinner together. Cherry spots a statue placed atop an altar. A gold medallion resembling the one Stephane wears is visible on the sculpture. The medallion contains a symbol of the Heart of Erzulie, the goddess of love.

Brock and Cherry return to the Temple of Erzulie and watch a voodoo ceremony. During the ceremony, Jeremiah Priest draws an image of the Heart of Erzulie in the dirt. A "possessed" woman then puts a hex on Brock. One of Stephane's friends, Jacob, tells Brock and Cherry to accompany him when the ceremony is over. When they follow Jacob backstage, Brock is knocked out.

When Brock comes to, he finds that he and Cherry are being held captive in a van. They are taken to Emo Tuff's residence and are held in a barn. When they are left alone, Brock removes a knife that he keeps hidden inside his belt. The hoods return and bring Bond and Chery to Tuff.

Tuff explains that human sacrifices are practiced in his religion and that Stephane had previously been offered as a sacrifice as part of a rite. Tuff informs Brock and Cherry that they will take part in a ritual sacrifice. Brock realizes that Tuff is responsible for the spate of missing persons. Tuff instructs Jacob and another follower named Eli to tie Brock and Cherry to a tree. Brock frees himself, takes a gun from Eli's trousers, shoots him, and then overpowers Jacob. Tuff shoots at Brock, who returns fire and kills Tuff. After Brock gets the drop on Priest, Cherry calls the police.

Weeks later, Brock employs Cherry as his new housekeeper. However, their relationship will not be strictly professional.

Commentary: In 2001, between writing *Never Dream of Dying* and *The Man with the Red Tattoo*, Raymond Benson kept himself busy by writing the short story "The Heart of Erzulie." According to Benson, Glidrose did not think his piece was up to snuff, so they declined to publish it. For over a decade, Benson kept "The Heart of Erzulie" in his proverbial desk drawer. In 2015, he revised the story, removed all references to Bond, and published the story under the same name in his short-story collection *12+1: Twelve Short Thrillers and a Play.* One does not need to be a Bondologist to see how the revised "Heart of Erzulie" would function as a short story featuring 007.

In the revised story, Brock Fuller, a former CIA agent with a second home in Haiti, serves as an obvious stand-in for Bond, an active SIS agent with a residence in Jamaica, in the altered plot. Bond's blue-grey eyes are changed to green; his Ronson lighter has been swapped out for an S.T. Dupont lighter, and his residence,

“Shamelady,” has been altered to “Metropolis.” Shamelady/Metropolis are clear references to Ian Fleming’s Jamaican home, Goldeneye. Benson’s assertion that Metropolis was built in the 1940s is a reference to Fleming’s acquisition of Goldeneye in 1946, and solidifies the connection between the two properties.

As with Benson’s Bond, Fuller has a belt that contains a hidden blade. Both Bond and Brock enjoy swimming in the waters outside their home and they both carry their smokes in a gunmetal cigarette case. When Brock introduces himself, he even does so in a manner that is familiar to Bond fans; he says, “My name is Fuller, Brock Fuller.”

If we were to read “The Heart of Erzulie” as a Bond story, then it’s one in which the agent is retired. The narrative could provide a glimpse into Bond’s life following his life as a spy. It would also anticipate Bond’s retirement and life in Jamaica in the movie *No Time to Die*. However, I don’t think we should assume that Bond would have been retired in Benson’s original version of the story. It's also possible that Benson created Fuller as a retired agent as a tactic to distinguish Fuller from Bond.

THE MAN WITH THE RED TATTOO (2002)

Author: Raymond Benson

In Brief: Bond journeys to Japan to stop a deadly virus spread by mosquitoes from killing world leaders at a summit. There, Bond is reunited with his old friend Tiger Tanaka.

Meaning of Title: Reference to a red tattoo that covers most of the villains' body.

Chronology: Contemporary. After the events of *Never Dream of Dying*.

Operation: Red Window Dawn.

Bastard Meter: None that relates to Bond.

Eggs: Only mosquito eggs that the villain is using to spread a virulent disease.

Insight into Bond: "All the women whom he had loved had come to a bad end. Was this his fate, to be forever alone because whatever he touched turned to dust."

Summary: A plane transports Kyoko McMahon from Japan to London. After becoming violently sick, Kyoko passes away from an unknown ailment. Kyoko had just spent some time with her father, Peter McMahon, head of the pharmaceutical firm CureLab. The unidentified ailment that killed Kyoko also claims her father and mother, leaving only her sister, Mayumi, alive.

Back in London, Major Boothroyd briefs James Bond and the Double Os on his latest gadgets. Boothroyd's new inventions are antacids that can be used as smoke bombs and a Palm Pilot that can be turned into an incendiary device.

Bond and his secretary Nigel Smith discuss the upcoming G8 summit, a gathering of representatives of the United States, the United Kingdom, Japan, France, Germany, Italy, Canada, and Russia. Bond worries that Goro Yoshida, a terrorist who he faced in the past, is on the loose and might disrupt the summit.

M informs 007 that although they are unsure of what could have killed the McMahon family, the Japanese police suspect foul play. Control of McMahon's company will now go to his daughter;

however, she is missing. M instructs Bond to go to Japan and investigate the death of the McMahon family. During the summit, Bond will also serve as the Prime Minister's bodyguard.

Before his trip, Bond inspects Kyoko McMahon's body at the mortuary. The pathologist tells Bond that Kyoko's body had a few mosquito bites but it's unlikely that the mosquitos caused her death. Two Japanese men arrive and try to steal Kyoko's body, but Bond disrupts their plans and kills them. When Bond inspects one of the Japanese men's bodies, he notices tattoos of dragons and waterfalls, an indication that he is a member of the Yakuza, the Japanese mafia.

In Japan, Yasutake Tsukamoto, an official leader of the Yakuza gang Ryujin-kai and one of the board of directors of Yonai Enterprises, meets with Goro Yoshida, the unofficial head of the Yakuza. Tsukamoto explains that Peter McMahon's stock in CureLab will go to his daughter, who works for them. Yoshida orders the daughter's death. Later, Yoshida discusses his imminent place to attack the West.

Bond goes to Japan, where he meets Reiko Tamura, of the Public Security Investigation Agency, and his old friend, Tiger Tanaka of the Japanese secret service. Tiger gives Bond a local mobile phone, with a homing device in it. They discuss the possibility that Yonai Enterprises hired the Yakuza to kill the entire McMahon family so that they can gain control of CureLab. Tiger tells Bond that a surviving member of the Fujimoto family is Shinji, the vice president of CureLab. Tiger also suggests that they can find the youngest McMahon daughter, Mayumi, through her friends and relatives.

Tiger gets news that Mayumi's old boyfriend, Kenji Umeki, knows where Mayumi is and for a price, he will reveal her location. Bond and Tiger go to the house where the McMahons were killed. There, they meet Shinji Fujimoto, vice president of Cure Labs. They discover a mosquito-filled garden and a small electric-powered fountain. Bond instructs Tiger to have the fountain analyzed. Fujimoto tells Bond that 80% of CureLab stock is owned by the family and that the other 20% is privately held. Until Mayumi is found, Fujimoto will serve as CureLab's president.

Tiger receives a call indicating that Umeki, Mayumi's old boyfriend, was murdered. Bond, Tiger, and Reiko investigate Kenji's death and note that his fingers were cut off, an indication that he was the victim of the Yakuza. Tiger theorizes that Kenji was killed to prevent him from sharing Mayumi's whereabouts. They search the body and find a bag of pachinko winnings, a sign that he was gambling nearby.

Bond and Reiko investigate the local pachinko parlors, where they find a boy who knew Kenji. The boy, a member of the Yakuza, tells them that Kenji used to come to the pachinko parlor regularly. Bond and Reiko are attacked by men on motorcycles who tell the agents not to return.

The next day, Reiko remembers that one of the motorcycle assailants is a Yakuza member named Noburo Ichihar. Bond and Reiko go to the fish market to meet Takuya Abo, Mayumi's cousin. Abo says that Mayumi works in Sapporo as a sort of masseuse referred to as a Soaplands girl. Abo theorizes that a creature from Japanese folklore, a "kappa," killed Umeki, Mayumi's old boyfriend. Abo also reveals that Goro Yoshida is planning something big. Before he can reveal more, Abo is shot to death by Noburo Ichihara. Bond chases Ichihara into a Kabuki theater, where Bond and Ichihara fight with swords but Ichihara gets away.

Bond visits the Ginza headquarters of CureLab with Shinji Fujimoto, its vice president. At the headquarters, Bond is knocked unconscious. When he awakens, he sees Noburo Ichihara, one of the members of the Yakuza. Bond accuses Fujimoto of killing the McMahons. Fujimoto makes an oblique reference to an upcoming meeting near the Great Buddha, in Kamakura, Japan. He then instructs Ichihara to kill Bond and hide his body. After Fujimoto's minions put Bond in a dumpster, Bond escapes by using Boothroyd's gadgets.

Bond sneaks around Fujimoto's headquarters and spots mosquitoes and a miniature bonsai waterfall, similar to the one in the McMahon's residence. Snooping around, Bond downloads computer files and then spots the missing molecular biologist, Fujio Aida.

Later, Bond meets up with Tiger. Tiger tells Bond that Fujimoto has a home in Kamakura, near the location of the Great Buddha. The next day, the agents travel to Kamakura, where they witness Fujimoto meeting with Masuzo Kano, president of Yonai Enterprises, and Junji Kon, a dwarf who is holding a briefcase full of money. Bond points out that the dwarf resembles a kappa, the creature from the fairy tales that Abo spoke about earlier. Shortly after that, Fujimoto is holding the case full of money, a payoff from Masuzo Kano. Bond discovers that the kappa killed Kano and left a miniature Buddha at the crime scene as a calling card.

The next day, Tiger and Bond learn that Shinji Fujimoto divested his shares in CureLab the day before he was murdered and that Yonai Enterprises board of directors control 20% of CureLab. A televised news report announces the merger of CureLab and Yonai Enterprises. Bond suspects that the Yakuza is involved in the murder of the McMahons and that the mosquitoes are being used to deliver a deadly biological agent.

Bond and Reiko visit an entomologist who informs them about a newly discovered process that allows mosquitoes to transfer diseases through their offspring. Later, Bond learns that the Kappa (whose real name is Junji Kon) is a hitman for the Yakuza. Tiger tells Bond that Naoshima Island will be the site of a an upcoming G8 conference.

Bond and Reiko travel by train to try to find Mayumi McMahon. On the train, Bond and Reiko make love. Later, they spot Kappa. Bond and Reiko inspect Kappa's room and find a jar of live mosquitoes. After locking them in, Kappa uses a remote radio transmitter to open the jar so that the virus-carrying mosquitoes can escape and attack Bond. Bond uses a gadget to escape the locked compartment and then he chases after Kappa, who is hiding somewhere in the train tunnels. Bond catches up to the killer and they fight. The Kappa knocks Bond out and suspends him over the tracks. Bond escapes before the train can barrel into him.

Bond discovers that Reiko and three train passengers were bitten by a mosquito and are brought to the hospital. Later, Reiko dies from the virus. Tiger tells Bond to go to the Sapporo Beer Garden and meet his contact Ikuo Yamamaru.

At the Garden, Bond meets Yamamaru, who provides the spy with Mayumi McMahon's location. Yamamaru tells Bond that Mayumi is working as a Soaplands girl in the Casanova Club, an establishment run by the Yakuza.

At the Casanova Club, Bond tells Mayumi that the Yakuza killed her brother and that mosquitoes are being used as murder weapons. Mayumi tells Bond to go to Noboribetsu, Japan where he can find tanks filled with mosquitoes at CureLab's site. Bond offers to protect Mayumi and agrees to meet at the Tokei-dai clock tower the next day.

Bond and Mayumi sneak into CureLab to inspect the mosquito tanks. Once inside, Mayumi blows their cover. They are captured and locked in the mosquito tank. Yasutake Tsukamoto, the apparent leader of the Yakuza, and Goro Yoshida, the actual leader of the Yakuza arrive. Yoshida admits to killing the McMahons with mosquitos that were released from a hidden compartment contained inside a bonsai waterfall device. Yoshida tells 007 that he will unleash the mosquitos at the G8 conference. Using Boothroyd's equipment, Bond causes an explosion and allows 007 and Mayumi to escape.

Days later, Bond and Tanaka travel to Naoshima to attend the G8 Summit. Bond and Tanaka survey the building for any threats to the dignitary's safety. They inspect the flower pots but do not see any signs of mosquitoes. Bond also surveys the art, including a large plaster "heart" made out of plaster but he does not detect the Kappa, who is hiding inside. When no one is looking, the Kappa places mosquito eggs in the pots and planters and then returns to his hiding place.

The US president and the UK prime minister are among the visiting world leaders. As the summit begins, Tiger spots the mosquitoes in the plants. Before he can notify anyone, Tanaka, who recently has had problems, suffers a heart attack. Bond races to Tanaka and calls for a medic.

A member of the delegation swats a mosquito. Realizing that the summit is under attack, Bond clears the area and disposes of the mosquitoes. Bond surveys the room and realizes that the Kappa has been hiding in the plaster heart. Bond and the Kappa fight. Bond gets the better of the assassin, who confesses that twenty members of the Yakuza will disperse virus-carrying mosquitoes around the world. Bond alerts the authorities who track down all twenty members and their deadly cargo. Bond and Nakayama lead raids on Goro Yoshida's terrorist operations. However, Yoshida's body has not been recovered.

As a thank you for keeping her safe, Mayumi presents Bond with a katana. Bond hands a letter to Mayumi from her father, explaining that he was a reluctant instrument of the Yakuza. Her father only went along with them to keep Mayumi safe. Before Bond leaves, Mayumi and Bond get to know each other much better.

Later that night, Bond senses danger and investigates. Goro Yoshida and Yasutake Tsukamoto enter. Yoshida draws his sword, Bond picks up his katana, and they battle. Yoshida seems to be getting the better of Bond when Mayumi fires a warning shot at him. Acknowledging defeat, Yoshida commits ritual suicide. Nakayama arrives and arrests Tsukamoto. Mayumi informs Bond that she plans to sell her stock in the company and start over.

Commentary: James Bond is plagued by guilt and his sense of accountability is not unwarranted. He feels personally accountable for the demise of the several women who died after meeting him. Many of his lovers have met grim ends because of their association with him. Vesper Lynd commits suicide. Shortly after marrying Bond, Tracy di Vicenzo was killed by Blofeld and Irma Bunt. Benson increases the number of slain women to include Helena Marksbury, Bond's secretary-turned-lover, Dr. Kimberly Feare, a neurologist-turned-lover, and Reiko Tamura, a Japanese agent-turned-lover. Bond is forced to confront those feelings in Benson's final original Bond novel *The Man with the Red Tattoo.*

Bond wielding off an attacker with a Katana
in *The Man with the Red Tattoo.*
Illustration by Pat Carbajal

When M assigns Bond to a mission in Japan, those unsettling feelings come to the surface. After all, Fleming's Bond has a personal history with the country. In *You Only Live Twice*, Bond went to Japan to find Blofeld and avenge Tracy's death. After killing Blofeld, Bond fell in love with Kissy Suzuki. Without realizing Suzuki is expecting his child, Bond leaves Japan. In the short story, "Blast From The Past," Benson reveals that she had a son, James Suzuki, who would stay in touch with, and occasionally see, his father although they were not particularly close. Benson concludes "Bond had never had a chance to know [his son]." Bond would never bridge that gap; his son would be murdered by Blunt.

When Bond initially arrives in Japan, he is unaware of the pain he is feeling. However, as the plot develops, Bond is unable to get away from the nearly overwhelming guilt he experiences over the deaths of the women that he's loved. When Reiko Tamura, the Japanese agent for whom he has grown to care, is murdered, Bond wonders, "Was this the price he had to pay for the lives he had taken throughout his career? Was this his fate, to be forever alone because whatever he touched turned to dust?"

In an unexpected way, Benson provides Bond with a measure of comfort. In the chapter appropriately titled, "Old Ghosts," Bond sees a vision of Kissy Suzuki, his dead lover and the mother of his deceased son. This ghost-like apparition comforts Bond and assuages some of his guilt. Kissy's ghost explains to Bond that it is not his fault that the people he cares about die. She recommends that he not stray from the life he has chosen. Bond takes her words to heart. In the end, Kissy helps to "lay the ghosts of the past to rest."

Continuity Nod: Benson references Bond's previous trip to Japan where he played a game of Scissors, Pay, Stone with Tiger Tanaka; confronted and killed Blofeld; and formed a relationship with Kissy Suzuki, who later gave birth to his son (*You Only Live Twice*). Bond also thinks about Vesper and Tracy. Further, Benson alludes to the short story "Quantum of Solace" where Bond once joked, "I've always thought that if I ever married, I would marry an air hostess."

Benson acknowledges his own books as well. Bond is still feeling the impact of the injuries he sustained in *High Time to Kill*. Bond saved the Prime Minister's life in *DoubleShot*. So when they meet again in *The Man with the Red Tattoo*, the Prime Minister remembers Bond from their previous encounter.

Bond's History: In the past, Bond has gone undercover as a wealthy, pleasure-seeking businessman. When he does so, he can travel first class and stay in the best hotels.

Bond's Personal Life: Bond starts each day with exercise.

Bond's Inner Life: Bond acknowledges that he is relatively content in life or about "as happy as a civil servant can be." Concerning his religious beliefs, Bond observes, "The gods don't have much use for me" and does not have much of a spiritual side. He concedes that he might not have much use for religion, until he finds it, like others do, on their death bed. Still, Bond does wonder if Junji Kon, a killer who seems to disappear and reappear at will, has supernatural abilities.

Bond's Tastes: Bond sometimes grows weary of keeping the comma of hair in place. So occasionally, as he does in *Red Tattoo*, he lets it fall. Bond prefers his Aston Martin to his Bentley. As he does in Fleming's works, Bond asks, "What's the score?" several times during the book.

Bond's Work Methods: Bond must attend formal equipment briefings that are conducted by Major Boothroyd. Other field and Double O agents, including 004 and 0010, are in attendance. However, those are not the only active Double Os, the rest are on assignment or killed in action. For a secret agent, everything in his surroundings is a possible weapon. At a fish market, Bond uses a ten-pound octopus to throw an attacker off balance. Bond's extremely high pain tolerance comes in handy in a few instances, such as when he is punched in the face by a thug for several minutes straight.

Assorted Observations:

- Bond gives a gentle rebuke to the *Daily Express,* which is also the paper that initially printed the Bond comic strips.
- Benson's Union Trilogy consists of *High Time to Kill, DoubleShot,* and *Never Dream of Dying*. Yet, *The Man from the Red Tattoo* is connected by a villain from *Never Dream of Dying.* As such, perhaps those series of books be referred to as Benson's Union Tetralogy.
- In 2005, The 007 Man With the Red Tattoo Museum opened; it was a museum on Naoshima Island devoted to Benson's book in particular and Bond in general. After being open for 12 years, the museum closed in 2017.

DIE ANOTHER DAY (2002)

Author: Raymond Benson

In Brief: Bond looks into a powerful and well-liked industrialist who is developing a solar-powered weapon that fires a heat beam.

Meaning of Title: Bond will survive his mission and live to die another day.

Chronology: Contemporary. Three years after the events of the *Tomorrow Never Dies* novelization.

Operation: Not applicable.

Bastard Meter: Unmentioned.

Eggs: Quail eggs.

Insight into Bond: "A Double O agent. A wild one—as I witnessed today. Will light the fuse on any explosive situation. Kill first, ask questions later. A danger to himself and others. A blunt instrument whose primary method is to provoke and confront. A womanizer."

Summary: Bond and two agents surf to Pukchong Beach in Malaysia. After reaching dry ground, they intercept a diamond trader named Van Bierk. Bond snatches a case filled with diamonds from Van Bierk. Then, he travels to North Korea in a helicopter. On board, Bond plants explosives in the case.

In North Korea, Colonel Tan-Gun Moon waits for Van Bierk. Posing as Van Bierk, Bond trades the diamonds for weapons. Colonel Moon's enforcer, Zao, discovers that Bond is an imposter. Before Moon and Zao can kill the spy, Bond pushes a button on his watch and the case explodes. When Colonel Moon flees in a hovercraft, Bond chases after him in another hovercraft. Moon's craft topples over a waterfall, apparently killing him. Bond is captured by Moon's father, General Moon.

General Moon imprisons and tortures Bond. After 14 months in prison, Moon demands that Bond reveal MI6's secrets. When Bond refuses, Moon threatens to kill the spy. Bond is brought to the Demilitarized Zone where he is traded for Zao. A syringe is used to subdue Bond after he is taken into custody.

Bond wakes up in a hospital, now a prisoner of his own government. M visits Bond and tells him that she received intelligence that Bond was leaking secrets. Bond insists on his innocence and says the enemy has been receiving intelligence from a spy inside the service. Bond believes that he was set up to free Zao from prison. When M leaves, Bond escapes to prove his innocence and find Zao.

With the help of a sailor, Bond hides on a ship heading for Hong Kong. In Hong Kong, Bond checks into a hotel and meets Mr. Chang, the hotel's manager and Chinese intelligence agent. Chang reveals that Zao has gone to Havana.

Bond travels to Cuba, goes to a cigar factory and meets a contact named Raoul. Raoul tells Bond that he might find Zao in Los Organos at a clinic that specializes in gene therapy. Bond goes to Los Organos and meets a beautiful woman who goes by the name Jinx.

Bond travels to Isla Organos and sneaks into the institute. In the clinic, Bond learns that Zao is undergoing a DNA replacement treatment with a device called the Dream Machine. During their battle, Bond snatches up a pendant that Zao is wearing. Elsewhere in the clinic, Jinx talks with the head of the clinic, Dr. Alvarez. Jinx steals a disk from the doctor's safe and sets an explosive. The explosive goes off and kills Alvarez but Zao gets away. Bond spots Jinx but she escapes by performing a two-hundred-foot dive into the water below. Bond examines Zao's pendant and discovers a diamond inside.

Bond returns to his local contact Raoul. A closer look at the diamond reveals that it came from the mines owned by wealthy English industrialist Gustav Graves.

In England, Graves talks to the press about his mysterious Icarus space program. Then, Graves goes to a private club in London with his press secretary, Miranda Frost. At the club, Graves practices fencing and challenges Bond to a duel. Bond wins the match, humiliating Graves. Graves invites Bond to join him in Iceland where he will demonstrate the power of his Icarus project. On his way out, a concierge gives Bond an envelope that contains a key.

Bond uses the key to enter an abandoned train station that has doubled as secret MI6 offices. Bond meets with M and expresses his suspicions about Graves. Then, Bond meets Q who provides Bond with a ring that emits an ultra-high frequency signal that can break glass. Q also gives Bond a car with a cloaking device that can render it nearly invisible. Elsewhere, M meets with Miranda Frost who is revealed to be an MI6 operative and not just Graves' press secretary. M instructs Frost to assist Bond in his assignment.

Bond travels to Iceland to stay at Graves' Ice Hotel. At the hotel's bar, Bond meets Jinx, and they go outside to watch the Icarus demonstration. They learn that Icarus is a satellite that can harness the power of the sun and redirect it as a powerful beam. Bond spots a dome near the Ice Hotel. Bond and Miranda break into the dome that is said to contain Graves' diamond mine.

Bond and Miranda make love. Taking the gun that Bond left on the bed, he tells Miranda that he is going to investigate the dome.

Inside the dome, Graves is using the Dream Machine. It is revealed that Colonel Moon underwent substantial DNA facial repair surgery after surviving his fall into the waterfall and emerged as Gustav Graves. Jinx breaks into the dome and is captured but Bond manages to find and free her. Jinx reveals that she is a member of the National Security Agency.

Bond confronts Graves at his office. Graves asks Bond if he ever figured out the identity of the mole inside MI6. Miranda appears and confesses that she has been working with Graves. Bond tries to shoot Graves, but his gun is empty; Miranda removed all the bullets after they made love. Bond escapes and he and Zao engage in a car chase, which ends in Zao getting impaled by the chandelier. Bond then rescues Jinx, saving her from drowning in the melted Ice Palace.

Graves and Miranda fly to North Korea, followed by Bond and Jinx who fly to the North Korean air base where Graves' aircraft is stationed and board it. They discover that Graves' father General Moon is also on board. Bond tells General Moon that Graves is his son. Graves explains that he intends to use the laser to destroy the boundary between North and Sea Korea, uniting the separate countries and possibly triggering World War III. General Moon pleads with Graves not to use the Icarus weapon. In response, Graves shoots and kills his father. Bond and Graves fight while Miranda and Jinx square off. Bond and Jinx vanquish their foes and then they destroy the Icarus.

Bond and Jinx make love and decide to spend the next few days together before they are each called away for their next mission.

Commentary: Raymond Benson's *Die Another Day* novelization closely follows the plot of the movie and the screenplay by Neil Purvis and Robert Wade. Benson takes fewer liberties with the movie than he did in his *Tomorrow Never Dies* novelization. As he did with the other movie tie-ins, Benson fleshes out the characters and fills in details about events that are implied but not depicted. In the movie, Bond breaks out of the hospital in South Korea and arrives at the harbor in Hong Kong. Some moviegoers might have wondered how the pajama-clad Bond made the journey. In the novelization, Benson outlines the steps that Bond took to get to Hong Kong. In Benson's account, Bond starts with just $3 in his pocket. Then, he goes to a local bar called the Top Hat and identifies his mark, a local pimp. Pretending to be drunk, Bond bumps into the pimp and takes his money. Using the pimp's money, Bond buys new clothes and food to eat. Then he goes to another bar and makes a deal with a sailor to stow away on his boat. The sequence serves as a showcase for Bond's resourcefulness.

Benson goes into more detail on the 14 months of torment that Bond endured at the General's hands. In the Eon film, Bond's torture lasted the length of Madonna's theme song. Benson devotes roughly half a chapter to Bond's torment. Benson also details how Colonel Moon became radicalized and broke away from his father's more moderate leanings. Setting up their estrangement makes the moment when Moon kills his father more effective.

Miranda Frost, the British agent who is revealed to be in league with Moon, also had a difficult relationship with her father. When Frost was fourteen, she killed her father by trapping him in a car with a swarm of bees. Moon and Miranda Frost met at Harvard and formed a bond of mutual respect. Later, she became an Olympic fencer. Moon poisoned Frost's opponent, allowing her to take the gold. Benson sums up their alliance thusly, "Moon liked to rule and Miranda liked to win."

Die Another Day is the twentieth Eon Bond movie, and, as it marked the 40th anniversary of the movie franchise, it is filled with references to previous Bond films. Benson retains most of those references and adds a few more. For instance, in Benson's work, Bond tells Jinx that he has experience boarding planes after they are already in motion. 007 has done just that in *GoldenEye* and *Octopussy*. Benson also has his Bond jokingly longing for the cello case from *The Living Daylights* so that he can use it for an escape. Bond reads *Tomorrow*, the newspaper featured in *Tomorrow Never Dies* and hears a cover version of "California Girls," the Beach Boys Song that was featured in *A View to a Kill*'s pre-title sequence.

Continuity Nod: In prison, Bond thinks about past loves, such as Solitaire, Tatiana, Tiffany, Honey, Domino, Kissy, and, of course, his deceased wife Tracy. However, he does not think about Gala Brand, a character that the literary Bond has encountered but the movie Bond has not. Bond also reflects on past foes, such as Blofeld, Goldfinger, Dr. No, and Drax, as well as allies like Felix Leiter, Darko Kerim Bey, and Tiger Tanaka. When Bond is in Cuba, he recalls the Hemingway House in Key West, Florida (*Licence to Kill*).

Bond's History: When he is trapped in prison, Bond thinks about his teenage years at school and being raised by his Aunt who was "worried that he was becoming anti-social;" he concludes that "she was probably right." His memories of his youth, family, friends, and colleagues help Bond endure isolation and torture. Benson observes that the "memories kept him lucid, and they kept him strong."

Personal Life: Bond has a working knowledge of many foreign languages. However, he knows very little Korean. After spending over a year in a North Korean prison, Bond presumably picks up a little more of the language. Bond is a light sleeper, which seems like a necessary skill for an agent. Like the literary Bond, 007 lives off King's Road.

Bond's Work Methods: Bond can withstand pain longer than any other Double O agent. Bond's ability to focus on his heartbeat helps him endure more than a year of continuous agony. He possesses a special talent that allows him to dramatically reduce his pulse rate, fooling a heart monitor into thinking he is dead.

Assorted Observations:

- Colonel Moon's name is a reworking of Colon Sun, the adversary in Kingsley Amis' novel of the same name.
- As in the Eon movie, Benson uses Jinx's real name, Giacinta. Whereas in the movie her last name is Johnson, Benson does not provide any last name for the character.

Benson's final work, the *Die Another Day* novelization, marks the end of the first era of Bond continuation novels. This 37-year period saw the publication of 1 continuation novel by Amis, 14 original novels by Gardner, 6 novels by Benson, 2 novelizations by Wood, 1 spin-off work by Calder-Marshall, as well as 5 other novelizations, and a few short stories.

The end of the Benson era also concludes the first part of my exploration of the Bond continuation novels. Part two will pick up in the second era and charts Bond continuation novels by Sebastian Faulks, Jeffery Deaver, William Boyd, and Anthony Horowitz. It also explores Charlie Higson and Steve Cole's *Young Bond* series, about the agent's teen years, Samantha Weinberg's *The Moneypenny Diaries*, about M's secretary, and Kim Sherwood's series, about other agents in the Double O division.

THE ERA OF SPIN-OFFS

"He says that courage is a capital sum reduced by expenditure."
IAN FLEMING, *Dr. No*

INTRODUCTION TO THE YOUNG BOND YEARS

On its surface, a series of books about James Bond's teenage years seems like an ill-conceived idea. After all, Ian Fleming's novels are aimed at adults and are at odds with family-friendly fare. Moreover, Fleming intended Bond to be a cipher. Telling the story of his boyhood exploits could diffuse his mystique. Still, Fleming left the reader clues about Bond's childhood. Fleming provided the reader with critical information regarding the death of his parents, the orphaned Bond's upbringing by his Aunt Charmian, and his education at Eton in England and Fettles College in Scotland. These scant details would become the foundation of the Yong Bond series.

A series aimed at younger readers might be a way to successfully introduce them to Fleming's character and eventually to Fleming's novels. Of course, Fleming himself wrote a children's book, *Chitty Chitty Bang Bang: The Magical Car*, the 1964 story about a magical car for his son, Caspar. So the notion of Fleming and children's work shouldn't be anathema.

The first Young Bond book, *SilverFin*, was published four months before the release of the sixth book in J. K. Rowling's best-selling series, *Harry Potter and the Half-Blood Prince*. In some ways, a book series about the young Bond was inevitable; after all, the publishing industry at that time was dominated by tales of a boy wizard. J. K. Rowling made it clear that both youngsters and adults could appreciate children's fiction with her seven-book Harry Potter series. It was within this publishing landscape that the Young Bond series was born.

CHARLIE HIGSON'S TENURE—PART ONE 2005–2009

Charlie Higson wrote the Young Bond novels *SilverFin* (2005), *Blood Fever* (2006), *Double or Die* (2007), *Hurricane Gold* (2007), and *By Royal Command* (2008), and the short story "A Hard Man to Kill" (2009). Higson also wrote the Bond continuation novella *On His Majesty's Secret Service* (2023).

SILVERFIN (2005)

Author: Charlie Higson

In Brief: James Bond, then 13 years old, is in his first year at Eton College when he learns about Lord Hellebore's scheme to give soldiers a serum that will make them superhuman.

Meaning of Title: SilverFin is the name of a loch in Scotland, and it is also the name of the villain's secret plan.

Chronology: Period. Set in 1933. Bond is 13 years old.

Operation: Not applicable.

Bastard Meter: None.

Eggs: Fried and scrambled.

Insight into Bond: "Nobody can hold a Bond forever. There was always a way out of any situation, no matter how bleak it seemed. You just had to find it."

Summary: In the 1930s, a boy named Alfie Kelly goes fishing in Loch SilverFin, Scotland. While fishing, Alfie catches his thumb on the hook and draws blood. Eels, who are attracted to the blood, attack him. Alfie spots someone on dry land but then he blacks out.

Thirteen-year-old James Bond begins his first day at Eton College, the boarding school in Windsor, England. James meets his roommates Pritpal Nandra from India, Tommy Chong from Hong Kong, and Freddie Meyer, a German-Jewish student. James inadvertently bumps into George Hellebore, an American school bully, and two of his mates. Later, Bond meets George's father, Lord Randolf Hellebore, an armaments salesman who has been funding experimental medical and science research. Hellebore used to know James' late father, Andrew Bond.

Bond's teacher Mr. Merriot tells him about a new Eton competition that George's father, Lord Hellebore, is sponsoring. Mr. Merriot encourages Bond to enter the race. James prepares for the upcoming competition by swimming in the river. He is harassed by George who demands that James compete in a race against fellow student Leo Butcher. Reluctantly, James enters the competition and loses. After the race, Butcher explains that since he plays the trumpet, he has enhanced lung capacity and is a strong swimmer as a result. Butcher agrees to teach James how to increase his lung capacity.

The three-part school competition begins; it includes shooting, swimming, and running segments. James comes in second in the shooting contest; George and Andrew Carlton, another student, tie for first. Between events, Lord Hellebore surreptitiously gives his son George performance-enhancing pills. During the swimming competition, George is nearly disqualified for several false starts. However, in deference to his father's status, George is allowed to continue the competition. Another boy comes in first and Andrew Carlton comes in second place. The last segment is the foot race, in which George will need to come in first, to win the overall competition. When James tries to stop George from cheating and taking a shortcut, George attack him. James gets away from the school bully. Carlton wins the race. Lord Hellebore is furious about his son's poor placement.

James receives a letter from his Aunt Charmian indicating that his Uncle Max is in poor health. Charmian invites James to spend the Easter Holidays with them at their home in Keithley, Scotland.

While waiting for the train to Scotland, James meets a boy named Red Kelly, who is looking for his missing cousin, Alfie. Red cannot afford to buy a train ticket, so James helps him sneak on board. During the train ride, James encounters George who is still sore at James. When George threatens to beat James, Red stands up to the bully, who backs off.

Aunt Charmian picks James up at the train station and drives him home in her Bentley. At the house, James is greeted by Uncle Max, whose health is failing. Later, Max teaches James how to fish and teaches Bond how to drive his Bamford and Martin. James is intrigued when Max reveals that he was a spy during World War I.

Charmian takes James to the circus. There, James runs into Red Kelly, who is still looking for his missing cousin. James agrees to help Red in his search. School bully George pays two local farm boys to attack Bond and Red. James can hold his own, but Red is the more skilled pugilist. Red agrees to give Bond boxing lessons.

The next day, James and Red search the countryside for Alfie. Along the way, they meet a local girl named Wilder Lawless riding her horse, Martini. Wilder reveals that she previously spotted Alfie by the Loch and reported Alfie's sighting to Lord Hellebore, who promised to inform the police about Alfie's whereabouts.

During their search, James and Red meet a Pinkerton Detective agent, Mike Moran. Morgan has been hired by Lord Hellebore's ex-wife, Maude Randolph, to locate Lord Hellebore's missing brother, Algar. James, Red, and Morgan investigate Lord Hellebore's property and make note of the unexpectedly high security, fencing, and dam that are designed to keep animals inside Hellebore's property. They also discover a footprint that may be Alfie's.

A few days later, James encounters Wilder Lawless who says that she went to the police and learned that Lord Hellebore never notified them she spotted Alfie. Morgan vows to continue his investigation into Hellebore. Later, James and Red search for Morgan and discover his dead body, which has been attacked by eels.

Preparing for trouble, James inserts a small folding knife into a newly fashioned secret compartment in the heel of his shoe. James and Red sneak into the back of a truck that is entering Hellebore's grounds. They try to enter the castle through a window, which can only be accessed by climbing a tree. James is able to successfully navigate the tree but Red falls from it and injures his leg. Red beseeches Bond to continue without him. Once inside the castle, Bond is knocked out.

When James wakes up, he discovers that he is in Hellebore's laboratory. Hellebore demands to know what James is doing in his castle. Bluffing, James claims that he is paying a visit to Hellebore's son, George. When summoned, George refuses to vouch for James.

Lord Hellebore explains that he has been experimenting with a formula to turn soldiers into super beings. Hellebore has been giving his brother Algar the formula, known as SilverFin, which has transformed him into a hulking monster. Lord Hellebore also tested the formula on Alfie Kelley, Red's cousin. Alfie died after his first injection. Now, Hellebore needs a new guinea pig and Young Bond will do. Hellebore gives James his first injection and promises to return for additional rounds.

James removes the knife from the secret compartment of his shoe and uses it to gain access to a shaft. The shaft takes James to a tunnel filled with cold water. To escape the castle, James will need to swim underwater for a great distance. Using the breathing methods that he learned from Butcher, James swims the length of the tunnel and escapes the castle.

Bond finds Red. Together, they steal a lorry and burst through the front gate. Hellebore catches up to James and strikes him across the face with a riding crop. Just then, Wilder shows up on her horse. They get away from Hellebore and run into George Hellebore, who regrets betraying Bond and wants to stop his father.

George helps Bond sneak back into the castle. Once inside, James and George set fire to Hellebore's laboratory, papers, and super soldier serum. They come upon Hellebore's brother, Algar who is locked up in a cage, and set him free. Lord Hellebore arrives and aims his gun at James and George. Before Hellebore can kill James, Algar arrives. Hellebore and Algar fight, eventually killing each other.

Ten days later, James wakes up in bed. Aunt Charmian, who has been nursing James back to health, reveals that Max has died. Charmian and James attend a memorial service for Max. When James recovers, he returns to Eton. At Eton, he is no longer afraid of the school bullies; his adventure has changed him.

Commentary: Ian Fleming largely avoided writing about James Bond's childhood. From Fleming's works we know that after Bond's parents died in a mountain climbing accident, his Aunt Charmian took him in and enrolled him at Eton College, a boarding school in Windsor England. Bond's stay in Eton was brief. He was kicked out of school for an incident involving a maid. Charlie Higson took the limited information that Fleming provided and weaved it into five books about Bond's teen years.

In *SilverFin*, Higson focuses on James' first term in Eton. Through flashbacks, Higson recalls how the 13-year-old Bond learned about his parents' death and how he came to live with his Aunt. More than that, Higson depicts Bond's first big adventure, an encounter with a villain developing a super soldier serum.

Higson explains how Bond acquired some of his particular set of skills. In *SilverFin*, Bond's Uncle Max teaches him how to drive; his classmate Leo Butcher teaches him how to hold his breath for long periods; and his new friend Red Kelly instructs Bond on how to fight. The implication is that any time in the Fleming novels, when Bond drives, swims, or fights, some of those abilities came from his time in *SilverFin.*

Bond also experiences his first romantic kiss. At the end of the novel, Wilder kisses James goodbye. The adult Bond would welcome the kiss, but the teenage Bond is less enthusiastic about the smooch.

At first glance, it seems that Higson also offers the origin of Bond's facial scar. In the novel, Lord Hellebore slashes Bond in the face with his riding crop. It seems that the resulting injury would leave a scar. However, a close read of Fleming's novels, suggests that Bond was scar-free until the age of seventeen.[120] So, the incident foreshadows things to come.

Higson is generally careful with the amount and nature of references to other Bond books and films. Having established that, I would like to draw your attention to one allusion, as it illustrates some of the challenges that Higson faced. In Fleming's novels, Bond drinks a martini, in part, because it reminds him of Vesper Lynd, the woman he loved but who betrayed him in *Casino Royale*. In *SilverFin,* Bond encounters Wilder Lawless, a teenager who rides a horse named Martini. Wilder and James form a friendship and the young girl saves his life. The unstated implication is that when the adult Bond drinks a martini, he is not only thinking of Vesper, but he's also drawing on his memories of Wilder. Some readers will get a kick out of the references to Bond's preferred beverage. Others might find that having two different associations is a weaker choice than having one. Ultimately, it comes down to the reader's taste.

James enters school as a wounded adolescent who is intimidated by bullies. In the end, James discovers that the fear bullies may induce in him pales in comparison to the other horrors in the world. Even the bullies see something "cold and terrifying in his eyes" resolve not to harass James in the future. As a result, in future books, school bullies learn to stay away from James and find other, more vulnerable targets.

Higson movingly writes about the time that Aunt Charmian let Bond know that his parents died. It's a heartbreaking chapter, told in flashbacks. Readers learn that Bond was quite close with his mother Monique. James and Monique would spend large parts of the year together while his father Andrew was away working. James and his father didn't have a very close relationship. Bond seems to feel that he disappointed his father. It's a wound that the adult Bond will never quite heal from.

Higson also introduces readers to Max, Bond's uncle. Max has several important functions in the story. Beyond teaching James about driving, Max quickly becomes a quasi-father figure to the boy. Max is a role model who confesses to James that he served as a spy during the war. James is no doubt inspired to follow in Max's footsteps. Bond's decision to become a spy is a tribute in some ways to his time with Max.

Higson also uses Max as a way to keep James in a state of loneliness and despair. At first, under the care of Charmian and Max, James has a "whole" traditional family again, an ersatz mother and father to keep him safe and provide him with love. When Max dies of cancer, Bond's world is destabilized once again. Moreover, James never got to say a proper goodbye to Max, who he knew was sick. In fact, James feels a certain guilt about the death. Max wanted to take James for driving lessons, but James declined and instead wanted to look into the disappearance of the missing boy. So James feels his last moments with Max were a disappointment in some ways. Of course, James did nothing wrong by declining Max's invitation. Yet, James will have to live with those unresolved feelings.

Despite all the pitfalls of writing about a young Bond, Higson delivers a satisfying and exciting yarn. Higson's *SilverFin* is a wonderful adventure novel that introduces the reader to a critical period in Bond's life.

Continuity Nod: In *SilverFin,* Aunt Charmian drives a four-and-a-half liter, four-cylinder Bentley, the same model that the adult Bond drives. Bond's Uncle Max drives a Bamford and Martin, which he eventually wills to James. Bamford and Martin would later change its company's name to Aston Martin. While Aston Martin is more closely associated with the movie Bond, the literary one occasionally drives one in *Goldfinger.* Aunt Charmian hates tea and thinks that continued tea drinking will result in the end of the British Empire. Charmian's thoughts echo a similar passage in *Goldfinger.* Before Uncle Max dies, he recites a credo from Jack London, "I shall not waste my days in trying to prolong them. I shall use my time." That same quote appeared in Bond's obituary in *You Only Live Twice* and would also be quoted in the movie *No Time to Die.*

Bond's History: James was born in Zurich, and lived in Switzerland, France, Italy, and London. Family activities usually include skiing, climbing, or sailing. He learned to swim in Jamaica, ride a horse, and shoot a gun in Italy. Bond's father Andrew is described as a man's man and a restless soul. Bond's mother Monique is the primary caregiver, as Andrew is often traveling for work. Monique sometimes finds herself torn between her love for her husband and her son.

Bond's Inner Life: James has anxiety dreams about his deceased parents. He's also quite lonely; he feels like an outsider at Eton. James bristles at all the rules that he is expected to follow. James is a people watcher; for fun, he'll identify strangers on the street and make up stories about them. He finds shooting a .22 Browning rifle to be rather exciting. When he grows up, James considers becoming an explorer or perhaps even a spy, like his Uncle Max.

Bond's Personal Life: James excels in his French class, but he struggles in Latin.

Bond's Tastes: His school dorm is decorated with images of a naval battle, a portrait of King George, and an island in the South Seas. James likes reading H. C. McNeile's novels about the gentleman adventurer Bulldog Drummond. Like Bond, Fleming was also a Drummond fan. As Bond expert Jack Lugo points out, James adopts some of Aunt Charmian's "attitudes and predilections such as her preference for coffee over tea."[121]

Bond's Work Methods: Bond learns that there are no rules in fighting; the only goal is to defeat your opponent. As such, when selecting a target on your opponent, no parts are off limits.

Comic Book Adaptions: *SilverFin* has been adapted into two different graphic novels. The first *SilverFin* graphic novel was published by Disney's Hyperion Books in 2008; the 160-page volume is adapted by Higson, illustrated by Kev Walker, and scripted by both Higson and Walker. Given the fact that Higson adapted his own book, it is not necessarily surprising that the *SilverFin* graphic novel is so faithful to the source material. However, what might be unexpected is the fact that the work captures the pace and the spirit of the original. The graphic novel does not rush from action beat to action beat. Instead, while not skimping on thrills, it retains many of the character-based elements of the novel.

By contrast, the second comic is a more modest effort. It is 64 pages long and the size of the book is 5" x 7.75", fairly small. The 2020 volume is adapted by Hannah Fish. The interior art is credited not to an artist but to a company Dynamo Ltd., a business that creates illustrations for licensed properties. The comic is intended as a learning aid for those for whom English is a second language. As such, the language-acquisition tool includes comprehension questions, homework exercises, and a glossary of words. Readers can access an audio and digital version of the book by visiting the publisher's website and entering the code which is imprinted on the inside back cover.

The 2008 adaptation retains the structure of Higson's book. It begins with a prologue and the rest of the comic is divided into three sections. Eton, Scotland, and SilverFin changed from "The Castle."

The 2020 edition moves the events in the prologue to the body of the story. It is divided into four parts—"Blood in the Water," "Eton College," "Scotland," and "Castle Hellebore."

Assorted Observations:

- James comes across a sign that reads "Trespassers Will Be Shot," a possible reference to a similar sign posted at a crocodile farm in the film *Live and Let Die* that reads, "Trespassers Will Be Eaten."
- Higson anticipates a scene from Eon's *Skyfall*. In *Skyfall*, the villain Raoul Silva tells Bond a story about trapping a hoard of rats in a drum. Silva explains that the rats eat each other until there are only two left. Similarly in *SilverFin*, Lord Hellebore tells a comparable tale about putting ten eels in a tank and watching the eels eat each other until only one remains.
- Similar to *Colonel Sun*, which is the only Bond continuation or spinoff book to be adapted into a comic strip, *SilverFin* is the only one to be made into a graphic novel.
- The *SilverFin* audiobook is narrated by Charlie Higson, making him the first Bond author to provide narration for his own book. Higson, an actor from the UK comedy sketch series *The Fast Show*, would continue to provide narration for all five of his Young Bond books, as well as his Bond novella *On His Majesty's Secret Service*.

BLOOD FEVER (2006)

Author: Charlie Higson

In Brief: While on a school trip and visiting his cousin in Sardinia, James Bond investigates a secret society, the Millenaria, that is establishing an international crime syndicate based on the principles of the Roman Empire.

Meaning of Title: Double meaning. One, after getting bitten by mosquitoes carrying malaria, Bond experiences vivid fever dreams. Two, according to Hungarian folklore, they could defeat their foe if they drank bull's blood.

Chronology: Period. Set after the events of *SilverFin*. In 1933.

Operation: Not applicable.

Bastard Meter: None.

Eggs: None.

Insight into Bond: "I know you, James. You like a spot of danger. It adds pepper to your soup."

Summary: Amy Goodenough, a teenage girl, and her father are traveling on a yacht in the Mediterranean. Hungarian pirate, Zoltan the Magyar, and his men board the boat and kill Amy's father. Seeking revenge, Amy stabs Zoltan. The wounded Zoltan orders his men to steal a small bronze statue, kidnap Amy, and burn the yacht.

James, who is still in his first year at Eton, joins his friends for a meeting of their covert club, The Danger Society, on the roof of a school building. Amy's brother, Mark Goodenough, is among the Society's members. The meeting ends early when school officials happen upon the club.

James overhears two men conversing in Latin as he makes his way back to his room. The men are in a chamber with a strange altar, a bowl of blood, and a painting of a man in a Roman toga that is enclosed in a frame with the letters UCMM at the bottom of it. There is also a book and a box that have "MM" written on them in red letters.

The following week, James meets up with his friends Pritpal Nandra and Tommy Chong. They run into Mark Goodenough, who has since learned that his sister, Amy, is missing. A panicked Mark asks

James to give him his car. Given Mark's agitated state, James refuses the request.

While walking with his Aunt Charmian, James sees his teacher Mr. Merriot and the president of Eton's classic society, John Cooper-ffrench. Then, Perry informs James that Mark is planning to steal James' car. James catches up with Mark who explains that he's upset because his father has been killed and his sister Amy is missing. Soon after, James learns of an art theft.

Bond's teacher Peter Haight invites James on the upcoming school trip to Sardinia, an island in the Mediterranean Sea. Later, James sees that the school bully Tony Fitzpaine is harassing Pritpal, a friend of James. James comes to Pritpal's rescue and punches Tony out. Then, James recognizes a nearby building where the two men were speaking Latin. James looks into the window and sees Cooper-ffrench, the Latin teacher, and a man with scars on his face and a tattoo of the letter "M" on each hand. James dubs the man Smiler. James asks Mr. Merriot what the double "M" could mean. Merriot doesn't know but tells James that he'll look into it.

James visits his Aunt Charmian in Kent. Charmian tells James to go on the school trip to Sardinia and, while he's there, visit his cousin Victor Delacroix who lives in Capo D'orso, a province on the northern coast. Elsewhere, Zoltan the Magyar continues to keep Amy Goodenough and her tutor hostage. Zoltan plans to hold Amy for ransom.

While in Sardinia, James receives a letter from Mr. Merriot, his classical teacher at Eton. Merriot tells Bond that Cooper-ffrench was talking about a secret Italian society known as the Millenaria, which is known by the double Roman Numerals. The now-defunct society is believed to be linked to fascists including Benito Mussolini, the Prime Minister of Italy; the group spoke Latin in their meetings.

James tells Haight about the Millenaria and suggests that the two men who were speaking Latin at Eton might be linked to the society. Haight is dubious of James' claims and, after giving him some water to drink, Haight tells James to explore a nearby tower. On his way up the tower, James is overcome with nausea and dizziness and nearly falls off. James passes out. When he wakes up, a worried Haight tells James that he saved him from plummeting to his death. Cooper-ffrench joins the school trip.

Bond travels to the northern part of Sardinia to meet his cousin. Once there, he's picked up by a local boy named Mauro Benetutti, who drives James to Victor's home. At the house, James meets an eccentric painter Poliponi. Bond notices that the residence is filled with valuable art. Twenty miles away, Zoltan the Magyar meets with Smiler, the man with the scars who was talking to Cooper-ffrench at Eton. Smiler is there to facilitate the delivery of Zoltan's crates.

Victor lends Bond a snorkel, goggles, and swimming fins so that he can swim in the Mediterranean Sea. While swimming, James spots Zoltan's boat a seaplane arriving with Count Ugo Carnifex, a local man who controls the mining industry, and his sister Contessa, Jana Carnifex. Ugo and Jana eat dinner with James, his cousin, and the painter. Over dinner, James learns Ugo controls a dam and that his vast palazzo is located above his silver mine. Ugo invites the trio to his carnival which is being held in the mountains.

Nearby, Zoltan and Smiler deliver the crates to Ugo but Ugo doesn't immediately pay Zoltan for his services. Ugo says he wants to buy Amy, but Zoltan declines the offer since he has feelings for his prisoner. Ugo orders his men to capture Amy. Amy is locked up behind steel bars.

James, Victor, and Poliponi meet Ugo who invites them to attend his carnival. At the carnival, James runs into Stefano and Zoltan. Victor, an engineer, tells Bond that Ugo made a grave mistake in the placement of his dam, as it is poorly constructed and unstable. James runs into his schoolmates at the festival, along with Eton professors Haight and Cooper-ffrench. James discovers that Ugo has built a replica of the Roman Colosseum. Zoltan and Ugo make a bet; they will each choose someone to fight for them. Ugo chooses Fitzpaine, the school bully, and Zoltan selects James as his champion. Zoltan gives James pointers on how to fight; James implements Zoltan's fighting strategy and knocks Fitzpaine out.

Elsewhere, Mauro walks into the woods and encounters a masked rider on a horse. The rider draws a sword and strikes Mauro down. That night, James spots Smiler and follows him. Smiler boards the railway car on Ugo's funicular-railway track, the only means to get to Ugo's palazzo. James jumps on the roof of the train car and gains access to Ugo's residence.

Bond discovers that Millenaria is holding a secret meeting with Smiler, Zoltan, and their leader, Ugo. Ugo announces that he wants to form an international crime syndicate that will communicate with each other in Latin. They toast with the blood of the bull. Afterward, Zoltan tells Ugo that he doesn't want any part of this plan.

While searching for Ugo's residence, Bond runs into Stefano, a local boy who is in charge of bringing Amy food. Stefano tells Bond that Amy is being held prisoner on Ugo's property. Bond locates Amy in her cell, but he doesn't have the tools to free her. Bond seeks help and finds his teacher, Peter Haight. After learning about Amy's predicament, Haight tells James that they need to get out of there. However, it's a trick; Haight is part of the cabal.

Haight brings James to Ugo. Ugo tells Haight that they need to find out if James told anyone about their schemes. Soon after, Haight sees Cooper-ffrench who has figured out that Ugo is up to no good. Haight pushes Cooper-ffrench off a tall ledge, killing him.

Ugo tells James that he steals the art so that he can ransom it back to its owners. Ugo intends to use the money to fund his scheme of becoming the new Caesar. Ugo brings James to a nearby bog and ties him down while mosquitoes who are carrying malaria bite him. Ugo demands that James tell him who betrayed him. James lies and claims that Zoltan is disloyal. Ugo departs. Later, Haight arrives and tells Bond that he and Ugo share their love of emperors. James realizes that Haight, who has been trying to kill him all along, was the one who drugged his water bottle at the tower.

As the malaria-carrying mosquitoes continue to attack Bond, Haight departs. James starts to hallucinate but is saved by Vendetta Benetutti, the sister of the boy who was killed by the rider on the horse. Vendetta nurses James back to health at a nearby village. Ugo sends Smiler to the village to eliminate James. Before Smiler can kill James, he is killed by one of Zoltan's men, Tree-Trunk. Zoltan explains that Ugo has refused to pay him for the art that he brought. Therefore, Ugo is now Zoltan's sworn enemy. Zoltan tells James that tomorrow he and his men will attack Ugo's compound and save Amy.

James decides that he needs to reach Amy before Zoltan gets to her. James and Vendetta agree to sneak into Ugo's residence via the aqueduct. James and Vendetta get to Ugo's palazzo and free Amy. Zoltan's men arrive shortly after. A battle rages between Zoltan and Ugo's army. James worries that Zoltan is going to destroy the dam, an act that will kill innocent civilians. James decides that the only way to stop him is to go to the caves beneath the palazzo. When they arrive at the caves, James and Amy discover that Zoltan is there waiting for them. The dam breaks and floods the palazzo. Ugo is killed when the rushing waters of the flood cause his seaplane to come crashing into him. However, Ugo's sister Jana survives and vows revenge against James.

James, Amy, Vendetta, and Zoltan flee the area. A masked rider attacks Zoltan. Zoltan is grievously injured but kills the rider, who is revealed to be Peter Haight, the teacher from Eton. Bond, Amy, and Zoltan take a boat to safety. Zoltan dies in transit and James returns to his cousin's villa. Ugo's sister Jana is there, and she tries to kill James. James and Amy jump into the water and swim to safety. Jana tries to pursue them, but she is stung to death by sea urchins. Amy is also stung by the urchins, but James saves her by sucking out the poison.

Commentary: In his first Young Bond novel, *SilverFin*, Charlie Higson wrote about many of the biggest touchstones in Bond's life. Higson covered Bond's parents' death, his life with Aunt Charmian, his first term at Eton, how he learned to drive, and his first kiss. So when it came time to craft his second Young Bond book *Blood Fever*, Higson could no longer rely on depicting the seminal firsts. Instead, Higson would have to cover new ground and take a different approach. So, with *Blood Fever*, he had to create a compelling, action-packed adventure that would reasonably fit within the life of a schoolboy. If *SilverFin* is an origin story, then *Blood Fever* is more akin to Bond's next big case. As a whole, *Blood Fever* is less dependent on drawing on Bond lore.

That's not to say that Higson completely avoids "firsts." It's just that this time—with two notable exceptions—the firsts are not life-changing events for Bond. Instead, for the most part, they are smaller moments that many teenagers might experience. *Blood Fever* depicts the first time that Bond goes snorkeling, fires a Tommy Gun, and learns how to be a better fighter. Zoltan the Magyar, a charismatic but dangerous pirate, teaches Bond how to throw a punch. Equally important is that Zoltan's techniques are specifically targeted to circumstances when Bond is fighting a bigger and stronger opponent. Zoltan cautions, "Be a dancer not a fighter. Keep moving." As the adult Bond will face off with killers like Oddjob and Red Grant, knowing how to get the best of an oversized brute is useful advice.

Bond also gets his first taste of an organized, multi-national criminal organization. The Millenaria are only in their initial stages of forming. Ugo's plans call to unite a group of criminals who "will work together, from within, undermining society, overthrowing governments." If they can do then, then they will get untold riches and they will be an "underground empire of criminals." Fortunately for James, the Millenaria are not quite in SPECTRE's league. By the end of *Blood Fever*, James has defeated them.

There is a surprising other first depicted. It's the first time that Bond will use his sexuality to manipulate a woman. In *Blood Fever*, James must leave behind Vendetta Benetutti, a local Sardinian girl, who shows a little jealousy about Bond's attempts to save Amy Goodenough from the clutches of Count Ugo Carnifex. However, Vendetta wants to accompany James on his mission. He tells her to wait for him. Uncertain that she will, he makes a fateful choice, "He took four steps, then ran back and kissed her hard on the mouth." It's a revealing moment because Higson had previously established that James isn't interested in girls, at least not yet. Earlier in the book, he told Vendetta, "I'm not looking for one [a girlfriend]." Moments before the kiss, James tells Vendetta, "I don't love [Amy]. I don't love you." That's not to say that James is indifferent to Vendetta; one could argue that Bond doth protest too much. However, his feeling for Vendetta is not entirely the point. The fact that he kisses her to influence her actions is notable.

Beyond telling readers about a young Bond's early exploits, Higson is interested in teaching his young and impressionable readers. As Fleming did, Higson is interested in describing a variety of subjects, including historical events and how things work. During *Blood Fever*, Higson provides information on how Tommy Guns work, how mosquitos pass on malaria via parasites that live in their body, Greek mythology, and Roman history.

Wealth and social status are a part of Higson's books. Bond goes to a posh school, but he's constantly reminded that he's not as wealthy as his schoolmates. Although he has a variety of friends, some students treat him poorly simply because he doesn't have their means. Additionally, Higson weaves the pitfalls of wealth and status into the villain's back story and even their demise. For instance, Count Ugo Carnifex is not nearly as wealthy as he pretends to be. Nor is he a Count. In actuality. Ugo is the son of a goat herder who just gave himself the title. Fittingly, Ugo is killed when his seaplane, a status symbol, crushes into him. Ugo's sister, Jana, is similarly hoisted by her own petard. Jana meets her end when she falls onto deadly urchins. Had she not been wearing such ridiculously high shoes and ridiculously long fake fingernails she would have been able to grab onto something to secure herself if her.

Higson alludes to the future by saying that the number seven will play a significant role in Bond's life. In *Blood Fever*, an artist performs a mentalism trick on James and says, "Seven is your number; it will be a very important number in your life. Seven is the luckiest of numbers."

The mentalism trick isn't all good news. The artist also tells Bond that "Death will walk by your side through your life." James dismisses it but the reader knows that it is deadly accurate. Elsewhere, Zoltan tells James that, in the future, he might need to enroll in the war and kill a man. To do so, Zoltan instructs Bond to harden his heart. Higson explains that James has a "reckless side to his nature and one day it was going to get him into big trouble."

Higson is careful not to overload the book with too many references to Bond's future. For these books to succeed, they need to deliver a satisfying story that is not dependent on referencing other Bond books and movies.

Along the way, James gets some life lessons that he'll take to heart. His cousin Victor advises, "Life should be for pleasure, not for war." As an adult, James will heed the first bit of advice but ignore the second part. Higson makes sure to remind the reader that James is just a boy. So, when Bond gets particularly frustrated, he breaks down in tears.

The way that Harry Potter books are structured is that each book represents a different school year at Hogwarts. Higson and Ian Fleming Publications did not follow suit. If they had, *Blood Fever* would have been set during Bond's second year at Eton. Instead, it's set at the end of his first term and during the summer holidays. This approach allows for the potential of more books to be set during Bond's teenage years. If the Young Bond books followed a one-book-per-year approach, then James would age out of school faster and there would be fewer Young Bond books.

Continuity Nod: Higson makes several homages to Ian Fleming and his writing. One character says that Bond's name is dull and blunt. One character cautions, "You only live once," a rephrasing of the title *You Only Live Twice*. Elsewhere, a character speaks about "sadism before supper." Fleming's writing has been criticized for, in addition to sexism and snobbery, its sadism. When James steps on a poisonous sea urchin, Mauro helps Bond by sucking out the poison. In the final moments of the book, Amy steps on an urchin but this time, Bond sucks out the poison. Years later, when Domino treads on a sea-egg spine in *Thunderball*, Bond will use this technique to assist her too. Higson includes another reference to Fleming's ninth novel. Count Lippe is the name of a SPECTRE enforcer in *Thunderball*. Lippe is likely the descendent of *Blood Fever*'s Armando Lippe, one of the men who Zoltan recruits to join his crime syndicate.

Bond's Inner Life: Even at an early age, James had a yearning to be free and independent. Even sitting still in class is a bit of a struggle for James. Higson explains that James "hated feeling trapped. Whenever he was, he always wanted to know there was a way out" and elsewhere, the most important thing for James "was to be free, to be in charge of his own life. When life becomes a routine for him, boredom easily creeps in."

James is a decent and moral boy but he's not above reproach. In *Blood Fever*, James and Fitzpaine, the school bully, compete in a boxing match. After a tough bout, James knocks Fitzpaine out. As

Fitzpaine is falling, James throws another punch for good measure. It wasn't necessary but James felt compelled to finish him off. Later, James apologizes and admits that his second punch was cruel. Still, James can be forgiven, Fitzpaine cheated by stuffing his gloves with a heavy object so that he could pack a bigger blow.

Elsewhere in the book, we see other examples of Bond's compassion. During the final raid, where Zoltan's men attack Ugo's warriors, Bond feels "desperately sorry" for the men who were killed in the battle. He knows that they are locals and that "this fight was nothing to do with" them.

Bond's Personal Life: Bond is a member of the Danger Society, a group of kids who break curfew and sneak around on rooftops at night. Bond is still friends with Pritpal Nandra and Tommy Chong, who were introduced in *SilverFin*, but neither plays a major part in the story. Pritpal fans need not worry, as he will have a significantly bigger part in Higson's next book *Double or Die.* Bond's classes include Latin, and the classics in general (Greek, Roman life).

Bond's Work Methods: When his adrenaline is up, Bond possesses the amazing ability to not only withstand pain but also to not fully experience it.

Bond's Family Tree: The Bond family tree continued to expand. In Higson's first Young Bond, *SilverFin*, readers are introduced to Bond's family on his father's side. In *Blood Fever*, Higson expands his mother's family by introducing Victor, a cousin in Sardinia. Higson fleshes out Aunt Charmian's backstory and explains that she used to make a living a living as an anthropologist, globetrotting and learning about different civilizations. Charmian has been to Greenland, Sahara, Papua New Guinea, and Burma. She is currently planning to go to the Amazon. Of course, when James grows up, his job will take him around the world and his understanding of different customs will hold him in good stead. Charmian's role in *Blood Fever* is considerably reduced from the part she played in *SilverFin*, where readers first got to know her.

Assorted Observations:

- The symbol of the villains is a double M. Of course, another M will play a crucial role in James' life when he grows up and becomes a spy. An inverted M with a tail is the calling card of SMERSH which is carved into Bond's hand in *Casino Royale*.

DOUBLE OR DIE (2007)

Author: Charlie Higson

In Brief: James Bond must decipher a series of clues to locate his kidnapped professor, and this leads him to the discovery of a coding-cracking device that the Soviets are developing to beat the United Kingdom in the war.

Meaning of Title: If Bond doesn't decipher the codes, which have double meanings, innocent people will die.

Chronology: Period. Set following the events of *Blood Fever*, in 1933, over six days in December. Also, a notable postscript, 12 years later.

Operation: Not applicable.

Bastard Meter: Not applicable.

Eggs: The best scrambled eggs that Bond has ever consumed.

Insight into Bond: "Despite what he said to the Head Master, he knew that he could never keep out of trouble."

Summary: In England, Eton math professor Alexis Fairburn is kidnapped while visiting a graveyard. At Eton, Bond is playing a game of hearts with his friend Pritpal Nandra. Their card game is interrupted by school officials, including House Master Cecil Codrose, who want to talk to James and Pritpal about two letters that they've received from Fairburn, their math teacher. The first letter is addressed to Codrose and it's a letter of resignation; Pritpal is the recipient of the second letter. Pritpal and Bond tell the school officials that they don't understand Fairburn's letter, which is filled with obvious factual errors. After talking with the boys, Codrose secures the letter in his study. Later, Pritpal realizes that Fairburn's letter contains a coded message that includes seven clues for them to solve.

With the help of his friends, Bond breaks into Codrose's office, and photographs Fairburn's letter so that they can examine it more closely. Using Fairburn's letter, the boys eventually figure that they need to attend the next meeting of the Crossword Society and find a Cambridge professor, code-named Gordius, who will be in attendance.

At the Crossword Society, James and Pritpal locate Gordius, whose real name is Professor Ivar Peterson. James decides that

Gordius isn't trustworthy. As the boys leave the Crossword Society meeting, James is nearly run down. James suspects that Gordius is lying about being Professor Peterson. James and Pritpal agree to go to Cambridge so that they can confirm Peterson's identity.

Bond meets up with his friend Perry Mandeville, who tells James about a dilapidated Bentley. Perry suggests that they buy and restore the car, but that plan is put on hold as neither student has sufficient funds to make the purchase.

James and Perry go to Cambridge in an attempt to locate Professor Ivar Peterson. At Cambridge, they meet Alan Turing, a mathematician and computer scientist. James enters Peterson's office and discovers that the real Professor Peterson has been murdered. Before he was killed, Peterson was writing a coded letter. Among Peterson's belongings, James notices a photograph of Peterson with Professor Fairburn and a third man named John Charnage. James takes the letter and the photograph.

Once outside, James realizes that two men, Wolfgang and Ludwig Smith, are following him. Ludwig's skin appears to be translucent. James jumps in his car and tries to get away. Wolfgang and Ludwig speed after James, forcing him off the road and destroying the car that he inherited from his Uncle Max.

An injured Bond wakes up in the hospital. James finds his way to Perry's house. Perry welcomes his friend. James decides he wants to visit John Charnage, the man from Peterson's photograph.

James and Perry go to Sir John Charnage's house and discover that Charnage is the man who was posing as Gordius at the Crossword Society event. They also discover that Charnage has a vast collection of poisons and a copy of Fairburn's letter, which he must have stolen from Eton. When James accuses Charnage of lying, Charnage leaves the room to call the police to tell them that Bond was spotted fleeing the scene of Peterson's murder. James and Perry run away.

James and Perry meet up with Pritpal and show him Peterson's coded note which is filled with ones and zeros. Pritpal explains that the ones and zeros are part of a binary code. James deciphers the note and learns that Fairburn has been kidnapped and will be taken out of London the next day. Other clues direct them to go to Highgate Cemetery in North London, refer to the creation of something called Nemesis, and instruct them to go to the Royal College of Surgeons and locate room five. At the Royal College, they find a collection of brains preserved in jars. One of the brains belongs to Charles Babbage, an 1857 mathematician who was working on an early computer.

James and Pritpal go to Highgate Cemetery where they need to find an Egyptian tomb. The boys enter the tomb and meet a homeless man named Theo. Theo helps them find the next item on their list, a lion. Theo explains that a statue of a lion marks the grave of George Wombwell, a Victorian showman whose traveling circus also contained an animal exhibit. James finds a piece of paper next to the lion. Before James can figure out the importance of his discovery, Wolfgang and Ludwig Smith appear. They kill Theo, but James and Pritpal escape. James hides in the trunk of Wolfgang and Ludwig's car.

Wolfgang and Ludwig drive to John Charnage's factory, Charnage Chemical Company factory. James sneaks out of the car and explores the factory, which is filled with poisonous chemicals. James pockets a bottle of the chemical potassium. As he continues to explore the vast space, he discovers that the factory is home to a secret nightclub and casino called the Paradise Club.

Bond enters the casino and meets a mobster named Dutch Flegenheimer, who demands that James pick his roulette numbers. James suggests a number and Dutch wins. As a reward, Dutch offers to give James a cut of the haul.

Ludwig grabs James and takes him to Charnage, who demands that James tell him what he's learned about his operation. When James refuses, Charnage forces James to drink vast amounts of gin until he passes out. Later James comes to and discovers that he's in a boat piloted by Wolfgang and Ludwig. They plan to drown James. James throws the bottle of potassium at the boat's wheelhouse, causing an explosion and injuring Wolfgang. James flees to safety but passes out when he reaches dry land. When he awakens, he learns that he's been taken in by a gang of girls who call themselves the Monstrous Regiment. The head of the Monstrous Regiment is Kelly, the sister of Red, the boy he befriended in Scotland (*SilverFin*). Red vouches for James.

James calls Pritpal who speculates that the machines that are being built must be massive and would need to travel from England to Russia via ship. If that's the case, Fairburn would also be found on the ship. Using an underground pneumatic railway, James, Red, and Kelly travel to the docks. They sneak onto the ship and locate a room housing the Nemesis machine, a computer that can be used to break enemy codes. Then, they find Fairburn who explains that Charnage isn't the head of the operation; Colonel Irena Sedova is in charge. Fairburn, Kelly, and James escape to a nearby boat and hide there. Sedova orders her men to kill Charnage and find Fairburn.

Sedova's men locate James, Kelly, and Fairburn. Red arrives with his gang, the Monstrous Regiment and a battle ensues between the Regiment and Sedova's forces. James locates the dying Charnage who tells him how to destroy the Nemesis machine. Suddenly, Ludwig and Colonel Sedova arrive. Ludwig attacks James but he's sucked into a fan and killed. James has the opportunity to shoot Sedova, but he refuses to shoot someone in cold blood. Sedova escapes and the boys destroy the machine.

Back at Eton, Bond decides that he is going to use his winnings from the underground casino to purchase and restore the dilapidated Bentley.

The postscript is set twelve years later. World War II is ending because of the efforts of the code breakers and scientists who decrypt German transmissions. An adult James Bond is tasked with taking an unnamed codebreaker to London. When Bond arrives on the site, he recognizes Alexis Fairburn, the man Bond saved when he was only a teenager.

Commentary: What did you do this week? I'll wager that Young Bond had a busier week than you did. Over the course of six days, Bond discovers that one of his teachers has been abducted, deciphers a string of clues, crashes his deceased uncle's car while experiencing his first car chase, drinks copious amounts of alcohol against his will, throws a chemical at a thug that caused him to lose four fingers, and, for the first time, dances with a girl. It's enough to make the rest of us feel a tad lazy. Moreover, the bulk of those events took place over an action-packed three days.

Keeping the events limited to a brief period keeps the tension high and the pace fast. Moreover, Fleming established that Bond only spent two terms at Eton. By having the key events play out in less than a week, Higson avoids using up another year of Bond's brief tenure at Eton. Both *Blood Fever* and *Double or Die* are set during James' summer vacation and before his second term begins. This strategy ensures that future Young Bond stories could retain the Eton setting.

Higson departs from the boy's action-adventure genre of his first two Young Bond novels and, in *Double or Die*, ensnares James in a *The DaVinci Code*-style mystery. In *Double or Die*, Bond must solve a series of seven clues so that he can locate his missing teacher and stop a plot by the Russians to gain access to a supercomputer that will create an unbreakable code.

As with *SilverFin* and *Blood Fever*, James experiences a few firsts in *Double or Die*. Some of the events that happen to James are universal to many teenagers. For instance, James suffers through his first hangover and dances with a girl. The circumstances surrounding these occurrences, however, are anything but normal. Bond's hangover is the result of the villain forcing James to drink gin, as a means of torture. And the dance occurs in an abandoned ship that James is hiding in while he's on the run from the enemy.

Higson further develops Bond's character in *Double or Die*. Bond begins to foster a sense of humor. He uses his humor to entertain his friends, antagonize his enemies, and diffuse the tension of a situation. James begins to learn that humor can be a tool for gaining an advantage.

Bond's reputation begins to precede him. The adult James Bond is well-known to foreign intelligence agencies. There are dossiers filled with personal details about the adult spy. Young James Bond has not earned that status. However, word is starting to get out. He has become something of a legend in the East End of London, where tales of his exploits of *SilverFin* have been passed around. One boy is honored to have James sleep in his bed.

James has a way to go before he's emotionally equipped to be a secret agent. In *Double or Die*, James has the opportunity to shoot Colonel Sedova. However, Sedova is without a weapon and James is not prepared to fire upon an unarmed person. The rest of the Young Bond series will continue to explore his reluctance to commit cold-blooded murder.

Continuity Nod: James Bond uses his gambling winnings to purchase a run-down Bentley; the literary Bond's preferred vehicle. While visiting London, James drives by the Universal Exports building, the import-export company that serves as a cover for SIS. The villain, Sir John Charnage, tells Bond about his gambling escapades in Royales-les-Eaux, France (*Casino Royale*). James references a Fleming short story when he indicates that the clues from their missing professor are "for our eyes only." There is also a reference to Bond's trip to Sardinia (*Blood Fever*).

Bond's Inner Life: After two major previous adventures, James is beginning to recognize that trouble will find him, or he will find trouble. He also understands that although he is not the biggest or smartest or most capable boy, he won't stop trying until he accomplishes what he wants, "I'm not the type to give up" and that he'll "keep chipping away" until his problem is solved.

Bond's friends are starting to notice a change in him. He's come into his own, is "utterly fearless," and has a blatant disregard for rules. His

friends describe him as "a man of action" and, using Fleming's wording, a "blunt object."
Despite all these adult adventures, Bond is still just a teen. And when he gets overwhelmed, he cries. Sometimes out of frustration. He's also scared throughout the book. He recognizes that he's in over his head but something about James forces him to set that aside and persist, nonetheless.

Bond's Personal Life: Bond is distracted at school and his work is starting to suffer. His courses include science and history, where he is studying the Napoleonic wars. He's read *Kidnapped* by Robert Louis Stevenson, possibly for pleasure. Bond and his friends play Field Game, a combination of American football and rugby, and that's only played at Eton. Bond is a natural player who helps his team win.

Bond's Work Methods: Bond's system for solving problems and defeating adversaries (either on the playing field or in combat) is to "shoot the moon." It's a risky maneuver with a high probability of failure but where the rewards are plentiful.

Assorted Observations:

- James uses the alias John Bryce for the first time. The adult Bond will use the same alias in Fleming's *Live and Let Die* and Benson's *The Facts of Death*.
- Aunt Charmian is referenced but she does not appear in *Double or Die*.
- The adult Bond depicted in the book is in his mid-twenties, circa 25 years old.

HURRICANE GOLD (2007)

Author: Charlie Higson

In Brief: Young Bond joins a gang to rescue two children who have been kidnapped. Things take a turn for the worse when James is trapped on an island that is being used as a hideout by criminals on the run.

Meaning of Title: Multiple meanings. One, it is a reference to a treasure that brings bad luck to those who possess it. Two, the main villain El Huracán, the hurricane, forces the inhabitants of his island to sieve for gold. Three, a hurricane ravages Mexico.

Chronology: Period. Late 1933 and early 1934. Set after the events of *Double or Die*. Roughly one year after James first enrolled in Eton.

Operation: Not applicable.

Bastard Meter: None.

Eggs: Eggs are used as an ingredient in a paste that is created to repel snakes and lizards.

Insight into Bond: "He was damned if he was going to give up without a fight."

Summary: Mexican aristocrat El Huracán is the leader of the Caribbean island Lagrimas Negras. The secluded island is populated by criminals who are hiding from the law. To stay on the island, criminals must follow El Huracán's laws, such as no contact with the outside world. El Huracán discovers that an American con artist named Robert King has violated the rules by trying to send letters to the mainland. As punishment, El Huracán places King in his "rat run," an obstacle course filled with dangerous animals and lethal traps. El Huracán promises that if King reaches the end of the course, he will be granted freedom. Halfway through, a panther devours King.

In Mexico, young James Bond is accompanying his Aunt Charmian on an expedition. While James and Charmian take in the sights, a thief named Angel Corona steals Charmian's pocketbook. James runs after the thief and retrieves Charmian's purse.

James and Charmian travel to Jack Stone's ostentatious house. James is going to stay there while Charmian continues her expedition in Southern Mexico. At the house, they meet Stone's two children, Precious, a spoiled teenager and Jack Junior, aka JJ, her seven-year-old brother. Stone informs Charmian that a storm is coming and that he will need to fly her to the expedition on his private plane. In Stone's absence, James will look after the children. Stone and Charmian depart for the airport.

That night, while a hurricane rages, a gang tries to break into Stone's house. Theda Glass is the leader of the gang, and her crew is Sakata, Manny, Whatzat, and Strabo. The gang locates Stone's safe and attempts to open it. James throws Manny out the window before hiding Precious and JJ in the old icehouse.

When the storm passes, the thieves try to break into Stone's safe. Since they are unable to open the safe, they take it with them. Meanwhile, James and the kids make their way to the town and discover that it has been destroyed by the storm. They meet Garcia, who works for Stone. Garcia reveals that Stone and Charmian are safe and are staying at the Mayan city Palenque. However, given the treacherous roads, they can't immediately return. Meanwhile, JJ is starting to get sick.

James leaves the children to see if he can find transportation to safety. By the time he returns, he discovers that the gang's vehicle is broken, and they have kidnapped Precious and JJ. James hatches a plan to save the kids; he introduces himself as Angel and offers to transport the thieves to the next town. The thieves agree, and James drives them and the kids.

As the drive continues, James gains the trust of the gang. He learns that the gang plans to find a way to break into the seemingly impenetrable safe and retrieve the unidentified object they are seeking, or ransom off the children in exchange for the combo to the safe. Later, their truck breaks down. A group of soldiers stop and offer assistance but the crooks gun them down. Bond and company arrive at an oilfield, where Strabo procures dynamite. They use the nitroglycerine from the dynamite to blow the lock off the safe. Soon after, James sees his chance to escape; he coldcocks Whatzat. When the goon won't go down, James throws lime in his face. Whatzat stumbles and falls in mud and water, drowning.

JJ's condition worsens. Garcia grabs JJ and tries to take him to the hospital. Strabo shoots and kills Garcia. Mrs. Theda Glass taunts Precious and tells her that her father, Jack Stone, wasn't nearly as wealthy as he pretended to be. Glass claims that Stone is a crook and smuggler who recently came into possession of United States naval secrets; Stone plans to betray his country and sell the documents to the Japanese. Glass opens the safe and learns that the documents are missing.

James and Sakata talk and enjoy each other's company. James tells Sakata that he's no different than the rest of the gang who hurt people. After reflecting on Bond's advice, Sakata sneaks away with JJ and takes him to the hospital. With Sakata gone, only James, Precious, Strabo, and Glass remain.

Glass decides that they need to go to a safe location. So she makes plans to go to El Huracán's island, where Glass will ransom Precious for the naval secrets. Bond and Precious escape from Glass. As they search for safety they run into Manny, the goon who Bond pushed out the window at Precious' house. Due to a brain injury, Manny mistakes James for his deceased brother Louis. James and Precious push Manny out of a moving car and escape.

James and Precious continue their journey and meet up with Stone's co-pilot, Beto, who tells them that JJ is safe. James and Precious find Stone's place and locate the naval secrets. Glass catches up with them and steals the documents.

Glass and Manny take James and Precious to Lagrimas Negras, the island where crooks live. When they arrive, El Huracán forces James and Precious to join his workforce and contribute to the maintenance of the island. James and Precious are told that they can never leave Lagrimas Negras but if they work hard, they won't be harmed. They learn about El Huracán's obstacle course, which is called La Avenida de Muerte, aka The Avenue of Death.

After discovering design plans for The Avenue of Death, James and Precious train in ways to defeat each stage of the obstacle course. When they are confident that they can successfully navigate the course, James and Precious deliberately get caught passing a message to the outside world. El Huracán is disappointed in James, who he had hoped would take over the island one day. El Huracán tells James and Precious that if they get through the obstacle course, they will be freed.

James and Precious enter The Avenue of Death and face close calls as they avoid panthers, army ants, and spinning stones that could crush them. In the final stage, a crocodile closes in on James and Precious. A bomb they had earlier planted detonates and blows up the course, freeing James and Precious.

El Huracán agrees to let Bond and Precious leave the island. In exchange for their silence, El Huracán returns the naval secret to James. Later, James and Precious reunite with her father Jack Stone. Precious tells her father to reform and return the naval secrets to the

United States. Stone agrees, and the trio travels back to the mainland, where James will reunite with Charmian.

Commentary: Not every aspect of James Bond's life and iconography warrants a backstory. For instance, one might not assume that the shampoo he used in *On Her Majesty's Secret Service* would merit one. Yet, Charlie Higson disagrees. A little context is necessary. In *Hurricane Gold*, James suffers through an ordeal. While a storm ranges, a gang breaks into a home where Bond is looking after two children. James evades the gang while simultaneously keeping the two children safe. When the hoods kidnap the children, Bond comes to their rescue. He's taken prisoner and forced to travel to an island compromised by criminals. James enjoys a shower on the island where he cleans off the grime he's gathered over the past few days. There is a bottle of Pinaud Elixir in the shower. It's a good shower and even better shampoo. James takes note of the product's name and "promised himself that he would only ever use that brand from now on in memory of the best shower he had ever had." The adult Bond makes good on the promise, which is how 007 finds himself using Pinaud Elixir, the "prince among shampoos," in *On Her Majesty's Secret Service*.

Bond's shampoo usage is reminiscent of the reasoning behind his Vesper martinis. When James drinks a martini in the later novels, it reminds him of the time he spent with Vesper Lynd in Casino Royale. Similarly, when the adult Bond uses Pinaud Elixir in On Her Majesty's Secret Service, he recalls his ordeal in Mexico in Hurricane Gold.

I kid. In truth, the Pinaud Elixir is just a wink to Bond fans who are intimately familiar with Fleming's books. Fleming only mentions the product in one novel. Higson is not suggesting that the shampoo is as important as Bond's cigarette brand or car manufacturer. The shampoo incident underscores the challenges that Higson faced while writing his Young Bond novels. As noted, he's already covered, so many important Bond firsts in the first three novels, that Higson needs to mine different territories. So for this fourth story, Higson charts Bond's emotional development.

We see further instances of when James chooses to put his life on the line to help others. For example, James steps up to defend Precious and JJ Stone, when a band of thugs burst into their house. Later, James spots JJ holding onto the roof of a car that is being swept away by a raging flood. James disregards his own safety and rescues the young boy.

Higson also shows James's burgeoning interest in girls. In the previous books, James has kissed girls—or rather, girls have kissed

James. James wasn't necessarily all that keen on the experience. In *Hurricane Gold*, James seems to finally enjoy the moment when Precious gives him a smooch. He likens it to "being kissed by an angel." In the last line of the book, an appreciative James puts his arm around her and together they watch the sunset. Previously, James was closed off to romantic relationships. He's finally opening himself up to the possibility of love. There's still room to grow.

Whereas the adult Bond is a loner, the teenager James works well in groups. In each novel, as he does in *Hurricane Gold*, he relies on other people to survive his ordeals. It seems that the only way he survived El Huracán's obstacle course is because Bond relied on Precious. Without her, Bond would have been worm food.

The adult Bond hates bullies and seems to have a disdain for the rich and the privileged. In *Hurricane Gold*, Higson continues to explore where James became sensitive to class issues. James sees how the rich kids treat their servants and James is always ready to lend a helping hand and ease their load. When he's brought to El Huracán's island, James feels special empathy for the workers, who have to cater to their boss's every whim. James develops his sense of justice in Higson's Young Bond novels that will carry over until his missions as a mature secret agent.

The villains often meet terrible ends but not by Bond's direct hand. Instead, the baddies will do something that will cause their own demise. For instance, when Strabo tries to shoot Bond, he misses and hits a wasp nest instead. In turn, the wasps sting Strabo, causing him to fall into a hoard of insects, that fatally sting him. Later, another villain falls into muddy waters and drowns. These deaths—where the villains often get hoisted by their own petard—are useful ways to eliminate the bad guy but keep the teenage James' hands clean and retain his innocence.

Higson continues to play with the form of the Young Bond novels. In the first three books, Bond's threats were largely of the human variety. While James does face his fair share of evildoers, a substantial number of the threats are from nature. The course is filled with a series of traps, which are often related to some dangerous animal. There are scorpions, alligators, and army ants, among other pesky and lethal critters. Higson's choice is also consistent with the Bond of the Fleming books, who faced off against a squid, a centipede, and poisonous spiders, and whose friend, Felix Leiter, was mauled by sharks.

In addition to the animals that Bond must deal with in El Huracán's traps, Bond also has to contend with the titular hurricane, its aftermath, floods, and a harrowing trek through the jungle. Higson makes a wise choice in mixing up the threats. The adult Bond has a reason for facing death frequently—his job requires it. The same does not hold true for a teenager. So veering away from criminals and leaning into the explosive power of mother nature, is a shrewd and practical decision. Higson's intended audience, younger readers, may more easily relate to these kinds of threats.

Higson also brings Aunt Charmian back into the fold. Charmian had a significant role in *SilverFin* but a reduced one in *Blood Fever* and in *Double or Die*, she did not appear at all. In *Hurricane Gold*, her part is small but still impactful. Seeing Charmian, even briefly, is one of the highlights of the series. Charmian is not the wallflower that some readers might have assumed. She's an independent woman who bravely travels the world alone, a task all the more impressive in the 1930s.

Hurricane Gold is a fun adventure story with a great conceit—Bond must escape from an island comprised of criminals. The premise of an island filled with crooks on the lamb is furtive ground for a story, and Higson gives writer Jim Thompson the credit for proffering into his 1958 crime novel *The Getaway.*

In a clever bit of cross-promotion, when the movie *Thunderball* was released in theaters, Pan Books republished Fleming's novel with a promotional letter from Domino Vitali to James Bond inserted into copies of the book. Higson takes a similar tack in *Hurricane Gold* and includes three letters to Bond in the book. The minor difference is that Fleming's letters were placed into copies and Higson's are printed inside the book. Two of the letters are from his friends Percy and Pritpal and the third letter is from his classics tutor, Michael Merriot. In his note, Pritpal informs James that the Bentley that Bond and he recently purchased is being restored, that Theo Bentinck is the new school bully, and that there is a new maid named Roan. Perry also reveals that he has been kicked out of school and that the Danger Society has been disbanded. In a letter, Merriot invites Bond to join the school's Easter vacation trip to Kitzbühel, Austria. Because none of *Hurricane Gold* takes place in Eton, the letters serve as a means to keep the reader updated about life at the school. They also set up plot points that will pay off in Higson's next Young Bond novel, *By Royal Command.*

Continuity Nod: The Japanese gang member named Sakata is named after Harold Sakata, the actor, and weightlifter who played Oddjob in *Goldfinger*. In the film *Moonraker*, the adult Bond drives a gondola on dry land as if it were a car. In *Hurricane Gold*, Young Bond's car gets swept up by a raging river and he needs to pilot his car as if it were a boat. The obstacle course that Young Bond navigates recalls a similar gauntlet in the novel *Dr. No*.

Bond's History: As a child, Bond loved going to the beach and digging up the sand to make little dams.

Bond's Inner Life: Young James Bond is impulsive; he acts without considering the consequences and often winds up in trouble for it. For instance, he chases a boy who stole his aunt's pocketbook. The boy, armed with a knife, draws the unarmed James into a trap.
James is appropriately emotional for a teenager. However, his reactions are in stark contrast to his adult self. When Bond gets overwhelmed, he will cry or laugh hysterically. This is an aspect of Bond's character that we've seen in Higson's previous offering as well.

Bond's Personal Life: Bond owns a telescope and is reading a Doctor Fu Manchu novel. Fu Manchu is an evil genius and Fleming's Doctor Julius No was partially inspired by Sax Rohmer's fictional character.

Bond's Tastes: James starts to get an idea of how he wants his apartment to appear when he's an adult: it should be spacious and unadorned. James forms this opinion after seeing his cousin's ostentatious dwellings.

Bond's Work Methods: Sakata befriends James and teaches him jujitsu. Sakata instructs James on how to use his enemy's body against them. He also advises James not to stiffen up when squaring off against an opponent; instead, James should remain willowy. James is learning to respond to danger instinctively and not to overthink his response.

Assorted Observations:

- Mr. Merriot, Bond's classics tutor who has appeared in the previous three Young Bond books has finally been given a first name—Michael.
- James sees his first dead body, a victim of the storm. It would be one of many that he comes across.

BY ROYAL COMMAND (2008)

Author: Charlie Higson

In Brief: Bond must thwart the assassination of King George and evade two dangerous villains from his past.

Meaning of Title: Two meanings. One, James meets two young girls whose toy shuttlecock is struck in a tree. The girls, who turn out to be Princesses Elizabeth and Margaret, ask or "command" James to retrieve their toy. Two, James accepts his first mission from Her Majesty's Secret Service.

Chronology: Period. Set in 1934, shortly after the events of *Hurricane Gold.*

Operation: Not applicable.

Bastard Meter: Not applicable.

Eggs: Scrambled and cooked by his pal.

Insight into Bond: "The life of a spy consisted of long periods of boredom punctuated by brief intense moments of fear and death."

Summary: In Lisbon, Colonel Irena Sedova searches for Martinho Ferreira at his bookstore, a front for a spy cell with ties to Moscow. Sedova gets shot by Ferreira's associate but she is protected by her bulletproof corset. She kills the associate and finds a scrap of paper with James Bond's name on it.

In Germany, Graf von Schlick and his mistress Liesl are driving through the countryside. They stop to help two men in a stuck car. When Graf von Schlick approaches the car, it explodes.

On a train in Austria for a school trip, young James Bond plays cards with German boys who are revealed to be Hitler Youth. The Germans accuse James of cheating when he wins. Then the boys attack James but he repels them. Later, in Kitzbühel. James has lunch with his friend Andrew Carlton. James is unaware that a man in a Trilby hat is following him.

The next day, James speaks with Eton's schoolmaster. Michael Merriot and takes skiing lessons with Hannes Oberhauser. Later, Bond spots classmate Miles Langton-Herring, a fellow student skiing in the wrong direction so he pursues him. When Miles breaks his leg, James tries to help him down the mountain but before long, an avalanche buries the boys in the snow. They dig themselves free and make their way down the mountain.

Frieda von Schlick goes to the Vienna opera, while her husband, Graf Otto von Schlick, is still undergoing treatment in the hospital for injuries he received in an automobile explosion. An unidentified assailant kills Frieda by throwing her out of her opera box.

Hannes Oberhauser takes James and Miles to a nearby hospital. At the clinic, James notices a sick patient (later revealed to be Graf Otto von Schlick) who is muttering that someone is trying to kill his cousin, Jürgen.

Later, Hannes Oberhauser and Michael Merriot collect Bond from the clinic. James is too sick to continue the school trip so Oberhauser lets James recover at his home, with his wife Helga. A week later, James returns to the school trip. He's unaware that the man in a Trilby hat is watching them. When the vacation ends, Hannes invites James to stay with his family in Vienna.

Back at Eton, James spends time with friends Pritpal Nandra and Tommy Chong. The new House Captain Theo Bentinck tries to intimidate James. James meets the new maid, Roan Power, who all the boys fancy.

Two Russians, Emerald and Amethyst, discuss Operation Snow-Blind and their plans to kill James. Elsewhere, James practices his sculling, a form of competitive boat racing. Roan asks James for a ride. Theo catches the two and reproaches James for consorting with a maid. As punishment, Theo canes James.

Merriot tells James that his grades are slipping. During their talk, James spots a man spying on him. Later, James sees the man again and chases after him, but the man gets away. James runs into Miles Langton-Herring, who has been released from the clinic. Miles invites James to a party at his house. Then, Roan invites James to a picnic that Sunday. James wonders if he's developing feelings for her.

On Sunday, James meets with his friend Andrew Carlton in a garage that holds a 4 ½ litre Bentley, the car that James and Andrew purchased with their gambling winnings (*Double or Die*). Then, James goes to Windsor Great Park for his picnic with Roan. When he arrives, James discovers that Roan brought her male friend, Dandy O'Keefe, a gardener at Eton. At the park, James notices that two little girls (later revealed to be Princesses Elizabeth and Margaret) have lost their toy shuttlecock. James helps them retrieve it.

James goes to Miles' house for the party. At the party, James meets Miles' father, Mr. Langton-Herring. Also in attendance is the future King of England, Prince Edward and Graf von Schlick.

Expressing his gratitude for rescuing his son, Langton-Herring presents James with a lavish gift, a diving watch. Then, James meets Prince Edward who tells James that his father King George V will be visiting Eton on June 4th, the birthday of King George. Graf von Schlick joins their conversation. James tells von Schlick that they were both at the clinic at the same time and that he heard him crying out for his cousin Jürgen. A flustered, von Schlick tells James that he's mistaken.

A few days later, James meets up with Roan's friend, Dandy who expresses his disdain for the monarchy and praises communist ideals. James realizes that his attraction for Roan is growing.

In town, Bond spots someone he thinks looks like Colonel Irena Sedova (whom he first encountered in *Double or Die*). James convinces himself that he's mistaken. In class, Bond's science teacher explains how you can use common items, such as weed killers, to create a bomb. James realizes that Roan's friend Dandy is going to kill the King at Eton's Chapel with a homemade bomb. Bond searches for and discovers the bomb in the chapel's crypt. Before he can defuse it, Roan knocks him out.

When James comes to, Dandy reveals that he's going to kill the King and frame Bond. Roan lights the fuse and leaves Bond to die. Using a razorblade that he previously hid in his coat, James cuts out of his binds and snuffs out the flame, eliminating the threat. James chases after Dandy. Dandy grabs Bond and tries to cut him with a knife. The man in the Trilby hat arrives on the scene and shoots Dandy. A car pulls up, the man in the hat and James get in and are taken to a nearby house where James meets his teacher, Merriot.

Merriot explains that the man in the Trilby hat, Captain Dan Nevin, is a member of the Secret Intelligence Service, who has been assigned to protect James. Merriot reveals that he too is a spy and now he acts as a lookout for potential recruits, such as James. Merriot reveals Roan and Dandy are spies working for the communists and instructs James to feed Roan false information. For Bond, that just means lying to someone he cares about.

Following Merriot's orders, James meets up with Roan and tells her that he knows that Dandy is trying to kill the King. Roan tells James that she didn't believe in Dandy's cause but was forced to go along with it. If she didn't help Dandy, he would have hurt her. Roan explains that Dandy was working on a secret plan known as Operation Snow-Blind and that Dandy, through intermediaries, is working for Martinho Ferreira, who runs the bookshop in Portugal. Ferreira reports to someone by the code name of Obsidian.

Later, a lovestruck Bond meets up with Roan and confesses that he's been lying to her and that he's been working for Merriot.

James offers to help Roan escape from Eton. By betraying his country, James will never be able to return to England or see his loved ones again.

James and Roan fly to Austria, where James hopes that ski instructor Hannes Oberhauser will take them in. Once there, Oberhauser welcomes them warmly and treats James as an extended member of the family. Still, James feels restless.

One day while hiking, James and Roan encounter a group of Russians. The Russians take James to Doctor Perseus Friend, a German scientist who he previously encountered at Loch Silverfin (*SilverFin*). Friend has recovered from his burns with the help of a secret formula. Now, Friend has partnered with the Russians to exact revenge on the United Kingdom. As part of his plan, Friend is posing as a distant relative of the royals, Graf von Schlick, to get close to Prince Edward. Friend explains that he is the one called Obsidian, the head of Operation Snow-Blind, and that he is actually a Nazi. Roan, a communist, is shocked to learn that she'd unknowingly been working on behalf of a fascist. Friend explains that Colonel Sedova has figured out Friend's plans and has been working to stop him. Friend plans to skin James alive and use the skin to transplant it onto Friend's body.

James and Roan are brought to their rooms where Roan confesses that she was deliberately leading Bond into a trap; she knew all about Operation Snow-Blind. James feels betrayed. James breaks out of his room, overcomes a security guard, and frees Roan and Graf von Schlick's wife, who have also been kidnapped.

James and Roan make their way to the operating theater where the skin graft surgery was to take place and James destroys the room. Friend's henchman, Vladimir Wrangle, locates Bond and the two of them struggle. Wrangle is getting the better of James when Roan intervenes, saves James, and kills Wrangle.

Friend spots James and starts firing at him, narrowly missing. Colonel Sedova arrives and shoots and kills Friend. Roan tells Sedova that she'll join him in Moscow and help contribute to the communist cause. When Sedova fires at Bond, Roan throws herself in the bullet's path, saving Bond, but suffering a fatal wound in the process. James grabs a nearby gun and shoots Sedova but she survives because she is wearing a bulletproof corset. British agents arrive and rescue Bond. James professes his love to the wounded Roan. Roan confesses that Dandy wasn't just her friend; they were husband and wife. Roan dies in Bond's arms.

Merriot arrives and reports that Colonel Sedova got away. Moreover, Bond cannot return to school at Eton; instead, he will have to go to Fettes. Merriot cautions James that he is now part of a bigger world of spies and villains. Hannes Oberhauser takes James back to his home where he will get a home-cooked meal and care.

Commentary: Here, everything changes for James Bond. This is where Higson was heading all along. *By Royal Command* depicts Bond's first assignment from His Majesty's Secret Service. It's the turning point in a young Bond's life—Higson poignantly captures the transition from an open-hearted boy to a young man. It's when Bond falls in love for the first time and experiences the ensuing heartbreak. It's when James is prepared to leave his family and friends behind for a woman he loves. It's when he's betrayed. *By Royal Command* is Higson's endgame.

Higson had been subtly tracing Bond's development over the course of the previous four novels. Each book represented a small step in Bond's development. Higson sensitively and carefully portrayed Bond's formative childhood experiences, including his first kiss, his first time operating a vehicle, playing cards with pals, his boredom at school, and his desire for more. In *By Royal Command*, Bond takes a giant step towards his destiny and his life as a secret agent.

In the first four books, James stumbled into a misadventure by chance. It's as though Eton was a trouble magnet. Teachers were kidnapped. School vacations were fraught with danger. There can only be so many coincidences before the idea strains credulity. So Higson changes tactics in his fifth book, Bond's past comes back to haunt him in *By Royal Command*. Dr. Friend from *SilverFin* and Irena Sedova from *Double or Die* are back in *By Royal Command*. Both want revenge on James for foiling their plans.

In addition to avoiding the trap of convenient coincidences, the return of these two villains serves another function. Bond's past *decisions* and *actions* come back to haunt him. If James didn't interfere with Friend's plans in *SilverFin*, then the evil doctor wouldn't have wanted to torture Bond in *By Royal Command*. The appearance of Sedova is even more layered. In *Double or Die*, James had the opportunity to kill her. Instead, James spared her life. It was a potentially deadly mistake for James to make. Had he been more professional or hardened his heart two books ago, then James would have been a lot safer in the fifth one. It's a life lesson that he won't soon forget.

It makes sense why Bond let Sedova live in *Double or Die*. If he had killed her, it would have been cold-blooded murder. James had also thwarted her plans; thus she was no longer a direct threat to him. Let's not forget that James is just a teen and not an adult, seasoned agent. By the time *By Royal Command* reaches its climax, James has changed. Now, he tries to kill Sedova who only manages to survive because she is donning a bulletproof corset. The fact that she lives helps James retain a little of his innocence. It's also beside the point, James is prepared to kill; he is one step closer to becoming the blunt instrument of Fleming's novels.

In *By Royal Command,* Higson reveals that Bond's classical tutor, Michael Merriot, is not simply an employee of Eton. Instead, Merriot works for the British government. His job is to identify young people who have the skill and aptitude to be spies. Merriot reveals his true motives to James and sends the young man on his first mission. James is not tricked into or forced into working for the Secret Intelligence Service; he does so willingly, albeit begrudgingly. Merriot's true identity is a surprise twist, but one that Higson set up in *SilverFin* when he established that Merriot had previously worked as a runner for the Royal Navy.

Bond is called upon to deceive Roan while collaborating with Merriot in order to uncover the gardener Dandy O'Keefe's schemes. Even worse, Bond learns that Roan—the first woman he ever loved—lied to him in order to win his confidence. Bond is unable to tell his loved ones the whole truth about what transpired, not even when the villain's scheme is exposed. The notion fills Bond with dread.

The devastating impact of working in the spy game is that James is forced to lie to his friends and his beloved Aunt Charmian. For the honorable and principled James, deceiving those he cares about and being deceived is almost too much to bear. Moreover, James, who lost his parents a few years back, is in desperate need of love and support. In the end, deceiving loved ones will cause him to become disconnected. James is further isolated because he doesn't want any harm to befall his friends. So to keep them safe, James begins to avoid emotionally intimate relations with others. By the book's end, James is ready to leave his friends and family behind.

In *By Royal* Command, Higson involves James with two significant characters in his life—a maid from Eton, Roan Power, and a ski instructor, Hannes Oberhauser—both of whom are Fleming creations. In "Octopussy," the adult Bond describes Oberhauser as a "wonderful man. He was something of a father to me at a time when I happened to need one." Fleming inserted this critical piece of Bond's personal history into the short story. So when Oberhauser is introduced as Bond's ski instructor and mountain guide in *By Royal Command*, Bondologist's collective ears perk up.

Higson depicts Oberhauser to be a kind and caring man who takes Bond in when the young boy has no place to go. In the last chapter of *By Royal Command*, Higson suggests the simple activities that they did together—family meals and exploring the mountains—made Bond feel like he had a family who cared for him. Over time, Oberhauser becomes a father figure to Bond, who is longing for one.

Despite Oberhauser's kindness and Aunt Charmian's welcome return, it's not a completely happy ending for James. James feels a little empty and hollow inside. Ultimately, James realizes that he is alone and that there is no one else in the world he can rely on. For James, the idea is not a completely chilling one. Instead, James makes peace with it and concludes, "There was nothing wrong with being alone."

Fleming briefly mentions Roan Power (but not by name) in Bond's obit in *You Only Live Twice*. Fleming writes that Bond was kicked out of Eton after "some alleged trouble with one of the boys' maids." The suggestion was that James had a dalliance with her. Higson doesn't dispute Fleming's account, but he does recontextualize it. Young James isn't a lothario; he's a love-struck kid who pines for this beautiful, slightly older girl. Roan is charming, independent, and strong-willed; everything that James finds attractive in a woman. So, for the first time in Higson's Young Bond novels, James falls in love. Previously, James was indifferent and sometimes hostile towards girls. In *By Royal Command*, James is smitten and over his heels in love with Roan.

Sometimes love makes you do strange things. And such is the case here. When James belatedly learns that Roan is not a maid but an enemy of the British government, he ignores his better instincts and helps get her out of the country. It's an act that not only will get Bond kicked out of his school, but it also forces him to leave all of his friends and Aunt Charmian behind. And it makes him a fugitive and an enemy of the state. Nevertheless, James is in love, and he misguidedly follows his heart. He believes Roan is an unwitting pawn in a sinister game. Unfortunately, for James, he's wrong. Roan purposefully set Bond up, duped him into betraying his country, and came dangerously close to getting him killed. Even after James sacrifices his standing and his country for Roan, she betrays him again. In the end, Roan sacrifices her life to save Bond. The relationship is intended to echo his short-lived romance with Vesper Lynd in *Casino Royale*.

Higson's books are so rich, that I wish he had written another that he set between *Hurricane Gold* and *By Royal Command*. In the first four books, Higson judiciously incorporates Fleming's lore into his stories. Higson's work never feels like he's making distracting references to Fleming's work. Instead, he carefully and methodically distributed Bond's seminal life events throughout the first four books. So, for me, it's somewhat unexpected that Roan and Oberhauser appear in the same narrative. I would have assumed that the incident with the maid that caused him to be expelled from Eton and his time spent with Oberhauser would each be covered in two different narratives. Because *By Royal Command* would be Higson's last Young Bond book, it was his last chance to include these two seminal characters.

Surprisingly, even after five Young Bond novels, Higson still seemed to have more Bond stories to tell. Higson left the series with the axiom, always leave them wanting more. The five Young Bond books by Higson are skillfully brought to a satisfying and enjoyable end with the resolution of Bond's character arc. As Higson puts it, "He was no longer a schoolboy, he had grown into a young man."

Continuity Nod: Higson makes references to Bond's parents and their death while mountain climbing and the incident with the maid that Fleming blithely mentions in *You Only Live Twice* becomes a central plot of *By Royal Command.* A lorry driver tells Bond that he "scared the living daylights out of" him; a reference to Fleming's short story "The Living Daylights." Higson also alludes to Bond's adventures in Mexico and to the Danger Society (*Blood Fever*, *Double or Die*, *Hurricane Gold*). Dr. Perseus Friend and Colonel Sedova are returning characters who first appeared in *SilverFin* and *Double or Die*, respectively. Bond's Uncle Max (*SilverFin*) is also brought up throughout the book.

Bond's History: Bond's trip to Kitzbühel reminds him of his childhood in Switzerland and the time he spent with his parents.

Bond's Inner Life: Young Bond has been changed by the events of the past four novels. Bullies no longer hold any power over him. He's seen too much, now, "nothing could scare him." James uses that realization to enjoy his time at school and to appreciate the freedom that can come with it. For a time, he's uncharacteristically carefree.

Even still, James knows that he's not a typical teenager; he's an "outsider." His friends recognize that he requires "trouble," "excitement," and "danger" in his life, while they try to avoid them. Even though James is not yet a spy, his adventures are taking a toll on him. He realizes "how lonely it was to have secrets." And when Roan betrays him, something fractures inside. He is no longer sure who he can trust. James realizes that he is now fated to live in a "world of half-truths and half-lies." However, James has a more chilling realization, it's not just everyone else who is lying, he too is guilty of deceit.

"Nobody was who they had seemed to be, and nobody was telling the whole truth. Not even him."

At first, James refuses the hero's call. James shirks Mr. Merriot's call to become a "great hero or a great villain" and instead he seeks to enjoy the ordinary things that life has to offer. Instead of looking forward, Bond prefers to stay in the moment and "not worry about what tomorrow might bring." When he gets everything that he ostensibly wants, such as a family (with Oberhauser serving as a father figure) and love (with Roan, for a while), he feels empty inside. The soft life doesn't suit him, and he quickly grows bored.

Bond's Personal Life: James's proficiency at cards in his adult life is due, in part, because his school chum Tommy Chong served as his de facto instructor. James' unofficial motto when it comes to gambling is, "If you are not prepared to lose with good grace, don't play cards for money." He enjoys swimming but isn't doing well in Latin and Greek. Hannes Oberhauser teaches James to ski with "safety and with style." One bit of advice Oberhauser offers is that James "must turn off your brain and let your body guide you."

James still desperately misses his deceased parents. When he thinks of them, he has to hold back the tears. Mostly, he misses their kindness. He wants to be hugged and comforted by them. If his father were alive, he might have followed in his footsteps and worked for an armament company. For James, not having any parents also means that nobody "really expects anything of" him and without those guard rails his "future is a little more uncertain" than that of his friends.

His longing for love makes Bond particularly susceptible to Roan's charms. For the first time in a Young Bond novel, James falls in love. At first, Bond tries to convince himself that "love was for saps" but he's enchanted by Roan. He feels a "powerful urge to lean forward and kiss" a girl." That urge only increases and his feelings for Roan deepen. Eventually, Bond is willing to give up his country, his friends, and his remaining family to be with Roan.

It wasn't chance that brought him to Eton; Michael Merriot, who was recruited from the SIS and who knew Bond's uncle, arranged for Bond to be accepted. Bond's father Andrew was not a spy, but he did use his position as an armaments salesman to gather intelligence.

Bond's Tastes: For James, the scent of hot oil and petrol from his car is the "sweetest perfume."

Bond's Work Methods: MI6 operatives know that "the life of a spy consisted of long periods of boredom punctuated by brief intense moments of fear and death."

Bond already understands he can push his body beyond normal limits if he sets his mind to it. While being lashed by one of the students in his school, James withstands the torture by thinking about Roan.

In the lining of his coat, James keeps a penknife, a pencil, slips of paper, a book of matches, and a lock pick hidden away in five secret pockets.

A year after Higson completed his five Young Bond novels, he returned to write "A Hard Man to Kill," which was included in the non-fiction companion book to the Young Bond series, The Young Bond Dossier Danger Society

"A HARD MAN TO KILL" (2009)

Author: Charlie Higson

In Brief: Aboard an ocean liner, Young James Bond encounters a villain named General Charles Caiboche whose men conspire to free him from police custody.

Meaning of Title: The villain is referred to as a hard man to kill.

Chronology: Period. Set between the events of *Hurricane Gold* and *By Royal Command*.

Operation: Not applicable.

Bastard Meter: None.

Eggs: None

Insight into Bond: "Trouble seemed to follow him around like a sick dog."

Summary: In Venezuela, a criminal named Emil Lefebvre observes teenager Wilder Lawless loading horses onto the ship *Columbie*, which is sailing from to Europe. Emil's confederates, Maury and Argente, have tied up a customs inspector.

Young James Bond and his Aunt Charmian are sailing on a yacht from the Caribbean to Pointe-à-Pitre, a French island, where the *Columbie* has recently anchored.

When James and Charmian board the ship, they discover that General Charles Caiboche, a former French Legionnaire turned gangster, is being held by the French police. Caiboche is being taken to France to stand trial for his crimes.

The *Columbie* boat sets sail for France. James meets members of the French security forces including a young military officer named René Mathis. Mathis explains that the Cuban army caught Caiboche and handed him over to the French.

On the third night of the trip, James and Charmian eat dinner at the captain's table with first officer, Dumas, and Italian opera singer, Eduardo Ponzi. After dinner, James and Charmian play bridge with Ponzi and the manager of the French gymnastics team, Emil Lefebvre. The majority of the players are critical of Caiboche, but Emil stands up for him. He contends that the war criminal is revered by others as a hero. Later, Bond bumps into Wilder Lawless, the girl he previously met at Loch SilverFin (*SilverFin*). Wilder tells Bond that she and her father are transporting horses across the Atlantic.

Bond and Wilder spend the next day together. The pair go to the ship's stables to look at Wilder's horses. At the stables, they see Emil and his two cronies Maury and Argente. While Maury stands guard, Emil and Argente use a crowbar to break into the crates. A crew member stumbles upon the scene, and Maury bashes him on the head with a crowbar. But when he raises it to deliver the finishing blow, James intervenes and knocks Maury out.

James inspects the crates and discovers that one of them contains guns and the other holds bullets, concluding that Emil must have already stolen the guns. James reasons that if he can hide the bullets, then the guns would be useless, and his fellow passengers would be safe. James instructs Wilder to get help, while he disposes of the ammunition.

James runs to the deck and throws the bullets into the ocean. Spotting Dumas, the first officer, James asks for help. Dumas instructs James to seek refuge in the lounge.

When Bond enters the lounge, he sees Dumas and Emil, who reveal that they are in league with Caiboche and that they've taken Wilder hostage. They plan to free General Caiboche and have him escape on another boat that is arriving shortly. Emil demands to know where the bullets are. When Bond refuses to talk, Emil threatens to hurt Wilder. James bluffs and tells Emil that he will take him to the hiding spot for the bullets.

James brings Emil to a lifeboat. There, James takes out a knife and stabs Emil in the foot, pinning him to the boat.

James seeks help from the French police, but he discovers that they've been murdered. Caiboche grabs James and throws him across the room. James runs into the bathroom for safety and finds René Mathis hiding in the shower. James and René decide to take on Caiboche together but when they leave the bathroom, they discover that Caiboche is gone.

James and Mathis stake out the lounge where Wilder is being held captive. To create a diversion, Mathis fires his rifle. James grabs Wilder and they flee to safety on the promenade deck. Crew members carrying clubs raid the lounge and retake control of the ship. Caiboche evades capture by jumping overboard.

Later, James and Wilder go over the events of the day and surmise that Caiboche must have drowned. Elsewhere in the Atlantic Ocean, a submarine arrives and rescues Caiboche.

Commentary: *The Danger Society: The Young Bond Dossier* is a 2009 guide to Charlie Higson's Young Bond series. *The Young Bond Dossier* is divided into chapters that highlight the young Bond's villains, vehicles, people, places visited, and weaponry used. The highlight of the guidebook is "A Hard Man to Kill," a 69-page short story with illustrations by Kev Walker.

As a general rule, Higson's inspirations in the Young Bond series seem to be Fleming's works and not the Eon films. However, occasionally Higson will slip in a Bond movie reference or two, as he does in "A Hard Man to Kill." In one scene, James jumps into the fray to save a crew member's life from a hood named Maury. Maury threatens James with a knife, threatening to gut him like a fish. But first, Maury wants to find out the young intruder's name. James introduces himself, "The name's Bond, James Bond." Then, he adds, "And you've got four seconds to put down that knife before I break your hand." In moments like this, Higson frames James less like a frightened boy from his books and more like a hero from the movies. Readers can almost hear the Bond theme.

Higson tempers these movie-friendly scenes with instances that reinforce that James is still a kid with a long way to go before he's the hero of Fleming's novels. For instance, after James escapes from one thug, he needs a moment to compose himself and to counteract the "tension" and "dizziness" that he is experiencing.

"A Hard Man to Kill" functions outside of the Young Bond series. The short story was written, in part, to entice readers to pick up the guidebook. Here, Higson isn't depicting Young Bond's development from boy to man to spy. Instead, he's offering a spirited adventure and enjoyable interlude to his novels. Bond's wins are often tempered with an emotional cost to him in the main series; even if it's just a further loss of his innocence. In "A Hard Man to Kill," James registers a win, largely free of complications with only one wrinkle—the criminal gets away. That's a problem for another adventure and it doesn't seem to weigh heavily on Bond. Overall, it's nice to see James prosper in this escapade.

Bond's History: Just before the story begins, James had been crewing a yacht on vacation with his Aunt Charmian in the Caribbean.

Continuity Nod: Higson's Bond meets a young René Mathis, the French intelligence agent who appeared in three Fleming novels, as well as in *Benson's Never Dream of Dying* and *Devil May Care*. There are allusions to the first four Young Bond books. Wilder Lawless, the heroine of *SilverFin*, is a key figure in the short story, and James' adventures in *Double or Die* are mentioned. Higson alludes to Bond's forthcoming trip to the Austrian Alps (*By Royal Command*). He also references Bond's meeting with Precious Stone and his battle with American gangsters in Mexico (*Hurricane Gold*). The vacation was a gift for James and his Aunt from Stone's father for saving her life. However, no good deed goes unpunished—James and Charmian couldn't have afforded the trip which caused James to go through his ordeal with Caiboche.

Bond's Personal Life: James lets loose a little while on vacation; he dances, goes shopping, and enjoys live music. Because he is fluent in French, James has a basic understanding of Creole. He has read P. C. Wren's adventure book *Beau Geste*, which is about three English brothers who enlist in the French Foreign Legion.

Bond's Inner Life: James acknowledges that he doesn't thrive in the rigid structure of school. He also worries if anything he will experience in the future will be as thrilling as his past adventures. He needn't worry; there are more thrills to come.

Bond's Tastes: James loves the Caribbean, and doesn't trust horses. James enjoys playing bridge, a card game that his Aunt taught him. The adult Bond will put his bridge skills to the test when he faces off against Drax at Blades (*Moonraker*).

Assorted Observations:

- When describing the arch-villain, Higson evokes Fleming's style when he writes, "He was a man of rectangles, there was nothing round about him."
- Not only did Kev Walker provide the illustrations for *The Danger Society*, but he also illustrated the entire Young Bond series, the graphic novel adaptation of *SilverFin,* and the covers for the twelve-issue comic series *James Bond Origin* comic (2018-2019).
- "A Hard Man to Kill" was released as an e-book in 2018.

SAMANTHA WEINBERG'S TENURE 2005–2008

Samantha Weinberg wrote three books in *The Moneypenny Diaries series—Guardian Angel* (2005), *Secret Servant* (2006), and *Final Fling* (2008), as well as the 2006 short stories "For Your Eyes Only, James' and "Moneypenny's First Date With Bond."

THE MONEYPENNY DIARIES: GUARDIAN ANGEL (2005)

Author: Samantha Weinberg

Pseudonym: Kate Westbrook

In Brief: While searching for clues about her father's mysterious death, Miss Moneypenny faces danger when an enemy agent tries to compel her to share government secrets. Moneypenny also accompanies 007 on a trip to Cuba to avert a war between the United States and Cuba.

Meaning of Title: After saving Bond's life, 007 refers to Moneypenny as his "guardian angel."

Chronology: Period and contemporary. Two timelines. Set in 1962 after *On Her Majesty's Secret Service* and in 2005.

Operation: Not applicable.

Bastard Meter: None.

Eggs: When Bond is presumed dead, a memorial service is held in his honor; egg and cucumber sandwiches are served.

Insight into Bond: "He is not a man to lose one's heart to—though it is not hard to imagine how one could. He is tough on the outside, but I've always thought surprisingly vulnerable within."

Summary: The passages from 2005 are told from Kate Westbrook's perspective and the passages from 1962 are taken from Jane Moneypenny's diaries.

In 2005, academic Kate Westbrook receives a package that contains diaries from her Aunt Jane Moneypenny, a secretary at the Secret

Intelligence Services. The diaries were sent to Westbrook ten years after Moneypenny's passing, as per her wishes. The package also includes a note from Moneypenny explaining that Ian Fleming's Bond novels were based on actual events, Bond was a real person but didn't go by that name, and Jane was the inspiration for the character Miss Moneypenny. Westbrook's grandfather, Hugh Moneypenny, worked with Fleming in naval intelligence during World War II.

January 1962: Moneypenny is dating an architect named Richard Hamilton. James Bond is mourning the death of his wife who was recently gunned down by Ernst Stavro Blofeld and Irma Bunt (*On Her Majesty's Secret Service*). Blofeld's whereabouts are unknown, and Bond is on a bender, depressed. Moneypenny learns that the wife of the Head of Munich Station was killed in a car crash. Moneypenny remembers her father who she believes was killed during World War II. At work, M has called a summit to discuss Cuba, which since John Kennedy's failed Bay of Pigs invasion, has become politically volatile.

February 1962 [Personal Life]: Moneypenny continues to date Richard Hamilton. Moneypenny meets with the head of security, Captain Troop. Troop tells Moneypenny that she violated security protocol by not informing security about her relationship with Hamilton. Moneypenny meets M's wartime friend Sydney Cotton, a man who knew her father. Afterward, Moneypenny pulls Cotton's file and discovers that Cotton, like her father, was involved in naval intelligence. Cotton tells Moneypenny that he is going to have dinner at Blades with someone who knew her father. Later, Moneypenny calls Rodney Porterfield, the butler at Blades, who reveals that Cotton is dining with Commander Patrick Derring-Jones. Because Derring-Jones knew Moneypenny's missing father, Moneypenny wants to know more about him.

[Work Life]: M advises the Cuba Group that President Kennedy will need to show his strength after the Bay of Pigs debacle.

[Bond]: Mary Goodnight and Moneypenny worry about Bond's mental health. Bond and Moneypenny go to lunch together.

March 2005: Westbrook learns more about Moneypenny's childhood in Nairobi. Jane and her sister Helena were close to their father Hugh and were devastated that he had to return to England to fight in the war. Hugh was friends with other naval intelligence officers including author Ian Fleming.

March 1962: Bond's depression deepens; he's drinking more and not concentrating on his work.

[Personal Life]: Jane continues to date Richard but one night, she finds Richard rummaging through her desk. Richard provides an inadequate excuse for why he's searching through her possessions. At work, Captain Troop won't disclose how the vetting of Richard is going. Jane's suspicions about Richard deepen. Moneypenny goes to the orchestra where she meets a man named David Zach, who asks her out on a date.

[Work Life]: The Cuba Group learn that suspicious cargo is being transported into Cuba by freight.

[Search for Father]: Moneypenny pulls the file on Commander Derring-Jones, who knew her father. Jane contacts Derring-Jones who invites her to visit Scotland so that they can discuss her father.

[Bond]: Bond travels to Madrid to search for Blofeld. In Madrid, Bond kills Blofeld's bodyguard but Blofeld gets away. Bond learns that Blofeld is heading for Singapore.

April 1962 [Personal Life]: Jane goes out on a date with David Zach, the man she met at the orchestra. Jane also continues seeing Richard Hamilton. Richard has been cleared by Captain Troop, but Moneypenny still has her doubts.

[Search for Father]: Jane meets with Patrick Derring-Jones, who served with Hugh Moneypenny. Derring-Jones said that he last saw Hugh during the Operation Ruthless mission, a gambit to steal a code book from the Germans. During the mission, Hugh Moneypenny sacrificed himself so that Derring-Jones, Peter Smithers, and Fleming could get away. Nobody knows what happened to Hugh Moneypenny.

[Bond]: Bond remains uninterested in his job. M assigns him to go to Casablanca to investigate former Nazis who are working as hired assassins.

May 2005: Westbrook learns that Derring-Jones died in October 2003 and that he might be the true-life inspiration for Fleming's fictionalized version of the real. Westbrook searches for Peter Smithers, who served with Hugh. Westbrook travels to Switzerland to meet Smithers who does not know anything else about Hugh's ultimate fate.

May 1962 [Personal Life]: Moneypenny's flat is broken into. She wonders if the intruder was looking for her diaries. Later, Moneypenny goes on a date with Zach, who claims to know something about her father. Still later, Richard tells Moneypenny that he's moving to West Berlin for work; they part ways. Soon thereafter, Zach tells Moneypenny that he has reason to believe that Hugh survived Operation Ruthless, but he was taken to Germany and held as a prisoner in Berlin. Zach promises to find out more information about Hugh's fate but only if Moneypenny agrees to betray her country and provide him with secret intelligence.

[Work]: Jane takes gun lessons at SIS's firing range. Clive Mostyn, the head of Northern Europe, commits suicide, leading SIS to suspect that Mostyn is the mole.

June 1962 [Personal Life/Search for Father]: Moneypenny goes on a date with Zach. Zach explains that if Moneypenny wants information about her missing father, then she needs to provide information about Britain's operation in Cuba. Moneypenny is instructed to copy the reports and deliver them in a week to the Brompton Oratory, a church. Jane realizes that Zach has been playing her from the start. Using SIS's resources, she attempts to learn more about Zach. Jane goes to the church and leaves a letter indicating that she won't betray her country.

[Bond]: Bond returns from Casablanca. Bond and Jane dance together at Loelia Ponsonby's wedding.

July 1962 [Search for Father]: Jane receives a call at her home from an unknown person instructing her to steal government secrets. She refuses. Jane realizes that she's in over her head and is going to need the help of SIS to get her out of this situation.

[Work]: Two CIA agents who were working undercover in Cuba are assassinated. The dead agents were in charge of Caballo, a Cuban-double agent working for the CIA. Bond is sent to Cuba to determine if Caballo is loyal to the CIA or if his allegiances are to Castro.

August 2005: Kate Westbrook visits the Gelman Library at George Washington University to look into the CIA's files on Cuba. The now-public files confirm the veracity of Moneypenny's diaries.

August 1962 [Search for Father]: Jane has lunch with Bill Tanner, M's chief of staff. Over lunch, Moneypenny tells Tanner about Zach's attempt to get her to betray her country. Tanner vows to catch the men who are pressuring Moneypenny. Tanner reveals that there might still be a mole in the department.

[Bond]: Bond remains in Cuba where he's searching for Caballo, the double agent who might have been responsible for the death of two CIA agents. Bond reports that the Russians are transporting unknown cargo into Cuba. M wants to know precisely what the cargo consists of. Bond's cover is blown and there is no way to send him a coded message warning him that he's in danger. M informs Moneypenny that she is going to join him on a trip to Washington, DC, where M and Moneypenny meet with Attorney General Robert Kennedy. M tells Kennedy that he believes that Caballo is in league with Castro.

M and Moneypenny meet with President John F. Kennedy. President Kennedy tells M that he wants more intel on Castro's relationship with the Russians. Kennedy asks M to travel to Miami so that he can brief Brigadier Lansdale about Caballo.

In Miami, M meets with Lansdale. The service receives word that Bond is requesting a radio transmitter so that he can send secure messages to SIS. 006 instructs Moneypenny to take the transmitter to give it to their contact at the Miami Bay marina. The contact, in turn, will take the device to Cuba. Moneypenny goes to the marina with the transmitter, but the contact never shows.

September 1962 [Work]: Moneypenny hires a fisherman to take her and the transmitter to Cuba. Once she arrives in Cuba, Moneypenny learns that Bond was forcibly taken to the vessel named the *Omsk*. Moneypenny stakes out the *Omsk* and sees that Bond is being held captive. (Moneypenny later finds out that Bond was chasing the head of Fidel Castro's secret intelligence unit and the possible true identity of Caballo, Major-General Geraldo Gil.) Moneypenny decides that she needs to save Bond. So, she sneaks onto the boat and uses her scarf as a garrote to overcome one of the guards. Moneypenny locates Bond and they jump off the boat. Once in the water, Bond shoots at the fuel tanks and the boat explodes. After reaching land, the two take a flight to London.

Back in London, Bond and Moneypenny report that they saw large cylindrical objects being unloaded from Russian vessels and placed in Cuban vehicles. However, there is no proof that the sixty-foot metal tubes contain missiles.

Later, President Kennedy sends Calvin Petersham to London to talk to M, Bond, and Moneypenny. The US government wants to know more about the metal tubes that she saw coming from Russia. Petersham requests that Bond and Moneypenny return to Cuba to photograph the tubes and find out whether Russia is supplying Cuba missiles.

[Search for Father]: Bill Tanner and Jane go to dinner. Tanner tells her that they haven't been able to locate David Zach, the man who is pressuring Moneypenny to spy on her country. Later, Tanner reports that Zach might be a Stasi agent, a member of the German security service.

[Bond]: Bond is once again feeling despondent.

October 1962 [Work]: Bond and Jane return to Cuba. Once there, they retrieve the radio that Moneypenny hid on their last trip. The metal tubes are not present when Bond arrives at the dock area where Moneypenny had last seen them. Later, Bond finds a construction site that might contain the tubes. M sends word that Bond needs to provide photographic evidence that the tubes contain missiles. Bond steals a helicopter to get an aerial shot of the missiles. Jane drives to the location while claiming to be carrying out Caballo's instructions to bring a military jeep. She is taken to the superiors on the site, where she meets General Igor, Cuba's agricultural adviser. There is a disturbance that demands General Igor's attention. Finding herself alone, Jane photographs the blueprints of missiles and military maps. Then, Janes leaves the site and takes a train out of town and to Havana. Bond and Moneypenny meet up and fly home, where they hand over the photos to SIS who will share the evidence with the United States.

Moneypenny learns that the mole was the Head of Southern Africa, Bobby Prenderghast. Later, Jane learns that the photos provided proof that the missiles were nuclear. The implication is that the Soviets, working through Cuba, will attack the United States. Later that month, President Kennedy announces that the United States has evidence that Cuba has nuclear missiles. As a result, Kennedy calls for a blockade that prevents additional ships from entering Cuba. It appears as though a world war may break out as the Cuban Missile

Crisis gets underway. However, via diplomatic efforts, Soviet Premier Nikita Khrushchev gives Cuba the order to destroy all nuclear weapons.

November 2005: Kate Westbrook meets with the elderly and retired Bill Tanner. Westbrook reveals her plans to publish Moneypenny's diaries. Tanner speaks very fondly of Jane.

November 1962: Moneypenny goes to an art gallery and runs into Zach who tells her that he will call her later in the week. Jane reports the meeting with Zach to Tanner, who tells her to go forward with the meeting.

[Bond]: Bond learns that his next assignment will take him to Japan (*You Only Live Twice*).

[Work]: President Kennedy's attaché presents Bond and Moneypenny with the Orange Star, an award given to foreign nationals. However, given the secretive nature of their work, Bond and Moneypenny must decline.

December 1962 [Bond]: Moneypenny learns Bond, who was last seen in Japan, is now missing.

[Personal Life]: Tanner tells Moneypenny that they have planted listening devices all over her flat. So, when Zach pays a visit, Tanner can eavesdrop on their conversation and catch him. Jane meets with Major Boothroyd, who gives her a gun hidden in a book. If things go sideways with Zach, Jane can protect herself. When Jane gets home, she finds a strange man hiding in her home. The intruder identifies himself as Zach's friend, Boris. Boris says that he has information about Jane's father. Jane attacks Boris but he subdues her and ties Jane to her bed. When Boris leaves the room, Jane frees herself and retrieves her gun. Richard arrives and attacks Boris, but Boris shoots him. Jane shoots Boris and then calls for assistance. Richard is taken to the hospital. Later, Jane learns that Zach was last seen going to Istanbul. She questions how Tanner's plan to capture Zach reached Zach and Boris and concludes that SIS has a mole who tipped them off. Richard survives and reveals that he's a member of the Security Service.

[Bond]: Bond is still missing. Later in the month, they receive a report that Bond died while killing Blofeld and Blunt.

[Final Entry]: Richard tells Moneypenny that her father wasn't killed during World War II. Instead, he was captured and held prisoner. Filled with hope, Moneypenny concludes that if her father survived the war, then perhaps Bond is alive as well. She vows to find out the fate of both her father and Bond.

Commentary: Just as Bond purists initially dismissed the Young Bond books as kid's fare, some fans incorrectly assumed that *The Moneypenny Diaries* series would be romance novels. *The Moneypenny Diaries* was released in 2005, just a few years after *The Nanny Diaries* (2002), a best-seller about elite Manhattan caregivers was published. With its soundalike title, *The Nanny Diaries* is sometimes classified as "chick-lit" or even "humor," so the comparisons were inevitable. *The Moneypenny Diaries: Guardian Angel* shouldn't be dismissed on those, or any, grounds. Samantha Weinberg's book is an entertaining, fast-paced spy thriller.

The Young Bond novels were written to develop a new market for Bond fans, young readers. Similarly, *The Moneypenny Diaries: Guardian Angel* was likely intended to bring more female readers into the fold. Romance novels are a billion-dollar industry and its readers, who are largely women, are voracious readers. One study found that romance readers make up 23% of the marketplace.[122] Therefore, it made sense from a financial perspective for Ian Fleming Publications to pursue that untapped market. However, IFP also had to maintain the integrity of its character to avoid diluting its core brand. The publication of *Guardian Angel* upheld both mandates for IFP.

The Moneypenny Diaries: Guardian Angel is not a typical Bond novel. In fact, it's not a traditional novel at all. Instead, it takes the form of Moneypenny's diary entries. Weinberg's premise is that Moneypenny was a real person and that all of the stories about Bond and the service, as written by Fleming, were a slightly disguised version of actual events. Additionally, Moneypenny's diaries are reported to be authentic. To bolster the charade, Weinberg's name doesn't appear on the cover of the book. Instead, *Guardian Angel* is said to be written by Moneypenny's niece Kate Westbrook.

The book is set largely in two distinct periods—the 1960s and 2000s. The first period coincides with one full year of Moneypenny's journal entries that start in January 1962 and end in December. This term involves Moneypenny's work at SIS, and it sends the secretary on a dangerous mission. The second period is set in the early-to-mid 2000s and it covers Kate Wesbrook's quest to learn what happened to Moneypenny. The diary itself is said to be "published" in 2005.

Weinberg keeps Bond present throughout *Guardian Angel.* The agent is not just a shadowy, felt-but-never-seen figure. Instead, he's very much central to the plot. In fact, 1962 is a very busy year for 007. During that period, Moneypenny is depicted as an active witness to the agent's personal and professional life. Bond marries Tracy, who is slain on their way to their honeymoon. Bond then goes on a bender, undertakes two missions that are alluded to but not depicted in *You Only Live Twice,* and hunts down and kills Blofeld. *Guardian Angel* concludes with Bond missing, presumed dead by the service.

Moneypenny also has a personal mystery to solve. Moneypenny's father Hugh Moneypenny fought in World War II and she believed that he was killed in action. However, through the course of the book, Moneypenny learns that her father might be an intelligence officer who survived the war. As the diary ends, Moneypenny vows to find out her father's fate. Westbrook, Moneypenny's niece, is drawn into the mystery, which she hopes will be revealed in her aunt's journals for 1963, the subject of Weinberg's next book, *The Moneypenny Diaries: Secret Servant.*

Weinberg takes many incidents that are alluded to in Fleming's novels, fills in the details, and spins original tales about them. For instance, in *You Only Live Twice*, M mentions that Bond has recently been on and cocked up two missions. Weinberg describes these missions and believably finds a reason to include Moneypenny in them. On one mission, Moneypenny must go to Cuba to deliver a coding machine to Bond, whose cover has been blown. While there, she saves Bond's life, but in doing so, she needs to hide the device. Moneypenny and Bond barely escape Cuba with their lives. The two are forced to return to Cuba to locate the unit and to take photographs of Russian weapons, a mission that is tied to the real-life events of the Cuban Missile Crisis.

Not only is Bond a character in *Guardian Angel*, but so is Ian Fleming. In it, Jane's father worked with Ian Fleming in Naval Intelligence. It was Fleming who planned out some of the service's missions. Fleming's published novels are a "near-accurate record" of what happened.

Weinberg gives Moneypenny a backstory and, of course, a full name—Jane Vivien Moneypenny was born in Nairobi, Kenya to Hugh and Irene; she has a sister named Helena. After her father was presumably killed in action and her mother was murdered as a result of a dispute between warring tribes, she and her sister Helena were sent to London. Once in London, Moneypenny found work as a junior cipher clerk in the Secret Intelligence Service. She had a dog named Rafiki, but when he died, she found another one named Uhuru.

Weinberg dramatizes Moneypenny's childhood, how she started working for the service, how she came to meet M, her flirtation with Bond, and the inner workings of the Double O Section.

Moneypenny has a few romances, one with Richard Hamilton, who she comes to suspect is a spy. The other is with David Zach, who winds up using information about the fate of Moneypenny's father to blackmail Jane. Moneypenny is besotted with 007 but she also knows that a relationship with him wouldn't work. However, Bond and Jane do kiss once. Briefly and unexpectedly, during the intensity of their mission in Cuba when they are paired together. However, even though Bond muses that he wishes he could have a relationship with someone like Moneypenny, no romance develops.

Weinberg also provides insight into Jane's character. Writing as Westbrook, Weinberg describes Jane as "a dash of flamboyance in a discreet shell." Moneypenny is Jewish and faced antisemitism, which sometimes prevented her professional advancement.

Moneypenny loves her work with the service; it brings her tremendous happiness. Unlike Bond, Jane tries to find a balance between work and love/family; she seeks both. And like Bond, she must ask herself the question, "What is more important to me, my career and country, or my flesh and blood." Like Bond, she ultimately chooses her country. The success of *The Moneypenny Diaries: Guardian Angel* lies in Samantha Weinberg's ability to set her spin-off novel so convincingly in Fleming's world.

Continuity Nods: *Guardian Angel* runs parallel to and intersects with Fleming's *On Her Majesty's Secret Service* and *You Only Live Twice*. As such, Weinberg writes about the fallout of Tracy's death, Bond's depression, the hunt for Blofeld, and 007's eventual disappearance. There are plenty of references to Bond's past loves (Vesper, Tracy, Jill Masterton, Solitaire, Tiffany, Tatiana Romanova), friends (Darko Kerim, Felix Leiter), and foes (Goldfinger, Rosa Klebb, Mr. Big, Dr. No, Scaramanga, SMERSH, SPECTRE) as well as incidents in Fleming's novel (Bond's visit to Shrublands, his obituary). Bond remains in touch with Honeychile Rider, who still sends the spy holiday cards. As established by Fleming, Bond takes yearly visits to Vesper's grave in France. The reference to Bond's uncle is likely an allusion to the Young Bond novel *SilverFin*, which was published earlier that same year.

Bond's History: Bond's housekeeper May used to look after Bond's dying uncle, and has known Bond since he was a child.

Bond's Inner Life: Weinberg details the depression that Bond falls into after Tracy's death. Bond, who was already a prodigious drinker, goes on a bender. The spy downs a whole bottle of Scotch in one sitting and keeps a bottle of whisky in his office. Inebriated Bond screams and rants while ranting against the world and no one in particular. To be able to drink while working, he keeps a bottle of whisky in his office. Beyond his current state of despair, Moneypenny is concerned about the "trauma he must have suffered from seeing so many people he knew and cared about blown to oblivion." To combat depression, Bond sees a therapist and undergoes acupuncture. Despite these efforts, 007 "seemed resigned to death, almost to be choosing it." Bond explains his reasoning for marrying Tracy. "I love the job, of course I do, but one can't keep living like a cowboy forever." Moneypenny speculates that Bond's attraction to his vocation is due to the "addictive lure of adrenalin" he experiences while on a mission.

Bond's Personal Life: Moneypenny affectionately describes Bond as a "professional flirt." She always thinks that he is "surprisingly vulnerable" and funny. Bond comes to doubt his approach to relationships. "I can't face the tedium of that cycle of flirtation, capitulation, and retreat." The agent sleeps with a gun under his pillow. Bond scatters Tracy Bond's ashes at Royale, which is also where Vesper is buried. Bond dances with Moneypenny at Loelia Ponsonby's wedding. And later, on a mission, they share a kiss, albeit a brief one.

Bond's Tastes: Bond takes pride in his well-maintained Bentley, which he has nick-named the Locomotive.

Bond's Work Methods: Weinberg reports that there has never been a married Double O agent. The demands of the job and the agent's character have precluded marriage, even though SIS policy does not forbid it. Or as Bond says, "Don't try to combine love and this kind of work. It can only end in tears." Occasionally, work romances occur, such as Mary Goodnight's fling with 006. When employees start romantic relationships, they must disclose their relationship status to Captain Troop, Head of Security at MI6. Once he has the information, Troop will vet them and make sure that they are not a security risk.

Bond is in charge of 006 and 009, the other Double O agents. Bond is seen to have a lesser war record than 006. Bond was in the Royal Navy Volunteer Reserve and 006 served as a marine commando, which is a more prestigious unit. Later, Bond is promoted out of the Double O division and becomes agent 7777.

The average term for an agent is three years; Bond has already been a Double O agent for ten. When agents are on assignment, they are responsible for submitting field reports every Friday. The communications center on the eighth floor fields the reports and relays the information to the appropriate party. After an agent returns from a dangerous mission, there is usually an informal celebration, an impromptu office party in which war stories are told.

An informal aspect of Moneypenny's job is mending (or breaking) the hearts of Bond's past lovers. For instance, she is forced to give the brush off to Ruby Windsor, a woman that fell in love with Bond on his mission in *On Her Majesty's Secret Service.* More precisely, Ruby fell for Bond's cover identity, Sir Hilary Bray.

Assorted Observations:

- Some of Bond's field reports, first-hand accounts of his dangerous missions, are included in *Guardian Angel.*
- In keeping with Fleming, M's office is located on the 8th floor and Bond's is on the 7th.
- Weinberg brings the reader up to date about some of Bond's friends and allies. As of the early 2000s, Bill Tanner is still alive but M, Boothroyd, Loelia Ponsonby, and Moneypenny have all passed. Mary Goodnight is living in Jamaica. 006 moved to South Africa after retirement and formed a security company. 009 resides on a farm near Wales and gives military lectures to the army at Hereford.
- M has a niece named Melinda.

"MONEYPENNY'S FIRST DATE WITH BOND" (2006)

Author: Samantha Weinberg

In Brief: James Bond takes out Jane Moneypenny for a romantic evening.

Alternate Title: "First Date"

Meaning of Title: Refers to Moneypenny's first date with James Bond.

Chronology: Period. Set two days after Bond killed a man in Stockholm, which led to him earning his Double O status.

Operation: Not applicable.

Bastard Meter: None

Eggs: None

Insight into Bond: "There was something about Bond that I found unsettling; his confidence, possibly, the touch of menace that clung subtly to him like his well-cut suits."

Summary: It's Jane Moneypenny's first day of work as the secretary to the head of MI6, M. Moneypenny's new boss instructs her to summon James Bond. Bond arrives, meets Moneypenny, and enters M's office. Moneypenny overhears M welcoming Bond to the Double O Division. The newly minted 007 invites Moneypenny out for drinks.

Bond and Moneypenny enjoy oysters and pink champagne that evening at Scott's as they toast the successful completion of his two assignments. 007 regales Moneypenny with stories of his past adventures and reveals how he earned his Double O status. They agree to see each other again.

A few days later, Moneypenny overhears two colleagues talking about their dates with Bond. When Bond arrives for his meeting with M, the agent asks Moneypenny out. Not wanting to be another conquest, she declines Bond's invitation. However, Moneypenny instructs 007 to keep wooing her.

Commentary: "Moneypenny's First Date with Bond" is unlike most other Bond short stories in that it does not depict a mission. Instead, it focuses on a few key moments in 007's relationship with Miss

Moneypenny. In it, Weinberg describes Moneypenny's first day as M's secretary, the first time Bond met Moneypenny, the first time the agent called the secretary by her nickname, and their first date.

The story also describes how Moneypenny came to set the terms and boundaries of their flirtatious relationship. Moneypenny welcomes Bond's attention, but she makes it clear that their relationship will never take on a more physical nature.

"First Date" sits slightly outside Weinberg's trilogy of Moneypenny books. The short story was written to publicize *Secret Servant.* So, it wasn't intended to continue her series as much as it was designed to attract new readers. As such, Weinberg makes small adjustments to her approach to capturing Moneypenny's world. For instance, Weinberg doesn't reference Moneypenny's first name; instead, she only refers to M's secretary as "Miss Moneypenny," as she is most commonly known to the general public. "First Date" doesn't have most of the hallmarks of a journal entry that appears in Weinberg's previous books. For instance, unlike the novels in the series, "First Date" does not cite the day, month, or year. Yet, the story is told in the first person, suggesting that it could be an entry.

Bond's History: Bond tells Moneypenny about his service in the Naval Intelligence branch as well as his various assignments in Egypt, the Caribbean, and the South China Seas.

Continuity Nod: Bond explains that he became a Double O agent by killing a cipher expert in New York City and a Norwegian double agent in Stockholm (*Casino Royale*).

Bond's Inner Life: Bond feels a measure of guilt for killing the two men that earned him his Double O status. It's not that they didn't deserve to die, it's just that he's affected by their death. Bond is particularly troubled by the slow death of the Norwegian double agent whose throat he slit.

Bond's Tastes: Bond celebrates his appointment to the Double O Division with oysters and champagne. He wears well-cut suits.

Assorted Observations:

- The 2006 short story first appeared in *The Spectator* and was titled "Moneypenny's First Date with Bond."
- In 2020, the story was retitled "First Date" and published in the eBook *The Moneypenny Diaries: Secret Chapters*.

"FOR YOUR EYES ONLY, JAMES" (2006)

Author: Samantha Weinberg

In Brief: Miss Moneypenny accompanies Bond on a mission to eliminate a mole at the casino in Royale-les-Eaux.

Meaning of Title: Moneypenny and Bond pretend to engage in a romantic relationship for the benefit of the enemy who is surveying them.

Chronology: Period. Set in September 1956, after *Diamonds Are Forever* and before *From Russia with Love.*

Operation: Not applicable.

Bastard Meter: None

Eggs: None

Insight into Bond: "Women are attracted to him like bees to a lavender field, a fact about which he is too well aware."

Summary: Miss Moneypenny and James Bond arrive at the entrance to the Hôtel Splendide in France. At the registration desk, they check in as a couple but opt for two different rooms. After Bond's swim and massage, they meet for dinner at the Casino Royale. Bond spots his target, a man in a white dinner jacket, flanked by two Slavic bodyguards. Bond spends a few hours drinking and gambling.

Bond drives Moneypenny back to their hotel. Along the way, Bond explains that René Mathis has informed them that their hotel room has been bugged. So once they arrive at the room, Bond and Moneypenny will need to pretend to be a couple. As they go over the plan, Moneypenny recalls a recent meeting with M in which he requested her help on the assignment. One of their agents is now working for the communists. Moneypenny's role is to accompany Bond on his mission where he will eliminate the turncoat.

For the benefit of the listening devices, Moneypenny and Bond kiss on the balcony before retiring to the bed where they pretend to make love. Then, while Bond gathers his rifle and slips out of the room, Moneypenny plays a tape that has pre-recorded conversation between her and Bond. The tape machine creates the illusion that

Bond hasn't left the room. In fact, Bond is on his way to eliminate the turncoat.

An hour and twenty minutes later, Bond still hasn't returned. Moneypenny grows nervous that he is taking too long. Suddenly, there is a knock on the door; it's the hotel manager, the target's bodyguards, and the police. The manager explains that there has been a murder and Bond has been spotted near the victim's room. The authorities demand to see Bond and force themselves inside the room. At that moment, Bond comes out of the bathroom, creating the impression that he's never left. Satisfied that Bond is not involved, the authorities leave. Bond jokingly invites Moneypenny to continue their charade, but he quickly falls asleep.

Commentary: Samantha Weinberg's *Moneypenny Diaries* novels successfully capture Fleming's world of James Bond and spy craft in the 1960s. Weinberg's books are designed to appeal to Fleming purists, as well as to the general public who might not as of yet have picked up one of the Bond novels. "For Your Eyes Only, James" functions differently. This short story is more of a romp.

The danger of James Bond and Jane Moneypenny's job is contrasted by the romance and the interplay between Bond and Moneypenny is heightened. "For Your Eyes Only, James" was published on the eve of Weinberg's second spin-off book "Secret Servant" and its purpose is to interest readers in the series, in the hopes of boosting sales. As a result, the story is jauntier and more playful than the rest of the series. Another signal that this is not the typical story from *The Moneypenny Diaries* is that Moneypenny's first name is not used. She is only referred to as "Miss Moneypenny" or, adopting Bond's nickname, "Penny," as the general public knows her. "For Your Eyes Only, James" also serves to illustrate Weinberg's ability to play with tone and bend her (and Fleming's) world to serve the function of the story (as a sales tool), without betraying her own three book series.

Continuity Nod: Weinberg refers to Vesper Lynd and Le Chiffre in *Casino Royale*; the diamond smuggling operation in *Diamonds Are Forever*; and Tatiana Romanova and the Spektor decoding machine in *From Russa with Love*. Bond's friend and colleague René Mathis, who appears in three of Fleming's novels, is also mentioned.

Bond's History: Bond has spent many years gambling at the Casino Royale, along the way he's made some friends at the tables. He's been to the Hôtel Splendide enough times that he knows the manager, Maurice, by name.

Bond's Inner Life: The sight of Moneypenny in a black velvet dress reminds Bond of Vesper wearing a similar outfit. The memory causes him a little pain. Moneypenny observes that Bond is a little too aware of his impact on women.

Bond's Tastes: When Bond has a few hours to himself, he goes for a swim and books himself a massage. Bond's fondness for gambling is cited; for Bond, the act of gambling is a joy unto itself, irrespective of whether he wins or not.

Bond's Work Methods: This is a routine elimination assignment for Bond. He does not need to gather intelligence; he only needs to function as an assassin and kill a man. Before using his .308 caliber Winchester International Experimental Target rifle in the field, Bond spent three days practicing with it at the SIS gun range in Bisley, a village in Surrey, England.

THE MONEYPENNY DIARIES: SECRET SERVANT (2006)

Author: Samantha Weinberg

Pseudonym: Kate Westbrook

In Brief: Jane Moneypenny goes behind the Iron Curtain to persuade a Soviet double agent and his wife to return to England.

Alternate Title: *Secret Servant*

Meaning of Title: Refers to the fact that Jane Moneypenny is a civil servant who is called upon to perform the duties of a secret agent.

Chronology: Period and contemporary; multiple timelines. Timeline one is set in 2006 and timeline two spans January 1963 to April 1964. *Secret Servant* is set after *Guardian Angel* and *You Only Live Twice,* and around the events of *The Man with the Golden Gun.*

Operation: Not applicable.

Bastard Meter: None in reference to Bond.

Eggs: Egg and cucumber sandwiches are served at Bond's memorial service.

Insight into Bond: "He didn't always obey orders, but he certainly got results."

Summary: In 2006, Kate Westbrook is getting ready to publish *The Moneypenny Diaries*, a collection of private journals her Aunt Jane Moneypenny wrote while serving as M's personal assistant. The diaries detail Moneypenny's work at MI6 and her search for her father Hugh Moneypenny, who went missing while completing a mission during World War II and is now presumed dead. Westbrook receives a letter from her employer, Cambridge University, firing her from her position as a professor. Her university objects to Westbrook's decision to publish the diaries.

***January to July 1963*:** Previously, James Bond went to Japan, discovered Ernst Stavro Blofeld's whereabouts, and killed him. Now, he's missing and pronounced dead. Harold Adrian Russel "Kim" Philby is the former Head of the Soviet Section, but, after it was discovered that he was a double agent for the Soviet Union, he vanished. Moneypenny's boyfriend Richard Hamilton, an MI5 agent, is in hospital, mending from an injury he sustained while trying to protect her.

After Richard's recovery, Moneypenny and Richard take a romantic holiday to Scotland. In Scotland, Richard explains to Moneypenny that he wants to assist in getting her information about her missing father, Hugh. Later, Moneypenny learns that Boris, the man who tried to kill her (*Guardian Angel*) is in Moscow. Still later, Moneypenny learns that Philby is also in Moscow. A memorial service is held in Bond's honor. M and Felix Leiter give speeches about their fallen comrade.

Later, MI6 learns that the KGB has captured an English spy, who might be 007. M asks Moneypenny to befriend Eleanor Philby, the wife of the double agent, who still resides in England.

***August 1963*:** A man claiming to be the presumed-dead Bond calls MI6. At first, M assumes the man is a fraud, but MI6 finds a match between the man's fingerprints and Bond's. Bond meets with M and tries to kill him (*The Man with the Golden Gun*). When Bond fails, he is captured and taken to see renowned neurologist Sir James Molony. After determining that Bond was brainwashed by the KGB to kill M, Molony deprograms Bond.

Following M's orders, Moneypenny meets with Eleanor Philby, the wife of the agent who betrayed MI6. Moneypenny believes that Eleanor had no idea that her husband Kim was a spy. Tanner tells Moneypenny that MI6 doesn't want Kim Philby to spill any secrets to the Russians. If Philby returns to England, he will be given immunity. Moneypenny realizes that she's been asked to befriend Philby's wife so that she can manipulate her into luring her husband back to England.

***September 2006*:** Kate Westbrook meets with the retired Bill Tanner. Tanner tells Westbrook that they never found the mole in MI6. Then, Westbrook meets Britain's most well-known Russian defector, Oleg Gordievsky, and inquiries about Russian agents who have infiltrated SIS in the 1960s. Gordievsky confirms there was a mole, but he doesn't know their identity. Soon thereafter, Westbrook runs into a coworker who reveals that he knows she is investigating MI6 and advises her against doing so.

***September 1963*:** Moneypenny visits Bond who is making a recovery and who wants to return to work. Still later, Richard tells Moneypenny that he believes he's being followed. According to Richard, the man who attacked Moneypenny, Colonel Boris, is on the loose and she won't be safe until Boris is out of the picture. As such, Richard intends to go to Moscow to find Boris. Later, Moneypenny meets with Eleanor Philby. Eleanor still believes her husband wasn't a traitor and she announces that she is going to move to Moscow to be with him. Moneypenny advises Eleanor to send her a letter and include the phrase "I hope your sister is well" if she ever needs assistance. Shortly after that, Eleanor leaves England.

Jane Moneypenny.
Illustration by Pat Carbajal

October 1963: Moneypenny has dinner with Bond and, later, visits the agent at his home in Chelsea. They discuss Colonel Boris, who had programmed Bond to try to kill M. Later, Moneypenny receives a parcel from Richard who has information about her father, Hugh Moneypenny. Hugh sometimes went by the cover name Hugh Sterling and participated in Operation Ruthless, a mission to obtain a decoding machine. When the operation failed, Hugh was brought to a POW camp at Colditz Castle in Germany. Hoping to learn more about her father's fate, Moneypenny reads a book on Colditz by Major Roddy

Parks. The book includes a reference to a prisoner named Hugh Sterling.

***November 2006*:** Kate Westbrook decides to fly to Germany so that she can visit the POW camp where her father was held.

***November 1963*:** M sends Bond on a mission involving Francisco Scaramanga. MI6 makes plans to extract Kim Philby from Moscow. However, the mission, led by 009 fails; M believes that there is a mole in MI6 who is relaying sensitive intelligence to the KGB.

Moneypenny meets with Major Roddy Parks, the author of the book about Colditz. Parks reports that Hugh arrived at Colditz, but he escaped before the POW camp was liberated. Parks advises Kate to contact Hugh's friend Miles Pitman, who lives in Kenya and might know what happened to Hugh.

***December 2006*:** To find out who the mole in MI6 was, Kate Westbrook meets with Oleg Gordievsky, a Russian who defected to England. Gordievsky reveals that there was a mole and that he told SIS about it.

***December 1963*:** Moneypenny suspects that she's being followed. Moneypenny learns that Bond killed Scaramanga in Jamaica, but that the spy was wounded in the process. Soon, Moneypenny learns even more heartbreaking news; Richard was killed while on the trail of Boris. Before Richard was murdered, he learned that Boris' real name is Vladimir Ilyich Grushenko, the stepson of the former head of the KGB. Gutted by Richard's death, Moneypenny decides to visit her sister in Kenya, where Moneypenny grew up.

Once in Kenya, Moneypenny tracks down Miles Pitman, the pilot who knew her father. Pitman tells Moneypenny that her father never made it out of Germany.

Moneypenny returns to London. She visits M at his home. M produces a letter from Eleanor Philby to Moneypenny asking for help. M believes that Eleanor wants to return to England but that she can't convince her husband to join her. M asks Moneypenny to go to Berlin and bring Philby home.

***January 1964*:** Moneypenny flies to Moscow. Per her instructions, she goes to the post office and finds Eleanor there with a woman named Melinda Maclean. Moneypenny surreptitiously lets Eleanor know that she will be at the Tretyakov Gallery the following day.

***February 2006*:** Kate Westbrook learns that her college is not the one who instigated her dismissal from her work; instead, Moneypenny's former colleagues at SIS are somehow responsible.

***February 1964*:** Moneypenny meets Eleanor Philby at the gallery. Eleanor explains that her husband Kim is under constant surveillance. Eleanor reveals that the woman that accompanied her to the post office is Melinda Maclean, the wife of another traitor. Eleanor worries that once Kim supplies the KGB with all the information that he has, they will kill him. Eleanor asks Moneypenny for help in persuading Kim to return to England. Moneypenny has dinner with Eleanor and Kim at their house.

Moneypenny spends time with the Philbys and Macleans; she sees Melinda flirt with Kim. Moneypenny goes to the Bolshoi Ballet with Eleanor and Kim. At the ballet, Moneypenny suspects that she's being watched. Moneypenny and Eleanor go to a Russian bathhouse. Moneypenny offers to bring Eleanor back to London, but Eleanor won't leave without her husband. When Moneypenny returns to her hotel, she sees signs that someone searched her room.

On the way to the train station, Moneypenny encounters Kim Philby. Kim asks for Moneypenny's help in going back to London. Moneypenny worries that it might be a trap, but MI6 sends word that Moneypenny should help Philby escape. Moneypenny tells Philby that she will help him get back to England. Philby demands that they leave Moscow via train.

***March 2006*:** Kate Westbrook has dinner with a friend who knows Kim Philby's fourth wife, Rufina, and offers to introduce Westbrook to her. Later, Rufina tells Westbrook that Kim remained a devoted member of the communist party for all of his life.

***March 1964*:** Moneypenny meets Kim Philby at the train station. Together, they board the midnight train out of Moscow to Leningrad. When the train arrives in Leningrad, a driver takes Philby and Moneypenny to a safe house where they meet a contact named Gerry. Gerry gives Moneypenny a glass of milk, which turns out to be drugged. When Moneypenny wakes up, she discovers that she's been tied to the bed and that Colonel Boris is present. Boris questions Moneypenny about MI6's operations but Moneypenny refuses to break. Boris gives Moneypenny a deal—tell him what he wants to know, and he will reveal what happened to Moneypenny's father. Boris and Moneypenny drive from Moscow towards the Arctic Circle. Moneypenny figures out that Boris is not operating under the KGB's authority. Instead, he's a disgraced agent who is trying to get back into the KGB's favor by delivering intelligence about MI6. Eventually, Boris takes Moneypenny to her father's grave. Boris and Moneypenny continue the drive north when their car is attacked. Shots ring out and an unidentified man fights with Boris. The man gets the better of Boris and reveals himself to be Bill Tanner. Tanner explains that he was worried about Moneypenny and tracked her down. Tanner puts Boris in the trunk of his car and crosses the border, escaping the Iron Curtain. Bill and Moneypenny return to London. Moneypenny makes peace with the fact that while she failed in her mission to bring Philby back to London, at least she knows what happened to her father.

April 2006: Kate Westbrook learns that Eleanor Philby left her husband Kim and moved out of Moscow when she found out that Kim and Melinda Maclean were having an affair.

April 1964: Moneypenny and Bill Tanner continue to spend time together. Tanner reveals that Colonel Boris is currently in Finland, but he will be brought back to London for questioning. Moneypenny attends the wedding of her sister, Helena.

M meets with Moneypenny and tells her that Colonel Boris wants to defect to England. It turns out that he wanted to leave Moscow and he used the SIS to escape. M informs Moneypenny that Boris wants to meet her.

Moneypenny goes to a Victorian mansion, where Boris is being held. Boris tells Moneypenny that after her father, Hugh, escaped from Colditz prison camp in German clothes, he was apprehended by the Russian army, who mistook Hugh for a Nazi spy. The Russian army handed Hugh over to SMERSH. Hugh managed to escape SMERSH's clutches and then made his way to Leningrad where he was taken in by a family of peasant farmers. Hugh suffered from pneumonia and died on their farm in August 1945. Later, M decides to send Boris back to Moscow.

Dikko Henderson, the Head of Station J (Japan), informs M that he has located Kissy Suzuki, the woman Bond was living with after developing amnesia (*You Only Live Twice*). Henderson reports that Suzuki had a son and Bond is the father. Tanner makes the decision not to tell Bond about his child. The next day, Bond prepares to leave for Casablanca for a new mission.

Afterword: Kate Westbrook meets with Ferdy Macintyre who works at MI6. Macintyre claims that there were no additional moles at the SIS during Moneypenny's tenure. Westbrook visits Bill Tanner who reveals that Moneypenny died in a boating accident during a storm. Tanner wonders if Moneypenny was murdered. Westbrook believes that Moneypenny might have figured out the mole's identity and was killed to keep the traitor's identity a secret. Westbrook vows to find out the truth behind Moneypenny's death.

Commentary: James Bond has a son. It is arguably the most significant revelation made in any of the continuation novels. Kissy Suzuki was carrying Bond's child, at the conclusion of *You Only Live Twice*. In his next and final book, *The Man with the Golden Gun*, Fleming chose not to elaborate on that plot point or confirm the child's existence. As a result, Bond fans have speculated about what happened to the child for years.

John Gardner wanted to provide answers and incorporate Bond's son into his novels. Yet, Ian Fleming Publications vetoed the idea as only Eon Productions have the right to use Bond's offspring in the novels. Raymond Benson was able to skirt the issue in his short story "Blast from the Past" by killing off Bond Jr. All that was left was a corpse. In *Secret Servant*, Bond's baby is alive and well, albeit he's quite young; just five months old.

Although Bond might be a carefree bachelor, he is not an irresponsible father; 007 simply doesn't know that he has a son. M and Bill Tanner make the decision not to inform Bond about his progeny. Tanner rationalizes that "James isn't exactly going to drop his 00" status and return to Kuro island to raise the child. Given that, they rationalize that keeping Bond in the dark would better serve him and SIS. Conflicted, Moneypenny agrees with Henderson's assessment of Bond's lack of paternal instincts but argues that Bond still has the right to know. However, Tanner would rather continue to use Bond as a blunt instrument, while he still can. Furthermore, Tanner suggests (without humor) that Bond probably has other children of which is not aware. Tanner may be correct, even though it's an unsavory idea that does not reflect well on Bond, especially given the status of contraception in the 1950s and 1960s.

Secret Servant continues with the conceit that the reader is perusing Moneypenny's actual diaries. However, the approach is slightly toned down from *Guardian Angel*. In her previous book, Weinberg seemed to have a little more freedom to pull in a variety of "sources." In addition to the entries in Moneypenny's diary, Weinberg created additional cables, field guides, mission reports, and even a large number of footnotes to support the idea that the fictitious Kate Westbrook is a historian and "editor" who was bringing in real historical documents to tell Moneypenny's full story. In *Secret Servant*,

Weinberg continues the strategy but not to the same extent. She draws from fewer fictional texts and footnotes and instead relies on the diaries. Both books are equally riveting. It's important to note that she took a different tack in the second book.

Weinberg ends *Secret Servant* on a doozy of a cliffhanger. Over the course of two books, the reader likely assumed that Moneypenny died of old age. However, in the afterword to *Secret Servant*, Moneypenny's niece learns that her Aunt might have learned the identity of a mole at MI6 and that the traitor killed Moneypenny so that their identity would remain a secret. The third book promised to reveal the answer and conclude the story. Readers would have to wait two years before all would be revealed.

Continuity Nod: *Secret Servant* is set after Weinberg's *Guardian Angel*, Fleming's *You Only Live Twice*, and during *The Man with the Golden Gun,* so there are numerous references to all three books. Other noteworthy allusions include Felix Leiter's run-in with the shark in Florida and a passing reference to Mr. Big (both *Live and Let Die*). Weinberg reveals that when Bond was injured by Rosa Klebb (*From Russia with Love*), Moneypenny spent a lot of time at the hospital caring for the injured agent. Bond went to a mud bath in upstate New York (*Diamonds Are Forever*).

Bond's Personal Life: Bond's memorial service is attended almost exclusively by an "obtrusive cluster of glamorous women," many of whom are married. Honey Rider, who is now married and goes by the name Honey Levin, is also present. Bond and Rider stayed in touch and Rider would send the agent yearly holiday cards. Although unable to attend the service, Kissy Suzuki is suitably distraught when 006 notifies her that Bond is believed to be dead. Bond's housekeeper, May, never lost faith that her employer was somehow alive. In his absence, May took a cooking class and intended to surprise him with a new dish or two. She was presumably no slouch before enrolling in the course.

Bond and Moneypenny's relationship extends beyond the banter and flirtation that is depicted in the movies. Weinberg confirms that there is a mutual affection between the two. Their relationship involves lively repartee, dinners, and even a kiss or two. Still, Moneypenny acknowledges that Bond is "coldly darkly handsome, with a hint of reserve that makes one want to discover more." Moneypenny also chides that Bond is "about as cerebral as a football," and observes that they are both orphans. Ultimately, their relationship is one of mutual respect.

At the end of *The Man with the Golden Gun*, there is a faint possibility that Bond's relationship with Mary Goodnight might continue. In *Secret Servant*, Bond notes that Goodnight would make someone a wonderful wife. In the end, Bond decides that Goodnight is not the ideal woman for him. For her part, Moneypenny feels that 007 is "destined to remain one of life's bachelors—desired but never contained."

Under doctor's orders, Bond is trying to limit his cigarette intake. So he smokes about 25 cigarettes a day, down from his usual 60 to 70.

Bond's Inner Life: Moneypenny acknowledges that many people describe Bond as having a cruel face, but she counters, "If you get to know him it's not hard to locate the emotion behind the surface froideur [coolness]."

Bond's Tastes: Bond is particularly fond of the martinis that Joe the bartender makes at the Savoy Hotel. Bond's recipe for an ideal martini is described.

Bond's Work Methods: Even though Bond has a nearly unlimited budget while he is on missions, he still needs to file expense reports. Moneypenny implies that Bond's discretionary spending is the highest in the department.

When Bond is presumed to have been killed in action, 006 becomes the head Double O agent. The secretaries at MI6 often get together for an after-work drink at a bar named Bully's. The crowd includes Mary Goodnight, 006's secretary, Moneypenny, and Jo Comely who will take over Goodnight's position when Mary goes to Jamaica.

Assorted Commentary:

- Even though there are only three *Moneypenny Diaries*, Jane Moneypenny kept 40 volumes of her personal journals.
- After M was forced out of the service, he spent his time painting, growing orchids, and completing jigsaw puzzles that depict naval battles. However, he also became paranoid and believed that the Communist agents were after him, and were even poisoning him.
- When Bond recounts the events that took place in *You Only Live Twice*, he acknowledges that his story "sounds like the product of a fevered imagination." It's a winking reference to Fleming.

THE MONEYPENNY DIARIES: FINAL FLING (2008)

Author: Samantha Weinberg

Pseudonym: Kate Westbrook

In Brief: Jane Moneypenny risks her life and career to keep a promise to M to discover the identity of the mole working inside SIS.

Meaning of Title: *Final Fling* is the final book in the *Moneypenny Diaries* series, and it is Moneypenny's final mission.

Chronology: Period and contemporary. Most of the book takes place from July 1964 to February 1965 and is set after Weinberg's *Secret Servant* and Fleming's *The Man with the Golden Gun*. The rest takes place in September and October 1990 and one chapter is set in 2007.

Operation: Not applicable.

Bastard Meter: None that relates to Bond.

Eggs: None.

Insight into Bond: "Despite his women and apparent independence, James lives for his job."

Summary: In 2007, Kate Westbrook is still struggling with the notion that her Aunt Jane Moneypenny might have been killed to prevent her from learning the identity of a mole who was working at SIS in 1964. Westbrook is trying to determine whether Moneypenny's death was due to a boating accident or if she was murdered. To search for clues, Westbrook reads her Aunt's diaries.

July 1964: Jane Moneypenny is called into M's office. M temporarily transfers Moneypenny to Jamaica so that she can help Mary Goodnight with administration. In Moneypenny's absence, Jo Comely will serve as M's secretary. Before Moneypenny leaves, she has dinner with Bill Tanner, M's Chief of Staff. They discuss the possibility of a mole at SIS, but Tanner rejects the idea.

Moneypenny learns that 009 was going to facilitate the defection of a KGB colonel. However, the colonel has been murdered and 009 has gone missing. SIS believes that someone tipped the Russians off; the only people who knew about the defection were M,

Bill Tanner, Deputy Chief Christopher Hunter, Deputy Cabinet Office Secretary Percy Warren, Chief of Soviet Section, Chief of Central Europe, and Dorothy Fields, all high-level and trusted personnel.

While on a mission in Tangier, Bond discovers that Professor Jacques Marchès is researching a deadly virus that can be spread through drinking water and was initially discovered in monkeys in the Congo.

August 1964: In Jamaica, Moneypenny enjoys her professional and social lives. Yet, she wonders if she was forced out of London. James Bond comes to Jamaica so that he can attend Goodnight's wedding, and give the bride away. Bond and Moneypenny receive word that 009 has been found; he's now in a coma in a hospital in Vienna.

September 1964: Moneypenny and Bond return to London and learn that 009 has died and toxicology tests will determine the cause of death. M tells Moneypenny that Jo Comely is going to stay on as his personal secretary. Moneypenny will now work for Deputy Chief Kit Hunter. Moneypenny is hurt that she can't return to her old position; she discovers that she and her new boss, Hunter, do not get along.

While going on a walk, Moneypenny bumps into Hilary Quartermayne, who also works at SIS. Hilary confesses that she's inadvertently responsible for 009's death. Hilary explains that she went to a party and met a man from Moscow named Nico. Over time, Hilary learned that Nico is being hunted by the KGB and that he has a wife and child who still live in Moscow. Hilary told Nico that one of her colleagues was currently in Vienna and was about to meet with a KGB colonel. Hilary wonders if Nico told the KGB about the colleague who, in turn, killed the colonel and harmed 009. Now, Nico has gone missing.

Dorothy Fields, the resident mole hunter, tells Moneypenny that the KGB was already onto 009 long before Hilary said anything. As a precaution, Dorothy transfers Hilary out of SIS but she's convinced that there's a mole at SIS.

October 1964: Moneypenny is mugged, and her pocketbook is stolen. She reports what happened to Bill Tanner but instead of comforting her, Tanner scolds Moneypenny for leaving Jamaica. Warren, Hunter, and other members of SIS believe that M is obsessed with finding a mole, when none exists. They wonder if it's time for M to step down.

Bond steals a sample of the deadly virus from Professor Jacques Marchès' laboratory. The Russians are also after the virus and now Professor Jacques Marchès has gone missing.

A few days later, Bond is forcefully removed from M's office. Moneypenny learns that 007, who is suspended and is the subject of an internal investigation, has left town.

While walking through the park, Jane meets Nikolai "Nico" Petrovic, the man from Moscow who befriended Moneypenny's colleague and then disappeared.

November 1964: Moneypenny reports her encounter with Nico to mole hunter Dorothy Fields who tells Jane to continue to meet with him. Moneypenny goes to the park and sees Nico who says that the KGB are after him and requests Moneypenny's help in arranging protection. Nico reveals that the KGB has a mole in the service who goes by the code name Colin. Moneypenny worries that Bill Tanner, who has a brother named Colin, could be the mole. Moneypenny reports her findings to Dorothy but withholds the information about Tanner. Soon after, Dorothy tells Moneypenny that it's time to bring M up to speed about Nico. Later, Moneypenny goes into her office and sees her boss, Hunter, rifling through her bag. When Hunter provides an unconvincing reason for being in her office Moneypenny knows that she's under suspicion.

Days later, Moneypenny learns that Nico has been exposed to the same virus that killed 009. Later, Moneypenny sneaks into M's office and removes the file containing information about the virus that killed 009. She learns that the virus has its origins in African green monkeys. Soon thereafter, Nico dies. Later, Nico's doctor, Miles Shepard, asks Moneypenny out on a date. Dr. Shepard wonders if Nico was recently in contact with African primates, as his virus suggests that he was. Then, SIS learns that the KGB didn't kill Nico. If the KGB didn't kill him, who did?

December 1964: Moneypenny decides to resign from SIS; the pressure and duplicity of the job have taken a toll. Moneypenny breaks the news to M, who readily accepts her resignation. While saying goodbye, M slips Moneypenny a piece of paper that contains an address in London. Later that night, Moneypenny goes to the address and finds M and Bond waiting for her. M tells her that he believes a mole in the office is responsible for Nico and 009's deaths. Now, M wants to install Moneypenny in the office of Deputy Cabinet Office Secretary, Percy Warren. M explains that 007 was only kicked out of the service as part of M's plan to uncover the mole. M wants people to think that the disgraced Bond is selling a sample of the virus to the highest bidder.

Moneypenny goes to dinner with Bond who reveals that M's secretary Jo Comely and Moneypenny's boss, Hunter, are having an affair. Moneypenny meets up with Jo who fantasizes about marrying Hunter. Moneypenny realizes that you can spell the mole's name, Colin, with the letters from her boss's name, <u>C</u>hrist<u>o</u>pher <u>Lin</u>ford-Hunter.

December 1964: Moneypenny tells Jo that she's going on a date with Bond, but it's a test to see if Jo will tell Hunter. Moneypenny and Bond have dinner together. Bond also reveals that someone was tailing him that night. The tail suggests that Jo told Hunter about the date.

January 1965: Moneypenny continues her work as Percy Warren's secretary. Warren tells Moneypenny that he knows she's been talking to Bond, who is believed to be a traitor who is selling the virus to the highest bidder. Worried that she's in deep trouble, Moneypenny confesses that she, Bond, and M are working together to ferret out the leak. Moneypenny tells Percy nearly everything. However, she doesn't reveal her suspicions that Hunter might be the mole.

February 1965: At home, Moneypenny feels poorly and wonders if she's been exposed to the deadly virus via the tea that she's drinking. She's suspicious of everyone and when she sees Tanner, she believes that he's trying to kill her. However, Tanner explains that she is simply suffering from pneumonia. Tanner laments that M is now obsessed with the mole and that M's job is in danger.

Four days later, M resigns from SIS; he's been forced out of the service. Over lunch with Moneypenny, Bond thinks that M was wrong about the mole and it was time for M to step down.

May 2007: Kate Westbrook receives an invitation to have lunch with Ferdy Macintyre, who works at MI6 and who instructed Westbrook not to publish Moneypenny's diaries. Macintyre admonishes Westbrook to discontinue her search for the mole. Westbrook is attracted to Macintrye, but she ignores his warning and persists.

Westbrook visits her deceased Aunt's home in North Uist, a Scottish Island. Westbrook goes to the police station to talk to the constable who investigated Moneypenny's death, Robbie Gordon. Gordon says that Moneypenny's death was considered a boating accident. At the time of Jane's demise, Gordon received a call from London indicating that the post-mortem would be conducted in London and not locally, as is customary. Gordon reveals that there was a second body found but the identity of that victim was unknown. He explains that Moneypenny's friend and fellow islander Randy Macallan found the entire affair to be a bit suspicious.

Bond living life under the identity of
Randy Macallan in *The Moneypenny Diaries.*
Illustration by Pat Carbajal

Westbrook meets Randy, who Westbrook briefly met at her aunt's memorial service (*Secret Servant*). Randy reveals that the day before Moneypenny death, she was seen talking to an unfamiliar man. Randy also reveals that Moneypenny was not using her own boat when she drowned; instead, she was using one that she rented from Lachlan Campbell. Westbrook suspects that Randy and Moneypenny were lovers. Westbrook unsuccessfully tries to contact Campbell.

Westbrook meets with Tanner who tells her that at the time of Moneypenny's death in 1990 that Christopher Hunter, Dorothy Fields, and Percy Warren were all alive, and therefore still count as suspects. Westbrook has lunch with Hunter, who reveals that he married Joanna Comely, M's new secretary, and that he doesn't think there was a mole at SIS. Next, Westbrook meets with Fields who says that she believes that there was a leak. Fields theorizes that shortly before M's death, he gave Moneypenny his mole file, which could contain clues to the mole's identity.

Westbrook returns home and goes through the files that Moneypenny sent her. She finds an article about a scientist named O'Connell, who traced the origins of the first case of HIV to Congolese monkeys. She examines a photo of Professor Marchès, one of the inventors of the deadly virus that killed 009 and Nico. She concludes that O'Connell and Marchès are the same person. Westbrook wonders if Moneypenny was killed to prevent her from exposing Marchès' real identity and role in 009's death.

Westbrook asks Macintyre to look into Professor Marchès. Later, Westbrook receives a file from Macintyre indicating that Professor Marchès died decades ago and therefore, couldn't be involved in Moneypenny's death.

Westbrook returns to North Uist, Moneypenny's home, and meets Randy Macallan. Randy admits that he worked with Bill Tanner during the war. Later, Westbrook located Lachlan Campbell, the man who lent the boat to Moneypenny. Campbell remembers seeing Moneypenny with a strange man named Colin.

Westbrook returns to London and meets up with Macintyre. They are chased by unknown operatives but escape. Macintyre tells Westbrook that she's under surveillance and that she shouldn't return home until it's safe. Days later, Westbrook receives a letter from Macintyre that includes a coded treasure map. She follows the map, which takes her to the hidden location of Moneypenny's last diary, this one is dated from the 1990s, shortly before her death.

September 1990: Moneypenny visits the dying M and promises to uncover the identity of the mole. Soon thereafter, M dies.

October 1990: Moneypenny receives a package containing M's file on the mole. After reading it carefully, Moneypenny concludes that Percy Warren is the mole. Moneypenny writes Warren a letter and suggests that they meet. At Moneypenny's home on the isle of North Uist, Moneypenny confronts Warren and accuses him of being the mole. Warren admits to being a leak but argues that if Moneypenny makes the information public, SIS will lose all credibility. Moneypenny suggests that they discuss the matter the next day while sailing.

2007: Kate Westbrook reads the final diary entry in which Moneypenny implies that she is going to put an end to Warren, but must first say goodbye to someone known as "J." Westbrook realizes that her Aunt sabotaged the boat so that it would sink and kill Warren. Moneypenny knew that she would die in the process. Westbrook goes to Randy Macallan's home. Randy confesses that he knew

Moneypenny's plan and he helped hide the evidence that implicated Moneypenny in Warren's murder. Moneypenny's actions ensured that SIS's reputation was upheld.

Westbrook returns to London and visits the lawyer who represents her Aunt's estate. The lawyer hands Westbrook a package, which contains a letter from Moneypenny, giving Westbrook the option to publish or keep them secret.

Westbrook meets with Macintyre who informs Kate that she is out of danger; he has seen to it that all threats to her have been neutralized. Westbrook decides to publish the diaries. Westbrook concludes that Tanner had romantic feelings for Moneypenny but that they were not reciprocated. She did, however, love Tanner as a friend. Westbrook asks Tanner if he knows the identity of the "J" that her Aunt had to say goodbye to before her death. Tanner reveals that the "J' is James Bond and that, through the course of investigating Moneypenny, Westbrook already met him.

Commentary: A good who-done-it will lay down all the facts and evidence about the identity of the killer and their motives and allow its readers to draw their conclusions. The reader will knowingly and confidently believe that they are a few steps ahead of the author and that they have solved the mystery. If the writer is successful, the reader will draw the wrong conclusion about the killer's identity. In the best mysteries, the author has left breadcrumbs leading down the primrose path, only to pull the rug out from under them at the very end. And that's exactly what Samantha Weinberg does in *The Moneypenny Diaries: Final Fling*. The twist at the end of the *Final Fling* not only forces the reader to reevaluate their assumptions about the plot of that book, but it also forces the reader to re-evaluate the first two books in the series, *Guardian Angel* and *Secret Servant.*

For all of *Final Fling,* readers had to repeatedly ask themselves two questions—Who killed Miss Moneypenny, and why? The why might seem self-evident; Moneypenny was apparently killed to prevent her from revealing the identity of the mole in SIS. Who killed her was an open question. There were various suspects, as they usually are. The list of potential baddies was limited to the people who had information about SIS's secret operations. That small list included even M, who is normally considered above reproach, and his trusted Chief of Staff, Bill Tanner.

Weinberg does an admirable job of making a case that Tanner could be the guilty party. However, it would not have been a satisfactory conclusion if Tanner, a well-liked character, had turned out to betray Moneypenny, the service, and his nation. It's not that Tanner is a beloved literary figure; rather, Weinberg makes me care for and root for him. Other suspects included mole hunter, Dorothy Fields. As it is her job to uncover leaks, she is arguably best equipped to cover her tracks. Deputy Chief Christopher Hunter and Cabinet Office Secretary Percy Warren, are both men who have little respect for M. And because Hunter and Warren don't like M, the reader doesn't like them.

While not officially a suspect, I had my doubts about Jo Comely, the secretary who took over Moneypenny's position as secretary to M. Comely is also Hunter's secret lover, so she had access to classified information. It would have been thematically fitting for Comely to be the killer. After all, the series is about an overlooked secretary (Moneypenny) who has little agency in the Bond novels. So it would have made sense for another secretary (Comely) to be the key to solving the mystery.

Alas, Comely is not the mole. Nor is M, Tanner, or even Comely's lover Hunter. Instead, it's Percy Warren, Moneypenny's new boss. Weinberg reveals that Warren is the traitor long before the story ends. So, the reader might let down their guard and be caught off guard by the book's additional twists.

Even though Moneypenny has correctly and conclusively identified the mole, she is unable to bring him to justice. If she does reveal that Warren, a high-placed officer in SIS was a mole, she will cause the American government to lose their faith in British intelligence. As a result, America will no longer trust the SIS with their secrets and the special relationship with the two countries will be severed or badly broken. Moreover, the United Kingdom and Russia have established a fragile peace and a revelation of such a nature could send the two countries to war with each other. Still, Moneypenny can't let the mole escape without consequences. Moneypenny is not a killer. She has had some self-defense training but unlike Bond, she is not equipped to kill in cold blood. She does, however, know how to pilot a boat. So she takes the mole out on a boat, sabotages it, and when the boat sinks, the mole drowns. Tragically, Moneypenny drowns too. She knew that her death was an unavoidable part of meting out justice for this man who betrayed his country and led to the demise of people that Moneypenny knew and cared about.

Let's return to the question: Who killed Moneypenny? The answer is no one killer her. It turns out that the reader was asking the wrong question. That question makes Moneypenny a victim, and merely a plot device, whose death in an inciting incident and a device meant to jump-start the plot. The question should have been: Why did Moneypenny kill the mole and allow herself to perish in the process?

The answer is, of course, for duty, honor, and country; she needed to protect the institution that she, M, and Bond dedicated their lives to. And in the process, Moneypenny gets a greater appreciation for Bond's sacrifices. In turn, the reader gets deep insight into the lives of civil servants who devote their lives to a higher cause, even if their duties aren't nearly as glamorous as Bond's. In the end, Weinberg turned the tables and reframed the narrative. In doing so, Moneypenny can longer be considered the victim in her own story. She's the hero.

Continuity Nod: There are references to Bond's adventures in Jamaica with Scaramanga (*Man with the Golden Gun).* Weinberg also recaps the events of her previous books *Guardian Angel* and *Secret Servant.*

Bond's History: Moneypenny describes Jamaica as Bond's "version of paradise." Bond first visited Jamaica after the war and spent a great deal of time fishing. He declared Jamaica to be the "most beautiful place" he'd ever seen.

Bond's Future: Most Bond novels don't look into Bond's future; they only explore his present mission and drop breadcrumbs about his past. Similarly, the bulk of *The Moneypenny Diaries* focuses on Moneypenny and Bond's adventures in the 1960s. Another portion of the book is set in the mid-2000s, the time that the book was published. It's in this period that Weinberg is able to reveal Bond's life beyond the service.

Following his retirement from the Secret Service, James Bond is alive and well; he's living in North Uist, a Scottish isle. And he's baking shortbread. He's mostly happy. Or, at least, content. He's enjoying his life by the sea, living in a house that he likely built himself. His life is simple. He tends to his garden (roses abound) and cooks goat curry. There are also apple trees on his property and he keeps his home-grown herbs in pots. It might be the sea air, or it might be too much hard living, but Bond now has a "craggy face." Still handsome, though.

He doesn't go by the name Bond anymore. These days, he answers to the name Randy Macallan. Aside from Pearson's *The Authorized Biography of 007*, *Final Fling* offers the only glimpse into Bond's later years. Bond is not the main protagonist in this novel. Instead, Moneypenny's life takes center stage.

Bond's Personal Life: At the end of *The Man with the Golden Gun*, Bond and Mary Goodnight entertain a possible future together.

Weinberg reveals that their relationship fizzled when Goodnight caught Bond flirting with a nurse who was helping him recuperate from Scaramanga's bullet. Since then, Bond has continued to pursue married women. It is Bond's devil-may-care attitude towards women that causes Moneypenny to observe that Bond is "licensed to shoot through the heart."

Weinberg never conclusively reveals if Bond and Moneypenny were intimate. However, she does indicate that while working together in the 1960s, they did kiss a few times. Kate Westbrook, Moneypenny's niece, believes that Bond did love her Aunt. In their later years, Bond and Moneypenny lived near each other on a remote Scottish isle. They were as close as a man as a wife, even if their relationship was not primarily physical. Bond himself acknowledges, "I'm not sure anyone would live with me anymore. I've never been much good at it, to tell you the truth. And I'm tired now. I've seen too much, loved too many."

Bill Tanner is often described as 007's best friend in the service. Here, Weinberg reveals that he's Bond's closest friend, in or out of work. Bond continues his yearly pilgrimage to Royale where he visits Vesper's grave.

Bond's Inner Life: Bill Tanner jokes, I fear that James is immortal." Tanner's opinion aside, Bond is quite aware of his own mortality. Given the nature of his business, he laments that "there's no great history of Double O's making it to retirement age."

The life of a secret agent takes its toll on Bond. To be effective at his job, Bond admits that "you've got to believe that there are genuine spooks luring in every crevice, but if you do, you're already halfway down the road to madness." Despite the toll it took on Bond, he was proud to serve his country.

Moneypenny views Bond in a way that most people don't. She thinks he has a terrific sense of humor, something that Fleming never emphasized. Moneypenny concludes that Bond is an "extraordinary man, funny and clever, yet with what must be a whole cabinet of sadness locked out of sight somewhere."

Bond's Tastes: As much as he loved his martinis, the retired Bond now appreciates a great double whisky. When Bond is sitting by a fire with a drink in hand and dressed in a dark suit and black polo jersey, Moneypenny remarks that he kind of looks like the devil. He's reading a spy novel called *The Lifeline* by Phyllis Bottome. As Bond scholar Alan J Porter points out, as well as being an established author in the

1930s, Bottome was Fleming's tutor at his school in Austria. She is also credited as being the first person to encourage Fleming to write.

Bond's Work Life: In *Final Fling*, Bond is sent to Tangier, where he's posing as an arms dealer, hoping to get the better of mercenaries who are selling weapons. M doesn't shake hands and rarely calls subordinates by their first name but when he does, it's usually for a strategic purpose. M has only referred to Moneypenny by her first name twice. The second time was when he was on his deathbed and asking her to find the mole. M died in 1989 and Moneypenny died a year later. M's successor was Sir Jack Gavascon, a former diplomat. Out of deference to Sir Miles Messervy, Gavascon opted to be called M, even though most chiefs use the initial C.

Assorted Observations:

- 009's first name is revealed as Mark.
- Starting with the first Moneypenny book, Kate Westbrook's fictional biography lists two unpublished novels. The details remain unchanged throughout the series. It's a shame that the popularity of Westbrook's work on her Aunt Jane's journals didn't lead to an opportunity to get her work published.
- Lois Maxwell, who played Miss Moneypenny in the films, wrote a column for *The Toronto Sun* from 1979–1994. The column, which included anecdotes about her time making movies and her personal life, was titled "Moneypenny."[123]

THE ERA OF ONE SHOTS

"He was a secret agent, and still alive thanks to his
exact attention to the detail of his profession."
IAN FLEMING, *Casino Royale*

Bond readers were accustomed to authors writing a series of books. Gardner wrote 14 original Bond novels and Benson authored six. Writing a series has its advantages; it allows authors to understand the character and the world in which he inhabits. Additionally, it gives the author and Ian Fleming Publications the time to build trust and develop a strong working relationship. It also gives readers a chance to understand the author's approach to 007, which might differ slightly (or significantly) from Fleming's. From 2008 to 2013, Ian Fleming Publications changed its publishing strategy. Instead of a series of novels, the next three Bond novelists would write one-off adventures. In addition to works by Sebastian Faulks, Jeffery Deaver, and William Boyd, this period also marked Charlie Higson's first return.

SEBASTIAN FAULKS' TENURE
2008

Sebastian Faulks wrote the Bond continuation novel *Devil May Care* (2008). Separate from his work with Ian Fleming Publications, Faulks wrote two parody short stories "James Bond Goes to Sainsbury's" (2002) and "Ian Fleming Thinks Even James Bond Goes Shopping" (2006).

"JAMES BOND GOES TO SAINSBURY'S" (2002)
"IAN FLEMING THINKS EVEN JAMES BOND GOES SHOPPING" (2006)

Author: Sebastian Faulks

Background: Neither story was authorized by Ian Fleming Publications and, therefore, falls outside of the remit of this volume. However, since Faulks wrote the continuation novel *Devil May Care*, it seemed appropriate to include this earlier effort.

In Brief: James Bond goes to the supermarket.

Meaning of Title: A succinct summary of the plot.

Chronology: Contemporary. Unconnected to any story published by Ian Fleming Publications.

Operation: Not applicable.

Bastard Meter: None.

Eggs: None, despite the grocery store setting.

Insight into Bond: "It was part of Bond's profession to kill people. He never liked doing it, but, he reflected as he fitted the silencer to his .25 Beretta, regret was unprofessional."

Summary: Bond sneaks into a grocery store; kills an employee for not carrying a decent wine, shops for groceries, joins the check-out line, eliminates the three people ahead of him in line, and discovers that Moneypenny is working the register.

Commentary: Before Ian Fleming Publications engaged Sebastian Faulks to write an official continuation novel, Faulks had already written two Bond parody pieces in which he approximated Fleming's literary voice. Faulks was a panelist on the BBC 4 radio quiz show *The Write Stuff.* Fleming was the author of the week on the April 4, 2002 edition of the program. In that episode, Faulks read a passage from *Goldfinger* where Fleming lists the names of various crime chiefs who are going to join forces to conduct the operation. As part of the game, writers would contribute a piece in the style of a renowned author. The panelists were instructed to write a Fleming pastiche that puts Bond in "uncharacteristically mundane surroundings."[124]

Faulks wrote a short piece called "James Bond Goes to Sainsbury's," in which the agent goes to the grocery store. In it, Bond employs a nerve gas that was hidden in his trolley to eliminate the long line of customers. The bit ends with Bond greeting Moneypenny, who is staffing the register. A surprised Bond queries, "Ah Moneypenny, are you licensed to till?" It's unlikely that Faulks' roughly 200-word short story got him the Bond writing gig. However, it does suggest that he had a passion and facility for writing in other writers' voices.

"James Bond Goes to Sainsbury's" was slightly expanded from the quiz show, retitled "Ian Fleming Thinks Even James Bond Goes Shopping," and published in the book *Pistache,* a 2006 volume of Faulks' parody pieces. The revised version ends with Bond purchasing candy M&Ms for his boss M.

Bond's Inner Life: This pair of short stories depicts Bond at his most ruthless; he kills a grocery store employee for not carrying high-quality wine and he disposes of three innocent customers to avoid waiting in line. Bond takes no pleasure in killing; nor does it consume him with grief or regret.

Bond's Personal Life: Bond smokes Morland cigarettes with three gold rings and he drives a 4½-litre Bentley. Bond's Sottish housekeeper, May, oversees Bond's flat in Chelsea, as she does in Fleming's novels.

Bond's Work Methods: Bond uses a .25 Beretta and, when necessary, a silencer.

DEVIL MAY CARE (2008)

Author: Sebastian Faulks

In Brief: James Bond must stop chemist Dr. Julius Gorner from industrializing the production of heroin and starting a war between the Soviet Union and the United Kingdom. 007 also agrees to help rescue a beautiful woman's twin sister who is said to be under Gorner's evil spell.

Meaning of Title: Bond possesses a devil-may-care attitude. The title also alludes to the idea that while nobody seems to care about the dirty business of being a secret agent, the devil might.

Chronology: Period. Set in 1967, after *The Man with the Golden Gun.*

Operation: Not applicable.

Bastard Meter: Cold

Eggs: Scrambled and Benedict.

Insight into Bond: "He found himself anxious to impress M."

Summary: In Paris, an Algerian drug courier named Yusuf Hashim is killed by an unidentified assailant. The assailant removes Hashim's tongue with a pair of pliers. Soon after, René Mathis, a member of France's military intelligence agency, is called away to look into the murder.

James Bond is in Italy, where he is spending part of his forced-three month sabbatical. He is still recuperating from the injuries sustained while battling Francisco Scaramanga (*The Man with the Golden Gun*). Bond meets Larissa Rossi, a married woman traveling with her husband. Bond has drinks with Rossi but declines her invitation to sleep together, a choice that surprises Bond himself. Bond is called back to duty.

Back in London, Bond goes to his office where he catches up with Moneypenny and is briefed by M about Dr. Julius Gorner, a businessman who operates a pharmaceutical business that produces legal opiate drugs for medical procedures. M explains that England is on the verge of a drug epidemic that could destabilize its economy. M orders Bond to find out more about Gorner. As a first step, Bond should go to Paris and speak to René Mathis.

In Paris, Bond runs into Larissa Rossi, the woman he met in Italy. She informs Bond that her real name is Scarlett Papava, an investment banker, who is searching for her missing sister, Poppy. Felix Leiter told her that Bond could help locate her drug-addicted sister who is under Gorner's influence. Scarlett tells Bond that she will arrange a meeting with Gorner at a private tennis club. Later, Bond asks Mathis to find out if Scarlett is an enemy agent.

Bond and Scarlett go to the club where Bond and Gorner play tennis. It's a fierce match, and Gorner consistently gets the upper hand on Bond. Suddenly, Bond starts winning but he's not quite sure why his luck changed. After the match, Scarlett tells Bond that she discovered the secret to Gorner's tennis success—he cheats. In a private room, Gorner's enforcer, Chagrin controls the height of the net, raising or lowering it to his boss' advantage. Scarlett found out and stopped Chagrin from adjusting the net, allowing Bond to best his opponent.

At lunch, Scarlett tells Bond that Gorner was a student of her father. Gorner was a bright pupil, but he cheated on exams and alienated people. More recently, Gorner met and befriended Poppy, Scarlett's sister. Now, Poppy is addicted to the opium that the pharmaceutical boss supplies. Bond learns that Gorner is heading to Tehran, Persia.

In Persia, Bond meets Darius Alizadeh, the local head of station. Darius briefs Bond on Gorner, who has a boat building yard in Noshahr. Darius shows Bond around the country which includes a trip to the Paradise Club, a local bathhouse. At the Paradise Club, Bond meets CIA agent J.D. Silver. Silver warns Bond to stay away from Gorner who has some sort of drug connection to the Soviet Union. Bond can't figure out how Gorner can transport the drugs from the remote Persian desert to the Soviet Union. Bond rules out a trip by air, as a small plane wouldn't have sufficient fuel to make the trip and a large plane would be detected by the Soviet Union.

In his hotel room, Bond sees a woman who he thinks is Scarlett but is revealed to be her twin sister, Poppy. The Papava sisters are nearly identical, but Poppy has a strawberry-shaped birthmark on her thigh and Scarlett does not. They also have different colored eyes. Poppy warns Bond that Gorner knows that he's in Persia.

Bond travels to Noshahr and breaks into Gorner's boat-building yard. He discovers an Ekranoplan, a giant aircraft that can operate on the water or in the skies. The vessel appears to be Soviet made but, for reasons that Bond can't determine, the image of a British flag has been painted on the vessel.

The next day, Bond goes back to the building so that he can take pictures of the craft. A guard catches him and knocks him out. When Bond awakens, he discovers Scarlett has also been taken prisoner. Gorner explains that he has seen the horrors of war and the pain that injured soldiers endure on the battlefield. His opiates alleviate their suffering. Gorner reveals that he has developed a process for the mass production of heroin. He will transport the drugs on a route ominously called The Hellfire Pass and Bond will be forced to take part in a test run for his ultimate plan.

Bond is taken to Afghanistan. There, Gorner's men pay off Afghan soldiers and pick up a large shipment of opium. After Gorner's men have taken control of the opium, Chagrin orders Bond to take a jeep and drive away. Bond thinks this might be his opportunity to escape but he doesn't get far; a grenade blows up the jeep and sends Bond soaring through the air. It turns out that Bond was simply a decoy who was meant to draw enemy fire and allow Gorner's men to safely flee with their opium supply.

Gorner tells Bond that he will put his main plan into effect the next day. As part of the plan, the Ekranoplan will drop nuclear warheads onto Russia's largest stockpile of nuclear weapons. As a diversion, a stolen British airliner will conduct another attack on Stalingrad. Britain will be blamed and will be drawn into a war. In turn, the Soviets would fire their nuclear missiles at London. Gorner informs Bond that he will be flying the plane that will attack the Soviet Union.

Bond is sent to his jail cell where he and Scarlett hatch a plan to escape. Scarlett screams and tells the guards that Bond has been taken ill. When they enter the cell to investigate, Bond overcomes the guards and slips out. Bond infiltrates Gorner's office, pretends to use his computer, and allows himself to be caught. Bond's distraction gives Scarlett enough time to get away and hide in the plane that Bond will be flying.

The next day, Bond is brought to the Vickers VC10 airplane that he will be forced to pilot. Bond meets pilot Ken Mitchell who is working for Gorner under duress.

Meanwhile, Felix Leiter, head of station Darius, and CIA agent Silver devise a plan to defeat Gorner. Darius receives a phone call with the coordinates of the plane. When Silver leaves the room, Leiter and Darius realize that he is up to no good, so they chase after him. Darius stops at a phone booth to inform MI6 of Gorner's plan. As soon as the critical intelligence is transmitted, Silver shoots Darius, who dies in Leiter's arms. Silver proclaims that if Gorner's scheme is successful, then the United Kingdom will be forced to join the Vietnam War. Darius' driver kills Silver before he can kill Leiter.

On the airplane, Bond tells Mitchell about Gorner's plan to drop the explosives on Zlatoust-36, a city that's near the Soviet's stockpile of nuclear weapons. Mitchell is aghast and doesn't want to kill innocent people. Bond attacks one of Gorner's guards. During the chaos, Scarlett gets a gun and fires it at a guard. A mid-air gunfight ensues. A stray bullet hits the window, causing the cabin to lose pressure. Bond finds a single parachute and gives it to Scarlett, who puts it on. Scarlett jumps out of the plane with Bond hanging on to her. Bond and Scarlett land safely nearby. Elsewhere, the Royal Air Force shoots down the Ekranoplan.

Bond and Scarlett escape the Soviet Union by hitchhiking to Moscow, taking a train to Leningrad, and then traveling by boat to Helsinki. Along the way, they are intercepted by Chagrin who attacks Bond. After a vicious fight, Bond kills him.

Bond and Scarlett eventually arrive in Paris. During a phone call, M tells Bond that he will arrange for 007 to meet the new 004. When Gorner catches up with Bond, the two men battle. Gorner tries to escape by jumping into the nearby river. However, he becomes intertwined in the boat's giant paddle and dies.

Later, Bond meets up with Scarlett who reveals that she is the newly minted 004 and that supporting Bond in the field was her first assignment. At first, Bond is angry that M didn't disclose Scarlett's true identity. He understands that Scarlett has been a tremendous asset and that he wouldn't have been able to complete the mission without her. Bond and Scarlett embrace.

Commentary: Ian Fleming Publications hired Sebastian Faulks to write *Devil May Care*, which was published on the 100th anniversary of Fleming's birth. Faulks' novel ignores the modern period established by Gardner and Benson and sets *Devil May Care* in the 1960s. The book begins a few years after the events of Fleming's last book, *The Man with the Golden Gun*.

The front cover of *Devil May Care* announces that Faulks was "writing as Ian Fleming." It's an unusual claim and it requires some context. As the book was published on Fleming's centenary, as a tribute, Faulks' remit was to write in Fleming's style. Faulks had both the experience and facility for adopting another author's voice and as previously discussed, he had already written two Fleming pastiches—"James Bond Goes to Sainsbury's" (2002) and "Ian Fleming Thinks Even James Bond Goes Shopping" (2006)." So Faulks attempted to write a fast-paced adventure, without unnecessary flourishes in Fleming's journalistic style. As Faulk's put it, the style consists of "short sentences, a lot of active verbs, no semicolons."[125]

Faulks was not only aiming to capture Fleming's technique, but he also sought to emulate the spirit of Fleming. Faulks explained, "What I want to write is the book that Fleming himself would have written had he lived a bit longer. Suppose Fleming lived five years longer and he rather recovered his enjoyment of writing and his enjoyment of the character, he might have written another really top-notch Bond adventure... This is the book I really tried to do. The very best of Bond if you like."[126]

For Faulks, the best of Bond meant creating villains in Fleming's mold. Dr. Julius Gorner, a chemist and the owner of a pharmaceutical company, is the main villain. He shares some traits with other Fleming baddies. Drax cheats at cards; Goldfinger cheats at golf; and Gorner cheats at tennis. Both Dr. No and Gorner have physical deformities. Dr. No has steel pinchers for hands and Gorner's hand is like a monkey's paw, a hand that resembles that of a chimpanzee and whose hair extends beyond his wrist. Gorner is aided by his henchman Pham Sinh Quoc, who goes by the name Chagrin. He wears a French legionnaire's hat, to cover an exposed part of his skull, a result of a surgery that Chagrin undertook on his temporal lobe. The unintended side effect is that Chagrin feels no emotion, no empathy, and essentially no pain. Chagrin uses an ordinary pair of chopsticks as a weapon. When given the chance, Chagrin puts the chopsticks in his victim's ears and then boxes them.

Bond is not left to his own devices. He's aided by René Mathis, a member of France's military intelligence agency. Felix Leiter, Bond's friend, and ex-CIA agent, is still working for the Pinkerton detective agency, as was established in the chapter "The Eye That Never Sleeps" in *Diamonds Are Forever*. The Texan is now living in Santa Monica. Leiter is still willing to, at a moment's notice, drop everything and help his old pal. Leiter describes Bond as his blood brother. Leiter isn't effective in a gun battle. His right hand, now sporting a hook, was his firing hand. Felix will either need to learn to shoot with his left hand or he'll need to find other ways to protect himself in the field.

Scarlett Papava is Bond's main love interest and a newly minted Double O agent. She's been sent by M to help Bond complete his assignment. M didn't have the confidence in a burnt-out 007 or a novice 004 to complete the mission on their own. Instead, M thought it would take both of them, working together, to bring down Gorner. Turns out M was right. Scarlett is a resourceful ally who single-handedly figures out that Gorner is cheating at tennis and enables Bond to defeat him.

Scarlett it turns out is a master of disguise. During the book, she appears to Bond as three different people, Larissa Rossi, Scarlett

Papava, and her sister Poppy. Just as Bond is taken in by her disguise, so are the readers. But, during the first reading, Scarlett seemed like a capable but not necessarily self-sufficient love interest for Bond. However, after she is revealed to be the new 004, it's necessary to completely reevaluate her character from the beginning. Scarlett is a bit of a mastermind, playing Bond and nudging him toward success. If it were not for 004, Bond would have failed the mission. Still, readers can debate if M needed to deceive Bond in this manner.

We are meant to believe that Bond fell in love with Scarlett during this adventure. In one scene, he picks up a miniature Eiffel Tower, and wonders if it would make a nice gift for her. Elsewhere, Bond thinks he might be dying but his only thoughts are of Scarlett. Bond wonders if he loves her.

The story's most significant emotional arc is Bond's loss of the swagger, confidence, and zip that are essential for him to excel at his dangerous job. Bond worries that because his "mind has run to fat" he will be removed from field work and regulated to office life. As such, he is steeling himself for a life of paperwork. The agent needn't have worried. As soon as Bond begins his mission, he starts to feel invigorated. By the end of the story, Bond has regained his zest for his work and is happy to be back in action.

Faulks' *Devil May Care* feels like it could have served as the first book in a new series. Bond and Scarlett begin an office romance that could have played out over the course of a few more books. I would have been curious to see how Faulks or another writer would have developed their relationship. The book's concluding paragraphs contain a character recap in which Bond's thoughts are briefly taken over by M, Loelia Ponsonby, Moneypenny, and Julian Burton, the psychological-fitness trainer at SIS. There is no narrative need for the reminder. Instead, it feels like a prelude to other Bond adventures.

But alas, Faulks would write only one Bond novel, and the next continuation author would wipe the slate clean and start a new storyline. Whatever the plans for these particular characters, they were never intended to include Faulks. When promoting *Devil May Care*, Faulks stated that he didn't plan to write a multi-part series and that his book was meant to be his solitary contribution to the Bond canon.

Continuity Nod: M acknowledges that, on the surface, this drug-related assignment doesn't seem as important as a probe into diamonds, an apparent reference to *Diamonds Are Forever.* While playing poker and *chemin de fer*, Bond recalls gambling with Le Chiffre (*Casino Royale*) and Hugo Drax (*Moonraker*), as well as the armorer's jibe that a Baretta is a lady's gun (*From Russia with Love*). During dinner with Scarlett Papava, Bond recalls his slain wife, Tracy di Vicenzo. There is also a passing reference to Kristatos, an informant, who Bond dealt with in Fleming's short story about drug smuggling, "Risico" and who also appears in the film *For Your Eyes Only*. The shark attack on Leiter in Florida in *Live and Let Die*, which left Bond's friend with a hook for a hand and without a right leg, is also referenced. There are also allusions to 007's battle with Blofeld in Japan (*You Only Live Twice*) and his attempt to assassinate M (*The Man with the Golden Gun*).

Bond's History: Bond dreams about taking a train in the Highlands as a kid and about his mother's voice. We learn that Bond visited Egypt as a young boy, most likely with his parents, but that he has limited memories of the experience.

Bond Inner Life: Faulks peppers the book with personal information about Bond throughout the narrative. For instance, while listening to the Pope's sermon, Bond envies those who follow religion and believe in God. He misses playing cards against a formidable opponent, without one, the game holds little interest to him.

While on his required three-month leave from office, Bond abstained from alcohol and sex and went to bed before ten. He also maintained a good exercise schedule that included tennis and swimming.

Bond's Tastes: Faulks' Bond, like Fleming's, takes strong showers, first using very hot water and then freezing water. Bond still wears a navy suit, black tie, and clean crisp shirt. For Bond, it is almost like wearing a comfortable uniform. Bond is still driving the Bentley that Fleming gave him. However, there are moments when, at work, he wishes that he were behind the wheel of an Aston Martin.

Bond loves to travel. For Bond, it's time that M, Moneypenny, and any paramours are unable to contact him. Instead, he can use that time for himself, to read about golf, or to drink a Blood Mary. His first drink in three months is two fingers of whiskey with equal parts ice and soda water.

Bond's Work Life: Loelia Ponsonby is still Bond's secretary. But she's now married and has two boys. 004 was killed in the line of duty, thrown under a moving train in East Germany. M has appointed a new agent to take his place. Bond knows the other Double O agents but, for security and safety reasons, they generally don't fraternize with one another.

At M's request, Bond picked up some chocolates for his superior in Italy. However, when Bond is displeased with his next assignment, Bond gives the sweets to Moneypenny instead. It's his informal protest. Still, despite his quiet protest, Bond greatly respects his boss and feels the need to impress him. In fact, elsewhere Faulks describes M as the "man he most respected in the world."[127]

At M's instructions, Bond talks to psychological-fitness trainer, Julian Burton, who goes by the name of R. 009 spoke to Burton and benefited from their conversations. As a calming technique, he teaches Bond how to take more breath into his lungs. This skill pays off later in the story when Bond must hold his breath to investigate Gorner's ship-plane.

Bond normally packs a Walther PPK, but he thinks that the more powerful Colt .45 will be needed for his present mission. He avoids using silencers as they can get caught on his clothes when he's attempting a quick draw, as it did in the novel *From Russia with Love*. The poison dart from Bond's Ronson Varaflame lighter may render an adversary immobile for up to six hours. As a rule, he steers clear of using gadgets.

Action: Chagrin's death is memorable. After overpowering Gorner's muscle, Bond and Scarlett attempt to throw him out the window. As they're doing so, their train enters a tunnel and the force of Chagrin's head hitting the tunnel causes an unintended decapitation. Faulks wisely resists the temptation to make a bad pun ("he lost his head") and instead has Scarlett break down and weep at the gruesome sight. By avoiding the cheap laugh, Faulks reinforces the stakes and the danger that Bond and Scarlett face.

Injury Report: Faulks puts Bond through his paces. In addition to dislocating his arm, Bond loses a tooth as a result of Chagrin's kick to the face.

Theme Song: As a unique promotion for *Devil May Care*, the publishers cooked up a contest that allowed bands to submit "theme songs" for the book. A Cardiff-based band named SAL won the contest. They beat out 500 other entries.[128]

JEFFERY DEAVER'S TENURE
2011

Jeffery Deaver wrote the Bond continuation novel *Carte Blanche* (2011).

CARTE BLANCHE (2011)

Author: Jeffery Deaver

In Brief: Bond is sent to investigate Severan Hydt, the owner of a rubbish and recycling operation, who is planning an attack on England.

Meaning of Title: Bond is normally given total freedom to complete his mission. In this assignment, the spy has to operate within the strict parameters of the local laws. Also, Bond concocts a recipe for a whiskey-based cocktail that he names Carte Blanche.

Chronology: Contemporary. Set in the then-present 2011.

Operation: Steel Cartridge and Incident Twenty.

Bastard Meter: Standard.

Eggs: Softly scrambled with Irish butter.

Insight into Bond: "But in the end, he now realized, such a woman, indeed any woman, could occupy but a small role in the peculiar reality in which he lived."

Summary: A train transporting scrap metal and deadly chemicals passes through Novi Sad, Serbia. Irishman Niall Dunne plans to derail the train, which would cause a chemical spill. James Bond catches sight of Dunne and thwarts their attack. After killing the Serbian local agents who Bond is working with, Dunne gets away. Bond searches Dunne's car and discovers and collects scraps of paper with notes on them.

Back in London, Bond is at his Chelsea flat where his housekeeper, May, prepares breakfast. Bond is an operative for the Overseas Development Group (ODG) and he works as a Double O agent in the O Branch. Bond's father Andrew Bond and mother Monique Delacroix were killed in a mountain climbing accident when

Bond was eleven. On Bond's mantle is a steel rifle cartridge that was discovered near his father's body.

Later at ODG, Bond talks to intelligence analyst, Ophelia "Philly" Maidenstone, and then he meets with M who oversees the entire division. M tasks Bond with tracking down Dunne and Noah and uncovering their master plan.

Severan Hydt, the head of Green Way International Disposal and Recycling, receives word that the total dead for tomorrow's unspecified event will be nearly 100. Hydt receives a report from Dunne regarding the operation in Serbia.

Bond reviews intelligence signals that mention a Russian initiative dubbed Steel Cartridge, an operation that is unrelated to Hydt. Bond instructs Philly to investigate Steel Cartridge. Bond meets with Percy Osborne-Smith, the deputy senior director of field operations for MI6. Osborne-Smith tries to decode the message on Dunne's papers that refers to "a meeting at Noah's office" and "Boots—March. 17. No later than that." Osborne-Smith believes that Boots may refer to the pharmacy chain of the same name. Bond recalls that there is also a Boots Road, the home of an old army base, and the 17th can mean that the attack will take place on the 17th of the month, which is the next day. Bond doesn't trust Osborne-Smith so he tricks him into looking into the pharmacy lead, which 007 suspects will not yield results.

Bond travels to Boots Road to investigate the abandoned army base in March, England. Bond breaks in and discovers that the plant has been rigged for demolition. Hydt watches the building blow up.

Later, Tanner tells Bond that the old base now belongs to Hydt's company Green Way International. Years ago, Hydt was in his university's sailing club and went by the nickname Noah, the name on the scrap of paper. Tanner reports that Incident 20, Hydt's operation, is also known as the Gehenna plan. Philly informs Bond that Operation Steel Cartridge was the targeted killing of SIS operatives who were tracking Russian spies.

Bond dines with Philly who explains that the metal from the train attack were identified as titanium-steel laminate, a rare substance. Later, René Mathis phones Bond and tells him that Hydt is leaving the country.

Bond follows Hydt, Dunne, and Hydt's lover Jessica Barnes to the airport, where they board a plane to Dubai. Bond takes a separate flight to Dubai. Once in Dubai, Bond senses that he's being followed. Bond meets Felix Leiter at a local café just outside the hotel where Hydt and Dunne are staying. There, Bond is introduced to Yusuf

Nasad, Felix's local asset. The trio spots Hydt and Dunne leaving their hotel and trails them.

Severan Hydt and Dunne travel to an industrial complex in the Deira, an area between Dubai Creek and the Gulf. They meet Mahdi al-Fulan, an MIT-educated entrepreneur, and Stella Kirkpatrick, al-Fulan's research assistant. Hydt is in attendance on behalf of Green Way International Disposal and Recycling, his legitimate business, to watch a demonstration of a machine that is designed to destroy computer data storage devices. Hydt and al-Fulan leave the site and head towards the site of their planned attack, The Museum of the Emirates.

Bond follows Hydt to the museum and discovers that Hydt is there to see an exhibition called "Death in the Sand" about a tribe of nomads who were slaughtered a thousand years ago. Hydt experiences an almost sexual pleasure looking at the dead bodies. Still, Bond is convinced that Dunne's note described an attack, even if the museum is not the intended target. Bond overhears Hydt telling al-Fulan that Dunne is going to kill Stella Kirkpatrick. Bond calls Felix Leiter to tell him to save Stella but Leiter doesn't answer. Worried about Leiter, Bond returns to al-Fulan's warehouse. At the warehouse, 007 spots one of al-Fulan's men dragging Leiter's unconscious body towards the waste disposal machine. 007 saves Leiter but discovers that their ally, Yusuf Nasad, has been killed.

Back at the hotel, Bond bribes a limo driver into revealing that Hydt is going to Cape Town, South Africa. After Bond and Leiter arrive in Cape Town, Tanner suggests that Bond meet Captain Bheka Jordaan of the South African Police Service. Jordaan lets Bond know that Hydt and Dunne are in Cape Town. Bond tells Jordaan that he's going to stop Hydt from pulling off his plan by any means necessary. Jordaan warns Bond that he must operate within the law; he doesn't have carte blanche.

Bond poses as Gene Theron, an Afrikaner from Durban, and arranges a meeting with Hydt. In the meeting, Bond claims that he works at a security company but has been to known supply arms and troops in areas of conflict. Bond explains that there is a significant amount of land that cannot be developed because the locals don't want to build on the mass graves. Bond offers to remove the bodies and relocate the remains. Hydt agrees to partner with Bond and asks to see a picture of the killing fields. Hydt invites Bond to a charity event that he's attending that night.

Bond meets Gregory Lamb, an MI6 operative in Cape Town who Tanner doesn't trust. Lamb tells Bond that he's being followed by a tall, slim, man with a gold earring.

Bond receives a coded message from Philly about Operation Steel Cartridge. Philly explains the Soviet Union measure involved killing MI6 and CIA agents. Bond suspects that his late father might have been killed as part of the initiative. If the report is true, then Bond's father was an enemy spy.

Bond goes to the Lodge Club for the charity event in support of the International Organization Against Hunger. There, he sees Hydt and his companion Jessica Barnes. Bond meets the managing director of the charity, Felicity Willing. After the event ends, Bond accompanies Felicity to a food bank. Then, the two go to a hotel and spend an intimate evening together.

The next day, Hydt tells Bond more about his legitimate disposal operation as they tour the grounds. Hydt brings Bond to a petty thief and tells Bond that if he kills the thief in cold blood, then they can work together. After Dunne hands Bond a rifle, 007 shoots the man, apparently killing him. It's revealed that the rifle was loaded with non-lethal wax bullets, a fact that 007 already figured out on his own. Having passed the loyalty test, Hydt offers to introduce Bond to his three partners in the operation.

On Bond's way out, he runs into Jessica Barnes, Hydt's lover. Jessica accepts Bond's offer to drive her into town. Jessica reveals that Hydt is very controlling and that she's trapped in the relationship. After she leaves, Bond wonders if Jessica is a potential ally or a threat.

In London, the Joint Intelligence Committee tells M that Bond's investigation of Hydt is distracting them from investigating the real threat. Back in South Africa, Bond spots the man who has been following him. Bond confronts the man and learns that he's Nicholas Rathko, a member of the Serbian paramilitary group, who blames Bond for the death of his brother in Dubai.

Bond goes to Hydt's plant and uses a listening device to eavesdrop on Dunne's conversation. Bond learns that the attack will take place in York at 10:30 a.m. that same day. Bond calls Percy Osborne-Smith and tells him what he knows. Percy doesn't trust Bond's intel. Bond realizes that he's on his own and that he only has two and a half hours to stop the attack.

Bond enters the plant and discovers photographs of an experimental lethal weapon known as the Cutter. The Cutter can fire hundreds of blades at a high velocity at its target. Bond deduces that Hydt has made the Cutter and that the purpose of the attack on the train in Novi Sad was unrelated to the deadly chemicals it was transporting. Instead, Hydt's operatives wanted to obtain the scrap metal materials in the train wagons so that he could build the Cutter. Bond figures out that Hydt's plan actually has two separate targets—a particular individual and members of the general public. Bond suspects that the attack on the public is only intended to obscure the real target, the individual. Before he can learn more, Hydt's security captures Bond.

Bond is brought to Hydt who explains that a researcher in York is developing a new drug that will aggressively fight cancer. The researcher will be in York at the same time that a human rights activist is teaching. Intelligence communities and the public will believe that the human rights activist is the intended target. However, Hydt's real aim is to kill the researcher working on the cancer drug. He has been hired by the president of a rival drug company in North Carolina to eliminate the competition.

After Hydt puts his plan into action, a news report airs about an explosion in York; Hydt's plan is apparently successful. However, shortly before the explosion, Bond had notified the authorities and prevented any serious injuries. Bond escapes from Hydt's clutches. Bheka Jordaan arrives with reinforcements and arrests Hydt. Dunne then shoots Hydt, stopping him from revealing anything about their plans.

Later Jordaan says that Hydt's three associates will be arrested and that the drug company president who hired Hydt will be brought to justice. M tells Bond that the Oversees Development Group will temporarily continue running Hydt's enterprises, as a way to ferret out other bad actors. The case seems closed, but Bond suspects that there is more to learn. He wonders if Gregory Lamb is somehow involved with Hydt.

Bond reveals to Felicity Willing that he's working with the British government and inquiries about Gregory Lamb. Felicity tells Bond that Lamb's nickname is Noah, the same name that appeared in Dunne's papers. Bond explains that intelligence reveals that Lamb has a secret meeting with someone at a deserted inn.

Bond goes to the inn and finds that Felicity is there, apparently shot by a police officer on orders by Lamb. Bond tells Felicity that she was the target of Incident 20. But when Bond attempts to call for help, Felicity pulls a gun on him and confesses that she set up Lamb and that Noah is not a person; it's an anacronym for the original name of the organization, NOAH, National Organization Against Hunger. It turns out that Felicity, not Hydt, is the head of the operation and that Dunne works for her. Felicity explains that Incident 20 and Gehenna are two separate operations. Incident 20 was Hydt's operation, and it involved the Cutter weapon. Gehenna was hers. Felicity's food organization controls a third of the food coming into South Africa, and it provides food aid in Latin America, India, and Southeast Asia.

Felicity can make money by controlling the food supply and sending it to armies so that they can win wars. Her first display of power will be an invasion of eastern Sudan by the central authority in Khartoum, an operation that will commence in 90 minutes. The entire plan has been financed by the Chinese government so that they can be the beneficiaries of the region's oil supply.

Gregory Lamb and Bheka Jordaan, who have been secretly monitoring the conversation, arrive and arrest Felicity. Dunne appears and tries to kill Bond, Bheka, and Lamb. Bond and Jordaan chase after Dunne and terminate him. Later, Tanner tells Bond that the forces outside of Sudan have stood down and the immediate threat to the country has passed.

Bond has dinner with Philly Maidenstone. Over dinner, Bond learns that his father was neither a secret agent nor a traitor, but his mother was a well-regarded spy. She was murdered by the KGB to prevent her from identifying Russian moles in the Secret Intelligence Service. Bond pledges to find the identity of her killer and those who ordered it. Philly tells Bond that she's getting back together with her fiancé. Later, Bond dines with Bheka Jordaan. But he knows that the relationship with Jordaan will not progress into anything romantic; he will always be alone.

Commentary: *Carte Blanche* breaks from other post-Fleming novels in that Deaver is not *continuing* Bond's story and career. Instead, Deaver's *starting* it. In *Carte Blanche*, James Bond, a veteran of the Afghan Wars, is in his early thirties. He has not yet battled Goldfinger, Drax, or encountered SPECTRE. Instead, Bond is only a couple of years into his tenure as a Double O agent.

Equally notable is that Deaver's novel is not a period piece; instead, it's set in the present day. Instead of cables, Bond reads emails and texts. Bond makes use of the most advanced technology available today, such as an encrypted smartphone that has been outfitted with facial-recognition software that allows him to identify foes and then follow their movements with the aid of satellites. Fleming purists might bump up against Deaver's decision to set the novel in the 21st Century. But the author told me that Fleming's novels were not period pieces so his should not be either.[129]

Fleming made frequent references to the news and cultural events of the day. Similarly, Deaver writes about contemporary topics, such as Taliban and Al-Qaeda and alludes to actors Matt Damon, Leonardo DiCaprio, and Kate Winslet (who Bond's colleague Ophelia Maidenstone resembles), as well as *Doctor Who*, the sci-fi series about a Time Lord.

Deaver does not assume that his readers are well-versed in Fleming's novels or the recurring characters in Bond's orbit. As such, he provides backstories for M, Bill Tanner, Moneypenny, Goodnight, and others and he clearly explains their jobs and their particular relationship to Bond. Deaver's Felix Leiter is a former Marine and he is a member of the National Clandestine Service, a department in the CIA. M is a card player, a fisherman, a watercolorist who prefers to paint flowers and lives in a Regency manor house. He is known as the Admiral. Moneypenny has a military background; she left the Royal Navy to work with M. Bill Tanner is a retired army officer who has achieved the rank of lieutenant-colonel. Bill Tanner mentored Bond when he was a young agent. They have developed a friendship and they play golf together every few weeks.

Deaver also revamps the Double O Section, which in Fleming's novels, was a part of SIS. In *Carte Blanche*, Bond is an agent for Britain's Special Operations Executive, an espionage and sabotage group formed by Winston Churchill at the start of World War II. The Special Operations Executive (SOE), in turn, reports to the Overseas Development Group (ODG) and M, who is its director-general. As part of ODG's cover, they help British companies with their foreign operations. As such, Bond can travel the world playing the part of a security and integrity analyst. In many ways, this new infrastructure differs from Fleming's. However, Pearson, the Fleming biographer (and continuation author) suggests that Fleming was partially inspired by the SOE and that Fleming's brother Peter was recruited by the organization.[130]

Deaver also details the events that led to Bond becoming a Double O agent. After leaving the Royal Naval Reserve, Bond didn't have a clear view of what he wanted to do in life. But a pal suggested that Bond take a stab at Defense Intelligence. Bond took to it, but he also wanted to get his hands dirty. After expressing his desire that he was craving more excitement, Bond received a handwritten note to attend lunch at the Travelers Club. At the club, Bond met the Admiral. The Admiral invited Bond to join Special Operations Executive (SOE) a secret agency that isn't part of MI6. The SOE agency won't be constrained by the rules of the other organizations. Their only goal is to protect British interest "by any means necessary." The Admiral, of course, is later identified as M and Bond immediately accepts his invitation.

Arguably, the most discussed element of the book is the subplot in which Bond investigates the circumstances that led to his parent's death. Fleming established that they were killed in a mountain climbing accident. Deaver retains that backstory but adds a twist. In

Carte Blanche, Bond suspects that his parents were murdered. At first, evidence suggests that his father, an armaments salesman, was actually a mole for the Russians and that he was killed before his identity could be discovered. Deaver weaves this mystery throughout the book and allows the revelations to disturb Bond, as the agent worries about his parents' loyalties. Ultimately, the revelation that his father was innocent and that his mother was a spy, like him, brings Bond closer to his parents.

The moral quandary of whether the death of one innocent person may ever be justified if it saves many lives recurs throughout *Carte Blanche*. In one instance, Leiter suggests that Bond should let Hydt conduct his initial attack on 90 people so that Bond can capture him before he plans a major attack which would kill thousands. Bond rejects the idea. In that instance, Bond believes he can save the people and foil Hydt's even more evil ambitions, therefore he is spared from having to make a moral decision. More than that, Bond can't bear the thought of sacrificing any lives.

Later, Hydt tells Bond to kill an innocent man by shooting him with a rifle. If Bond kills the man, he would have gained Hydt's trust. In the story, Bond fires at the man and seems to kill him. But it's revealed that the rifle contained wax bullets. Furthermore, Bond knew that he was firing a non-lethal round. As a result, Bond was able to avoid making this moral decision. But it's safe to bet that Deaver's Bond would not have killed an innocent man, even if it would have helped him accomplish his mission. He would have found a solution to save everyone.

As a Double O agent, 007 often has carte blanche to carry out his assignment. Deaver argues that agents need to feel that they are entitled to the moral authority that comes with carte blanche. Deaver suggests that it's essential for agents to believe "that they were different, that they were allowed to—no required to—operate outside the law." However, when he arrives in South Africa, he is forced to operate under their laws, a prospect that Bond bristles at.

Deaver's Bond used to long to find a woman with whom he could "share all secrets—could share his life." Bond has come to realize that finding such a woman would be impossible, given his profession. Instead, he has mostly resigned himself to the notion that his profession would be a higher priority. Still, Bond develops romantic feelings for his colleague Ophelia "Philly" Maidenstone, MI6's liaison officer. Philly is a married woman estranged from her husband. As their relationship develops, Bond wonders if they can share a life together. Philly reconciles with her fiancé in the end. This unrequited love is something that Fleming's Bond has gone through, most notably with Gala Brand in *Moonraker*. And without a woman, Bond understands that he will be "traveling forever alone."

Bond's History: Deaver details significant events in Bond's life as Fleming originally portrayed them, including his parent's death, his childhood with Aunt Charmian, and his education at Eton and Fettes. Deaver also adds to the tapestry of Bond's life. As a fifteen-year-old at Fettes, Deaver's Bond trained in close combat fighting techniques, formed a climbing club, and practiced in the Highlands. Before becoming a Double O agent, he worked in Defense Intelligence and was a member of the Naval Reserve. Bond has been to Dubai on a previous mission, and he appreciates the diversity of cultures and religions in Dubai that co-exist peacefully. He also enjoys Dubai's topography, because it's so unlike the landscapes of Kent, where he grew up. He's conducted operations in Belgrade and North Korea, where he rescued a captured MI6 asset from prison.

Bond's Personal Life: Bond is a member of a private club in Berkeley Square, the Commodore, that he goes to for gambling and where he often loses money at the tables. His frequent gambling companion is a Jordanian named Fouad Kharaz. Bond's living room hardly has furniture. But it does contain a few items that he inherited from his deceased parents, including a desk, chairs, lamps, and a sound system, which Bond uses infrequently. Photos of his parents, grandparents, and Aunt Charmian are on display.

Bond driving a Bentley Continental GT
in *Carte Blanche.*
Illustration by Pat Carbajal

Bond's Tastes: Even though he keeps a clock by his bed, Bond wakes up by the alarm on his mobile phone; he sleeps naked. Bond takes freezing cold showers, shaves with a double razor, and dresses in a navy blue suit, white shirt, a burgundy-grenadine tie, and slip-on shoes without laces. He no longer smokes and prefers to have breakfast at a nearby hotel, which includes three scrambled eggs, bacon, and toast with Irish butter and marmalade. Bond tells an attractive woman that his second favorite method to wake up is by the popping sound of a champagne cork. His favorite is presumably far more risqué.

Bond drives a Bentley Continental GT, estimated to be worth £125,000. Deaver notes that the car was featured on the UK show *Top Gear*, a possible reference to an episode that they aired on the vehicles used in Eon's films. Bond has a passion for Formula One cars and racing. Even on assignment in Dubai, Bond picks up the *National* newspaper so that he can read their coverage of the latest race.

Bond's Inner-Life: Deaver notes that Bond is not a patient man. However, tolerance is often required for his job. So, Bond manages to temper his impatience. Bond acknowledges that continual exposure to genuine threats causes him to fear phantom ones. He also accepts that he will likely be killed in the line of duty.

Bond's Work-Life: Bond must go through two devices that scan his eyes and confirm his identity before he can enter his office. To maintain peak physical fitness, he goes to the gym for at least an hour a day, and he enjoys daily jogs in Regent's Park. Bond tries to have a working knowledge of as many languages as possible but has never been able to replicate any of the clickings that are used in some African languages. He knows a bit of Serbo-Croatian. Q Branch devised a microphone that was hidden in an ordinary house fly. Or as Bond surmises, it's a "bug in a bug." Bond is also given an inhaler with a hidden camera. Bond's iPhone is jokingly referred to as an "iQphone." Bond and Leiter will never drink to a fallen colleague, although they might be tempted to raise a glass. By tradition, it's forbidden.

Bond's Training and Tradecraft: Deaver provides details on Bond's training at Fort Monckton's Special Training Center. Throughout the story, Deaver sprinkles in advice that his instructions provide. Tips from the instructors include "Small clues save you. Small errors kill;" "Your enemy's purpose will dictate your response;" and "You wear your cover to the grave." Other bits of advice include, "With many opportunities come many operatives."

Bond also learned to never try to fake his own handwriting as he will eventually fail at it and that ignoring his intuition will get him killed. He was taught that when he has the drop on an adversary, he should ignore their words as they monologue and instead pay careful attention to their hand movements and body language. Elsewhere, Deaver outlines the importance of seduction in tradecraft and explains how it works best. In those situations, seduction is most effective when the spy does not appear to chase their target but, instead, lets the target come to them.

Bond's training at Fort Monckton was both physical and psychological. Instructors were there to get agents into the mindset of being a spy. As such, an instructor argues, "Combatting evil sometimes requires a suspension of accepted values." It was important for agents to feel that they had the moral authority to wield their Double O status like a sword or shield and that they are empowered to exercise it as they see fit. When it comes to assassinations, agents learn that it's just another aspect of their profession and that it is no different than surveillance or learning how to do a proper dead-drop. It's a tool of the trade, no more odious than any of his other duties. This moral authority is essential if Bond is going to follow M's admonishment that, as a Double O agent, "Our mission is simple. We protect the Realm...by any means necessary."

Bond's Parents: Deaver supplies information about Bond's parents Andrew and Monique. Monique is given the profession of a freelance journalist. Andrew was a fan of car racing, and he collected old newspaper photos of H. M. Bentley and W. O. Bentley, the brothers who founded Bentley Motors. We can infer that Bond's interest in car racing and his personal Bentley are links to his dad, who Bond dearly loved. Andrew was a quiet but dependable man who, in addition to collecting stamps and photographs of cars, loved repairing and driving them.

As a child, Bond traveled with his parents. From those trips, Bond picked up his love for traveling, local food, living in hotels, and facility for foreign languages. His openness to foreign customs and cultures would later serve him well as a secret agent.

Deaver fleshes out the details of the circumstances around the death of Bond's parents. Bond recalls that he was dropped off at his Aunt's house just before Christmas in 1990, so that they could go to Mont Blanc for a five-day skiing and climbing vacation. They were to return to Bond by December 25th to celebrate the holiday as a family. The ice-climbing accident shattered those plans and Bond's childhood. Bond keeps a bullet on his mantelpiece that was discovered close to his father's body. A subplot in the book centers on Bond's search for the bullet's provenance and its significance.

An encrypted email from Philly informs Bond about Steel Cartridge, a joint KGB and Russian Foreign Intelligence Service operation to kill MI6 agents in the late 1980s and early 1990s—covering the time of his parents' death—causing Bond to suspect that his father was a spy. Later, Philly tells Bond that the Steel Cartridge operation was an effort to kill moles in MI6. This new information forces Bond to consider the possibility that his father was not only a spy but a traitor.

As the evidence against Bond's father mounts, Bond's own investigation suggests that the mountain's face was a challenging but not particularly dangerous ascent. Moreover, the slope wasn't so steep that a fall would be fatal. Bond also can't figure out why his Aunt Charmian received frequent cash wire transfers unrelated to any insurance-related death benefits. The frequency and mysterious source of those wire transfers fuels Bond's suspicion. Throughout the book, Bond increasingly suspects his dad of espionage. Bond recalls that his Aunt said that Andrew would never draw attention to himself and wouldn't stand out in a crowd. Good qualities for a secret agent. It weighs on Bond.

Eventually, Bond learns that his father wasn't a spy but his mother Monique was. Her job as a freelance journalist was perfect cover to travel to different countries. Her frequent trips without her son cause young James to feel rejected. But through his investigation, the adult Bond comes to a realization—the reason she left James behind when she traveled. It wasn't because she didn't want to spend time with him; it was to keep him safe.

Unwritten Sequel: As noted, Bond learns that his mother was a spy. However, he doesn't know who killed her or why. But Deaver suggests that Bond will look into the matter. Presumably, Deaver left this plot thread for a follow-up book that either he or another writer could pick up. However, the next Bond book would be set in the Sixties and not in the present day. So any possibility of figuring out the circumstances of Monique Bond's death would have to be abandoned.

Assorted Observations:

- Bond's cover is Gene Theron, an Afrikaner mercenary from Durban. Toby Stephens, who played James Bond in nine radio plays for the BBC, reads the audiobook. As a result, Stephens speaks most of Bond's dialogue with a slight Afrikaner accent.
- Durban has another connection to Bond lore. The Durban Repertory Theatre adapted Fleming's novel Moonraker into a radio play in 1958.

WILLIAM BOYD'S TENURE
2013

William Boyd wrote the Bond continuation novel *Solo* (2013). To commemorate the release of Boyd's *Solo*, the author wrote a pair of short stories, "William Boyd Interviews James Bond" and "William Boyd Q&A with James Bond." The companion pieces were both published in *The Guardian* on September 28, 2013, the week that *Solo* launched.

SOLO (2013)

Author: William Boyd

In Brief: Bond is dispatched to the West African nation of Zanzarim, where a civil war is raging, to kill the leader of the resistance, Brigadier Solomon Adeka.

Meaning of Title: Bond goes "solo" when, on his own initiative, he hunts down Kobus Breed, a mercenary, and Blessing Ogilvy-Grant, the woman who apparently betrayed and shot him.

Chronology: Period. Set in 1969, five years after Fleming's *The Man with the Golden Gun* and, presumably, two years after Faulk's *Devil May Care.*

Operation: Not applicable.

Bastard Meter: Devious Bastard.

Eggs: Scrambled and served as an overcooked omelet.

Insight into Bond: "He grew angry with himself. What was he doing thinking about the future? It was the hero and now that intrigued and fulfilled him."

Summary: On James Bond's forty-fifth birthday, he wakes up in a hotel casino and then meets a beautiful woman named Bryce Fitzjohn, an actress who is celebrating the fourth anniversary of her divorce. Bryce invites Bond to a cocktail party at her home. Bond declines and returns to his flat in Chelsea where he greets his new housekeeper Donalda, May's niece and replacement. Bond wonders if his encounter with Bryce was chance or if she's a possible threat. To find out, Bond sneaks into Bryce's house and confirms that she is who she claims to be.

Bond goes to his office, talks with Moneypenny, and then meets with M. M tells Bond about a civil war in a West African country named Zanzarim. The conflict is between the powerful Zanzarim army, and a new independent government called the Democratic Republic of Dahum. M orders Bond to go to Zanzarim and kill the head of the resistance, Brigadier Solomon Adeka. Adeka's death would end the war, unify the country, and save the lives of thousands of civilians.

Before heading to Africa, Bond visits Solomon Adeka's estranged brother, Gabriel Adeka. Gabriel is a founder of a charity called AfricaKIN that supports the people of Dahum. Gabriel tells Bond that the winner of the war between Zanzarim and Dahum will control the oil beneath the Zanza River Delta.

Bond flies to Zanzarim and meets Christmas, his driver, and the local head of station, E. B. "Blessing" Ogily-Grant. As part of his cover, Bond poses as a journalist from Agence Presse Libre. At the hotel bar, Bond meets a group of journalists, including the insufferable Geoffrey Letham.

The next day, Bond and Blessing begin their journey to Dahum to find Solomon Adeka. Along the way, they stop at a hotel and make love. When Bond wakes up, he's confronted by a mercenary named Jakobus "Kobus" Breed. Breed's superiors think that Bond has been sent by the British government to help the Dahum opposition. Breed takes Bond and Blessing hostage.

On a trek through the forest, Breed and his men get into a firefight with the Zanzarim army. Bond and Blessing escape in the confusion but Blessing panics, runs away, and is apparently mowed down by enemy gunfire. Bond is eventually recaptured by Breed who lets Bond go once he's persuaded that Bond is a journalist.

The next day Bond meets his assistant, Sunday. Bond attempts to interview Brigadier Adeka but he's told that Adeka doesn't grant interviews. Later, Bond meets Hulbert Linck, a wealthy businessman who is supporting Zanza's resistance movement.

Bond watches a ritual where "fetish priest" Dr. Tony Msour performs a ceremony that blesses the soldiers. After the ceremony, the soldiers are in the right frame of mind to go into battle. Using his cover as a journalist, Bond embeds with the Dahumian army, who have lost control of a local village to Zanza forces. In exchange for an interview with Adeka, Bond provides a military strategy that allows Dahum to win the skirmish.

Bond is brought to a private home for his interview with Adeka. There, he encounters a high-ranking member of the Dahumian army named Colonel Denga. Then, Bond meets Adeka, who is suffering from aggressive cancer. Realizing that Adeka is about to die, Bond elects not to terminate him. Soon thereafter, Adeka dies, and Colonel Denga is announced as his successor.

Bond files a report with M who, in turn, instructs the spy to stay in Zanzarim and monitor the developing situation. Bond goes to Tony Msour's house and kidnaps him, and administers a drug that will keep the priest out of commission for 48 hours. Without their priest, the Dahumian army will be less motivated to fight the Zanza forces. Kobus Breed accuses Bond of kidnapping Msour. The presumed dead Blessing Ogilvy-Grant appears; she is apparently in league with the enemy. Kobus is about to kill Bond but Blessing shoots Bond first. An injured Bond passes out.

Bond convalesces in a military hospital for five weeks. M visits Bond in the hospital and explains that the person who claimed to be Blessing Ogilvy-Grant was actually Blessing's secretary whose real name is Aleesha Belem. Bond decides to "go solo" and track down Kobus Breed and Belem.

Bond returns to his flat in Chelsea where he discovers that Donalda has been attacked. Bond's previous housekeeper, May, comes to help.

Bond discovers that the AfricaKIN offices have been moved to Washington, DC. Bond goes to DC and stakes it out. He spots Colonel Denga and Belem and follows Belem to her hotel. At the hotel, Bond is confronted by two CIA agents, Brigham Leiter, Felix's nephew, and Luke Bassinette, who tell Bond that Belem works with the CIA. The CIA gives Bond 48 hours to leave the country.

Bond meets with Belem who explains that she shot Bond to save his life. If she hadn't, Breed would have killed them both. Belem tells Bond that Gabriel Adeka is in Virginia with her charity. After pretending to exit the country to throw the CIA off his trail, Bond doubles back, eventually returning to Belem's room, where he discovers that she's been killed by Breed.

Bond travels to a clinic that Gabriel Adeka operates. There, Bond crushes Breed's head with a stone. Bond discovers that Adeka is being held captive and has been drugged. Hulbert Linck appears and tells Bond that Adeka and Breed are using the AfricaKIN charity to smuggle heroin into the United States. CIA agent Massinette arrives and kills Linck, just as he is surrendering to Bond. Bond believes Linck was slain because the CIA wanted to silence him because he knew too much. Felix Leiter arrives to provide backup for Bond. Korbus

Breed's body cannot be found. Bond wonders if Breed somehow survived or if his dead body was hidden as part of a cover up.

Later, Bond tells Leiter that Solomon Adeka has been posing as his brother Gabriel. Bond and Felix travel to Zanzarim and dig up the grave where Solomon was supposedly buried, and discover an empty coffin. Leiter reveals that in exchange for Linck's military aid to the Dahum cause, Linck would be given the oil rights. However, Solomon Adeka couldn't authorize the deal, only his brother Gabriel could. So the pair conspired, faked Solomon's death, and installed Gabriel as head of AfricaKIN, ensuring that the oil deal went through. In the end, the oil deal benefited both the United Kingdom and the United States.

Back in London, M congratulates Bond on helping to bring an end to a blood war. Bond suspects that ensuring the successful completion of the oil deal was really what his superiors wanted all along.

Bond goes to Bryce's home to return her passport and to pursue a relationship with her. Hearing a car speed away, Bond wonders if it was a possible threat to Bryce. Either way, Bond knows that a relationship with Bryce would endanger her. Bond ends the relationship and leaves the house; he knows he must always be alone.

Commentary: Happy Birthday, 007. *Solo* takes place in 1969 on Bond's birthday. As such, Boyd needed to determine 007's age and figure out how many candles to put on Bond's cake. However, Boyd couldn't get a reliable date of birth from Fleming, who was not fastidious about such matters. Bond's age fluctuates between novels. Boyd relied on a passage in *You Only Live Twice* to provide a clue. In Fleming's second to last novel, M mistakenly thinks that 007 is dead, so he writes an obituary to be published in *The Times.* In it, M (and Fleming) gave Bond the birthdate of 1924. In the intro to *Solo*, Boyd reasons that the obituary represented the "key facts about Bond and his life that [Fleming] wanted to be in the public domain—facts that would cancel out various anomalies and illogicalities that had appeared in the earlier novels."[131] Given that, Boyd's Bond is 45.

Solo is set in the late 1960s. There are a few moments where Bond, a figure of the 1950s, is out of step with the times. In one scene, Bond toys with changing his hairstyle so that it's more *au current* but decides against it. In keeping with the Sixties-setting, Bond goes to the cinema to see *Bob & Carol & Ted & Alice*, the 1969 film about wife-swapping. Bond leaves before the film's climax but this decision is likely motivated by his focus on his mission and less about the film's merits.

It's not just the times that are a-changin', it's also the people in Bond's life. Bond's longstanding housekeeper, May, retired. May's arthritis played a role in her choice to resign, and Bond was undoubtedly sad to see her go. Her niece Donalda has taken her place. Donalda doesn't know much about Bond's chosen profession. However, he does give Donalda a secret way to contact him that would go unnoticed by prying eyes. Donalda performs her duties exactly as May did. The changing of the guard is so seamless that Bond hardly even notices it.

Because Donalda's presence causes Bond no discernable discomfort and it does not break up his routine, she may have been included in the narrative to serve as the "sacrificial lamb." The term sacrificial lamb was originated by John Brosnan in his 1972 book *James Bond in Cinema* to refer to a character who is killed off for helping Bond. Because Bond can't die, bumping off another character can add stakes to the proceedings. Donalda serves as *Solo*'s sacrificial lamb, even though she survives the attack. It's possible that Boyd felt that readers would have rejected an assault on May, an enduring character, so he created Donalda as a stand-in. Or perhaps her inclusion in the story simply underscores the passage of time.

Bond dreams throughout the book. The dreams provide a way to provide insight into Bond's character and reveal aspects of his life before he was a secret agent. In his dreams, he's in Normandy, on D-Day, as he was during the war. Bond was 19 years old at the time; a lieutenant in the Special Branch of the Royal Naval. In one mission, Bond is tasked with recovering a German cipher machine. In one dream, as Bond and an enemy soldier faced off, they both reached for their weapons. When Bond's weapon malfunctioned, it seems that he will be killed. At the last moment, a British soldier executes the enemy. This event marks the first time that Bond "stared death in the face."

Bond might be at the spy game too long, as it seems to be making him paranoid. A chance encounter with a beautiful and interesting woman causes Bond to feel overly suspicious. He wonders if he's being set up by the enemy. Bond can't shake the feeling, so he breaks into the innocent woman's house and snoops around.

The cinematic Bond has gone rogue on several occasions, including in *Licence to Kill*, *Quantum of Solace*, and *Spectre*. The literary Bond generally sticks to M's general orders, even if he executes them in an unorthodox method. In *Solo*, Bond conducts a mission for his personal vendetta. As such, Bond does not have the support or resources of MI6. Despite being aware of the "Draconian" punishments that he could face for going solo, Bond is not reprimanded. Instead, after he satisfies his thirst for revenge, M commends Bond. Contrary to what he was told, the surprised spy doesn't think he was deployed to aid in the reunification of a warring nation for humanitarian purposes. Instead, Bond thinks he was sent to Zanzarim to help his nation gain control of its oil. Being a pawn of the government leaves a bitter taste in his mouth.

The title has a double meaning, as noted. Not only does Bond go rogue to accomplish his mission, but he also winds up solo, or alone. Part of him wants to start a relationship with Bryce Fitzjohn. However, after realizing that being with him would put Bryce in danger, he leaves her. Boyd writes, "And where would he ever find someone like her again? He wondered, with some bitterness. That was the price he paid for the job he did, he supposed. Falling in love with a beautiful woman wasn't recommended."

Continuity Nod: Bond recalls his train trip from New York to Florida and the mission with Felix Leiter that cost his ally his limbs (*Live and Let Die*). Felix Leiter makes a late appearance in the novel, as does a new character, CIA operative Brig Leiter, Leiter's nephew. M reveals that French intelligence officer, René Mathis (*Casino Royale*) helped arrange Bond's cover story by procuring press credentials from a French newspaper. Bond meets a woman name Bryce Fitzjohn, whose name is a variation on John Bryce, the alias that Bond used in Fleming's second novel. Bond uses a Walther, but he misses his beloved Beretta, the gun he was forced to surrender after the events in *From Russia with Love*.

Bond's History: At Fettes, Bond formed the Judo Society and recruited fellow student "Bloater" McHarg. Despite Bloater's skill and help in securing a win in the South of Scotland Judo League, Bond does not hold Bloater in high regard. In fact, Bond doesn't even know his classmate's first name, which is Turnbull. Bond has such contempt for Bloater, that he even uses him as an unwitting decoy, in his mission to infiltrate Rowanoak Hall. During the war, Bond performed desk work at the Admiralty House in Westminster. He fought in Ardennes and Normandy in 1944 and Berlin in 1945.

The scent of Shalimar perfume always reminds Bond of his mother. The fact that Bond's mother was Swiss, and his father Scottish was not a cause of friction between the couple. Instead, it helped create a bond between them. The smell of a bonfire also causes Bond to remember the war. Bond served in Beirut. His time in Beirut was monotonous, possibly because he saw little action.

Bond's Inner Life: When Bond is about to start a mission, he feels the "heart-thump of excitement" and he's able to compartmentalize his personal life. He's able to "cast aside" his romantic feelings for a woman until the mission is over.

Jensen FF from *Solo.*
Illustration by Pat Carbajal

Bond's Personal Life: Bond is still driving his Bentley. However, the car is showing signs of age; it needs a new gearbox and isn't fit for driving. So he tests a gunmetal silver Jensen FF, manufactured in Britain by Jensen Motors. Bond has a quasi-sensual response to sitting in the new car and smelling its leather. He still lives in the same flat in Chelsea. His long-term lease on the flat will end when he's 89 years old. However, after many years of the status quo, Bond is getting his place renovated. Hidden behind his radiator, Bond keeps a weapon, currency, and a list of contacts that he can call in case of an emergency, as well as keys to a safe house in Maida Vale, a residential neighborhood in West London. He sleeps in his pyjamas, as Fleming described. Bond has read Charles Dickens' work and Graham Green's *The Heart of the Matter*, the 1948 novel set in West Africa.

Bond's Romantic Life: Bond develops feelings for two women, Bryce Fitzjohn and Blessing Ogilvy-Grant (aka Aleesha Belem). Bryce stirs emotions in James that he hasn't felt for a long time. When Blessing apparently betrays him, 007 is emotionally wounded. After all, Blessing was someone he had "made love to in all openness and generosity of spirit." When she dies, Bond cries. Fleming's Bond doesn't cry often;

the first time in his adult life that Bond cried was when he saw that his friend, Quarrel, had survived a shark and barracuda attack (*Live and Let Die*).

Bond's Tastes: Bond gambles at a private casino called Fielding's, where he drinks freely (martinis and champagne) and loses with even more abandon. He also enjoys pudding after a meal. Bond finds that whisky can be a useful sleep aid. For breakfast, Bond eats four scrambled eggs and well-cooked bacon, believing it's essential to start each day with a good breakfast. Bond finds that he should limit his intake of American coffee, as it's a surprisingly potent diuretic. Bond enjoys staying at the Dorchester hotel because he likes its forceful showers. It's not all caviar and champagne for Bond. While in Washington, DC, Bond dines on a simple ham and cheese sandwich, which he pairs with a poorly made martini.

Bond's Work-Life: Sometimes, Bond grows weary of his banter with Moneypenny. His secretary's name is Araminta Beauchamp, who he dubs "Minty." While on a stakeout, Bond considers different disguises, including shaving his head and growing a beard. Instead of a full disguise, he opts to "focus attention on one or two elements of the disguise so that they obscured the other more familiar ones." (Fleming's Bond didn't use disguises.) When trying to remain incognito in a foreign city, it's sometimes useful to have two separate hotel rooms in two different hotels; this way you double your chances of losing a tail. When trying to gain access to a hotel room occupied by a person of interest, it's better to identify yourself as from the "maintenance" department rather than "room service."

Assorted Observations:

- There are some disturbing sequences in the book, such as when Bond comes across a hut full of dead children. In these moments, Boyd uses his novel to highlight some of the atrocities in South Africa.
- In another sequence, Bond commands the resistance. The film Bond often leads groups of soldiers in battle (see *You Only Live Twice*, *Spy Who Loved Me*, and *Moonraker*) but the literary one doesn't often get to demonstrate his military abilities.
- The fictional country at the center of the conflict is Zanzarim. However, some of the advanced press materials identified the country as Voltazia.

"WILLIAM BOYD INTERVIEWS JAMES BOND" (2013)

Author: William Boyd

In Brief: William Boyd, the author of the James Bond continuation novel *Solo*, travels back to 1969 London to meet the subject of his book.

Meaning of Title: The author of a Bond continuation novel interviews the agent.

Chronology: Period. Shortly after *Solo*.

Operation: Not applicable.

Bastard Meter: None.

Eggs: None.

Insight into Bond: "I see myself as a civil servant with a decent salary and a pension."

Summary: Author William Boyd travels back in time from 2013 to 1967. Boyd's assignment is to interview special agent James Bond for a newspaper article. Boyd visits Bond's flat in Chelsea and meets Bond's new housekeeper, Donalda. Then, Bond and Boyd go to a nearby restaurant for the interview. Afterwards, Bond and Boyd go their separate ways.

Bond's History: As a child, Bond was introduced to the saying, "Le lune ne garde aucune rancune," which roughly translates to "The moon bears no grudge." The quotation is credited to T.S. Elliot, who repurposed the original French poet Jules Laforgue's words..

Continuity Nod: Bond references his mission in Africa (*Solo*).

Bond's Personal Life: Bond has no family, no siblings, and he lives a solitary existence. He is 45 years old. He describes himself as a Scottish peasant, as he did in *The Man with the Golden Gun*.

Bond's Inner Life: Bond offers a reason why he's a gourmand. "We have to eat to live. We might as well take some trouble over what goes down your throat."

Bond's Tastes: According to Boyd, Bond lives on a posh street in an area of town that has seen better days. From Bond's point of view, nowadays, it's a little too trendy. He's been living there since before 1953 and has recently redecorated it. May has retired and her niece Donalda is now his housekeeper. Bond's flat is outfitted with a Persian rug, two walls filled with books, and no television. He's a fan of Ralph Waldo Emerson's poems and dog-ears his favorite passages. His bar is stocked with Dimple Haig whisky, Gordon's gin, and Jim Beam. When toasting, Bond says, "Slàinte mhaith," which is the Scottish expression meaning "Good health." He is a constant smoker, probably still consuming 70 cigarettes a day.

Bond's Work Methods: Even when Bond is off-duty and on his home turf, he still routinely checks his surroundings to make sure that he's not being followed. Even though he is at the mandatory retirement age, Bond suspects that he won't be forced out of the service.

"WILLIAM BOYD Q&A WITH JAMES BOND" (2013)

Author: William Boyd

In Brief: James Bond submits to an interview with a Bond continuation novelist.

Meaning of Title: The author of a Bond continuation novel interviews the agent.

Chronology: Period. Follows *Solo* and concurrent with "William Boyd Interviews James Bond" (2013).

Operation: Not applicable.

Bastard Meter: None.

Eggs: None.

Insight into Bond: "For a man in my profession, I shed tears far too easily."

Summary: James Bond submits to a 32-question Q&A with a journalist.

Commentary about both short stories: The two stories use slightly different forms. "William Boyd Interviews James Bond" is more of a traditional short story, with a beginning, middle, and end; "William Boyd Q&A with James Bond" takes the form of a newspaper article. At about 816 words, "William Boyd Q&A with James Bond" might be the shortest Bond story. "Moneypenny's First Date with Bond," is a close second at roughly 1,131 words.

Neither "William Boyd Interviews James Bond" nor "William Boyd Q&A with James Bond" should be considered canon. There's no reason to believe that the events depicted in either short story should be taken too seriously. After all, the stories not only include a Bond continuation author interviewing his subject but also time travel, in which Boyd travels from 2013 to 1969 to meet 007. Nor does Boyd explain why the secret agent would agree to an interview. Instead, the short stories are offered as ephemera, a lark to draw attention to Boyd's new Bond novel. To date, neither story has been reprinted.

Unconnected to the launch of *Solo*, Boyd also authored an article for the *Times Literary Supplement* on July 12, 2020, titled "The

Spies Who Lived Here: How I Found James Bond's Precise Address." [132] The article was intended to drum up some press for Boyd's novel *Trio*, which was published later that year. The pieces, as the subtitle suggests, are about Boyd's effort to locate the exact location of Bond's flat in Wellington Square. According to Boyd, he has successfully identified the address—Number 25, Wellington Square.

Continuity Nod: Bond brings up Tracy, Tiffany Case, and the mercenary Kobus Breed (*Solo*).

Bond's History: Bond's earliest memory is the mountains in Switzerland.

Bond's Personal Life: Bond's greatest love is Tracy.

Bond's Inner Life: Bond says that he was happiest when he was living with Tiffany Case. According to Bond, his biggest fear is dying in a plane crash.

Bond's Tastes: His favorite smell is Guerlain's Shalimar, which is the perfume that his mother's used. He considers himself more of a dog person than a cat person. At his funeral, he would want mourners to hear Judy Garland or Ella Fitzgerald's version of "After You've Gone."

THE RETURN OF THE YOUNG BOND ERA

"Never say no to adventures. Always say yes,
otherwise you'll lead a very dull life."
IAN FLEMING, *Chitty Chitty Bang Bang: The Magical Car*

After three Bond novels by three different authors were published, Ian Fleming Publications turned their attention back to the Young Bond series.

STEVE COLE'S TENURE 2014-2017

Steve Cole wrote four Young Bond books, *Shoot to Kill* (2014), *Heads You Die* (2016), *Strike Lightning* (2016), and *Red Nemesis* (2017)

SHOOT TO KILL (2014)

Author: Steve Cole

In Brief: Young James Bond is on a field trip to Hollywood with his progressive school where he discovers a blackmail scheme involving crimes that have been caught on camera.

Meaning of Title: Beyond the reference to shooting someone to death, the term also refers to a film camera that shoots, or records, a murder.

Chronology: Period. Set in the summer of 1934, after the events of *By Royal Command.*

Operation: Not applicable.

Bastard Meter: None.

Eggs: Bond orders his eggs sunny side up but they are served fried instead.

Insight into Bond: "James found himself wondering why he felt this endless compulsion to take risks. There had to be some other, kinder way to bring colour to life."

Summary: In Los Angeles, a criminal known as "the Kid" pays a small-time crook to film people engaging in illegal or compromising activity so that he can use the footage to blackmail the subjects. One of the reels, containing violent crimes and murders, has gone missing. The Kid is now looking for the film reel.

In England, young James Bond is enrolled at a progressive school named Dartington Hall. James intends to complete his summer coursework at Dartington before starting at Fettes in the fall. His classmates include Boudicca "Boody" Pryce and Hugo Grande. One day, a school official invites Bond to go on a school trip to Hollywood. The students will meet Dr. Tobias Leaver, an experimental educator and philanthropist who might make a sizable donation to the school. Leaver's work is being bankrolled by movie mogul, Anton Kostler. School bully Beatrice Judge accuses James of taking her place on the trip after learning that James is going.

James attends a meeting of the school's movie club. Fellow student Dan Sloman announces that he pilfered this week's film from the projectionist at his father's movie theater. The kids watch the film and discover that it's not a Hollywood movie; instead, it's a snuff film, depicting actual murders and acts of violence.

When James, Hugo, and Dan return the film reel to the theater, they find the dead body of the projectionist. James hears a noise and realizes that the murderers are still in the theater. Holding onto the film reel, James and his friends fend off attacks from the intruders and escape.

That night, James receives a letter signed by his friend Hugo instructing him to go to Queen's Marsh brook. When James arrives at the brook, he realizes that he's been set up. Beatrice's brother ambushes James. James realizes that if he's injured, then Beatrice can take his place on the trip to Hollywood. James seizes one of the men's air guns after they attack him. James is knocked out in the scuffle.

James wakes up in an ambulance, steals the vehicle, and races to the airfield where the Zeppelin airship is preparing to take the students to America. Much to Beatrice's disappointment, James arrives in time.

James boards the Zeppelin and meets Dan's uncle and aspiring screenwriter, Stuart Sloman. En route to Hollywood, James meets Lenny Vasquez, an employee of Kostler studios, and a hat-wearing German movie producer named Rudolf Dürr, who James dubs the Fedora Man. James becomes suspicious of the Fedora Man when the German man says a phrase with an English accent.

The airship arrives in California. Dan tells James that he sent the film reel back to London. James and his friends visit Allworld Studios and meet George Barron, head of security. During the tour of the studio, James steals ball bearings so he can use them as ammunition in his air gun.

James and friends meet Anton Kostler, head of the studio. At first, Kostler is welcoming but then he ends the tour abruptly so that he can talk to Dan's screenwriting uncle about something in private.

Barron, the head of security, arranges for James and his friends to be driven back to the hotel. Along the way, they witness a demonstration escalate into a riot. James spots the Fedora Man and overhears a conversation between two hoods about filming the riot for Martyn, aka the Kid. When the hoods escape in a car, James notes the license plate number.

Bond goes to a drugstore to purchase iodine to clean up his bruises. There, Bond overhears a phone call between reporter Victoria "Tori" Wo and her newspaper editor. After the call, Tori and James discuss the riot and Bond tells her that the thug's license plate ends in "ILL 30." Tori tells Bond that ILL stands for Illinois Tori explains that Hollywood's connection to gangsters goes way back, and the hoods' appearance at the riot proves that Anton Kostler is connected to the Chicago mob.

The next day, James and his friends go to the film school, Kostler Allworld Academy. At the academy, they meet the director of education, Dr. Tobias Leaver. He explains that the students will participate in intelligence tests so that they can study the impact of different educational styles on children and determine which approach yields the greatest achievements.

Anton Kostler's son, Martyn, aka "the Kid," gives James a tour of the school. During the tour, Martyn, a budding filmmaker, fires the actors in his student film. Aspiring actor Dan offers to step in and take their place. In the parking lot, James notices that Martyn's car has Illinois license plates.

James meets up with Tori Wo, the journalist, who tells James she's going to a party at Anton Kostler's mansion that night. James and Hugo return to the hotel and discover that the film reel has been delivered to Stuart Sloman. Dan lied when he said that he sent it back to London. James decides to go to Koster's party and give Tori the film reel.

James sneaks into the party and locates Tori in Kostler's office. Tori and James discover that Kostler's study is filled with folders that contain dirt on Hollywood luminaries, which he uses for blackmail purposes. James learns that Lenny Vasquez isn't merely a Hollywood promoter, he's also a murderer and extortionist. James and Tori return to the party.

Young Bond at Fettes College
in the Young Bond series.
Illustration by Pat Carbajal

At the party, Dan reveals that Martyn is going to help turn him into a movie star. James thinks that Martyn only wants to use Dan to find out where the film reel is hidden. When security closes in on James and Tori, they steal a car and high tail it out of there. Kostler's thugs chase after them, but James and Tori get away. Tori takes the film reel and tells James to go to the police. Later, James picks up the air gun that one of his friends repaired and dubbed Queensmarsh, after the swamp in which he acquired it.

James locates Dr. Leaver who explains that Kostler has been blackmailing him and forcing him to do his bidding. James is captured by Kostler's men and brought to him. Kostler explains that Sloman, an aspiring writer, was mistakenly sent the film reel. Sloman attempted to use the reel to blackmail Kostler into giving him a career in show business.

James and his friends are taken to a giant soundstage made to look like a Western saloon. Kostler announces his plans to kill the students, film their deaths, and sell the bloody footage. Kostler shoots Stuart Sloman, killing him. Suddenly, the Fedora Man arrives and helps James and his friends escape. The Fedora Man identifies himself as a member of the British Secret Intelligence Service named Adam Elmhirst. Elmhirst had been sent to investigate Kostler and keep James safe. Elmhirst kills Vasquez but is shot in the chest by Barron. Because he's wearing a bulletproof vest, Elmhirst survives.

Kostler and Barron take Boody hostage and escape in his aircraft. Bond chases after them and boards the ship before it can get away. Bond and Barron battle while Kostler films them. Dr. Leaver fires a gun into the zeppelin, resulting in an explosion, killing both Leaver and Kostler's son Martyn. Bond grabs his air gun and fires it into Kostler's ear, causing Kostler to let go of him. Bond and Boody escape from the blazing aircraft. Kostler goes down with the ship.

James recovers from his ordeal at the hospital. He bids his new friends farewell as he is leaving Dartington and enrolling in Fettes. Boody gives James a goodbye kiss. Elsewhere, SIS agent Adam Elmhirst considers the Bond family's long history of spying. Not only was Bond's Uncle Max a spy, but so was Andrew, Bond's father.

Commentary: When Aaron Sorkin left *The West Wing,* the political drama that he created, he wanted to leave certain story threads unresolved. Sorkin reasoned that it would be easier for the next writer to resolve those plot points rather than start from scratch. Sorkin used a pool analogy to explain this tactic. He compared it to leaving a few pool balls on the table—each ball represented a different story point that was still in play. Similarly, when Charlie Higson stopped writing the Young Bond series, he left some plot lines hanging.

At the end of Higson's *By Royal Command*, James is now a SIS asset, and he can go on sanctioned missions for the government. In future books, James wouldn't need to stumble upon adventures, as he continuously did in Higson's series. Instead, the SIS could identify threats and employ James. This would been an effective way to remove coincidence from the series. Cole opts not to employ this idea. Instead, once again, James finds a mystery by chance in *Shoot to Kill*.

Cole also had the option of developing Bond's relationship with his father-figure Hannes Oberhauser, having Bond track down Colonel Irena Sedova, the murderer of his girlfriend Roan Power, or even killing off Aunt Charmian (heaven forbid!). However, Steve Cole didn't want to play with Higson's pool balls; he wanted to clear the table and stack his own.

As such, Cole's *Shoot to Kill* is less of a continuation of the previous Young Bond novels written by Higson than it is a largely new series featuring the same main character. Without skimping on the excitement, Higson's books carefully charted young Bond's emotional growth. With *Shoot to Kill,* Cole has taken a different approach and writes an adventure book for young teenagers. As Bond expert Ajay Chowdhury characterizes the differences in the tenures, Higson and Cole are, respectively, "the Sean Connery and Roger Moore of the Young Bond authors."[133]

Fans of Higson's series might not have been quite prepared for this tonal shift. It's only natural that the Young Bond series would undergo a change in style when Higson left and Cole took over. Having one author trying to mimic another one is most assuredly a recipe for disaster that would yield disappointing results. Starting a new school with largely new friends gives Cole a fresh start.

It's also important to remember that there was a six-year gap between Higson's last book, *By Royal Command* (2008), and Cole's first book, *Shoot to Kill* (2014). Even though fans today might read Higson and Cole's books in immediate succession, it would be unreasonable for the publisher to assume that readers would have closely held the events of the previous author's book in their heads. Also, the young teenagers of Higson's years had grown up in the intervening six years. Higson's 13-year-old readers were now 19-year-old college students and presumably a different audience than those targeted in Cole's books. In many ways, it was essential for Cole to wipe the slate clean and start fresh.

As noted, in the previous novel, Higson established that James now has a contact in the intelligence community and that he might be called on again if the country needed him. Cole largely eschews that plot device and has James stumbling onto his next adventure yet again. Still, Cole doesn't completely abandon the notion that the SIS have their eyes on Bond. Cole introduces readers to Adam Elmhirst, an agent who has been assigned to keep a watchful eye on James and make sure that no harm comes to the child. Cole also introduces the idea into the series that not only was Uncle Max a spy, but so was Bond's father. It's almost as if joining the family business was inevitable. Years later, in *Spectre*, Craig's Bond will express a similar sentiment when he laments, "I'm not sure that I ever had a choice" except to become a spy.

Shoot to Kill is aimed squarely at the pre-teen set. Young James steals an ambulance, crashes a party, and sees how movies are made. He is brave beyond his years. When his friends are in the same movie theater as a pair of killers, James tells his friends to stay hidden and that he will try to draw the killers away from them. Even though James is becoming a true man of action, he does have his weaknesses. After a hairy encounter, an over-exerted James vomits.

Fleming established that after Bond attended Eton he was enrolled in Fettes. Cole doesn't dispute those facts, but he does set *Shoot to Kill* during the period *between* both schools. Cole implies that the adult Bond would not remember much about his time at Dartington Hall, except that it was sunny. Dartington Hall is a progressive school with few rules and regulations. James doesn't have to adhere to a school dress code. Because James chafes at structure and discipline, putting him at a school where he can't rebel is an interesting creative choice.

Shoot to Kill takes James to Hollywood, an entirely new locale for the series, where Bond investigates a movie producer who commissions the creation of snuff films—murders that are deliberately recorded.

James experiences shooting a person for the first time. In the book's climax, Kostler is attempting to strangle Bond to death. It seems like Kostler will succeed until James remembers that he's still carrying Queensmarsh, his air gun. It's no toy; the weapon is loaded with ball bearings and James fires it into Kostler's ear. James didn't kill Kostler. Firing ball bearings into another human's flesh, even for survival, isn't an experience that the teenager won't soon forget.

If there is a theme to the book, it might be acceptance. James learns to accept his fate as a man who craves danger and will combat evil in its many forms. He knows that his life will be a difficult one. As a way to brace himself against the hazards that are undoubtedly facing him, he embraces luxury and friendship, when he can find it.

Continuity Nod: Cole alludes to a few moments from Higson's books, including when James is plied with alcohol and his acquisition of a Bentley Mark IV (*Double or Die*). When an adult in a fancy hotel orders a martini for himself and a lime Rickey for the kids, James thinks to himself that he's developing a "taste for cocktails." Cole references Fleming's short story when he notes that something scared "the living daylights" out of Bond's friend Hugo. Later, when James is recovering in a hospital, a friend offers him a martini as a reward for his heroics. James cautions a friend to never say never, possibly a reference to Sean Connery's seventh Bond film, *Never Say Never Again*.

Bond's Personal Life: James avoids friendships because "friendship meant trust, and trust could be betrayed." During the book, James slowly learns to trust and rely on his friends. Bond's trust was previously repeatedly broken in Higson's books and the adult Bond will find betrayal to be a professional hazard. Bond's new friends largely come through for him at this moment. One of James' new friends describes him as "Cool and clear-headed, and a talent for trouble." An apt description.

Bond's Inner Life: Without danger, James feels that he's "grown soft." It's only on missions, that he feels "real purpose." He has started to welcome that risk and intrigue will be a part of his life. James muses, "What's life without a little danger." In the final passages, James accepts that his life be a "long, difficult struggle against forces unknown."

Bond's Tastes: James enjoys watching movies. From Fred Astaire and Ginger Rogers musicals to action, Bond seems to enjoy them all. He also thinks that making a living as a star in action movies might be nice. However, his thoughts about starring in action movies might not reflect Bond's tastes. Since Bond's experiences will be transformed into action films, it's more likely to be some meta-commentary.

Assorted Observations:

- Ian Fleming Publications selected Cole to write the Young Bond novels, in part, because of the popularity of his *Doctor Who* novels. Cole also had tremendous success with *The Astrosaurs*, his children's book series with twenty-two titles about dinosaurs in space.
- Aunt Charmian is referenced but does not appear in the book. While Bond is off galivanting around, she's conducting anthropological work in Mexico.

HEADS YOU DIE (2016)

Author: Steve Cole

In Brief: Young Bond discovers that a villain plans to infect England with a poison that is transferred through paper currency.

Meaning of Title: When the baddie needs to decide whether to kill someone or not, he flips a coin. If it lands on heads, they die.

Chronology: Period. Set in the late summer of 1934, shortly after the events of *Shoot to Kill*.

Operation: Not applicable.

Bastard Meter: None.

Eggs: No edible ones, but the bad guy releases parasites that lay their eggs under a human's skin and can kill them.

Insight into Bond: "James Bond absently tossed the coin again. Even if he could catch every last light in the sky, he thought, it would never be enough."

Summary: In Cuba, arms dealer Sarila Karatan sneaks into a lab belonging to the biologist Audacto Solares, aka Scolopendra. Karatan steals a strongbox from Scolopendra's safe. When she's discovered, Karatan tries to escape in a boat. Scolopendra's men chase after her. Before they catch and kill her, the arms dealer throws the coveted strongbox into the water.

Elsewhere in Cuba, young James Bond chases after a pickpocket who has stolen a wallet belonging to a family friend and chemist, Gerald Hardiman. James retrieves the wallet and returns it to a grateful Hardiman. Over lunch, James learns that Hardiman is having financial trouble. James notices that the driver of a nearby Coupé de Ville is surveilling Hardiman.

After lunch, Bond spots a local girl, Maritsa, being confronted by two thugs, Ramón Mosqueda and El Puño, aka The Fist. James comes to Maritsa's aid. While the goons are distracted, Maritsa runs away.

Later, James is informed by Hardiman that Ramón and El Puo are employed by Scolopendra, a biologist who is also Hardiman's employer. That night, Scolopendra calls Hardiman and asks if he knows anything about the theft of his lab. Hardiman resigns from working on Scolopendra's secret project.

The next day, Bond and his friend Hugo Grande discover that Hardiman's house has been ransacked and that Hardiman is missing. Bond and Hugo go to the police with their theory that Scolopendra kidnapped Hardiman. The police don't believe the boys and counters that Hardiman owed a lot of money to various people and had it coming to him.

When James returns to Hardiman's apartment, he meets Maritsa and Scolopendra's daughter, Jagua. Jagua tells Bond that she and Hardiman planned to escape to Cuba together. Jagua reveals that her father has kidnapped Hardiman and is holding him on his vast estate. Hugo suggests that, to pay off his debts, Hardiman sold Scolopendra's secrets to Sarila Karatan, who stole the strongbox. However, the contents of the box remain a mystery.

Bond and Hugo break into Scolopendra Industries, and discover plans involving a tugboat that will transport timber from Cuba to the North Atlantic. Scolopendra's calendar reveals that he has a meeting at the Gran Casino soon with Chester MacLean, Scolopendra's former enforcer and current harbor master. The boys are discovered by Scolopendra's partner and lover La Velada, aka The Veil, so named because she wears a veil. La Velada shoots at James and Hugo, but they get away.

James and Hugo go to the Gran Casino where Scolopendra keeps a private suite. Bond and Hugo sneak into Scolopendra's suit and hide under his bed. Scolopendra, La Velada, and El Puño enter the suite with MacLean, the harbor master. Scolopendra tells MacLean that a large sum of money was deposited into MacLean's bank account. Scolopendra suspects that MacLean was in on Sarila Karatan's efforts to steal his box. MacLean accuses La Velada of being a part of The People's Commissariat for Internal Affairs, the Soviet Union's intelligence and law enforcement agency. After flipping a coin to decide MacLean's fate, Scolopendra kills the traitor.

James and friends search the harbor for the strongbox and find it. As they do so, they are attacked by another group of divers. James fends them off and makes it to a nearby beach. Once on dry land, he's chased again. Bond speeds off on a motorcycle. When he has a moment's respite, he opens the steel box and discovers yet another box inside. The police spot James and chase after him. James gets away but drops the box in the process. The police find the box and discover that it's full of money. El Puño kidnaps Jagua and takes her back to her father at his estate.

James goes to the harbor and locates Scolopendra's boat, which he intends to stowaway in to get to the location where Hardiman is being held captive. Before he can enact his plan, the police arrive, arrest James, and bring him back to the police station.

At the station, the police handle the money that they retrieved from the strongbox. After touching the money, which has been coated with a lethal substance, the policemen break out in blisters. El Puño sets fire to the station in an attempt to burn the evidence and collect the strongbox. In the chaos, James flees the building and meets up with Hugo. Ramón captures the two boys and takes them by boat to Scolopendra's laboratory.

At Scolopendra's lab, James is reunited with Gerald Hardiman. Bond and Hugo are sealed inside a room that is filled with botflies a species of parasite that is said to be fatal to humans. Scolopendra tells Hardiman that if the biologist doesn't tell Scolopendra what he knows about the arms dealer who stole the box, then the boys will die. Hardiman admits that he revealed Scolopendra's plans to Valentine Barbey, an agent at America's foreign intelligence service called The Corps of Intelligence Police (CIP). Barbey instructed Karatan to steal the strongbox and when that failed, he organized a team of divers to retrieve it from the bottom of the ocean.

In their holding cell, Bond and Hugo discover a journal from Lana Barbey, Valentine Barbey's sister and someone who worked for Scolopendra. Bond and Hugo get sick after they touch the journal. Whatever poisonous substance was on the money was also on the journal.

Scolopendra explains his master plan over dinner. Using his mill, Scolopendra created phony bank notes and coated them with a poisonous substance. He plans to transfer the money to England by tugboat and log raft. When the currency goes into circulation, anyone who handles it will come down with a mysterious illness. If Britain agrees to be governed by the Soviet Union, he will give them the antidote; if not, millions will die. Then, the money will circulate throughout the world and the rest of the world powers will have to pay for the antidote or they will suffer the same fate as England. Now, Scolopendra needs Hardiman to create the antidote.

After dinner, Jagua breaks James and Hugo out of their room. James rushes to the lab to find a possible antidote but it explodes before he can break in. El Puño and La Velada arrive. Le Velada confesses that she is working undercover for the Soviet Union and against Scolopendra. El Puño chases James to the mill where the counterfeit currency is being made. El Puño attempts to murder James but is killed when he stumbles into the shredder machine that was being used to make the counterfeit money.

Bond, Hugo, and Jagua fly in Scolopendra's seaplane to the tugboat and log raft that is transporting the poisoned currency. Bond and Jagua find Scolopendra and tell him that La Velada has betrayed him. Scolopendra doesn't believe them and thinks that it was Ramón who was disloyal. Feeling betrayed, Scolopendra shoots Ramón, and the ensuing gunfire ignites the seaplane's fuel. Scolopendra attempts to kill James, but he's stopped when Jagua stabs him with a knife. The wounded Scolopendra persists, but James fires a cannon into Scolopendra which sends the villain flying into a pile of poisoned money.

The raft that James and Hugo are on starts sinking. Hugo, who is caught in netting, begins to drown. James retrieves the knife from Scolopendra's back and uses it to free Hugo. Bond, Hugo, and Jagua get to safety and La Velada escapes. Hardiman gives Bond and Hugo a compound that will counteract the poison they were exposed to at Scolopendra's estate. In a few weeks, the fully recovered boys will return to school. James gazes up at the night sky and searches for the meaning of life and wonders if he will ever be satisfied.

Commentary: The villain's plot is an essential element of any good Bond book. Steve Cole raises the stakes and surpasses his first Young Bond novel with *Heads You Die*. The antagonist in *Shoot to Kill* is essentially a small-time blackmailer. Yet, in *Heads You Die*, the villain has ambitions to rule the world. Audacto "Scolopendra" Solares, has invented a poison that can be transferred via paper currency. Scolopendra has applied the poison to the currency that he's shipping to England. Anyone who touches the bills will get sick and die unless the British government pays an exorbitant sum for the antidote. Once the tainted currency is distributed throughout the globe, he will be able to hold the entire planet to ransom. Scolopendra's scheme is delightfully devious and is worthy of a Bond movie villain.

James gains more independence throughout *Heads You Die*. When Bond learns that he cannot turn to family, friends, or institutions for assistance, Cole causes Bond to transform. Instead, James discovers that he must rely on himself to defeat the enemy. It's an essential stage in Bond's independence and maturation. He's no longer running scared. When necessary, he is prepared to engage a villain in a direct fight. At the conclusion of the book, the teenage Bond realizes that "We can't always wait around for someone to slay our dragons... Sometimes we have to play St. George ourselves."

It could be argued that James murders a man for the first time. In the previous Young Bond books, villains would be hoisted by their own petard. In other words, James wouldn't directly kill them. Instead, they would often do something that would cause their own deaths. In *Heads You Die*, James registers what could be interpreted as his first kill. In the book's climax, Scolopendra is about to murder James. To defend himself, James fires a cannon at Scolopendra's legs and causes the villain to be sent flying into a pile of poisoned money. Then, the water rises, and Scolopendra sinks into a watery grave. One could argue that it was the water that actually took the villain's life or that he would have died anyway from exposure to the poison via the currency that he was lying on. Scolopendra's daughter stabs him so it's possible that those wounds would have been fatal. Even so, Bond's act of firing a canon at Scolopendra seems like young Bond's most ruthless, albeit necessary, act to date.

Continuity Nod: Cole gives a nod to the bird lover who inspired Fleming to name his spy James Bond when young James finds a copy of *A Field Guide to the Birds of the West Indies*, the 1936 book by ornithologist James Bond. Understandably, Cole deliberately doesn't mention the name of the author of the guidebook.

Bond's History: Cole provides another glimpse into Bond's childhood. The Bond family, or as Cole writes "The Bonds" had a close family friend named Gerald Hardiman, a biologist and chemist. When Aunt Charmian is working in Mexico, she arranges for James to spend time with Hardiman in Cuba. Hardiman was sufficiently close with Andrew Bond that he still keeps a photo of him in his wallet. The photo was taken outside the Bond family home in Switzerland, sometime in the 1920s.

The Bonds would ski with Hardiman in Chamonix-Mont-Blanc. When Andrew discovered that Hardiman had crashed into a tree on one of their ski runs, Andrew burst out laughing. James was only six at the time but he clearly remembers Andrew's reaction and it remains a warm memory of his father. Other continuation authors sometimes paint Andrew as being somewhat stern. So, it's nice that James has memories of his dad's lighter side.

Bond's Personal Life: Even though young Bond is largely indifferent toward girls, they have already begun to find him irresistible. His friend Hugo observes, "All the girls love you, James. You're a modern-day St. George, ready and willing to slay their dragons." In George's estimation, the girls are attracted to Bond because he's their savior.

This equation might have played a role in the adult Bond's decision to become a spy.

Bond's Inner Life: In Higson's books, James avoided danger whenever possible. In Cole's novels, James is starting to welcome it. Cole writes that James "knew that he would never get used to the thrill of danger. That was its allure. So much of life was routine and boring, but danger had no rules. It happened anywhere, could take so many forms." From now on, Bond would crave excitement and recognize it as a stimulant.

James is hardening and edging towards his destiny of being a blunt instrument. However, he still has his limits. James thinks to himself that he could never shoot a man in cold blood. Killing a man at point-blank range is understandably still a step too far for the teenager.

Young James is not what one might call a "happy" kid. He's already seeing that his life will have meaning but that it was also not completely fulfilling. As he marvels at the stars in the sky, he has an awareness that a part of him will always be unsatisfied. Cole explains "Even if he could catch every last light in the sky, he thought, it would never be enough."

Bond's Tastes: Young James enjoys playing poker with his friends. When he goes to a casino, he feels the thrill of being there. He responds to the glamour and luxury of the casino. He also appreciates the *sounds* that it produces like the "seductive patter of the croupiers" and the "rattle" of the roulette wheels.

Assorted Observations:

- In his first Young Bond novel, Cole introduced the idea that Andrew Bond was a spy. He doesn't develop the idea further in *Heads You Die*. Instead, he saves that for a later book.
- Young James already enjoys swimming but in *Heads You Die*, he experiences diving for the first time.
- The chase is on. Young Bond is chased by a car, a boat, police, and even underwater divers.
- A passage from Fleming's short tale "The Hildebrand Rarity," involving Bond underwater, served as the inspiration for a similar scenario in Cole's novel *Heads You Die*, according to the author's note in the Waterstone's hardback edition of the book.[134]

STRIKE LIGHTNING (2016)

Author: Steve Cole

In Brief: Young Bond discovers a villain's scheme to make armored exoskeleton suits with cutting-edge technology to help Germany win the inevitable war against the United Kingdom.

Meaning of Title: A high-voltage electrical test performed on a weapons system to determine its susceptibility to such an attack. It's also a reference to a lightning strike that allegedly killed young Bond's school friend.

Chronology: Period. After the event of *Heads You Die.* The action takes place from November 29 to December 23, 1934.

Operation: Not applicable.

Bastard Meter: Not registered.

Eggs: Scrambled and served on hot buttered toast.

Insight into Bond: "Giving in was never an option."

Summary: In Scotland, German weapons manufacturer Hepworth Blade oversees a test of an armored suit dubbed the Steel Shadow. A local boy enters the testing site and is accidentally killed. Blade gives the order to hide the boy's body.

Nearby in Edinburgh, Scotland, young James Bond attends school at Fettes College. James and his friend Perry Mandeville and Marcus Stephenson practice their judo skills. Later, Marcus goes missing. When James can't locate his friend, he checks Dr. Randolph Whittaker's lab, where Marcus has been assisting their science teacher on a secret demonstration.

As James approaches Whittaker's lab, he hears the grinding of a machine and senses that the air is charged with electricity. Through the lab door, James can make out the voices of Marcus, Whittaker, and an unknown girl. Marcus screams. James tries to gain access to the lab, but Whittaker orders James to leave. Later, James finds the severely injured Marcus lying on the ground; his skin is burnt. Marcus coughs out the words "Ruskie" and "twenty." Before he can learn more, James is sprayed with a substance that knocks him out.

Three days later, James wakes up in the school's hospital. Herta Axmann, a scientist who works with Dr. Whittaker, tells James that Marcus died from a lightning strike. James explains to his Aunt Charmian that Marcus was injured by electric shocks in Whittaker's lab, not lightning. James believes that the unconscious Marcus was moved from the lab and dumped on school grounds. Charmian doesn't buy Bond's theory. She explains that because James was discovered passed out and next to Marcus, most people at the school believe that Marcus was killed while pulling off a prank that he and James engineered. Instead of viewing Bond as a victim of wrongdoing, the school views him as the offender.

The next day, James meets Hepworth Blade, a weapons manufacturer and head of Blade-Rise Industries, a research and development center in the Netherlands. Blade's chauffeur is a man named Carrel. Blade reveals that he is suffering from Stone Man Syndrome, a rare disease that is effectively turning his soft tissues into stone. Bond learns that his friend Marcus was going to intern for Blade.

The following day, Whittaker's lab is cleared out. Later, while going for a run, James is attacked by four students who blame him for Marcus' death. A groundskeeper gives James first aid and reveals that Whittaker has a workshop located behind the school. That night, James goes to the workshop, but he can't get in. Instead, he finds a note that says "Predictable, Bond." James realizes that someone knows he is on their trail. Later, James finds out that the groundkeeper had to leave school for a sudden death in the family. James wonders if the groundskeeper was silenced.

James gains entry to Whittaker's workshop and finds a coded note. After decoding the note, James discovers that a demonstration will take place in Ruskie, a hamlet in Scotland or possibly Thornhill, a village in Scotland. Later, James learns that Dr. Whittaker and Herta have left Fettes.

During the December break, James and Perry search for Whittaker. Eventually, the boys locate him in Thornhill Abbey, a heavily protected estate. James and Perry jump on top of a lorry so that they can enter the grounds. Once inside, they see that Herta is trapped in the Steel Shadow, an iron suit that resembles high-tech medieval knight armor. They watch a demonstration that shows the suit's full firing power. Whitaker tells the onlookers that a battalion of soldiers wearing the outfit could win the war for England. The boys wonder if Whittaker is working on behalf of England or if there's something more sinister going on. James and Perry try to leave the area, but they are locked in a lorry and can't get out. The lorry boards a cargo ship, which sets sail.

On the ship, James and Perry find Whittaker and Herta and discover that a circuit board unit controls the Steel Shadow. James steals the circuit board. James overhears Whittaker talking about a party at the Hotel des Indes, in the Hague. Perry has relatives in Scheveningen, a nearby district.

The ship reaches port and Bond and Perry disembark and attempt to follow a lorry to Blade's headquarters, but Whitaker spots them. Bond and Perry get away and attempt to make it to Perry's relative's house. They run into Kitty Drift, Perry's old acquaintance. Kitty agrees to travel with the boys to Scheveningen since she is familiar with all the train routes. Along the way, Kitty explains that Konstantin Grünner, the German Ambassador to the Netherlands, is hosting their annual Christmas party at the Hotel des Indes. The boys realize that Whittaker will be at Grünner's party.

The trio makes it to Perry's relative's house in Scheveningen. At the house, James discovers that Perry's family has also been invited to Grünner's party. James decides to use the invitation to get into the event and spy on Whittaker and Herta and find out if they are in league with Grünner.

James sneaks into the party and watches Grünner give a speech about Holland's geographical importance and how it's strategically located between Germany, France, and Britain. If the Nazis want to expand their power, taking control of Holland could give them the leverage they need. James wonders if Blade intends to sell his weapon to the Nazis.

James eavesdrops on the meeting between Grünner, Whittaker, and Herta. He learns that the Steel Shadow will fail if high levels of electricity are used to combat it and that Dr. Whittaker's files on the creation of the weapon are in a safe at Blade's home in Wassenaar, Netherlands. James concludes that Blade is betraying Britain by working with Nazi Germany. Then, Grünner shoots and kills Whittaker who he suspects is double-crossing him.

James goes to Blade's house and attempts to steal Dr. Whittaker's files on the suit. After evading a trio of dogs, James sneaks into Blade's residence and searches for the safe. Inside, he overhears a fight between Carrel, Blade's chauffeur, and Herta. Herta takes out her gun and aims it at Carrel, but James stops her before she can pull the trigger. James knocks Herta out and then locates the Steel Shadow files in Blade's office. Before he can flee the house, James is seen by Blade. The revived Herta fires at James but misses as he takes off. James jumps into Blade's car and speeds away.

James returns to Perry's grandparents' house and finds Perry and Kitty, as well as Blade's bodyguard Van Diemen. Van Diemen demands that James return the files that he took from Blade's home. Perry knocks the bodyguard out by slamming a vase on his head. James, Perry, and Kitty leave the house and drive towards Rotterdam. On the drive, Kitty tells the boys about a Ghost Train, an unscheduled train that travels between Rotterdam and The Hague. James decides that they should follow the train to its final stop. Once they discover where it's going, they can alert the authorities.

James, Perry, and Kitty locate and board the Ghost Train. After a few hours, the train arrives at a factory, which is connected to a railway yard. They believe that the train will be loaded with arms that will then be sent to Germany to aid them in their war effort. The trio decides to sabotage the train. However, they are caught and put on a train heading near Düsseldorf. Herta reveals that Blade was going to supply the Germans with four Steel Shadow units. Herta sprays Bond with a nerve agent.

When James awakens, he finds that he's strapped inside one of the Steel Shadow units, which is being controlled by voice command by Grünner. Blade tells James that Germany is working on their own exoskeleton suits called the Blood Flag, which are more powerful than the Steel Shadows. Grünner announces a demonstration will take place the following day; in it, Steel Shadows and the Blood Flags will face off. The Steel Shadows will be piloted by James, Van Diemen, and Carrel. Kitty and Herta will be inside the Blood Flags.

The next day, James practices piloting his Steel Shadow exoskeleton suit. During the practice, Blade reveals that he's been working for the English government against Germany. Blade's ultimate goal is to locate the Nazi's weapon's research center and destroy it, setting Germany's war effort back years. Blade has concealed a radio transmitter in the Steel Shadows that will allow him to find Germany's research center. When the unit is brought to Germany, England will be able to locate and destroy the top-secret facilities. James is still not sure that he can trust Blade.

The demonstration begins and all five exoskeleton suits are put to the test. Blade's bodyguards are defeated and James and Herta square off for a final battle. James discovers that Blade has turned his suit into an electromagnet, which keeps Herta pinned down. Perry crashes his car through the demonstration and James and Kitty get in his car to escape to safety. Grünner chases after them in a Steel Shadow unit. James attempts to ram his car into Grünner but Grünner is able to use the suit's powerful arms to stop Bond's vehicle from making impact. Grünner is about to kill James, but Blade intervenes and explodes a mortar, killing Grünner, and sacrificing his own life in the process. As the factory burns down, James, Perry, and Kitty flee. Once safe, Kitty kisses James. Bond makes plans to return to Aunt Charmian in time for Christmas.

Commentary: Why does a loner with a mistrust of authority like James Bond serve the British government? James' reputation as a lone wolf has been stressed extensively throughout each previous Young Bond book, including those by Higson. Even team sports like rugby don't appeal to James. He prefers to act alone. Why would he grow up to work for the government and become a tool of the state, questions Steve Cole in *Strike Lightning*? The answer comes from an unlikely source, the book's apparent villain, Hepworth Blade.

Blade, a weapon manufacturer, is developing a super-powered exoskeleton suit that the English government can use to defeat Germany in the war. Blade makes the convincing argument that "weapons save lives." Blade believes that by creating and selling munitions he is keeping the world safe. Since Bond's father Andrew also worked in the munitions industry, he finds it difficult to reject the theory.

James begins to question if he is becoming a kind of weapon. He asks himself, "Is that what I'm becoming?" Readers know the answer. When he reaches adulthood, James will be a weapon or, as Fleming put it, "a blunt instrument." James will use countless weapons to kill others, in the name of saving lives. And the hand that will wield the weapon is England.

James needs to make peace with the decision, even if readers already know his fate. To best serve the British government, Bond must accept that he will need to be and/or use weapons. Even though Bond is willing to sacrifice his life for his country, he is still figuring out what he's prepared to do on its behalf. James doesn't know if he can kill someone in cold blood. He doesn't completely reject the idea but he's not yet sure if he's capable of it. For Cole's young Bond, it's an uncomfortable truth. In the end, Bond concedes that while spying is a "filthy occupation," it is still a necessary one and that dying for one's nation is "sweet and honorable" if the cause is just. So it's only fitting that his air pistol is named Queensmarsh as its name suggests "nobility and dirt."

Strike Lightning appears to perpetuate the trope of villains who have physical flaws. Blade suffers from a disorder called Blade Stone Man Syndrome, which causes the soft tissue in his body to harden. It's as if his organs are being turned into stone. Blade is so fragile that his body can't be touched. He can't even shake hands. His team covers the sharp edges of the furniture's surfaces with soft materials before he enters a room to protect him. His home is similarly fortified; his stairs, for instance, are covered in foam rubber. Cole subverts the trope. In the end, it's revealed that Blade isn't the bad guy; instead, he's working on behalf of the British government to undermine Germany's war efforts.

James does not have a familiar relationship with him, but Blade offers Bond a lot of fatherly advice. In various instances, Blade tells James "Use your time well, every last second. Whatever cards you're dealt, play them as best you can." Elsewhere, Blade tells James, "However hopeless things seem, you must *use* your time." It's unquestionably good advice, even if it's coming from someone who is presented as the book's villain.

Repeatedly throughout the book, Bond convinces himself to try to "wring full value" out of each moment because "all things pass," including the time he has with loved ones. Memories of his parents are largely "buried at the back of his mind" and they remain there until he chooses "to retrieve them." The pain of their memory is still raw, so he doesn't try to think of them too often. This notion of using time well echoes the thought that Bond's Uncle Max gave to him before he died. So Blade's advice resonates with James more than one might expect.

James is further isolated from his dwindling family in *Strike Lightning*, making him more likely to join the service, where he can become a part of a de facto family. James could rely on Aunt Charmian in the previous Young Bond. She was such a warm and appealing figure in Higson's books that James never felt truly alone. James was devastated by his parent's death, but Charmian's love and support blunted the loss. Cole uses Charmian differently.

James still has Charmian's backing, but she is no longer his most ardent advocate. School officials think James played a role in his friend's passing. They believe that Marcus and James were pulling off a prank when they were struck by lightning, leaving Marcus dead but James injured. In actuality, Marcus was killed by the bad guy. Charmian, though, finds it difficult to accept Bond's account. In the end, Charmian supports him, but their close relationship suffers. Worse yet, Charmian continues to enroll James in boarding schools. Eton came first, followed by Dartington Hall, and now Fettes. James feels as though he has no solid foundation because of these shifting schools. For him, home is the feeling that he gets when he faces danger.

Continuity Nod: When Bond thinks that he and Kitty are about to be killed he tells her, "We have all the time in the world." (*On Her Majesty's Secret Service*). Bond's adventures at Eton are mentioned (Higson's series), as are his adventures in Los Angles (*Shoot to Kill*) and Cuba (*Heads You Die*). Bond and his friend Perry are trying to get a judo club off the ground. Cole picked up this piece of Bond's biography from the obituary that appears in *You Only Live Twice.* The line from the Jack London poem that Mary Goodnight quoted at the conclusion of *You Only Live Twice* is referred to in Blade's admonition to Bond to make good use of his time—"I shall not waste my days in trying to prolong them. I shall use my time." The line is reprised at the end of *No Time to Die*.

Bond's Personal Life: Even though he's only fourteen years old. James can pass for being eighteen.

Bond's Inner Life: Young James tries not to be overly self-reflective. His belief that "self-analysis is a waste of time" will carry on into adulthood. Still, he is self-aware. For instance, he knows that once he starts something he will see it through to the end, damn the consequences or personal costs.

Bond's Tastes: Bond has already started smoking cigarettes. Of course, it's against school rules so he has to do it surreptitiously. As he did at Eton, James studies ancient Greek and Roman literature but it's science that he's most interested in. He's on the rugby team.

Bond's Work Methods: Bond starts to learn about his body's abilities and limits. He begins to understand when to push his endurance to the limit and when to hold back a little.

Octopussy's Tarzan Yell: Cole finds an in-universe justification for James Bond's Tarzan yell in *Octopussy.* In the Eon film, Moore's Bond swings across the jungle while bellowing Tarzan's signature call. Some Bond fans enjoyed the reference and others thought it was an easy joke that diminished the tension of the film. In *Strike Lightning*, James turns out to be a Tarzan fan. He and his pal Perry head to the cinemas to watch *Tarzan and His Mate* (1934), the second of twelve films that Johnny Weissmuller starred in. In Cole's first Young Bond novel, *Shoot to Kill*, James attended a lavish Hollywood party and caught a glimpse of the Olympic swimmer-turned-actor. So when Moore's Bond is performing the Tarzan call, he's not only channeling the King of the Apes, but he's also reliving a part of his youth.

Assorted Observations:

- In *Shoot to Kill*, Cole introduced the idea that Andrew Bond might be a spy. He didn't pursue that story plot in the last book, *Heads You Die*, and he doesn't follow it up in *Strike Lightning*. However, it will play out in his fourth and final book *Red Nemesis*.
- Bond and his friend Perry are a two-man crime spree; the duo steals three different cars throughout the book.

RED NEMESIS (2017)

Author: Steve Cole

In Brief: Young Bond must stop a villain who intends to assassinate King George and overthrow the British government. Simultaneously, an unearthed letter from Bond's deceased father forces him to contemplate the terrifying possibility that his father was a Soviet spy and that his parent's fatal climbing accident was a deliberate act of murder.

Meaning of Title: The bad guys are members of the Soviet Union, aka "Reds."

Chronology: Period. Set shortly after the events of *Strike Lightning*. End of summer, 1935.

Operation: Not applicable.

Bastard Meter: "Unhelpful bastard."

Eggs: Scrambled with Bologna sausage and dill.

Insight into Bond: "I learned to be tough when my parents died."

Summary: In the prologue, set in 1931, teenage ballerina Anya Kalashnikova drives in a car with her architect father, Ivan. After intentionally crashing their vehicle, Ivan checks and purposefully slams the car door on Anya's legs.

Four years later. In the summer of 1935, James Bond and his friends go on a treasure hunt. Later, Bond's Aunt Charmian gives James a recently discovered backpack that belonged to his late father Andrew, who died in a climbing accident with Bond's mother, Monique. James finds a coded note from Andrew to Bond's late Uncle Max (*SilverFin*) while inspecting the backpack.

James seeks advice from SIS operative, Adam Elmhirst (*Shoot to Kill*) but he is unable to contact so he leaves a message. James decodes a portion of the message that mentions the Mechta Academy for the Performing Arts. At the Public Record Office, he learns that the Academy's architectural plans were created by Ivan Kalashnikov, the man from the prologue. James decides to visit the academy and learn more.

At the Mechta Academy, James meets Madame Gaiana Radek, the assistant principal and dance instructor. Madame Radek is rehearsing a show that is scheduled to perform at the Royal Opera House. Demir, a security guard for the Academy, approaches James. James knocks Demir out cold and then snoops around the school. James overhears a boy in the basement discussing a special cargo. When the boy leaves, James finds a crate filled with explosives. The boy returns and knocks James out.

James wakes up in a police station. Madame Radek arrives and accuses James of being a spy. James learns that King George will attend Radek's upcoming performance at the Royal Opera House. Later, Elmhirst arrives at the jail. Elmhirst is attacked by a police sergeant. James and Elmhirst cold cock the officer and flee. Together, they agree to decipher the rest of the coded message. Elmhirst tells James that the SIS believes that Bond's father, Andrew, was working in Moscow as a mole for the Soviet Union. They believe that when Andrew's cover was blown, rather than face capture, Andrew and his wife, Monique, killed themselves.

James and Elmhirst fly to Moscow to clear Andrew's name. Elmhirst and James figure out that *The Trumpeter of Krakow*, a book on Bond's childhood bookcase, can be used to break the code. They purchase a copy of the book and head to Moscow's center, where they check into a hotel. At the hotel, Elmhirst receives a message from the SIS, but they are attacked by Andrei Karachan from Mechta Academy. Karachan grabs the backpack and tries to steal it. While James retrieves the backpack, Karachan escapes. Elmhirst and James wonder how Karachan knew that Andrew's coded message was hidden inside the backpack.

James and Elmhirst decipher more of the code and determine that La Velada (*Heads You Die*) is tied to the mystery. They also learn that Andrew Bond found evidence that the Soviets were mounting an attack on England, a move that would facilitate Hitler's expansion of his Nazi empire. Elmhirst hypothesizes that Andrew had to hide the information in Moscow since he was already overseas and could not transport it to England without getting captured by the Soviets.

At the hotel, James and Elmhirst are attacked by two men. James escapes but he's not sure if Elmhirst has survived the assault. Then, Karachan's men snatch James. James fights his way out, steals a bicycle, and then boards a tram. When James opens the bag, he finds a miniature version of St. Basil Cathedral. He inspects the replica and finds a concealed address for a residence in Moscow.

James goes to the address and encounters an old woman and a girl with a cane. The girl tells him to leave the house. James walks away without realizing a shadowy presence is watching him.

James returns and enters the house when he sees that the girl with a cane leave. Once inside, he discovers a blind old man who mistakes James for his father, Andrew. James learns that the man is Ivan Kalashnikov, the architect who designed the Mechta Academy. Ivan reveals that there is a covert undertaking tied to four buildings. Ivan confesses that he crippled his daughter Anya, who was a rising star in ballet, so that they could return home to Moscow.

When Anya returns, James demands that she helps him figure out more about the secret project that her father is involved with. Suddenly, James believes he hears Elmhirst's voice, so he rushes to him. However, instead of seeing Elmhirst, James discovers Ivan's dead body. James also sees the boy who attacked him at the Mechta Academy. The boy identifies himself as Mimic, as he can imitate any voice. When James fights Mimic, an oil lamp is kicked over in the melee and sets fire to the house. James and Anya flee. Anya theorizes that her father knew that Andrew was connected to the SIS so he likely tried to supply him with critical information that would help the British.

James and Anya are accosted by a Russian. Elmhirst saves James just in time. James tells Elmhirst about the model of St. Basil's Cathedral, which is located in Red Square. After following the clue to go to the Cathedral, Andrew's message directs them to a specific burial plot at a graveyard. They dig up the grave and find a satchel containing Andrew Bond's Beretta 418. They also find Anya's father's designs for the Mechta Academy. They realize that the four buildings that Anya's father mentioned are linked to the River Thames by subterranean passages. James wonders if Anya's father was tasked with causing a flood with the water from the Thames. Karachan and Mimic arrive at the graveyard. Mimic imitates Elmhirst threatening Andrew Bond. James realizes that Elmhirst is a double agent for the Soviet Union and that he murdered his father. Before James can attack Elmhirst, he's stuck with a needle and loses consciousness.

James comes to and learns that he's in a submarine in the North Sea. Elmhirst admits that Andrew Bond discovered the papers that would prevent the Soviet Union from conducting its secret scheme. James is brought to the top of the submarine, where he is keelhauled and asked to reveal the meaning of Andrew's messages. When James refuses, he's brought to Anya's cell. Elmhirst hits Anya on her injured legs with a metal tray and demands that James gives him the information he needs. James stops the assault on Anya by offering false information.

The submarine reaches England and enters the River Thames. Elmhirst explains that the sub can secretly dock in underground locations where they won't be detected. James and Anya realize that if they can find a way to flood the tunnels, they will thwart Elmhirst's plans and stop the Soviets.

The submarine docks at Mechta Academy where they meet Gaiana Radek, the assistant principal, who confesses that she's actually La Velada. Karachan explains that they are planning an attack on London. The Soviets will set off an explosion that will result in a tsunami, flooding England with water from the Thames. Then, the Soviets will install a new government. At first, the Soviets will rule by force but then they will use propaganda to convince the citizens of England that the Communists ways are the best.

Anya uses Bond's concealed Berretta while they are imprisoned in a room to shoot his handcuffs off. Karachan hears the noise and comes to investigate. James and Karachan fight, and during the struggle, Karachan is killed when a piece of window glass shatters and enmeshes itself in his neck.

James and Anya escape and head to the Opera House, where the Russian plan is taking place. Along the way, they discover crates filled with explosives. They realize that the secret project was focused on four buildings and that the tower isn't a building tower, it's a transmitter tower, which will be used to disseminate Soviet propaganda, with Mimic impersonating the voice of King George. They also spot a fuse connected to the crates filled with explosives.

James and Anya sneak into the Royal Opera House. At the Opera House, James sees King George V and the Prime Minister entering their private box, which is being guarded by Elmhirst. James overpowers a doorman, steals his uniform, and picks up a waiter's tray. James bluffs his way up the stairs and gets closer to the King by pretending to be a waiter. James tries to save the King, but Elmhirst is waiting for him. So James flees.

Enacting their plan to protect the King, Anya goes on stage and starts dancing, as if she were a member of the company. Then she takes out a gun, fires it into the air, and pretends to threaten the King. The King is quickly taken out of the Opera House and brought to safety.

James returns to the tunnels to prevent the fuse from being lit. There, James spots La Velada and Mimic. Before he can do anything to stop them, Demir gets the drop on James. La Velada pulls down her veil to reveal her face. The site of La Velada is enough to make Demir recoil. This momentary distraction gives James enough time to knock Demir out. La Velada pulls a gun on James. James decides to blow La

Velada and himself up to prevent her from causing the tsunami. The explosion kills La Velada. James puts out the fuse by throwing La Velada's corpse on it.

James and Anya use the explosives to safely flood the tunnels, preventing the plan from being conducted at a later date. James vows to kill Elmhirst, the man who made him an orphan. Then, James and Mimic fight. James breaks Mimic's jaw and ruptures his eardrums so that the boy can't imitate others. James finds Elmhirst at the radio tower. Elmhirst is about to escape by gliding down a cable but before Elmhirst can get away, James shoots him. Elmhirst falls to the ground, impaled on a radio mast.

Later, James bids Anya farewell. Then, as a means of closure, James buries his father's backpack at the Aiguilles Rouges but keeps the gun.

Commentary: Does young Bond have what it takes to kill a man in cold blood? It's the central issue of Steve Cole's tetralogy. He raises the question in *Shoot to Kill,* explores it in *Strike Lightning and Heads You Die,* and answers it in *Red Nemesis*. The Russian playwright, Anton Chekhov, popularized the theory that if a gun is introduced to the story in the first act, it must be fired before the play is over. In some ways, Cole's question about James is Chekhov's gun.

In Cole's first three books, Bond (and Cole) wonder if young Bond could shoot an unarmed man. In Cole's (and Higson's) previous adventures, young Bond didn't directly kill anyone. Instead, their deaths were the result of their own misdeeds and mistakes or James was simply acting in self-defense. Nevertheless, in *Red Nemesis*, James makes the conscious decision to kill a man in cold blood.

In the book's climax, James kills Adam Elmhirst, Bond's mentor, and a man who Bond's father trusted. However, Elmhirst double-crossed and killed Bond's parents. So rather than let Elmhirst escape and possibly kill others, James shoots the defenseless man. The decision to kill the man is deliberate, and it marks the end of Bond's character arc in Cole's series.

Red Nemesis also depicts the transformation of "James" into "Bond." Elmhirst beams, "Welcome to the job, Bond," as he welcomes the young guy to the world of espionage. It's a signal that Bond is pursuing his destiny to become a spy and a Double O agent. It's not Bond's last step in his evolution but it's a critical one. It's a sign that Bond is pursuing his destiny to work for the Double O organization as a spy.

Red Nemesis is also about mourning and putting the past in its proper context. In the previous seven Young Bond books (both Cole's and Higson's), the death of Bond's parents is an open wound that hasn't healed. Their death is Bond's central trauma. Through the events of the book, James learns to literally bury the past. In *Red Nemesis*, James is given a backpack that his father intended to deliver to him. The backpack contains a coded letter that James needed to solve to not only stop Elmhirst's plot but also to discover the mystery of who killed his father and why. Once Elmhirst is defeated and the world is safe again, Bond buries the backpack, symbolically laying his parents to rest. James will always mourn their loss, but he has now found a way to live with their absence.

Most of the continuation novels that address Bond's past do so fleetingly. Yet, Bond's personal history is a subject of *Red Nemesis*. In Cole's book, James must decode a message that his father Andrew sent his Uncle Max. Bond's childhood and his relationship with Andrew are brought to the fore throughout the book. For instance, his childhood bookcase was filled with books and records. Andrew would travel a lot for his work as a representative for Vickers Armaments. When he came home, Andrew would generally return from his travels with a souvenir, such as a book, a toy soldier, or some chocolate. For instance, as a child, James would play a treasure hunt game called Which Way Now? Usually, James and Andrew were successful in locating the hidden object, but one time his toy cavalry captain was never recovered.

The biggest blast from Bond's past comes through the villain Mimic, who can replicate any voice that he hears. Mimic was there when Adam Elmhirst murdered his parents. Mimic taunts James by repeating Andrew and Monique's final words. There are two unintended consequences for this. One, James finds out exactly how his parents met their end. He no longer needs to live his life with any confusion. Two, in a weird way, he gets to spend time with his parents one last time and hear his father bid him farewell. Using Andrew's voice, mimic says, "Goodbye, James." Of course, it's a sick game that Mimic is playing. Nonetheless, it does provide a kind of closure for James.

At first, Bond acknowledges that he never really understood his father, "I suppose I never got to listen to my father speak his innermost thoughts to his pillow at night." Andrew wasn't a particularly warm or nurturing father. When he was but a small boy and skinned his knee, his father offered scant comfort, "Don't make such a meal of things, James... Don't show it hurts." By the story's conclusion, Bond is consciously aware of how this adventure is bringing him closer to his father. James realizes that he "felt closer to his father than perhaps he ever had" and, elsewhere, standing in a spot his father once occupied, "James felt closer to him than ever."

James discovers a leather satchel in Moscow that his father had hidden. In it, is a Beretta 418 and a chamois-leather holster. In Fleming's novel *From Russia with Love* and *Dr. No*, The adult Bond will carry a .25 Beretta for fifteen years and used one in Fleming's novel *From Russia with Love* and *Dr. No*. The adult Bond is nearly killed by Rosa Klebb when the silencer catches on Bond's pants. The striking implication is that Bond almost dies by utilizing a weapon made by his father's chosen gun manufacturer.

Continuity Nod: In *Red Nemesis*, the villain La Velada from *Heads You Die* and the SIS agent Adam Elmhirst from *Shoot to Kill* both make a comeback. James finds a crate of explosives that was produced by Blade Industries, the fictional weapons manufacturer from *Strike Lightning*. Cole appears to be referring to the Eon films when Anya exclaims, "Oh, James."

Bond's History: Cole provides a date for Andrew and Monique's death—1932.

Bond's Personal Life: James has never played an instrument.

Bond's Inner Life: While comforting Anya, James reveals his philosophy of life, "I can see why you think nothing good lasts… But perhaps nothing bad will last either. What we have—all that we ever have—is right now." Still, James also believes that while might be through with the past that the past isn't through with us. He laments that "the past never stops burning."

Bond's Work Methods: Adam Elmhirst, the SIS agent who becomes a mentor to James, advises him to stop and devise a plan before acting. Elmhirst cautions James not to use multiple codes in one message.

THE UNEXPECTED TRILOGY

One day, and he accepted the fact he would be
brought to his knees by love or by luck."
IAN FLEMING, *Casino Royale*

ANTHONY HOROWITZ'S TENURE 2015–2022

Anthony Horowitz wrote the Bond continuation novels *Trigger Mortis* (2015), *Forever and a Day* (2018), and *With a Mind to Kill* (2022). Horowitz is also the author of the successful young adult spy series Alex Rider, whose last name is a variation on Honey Ryder, the Bond Woman from *Dr. No.* He wrote *The House of Silk: A Sherlock Holmes Novel* (2011) and *Moriarty* (2014), two mysteries inspired by the work of Arthur Conan Doyle.

TRIGGER MORTIS (2015)

Author: Anthony Horowitz

In Brief: Bond enter a motorsport race to protect an English racecar driver from being killed by the KGB. The case leads him to uncover a Russian plot to end America's space program.

Meaning of Title: A panic button known as Trigger Mortis can be used to destroy an errant rocket before it causes any damage. The term "trigger mortis" comes to mind when Bond is standing over the body of a dead attacker with his finger wrapped around the trigger of a pistol.

Chronology: Period. Set about two weeks after *Goldfinger*. In 1957.

Operation: Bernhard.

Bastard Meter: Standard issue "bastard," as described by both Pussy Galore and Jeopardy Lane.

Eggs: A single egg boiled and, for another meal, scrambled.

Insight into Bond: "Bond knew that there would come a time, a moment in a mission, when his luck would run out. It was a mathematical certainty."

Summary: In Virginia, USA, German rocket scientists Thomas Keller meets a man at a diner. The man gives Keller a suitcase full of $250 thousand in cash, payment for Keller's participation in sabotaging a rocket engine. Keller returns home to his wife, Gloria. Gloria stabs him to death, grabs the cash, sets fire to their home, and flees.

Pussy Galore has been staying in James Bond's flat in England for the past two weeks. They've been seeing each other since they thwarted Auric Goldfinger's efforts to steal the gold from Fort Knox (*Goldfinger*, of course). Now, their relationship is strained.

M informs Bond that SMERSH intends to win the German Grand Prix in the town of Nürburg, by using their driver Ivan Dimitrov to force English driver Lancy Smith off the track. M instructs Bond to pose as a driver, compete in the race, and stop Dimitrov.

When Bond returns home, Galore tells him that two men were following her. Then, an experienced female racer named Logan Fairfax coaches Bond in the sport. Later, Bond and Logan go to dinner and then retire to Logan's hotel for a little more privacy. At the hotel, Bond sees that Galore is being held captive in a car. The car speeds away and Bond and Logan chase after it. They follow the car to a stone circle in a forest. To his horror, Bond discovers that the thugs have chained Galore to a stone, and they are painting her body in gold. Bond realizes that Goldfinger's men are getting their revenge for Galore's betrayal of their boss. Bond kills the men and frees her. Logan and Bond bring Galore to the hospital. Later, Galore announces that she has struck up a romance with Logan and she's leaving Bond.

Bond goes to Nürburg, Germany for the race. There, he meets Lancy Smith, the English driver that Bond is sent to protect. At a local pub, Bond spots Russian driver Dimitrov talking to SMERSH operative Vladimir Gaspanov and Sin "Jason" Jai-Seong, a wealthy owner of a construction company and race fan. Bond questions why Sin, a seemingly legitimate businessman, would speak with two SMERSH agents.

On the day of the race, Bond instructs his pit crew to empty most of the fuel from his car. Bond's vehicle will be lighter and faster with less fuel. When the race begins, Dimitrov tries to cheat by throwing grit in Bond's face, obstructing his vision. Bond recovers and forces Dimitrov's car off the road, where it crashes and catches fire. Bond pulls the Russian driver out of the wreckage.

The afterparty is held at Jason Sin's water castle near Nürburg. At the party, Bond sees a SMERSH operative talking to Sin. He also meets Jeopardy Lane, who claims that she's a journalist for a motorsport magazine. Bond sneaks into Sin's private office. Once inside, Bond sidesteps the pressure alarm hidden under the rug. Bond finds a series of photographs of three Koreans surrounding a rocket ship somewhere in America. Jeopardy enters the room and accidentally triggers the alarm. Bond grabs the photos, and he and Jeopardy climb the tower on top of the castle. As the guards move in, Bond and Jeopardy jump into the water below and swim to safety.

Auto racing is "Murder on Wheels."
Illustration by Pat Carbajal

Sin interrogates a guard who failed to prevent Bond from sneaking into his office. Sin presents the guard a deck of cards, 45 of which predict a different gruesome manner of death and 3 are blank. If the guard draws a blank card, he will be set free. If he picks one of the other 45 cards, then he will have determined the manner of his own death. If he doesn't comply, Sin will slaughter his family. After drawing a card, the guard hangs himself.

At Bond's hotel, Bond tells Jeopardy that he knows that she's not a journalist, but she doesn't confirm the exact nature of her profession. Jeopardy reviews the photos that Bond stole from Sin's office and concludes that they depict a US-based rocket launch site.

Bond and Jeopardy agree to work together. When Bond leaves the room, Jeopardy steals Sin's photographs and slips away.

Bond meets with German SIS agent, Charles Henry Duggan, and they discuss the space race between Russia and America. Duggan theorizes that whoever controls space will control the world. Duggan wonders if the Russians are trying to win the space race by sabotaging the American space program. Duggan informs Bond that the next rocket launch in five days from Wallops Island, off Virginia.

Bond travels to Wallops Island to visit the Naval Research Center. There, Bond warns Navy Liaison Captain Eugene Lawrence about Sin's plans to redirect a rocket to crash into a U.S. city. Lawrence reassures Bond that there is no threat because the control room has a failsafe mechanism called trigger mortis that would cause it to explode before it could cause any harm. Lawrence produces the photographs that Bond stole from Sin, but he won't reveal how he came into possession of them.

On Bond's way out of the base, he strikes up a conversation with base manager Johnny Calhoun. Calhoun reveals that Keller, the German engineer killed by his wife, was one of his supervisors. Calhoun provides Bond with Keller's home address near Salisbury, Maryland. When Bond visits Salisbury, the local police tell him that Gloria Keller plotted to murder her husband for weeks; it wasn't an impulsive act. Bond finds it suspicious that Keller was killed weeks before the launch of the rocket.

When Bond returns to his motel, the manager tells Bond that Calhoun will come by the hotel the next day to speak to Bond. Bond suspects a trap because he never told Calhoun where he was staying. Bond tries to sneak away but enemy agents descend on him. Before the agents can grab Bond, Jeopardy arrives and helps Bond escape.

Jeopardy reveals that she is a US Secret Service agent working with the Department of Treasury. She is investigating the counterfeit money that Gloria Keller took from her dead husband. Later, they learn that Sin is now back in America, working out of his railway depot in Coney Island, New York.

Bond and Jeopardy go to Sin's depot. While Jeopardy distracts the guards, Bond enters a warehouse that houses a replica of the rocket ship that will be launched from Wallops Island. The replica, however, is missing a crucial component and cannot be launched. Sin's men capture Bond and Jeopardy and bring them to their boss.

Over dinner, Sin tells Bond and Jeopardy that the replica rocket is being taken to New York City by train. The replica will be packed with explosives and set off near the Empire State Building, causing the landmark building to collapse. Simultaneously, the authentic rocket will be sent off course. The public will assume that the rogue U.S. rocket traveled from Virginia to Manhattan and crashed into the Empire State Building. America's space program will be set back, and the Russians will win the space race.

Sin produces his deck of cards and instructs Bond to pick one. Bond uses his card sharp skills to pick the card which would free him. Assuming Bond is cheating, Sin selects another card for Bond; this one indicates that Bond will be buried alive. Jeopardy slips Bond a knife that she took from the dinner table. Bond is brought outside, where he is put in a box and buried alive. Sin's men leave Bond to die. Using the knife, Bond frees himself from this coffin and rescues Jeopardy.

Bond trying to free himself from
the coffin before air runs out.
Illustration by Pat Carbajal

Bond and Jeopardy locate Sin who is boarding the train carrying the replica rocket and explosives. After stealing a motorcycle, Bond and Jeopardy chase after the train. Bond leaps onto the train from his motorcycle. As Sin's train pulls into Manhattan, Bond finds the bomb and diffuses it. Bond and Sin fight each other in the tunnels. Sin seems to be getting the upper hand, but Bond manages to electrocute his opponent on the third rail. The genuine rocket launches from Wallops Island; it veers off course, and the technicians push the trigger mortis panic button, causing the rocket to self-destruct and fall harmlessly into the ocean.

Bond and Jeopardy spend one last night together. Bond would like to continue seeing Jeopardy, but she ends their relationship. On Bond's way to work, he is confronted by Dimitrov, the Russian race car driver. Dimitrov attempts to shoot Bond, but the spy is too fast, and he kills Dimitrov instead. Bond realizes that one day his luck will run out. For now, he's safe.

Commentary: So, you want to write a Bond continuation novel. Should it be a sequel or a prequel? That's the question that Ian Fleming Publications and Bond authors are faced with. That is to say, the continuation novel can take the form of a sequel, and be set after the events of Fleming's twelve novels. Or it can be a prequel, and cover Bond's history before his first mission as a Double O agent in *Casino Royale*. With *Trigger Mortis*, Anthony Horowitz eschews the issue and writes a story that is placed midway through Fleming's series.

Horowitz sets *Trigger Mortis* two weeks after Fleming's seventh novel, *Goldfinger.* After concluding that mission and defeating the gold-obsessed villain and his mute bowler-wearing henchman, the villain-turned-hero, Pussy Galore, has moved in with 007. At first, passion stokes the embers of their relationship. After a fiery start, their relationship cooled off. Clearly, this was a relationship that was not built to last. Bond always feels self-conscious introducing Galore to his acquaintances; he also feels that her first name seemed a bit puerile. Yet, it's not Bond who ends their time together; Galore makes the final decision. She meets another woman and leaves Bond in her wake.

By setting *Trigger Mortis* mid-point in Fleming's series, Horowitz has now deliberately and confidently boxed himself into a corner. At this point in his career, Bond is a seasoned Double O agent. He still retains a certain amount of verve for his job. He hasn't yet met Blofeld or fallen in love with Tracy, which would lead to the loss of his bride. Because most continuation novels are set after *The Man with the Golden Gun*, Bond is haunted by the death of his slain wife. Horowitz avoids writing about a depressed Bond who is hell-bent on revenge. Instead, he delivers a rousing classic Bond adventure. M gives Bond a mission; Bond tracks down the villain, competes in an exotic sport, is tortured, meets a woman, loses a woman, gets a woman, and vanquishes the foe—in short, Bond triumphs.

Horowitz delivers a typical Fleming antagonist, Sin "Jason" Jai-Seong or as the writer puts it, "sin by name, sin by nature." The destiny of Sin's victims is decided by a pack of cards. Each card offers a distinct grisly ending. Some playing cards demand that the victim ingest poison or slice their own wrists. A bullet to the head is a quick and relatively lenient alternative, but other punishments take days to carry out. Decapitation, electrocution, or suffocation are further options. Unlucky Sin presumes Bond is cheating when he draws a card that would free him, and maliciously decides he will bury Bond alive. In one especially terrifying scene, Bond is trapped underground in a coffin and must escape before the air supply runs out.

Horowitz was given a chance that no other author had ever received from Ian Fleming Publication. They let him read unpublished Fleming Bond stories so he could draw from them for his novel. They allowed him to read unreleased Bond writing by Fleming to take inspiration from them for his new story. He was presented with Fleming-authored outlines for episodes for a Bond television series that never materialized. In one, Bond is required to take part in a Formula One race and defend a driver from the Russians. It's a brilliant Fleming concept because Bond doesn't have to win the race to complete his objective. All he needs to do is stop the Russians from killing a specific driver. That's it. The plan is reminiscent of *Casino Royale*, in which James Bond is tasked with bankrupting an enemy. Horowitz would take this kernel of an idea and expand on it. In the end, the villain's plot is on a much bigger scale. Still, these kinds of plots are more realistic and plausible.

Horowitz, however, is not attempting to copy Fleming's writing. He is not "writing as" Fleming, as Faulks attempted (an unenviable task if there ever was one). Instead, Horowitz, who has a deep appreciation for 007, delivers the Bond novel that he would like to have read. He does not attempt to reinvent the book or the character for today's audience, although he is mindful to represent shared contemporary values and characters. In doing so, Horowitz delivers Bond as Fleming and his devoted readers might imagine.

Continuity Nod: Many of Bond's missions in Fleming's first seven novels are referenced. Horowitz cites Le Chiffre and the song "La Vie En Rose" (*Casino Royale*); Mr. Big (*Live and Let Die*); the race through Kent with Hugo Drax, the book that Bond reads to help him become a better card sharp, *Scarne on Cards*, being nearly incinerated by a rocket (*Moonraker*); reluctantly trading in his Beretta .25 for a Walther PPK, SMERSH's plan to target Bond (*From Russia with Love*); Julius No's base of operations in Crab Key, Jamaica (*Dr. No*); Auric Goldfinger's heist, Oddjob's demise by being sucked out of an airplane window, and Jill Masterton's murder by gold paint (*Goldfinger*).

Bond's History: Bond fondly recalls sneaking into his father's study as a kid to read his weapon-related files for Vickers Aviation, the arms business his father worked for. His father chuckled instead of reprimanding him when he was caught. When Bond was young and suffering from headaches, his Aunt would advise him to take a plant called houseleek, which she should grow in Scottland. As part of a school trip, he was taken to the home of poet John Keats in the London neighborhood of Hampstead. During his teenage years, his family took him skiing and climbing at Kitzbühel, Austria.

Bond wanted to join the Royal Naval, but he was too young; so he lied about his age. The notion that he was too young to join and needed to lie might be Horowitz's attempt to clean up a possible discrepancy in Fleming's timeline. Bond devotees have pointed out that by Fleming's accounting, Bond would have only been seventeen years old when he joined the navy, too young to enlist. Horowitz's suggestion that Bond needs to fib about his age is a graceful way to take all of Fleming's writing as sacrosanct and not simply label the accounting as a mistake. Other Bond authors, including Boyd, have also put forth this theory.

During basic training, Bond witnessed a sailor blowing himself up with explosives by failing to follow proper protocols. Bond also served on the T-class submarine, the *Trespasser*. The captain had mistaken a whale for the enemy's vessel, and he fired upon it; causing the crew to laugh at the captain's folly.

Bond has entered a handful of competitive races with his beloved Bentley, including ones at Goodwood, Silverstone, and Albi.

Bond's Personal Life: After his assignment in *Diamonds Are Forever*, Bond continued a brief romance with Tiffany Case. Horowitz claims that their relationship had turned into a series of small fights before they split. Case is only mentioned in passing, though, as Bond is already dating Goldfinger's pilot Pussy Galore at the beginning of *Trigger Mortis*. Galore makes Bond his requisite eggs for breakfast, but she makes him feel bad about being a creature of habit. Galore and May, Bond's Scottish housekeeper, do not get along.

Bond is deeply attracted to women who have a "need to be loved." For the most part, Bond doesn't socialize; he feels that it's a security risk. The mechanic who looks after Bond's Bentley is named Cranwell. Bond gets a copy of *The Times* delivered to his flat each morning. Horowitz doesn't indicate if Bond uses his real name for the subscription or an alias.

Horowitz gives Bond an old-war buddy, Charles Henry Duggan. Bond and Duggan served together during the Royal Navy. Dugan is now the head of Station G. He's an effective operative, a terrible dresser, and is, incidentally, gay. Despite his initial discomfort of knowing an openly gay man, Bond and Duggan get along quite well and Duggan can take the mickey out of 007, the way very few people can.

Bond's Inner Life: Bond's job, above all, provides purpose in his life and everything else "friendship, even love—was extraneous." For Bond, life is like a game of chance. It also means that he generally puts all of his chips on one color; win or lose.

Bond feels that death might be catching up with him and that he might fail this mission. "So many missions in the last ten years…Could he really have believed he would succeed in every one of them?" And later when Sin has the drop on the unarmed agent, "Bond knew it was over. This was it." It's Bond's skill and luck that have enabled him to survive in the Double O Division longer than any other agent.

Bond and the enemy who he is going to kill share an unexpected closeness. In fact, "there is no relationship in the world quite like the one between the man who intends to kill and the man who is about to die." Bond compares it to that of a snake and a rabbit. The rabbit must die so that the snake can eat. It's as simple as that. Later, Horowitz explains that killing is not personal to Bond and that 007 routinely snuffs "out their lives without even thinking of them as human beings at all." Still despite it all, Bond doesn't leave "an inch of his humanity behind" when he does what is necessary to escape death. However, by the time Horowitz's third Bond book concludes, that's not necessarily the case.

Bond's Bentley Mark VI in *Trigger Mortis.*
Illustration by Pat Carbajal

Bond's Tastes: Bond amusingly observes that to survive in America, all you need is a gun and a wallet. Bond has an appreciation for the plumbing in America and thinks it's vastly superior to that of England. Bond wears a Rolex Submariner watch but loses it while trying to escape from an early grave. When it rains, Bond doesn't use an umbrella; he thinks they are poorly designed inventions. Bond finds the sound of the rain on his Bentley to be comforting.

Bond's Work Methods: Bond is trained to fire a gun with either hand. He's nearly as quick to draw with his left hand as his right. To ensure that Bond's a sharpshooter, he practices for an hour in MI6's indoor shooting range. The rest of the day is devoted to paperwork. Bond's office is on the fifth floor, the Communications Room is on the seventh floor, and M's office is on the ninth.

The spy's smoking habit is beginning to impact his job performance. When Bond tries to run after a speeding train on foot but fails, he realizes that if he did not smoke so much, he probably would have succeeded. Instead, as Bond catches his breath, he futilely observes it speed away in the distance. Agents are advised to confuse their opponent when they are trapped by using "the least obvious course of action."

Assorted Observations:

- The UK Hardcover was designed so that the dust jacket could be cut up into six different parts and then reassembled as a Vanguard rocket ship.[135]

FOREVER AND A DAY (2018)

Author: Anthony Horowitz

In Brief: James Bond, a newly minted Double O agent, is assigned to find out why Agent 007, his predecessor, was killed.

Meaning of Title: It is the length of time that two lovers yearn to be together. Bond's lover adds an extra day because eternity isn't long enough.

Chronology: Set before *Casino Royale*, the first Bond novel.

Operation: Overlord and Mordonius.

Bastard Meter: Unaddressed, however, he is referred to as a "pig."

Eggs: Scrambled.

Insight into Bond: "They call you 007 because they know it will make it easier for you to kill brutally and without remorse. It matters to them that you should be a double zero. They have taken part of your humanity."

Summary: M and Bill Tanner discuss the death of 007, who has been murdered in the south of France while looking into the drug trade in the Corsican underworld. Before he was killed, 007 was preparing to meet Joanne Brochet, codenamed Madame 16, aka Sixteen. Now, there is a vacancy in the Double O division which needs to be filled. M decides that an up-and-coming operative named James Bond should be given a promotion.

When Bond first meets Loelia Ponsonby, his new secretary, she gives him a file on Jean-Paul Scipio, the Corsican underworld boss who 007 was looking into before he passed away. Then, Bond encounters M and his secretary Miss Moneypenny. M briefs Bond on Irwin Wolfe, head of Wolfe America company that makes film stock. M tells Bond that 007 had rented a flat in Nice, France. Bond is tasked with finding out who killed 007 and why. Bond assumes the designation of 007.

After flying to Nice, Bond investigates 007's flat but he doesn't find anything inside. He does discover a shed on the building's roof where 007 concealed a series of photographs, an invoice, and a postcard. Bond is attacked as he is going through 007's possessions.

After disabling the assailant, Bond learns that the man who struck him is a CIA agent named Reade Griffith. Realizing that their interests are aligned, Bond shows him 007's hidden stash. Griffith identifies Jean-Paul Scipio, the Corsican underworld member and Sixteen, the woman the late-007 was supposed to meet. The name and phone number of a woman named Monique are listed on the postcard and the bill is from Ferrix Chimique, a chemical company that operates out of Marseilles. Griffith tells Bond that he can find Sixteen at a casino in Monte Carlo.

Bond goes to Monte Carlo, finds Sixteen playing blackjack, and joins the game. Sixteen is an accomplished gambler but Bond beats her. Later, over drinks, Sixteen is questioned by Bond about 007, but she denies ever having met him. Sixteen invites Bond to attend a party that is being thrown the next day by Irwin Wolfe, head of a company that manufactures film stock. Bond and Griffith visit the site of 007's murder. They learn that the chemical company Ferrix Chimique is nearby.

The next day, Bond and Reede meet the managing director at Ferrix Chimique. Then, Bond sneaks into the records office and learns Irwin Wolf purchased a large supply of a chemical called acetic anhydride. Bond is discovered and knocked out. When Bond rouses, he finds that he has been bound to a chair by Jean-Paul Scipio, the Corsican mafia boss. Scipio threatens Bond with hydrochloric acid. Scipio appears to throw the acid on Bond's face and the agent screams in agony. However, the acid was substituted with water and Bond merely imagined the pain. Bond is let off with a warning and told to keep clear of Scipio's affairs.

Bond and Reade compare notes. Reade tells Bond that the chemical acetic anhydride found at Wolf's company is used to produce film stock. So, perhaps Wolfe's connection to Ferrix Chimique isn't that sinister after all. Reade suggests that Sixteen might have tipped Scipio off to their arrival at the factory.

That evening, Bond and Sixteen go to a party thrown by Irwin Wolfe, owner of the film stock company. Wolfe invites Bond to join him on his cruise liner, *The Mirabelle*. The next day, Bond traces a number he found on the back of the late 007's postcard to Monique de Troyes, an employee of Ferrix Chimique. Bond meets with Monique who knew 007 and fed him info about Wolfe's company. She tells Bond that the chemical on 007's invoice is used to make film stock. Shortly after the meeting, Monique is killed.

Bond and Sixteen spend the night together. She explains that Wolfe hired her to perform corporate espionage. Wolfe's company is number three in the film manufacturing business, and he wanted to create a better product that would drive Technicolor, a competitor, out of business.

Bond and Sixteen decide to investigate Wolfe's manufacturing plant. Posing as food-delivery workers, they infiltrate the plant. Inside, they discover a laboratory for the mass production of heroin and that Jean-Paul Scipio and Irwin Wolfe are in cahoots. Bond and Sixteen are caught.

Bond and Sixteen are brought to Wolfe's ship, which is being used illegally to smuggle heroin. Scipio and Wolf plan to flood the United States with high-grade and inexpensive heroin, a move that will create a nation of addicts. On board, Wolfe instructs the ship's doctor to inject Bond with a highly addictive batch of the narcotic.

Bond and Sixteen are brought back to the cabin. There, Sixteen lets out the blood in Bond's arm to diminish the full effect of the drug. Sixteen tricks the guards into believing that Bond overdosed. When the guards rush in, Bond and Sixteen overpower them and escape. Bond jury-rigs a bomb, sinks the ship, and kills Scipio. Sixteen goes down with the ship.

Back in London, M congratulates Bond on a job well done. Yet Bond thinks the mission isn't over because Wolfe, the man responsible for the death of the former 007, is still at large. M gives Bond tacit permission to kill Wolfe.

Bond breaks into Wolfe's residence and discovers that Wolfe has been killed by Reade Griffith, the CIA agent. Reade confesses that he was in league with Scipio but claims that Scipio killed the previous 007, not him. Reade insists that he prevented Scipio from killing Bond. Reade also admits that the chemical acetic anhydride, as he previously told Bond, is not just used to produce film; it's also used to make heroin. The CIA agent acknowledges that he wasn't completely truthful with Bond but insists that there was nothing sinister about his actions. Bond shoots Reade in the head because he believes he was partially responsible for the deaths of Sixteen and 007. Bond feels no remorse for his decision.

Commentary: *Forever and a Day* serves as a James Bond origin story perhaps even more so than *Casino Royale*. We are privy to numerous firsts in Bond's life. We watch as Bond meets Miss Moneypenny, Loelia Ponsonby, and M for the first time. We are privy to the moment Bond is given the 007 prefix and his first assignment as a Double O agent.

Bond has just finished a long-range killing in New York when *Forever and a Day* begins. He is now in Stockholm, where he has been tasked with killing Rolph Larsen, a double agent for the Nazis who is responsible for the death of two English intelligence offers. Before stabbing his second target to death with a knife, Bond wants to confirm that Larsen is actually responsible. Bond won't simply take M's word for it. If Bond is going to kill someone, he wants to feel justified. In this way, Bond isn't simply a tool of the government that can be wielded indiscriminately by whoever holds the whip. The confirmation that man is the guilty party gives Bond the "peace of mind" that he requires to carry out his orders. And with that information, Bond removes a knife and drives it into Larsen's skull.

In *Casino Royale*, Fleming made a passing reference to this mission and gave some general details: the Norwegian, the double agent, even the method of death—the knife. Horowitz, however, takes the sparse elements, develops them, and dramatizes them into an exciting short story that sheds light on Bond's personality. Determining what parts of Bond's past should be elaborated on and what parts should remain unknown is a delicate task. A Bond continuation author doesn't want to supply too much information that will dilute the mystery of a deliberately oblique figure. However, in this instance, Horowitz not only expands on the myth but also adds to it by revealing more about Bond's character.

Bond is still an unformed agent in *Forever and a Day*. He is not yet the hero he will one day be. The spy in command is Madame 16. Although she also goes by the name Sixteen, her real name is Joanne Brochet. She is just as accomplished at playing cards, as resourceful, and as skilled at skullduggery as Bond. She's an even better lover. The Bond of the movies and the continuation novels knows how to give a woman pleasure. During the events of *Forever and a Day*, Bond is still lacking in that department. Sixteen criticizes Bond's ability, "You make love like a schoolboy."

Each Bond author adds a little color to the characters in Bond's orbit. Horowitz establishes that Chief of Staff Bill Tanner is a former colonel in the Corps of Royal Engineers who identified Bond as a rising star and a suitable candidate for the Double O division. Tanner met Bond during the war, but they didn't become close friends until Bond joined the secret service. Bond has great admiration for M. While M can be gruff, he has never been impolite to Bond. When Bond verifies his target's culpability before executing him, M pretends to be frustrated with 007. However, M actually respects Bond's decision. When Bond and Loelia Ponsonby first met, he suggested the nickname Lil, which she rejected outright. May provides Bond with what he considers to be the best scrambled eggs he's ever eaten.

Horowitz not only tells an engaging story, but he also provides context and reasoning for some tenants of the Bond adventures.

Horowitz's Bond is given the number 007 for two reasons. One, Bond wants to use it as a tribute to the former 007, a man that Bond considered a friend. Two, he doesn't want the designation to go unused and to signal to the enemy that there was a death in the organization. Bond believes that if he's the next 007 it will seem like MI6 the opposition won't think they are a man down. Instead, it will be a signal of MI6's strength.

Before becoming an agent, Bond coveted the Double O status, it was something that "he wanted more than anything in the world." Sixteen points out that with his Double O status, Bond has the power to choose who lives and who dies. Sixteen argues that there are two kinds of people with that choice—secret agents and psychopaths. Elsewhere, Sixteen contends that when they gave Bond a number, they stripped him of his humanity.

Horowitz also explains why Bond doesn't usually use an alias. In *Forever and a Day,* the previous 007 used one and was killed anyway. In addition to that, Bond's cover is immediately blown, essentially at the start of his mission. Bond is recognized by the casino owner and his target, Sixteen.

Bond takes on aspects of Sixteen's preferences. From Sixteen, Bond picks up a habit of shaking and not stirring martinis. After Sixteen dies, Bond switches to Sixteen's preferred brand of cigarettes, Morlands of Grosvenor Street. Just as Bond drinks a Vesper Martini as a tribute to Vesper Lynd, it could be seen that Bond smokes his Morlands as a way of remembering Sixteen. While the Bond/Sixteen relationship isn't as significant as his relationship with Vesper, it is unquestionably vital. In one scene, Sixteen invites Bond to dinner and she instructs Bond to set the table. Horowitz's description of Bond setting the dinner table is one of the most intimate passages in any Bond continuation novel. While he's setting the table, Bond realizes that it's been years since anyone asked him to perform such a task. It's a throwaway line but it suggests Bond's increased isolation and his proclivity for living alone.

Continuity Nod: *Forever and a Day* is a prequel to *Casino Royale.* Thus, Horowitz is unable to make any allusions to most of the missions Fleming describes in his books because those stories take place after the events of *Forever and a Day*. Still, Horowitz can allude to Bond's preferences. For instance, Sixteen orders a vodka martini, shaken not stirred. He drinks coffee but never tea, something Fleming would expand on in *Goldfinger*. Bond lost his virginity when he was in his teens to a woman who was six years older than him ("From a View to a Kill").

A surprisingly intimate moment in which Bond sets the table for a dinner with Madame Sixteen.
Illustration by Pat Carbajal

Bond's History: Bond grew up near Canterbury in a small town called Pett Bottom. Until he reached eighteen, he had been living off a trust fund that his parents established before their deaths.

Bond's Inner Life: Bond's greatest professional asset is that he believes he's better and stronger than the enemy. This point of view gives him a psychological edge in the field. Horowitz's Bond knows that he will likely be killed in action. He accepts that it is a part of his job, and he's non-plussed by it. When death comes, Bond will learn its "secrets."

Bond's Personal Life: Bond loathes the opera, and he rarely goes to the movies. Breakfast is a ritual where he can think about the events of the day, which is why Bond puts so much thought into what he eats. If breakfast is a ritual, then "lunch was a pleasure, and dinner often a celebration."

Bond drives a Jaguar XK 120 because his beloved Mark II Continental Bentley was wrecked. Even though the Bentley can't be driven in its current condition, Bond foots the bill to store it in East London. His salary is meager, and Bond doesn't live lavishly. As with Fleming, Horowitz's Bond is financially solvent when on assignment. In the words of Horowitz, "A license to kill, it seemed, also came with an almost unlimited license to spend."

Work-Life: Before joining the Double O Division, Bond worked in the same building but on the third floor. Horowitz explains that the Double O Division was intentionally kept small. Only three members (007, 008, 0011) comprised it. The fact that there are no agents with lower numbers in the sequence (like 001) was intended to avoid patterns, something that an enemy can identify and exploit.

Assorted Observations:

- For the unproduced television series about 007, Fleming wrote an outline for an episode titled "Russian Roulette." Horowitz incorporates elements of the story into *Forever and a Day.*
- The villain's private villa is named Shame Lady, a reference to the flowers that grow near Fleming's Jamaican home.
- The previous 007 used the cover name Richard Blakeney.

WITH A MIND TO KILL (2022)

Author: Anthony Horowitz

In Brief: M sends Bond back to the Soviet Union to find out who brainwashed him. The Soviets, however, have their own plan to use Bond to assassinate the Soviet Premier.

Meaning of Title: The phrase "a mind to kill" refers to the fact that Bond had been brainwashed to kill M and, unbeknownst to 007, he is still a sleeper agent for the enemy.

Chronology: Set about two weeks after the events of *The Man with the Golden Gun*, Fleming's last novel.

Operation: Not applicable.

Bastard Meter: Not addressed.

Eggs: Bond daydreams about eating scrambled eggs but he's never served them.

Insight into Bond: "Luck had always been on his side, and he understood that luck has a way of moving on when it decides it had enough."

Summary: A funeral service is held for M, the head of the Secret Intelligence Service. However, M isn't dead; the funeral is a ruse to trick the Soviets into believing that a brainwashed James Bond killed his superior. What the Soviets don't know is that Bond failed, and he was deprogrammed by clinical psychologist Major Colin Cunningham at a facility known as The Park.

M tells Bond that he was brainwashed by the Steel Hand, who are comprised of members from the SMERSH, and the KGB. M tells Bond that the Steel Hand still believes Bond is under their influence; a fact that can be used against them. M instructs Bond to travel to Moscow, infiltrate the Steel Hand, find out their plan, and stop it.

The Steel Hand gathers in Moscow; its members include former SMERSH head, General Grubozaboyschikov and Colonel Boris, the man who brainwashed Bond (*The Man with the Golden Gun*). Colonel Boris performs a demonstration of his brainwashing program's effectiveness. He asks one of his men to jump out the window; the man complies and falls to his death. Boris explains that they have planted a similar "trigger" inside Bond's mind that neither Bond nor MI6 know of. As a result, even if Bond has been deprogrammed, the trigger remains, and Bond will be forced to do the Steel Hand's bidding. Impressed, the Steel Hand decides to use Bond to carry out their plan.

Back in England, Bond is still being held at The Park, continuing the fiction that he is an enemy of the state. Per M's instructions, Bond calls his contact in Moscow and lets him know that he's going to be transferred to the police station. During the transfer, Steel Hand fighters attack the convoy carrying Bond and free him.

Bond is flown to Moscow, where he is brought to Colonel Boris. Bond tries to gain Boris's confidence by pledging loyalty to the Soviet Union. Bond is tortured by Boris who distrusts the spy. Bond withstands the punishment and is declared fit to carry out the Hand's mission. Colonel Boris assigns Katya Leonova to be Bond's handler. Boris tells Katya to take Bond to Moscow via train and confirm that he's still loyal to the Soviet Union

When Bond and Katya are on the train, he spots two male KGB agents. Later, Bond hears Katya struggling in her compartment. Bond bursts in and dispatches the two men who are harming her.

Once in Moscow, Katya leaves her hotel and Bond follows her. As Bond spies on Katya, the Steal Hand spies on Bond. General Grubozaboyschikov and General Boris question Bond's loyalty. They receive a report that the man who previously killed their operative and Francisco Scaramanga is a British agent named Mark Hazard, Bond's alias (*The Man with the Golden Gun*). The Steel Hand arranges for Hal Garfinkel, who had previously met Bond in Jamaica, to pay Bond a surprise visit in order to determine whether Bond and Hazard are the same person.

Later, Katya tells Bond about her ex-boyfriend Dmitry who lost faith in the Communist Party. Being a good communist, Katya reported him, and Dmitry was given electric shock treatment that left him forever diminished. She regrets her decision.

Garfinkel goes to Bond's hotel. A man resembling Bond opens the door and identifies himself as Mark Hazard. Garfinkel reports to Boris that Hazard and Bond are different people. It turns out that shortly before Garfinkel arrived, Bill Tanner's friend, Margarita, warned Bond about Garfinkel's visit and provided a stand-in to trick Garfinkel. Soon after, Katya figures out that Bond is no longer under Boris's control.

Later, Colonel Boris gives Bond the rifle that he will need to complete his mission. The Steel Hand asks Bond to conduct a loyalty test by murdering a British cultural attaché named Zephyr. Bond agrees to conduct the assassination but grapples with the problem—kill an innocent man or blow his cover. Bond warns Zephyr about the assassination attempt. Then, he realizes that Zephyr is a Steel Hand agent and not a British attaché. Bond decides to kill Zephyr to protect his cover story. Zephyr stabs Bond and the spy retaliates by throwing Zephyr under a train.

Bond meets up with Katya who tends to his injury. Bond discovers that Colonel Boris is actually Katya's father. Bond tells Katya that he'll bring her back to London with him but once there, he will have nothing to do with her.

In East Berlin, Grubozaboyschikov orders Bond to go to the Berlin State Opera and kill the man who will be occupying Seat 12. The night of the opera, Bond realizes that his target is the head of the Soviet Union, Nikita Khrushchev. Before he can abort his mission, Colonel Boris activates his "trigger" and Bond is once again under Boris' command. To shock himself out of it, Bond stabs himself with a knife. Then, Bond kills Boris.

As Bond exits the opera, Katya approaches him and declares her love for him. Bond rebukes Katya as a change of heart soon after and thinks about pursuing a relationship with Katya. Before he can tell her, Kataya is gunned down. Bond feels responsible for Katya's death and decides to quit the Double O Division and move out of London.

Bond attempts to cross the border to West Berlin and safety. East German guards warn him to stop walking. The guards load their rifles, preparing to shoot Bond. Bond continues to walk, his future uncertain.

Commentary: Did Anthony Horowitz kill James Bond? In the final pages of *With a Mind to Kill*, Bond is disgusted with himself and his profession. Yet another woman who he cares about was gunned down in front of him. Now, Bond has decided to resign and start a new life. He must first pass through Checkpoint Charlie, which serves as a border crossing between the West and the East. As he begins the treacherous walk, the East German guards demand that Bond halt. He ignores them. The guards load their rifles. Bond knows that if he doesn't stop, he will be shot. He keeps walking. The book ends on this uncertain note. Readers are left with the unsettling question—was Bond gunned down?

If he was, it would be consistent with Ian Fleming's assertion that few Double O agents live beyond 45. Bond knows that someday he will likely be killed in action. As early as his first Bond novel, *Trigger Mortis*, Horowitz planted the idea that Bond would die in a future work. In it, he foretold "One day someone, somewhere would have the edge and it would be he lying there dead, flat-out in the rain. But not today." Aware of his own mortality, in *Forever and a Day*, a drugged-induced Bond wishes that he was "invulnerable" and that "he would live forever."

Still, Bond is not consumed by his own mortality. He is, however, fed up with his job in the secret service. 007 is seriously considering offering his resignation. He's ready to pursue the "alternative life" that he imagined for himself. It's a life that includes golf, gambling, women, and tinkering with his car. Additionally, after seeing the inside of the Soviet Union, he's disillusioned by his mission. He was taught that the Soviets were a strong superpower. Instead, he's discovered their people are starving and living gray lives in a gray city. He's also tired of being "M's gigolo."

Bond struggles with the notion of retirement. He knows that some part of him enjoys "living on the edge of a world that is forever out of his reach. Bond needs death, or the threat of death, as a constant companion. For him, it is the only way to live."

Despite his need for excitement, there are limits to how far he will go to complete his mission. He will freely break the law but will not go against his own rules of right and wrong. For instance, there are two scenes in which Bond's deception that he is still brainwashed could be exposed. In one, the Steel Hand attacks his convoy. Bond must decide if he's going to kill a junior agent to protect his cover. In another, the Hand orders him to assassinate a British cultural attaché named Zephyr. In both instances, Bond is willing to jeopardize the mission, and his life, to save the life of an innocent.

Despite his best intentions, there is a potential cost to Bond's actions. Compromising the mission could mean the deaths of many people. Faulks set up similar moral dilemmas for Bond in *Carte Blanche*. Faulks' Bond was able to skirt the issue because Faulks provided Bond with a convenient out. Bond knew the gun he was given contained wax bullets. So Bond never really faced the central problem. Horowitz's Bond is given no such out. The decisions he makes have consequences and when 007 fails to shoot the men on his side, Bond must face the repercussions and he is tortured because he failed the trust test. This Bond couldn't kill an innocent, even if it were to cost him his own life.

Forever and a Day is a direct prequel to Fleming's first Bond novel and *With a Mind to Kill* is a sequel to Fleming's last two Bond novels *You Only Live Twice* and *The Man with the Golden Gun*. To fully follow *With a Mind to Kill*, it's necessary to have a familiarity with the major events and some of the minor characters in the past two novels. Still, Horowitz makes sure that readers who are less familiar with Fleming's work are not lost. Horowitz not only weaves in pertinent information during the course of the book but there is a short recap of *You Only Live Twice* and *The Man with the Golden Gun* before it begins.

Horowitz seized on the gaps in Bond's history and dramatized them in *With a Mind to Kill*. *The Man with the Golden Gun* begins with a brainwashed Bond attempting to kill M by shooting him with a cyanide pistol. A quick-thinking M lowers a protective shield and thwarts Bond's strike. Bond is taken into custody, deprogrammed, and then sent out on his next mission. However, Fleming skipped over detailing a lot of the major events. Bond's brainwashing took place between the events of *You Only Live Twice* and *The Man with the Golden Gun*. Similarly, Fleming refers to Bond's deprogramming, but he doesn't depict it. Horowitz details the process of Bond's programming and subsequent deprogramming. Stating a character has been brainwashed is one thing; credibly conveying the complex process is quite another.

Of minor note, it's not only the readers who need to be convinced about the efficacy of brainwashing, so does Bond. In *Live and Let Die*, Bond falsely brags, "I'm not a good subject for suggestion or hypnotism." Fleming and Horowitz beg to differ.

Not only does Horowitz flesh out critical events in 007's life but he alludes to the emotional cost these events have on our hero. Bond's attack on M in *The Man with the Golden Gun* is still weighing on him. Even though 007 failed to kill his superior and father figure, there is an emotional cost. Even the enemy comments that when attempted to destroy M, he also destroyed a part of himself. Bond is also starting to feel self-disgust, a new emotion for him. He is no longer indifferent to the toll on himself and the woman that he loves. When she dies, knowing that she thinks he hates her, it's too much for Bond to bear.

With a Mind to Kill could serve as the last Bond novel. In the final moments of the book, Bond ignores the bullets that are being fired at him, seemingly unconcerned about his fate. If he lives, he lives. If he dies, he dies. Horowitz is deliberately vague about Bond's fate. He leaves it open to interpretation. Still, readers can reasonably conclude that Bond is killed. Even if that were the case, his death would occur after the book ends, not during its narrative. Either way, Horowitz is suggesting that Bond is not long for the world, or at least the Double O Division. *Trigger Mortis* ends with Bond acknowledging that one day his luck will run out. In *With a Mind to Kill*, Horowitz offers the possibility that it has.

Continuity Nod: Horowitz references most of the major Bond villains, including Blofeld, Scaramanga, Le Chiffre, Mr. Big, Hugo Drax, Rosa Klebb, and Dr. No. Tracy is alluded to on multiple occasions, but Vesper is not. The fact that Vesper is not mentioned could indicate that Horowitz's Bond has in some ways moved on and that he considers Tracy his one true love.

Bond's History: 007's Aunt Charmian practiced aromatherapy, using smells to influence thinking and feelings.

Bond's Inner Life: The villain describes 007 as a "spy, a womanizer, a killer' who has "no interest in books or great art or natural science." Bond's sardonic and sarcastic sense of humor tips off the enemy that he is no longer brainwashed.

Bond's Personal Life: Horowitz suggests that even if Tracy was not gunned down, their marriage would not have lasted. Eventually, he would have cheated on her. Horowitz also contends that it's not that Bond can't fall in love, he falls in love often, including in this novel, it's just that 007 is not able to commit himself fully to just one woman.

Bond's Tastes: Horowitz's Bond, like Fleming's, wears pyjamas. However, the ones issued in the Soviet Union are so abrasive against his skin that Bond is unable to wear them. Instead, he sleeps naked. Despite abhorring the opera, Bond has been to it twice. Both times on missions. Bond still lights his cigarettes with a Ronson lighter.

Bond's Work Methods: The Naval Intelligence taught Bond a rope climbing technique called break and squat. His instructor also touted that in a knife fight, there are no rules. Kill the other guy or he will kill you. Bond was also taught close-quarter combat and read instructional manuals on new fighting techniques.

Horowitz's Bond, like Fleming's, greatly respects M and admires him most in the world. M's position as head of the British Secret Intelligence Service is not simply a desk job; there are inherent dangers in holding the position. The last man to hold M's job was assassinated. Horowitz also argues that M was a father figure to Bond.

Schrödinger's Bond: *With a Mind to Kill* shares some surface similarities with Daniel Craig's final Bond film, *No Time to Die*. Both works concern Bond's apparent demise. In both, 007 has seen enough death and destruction. Craig's Bond is retired and Horowitz's 007 seriously considers a life outside the service. Horowitz's book and

Craig's film also share a similar scene. In the book, a betrayed 007 tells his lover that after he takes her to safety, she will never see him again. In Craig's film, 007 also tells his lover that after she gets to safety, they will never be reunited. Bond's death in *No Time to Die* is unambiguous; viewers see the missiles strike him down. Yet in *With a Mind to Kill*, readers don't actually witness Bond's death. In a literal sense, Horowitz leaves him alive, unharmed.

Assorted Observations:

- Sir James Molony is a character in the book who helps deprogram the brainwashed Bond. Molony previously appeared in *The Man with the Golden Gun* and in Gardner's *Scorpius* and Weinberg's *The Moneypenny Diaries: Secret Servant*.
- Sir Miles Messervy's wife is identified as Lady Frances Messervy. The head waiter at Blade, whose name is Porterfield, respected M enough to attend his staged funeral.
- Colonel Boris is known as the hammer because that is his weapon of choice.
- "Bond Goes to Jail" was the title that Fleming gave for an episode of his unmade television show about 007. Horowitz attempted to incorporate the episode's central premise of Bond in a jail cell, but he couldn't make it work to his satisfaction. So instead of having Bond attempting to escape from jail, Horowitz has Bond escape on the way to it.

THE ERA OF EXPERIMENTATION

"Why not make it for always?"
IAN FLEMING, *On Her Majesty's Secret Service*

KIM SHERWOOD'S TENURE
2022–

Kim Sherwood is the author of a planned trilogy of novels about the next generation of agents in the Double O division. The first two novels are *Double Or Nothing* (2022) and *A Spy Like Me* (2024).

DOUBLE OR NOTHING (2022)

Author: Kim Sherwood

In Brief: James Bond is missing and the next generation of Double O agents face new threats. As Joseph Dryden (004) investigates Sir Bertram Paradise, a tech billionaire, who claims his advanced technology can stop climate change, Johanna Harwood (003) and Sid Bashir (009) search for Paradise's missing scientist.

Meaning of Title: A reference to a bet that is repeated four times throughout the novel, twice by the villain and twice by a Double O agent.

Chronology: Contemporary.

Operation: Not applicable.

Bastard Meter: None about Bond.

Eggs: None for Bond.

Insight into Bond: "He never knew when to fall in love. And when not."

Summary: Aazar Siddig "Sid" Bashir, agent 009, is in Syria on a mission to rescue Johanna Harwood, agent 003, who has been taken hostage by the mercenary group Der Rattenfänger. Bashir sneaks into Rattenfänger's base and attempts to locate Harwood. Bashir encounters Colonel Mora who somehow knew he was coming. Mora gets the better of 009 and nearly kills him, but Harwood shoots the colonel and rescues Bashir.

Bashir and his ex-fiancé, Harwood, debrief in a hotel in Istanbul. Harwood claims that she didn't reveal any intelligence to the enemy. Harwood was captured while searching for James Bond, who has been missing for the past 17 months. They spend the night together.

Bashir and Hardwood return to London. Moneypenny, who oversees the Double O Division, sends Harwood to the Shrublands health clinic for observation and recovery. Moneypenny receives word that Mikhail Petrov, a climate scientist and the subject of Bond's last mission, is dead and his wife Anna Petrov is missing. Before Bond vanished, he was supposed to meet with Petrov in Barcelona and help facilitate his defection. Bashir's end of it was to shadow Bond.

Moneypenny meets with Joseph Dryden, 004. Dryden is effectively deaf, a result of a war injury, but thanks to an implant created by Q Branch, he can hear. The listening device also allows Q and Dryden to communicate with each other. Moneypenny and Dryden discuss tech billionaire Bertram Paradise whose geoengineering project Cloud Nine is designed to stop climate change. Paradise might be connected to the disappearance of Dr. Zofia Nowak, who designed his supercomputer and cloud-seeding technology, and head of security Robert Bull. Dryden's former lover and military buddy, Luke "Lucky Luke" Luck is the new head of Paradise's security force. Moneypenny wants Dryden to get to Paradise through Luke and find out what happened to Nowak and Bull. Before he leaves on his mission, Dryden boxes with Conrad Harthorp-Vane, Triple O.

Hardwood submits to an evaluation by MI6 psychiatrist Dr. Kowalczyk. Kowalczyk is assessing Harwood's mental state following her capture. Kowalczyk finds it suspicious that Harwood killed Colonel Mora when she should have captured him. The colonel knew who was funding Rattenfänger's operation and could have been of use to the service. Harwood admits that she went looking for the missing 007 without authorization.

Dryden meets with Lucky Luke and tells him that he's working for security work. Luke introduces Dryden to Bertram Paradise. Paradise offers Dryden a job on his security team, working under Luke. Paradise's Cloud Nine project will send satellites into the air that will chart the climatic crisis. Paradise's quantum computer, Celestial, will help predict the future and he will oversee the operation through his yacht *Ark*. His ultimate goal is to control the weather.

In London, M tells Bashir there is a mole in MI6, whose betrayal possibly led to Bond's capture and the death of other Double O agents. M cautions that Harwood might have turned while in captivity or, worse still, that she was always working for Rattenfänger. Bashir believes that Bond provided a clue to his safety in his last conversation with Bashir. However, Bashir is not certain what part of their interaction included the clue.

Paradise, Dryden, Luke, and Paradise's enforcer, Yuri Litvinnof, fly to Vozrozhdeniya Island, a former top secret testing ground for deadly pathogens like anthrax. Nearby is the Aral Sea, a now dried-up water source for Kazakhstan, Uzbekistan, and Turkmenistan. There, Paradise hosts a press conference and tells reporters about his plans for the rebirth of the area and his newest crop, which will provide food to the area.

Later, Paradise, Luke, Dryden, and Yuri check into the Cosmodrome, a former spaceport in Kazakhstan that the Russians used in the 1950s. Paradise acquired it so that he could launch his satellites into space. Later, after fending off an attack by homophobes, Luke and Dryden make love.

Moneypenny and Bill Tanner meet with Q Branch founder Mrs. Keator and Q Branch engineer Ibrahim Suleiman. Keator explains Dryden sent her copies of Paradise's men's passports. They've discovered that the passport belonging to Yuri is fake; his real name is Michael Dobra. Bond and Mary Ann Russell, Operative 765, encountered Yuri before, at a casino in Paris years ago.

Moneypenny pays a visit to Mary Ann to learn more. Mary Ann reveals that after Yuri tried to recruit Bond to Rattenfänger, she reported the meeting to Tanner. Moneypenny notes that Tanner kept the intelligence to himself. Mary Ann said that she observed Yuri's relationship with Paradise was strained. After the meeting, Moneypenny calls into Q branch and orders Dryden to get Yuri to reveal Paradise's relationship to Rattenfänger and then kill him.

Harwood and Bashir meet with human rights lawyer Ruqsana Choudhury, who is an old friend of Bashir. Choudhury says that Dr. Zofia Nowak was afraid of Robert Bull, Paradise's head of security and that she suspected Bull was bugging her phone. When Nowak was in Berlin, she started dating an American named Felix Leiter.

For the benefit of the international press, Paradise successfully tests his seeding device; among the onlookers is Elena Ilić, a journalist who is a strong opponent of Paradise.

Yuri confronts Dryden and injects the agent with anthrax. Yuri tells Dryden that he knows he has orders to kill him. Rattenfänger, who intends to profit from Paradise's inventions, has ordered Yuri to protect Paradise. However, lately, Paradise has been showing an independent streak that Rattenfänger doesn't approve of. After a fight, Dryden kills Yuri and then passes out.

When Dryden comes to, Paradise explains that the anthrax will not be fatal as it wasn't prepared properly. Dryden is informed by Paradise that he used Luke to recruit Dryden into the group in order for Dryden to murder Yuri. Luke is unaware that his old friend is being used as a pawn.

Moneypenny meets with Mrs. Keator who wonders why Tanner didn't include the information that Bond met Yuri in his report. Keator reveals that Tanner has been surreptitiously making trips to the town of Lewes.

Moneypenny tracks down Tanner in Lewes and asks him why he withheld information on his report about Bond's meeting with Yuri. Tanner evades the question and suggests that there is a leak in the department.

Harwood meets Felix Leiter, an old friend of Bond's who is stationed in Berlin. Harwood suspects that Leiter has Bull detained in an undisclosed location and she asks for permission to interrogate him.

Elsewhere in Berlin, Bashir and Choudhury meet Anya, a friend of the missing Dr. Nowak. While they are talking, Bashir spots two enemy agents spying on them. Bashir tells Anya to go to the American Embassy and find Felix Leiter.

Harwood is contacted by Rattenfänger, who arranges for her to meet Colonel Mora, the man who previously captured her. Harwood tells Mora that when she shot him, she deliberately missed his vital organs so that he could live. Harwood wants Mora's help in finding Dr. Nowak, who was going to tell the authorities that Rattenfänger was funding Paradise's efforts. Security officer Bull was instructed to silence her. Mora explains that Rattenfänger considers Paradise to be persona non grata.

Felix Leiter takes Harwood to the cell holding Paradise's security man Bull. Harwood poses as Paradise's operative and tricks Bull into revealing that Dr. Nowak can be found by locating her grandmother. Satisfied with the information, Harwood kills Bull.

Elsewhere, in an abandoned military complex in Germany, Colonel Mora has Bashir zip-tied to a chair and Ruqsana Choudhury is suffering from the effects of a poisonous injection Paradise gave her. Mora demands to know where Dr. Nowak is located. If Bashir doesn't provide the information, Chowdhury will die. Suddenly Harwood appears and it seems to Bashir that she is a double agent working for Mora. He doesn't realize that Harwood's a triple agent, working for MI6. She announces that Dr. Nowak is hiding under an assumed name in Frankfurt. Mora leaves to find Nowak in Frankfurt. Bashir knows that Harwood is bluffing; Nowak is still in Berlin. Leiter shoots Mora's men and frees Bashir.

In Germany, Leiter locates Dr. Nowak's biological mother, Mrs. Schulz, and he tells her that he wants to help keep her daughter safe. Mrs. Schulz reveals that her daughter was talking to a journalist but that she doesn't know the reporter's name. After the call, Dr. Nowak destroyed her phone and left the fragments hidden in the garden. Leiter retrieves the phone and gives it to Q Branch to retrieve data from it. Q Branch determines that the journalist's name is Elena Ilić, and she intends to meet Dr. Nowak on Bled Island on Lake Bled, Slovenia.

Harwood and Leiter go to Lake Bled and spot the journalist and Nowak. However, Mora and a sniper are lying in waiting. Along the way, the sniper shoots at Harwood. Leiter returns fire. The sniper shoots and kills the journalist and wounds Leiter. Mora and his men kidnap Nowak. Harwood rushes to give Leiter medical attention.

On the *Ark*, Dryden is placed in a tiger's cage; the tiger is restrained and just out of range of mauling Dryden. Paradise reveals that Dryden's earpiece was transmitting every word he said and heard to Rattenfänger, proving that MI6 has a mole. Paradise explains that he's going to use his technology to accelerate climate change. Paradise will control new trade routes when the ice melts and other oceans run dry.

Bashir and Leiter recover from their injuries at a hospital.

Back on the *Ark*, Dryden makes a bet with Paradise that will be decided with a flip of the coin—heads he turns off the machine and tails Dryden reveals Dr. Nowak's location. Paradise accepts but Dryden loses the bet. Dryden places and loses a series of bets. With each flip, the coin lands closer to the tiger's case. On the final bet, the tiger lunges at Paradise and mauls him. In the chaos, Dryden takes a gun from one of Paradise's men and uses it to shoot Paradise in the head. Paradise's guards are about to kill Dryden when Luke arrives.

Harwood and Bashir go to Syria, the likely location for Paradise's quantum computer. They find Dr. Nowak bound to a chair, near Paradise's computer and surrounded by his men.

Back in London, Mrs. Keator reveals that Moneypenny is inadvertently transmitting Harwood and Bashir's movements to the enemy. Aisha, one of Q's engineers, discovers a transmitting device planted in Moneypenny's office.

On the *Ark*, Lucky Luke kills Paradise's men and saves Dryden. Then, they make their way to the ship's engine room, and they overload the engine. As the circuits overload, a fire breaks out.

Colonel Mora's men capture Bashir. Mora taunts Bashir, who retaliates by biting off the tip of Mora's tongue. Then, Bashir strangles Mora. A gunfight ensues, and Harwood kills Mora's men. Harwood orders Dr. Nowak to shut Paradise's satellites down so that MI6 can locate the *Ark.* Nowak does as instructed and learns that Paradise's ship is in the Sea of Okhotsk. The still-living Mora grabs a gun and fires it at Harwood. Bashir throws himself in the bullet's trajectory.

On the *Ark,* Paradise's men start to overcome Dryden. At the last minute, friendly commandos, led by Japan's Secret Service agent Tiger Tanaka, arrive and kill Paradise's men. Dryden and Luke escape with Tanaka and Paradise's quantum computer sinks to the bottom of the ocean.

Harwood tries to save the gravely wounded Bashir. Realizing that Basir is about to die, they declare their love for each other and say their wedding vows. Shortly after that, Bashir dies. Harwood administers first aid to Mora so that she can extract information from him.

In London, M and Moneypenny discuss how the once-trusted Bill Tanner could have betrayed his country and colleagues. It turns out that Tanner had a son that was never disclosed to the Secret Service. The enemy learned that Tanner's son is a prisoner in England, and used the information to blackmail Tanner into helping them. His betrayal led to the death of the former 009 and Bashir, as well as Bond's capture. After being caught, Tanner kills himself.

In the Syrian caves, a task force arrives and captures Mora. Harwood searches the caves and finds an empty prison. The previous captive etched three numbers on the wall—007, giving hope that Bond might still be alive.

Commentary: "*Bond is missing,*" the cover of *Double or Die* declares. A key plot point of Kim Sherwood's novel is the search for 007 who has disappeared and is presumed dead. However, his presence is surprisingly palpable in a novel that is promoted as being sans Bond. In the same way that Marlon Brando's Don Corleone's presence is felt throughout *The Godfather Part II*, Bond casts a shadow over *Double Or Nothing.* Bond is mentioned frequently by the key characters, several of whom have relationships with him. He trains other Double O agents, while simultaneously performing missions with them. Moneypenny maintains her flirtatious relationship with him and when M retires, he hopes that Bond will replace him. It's not completely accurate to say that 007 doesn't appear in the book; he does but only in flashback sequences and in the characters' memories.

Bond, however, is not the hero of *Double Or Nothing*. That honor belongs to a new generation of Double O agents, including Johanna Harwood (003), who was studying to be a surgeon before she was recruited, Josephy Dryden (004), a veteran of the war in Afghanistan, and Aazar Siddig "Sid" Bashir (009), chess master and strategist. Sherwood also introduces Conrad Harthorp-Vane (000), privileged and tactless, and like Bond, an Etonian. Even the villain of the book, Colonel Mora, notices the change in protagonist and taunts Hardwood that she should forget about Bond. Mora tells Harwood, "Time to move on [from Bond.] You are the new hero of the Secret Service."

Mora is referring to Bond in the narrative and simultaneously breaking the fourth wall to refer to the fictional character and cultural figure. It's as if Mora is suggesting that Bond is no longer a relevant hero for modern audiences. Instead, he represents a bygone era when the British Empire was unstoppable, and colonialism was not questioned. Bond is described as "the poster boy for a waning empire." Paraphrasing Fleming in *From Russia with Love*, Mora taunts, "All of your country's strength lies in myth—the myth of the empire, the myth of Churchill, the myth of Scotland Yard and Sherlock Holmes. The myth of James Bond. Myths are built on heroic deeds and heroic people, perhaps. Or perhaps they were only ever fantasy."

Sherwood draws a direct line from James Bond, the literary figure, to Sherlock Holmes, who like Bond has been the hero of books, films, radio plays, comics, and audio dramas. The meta-commentary suggests that Bond is no longer as influential a cultural figure as he once was. Accepting the villain's (distasteful) premise, Sherwood's remit was to create new characters that would appeal to people of diverse backgrounds, identities, and experiences. While incorporating the typical Bond tropes, Sherwood also seems to be reinventing the series to ensure that it appeals to readers outside the Bond fan community.

On the surface, Harwood, Bashir, and Dryden are not like Bond at all. Harwood is a female agent, Bashir is Muslim, and Dryden is a gay Black man of Jamaican descent. Dryden suffered a war injury and requires a Q Branch-created listening device to hear. Thanks to Q Branch, his brain is effectively a super computer. Sherwood is opening up Bond's world to be more inclusive. She's allowing more readers to see themselves as heroes. Despite their apparent differences 003, 004, and 009 are similar to 007; they are all brave, selfless, and dedicated to Queen and Country. They can be framed using similar metaphors. If Bond is a "blunt" instrument, then Bashir is a "fine one" and Hardwood is a "scalpel."

Sherwood tips her hat to the Bond of the movies. Johanna Harwood is named after one of the screenwriters of *Dr. No* and *From Russia with Love.* The Harwood in *Double Or Nothing* is French-Irish and the real-life Harwood was born in Ireland and moved to France. Security officer Bob Simmons derives his name from the stunt performer who worked on many Eon Bond films and who appears as Bond in the gun barrel sequence in the first three Bond films. Bashir's name is a tip of the hat to Julian Bashir, the Starfleet officer in *Deep Space Nine*, who has a Bond movie-style adventure in the episode *Our Man Bashir.* Bond opts to refer to the head of the armory as Q, and not Major Boothroyd, as Fleming had. When considering historical Double O division traitors, Harwood recalls 006, who, like the character in the movie *Goldeneye*, betrayed the division.

Double Or Nothing is a stylish novel and Sherwood is unquestionably witty and filled with word play, playing one idea against another. To wit, if Bond is "not standing you *up* he's letting you *down.*;" Dryden distinguishes what "my brain *knows* and what my body *feels.*" Bond opines, " A man makes his own *luck.* A woman makes her own *choices.*' [Emphasis mine.] Sherwood writes that Triple O punches "come straight from childhood" and as if he's trying to take his opponent's "lunch money." A Q Branch science officer tells 004, "Give the demigod a kiss from us."

There is also plenty of romance in the novel. Dryden and Lucky Luke are romantically attracted to each other. Bashir and Harwood are also in love. One of Sherwood's most romantic lines occurs when 003 tells 009, "I love moving in time with you."

At 415 pages, *Double Or Nothing* is one of the longer Bond continuation novels. Faulks's Bond book is 295 pages, Boyd's is 322 pages, and Horowitz's are 304, 276, and 266. The only modern continuation novel that is longer is Deaver's at 428 pages. So Sherwood's book is more than 100 pages longer than the more recent efforts. Incidentally, both Deaver and Sherwood's books are set in the present.

It isn't entirely fair to compare the length of Sherwood's work to the other continuation novels. Readers are already rooting for Bond, a well-established character, before they even pick up a continuation novel. Sherwood doesn't have that luxury. Sherwood is introducing readers to a new cast of characters, and she needs the time and space to introduce them, reveal their backstories, put them on separate missions, and make readers care for them.

She also needs to establish a new villain for the Double O agents to battle. Sherwood invents Rattenfänger, a SPECTRE-like organization and pits her heroes against a tech-billionaire Sir Bertram Paradise who wants to use satellites to control the weather.

Sherwood must also establish the inner workings of the Double O Section, as it might exist today. Q is not a person; instead, it's the nickname for the service's super computer that is targeted to ferret out enemy action. Sherwood gives the security officer who operates the elevator a coded system to maneuver the lift between floors. Sherwood's creations include Mrs. Keator, the co-founder of Q Branch; two Q Branch engineers, Aisha Asante and Ibrahim Suleiman; and Sir Emery, as the new M. In keeping with the *Star Trek* connection, Sherwood revealed in interviews that Sir Emery's appearance is based, in part, on Patrick Stewart.[136] She also utilizes familiar faces; Moneypenny is running the Double O Section; Felix Leiter remains a crack-shot and a loyal friend to Bond; and Tiger Tanaka appears in a heroic third-act cameo.

The book, however, isn't truly a happy family reunion for all the legacy characters. Bond's best friend in the service, Bill Tanner, is revealed to be a traitor. Tanner never informed the Secret Service that he had a son, it turns out. The enemy utilized the fact that Tanner's hidden son is a prisoner as leverage to demand assistance from Tanner. Tanner's betrayal led to Bond's capture. The twist may anger some Bond aficionados who believe it to be a betrayal of the character. Here Sherwood is arguing that no person or institution is above reproach.

Double Or Nothing is the first book in Sherwood's trilogy and it's an implicit argument that other stories in Bond's universe are worth telling. As *The Washington Post* argues, "More than an addition to the canon, *Double Or Nothing* is an expansion of the universe and an exploration of how the Bond archetype can be channeled into other characters."[137] *Double Or Nothing* ends with Harwood finding proof that Bond might still be alive. The search for Bond continues in Sherwood's second book, *A Spy Like Me*. More crucially, Sherwood's first entry in a planned trilogy of novels ends on a thrilling note, and it extends an invitation to new readers to join the Bond literary community.

Continuity Nod: *Double Or Nothing* includes references to the Japanese cipher agent and the Norwegian double agent whom Bond killed to earn his Double O status, SMERSH, and the town Royale-les-Eaux, the fictional French town in *Casino Royale*. There are allusions to Bond and Tracy's trip past Rosenheim, Germany, and the visage of the white peaks ahead (*On Her Majesty's Secret Service*), and to Bond's expulsion from Eton (*You Only Live Twice*). Harwood visits

Shrublands (*Thunderball*) following her capture in Syria. Harwood knows that Felix Leiter once got the drop on Bond in New York and joked, "No good, James. The angels have got you" (*Diamonds Are Forever*) and again when Felix snuck into his hotel room (*Live and Let Die*). Bond participated in an op in France, which was dubbed Operation View to a Kill ("From a View to a Kill"). Sherwood uses the phrase "Icons are Forever," a reference to *Diamonds Are Forever.* Harwood and Felix encounter "Trigger," the sniper posing a cellist in "The Living Daylights."

Bond's Inner Life: Bond's philosophy is that "Life is nothing but a heap of six-to-four against, Penny. That doesn't mean I leave the table." The most fun part of any mission is the moment that it goes sideways.

Bond's Personal Life: Bond is older than 45, the mandatory retirement age, but he's still performing dangerous missions. Bond remains a bit of a cad, he spends more "nights in honeymoon suites than a onetime widower ought to." He still plays golf with Tanner; recently, he lost a game to Bill Tanner and owes his friend fifty pounds. Bond was in a relationship with Johanna Harwood. However, she left him and started dating 009. Harwood liked Bond because he was fun and made her laugh.

Bond's Tastes: Bond drives an Aston Martin. In keeping with Fleming, he likes gambling because he can become a master of luck and chance and not be a servant to them.

Bond's Work Life: After Miles Messervy retired, Sir Emery took over as head of MI6. Moneypenny runs the Double O Section and reports to Emery. Emery was initially something of an older brother figure to Bond. Yet later, like M, Emery became a father figure to 007. Bond is in charge of training the three agents in the division. He never knocks when entering Moneypenny's office; he just saunters in. Sherwood's M is a former Double O agent. Major Boothroyd has died; his headstone reads A Life in Service. Bill Tanner is divorced from his wife and had a son out of wedlock.

Life in the Double O Section is as dangerous as ever. 008 and 009 were both shot; 0011 is missing; 002, 0010, and 005 were all killed in action. The surviving agents sometimes blame themselves for their colleagues' misfortunes. Dryden blames himself for 005's death and Bashir feels like he failed to prevent 007 from falling into the enemy's hands. Double O agents are trained to hold their breath underwater for up to four minutes. Q Branch was founded by Major Boothroyd and Mrs. Keator.

Bond's Work Methods: Bond trains his recruits to believe that each agent has a "hurricane room" in their mind, that they can retreat to when the odds are insurmountable. The agents can take refuge there. He carries a Walther PPK. As Sherwood explained in her interview with David Zaritsky of *The Bond Experience*, the hurricane room is actually a Fleming invention.[138] Fleming used the term in *From Russia with Love* as a coping device that Bond uses when getting in stressful situations.

Moneypenny's New Job: Some Fleming purists pushed back on Sherwood's decision to make Moneypenny the head of the Double O division. Sherwood is not the only Bond luminary to believe that Moneypenny was due for a promotion. Upon Lois Maxwell's death, Sir Roger Moore suggested that perhaps the cinematic Moneypenny was also due a promotion, "It was a great pity that, after I moved out of Bond, they didn't take her on to continue in the Timothy Dalton films. I think it was a great disappointment to her that she had not been promoted to play M. She would have been a wonderful M."[139]

CHARLIE HIGSON'S TENURE—PART TWO
2023

ON HIS MAJESTY'S SECRET SERVICE (2023)

Author: Charlie Higson

In Brief: James Bond must prevent King Charles III's coronation from being thwarted by Æthelstan of Wessex, a wealthy eccentric who lays claim to the throne.

Meaning of Title: When King Charles III succeeded his mother Queen Elizabeth II, the Secret Service became his.

Chronology: Contemporary. Set between April and May 2023, a separate chronology from Higson's Young Bond series.

Operation: 848.

Bastard Meter: None for Bond. Although 007 refers to Æthelstan as a "cold, scheming bastard."

Eggs: Two scrambled eggs on wholemeal toast.

Insight into Bond: "There was only one person standing between them and chaos. James Bond."

Summary: May 4, 2023: Two days before the Coronation of Charles III, James Bond is assigned to protect the King. The King's aides include Flora Woodbridge. Bond scans the crowd for anyone who might be plotting to harm the monarch. The threat against Charles is linked to the death of 009, who was dating Miss Moneypenny until he was slain in Hungary. Bond has 26 minutes to figure out the identity of the traitor and stop the threat. He uses that time to recall the events that led him to this moment.

Flashback. M informs Bond that that a man who refers to himself as Æthelstan of Wessex, claims to be a descendent of King Alfred the Great and the rightful heir to the throne. Æthelstan might be using his private military force to disrupt the upcoming coronation. Earlier, 009 was dispatched to Hungary to infiltrate Æthelstan's castle. M thinks that before he was slain, 009 found something significant and hid it at the castle. M instructs Bond to go to the castle, locate the hidden item, and kill Æthelstan.

March 7: 2023: Sixty days before the Coronation. In Croatia, Marina Buehler is being driven in her car by her driver, Giorgio, and they are accompanied by a bodyguard named Carl. Three riders on motorcycles stop the vehicle and steal Marina's pocketbook and phone. Bond arrives on the scene, saves Marina, and scares off the attackers. Bond introduces himself as a security operative named Peter Sanbourne. Giving Marina his business card, "Sanbourne" encourages her to contact him if she ever needs a more capable security team.

March 23, 2023: Forty-four days before the Coronation. In Budapest, Bond is eating breakfast and is studying a fifty pence piece with a portrait of King Charles' profile engraved on it. Then, Bond takes a tram and looks out for any passengers who might be spying on him. A woman with a toddler and a couple of tough-looking men are among the passengers.

When Bond gets off and hides in a gift shop, he spots the woman from the tram on his tail. However, the woman is no longer carrying her child. Bond deduces that the child was just a prop to divert suspicion from her. Pretending to be a tourist, Bond approaches the phony mom and uses his Q Branch issued phone to clone the woman's phone.

Bond goes to the 360 Bar to meet his contact. Using information from the woman's phone, Bond learns that her name is Ragnheiður Ragnarsdóttir and she's in the security division of an investment fund named The White Dragon Sovereign Nation Institute. Bond's contact, Canner Lyle, arrives. Lyle is there on behalf of his boss, whose wife he rescued in Croatia. Lyle tells Bond that he has a job for him.

April 11, 2023: With 25 days until the Coronation, Bond goes to Æthelstan's castle, which is nestled in the Zemplén Mountains in Hungary. Upon arrival, he is greeted by Canner who tells Bond that he is invited to a dinner and a reception that night. Before the reception, Bond keeps an eye out for clues on where 009 would have hidden the information on Æthelstan that he discovered.

At the reception, Bond meets John Tyler, an extremist libertarian, an aristocrat named Lord Anthony Saxewell-Brooks, who has picked up the nickname Lord Bonkers, and Renaud Caiboche, an ex-French Foreign Legionnaire. Then, Bond greets Marina, whose life he recently saved. It turns out that Marina was never in danger; instead, Bond and three operatives from Special Operations staged the threat against her life to gain Marina's confidence. Ragnheiður arrives and greets Bond and then Æthelstan makes his entrance. Æthelstan addresses his guests and makes a speech suggesting that the greatest threat to England comes from its citizens with progressive agendas. He argues that it's time that the people take back control of the country and let its King properly rule the people. He threatens to disrupt the coronation and eventually shut down Buckingham Palace and Parliament. Æthelstan claims that he is the rightful next King of England.

Later that evening, Bond meets Æthelstan's, who welcomes him to Operation 848. The operation, about which Bond will be briefed tomorrow, involves an unspecified attack on London.

Ragnheiður visits Bond in his room and, for the sake of the hidden cameras, she pretends to seduce him. After using her robe to cover up the cameras, Ragnheiður hands Bond a slip of paper. The paper explains that she's also working to bring down Æthelstan. She provides Bond with 009's secret code word "Persimmon," a word once uttered to signal that 009 completely trusted her. Bond realizes that he wasn't looking for something, he was looking for someone, namely Ragnheiður.

April 12, 2023: With 24 days left until King Charles' coronation, Bond meets with Captain Nick Cornwell, an ally, to discuss how to thwart Operation 848. They discuss where they will put their explosive charges. Bond learns that Æthelstan's castle is outfitted to be a broadcasting center and it's filled with sophisticated computers and mainframes, as his attack will both be a physical war and a digital one. Bond and Cornwell coordinate their attack so that Bond goes after Æthelstan, and Cornwell's men go after the computer substation.

That night, there is a knock on Bond's door. When he answers it, he sees Ragnheiður, Lyle, Æthelstan, and his men, including Canner, the enforcer. They know that Bond is a spy and not a security expert. They take Bond to the broadcasting center, where he will record a video confession indicating that he's a spy. Before the recording takes place Æthelstan admits to Bond that he knows that he can't become King. However, for his plan to work, he just needs to fool the public into believing that he could be. His real plan actually involves ruining the British economy by disrupting the coronation, which bankers believe will help market forces. Once the British economy is in ruin, he will come in as its savior.

Bond begins to confess when an explosion goes off and the lights cut out. Ragnheiður cuts Bond free. Bond and Ragnheiður try to fight their way out. Ragnheiður gets knocked out and Bond overcomes

Canner. Æthelstan grabs a gun and shoots Bond in the leg. Desperate for a weapon, the otherwise unarmed Bond takes out the fifty-pence piece with King Charles' portrait on it and throws it to Æthelstan. When the coin knocks Æthelstan off balance, Bond overcomes and disarms him.

Bond and Ragnheiður watch as Æthelstan's men engage the British forces in combat. Æthelstan's flees in a car during the chaos. Bond and Ragnheiður commandeer a vehicle and chase after him. Meanwhile, Cornwell and his men destroy Æthelstan's mainframes.

When Bond catches up to Æthelstan's car, Ragnheiður shoots out his tires. Æthelstan tells Bond that even though he's caught, it's too late for Bond to stop his secret master plan. Bond kills Æthelstan by snapping his neck because he doesn't want him to live on as a symbol for his twisted cause.

May 4, 2013: Two days before the Coronation, Bond is on King Charles' protection detail, scanning the crowd for potential threats. Even though Æthelstan is dead, Bond is certain Æthelstan has a backup plan in effect. Bond wonders what the connection is between Operation 848 and Æthelstan's birthday, which is on May 4th, the date of the potential attack. Ragnheiður speculates the operation will be conducted at 8:48 a.m.

King Charles is taken into a safe room between the hours of 8:40 a.m. and 9 p.m. At 8:46 a.m., Bond receives a message from Ragnheiður, indicating that Æthelstan has a daughter named Christina Hayes, who has subsequently changed her name to Flora Woodbridge. Bond realizes that Flora matches the description of a person in the King's party who is carrying His Majesty's special pen. Bond detains Flora who tries to kill Bond by stabbing him with the poison pen. Bond disables Flora, ensuring King Charles' safety.

Two days later. With the King out of harm's way and the Coronation over, Bond and Ragnheiður continue with their relationship. However, both of them know that it won't lead anywhere.

Commentary: Charlie Higson's Young Bond books surprised adult readers by showing his knowledge and affinity for the character. So it's not surprising that since their publication, Bond fans have been clamoring for Higson to write more books set in 007's world. There had been a sustained and informal campaign on social media for him to write another book. Fans initially assumed that, if their prayers were answered, Higson's next book would either be set in Young Bond years or he might set the book during Bond's war service. Another possibility is that Higson would write about the adult Bond and set the books in the 1950s or 1960s as other continuation authors have done. Still, not all fan campaigns are successful. Most aren't.

So fans were delighted when on March 31, 2023, Ian Fleming Publications announced that Charlie Higson would write a new Bond work *On His Majesty's Secret Service,* and that it would be published on May 4, 2023, roughly five weeks later. The press release included several welcome surprises. Higson's story would not be a Young Bond work; it would be about the adult Bond. Perhaps more unexpected, it would not be a period piece; it would be set in the present. Finally, *On His Majesty's Secret Service* wouldn't be a novel or even a short story; instead, it would be a novella, a first in Bond literature.

On His Majesty's Secret Service was timed to be released on the eve of King Charles III's coronation. As such, it was only fitting that the story would be about a villain's sinister plan to disrupt the event. The novella is only 161 pages long. As such, the story is fairly lean. Nary a martini is served. Higson dispenses with the usual bells and whistles of the typical Bond novel and strips the story to its essence. There are a couple of relevant callbacks to Fleming's books but for the most part *On His Majesty's Secret Service* is devoid of references to Bond's past loves and villains. A passage of the book reads, "There was no room for finesse, for careful plotting, for negotiation. He was a bullet and he'd already been fired from the gun." Higson wrote this about the nature of Bond's fraught mission, but the same could be said for the plot itself.

The structure is also atypical for a Bond book. When the story opens, Bond is already on the main mission. He needs to identify the threat to King Charles and he only has 26 minutes before the villain's operation begins. So the bulk of the book is a flashback, with Bond going over the events that led him to that moment, to review the clues and thwart the potential killer. Other authors, including Fleming, have started with Bond mid-mission, but Higson might be the only one to kick off the book near the story's climax.

The eccentric and pretender to the throne, Æthelstan of Wessex, is Bond's main enemy. To win over supporters, the Æthelstan of Wessex resorts to hate speech and fascist rhetoric. Eventually, it becomes clear that his rhetoric was a smoke screen, a way to gain influence. Some fans pushed back at the perceived politics of the novella. However, Higson countered that his Bond is fighting extremism in all forms and not specifically criticizing the left or the right. Higson argues that Fleming's writing was political, citing passages from *Casino Royale* and *From Russia with Love* as instances of how 007's political beliefs are exposed. Higson also reminds us that Fleming stated in his 1962 *Playboy* interview, "I should think what politics [Bond] has are just a little bit left of center."[140]

On His Majesty's Secret Service was an unexpected hit for Ian Fleming Publications, it appeared on the *Times* best-seller list, and it quickly went into its second printing. Its success may have a lesson for us. As noted, the book wasn't what any of the Bond fans previously demanded or expected. It doesn't fit in any established mold in the Bond canon. Yet, it was embraced. The experiment may have shown us that the best way for Ian Fleming Publications to satisfy fans is not to give them what they believe they want, but rather what they didn't know they needed.

Continuity Nod: Bond already has a working knowledge of Coats of Arms and heraldry because he needed to study them in *On His Majesty's Secret Service.* In response to a question about how much time they have to foil Æthelstan's plans, Bond bemoans the fact that they don't have "all the time in the world." A character in the story is Ranaud Caiboche, who shares the same last name as General Charles Caiboche, the villain in Higson's short story "A Hard Man to Kill."

Bond's History: Bond has been stabbed in the stomach and had a section of his colon removed during life-saving surgery. He's been to Budapest before. One assignment took him to the Hungarian Opera House where he eliminated an enemy agent.

Bond's Personal Life: After Bond and Ragnheiður left Hungary they continued a romantic relationship, even though Bond is dating a woman named Yasmin. By mutual agreement, his relationship with Yasmin is strictly sexual; they don't discuss their private lives with each other. Yasmin is a lawyer who specializes in immigration law, and she believes that Bond works for the Foreign, Commonwealth & Development Office. Bond, like everyone in his office, has to notify his superiors when he's dating someone regularly. The person is vetted to make sure that they haven't been sent by the opposition to compromise the agent.

Bond's Inner Life: Bond typically experiences post-mission melancholy. Keeping busy in his personal life aids in warding off negative emotions. However, being assigned to another assignment is the only remedy.

Bond's Tastes: He likes good champagne but doesn't believe that there is a direct correlation between quality and price. He's not particular about the whiskey he drinks. He doesn't enjoy William Shakespeare's comedies, faux-medieval banquets, or modern dance and he's never read *Moby Dick.* He relies on the metric system and avoids using imperial measurements like feet and inches. Bond prefers to eat a light meal and he's mindful of his gut health, so he eats foods rich in fiber and fruit, including yogurt and kimchi. He plays squash and tennis, and he goes on runs and swims. He doesn't wear clothes with logos on them.

Bond's Work Methods: SIS's tech geniuses scrub the internet for any clue to Bond's identity and chosen profession. The techs can create a solid internet persona for him to support his cover story while he is on a mission. Agents have a private "safe word" that they only reveal to people they are certain they can trust. When another agent hears that safe term, they know that the person was deemed unimpeachable. When an agent is concealing information for another agent, the item should be hidden in plain sight rather than in an obscure place that will never be found. Since fist fights are painful, Bond will try to avoid them whenever possible. He will only fight as a last resort. Bond now carries a Glock 17 9mm.

Assorted Observations:

- Higson's *On His Majesty's Secret Service* is set a few years after the events of *On Her Majesty's Secret Service*, as if the events in Fleming's novel occurred in the 21st Century and not the 1960s.
- As he did for his Young Bond novels, Higson narrated the approximately four-and-a-half-hour-long audiobook.

AFTERWORD: PARTING SHOTS

I hesitate to attempt to encapsulate the entire Bond literary canon in a few scant paragraphs. In a follow-up volume, I will compare different tenures and assess the similarities and differences across the entire series. It will also include interviews with many of the continuation authors. But for now, I will say that each author has brought something distinctive and memorable to the literary Bond.

Amis established that other authors could do the seemingly impossible and follow in Ian Fleming's footsteps. Arthur Calder-Marshall introduced children to Bond's dangerous world. Christopher Wood brought the movie Bond closer to the literary hero. John Gardner introduced the character to modern times and kept 007 in print for nearly two decades. Raymond Benson combined his version of Fleming's spy with movie-style adventures and drew on his encyclopedic knowledge of all things 007.

Charlie Higson wrote a nuanced and revealing look at Bond's formative years. Steve Cole emphasized the fun and excitement of Bond's school days. Samantha Weinberg gave Miss Moneypenny a rich and complex inner life.

Sebastian Faulks experimented by writing an entire novel that aspired to capture Fleming's voice. Deaver brought Bond to the 21st century with his potboiler that could serve as an entry for new readers. William Boyd pulled back the layers on Bond's character and forced the spy to confront his 45th birthday. Anthony Horowitz's work spans his version of Bond's whole career as a Double O agent.

Kim Sherwood expanded Bond's world and invited new heroes to share the spotlight with him. Charlie Higson returned to write a piece that reflected the times and that defied expectations in both its form (a novella) and structure (told through flashbacks).

For over fifty years, Ian Fleming Publications has delivered an appealing variety of undeniable Bond stories.

Until we meet again, grab a Bond continuation novel—any one will do—and dive in. There's a Bond novel out there for all tastes and interests.

The James Bond Continuation Novels Will Return.

HISTORIC ADVERTISING AND PROMOTIONAL MATERIALS

Promotional piece for *Colonel Sun.*
Courtesy of Gary J. Firuta

Colonel Sun advertisement.
Courtesy of John Cox, The Book Bond

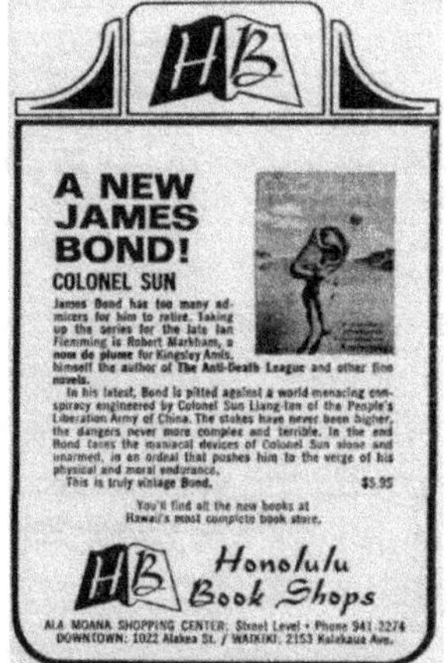

Colonel Sun advertisement.
Courtesy of John Cox, The Book Bond

Promotion piece for *Colonel Sun.*
Courtesy of Dave Tulley

Advertisement for
John Pearson's book excerpt
in the *Sunday Telegraph.*
Courtesy of Gary J. Firuta

MEMORANDUM

Back of the US hardcover edition of
John Pearson's "authorized biography."
Bond provides his thoughts on the book.
"Very good—I enjoyed it a lot. There are no errors..."
Courtesy of John Cox, The Book Bond

Promo for Christopher Wood's novelization.
Courtesy of Gary J. Firuta

Finally. . .
After Fourteen Long Years. . .
007 has had his
LICENSE RENEWED

IAN FLEMING'S
JAMES BOND
LICENSE RENEWED

A major new villain is capturing nuclear power plants all over the world. . .holding them for ransom. . .threatening the world with catastrophic meltdown. Who can save us? There is only one man: a man who treats his body like a finely honed tool that needs careful attention. . .a man who knows what he wants from machines, situations, and people, and knows how to get it. . .a man who has the morals of a hero, but is not afraid to kill for his country. . .a man so trusted by those in power he is the sole surviving British secret agent retaining his "Double-Oh" prefix number—his License to Kill. The world's greatest super-spy: James Bond, 007!

John Gardner, the author of many successful and acclaimed thrillers, has been selected by Ian Fleming's estate to carry on the fine tradition of transcribing the missions of James Bond, and he has brought his considerable talents to the task while retaining the wonderful Flemingesque touches of minute detail, lovingly particular description, and driving purposefulness. There is intelligent humor, thrilling gadgets, and wonderful women—and a horrible villain with a grim task.

ORDER TODAY FOR A SPECIAL DISCOUNT

Send Money Orders to the James Bond 007 Fan Club, PO Box 414, Bronxville, N.Y. 10708 USA
New York State residents add sales tax.

Name:
Address:
City: State:
Zip Code: Country:

Advertisement for *License Renewed,*
distributed to members of
Richard Schenkman's
James Bond 007 Fan Club.
Courtesy of Gary J. Firuta

Advertisement for
License Renewed.
Courtesy of Gary J. Firuta

"This equipment used by
James Bond in his latest spy novel,
License Renewed."
Courtesy of Gary J. Firuta

Saab advertisement.
Courtesy of Gary J. Firuta

Saab advertisement.
Courtesy of Gary J. Firuta

New York Post heralds their excerpt of *License Renewed.*
Courtesy of Gary J. Firuta

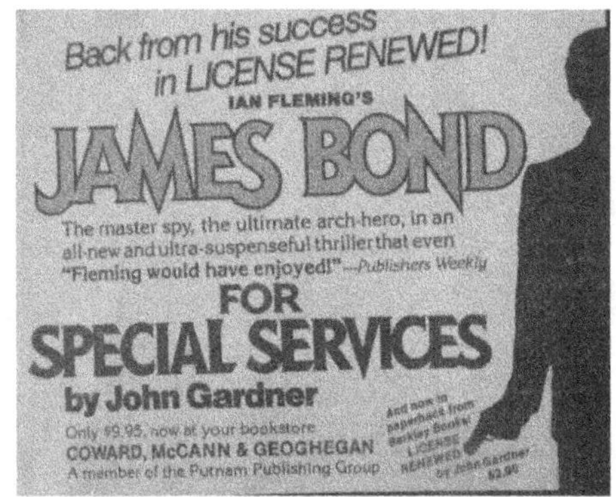

Advertisement for
For Special Services.
Courtesy of Gary J. Firuta

Advertisement for
For Special Services.
Courtesy of Gary J. Firuta

Advertisement for Bond books
by John Gardner & Ian Fleming.
Courtesy of Brendan Edwards

Ad for *Icebreaker* in
The Literary Guild,
a mail-order book club.
Courtesy of Gary J. Firuta

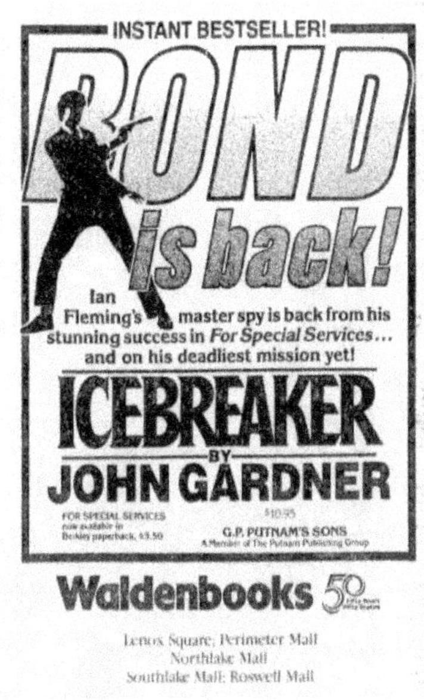

Icebreaker advertisement.
Courtesy of Gary G. Firuta

Role of Honour poster.
Courtesy of Robin Harbour

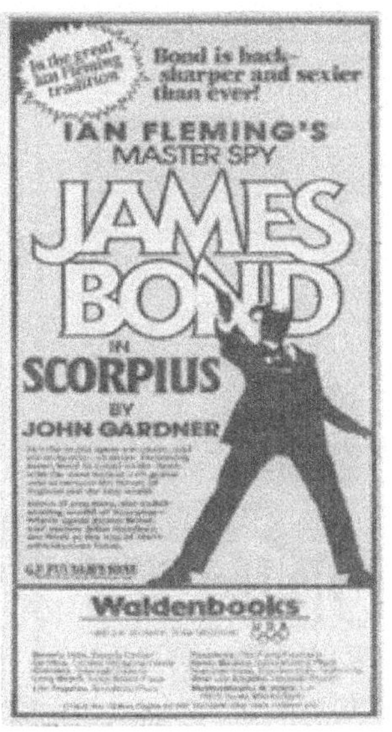

Scorpius advertisement.
Courtesy of John Cox, The Book Bond

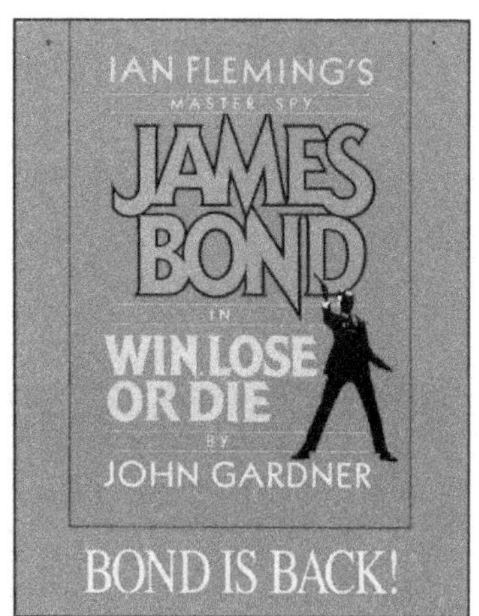

Win, Lose or Die promotional art.
Courtesy of Gary J. Firuta

Ad for *Win, Lose or Die,* in the *License to Kill* novelization.
Author Collection

Promotional fan for *Brokenclaw.*
Courtesy of a Bond fan

Uncorrected proof for *High Time to Kill.*
Courtesy of John Cox, The Book Bond

Pen and ink by Kev Walker
for a scene from *Blood Fever.*
Courtesy of John Cox, The Book Bond

UK proof edition of *Double or Die.*
Courtesy of John Cox, The Book

Young Bond collectors cards.
Courtesy of
John Cox, The Book Bond

Ad for Steve Cole's *Shoot to Kill* and the entire
Young Bond series up to that point.
Courtesy of Gary J. Firuta

Devil May Care ad campaign.
Courtesy of John Cox, The Book Bond

Promotional art for
Jeffery Deaver's
Carte Blanche.
Courtesy of Gary J. Firuta

Forever and a Day advertisement.
Courtesy of John Cox, The Book Bond

APPENDIX 1
JAMES BOND WORKS BY AUTHOR

The publication dates provided are for the United Kingdom. The dates in the United States are not necessarily the same year. As noted, Samantha Weinberg's *The Moneypenny Diaries: Guardian Angel* was published in the UK in 2005 but when it was released in the U.S. in 2008 it was called *The Moneypenny Diaries*. Kim Sherwood's *Double Or Nothing* was published in the UK in 2022 and in the U.S. in 2023.

By Ian Fleming
Casino Royale (1953)
Live And Let Die (1954)
Moonraker (1955)
Diamonds Are Forever (1956)
From Russia, With Love (1957)
Dr. No (1958)
Goldfinger (1959)
For Your Eyes Only (1960)
(Collecting the short stories "From A View To A Kill," "For Your Eyes Only," "Risico," "Quantum Of Solace," and "The Hildebrand Rarity")
Thunderball (1961)
The Spy Who Loved Me (1962)
On Her Majesty's Secret Service (1963)
"007 in New York" (1963)
You Only Live Twice (1964)
The Man With The Golden Gun (1965)
Octopussy and The Living Daylights (1966)

By Arthur Calder-Marshall
The Adventures of James Bond Junior 003½ (1967)

By Kingsley Amis
Colonel Sun (1968)

By John Pearson
James Bond: The Authorized Biography Of 007 (1973)

By Christopher Wood
James Bond, The Spy Who Loved Me (1977)
James Bond and Moonraker (1979)

By John Gardner
Licence Renewed (1981)
For Special Services (1982)
Icebreaker (1983)
Role of Honour (1984)
Nobody Lives For Ever (1986)
No Deals, Mr. Bond (1987)
Scorpius (1988)
Licence To Kill (1989)
Win, Lose or Die (1989)
Brokenclaw (1990)
The Man From Barbarossa (1991)
Death Is Forever (1992)
Never Send Flowers (1993)
SeaFire (1994)
GoldenEye (1995)
COLD (UK), Cold Fall (US) (1996)

By Raymond Benson
"Blast From The Past" (1997) (Short Story)
Zero Minus Ten (1997)
Tomorrow Never Dies (1997)
The Facts of Death (1998)
High Time To Kill (1999)
"A Midsummer's Night's Doom" (1999) (Short Story)
"Live At Five" (1999) (Short Story)
The World Is Not Enough (1999)
DoubleShot (2000)
Never Dream of Dying (2001)
"The Heart of Erzulie" (2001) (Short story, unpublished in its original form)
The Man with the Red Tattoo (2002)
Die Another Day (2002)

By Charlie Higson
SilverFin (2005)
Blood Fever (2006)
Double or Die (2007)
Hurricane Gold (2007)
By Royal Command (2008)
"A Hard Man To Kill" (2009)
On His Majesty's Secret Service (2023)

By Steve Cole
Shoot to Kill (2014)
Heads You Die (2016)
Strike Lightning (2016)
Red Nemesis (2017)

By Samantha Weinberg
Guardian Angel (2005)
Secret Servant (2006)
"Moneypenny's First Date with Bond" (2006; Short Story)
"For Your Eyes Only" (2006; Short Story)
Final Fling (2008)
Collection: The Moneypenny Diaries: Secret Chapters (2020) contains the 2006 "Moneypenny's First Date with Bond" and "For Your Eyes Only"

By Sebastian Faulks
Devil May Care (2008)

By Jeffery Deaver
Carte Blanche (2011)

By William Boyd
Solo (2013)

By Anthony Horowitz
Trigger Mortis (2015)
Forever and a Day (2018)
With a Mind to Kill (2022)

By Kim Sherwood
Double Or Nothing (2022)
A Spy Like Me (2024)

Other Notable Bond Stories
"Some Are Born Great" by two-time Bond screenwriter Johanna Harwood (1960)
The James Bond Dossier by Kingsley Amis (1965)
The Book of Bond or, Every Man His Own 007 by Kingsley Amis (1965)
Per Fine Ounce by Geoffrey Jenkins (1968, unpublished)
"James Bond Goes to Sainsbury's" by Sebastian Faulks (2002)
"Ian Fleming Thinks Even James Bond Goes Shopping" by Sebastian Faulks (2006).
Danger Society: The Young Bond Dossier (2009) with a short story by Charlie Higson
"William Boyd Interviews James Bond" (2013) by William Boyd.
"William Boyd Q&A with James Bond" (2013) by William Boyd.

APPENDIX 2:
RUNDOWN OF THE CONTINUATION WORKS

I thought it would be useful to offer a brief overview of each work, given the vast number of stories. I include a summary and break down the characters into several categories, including Heroine, Villian, and Love Interest. Drawing on Dr. Lisa Funnell's scholarship of gender and feminism in Bond, I wanted to avoid using the term "Bond Women" to describe the varied roles that women play. Instead, I wanted to distinguish between how each character functions. "Bond Women" can be villains, heroes, or love interests, among other roles and their function can change throughout the narrative. So categorizing them by their nature is imprecise and myopic. When the women represent more than one category, I include them in each.

The Adventures of James Bond Junior 003½
Premise: 007's nephew, James Bond Junior, suspects his new neighbor of stealing gold bullion and concealing it on his property.
Author: Arthur Calder-Marshall
Published: 1967
Heroine: Sheelagh Smith
Love Interest: Sheelagh Smith
Villain: Mr. Merck
Henchman: Donal

Colonel Sun
Premise: Bond must rescue M who has been kidnapped by the sadistic Colonel Sun Liang-tan of the People's Liberation Army.
Author: Kingsley Amis
Published: 1968
Heroine: Ariadne Alexandrou
Love Interest: Ariadne Alexandrou
Villain: Colonel Sun Liang-tan and Von Richter

James Bond: The Authorized Biography of 007
Premise: Bond tells a biographer his life story.
Author: John Pearson
Published: 1973
Love Interest: Honeychile Rider, current and Marthe de Brandt plus appearances by most of his previous romantic partners.
Villain: Irma Bunt current, plus appearances by nearly every major Bond baddie.

James Bond, The Spy Who Loved Me
Premise: Bond teams with Soviet agent Anya Amasova to retrieve two stolen nuclear submarines.
Author: Christopher Wood
Published: 1977
Heroine: Anya Amasova
Villain: Sigmund Stromberg
Henchman: Jaws

James Bond and Moonraker
Premise: Bond is sent to investigate the hijacking of Hugo Drax's space shuttle, the *Moonraker*.
Author: Christopher Wood
Published: 1979
Heroine: Holly Goodhead
Villain: Hugo Drax
Henchman: Jaws

Licence Renewed
Premise: James Bond is sent to investigate a physicist who is determined to set off six nuclear reactors if his ransom demands are not met.
Author: John Gardner
Published: 1981
Love Interest: Lavender Peacock
Villain: Anton Murik
Henchman: Caber

For Special Services
Premise: Bond must discover if Markus Bismaquer, a wealthy ice cream manufacturer, is connected to the newly reconstituted SPECTRE, which appears to be led by Ernst Stavro Blofeld. Bond is aided on this mission by Felix Leiter's daughter, Cedar Leiter.
Author: John Gardner
Published: 1982
Heroine: Cedar Leiter
Love Interest: Nena Bismaquer (later revealed to be Nena Blofeld)
Villain: Nena Blofeld and Markus Bismaquer
Henchman: Walter Luxor

Icebreaker
Premise: Bond teams up with agents from the CIA, KGB, and Mossad to stop the rise of a neo-Nazi group who are conducting assassinations and dispensing armaments from their hidden base on the Russia-Finland border.

Icebreaker (cont'd.)
Author: John Gardner
Published: 1983
Heroine: Paula Vacker
Love Interest: Rivke Ingber (aka Anni Tudeer)
Villain: Aarne Tudeer (aka Count Konrad von Glöda)

Role of Honour
Premise: Bond pretends to resign from SIS so that he can work for the enemy, a SPECTRE agent who is using computer games technology to execute criminal and terrorist enterprises.
Author: John Gardner
Published: 1984
Heroine: Cindy Chalmer
Love Interest: Persephone "Percy" Proud
Villain: Dr. Jay Autem Holy and Tamil Rahani

Nobody Lives For Ever (aka Nobody Lives Forever)
Premise: When SPECTRE puts out a contract on 007's life, Bond must evade numerous assassination attempts by the world's best hitmen. Bond must also rescue Miss Moneypenny and his housekeeper, May, from kidnappers.
Author: John Gardner
Published: 1986
Heroine: Nannette 'Nannie' Norrich (at least for a while)
Love Interest: Principessa Sukie Tempesta
Villain: Tamil Rahani
Henchman: Paul "the Rat" Cordava and Heinrich "The Hook" Osten

No Deals, Mr. Bond
Premise: After two assets are brutally murdered, Bond must protect the remaining members of Operation Cup Cake, an old initiative in which five German civilians attracted enemy operatives, learnt their secrets, and gave them to the British.
Author: John Gardner
Published: 1987
Love Interest: Ebbie Heritage
Villains: General Konstantin Nikolaevich Chernov and Heather Dare

Scorpius
Premise: Bond is dispatched to look into the murder of a well-connected woman who had recently joined the Meek Ones, a deadly religious cult that is run by the world's most dangerous armaments trader, Vladimir Scorpius.

Scorpius (cont'd.)
Author: John Gardner
Published: 1988
Heroine: Harriett Horner
Love Interest: Harriett Horner
Villain: Vladimir Scorpius/Father Valentine

Win, Lose or Die
Premise: Bond must defend a Royal Navy aircraft carrier holding a conference of international leaders from an attack by the terrorist group BAST.
Author: John Gardner
Published: 1989
Heroine: Beatrice Maria da Ricci
Love Interest: Beatrice Maria da Ricci and Nikola Ratinokov
Villains: Bassam Baradj, Abou Hamarik, and Saphii Boudai aka Clover Pennington

Licence to Kill
Premise: Bond goes rogue to get vengeance on the drug lord who mutilated his friend, Felix Leiter.
Author: John Gardner
Published: 1989
Heroine: Pam Bouvier
Villain: Franz Sanchez
Henchman: Dario

Brokenclaw
Premise: Bond is sent to investigate a possible connection between a charismatic mob boss who supplies information to Chinese Intelligence, Brokenclaw Lee, and the disappearance of naval experts working on a submarine detection system. Along the way, Bond discovers that Brokenclaw is working on a scheme to destabilize the American dollar by manipulating the stock market.
Author: John Gardner
Published: 1990
Heroine: Sue Chi-Ho, aka Chi-Chi Sue
Love Interest: Wanda Man Song Hing
Villain: Brokenclaw Lee/Lee Fu-Chu
Henchman: Bone Bender Ding

The Man from Barbarossa
Premise: James Bond and Mossad agent, Pete Natkowitz, are sent to infiltrate the Scales of Justice terrorist group who are putting a war criminal on trial as a

The Man from Barbarossa (cont'd.)
smokescreen for their true plans to destabilize the Soviet Union and install their own Soviet leader.
Author: John Gardner
Published: 1991
Heroine: Nina Bibikova
Love Interest: Nina Bibikova
Villain: General Yevgeny Yuskovitch

Death Is Forever
Premise: Bond teams with CIA agent, Easy St. John, to find out who is killing off a shuttered spy network. Along the way, Bond discovers a scheme to kill twelve world leaders as they ride a train through the Chunnel and install a Stalinist regime in their place.
Author: John Gardner
Published:1992
Heroine: Elizabeth "Easy" St. John
Love Interest: Elizabeth "Easy" St. John
Villain: Wolfgang Weisen

Never Send Flowers
Premise: Bond is dispatched to look into a string of brutal killings that appear to be related to a well-known actor. The serial killer must be stopped before he can target the Royal family at Euro Disney.
Author: John Gardner
Published:1993
Heroine: Fredericka "Flicka" von Grüsse
Love Interest: Fredericka "Flicka" von Grüsse
Villain: David Dragonpol

SeaFire
Premise: James Bond and Fredericka von Grüsse looks into Sir Maximilian Tarn, a philanthropist and industrialist who wants to revive the Nazi party.
Author: John Gardner
Published: 1994
Heroine: Fredericka "Flicka" von Grüsse
Love Interest: Fredericka "Flicka" von Grüsse
Villain: Tarn
Henchman: Mr. Archibald and Mr. Cuthbert, aka Anna and Caty

GoldenEye
Premise: When a mysterious figure known as Janus steals the GoldenEye technology, Bond is sent to recover it before Janus can use it to topple England's financial institutions.
Author: John Gardner
Published: 1995
Heroine: Natalya Simonova
Love Interest: Natalya Simonova
Villain: Alec Trevelyan, 006
Henchman: Xenia Onatopp

COLD (aka Cold Fall)
Premise: Bond must determine how a terrorist attack on an airline is connected to a new criminal organization called COLD, which is hell-bent on destabilizing the American government.
Author: John Gardner
Published:1996
Heroine: Beatrice Maria da Ricci
Love Interest: Fredericka "Flicka" von Grüsse,
Villains: General Brutus Clay and Sukie Tempesta

"Blast from the Past"
Premise: Bond investigates the death of his only son James Suzuki, who was killed by his old foe Irma Bunt.
Author: Raymond Benson
Published:1997
Heroine: Cheryl Haven
Love Interest: Cheryl Haven
Villain: Irma Bunt
Henchman: Hans and Josef

Zero Minus Ten
Premise: On the eve of the handover of Hong Kong to China, Bond is sent to Pearl of the Orient to see if a shipping firm named EurAsia Enterprises is connected to a series of terrorist attacks.
Author: Raymond Benson
Published: 1997
Heroine: Sunni Pei
Love Interest: Sunni Pei
Villain: Guy Thackeray
Henchmen: The Chang brothers, three albino twins, which Bond nicknames Tom, Dick, and Harry.

Tomorrow Never Dies
Premise: Bond and Chinese Agent Wai Lin join forces to bring down a media mogul who is trying to start a war between the British and Chinese governments.
Author: Raymond Benson
Published: 1997
Heroine: Wai Lin
Love Interest: Paris Carver
Villain: Elliot Carver
Henchman: Stamper

"The Facts of Death"
Premise: After M's boyfriend is killed, Bond travels to Austin and Greece to see if his death is connected to a series of terrorist attacks involving a deadly toxin that is connected to The Decada, a cult that is based on mathematical principles.
Published: 1998
Heroine: Niki Markos
Love Interest: Niki Markos
Villain: Konstantine Romanos and Hera Volopoulos
Henchman: Vassilis Romanos

"Midsummer Night's Doom"
Premise: James Bond must attend a party in the Playboy mansion to retrieve stolen secrets that are being sold to the Russian Mafia.
Author: Raymond Benson
Published: 1999
Love Interest: Lisa Dergan
Villain: Anton Redenius
Henchman: Estragon

High Time to Kill
Premise: Bond must climb the world's third-highest mountain in order to locate a plane that contains military secrets.
Author: Raymond Benson
Published: 1999
Heroine: Heather Dare
Love Interest: Helena Marksbury
Villain: Roland Marquis and The Union

"Live at Five"
Premise: Bond helps an Olympic skater from the U.S.S.R. defect on live television.
Author: Raymond Benson
Published: 1999

"Live at Five" (cont'd.)
Heroine: Janet Davies
Love Interest: Janet Davies
Villain: The Russians

The World Is Not Enough
Premise: Bond is sent to protect M's family friend Elektra King from a madman who once kidnapped her.
Author: Raymond Benson
Published: 1999
Heroine: Dr. Christmas Jones
Love Interest; Elektra King and Dr. Christmas Jones
Villain: Elektra King and Victor "Renard" Zokas

DoubleShot
Premise: James Bond must stop his doppelganger from carrying out a plot to kill the Prime Ministers of Britain and Spain during a peace conference. If he fails, an ex-bullfighter and current mafia leader will become the next Governor of Gibraltar and Bond will be blamed for the assassinations.
Author: Raymond Benson
Published:2000
Heroine: Heidi Taunt and Hedy Taunt
Love Interest: Heidi Taunt and Hedy Taunt
Villain: Le Gérant and Domingo Espada
Henchman: Margareta Piel, aka the Praying Mantis

Never Dream of Dying
Premise: 007 must stop Union head Le Gérant from carrying out a plot to blow up a movie premiere during the Cannes Film Festival; 007 also confronts his ex-father-in-law Marc-Ange Draco, who is trying to eliminate him.
Author: Raymond Benson
Published: 2001
Love Interest: Tylyn Mignonne
Villain: Le Gérant and Marc-Ange Draco

The Man with the Red Tattoo
Premise: Bond travels to Japan where mosquitoes carrying a deadly virus are being used to kill members of an international conference. Simultaneously, Bond reunites with his old friend Tiger Tanaka.
Author: Raymond Benson
Published: 2002
Heroine: Reiko Tamura
Love Interest: Reiko Tamura

The Man with the Red Tattoo (cont'd.)
Villain: Goro Yoshida and Shinji Fujimoto
Henchman: Junji Kon, aka Kappa.

Die Another Day
Premise: Bond investigates a wealthy and beloved industrialist who seems to be developing a space weapon called the Icarus for nefarious purposes.
Author: Raymond Benson
Published: 2002
Heroine: Giacinta 'Jinx' Johnson
Love Interest: Miranda Frost
Villain: Gustav Graves, Miranda Frost
Henchman: Zao

SilverFin
Premise: 13-year-old James Bond attends his first year at Eton College and uncovers Lord Hellebore's plan to inject a serum into soldiers as a way to make them superhuman.
Author: Charlie Higson
Published: 2005
Heroine: Wilder Lawless
Love Interest: Bond shares a brief kiss with Wilder Lawless, but he's not yet interested in girls.
Villain: Lord Randolf Hellebore
Henchman: Cleek MacSawney

The Moneypenny Diaries: Guardian Angel (aka The Moneypenny Diaries)
Premise: While searching for the fate of her presumed dead father, Miss Moneypenny comes into danger when an enemy agent tries to compel her to share government secrets. Simultaneously, Moneypenny accompanies 007 on a trip to Cuba to avert a war between the United States and Cuba,
Author: Kate Westbrook
Published: 2005
Heroine: Jane Moneypenny
Love Interest Moneypenny's suitors include Richard Hamilton and possibly Bill Tanner
Villains: David Zach, Geraldo Gil, aka Caballo, and Colonel Boris.

Blood Fever
Premise: While simultaneously participating in a school trip and visiting his cousin in Italy, Bond investigates a secret society called Millenaria, which tries to emulate the ancient Roman power structure and plans to form an organized multi-national criminal organization.

Blood Fever (cont'd.)
Author: Charlie Higson
Published: 2006
Heroines: Amy Goodenough, Vendetta
Love Interest: None, though he kisses Vendetta, young James isn't interested in girls.
Villains: Count Ugo Carnifex, Zoltan the Magyar
Henchmen: Smiler, Tree-Trunk

"For Your Eyes Only, James"
Premise: Miss Moneypenny accompanies Bond to the Casino Royale on a mission to kill a warlord.
Author: Samantha Weinberg
Published: 2006
Heroine: Jane Moneypenny
Love Interest: James Bond
Villain: Ahmen Khan Zadran

"Moneypenny's First Date With Bond"
Premise: On her first day of work at MI6, Jane Moneypenny accepts James Bond's invitation to dinner. After learning that Bond is a bit of a cad, she determines that she wants to keep their relationship platonic.
Author: Samantha Weinberg
Published:2006
Heroine: Jane Moneypenny
Love Interest: James Bond

The Moneypenny Diaries: Secret Servant
Premise: Jane Moneypenny goes behind the Iron Curtain to convince a Soviet double agent and his wife to return to England.
Author: Samantha Weinberg
Published: 2006
Heroine: Jane Moneypenny
Love Interest: Richard Hamilton and possibly Bill Tanner.
Villain: Colonel Boris

Double or Die
Premise: To find a kidnapped Eton professor, James Bond must decipher a series of codes, which leads him to the discovery of a calculating machine that the Soviets are building to help crack codes so that they can win any wars and defeat the United Kingdom.
Author: Charlie Higson
Published: 2007

Double or Die (cont'd.)
Heroine: Kelly Kelly
Love Interest: Kelly Kelly
Villain: Colonel Irena "The Grandmother" Sedova
Henchman: Ludwig and Wolfgang Smith

Hurricane Gold
Premise: After a gang kidnaps two children, Bond vows to keep them safe, but winds up on an island that is being used as a hideout for wealthy criminals.
Author: Charlie Higson
Published: 2007
Heroine: Precious Stone
Love Interest: Precious Stone
Villain: El Huracán, Theda Glass
Henchman: Strabo
Not So Evil Henchman: Sakata

The Moneypenny Diaries: Final Fling
Premise: Jane Moneypenny promises to fulfill M's last request that she find and expose the MI6 mole.
Author: Samantha Weinberg
Published:2008
Heroine: Jane Moneypenny
Love Interest: possibly James Bond for Moneypenny; Christopher Hunter for Kate Westbrook
Villain: Percy Warren

By Royal Command
Premise: Bond must thwart the assassination of King George while avoiding two villains from his past who are out to kill him.
Author: Charlie Higson
Published: 2008
Love Interest: Roan Power
Villains: Colonel Irena "the Grandmother" Sedova, Dr. Perseus Friend
Henchman: Vladimir Wrangler

Devil May Care
Premise: James Bond must stop Dr. Julius Gorner, a chemist, who wants to start a war between the Soviet Union and England, while simultaneously recovering a beautiful woman's twin sister who is under the villain's evil spell.
Author: Sebastian Faulks
Published: 2008
Heroine: Scarlett Papava

Devil May Care (cont'd.)
Love Interest: Scarlett Papava
Villain: Dr. Julius Gorner
Henchman: Chagrin

"A Hard Man to Kill"
Premise: While on a cruise, Young James Bond encounters a villain named General Charles Caiboche who is in the process of escaping police custody.
Author: Charlie Higson
Published: 2009
Heroine: Wilder Lawless
Love Interest: Wilder Lawless
Villain: General Charles Caiboche
Henchman: Emil Lefebvre

Carte Blanche
Premise: Bond is assigned to investigate and then stop Severan Hydt, an entrepreneur and owner of a rubbish and recycling operation, who is planning an attack on England.
Author: Jeffery Deaver
Published: 2011
Heroine: Felicity Willing
Love Interest: Ophelia Maidenstone
Villain: Severan Hydt

Solo
Premise: Bond is dispatched to kill rebel leader Brigadier Solomon Adeka in the West African nation of Zanzarim, which is engulfed in a civil war. He instead helps the resistance win the war but he's then shot by Blessing Ogilvy-Grant, a woman posing as his ally. After he recovers, Bond goes to America to seek revenge. In the process, he learns how the people of Zanzarim have been exploited to gain control of their oil.
Author: William Boyd
Published: 2013
Heroine: Blessing Ogilvy-Grant,
Love Interest: Bryce Fitzjohn
Villain: Brigadier Solomon Adeka

"William Boyd Interviews James Bond"
Premise: William Boyd, the author of a James Bond continuation novel, travels back to 1969 London to meet the subject of his book.
Author: William Boyd
Published: 2013

"William Boyd Q&A with James Bond"
Premise: James Bond submits to an interview with a Bond continuation novelist.
Author: William Boyd
Published: 2013
Love Interest: Teresa di Vicenzo and Tiffany Case (referenced)
Villain: Kobus Breed (referenced)

Shoot to Kill
Premise: Young James Bond starts a new school in England and then travels to Hollywood to investigate a series of crimes that are caught on film.
Author: Steve Cole
Published: 2014
Heroine: Boudicca "Boody" Pryce.
Love Interest: None
Villain: Anton Kostler

Heads You Die
Premise: Young Bond discovers that a villain plans to infect British citizens with a poison that is transferred through paper currency.
Author: Steve Cole
Published: 2016
Heroine: Jagua Solares
Love Interest: Jagua Solares
Villain: Scolopendra/Audacto Solares and La Velada/The Veil
Henchman: El Puño/The Fist

Strike Lightning
Premise: Young Bond stumbles on a villain's plot to aid Germany by building powerful exosuits.
Author: Steve Cole
Published: 2016
Heroine: Kitty Drift
Love Interest:
Villain: Konstantin Grünner and apparently Maximilian Blade
Henchman: Herta Axmann

Red Nemesis
Premise: After receiving a letter from his dead father, young Bond must stop a villain, who intends to assassinate King George and overthrow the British government.

Red Nemesis (cont'd.)
Author: Steve Cole
Published: 2017
Heroine: Anya Kalashnikova
Love Interest:
Villain: Adam Elmhirst, La Velada
Henchman: Mimic

Trigger Mortis
Premise: Bond must enter a race to protect an English racecar driver from being killed by the KGB. The case leads him to uncover a plot to end America's space program.
Author: Anthony Horowitz
Published: 2015
Heroine: Jeopardy Lane
Love Interest: Pussy Galore
Villain: Jason Sin

Forever and a Day
Premise: James Bond, a newly minted Double O agent, is assigned to find out why 007, his predecessor, was killed.
Author: Anthony Horowitz
Published: 2018
Heroine and Love Interest: Joanne Brochet aka Madame Sixtine
Villain: Jean-Paul Scipio and Irwin Wolfe

With a Mind to Kill
Premise: To get revenge on the Soviet organization that brainwashed Bond, M sends the newly deprogrammed, but vulnerable agent, into the heart of Moscow.
Author: Anthony Horowitz
Published: 2022
Love Interest: Katya Leonova
Villain: General Boris

Double Or Nothing
Premise: James Bond is missing and the next generation of Double O agents face new threats. As Joseph Dryden (004) investigates Sir Bertram Paradise, a tech billionaire, who claims his advanced technology can stop climate change, Johanna Harwood (003) and Sid Bashir (009) search for Paradise's missing scientist.
Author: Kim Sherwood
Published: 2022
Heroes: Johanna Harwood, Joseph Dryden, Sid Bashir

Double Or Nothing (cont'd.)
Love Interest: Luke Luck
Villain: Sir Bertram Paradis
Henchman: Yuri Litvinnof

On His Majesty's Secret Service
Premise: James Bond must thwart a plan to assassinate King Charles III during his coronation.
Author: Charlie Higson
Published: 2023
Heroine: Ragnheiður Ragnarsdóttir
Love Interest: Ragnheiður Ragnarsdóttir and Yasmin
Villain: Æthelstan of Wessex and Flora Woodbridge
Henchman: Canner Lyle

A Spy Like Me
Premise: As the search for James Bond continues, Double O agents investigate a smuggling network with terrorist ties.
Author: Kim Sherwood
Published: 2024
Heroes: Johanna Harwood, Joseph Dryden, Conrad Harthorp-Vane

ACKNOWLEDGMENTS

I should start by thanking all of the authors whose novels are the subject of this work. Those incredible writers include Arthur Calder-Marshall, Kingsley Amis, John Pearson, Christopher Wood, John Gardner, Raymond Benson, Charlie Higson, Sebastian Faulks, Jeffery Deaver, William Boyd, Steve Cole, Anthony Horowitz, and Kim Sherwood. From Ian Fleming Publications, I express my gratitude to the formidable Corinne Turner, who has played a critical role in overseeing numerous continuation novels of the modern era. My interviews with many of these figures will appear in the second and final volume.

I would like to thank David Zaritsky of *The Bond Experience*, James Page of *MI6-HQ.com,* David Lowbridge-Ellis of *License to Queer*, Andy Lane and Paul Simpson of *The Bond Files*, Joseph Darlington of *Being Bond*, Anders Frejdh of *From Sweden with Love*, John Cox of The Book Bond, Lennart Guldbrandsson of Writing Bond, Tom Cull of Artistic Licence Renewed, Dr. Lisa Funnell of *For His Eyes Only: The Women of James Bond*, Shane Whaley of Spybrary, Matt Spaiser of Bond Suits, Ajay Chowdhury of *Some Kind of Hero*, Andy Lane and Paul Simpson of *The Bond Files,* Mark O'Connell of *Catching Bullets*, Nicolas Suszczyk of *The Bond of the Millennium*, Gareth Owen of Bondstars, Remmert van Braam of the Bond Lifestyle, Wolfgang Thürauf of James Bond Club Deutschland, Steven Jay Rubin of *The James Bond Films*, Richard Schenkman of *Bondage*, Lee Pfeiffer of *The Incredible World of 007* and *Cinema Retro,* Tom Sears and Chris Wright at *James Bond Radio*, James Chapman of *Licensed to Thrill,* Bruce Scivally of *James Bond: The Legacy*, Thomas Nixdorf of The Nixdorf Collection, Llewella Chapman of *Fashioning James Bond*, Tim George and Graeme Bibby of The James Bond Cocktail Hour, the gang at Really, 007, Phil Noble Jr. who named my last book, *Archivo 007*, Greg Bechtlof of *MI6,* Thomas Felix Creighton of British Culture: Albion Never Dies, Jeffrey Marshall, Bill Koenig of *The Spy Command*, Peter Lorenz of the *Illustrated 007*, Matt Sherman of Bond Fan Events, Spencer Draper of Damn Fool Idealistic Crusader, Scott Hettrick of Hollywood in High-Def, Clinton Rawls of *Comics Royale*, and Calvin Dyson, for whom I hope this volume is of some use in the creation of his videos.

I would like to thank the members of the group James Bond Collectable Books Worldwide and all its members including Matthew Bradford, Tony Jelly, Peter Crush, Jochem Gr, Martin Welles, John Fairbrother, Gary Rosenfeld, David Lloyd, Ian Stubbs, Greg Williams, Tom Zielinski, Alan Tong, Ian Allison, Matthew Dewhurst-Grice, Bazeer Flumore, Robin Harbour, Pete Beaumont, Michael Fenemore, Paul Shields, Matthew Wood, David Alexander, Rebecca Andrews, Craig Arthur, Thomas Eagle, Brendan Edwards, Tim Kitchen, Simon Read, Richard Skillman, Gary Webster, and the rest of the gang. Thanks to fellow Bond fans Doug Redenius, Reuben Wakeman, Anthony Joseph, Paul Rowlands, Michael Poplawski, and Martijn Mulder.

I am incredibly grateful that John Peel agreed to write the foreword to this volume. John was incredibly generous to do so.

My appreciation also goes to Jon Gilbert, Simon Gardner, and Steve Clamp.

I raise my glass to Gary J. Firuta and offer cheers for supplying many of the advertisements and promotional material. For additional illustrations, I would like to thank Dave Tulley, Brendan Edwards, Robin Harbour, and, for the abundance of images, John Cox of The Book Bond.

Huge thanks to Elizabeth Belasco, a diligent, tireless, and affable editor.

I'd also like to thank all the readers who expressed their enthusiasm for my previous works. Some of those wonderful people include Mark Ashby, Cal David, Glenn Hewett, Darren Noble, David Stephens, Brian Dobson, Oscar Rubio, Martin Hrdr, Michael Gallipo, David Stephens, Victor Tapia, Howard Pieratt, Steve Brock, Sean Hannam, Marc Hernandez, Ihsan Amanatullah, Kyle Barbeau, and Anagnostis Karras.

I'm thrilled that Sean Longmore has designed the cover for this book. He came up with the poster for the ultimate continuation novel. I am delighted to include artist Pat Carbajal's remarkable illustrations in this volume. I am a huge fan of both of their work.

Huge thanks to Jack Lugo for all of his honest, astute, and constructive feedback. Brian McKaig of *The Bondologist Blog* has always been generous with his research and support. He loves to solve Bond-related mysteries and he is the biggest John Gardner fan I know. Jack and Brian's encouragement was unwavering. I would like to thank my Beta readers, Alan Porter, William Kanas, and Brad Frank. Their comments and feedback were invaluable. Additional thanks to Roland Hume for his encouragement.

I also want to thank my family and friends for all of their support. For my dear and beloved uncle Elliot Ravetz, who is my biggest writing advocate and booster. For my mom, the honorable Sandra Edlitz, who always encouraged me to follow my dreams. I'd also like to thank my wonderful sister Tracy, who is also a great aunt. Additional love and thanks go to the awesome Gail Ravetz, Mark Visceglia, Scott Edlitz, Katy Edlitz, George Berger, Doctor Joan Shapiro, and Doctor Irving Shapiro. I also want to remember my late father, Robert I. Edlitz.

Above all, I must thank Dr. Susan Shapiro, my sage, incredible, and beautiful wife, and Ben and Doug, my two amazing children who grow more impressive and wonderful each year. I can't wait to see your next phase and evolution. Whatever it is, it's perfect.

SOURCES

I have cited my sources in the notes. However, I would like to further acknowledge the following:

Non-Fiction Books

Andy Lane and Paul Simpson, *The Bond Files*, Virgin Publishing, 2001

Alan J. Porter and Gillian J. Porter, *The James Bond Lexicon*, White Rocket Books, 2021

Raymond Benson, *The James Bond Companion*, Dodd Mead; 1988

Ann Fleming (Author), Mark Amory (Editor), *The Letters of Ann Fleming,* Collins Harvill, 1985

Kingsley Amis (Author), Zachary Leader (Editor), *The Letters of Kingsley Amis*, HarperCollins, 2001

Ian Fleming (Author), Fergus Fleming (Editor), *The Man with the Golden Typewriter*

John Griswold, *Ian Fleming's James Bond: Annotations and Chronologies for Ian Fleming's Bond Stories*, AuthorHouse 2006.

Jon Gilbert, *Ian Fleming: The Bibliography*, Queen Anne Press, 2017

Jon Gilbert, *Ian Fleming and James Bond: Manuscripts in The Schøyen Collection*, Adrian Harrington, 2020

Nicholas Shakespeare, *Ian Fleming: The Complete Man*, Harvill Secker, 2023

Peter Haining, *James Bond: A Celebration*, W.H. Allen, 1987

Fiction Books

Ian Fleming, *Casino Royale*, Jonathan Cape, 1953

Ian Fleming, *Live And Let Die,* Jonathan Cape, 1954

Ian Fleming, *Moonraker,* Jonathan Cape, 1955

Ian Fleming, *Diamonds Are Forever,* Jonathan Cape, 1956

Ian Fleming, *From Russia, With Love,* Jonathan Cape, 1957

Ian Fleming, *Dr. No,* Jonathan Cape, 1958

Ian Fleming, *Goldfinger*, Jonathan Cape, 1959

Ian Fleming, *For Your Eyes Only,* Jonathan Cape, 1960

Ian Fleming, *Thunderball,* Jonathan Cape, 1961

Ian Fleming, *The Spy Who Loved Me,* Jonathan Cape, 1962

Ian Fleming, *On Her Majesty's Secret Service,* Jonathan Cape, 1963

Ian Fleming, *You Only Live Twice,* Jonathan Cape, *1964*

Ian Fleming, *The Man With The Golden Gun,* Jonathan Cape, 1965

Ian Fleming, *Octopussy and The Living Daylights,* Jonathan Cape, 1966

Kingsley Amis, *The James Bond Dossier*, Jonathan Cape, 1965

Kingsley Amis, *The Book of Bond or Every Man His Own 007*, Jonathan Cape, 1965

Kingsley Amis, *Colonel Sun*, Jonathan Cape, 1968

Arthur Calder-Marshall, *The Adventures of James Bond Junior 003½*, 1967

John Pearson, *James Bond: The Authorised Biography Of 007*, Sidgwick & Jackson, 1973

Christopher Wood, *James Bond, The Spy Who Loved Me*, Jonathan Cape, 1977

Christopher Wood, *James Bond and Moonraker*, Jonathan Cape, 1979

John Gardner, *Licence Renewed*, Jonathan Cape, 1981

John Gardner, *For Special Services*, Jonathan Cape, 1982
John Gardner, *Icebreaker*, Jonathan Cape, 1983
John Gardner, *Role of Honour*, Jonathan Cape, 1984
John Gardner, *Nobody Lives For Ever*, Jonathan Cape, 1986
John Gardner, *No Deals, Mr. Bond*, Jonathan Cape, 1987
John Gardner, *Scorpius*, Jonathan Cape, 1989
John Gardner, *Licence To Kill*, Coronet Books, 1989
John Gardner, *Win, Lose Or Die*, Jonathan Cape, 1989
John Gardner, *Brokenclaw*, Hodder & Stoughton, 1990
John Gardner, *The Man From Barbarossa*, Hodder & Stoughton, 1991
John Gardner, *Death Is Forever*, Hodder & Stoughton, 1992
John Gardner, *Never Send Flowers*, Hodder & Stoughton, 1993
John Gardner, *SeaFire*, Hodder & Stoughton, 1994
John Gardner, *GoldenEye*, Coronet Books, 1995
John Gardner, *Cold Fall*, Hodder & Stoughton, 1996
Raymond Benson, "Blast From The Past," Playboy, 1997
Raymond Benson, *Zero Minus Ten,* Hodder & Stoughton, 1997
Raymond Benson, *Tomorrow Never Dies*, Coronet Books, 1997
Raymond Benson, *The Facts of Death*, Hodder & Stoughton, 1998
Raymond Benson, "A Midsummer's Night's Doom," Playboy, 1999
Raymond Benson, *High Time To Kill*, Hodder & Stoughton, 1999
Raymond Benson, "Live At Five," TV Guide, 1999
Raymond Benson, *The World Is Not Enough*, Hodder & Stoughton,1999
Raymond Benson, *DoubleShot*, Hodder & Stoughton, 2000
Raymond Benson, *Never Dream of Dying*, Hodder & Stoughton, 2001
Raymond Benson, *The Man with the Red Tattoo*, Hodder & Stoughton, 2002
Raymond Benson, *Die Another Day,* Coronet Books, 2002
Charlie Higson, *SilverFin*, Puffin Books, 2005
Charlie Higson, *Blood Fever*, Puffin Books, 2006
Charlie Higson, *Double or Die*, Puffin Books, 2007
Charlie Higson, *Hurricane Gold*, Puffin Books, 2007
Charlie Higson, *By Royal Command*, Puffin Books, 2008
Charlie Higson, "A Hard Man To Kill," Puffin Books, 2009
Charlie Higson, *On His Majesty's Secret Service*, Ian Fleming Publications, 2023
Steve Cole, *Shoot to Kill*, Random House, 2014
Steve Cole, *Heads You Die*, Random House, 2016
Steve Cole, *Strike Lightning*, Random House, 2016
Steve Cole, *Red Nemesis*, Random House, 2017
Samantha Weinberg, *Guardian Angel*, John Murray, 2005
Samantha Weinberg, *Secret Servant*, John Murray, 2006
Samantha Weinberg, "First Date," The Spectator, 2006
Samantha Weinberg, "For Your Eyes Only," The Tatler, 2006
Samantha Weinberg, *Final Fling*, John Murray, 2008
Sebastian Faulks, *Devil May Care*, Penguin, 2008
Jeffery Deaver, *Carte Blanche*, Hodder & Stoughton, 2011
William Boyd, *Solo,* Jonathan Cape, 2013
Anthony Horowitz, *Trigger Mortis*, Orion Publishing, 2015
Anthony Horowitz, *Forever and a Day*, Jonathan Cape, 2018
Anthony Horowitz, *With a Mind to Kill*, Vintage Books, 2022
Kim Sherwood, *Double Or Nothing* Harper Collins, 2022

Websites
MI6-HQ.com: The Home of James Bond 007
The Book Bond
Absolutely James Bond
Artistic Licence Renewed
The Bondologist Blog

YouTube Channels
David Zaritsky
Calvin Dyson
David Lowbridge-Ellis

NOTES

[1] Paul Simpson, "Bond in Books," *James Bond: Octopussy,* Titan Press, 2004
[2] As highlighted by Mark O'Connell, "Catching the Cold Bullet – Reviewing Anthony Horowitz's new mind-Bonding novel, With a Mind to Kill," May 2022, https://markoconnell.co.uk/catching-the-cold-bullet-reviewing-anthony-horowitzs-new-bond-novel-with-a-mind-to-kill/
[3] Nicholas Shakespeare, *Ian Fleming: The Complete Man*, Harvill Secker, 2023, p453 and Jon Gilbert, *Ian Fleming: The Bibliography*, Queen Ann Press, 2012. p664
[4] Jon Gilbert, *Ian Fleming: The Bibliography*, Queen Ann Press, 2012. p665
[5] Nicholas Shakespeare, *Ian Fleming: The Complete Man*, p672, Harvill Secker, 2023
[6] Janet Shprintz, "Big Bond-Holder," Variety, May 29, 1999, https://variety.com/1999/film/news/big-bond-holder-1117492814/
[7] Edwin McDowell, "James Bond Making 'Wild' Comeback," New York Times, June 5, 1982, https://www.nytimes.com/1982/06/05/books/james-bond-making-wild-comeback.html
[8] Unknown Author, "Author Sells Himself," *New York Times*, March 23, 1964, https://www.nytimes.com/1964/03/23/archives/author-sells-himself.html
[9] Mrs. Ian Fleming: Widow to a Legend (The Cool Crazy Committed World of the Sixties, by Pierre Berton, 1966), found on MI6 Community.com, posted by Revelator.
[10] Unknown Author, "Author Sells Himself," *New York Times*, March 23, 1964, https://www.nytimes.com/1964/03/23/archives/author-sells-himself.html
[11] Unknown Author, "Author Sells Himself," *New York Times*, March 23, 1964, https://www.nytimes.com/1964/03/23/archives/author-sells-himself.html
[12] Jon Gilbert, *Ian Fleming: The Bibliography,* Queen Ann Press, 2012.
[13] Ian Fleming Publications, "A Tribute Peter Janson-Smith 1922-2016," IanFleming.com, April 20, 2016, https://www.ianfleming.com/a-tribute-to-peter-janson-smith-1922-2016/
[14] Ann Fleming (Author) and Mark Amory (Editor), *The Letters of Ann Fleming*, p372, Collins Harvill,1985
[15] "The Geoffrey Jenkins Letters," MI6, August 23, 2010, https://www.mi6-hq.com/sections/articles/literary_per_fine_ounce_letters1?s=literary&id=2648
[16] Pierre Berton, *The Cool Crazy Committed World of the Sixties: Twenty-One Television.* As spotted in MI6communiy.com by Revelator, April 2016
[17] Pierre Berton, *The Cool Crazy Committed World of the Sixties: Twenty-One Television.* As spotted in MI6communiy.com by Revelator, April 2016
[18] Duff Hart-Davis, *Peter Fleming: A Biography*, Oxford University Press, 1987 p374.
[19] Duff Hart-Davis, *Peter Fleming: A Biography*, Oxford University Press, 1987 p374.
[20] "People: Feb 4, 1966, *Time Magazine*, https://content.time.com/time/subscriber/article/0,33009,898943,00.html

[21] James Fleming, "Bond Behind the Iron Curtain: Guest post by James Fleming," Do You Write Under Your Own Name, December 4, 2021, http://doyouwriteunderyourownname.blogspot.com/2021/12/bond-behind-iron-curtain-guest-post-by.html
[22] Duff Hart-Davis, *Peter Fleming: A Biography*, Oxford University Press, 1987 p374.
[23] Duff Hart-Davis, *Peter Fleming: A Biography*, Oxford University Press, 1987 p374.
[24] Ann Fleming (Author) and Mark Amory (Editor), *The Letters of Ann Fleming*, Collins Harvill,1985
[25] Kingsley Amis (Author) and (Editor), *The Letters of Kingsley Amis*, Harper Collins, 2001
[26] Raymond Benson, "A Dialogue with Kingsley Amis," *Bondage*, Issue #13, 1984
[27] Ann Fleming, Mark Amory (editor), *The Letters of Ann Fleming,* p347, William Collins Sons, 1985
[28] Peter Haining, *James Bond: A Celebration*, W.H. Allen & Co Plc, p70, 1987
[29] Charlie Higson, BBC Radio 4, "Amis, Amis & Bond," July 17, 2007, as rediscovered by MI6.
[30] Charlie Higson, BBC Radio 4, "Amis, Amis & Bond," July 17, 2007, as rediscovered by MI6.
[31] Raymond Benson, "A Dialogue with Kingsley Amis," *Bondage*, Issue #13, 1984
[32] Duff Hart-Davis, *Peter Fleming: A Biography*, Oxford University Press, 1987 p375.
[33] Duff Hart-Davis, *Peter Fleming: A Biography*, Oxford University Press, 1987 p375.
[34] Raymond Benson, "Classified Dossier: James Bond's (literary) agent," *Crime Spree* Magazine, https://commanderbond.net/9854/classified-dossier-james-bonds-literary-agent.html
[35] Jeremy Dunns, *Need to Know: An Archive of Journalistic Pursuits,* 2021
[36] "John Gardner Interview," *007 Magazine*, July 1994, http://www.007magazine.co.uk/archive/john_gardner_interview.htm
[37] Raymond Benson, "Gardner's World,“ *007 Magazine*, #28, 1995
[38] John Cox, "Benson On Bond: An Interview with Raymond Benson," *Tied In: The Business History and Craft of Media Tie-In Writing*," edited by Lee Goldberg, 2010
[39] "James Bond Returns in Devil May Care," AP News, May 2008, https://abc7chicago.com/archive/6168718/
[40] Peter Kemp, "Exclusive: Sebastian Faulks Interview, Sunday Times, May 25, 2008, https://www.nytimes.com/2008/05/28/books/28masl.html
[41] Guy Dammann, "James Bond Smashes Sales Figures," June 4, 2008, The Guardian, https://www.theguardian.com/books/2008/jun/04/mediabusiness.sebastianfaulks
[42] Jack Crone, "New Bond author shoots down fellow 007 writers over too many plot twists which 'Fleming would never have done," September 6, 2015, https://www.dailymail.co.uk/news/article-3224029/Author-latest-Bond-book-dismissed-fellow-007-writers-adding-plot-twists-setting-action-wrong-country-Fleming-never-done.html

[43] "James Bond Returns in Devil May Care," AP News, May 2008, https://abc7chicago.com/archive/6168718/
[44] Peter Kemp, "Exclusive: Sebastian Faulks Interview, Sunday Times, May 25, 2008, https://www.nytimes.com/2008/05/28/books/28masl.html
[45] Patrick Cremona, "Double Or Nothing author on writing a Bond novel without James Bond," RadioTimes.com, May 10, 2023, https://www.radiotimes.com/movies/double-or-nothing-author-james-bond-novel-exclusive-newsupdate/
[46] John Cox, "Chris Moore's little known novelizations of Octopussy and A View to a Kill," The Book Bond.com, January 16,2023
[47] Kingsley Amis, writing as William Tanner, *The Book of Bond or Every Man His Own 007,* Jonathan Cape, p12, 1965.
[48] Kingsley Amis, writing as William Tanner, *The Book of Bond or Every Man His Own 007,* Jonathan Cape, p23, 1965.
[49] Kingsley Amis, writing as William Tanner, *The Book of Bond or Every Man His Own 007,* Jonathan Cape, p28, 1965.
[50] Charlie Higson, BBC Radio 4, "Amis, Amis & Bond," July 17, 2007, as rediscovered by MI6.
[51] Zachary Leader, *The Life of Kingsley Amis*, p. 524, Random House, 2006
[52] Zachary Leader, *The Life of Kingsley Amis*, p. 536-537, Random House, 2006
[53] Zachary Leader, *The Life of Kingsley Amis*, p. 542, Random House, 2006
[54] Kingsley Amis, writing as William Tanner, *The Book of Bond or Every Man His Own 007,* Jonathan Cape, p111, 1965.
[55] An earlier and abridged version of my essay appeared in *The Lost Adventures of James Bond.*
[56] Nick Kincaid, 007Forever.com, "The Search for RD Mascott (James Bond Junior 003 ½)" web.archive.org/web/20060617134228/http:/www.007forever.com/books/investigativereports004.html
[57] Jake Rossen, Mental Floss.com "No One Knows Who Wrote his James Bond Novel," November 6, 2015, https://www.mentalfloss.com/article/70751/no-one-knows-who-wrote-james-bond-novel
[58] R.D. Mascott, *003½: The Adventures of James Bond Junior*, Glidrose Productions ltd., Random House, 1968, p208
[59] Ian Fleming, *On Her Majesty's Secret Service*, Thomas & Mercer edition, 2012, p58
[60] Ian Fleming, *You Only Live Twice*, Thomas & Mercer edition, 2012, p206.
[61] R.D. Mascott, *003½: The Adventures of James Bond Junior*, Glidrose Productions ltd., Random House, 1968, p6
[62] R.D. Mascott, *003½: The Adventures of James Bond Junior*, Glidrose Productions ltd., Random House, 1968, p6
[63] Andy Lane and Paul Simpson, *The Bond Files*, Virgin Publishing, 2002, p127

[64] Unknown author, *The Bookseller*, July 22, 1967. I first learned about Saltzman's plans from Sean Egan "James Bond: The Secret History," John Blake Publishing, 2016, p192.
[65] Kingsley Amis (Author) and (Editor), *The Letters of Kingsley Amis*, Harper Collins, 2001
[66] Zachary Leader, *The Life of Kingsley Amis*, p. 553, Random House, 2006
[67] Zachary Leader, *The Life of Kingsley Amis*, p. 512, Random House, 2006
[68] "Tom Adams Obituary," The Guardian, Feb 3, 2020, https://www.theguardian.com/artanddesign/2020/feb/03/tom-adams-obituary
[69] James Page and James Wheatley, "The Genesis of Colonel Sun," *Colonel Sun*, Titan Books, 2005
[70] Jason Whiton, "Double 007 Design II," SpyVibe, May 15, 2013, https://spyvibe.blogspot.com/2013/05/double-007-design-ii.html
[71] "Colonel Sun II: Bond Had Never Liked Acapulco, BondFanEvents.com, March 19, 2018
[72] Jeremy Duns, *Need to Know: An Archive of Journalistic Pursuits,* 2021
[73] Jeremy Duns, *Need to Know: An Archive of Journalistic Pursuits,* 2021
[74] Jeremy Duns, *Need to Know: An Archive of Journalistic Pursuits,* 2021
[75] "Exclusive Interview with 'Per Fine Ounce' Author, Peter Vollmer," Artistic Licence Renewed, March 1, 2015, https://literary007.com/2015/03/01/exclusive-interview-with-per-fine-ounce-author-peter-vollmer/
[76] "The Geoffrey Jenkins Letters," MI6, August 23, 2010, https://www.mi6-hq.com/sections/articles/literary_per_fine_ounce_letters1?s=literary&id=2648
[77] Jeremy Duns, *Need to Know: An Archive of Journalistic Pursuits,* 2021
[78] "The Geoffrey Jenkins Letters," MI6, August 23, 2010, https://www.mi6-hq.com/sections/articles/literary_per_fine_ounce_letters1?s=literary&id=2648
[79] Jeremy Duns, *Need to Know: An Archive of Journalistic Pursuits,* 2021
[80] "The Geoffrey Jenkins Letters," MI6, August 23, 2010, https://www.mi6-hq.com/sections/articles/literary_per_fine_ounce_letters1?s=literary&id=2648
[81] Jeremy Duns, *Need to Know: An Archive of Journalistic Pursuits,* 2021
[82] Hank Reineke, "A lot of criminals are very dodgy people," *007 Magazine*, #49, 2006.
[83] David Leigh, "John Pearson Interview," March 4, 2013, MI6-HQ.com, https://www.mi6-hq.com/sections/articles/interview_john_pearson
[84] Hank Reineke, "A lot of criminals are very dodgy people," *007 Magazine*, #49, 2006.
[85] Raymond Benson, "Classified Dossier: James Bond's (literary) agent," *Crime Spree* Magazine, https://commanderbond.net/9854/classified-dossier-james-bonds-literary-agent.html
[86] Raymond Benson, "Classified Dossier: James Bond's (literary) agent," *Crime Spree* Magazine, https://commanderbond.net/9854/classified-dossier-james-bonds-literary-agent.html
[87] David Lowbridge-Ellis and Tom Mason, "Somewhat Fishy: The Deeply Strange Scripts for The Spy Who Loved Me," Licence to Queer, August 5, 2023, https://www.licencetoqueer.com/blog/something-fishy-the-deeply-strange-scripts-for-the-spy-who-loved-me

[88] General Nikitin's appearance in the novelization is spotted by Calvin Dyson. Calvin Dyson, "James Bond, The Spy Who Loved Me Novelization Book Review," December 7, 2019, "https://www.youtube.com/watch?v=v9jHFoNcRJc
[89] Wood, Spy Who Loved Me novelization.
[90] Spy Who Loved Me Script
[91] Wood, Spy Who Loved Me novelization.
[92] Calvin Dyson, "James Bond and *Moonraker* Novelization Book Review," YouTube.com, Jan 3, 2020, https://www.youtube.com/watch?v=m59wDn0GSMY
[93] Matthew Field and Ajay Chowdhury, *Some Kind of Hero: The Remarkable Story of the James Bond Films*, History Press, 2015
[94] Edwin McDowell, "Behind the Best Sellers: John Gardner," June 7, 1981, https://www.nytimes.com/1981/06/07/books/behind-the-best-sellers-john-gardner.html
[95] People, June 21, 1982, Fred Hauptfuhrer, interview with John Gardner; May 2, 1983, review of Icebreaker, p. 26. As quoted in,
[96] Edwin McDowell, "Behind the Best Sellers: John Gardner," June 7, 1981, https://www.nytimes.com/1981/06/07/books/behind-the-best-sellers-john-gardner.html
[97] Edwin McDowell, "Behind the Best Sellers: John Gardner," June 7, 1981, https://www.nytimes.com/1981/06/07/books/behind-the-best-sellers-john-gardner.html
[98] John Gardner, "In the Autumn of 1980," https://john-gardner.com/bond/
[99] "Licence Renewed," 007 Magazine, p43, 2004, originally appeared in the James Bond British Fan Club publication Vol 1, No. 6, 1983
[100] "Licence Renewed," 007 Magazine, p43, 2004, originally appeared in the James Bond British Fan Club publication Vol 1, No. 6, 1983
[101] Jim Lawrence and John McLusky, *The Paradise Plot*, Titan Books, 2008, as spotted by Paul Simpson.
[102]Jon Gilbert, Ian Fleming and James Bond. Manuscripts in the Schøyen Collection, p145, Royal Tunbridge Wells Adrian Harrington Ltd., 2020
[103] Raymond Benson, *Licence Renewed,* Introduction, Pegasus Books, 2011
[104] John Gardner, *For Special Services*, Afterword, Ian Fleming Publications, 1982
[105] Don Swain, *Book Beat Radio*, November 21, 1985, https://media.library.ohio.edu/digital/collection/donswaim/id/3620/rec/3?fbclid=IwAR1J3toS_eHC0MuNe16e_woUtUwCYqRXDgmLDuLLTKOK6-ZLuZpWuvOf2Kc
[106] Bob Hahn, "Books," *Cincinnati Post*, May 24, 1989
[107] John Gardner, *Licence to Kill*, Introduction, Armchair Detective Library Edition, 1990
[108] Raymond Benson, "Gardner's World," 007 Magazine, #28, 1995
[109] Calvin Dyson, 'Licence to Kill' Novelization Review | John Gardner Adapts Timothy Dalton's Bond for Book Form," January 8, 2023, Calvin Dyson's YouTube Channel, https://www.youtube.com/watch?v=bW4leK1hmmA
[110] As identified by Bill Kanas and reported by Adam Farrington-Williams, "Q&A with John Gardner," Universal Exprts.net https://www.universalexports.net/Books/renewed.shtml

[111] As spotted by Calvin Dyson, "'Win, Lose or Die' | 007 Saves Thatcher, Bush, and Gorbachev?! | John Gardner Book Review," YouTube.com, Nov 6, 2022, https://www.youtube.com/watch?v=gwK6HhRprnc
[112] As spotted by Calvin Dyson, "Death is Forever," Calvin Dyson's YouTube Channel, June 25, 2023, https://www.youtube.com/watch?v=N4_U0w28Ero&t=303s
[113] Raymond Benson, "Gardner's World," *007 Magazine*, October 1995, Issue 28 www.007magazine.co.uk
[114] Nicholas Shakespeare, *Ian Fleming: The Complete Man*, Harvill Secker, 2023, p590
[115] John Cox, "Raymond Benson on Writing the Bond Novels," International Association of Media Tie-In Writers, May 11, 2023, https://iamtw.org/raymond-benson-on-writing-the-bond-novels/
[116] Neal Purvis, Robert Wade, Bruce Feirstein, *The World Is Not Enough*, 1999, deleted scenes from MGM Home Video.
[117] Mark Edlitz, *The Many Lives of James Bond*, Lyons Press, 2019
[118] Neal Purvis, Robert Wade, Bruce Feirstein, *The World Is Not Enough*, 1999, deleted scenes from MGM Home Video.
[119] David de Keyser redubbed Gabriele Ferzetti's dialogue.
[120] Single-O-Seven, "What About James Bond's Scar," January 26, 2007, CommanderBond.net https://debrief.commanderbond.net/topic/38938-what-about-james-bonds-scar/
[121] Jack Lugo, "A Look at Silverfin by Charlie Higson," March 18, 2015, https://jackl0073.wordpress.com/2015/03/18/a-look-at-silverfin-by-charlie-higson/
[122] https://www.glamour.com/story/romance-is-a-billion-dollar-industry
[123] "Lois Maxwell Obituary," September 2007, For Your Eyes Only, https://www.for-your-eyes-only.com/Site/Lois_Maxwell_obit.html
[124] BBC Radio 4, "The Write Stuff," April 3, 2002, https://archive.org/details/BBC_Radio_4_Extra_20200709_080000?start=1401
[125]Bob Thompson, "Trenches to Trench Coats: Summing Up Sebastian Faulks, Washington Post, October 24, 2007, https://www.washingtonpost.com/wp-dyn/content/article/2007/10/24/AR2007102402689_4.html
[126] "Devil May Care - The New James Bond Novel - Sebastian Faulks," Random House Publishing, 2008 "https://www.youtube.com/watch?v=wHCEwIkNtkE
[127] Sebastian Faulks, *Devil May Care*, Penguin, 2008, p33
[128] Matt Weston, "SAL Wins 'Devil May Care' Theme Song Contest," CommanderBond.net, March 2008, https://commanderbond.net/4953/sal-wins-devil-may-care-theme-song-contest.html
[129] Jeffery Deaver author interview, 2023
[130] John Pearson, *The Life of Ian Fleming*, Jonathan Cape Ltd, 1967
[131] Boyd, *Solo*, Introduction
[132] William Boyd, "The Spies Who Lived Here," TLS, July 17, 2020, https://www.the-tls.co.uk/articles/the-spies-who-lived-here-essay-william-boyd/
[133] Ajay Chowdhury, October 27, 2023, https://twitter.com/ACEtoots
[134] Steve Cole, *Heads You Die*, "Author's Note: Taking the Plunge," Red Fox, Waterstone's Edition, 2016

[135] David Zaritsky, "Exclusive Interview with Anthony Horowitz | With a Mind to Kill," The Bond Experience, May 23, 2023, "https://www.youtube.com/watch?v=-FmXfnYs5_o&t=1258s
[136] David Ellis-Lowbridge, "Conversation with Kim Sherwood," Licence to Queer, August 31, 2002, https://www.youtube.com/watch?v=NeUdmGFXoug
[137] Anna Pitoniak, "Who Says 007 Needs to be White British and Male?" *The Washington Post*,
April 30, 2023, https://www.washingtonpost.com/books/2023/04/30/james-bond-double-nothing-sherwood/
[138] David Zaritsky, "James Bond is Missing! DOUBLE OR NOTHING...the Journey Continues with Kim Sherwood!" April 11, 2023, https://www.youtube.com/watch?v=MXcW6xj7bDM
[139] "Lois Maxwell (1927-2007)," September 30, 2007, MI6, https://www.mi6-hq.com/sections/articles/biography_lois_maxwell
[140] Ken Ferguson, *Ian Fleming: The Playboy Interview*, September 1962, republished 2012, Playboy Enterprises, Inc.

Portrait of Bond.
Illustration by Pat Carbajal

ABOUT THE ILLUSTRATOR

Artist Pat Carbajal started as a political cartoonist at various national newspapers in Argentina. He then moved on to portrait art, illustrations, children's books, comic books, and storyboards for commercials.

Pat started producing art for the American market in 2007 when he illustrated covers for *Timeline of The Planet of the Apes* by Rich Handley for Hasslein Books. In 2009, he painted covers for the Bluewater Productions biography series, which were based on the lives of influential American women. Rock stars were the next subject for Pat. Bob Dylan, Jim Morrison, and Jimi Hendrix were the legends who were featured in *Rock and Roll Comics: The Sixties*, followed by Ozzy Osborne, AC/DC, and Guns N' Roses in *Rock and Roll Comics: Rock Heroes.*

The first graphic novel that Pat completely illustrated was *Allan Quartermain,* which was written by Clay and Susan Griffith and was published by Bluewater. Together with Clay and Susan Griffith, he created the character of The Raven for Bluewater's *Vincent Price Presents*, a classic horror comic book that starred Hollywood screen legend Vincent Price. Pat made his debut as a writer in the following issue of the comic.

He illustrated the cover and interior art for *The James Bond Lexicon: The Unauthorized Guide to the World of 007 in Movies, Novels, and Comics.*

For Hasslein Books, Pat illustrated the covers and interior art for Lexicon of *The Planet of the Apes* and *Back to the Future*, as well as *Total Immersion: The Comprehensive Unauthorized Red Dwarf Encyclopaedia.*

Pat also creates exclusive designs for t-shirts with Rotten Cotton. He also produces comic books and cover artwork for Eibon Press, with a series of horror graphic novels based on cult movies, including *Maniac*, Lucio Fulci's *Zombie*, and *The Beyond.*

This is Pat's fourth book with Mark Edlitz. He also provided illustrations for *The Many Lives of James Bond*, *The Lost Adventures of James Bond*, and *Movies Go Fourth: 4th Films in Fantastic Franchises.*

Pat lives in Argentina.

ABOUT THE COVER DESIGNER

Sean Longmore is a freelance graphic designer from the UK. He currently works producing art for Blu-ray releases including Brosnan's *The Thomas Crown Affair*, Roger Moore's *Gold*, and various action films starring Michelle Yeoh, as well as producing Bond fan art when he finds time. He also works in the world of Doctor Who.

The first Bond film he saw in the cinema was *Die Another Day*, aged seven. His late grandmother watched alongside with her fingers in her ears because it was too loud; he still adores it to this day and now watches every Bond film just a little bit too loud...

Sean can be found on Instagram at @seanlongmore.

ABOUT THE AUTHOR

Mark Edlitz has worked as a writer and producer for ABC News, NBC-Uni, CNBC, Discovery ID, and National Geographic Channel's *Brain Games*.

Edlitz's writings about pop culture have appeared in *The Huffington Post*, *Los Angeles Times Hero Complex*, *Moviefone*, and *Empire* magazine online.

He wrote and directed the award-winning independent film *The Eden Myth* and directed *Jedi Junkies*, a documentary about extreme Star Wars fans.

Edlitz's first book, *How to Be a Superhero* includes interviews with actors who have played superheroes over the past seven decades.

His second book, *The Many Lives of James Bond* consists of original interviews with artists who have created James Bond movies, novels, television, radio dramas, comic books, and video games. It also includes a large collection of interviews who have played 007 in different media.

His third book, *The Lost Adventures of James Bond* uncovers different scenarios for Timothy Dalton's abandoned third and fourth Bond movies, questions Toby Stephens about playing 007 on the radio, delves into the unproduced *Casino Royale* play, and exposes the secret history of *James Bond Jr*, the animated series about 007's nephew.

His fourth book, *Movies Go Fourth: 4th Films in Fantastic Franchises* is a celebration of the fourth movies in the most popular film franchises of all time. It offers behind-the-scenes stories of fourth films from such beloved series as *Star Wars*, *Star Trek*, and *James Bond.* It also explores infamous fourth films, including *Jaws: The Revenge*, *Superman IV: The Quest for Peace*, and *Batman & Robin.* This riveting book reveals the inside scoop on some of the biggest films in horror (*Halloween*, *Nightmare on Elm Street*), sci-fi (*Highlander*, *Terminator, Planet of the Apes*), action (*James Bond*, *Die Hard*, *Rambo*), and comedy (*Police Academy, Home Alone*). It also examines notable unmade fourth films, such as *Francis Ford Coppola's The Godfather: Part IV and Sam Raimi's Spider-Man 4.*

Edlitz lives in New York with his wife and two children.

www.ingramcontent.com/pod-product-compliance
Lightning Source LLC
Chambersburg PA
CBHW080912190726
48294CB00009B/2061

* 9 7 8 1 7 3 5 4 6 1 6 3 2 *